HOUSE WITHOUT A ROOF

BOOKS BY MAURICE HINDUS

HOUSE WITHOUT A ROOF

CRISIS IN THE KREMLIN

MAGDA

IN SEARCH OF A FUTURE

THE BRIGHT PASSAGE

THE COSSACKS:
The Story of a Warrior People

MOTHER RUSSIA

RUSSIA AND JAPAN

HITLER CANNOT CONQUER RUSSIA

TO SING WITH THE ANGELS

SONS AND FATHERS

WE SHALL LIVE AGAIN

GREEN WORLDS

MOSCOW SKIES

THE GREAT OFFENSIVE

RED BREAD

HUMANITY UPROOTED

BROKEN EARTH

THE RUSSIAN PEASANT AND THE REVOLUTION

HOUSE WITHOUT A ROOF

Russia
after
Forty-three Years
of Revolution

BY MAURICE HINDUS

DOUBLEDAY & COMPANY, INC.
GARDEN CITY, NEW YORK
1961

Library of Congress Catalog Card Number 61–9516

IT IS PARTICULARLY IMPORTANT FOR WESTERN MINDS
TO UNDERSTAND THE NATIONAL ROOTS OF RUSSIAN COM-
MUNISM AND THE FACT THAT IT WAS RUSSIAN HISTORY
WHICH DETERMINED ITS LIMITS AND SHAPED ITS CHARAC-
TER. A KNOWLEDGE OF MARXISM WILL NOT HELP IN THIS.

Nikolai Berdyayev,
The Origin of Russian Communism

CONTENTS

FOREWORD

Since the death of Stalin I have made two visits to the Soviet Union, one in the summer of 1958, the other two years later. As I traveled about the country observing the progress and achievement, especially in industry, I began to feel that I was moving from room to room through a spacious house with no roof over it. Though the foundation was solidly constructed, walls were being torn down, rebuilt, or newly put up. Without permanent support no roof could be raised.

State ownership of the means of production, which is the foundation of Soviet society, has remained unshaken, But—the machine tractor stations which dominated the collective farms and which to Stalin were "fortresses of socialism" have vanished. The State Security Police has been stripped of its instruments of terror, but there is no assurance that these will remain in disuse. Management of industry and agriculture and the state apparatus have been largely decentralized, but the persistence of bureaucracy and parasitism make further reconstruction inevitable.

Stalin's policies of Russification, which had strengthened the nationalism of the minorities, have been softened, but the nationalist problem still awaits an equitable solution. "Socialist legality," the ideological term for the rule of law, has been reaffirmed and redefined but has not prevented party secretaries from violating the legal code. The Soviet village is in process of reconstruction, but Khrushchev's once abandoned project, now revived though not enjoined, of transforming the village into a rural town of multistoried houses is encountering stiff resistance and there is no reason to believe that it will ever be carried out on a nation-wide scale. Even the radically reconstructed school system must be regarded as still in an experimental stage, so educators told me.

And who now hears of "collective leadership"—another fortress of socialism—hastily improvised, as hastily scrapped, and perhaps as hastily to be put up again? The names of Kaganovich, Malenkov, Molotov, do not even appear in the newly published third edition of the *Malaya* ("Little") *Encyclopedia*.

The mightiest revolution in history is still unfinished, very much unfinished. The very expression "socialism in transition to communism," by which ideologists term the present state of the Soviet system, is more than an intimation of changes to come in the institutional and personal life of Soviet humanity.

In this book I have attempted to give a picture, necessarily limited in scope, of the Soviet Union as it has evolved during forty-three years of stormy history: of blood and terror, of sensational reversals in theory and practice, of education and construction, of great tragedy and great achievement. The most violent revolution ever engineered by man, it has also been spectacularly creative; else there would have been no sputniks, no cosmonaut, and Russia would not have become the super-power that it is, second only to America. But the creativeness has been achieved in a traditional Russian way, by iron rule from above and in complete disregard of human cost and the freedoms that the West cherishes.

Whatever the errors I may have committed in my books on the Soviet Union, I never had reason to retreat from my interpretation of the origins of the revolution—that it was neither international nor proletarian, but national and peasant, having exploded out of the realities of Russian life and the barbarisms of Russian history, more particularly out of the muzhik's centuries-old battle for land. This was the central theme of *The Russian Peasant and the Revolution*, published in 1920, the first book I wrote on the bolshevik upheaval.

Years later, in his *History of the Russian Revolution*, Leon Trotsky, despite his flaming proletarian internationalism, was constrained to write, "If the agrarian problem as a heritage of the barbarism of the old Russian history had been solved by the bourgeoisie . . . the Russian proletarian could not possibly have come to power."[1]

[1] Leon Trotsky, *History of the Russian Revolution* (Simon & Schuster, New York, 1937), I, 51.

The incontestable fact is that the struggle between the Communist and non-Communist countries, notably between America and the Kremlin dictatorship, is not over the capitalist industrialized nations in Europe or elsewhere, but over the underdeveloped or peasant countries in Asia, Africa, and Latin America. Having failed to persuade, beguile, or drive the proletarian in industrialized countries into revolutionary uprisings, the Kremlin leaders are concentrating their attention, now as never before, on the peasant in the backward areas of our planet. We are indeed living in an age not of proletarian but peasant revolutions.

Essentially this is a book not about doctrine, politics, economics, but about people. Born in a Russian village, I knew the people in my childhood and boyhood. I rediscovered them in the early twenties, when I returned to Russia as an American journalist. On and off I lived among them for lengthy periods at a time between 1923 and 1937. I knew them again during my three years as war correspondent in Moscow and became reacquainted with them during my last two journeys to the Soviet Union, when after Stalin's postwar dark years communication with old friends, with fellow passengers on trains and planes, with workers in factory districts, with peasants in villages, with young people everywhere, was comparatively free from outside interference. When interference arose, as it did in Moscow more than anywhere else, one might often find a way of side-stepping it. Actually, the farther one travels from Moscow, the easier communication becomes for the foreigner who is fluent in Russian. In Siberia, to me the most exciting territory in the Soviet Union, people appear rather glad to meet the foreign visitor.

Though nowadays travel for foreigners is restricted to certain territories, people are people, everywhere one goes, and one never knows when he will stumble onto somebody whose story or experience will prove more revealing than an interview with any Kremlin personage. I am probably the only foreign journalist who has lived in the Soviet Union for long periods at a time who never asked for an interview with any Kremlin leader, not even with Stalin and Khrushchev.

I have always believed that the Soviet Union is a country to hear rather than see. Russians are vivid and voluble in speech, and any Russian the foreigner meets is, to use a journalist's expression, a story, even as the foreigner is to the Russian. So here, as in other books I have written, I have made free use of dialogue, of talk with friends and strangers, young and old, high and low, and sometimes of chance bits of overheard conversation. I have never known a better way of reporting on the mind and the mood of Soviet humanity.

PART I

REACQUAINTANCE

_I._

A FRAGMENT OF RUSSIA

Sheets of torrential rain darkened the highway as the dilapidated
taxi carried me to the airport outside Helsinki for my plane to
Leningrad. Halfway along we jolted to a stop as though the ancient
vehicle, like a balky mule, had decided that this was no weather to
be out in. The driver let loose a string of imprecations as lurid as
any muleteer's, while I puffed nervously on a cigarette and pictured
the plane taking off without me. At last the engine sputtered into life
and we rattled off into the rain, the driver muttering angrily to himself all the way to the airport.

By the time we reached it the rain had settled into a steady drizzle.
But I had just made the plane, which despite a low ceiling was taking
off on schedule. With the other passengers I crossed the wet field
where it waited, and was surprised that no Russian official was at the
gateway to examine our visas. Nor did the Soviet hostess at the foot
of the ramp ask for our passports. The omission of the usual formality
cheered me; I interpreted it as a sign of relaxed vigilance on foreigners bound for Russia—not that anyone would be rash enough
to attempt to sneak into the Soviet Union illegally.

I took my seat and in a moment the heavy door slammed; Finland
and the West were shut out. Soon I felt the easy lift of the twin
engines, and like a homing bird, the gray plane slid through the mist
toward the frontier. For the first time since the end of the war I was
back again in the Soviet Union—in a little flying fragment of it.

I sat alone midship in the cabin. Up forward was a group of

young Americans, some of them college students, loaded with cameras, all of them laughing and chattering in expectation of the adventure ahead. In the very rear of the cabin half a dozen young Russians conversed in low voices, as subdued as in a classroom, quite oblivious to my ebullient fellow countrymen.

The most subdued person on the plane was the hostess, a short, buxom, pink-cheeked girl with dark eyes, her heavy hair coiled in a bun at the back of her head. Her small mouth was shiny with lipstick, her nails lacquered bright red. Her outfit in no way resembled the trim uniform of a Western hostess. She wore no cap, and the mannish jacket of her blue serge suit with its padded shoulders made her look plumper than she was. She was the most silent and unsmiling hostess I had ever encountered in years of plane travel; and she went about her duties with a stiff reserve that ill suited her youthful freshness.

But when I watched her with the Russians I discovered that she had two personalities—one for them and one for foreigners. With the Russians she was lively and unaffected; with us she was stiff and guarded; she acted as though to relax for one moment might betray something about herself that would rouse disapproval or derision or would break down the barrier she felt duty-bound to maintain between herself and foreign passengers.

No doubt she had been cautioned against close association with travelers from *zagranitsa* (abroad), and of the subtle machinations of the "class enemy" ever alert to lure innocent Soviet citizens into the paths of disloyalty. Soviet security organs have always known how to instill in their charges as deep a dread of foreign mischief makers as ever did muzhik mothers in their children, in the old days, of the Evil One with the tales they told of his wily and sinister depredations. Yet this girl had also been given lessons in deportment calculated to impress foreigners with her social decorum so she wouldn't be judged inferior to her sisters beyond the frontier. She was no doubt well educated; Soviet authorities do not select hostesses for their international airlines as perfunctorily as they choose salesgirls for grocery stores. In her own special province the hostess is an ambassadress for "the socialist Motherland": she offers the visitor his first glimpse of Soviet humanity and leaves an impression that may be lasting.

Yet for all her education and training, this not unattractive girl in the mannish jacket might have just come from some far-off province, so ill at ease did she appear in the urbane atmosphere of the plane. When she brought tea and biscuits she acknowledged our *spasibo* with no trace of a smile, no flicker of friendliness. Her girlish features remained as stony as a soldier's on guard duty. She was, I must say, an exception among Soviet hostesses, especially those on inland airlines, where the passengers are usually Russian and the hostesses freely join in the social informality that prevails there. But on this plane the foreigner couldn't help becoming instantly aware of the contrast between a Western hostess and the Soviet girl: the easy and impersonal friendliness of the one, the stiffness and taciturnity of the other.

When her enforced contact with foreigners was over, she rejoined the Russian group, where she became her natural, lively, and expansive self. I reflected that for her the plane was two worlds in one: her own familiar Russian world and the world of *zagranitsa*, and the moment she crossed the invisible borderline from the one to the other she froze into an automaton with not a glimmer of the vivacity she displayed before the Russians.

Once, happening to glance back to the Russian group, I saw our hostess break into a broad smile that disclosed the sparkle of a gold tooth. The gold tooth was a surprise. On previous visits to the Soviet Union I had rarely observed these dental embellishments, even among the highest-salaried people in the country. Stalin seemed to sit on his hoard of gold as jealously as a setting hen on her eggs, and steel teeth were then in favor—there was hardly any other choice. Dental hygiene never was and still is not as advanced in Russia as preventive medicine, and tooth decay is widespread. In the theater, at the ballet and the opera, I was often unpleasantly shocked at the sight of an attractive woman flashing a steely smile on her escort.

At first I thought that our hostess had merited her more precious dental adornment because of her position. But I learned later, after I had traveled around the country, that gold was universally supplanting steel for dental caps and crowns. In fact, gold teeth were the craze of the moment; and it was a Soviet dentist who told me that now and then a village youth who wants to show off will have a healthy tooth filed down and crowned with gold. This small piece of ostentation, I learned, went back to Stalin's postwar years; it was one of the few significant concessions that the formidable dictator had allowed to a widespread craving for personal adornment. But gold was expensive, and people didn't have as much money as they now have. Nowadays one buys a nugget in a state jewelry shop; the cost is nominal—about eight of the new rubles ($8.80)—and few are so poor that they cannot afford it, even if they have to borrow for it. The dental work is of course free. In consequence, even milk-maids and waitresses regard steel caps and crowns beneath their dignity, and Russian smiles are as glittering as any in the world.

When I met a young woman in Moscow who sported two gold crowns, and told her that Americans consider porcelain or plastic more aesthetic than gold, she was greatly surprised. Why would any-body want anything but gold? Only gold could give a reassuring feel-ing of opulence. Let nobody say that people in a Communist society disdain such ostentation. They would be mortified if they were to discover that the present rage for gold teeth is a resurgence of a *nouveau riche* aspect of the very *meshchanstvo* (middle-class tastes) that bolshevism had vowed to extirpate forever.

To while away the time on the flight, I picked up a copy of *Smena* ("Young Generation"), an illustrated bimonthly youth journal. As I leafed through it smiling faces flashed at me from cover to cover. Not an unsmiling face in the entire issue: everyone appeared as delighted as facial anatomy would allow. In Soviet publications the smile has caught up with, indeed has surpassed, the broadest capital-istic smiles in American refrigerator and soft-drink advertisements.

Next I turned to letters to the editor, a feature I always find interesting in publications everywhere. A young man, a steel worker in Stalino, named Vladimir Perebeynos, sent in this offering: "Mil-lions of people in all countries applaud the remarkable initiative of the Soviet Government [in its nuclear peace proposals]. The com-mon people on our earth perceive in it a bright ray of hope; it inspires them in their difficult struggle for the right to work, to freedom and peace." How Vladimir knows what goes on in the minds of the common people of Borneo, Dutch New Guinea, the Eskimos in Canada, the miners in West Virginia, he doesn't tell us.

Nor does the editor enlighten the reader on the source of his correspondent's omniscience.

From the Volga city of Saratov comes a letter from a girl named Violetta Ruzanova. She is just graduating from the ten-year school, she writes, and at first she was set on going to college. But while visiting a factory she was so enraptured by the sight of a slight girl expertly handling a complicated machine that after talking to the girl she abandoned her scholastic ambitions for the life of a factory worker. She wants to share her happiness in this new life with the readers of *Smena;* she wants them to know that before going to the factory all she knew about life was what she had read about in books. But the factory has disclosed to her her "inner inclinations and aspirations" and pointed out her "destined road to life."

Another proselyte to the life of a machine-tending worker is Valentina Turina, from the famed textile city of Ivanovo. She had enrolled in a pedagogical college but didn't like it because the book learning there was purposeless and she craved a life full of purpose. So she became a textile worker. Now: "I cannot even imagine how I could live without the factory. No, I cannot."

These letters were published several months before Khrushchev came out with his original proposal for the reconstruction of the public school system: the abolition of the academically advanced ten-year schools and the limitation of compulsory education to seven or eight years, after which boys and girls should go to work in factories or on farms, while those wishing to continue their education might do so through correspondence courses, in evening schools, or in the already established factory trade schools. But discussion of the uselessness of book learning divorced from work had already appeared in the press. And here was *Smena* publishing testimonials hailing the new dispensation as one of the great inspirations of the ages. Of the pain and the anger of mothers, which I was to hear over and over, at the prospect of sending fourteen- and fifteen-year-old sons and daughters to work on farms and in factories, *Smena* of course never published a single word.

Khrushchev's proposal was drastically modified. Not only fathers and mothers but well-known educators and boys and girls themselves stood up against it. But I never heard a boy or girl speak with such contempt of book learning and such rapture of machine tending as did *Smena*'s correspondents, the rapture of lost souls suddenly discovering the one road to redemption.

I put the journal aside and looked down on the green world of grassy swamp, fields, and forest that stretched from Helsinki to Leningrad. The rain had stopped but the sky was gray and murky, as it is much of the year above Leningrad. Then I turned back and looked at the Russians in the rear of the cabin, the hostess among them, drinking tea, chatting quietly, and oblivious to the loud gaiety of the American college students up forward. They appeared cheerful, reserved, well mannered, a planet away from the ecstasy and omniscience that overflowed the pages of the magazine I had been reading. I could only conclude, and not for the first time in my years of travel in Russia, that the Soviet press, daily and periodical, is one of the least reliable keys to the minds and hearts of the Russian people. The conclusion was reinforced when in Moscow about a week later I met the editor of *Smena*, Mr. Velichko, and several of his associates in the large modestly furnished editorial office. Mr. Velichko was a man in his late thirties, of medium height, lean, muscular, with a strong, expressive face and thick dark-brown hair touched with premature gray. His blue-gray eyes were both lively and reflective and his smile was unassuming, not the forced display of delight that flashes from the pages of his magazine. Nor was there any doctrinaire fatuity in his speech; when we spoke of Soviet living standards, he candidly admitted that there was less meat for consumers than in the prewar years. When I asked him how he reconciled the inflamed patriotism his journal propagates with proletarian internationalism, he appeared surprised that I found in the two doctrines one of the great contradictions in Soviet ideology. Blandly he assured me that a Soviet citizen could be both an ardent patriot and an ardent internationalist, but that a citizen of a capitalist country could not. Touching on the *Communist Manifesto*, I asked if he didn't think it dated because in the century since it was written history has invalidated the predictions of Karl Marx and Friedrich Engels. No, he thought that those predictions were as valid today as they were then. A lively discussion ensued but we got nowhere, because Holy Writ, which the *Communist Manifesto* is in the Soviet Union, admits of no doubts and to question any part of it is mortal sin. But in the arguing, neither the editor nor his associates assumed the attitude of lofty superiority and haughty omniscience or spoke in the flamboyant rhetoric that blazes out of the magazine they publish. In the flesh they were modest and unaffected, easygoing and genial, as Russians usually are. In no way did they resemble the perfervid crusaders and the paragons of self-righteousness in *Smena*'s pages.

At last the plane began to circle for a landing, and peering out of the window at the tilting earth, I saw through the blue mists that drifted over Leningrad cluster after cluster of gigantic hoisting cranes. Never before had I seen a sight like it in Leningrad or anywhere else in the country. The mechanical monsters were everywhere, signalizing the rise of new factories, new homes, new schools in the marshy land around Russia's second city. They broke up and darkened the beautiful skyline that had always been the glory of the onetime capital of the Czars. But they symbolized the energy and the sweep of new construction.

Indeed, construction on a gigantic scale is the one stupendous reality in the Soviet Union today; it was to hit my eyes and stir my mind wherever I traveled, in the Ukraine, in White Russia, in the Cossack Kuban, in Central Asia, above all in Siberia—Russia's least-known country and her most fabulous treasure house of natural resources. It proclaims an infinitely greater truth than all the high-flown words of self-congratulation and self-adulation in the Soviet press and in Soviet oratory. It is, in fact, the one incontrovertible and overwhelming truth about the Soviet Union.

2.

LENINGRAD
Citizenry on Parade

In Leningrad I stopped at the Europa Hotel, where I had often stayed in the prewar years. A tall, robust, ruddy-faced porter brought up my baggage, and after he set it down he straightened up and stood before me with an expression of expectancy. As I had not yet changed my dollars into rubles, I said, "I'm sorry, I have no Russian money, not a single ruble."

"I'm not asking for anything," he replied, but continued to stand before me grinning.

It was only in the early years of the revolution that Soviet serving personnel—doormen, porters, waiters, chambermaids, elevator operators, barbers, though not all of them—scorned tips as an insult to their person. But the idealism of those proud days has long ago vanished; and can anybody blame Soviet hotel attendants for reaching out for an extra ruble? Salaries are low, from forty to sixty of the new rubles a month (forty-four to sixty-six dollars at the official rate of exchange), and prices are high. So the capitalist custom of tipping has survived all Communist propaganda against it.

I unlocked a bag and came up with a cake of soap, which on all my previous visits to the Soviet Union hotel attendants had gratefully accepted. To my astonishment the burly porter frowned, mumbled a displeased *spasibo*, and stalked out of the room.

This was my first intimation that soap was no longer the prize gift it had once been. I was to discover that it was plentiful and of a better quality, though the price was still high—from the equivalent of twenty-five to fifty cents a cake. Westerners may take the universal availability of soap as much for granted as that of bread and salt, but in the Soviet Union even in the more comfortable prewar years the people were plagued by periodic shortages of it. The quality was so poor that often it would not lather up and it frequently irritated the skin. Now nobody needed to go without soap or curse the chemical industry for turning out an execrable product.

The Europa Hotel was built in Czarist times—solidly, spaciously, luxuriously—for a wealthy clientele. Its very name signified Western comforts and services. With the coming of the Soviets both had woefully deteriorated. I was not the only guest there who often discovered that "room with bath" might mean a bathroom with no tub, or tub with no plug, so that one had to contrive a stopper from anything at hand (I always used a wad of paper tied in a handkerchief). Now, at least in my room, nothing was missing, not a bulb, not even toilet paper; no faucet dripped; the toilet flushed, with no annoying after-gurgle of water into the bowl. If there was no plug in the washbasin, it is because Russians do not believe in washing up in dirty water. There was even a wastebasket in my room, soap in the bathroom, stationery on the table, a blotter, two inkpots, a penholder with a shiny new point. Never before had Intourist been so solicitous for the convenience of foreign visitors. If it didn't provide a telephone book it was because higher authority had ruled against it. But anybody who wishes to look up a telephone number may go to the post office and ask for the book. He will get it promptly without the need of producing a passport, with no trouble at all.

Though Intourist had refurbished the Europa and given it a Western look, it was conspicuously lacking in the taste and coziness I enjoyed in Helsinki's Vaakuna Hotel. An air of stuffiness breathed out of the heavy plush window draperies and out of the curtains around the bed, out of the huge shiny walnut wardrobe and the over-stuffed furniture. Nothing was missing for convenience and comfort, yet everything was heavily ornate and cheerlessly ostentatious. That was the way patrons in Czarist times must have loved it and that was the way Intourist chose to keep it, perhaps to persuade the foreign visitor that the thirty dollars a day he was paying (including meals and tourist services) was no extortionate price for the privilege of sharing the somber opulence of the rich and elite of Czarist times.

I didn't linger in my room. The street called me, as it always does when I arrive in a Russian community, where promenading is a popular diversion. I know of no more enlightening experience for a journalist, especially if he speaks Russian, than to join this parade immediately after his arrival, when his senses are freshly keyed to the passing scene. The appearance of the people, their voices, their gestures, their general demeanor, the casual words he catches, the incidents he observes, tell a story he will never read in Smena's or Pravda's pages.

I sauntered out on the Nevsky, Leningrad's and Russia's most majestic street. It was the month of June, a month of white nights, and a pale light lingered in the sky. The last time I had walked the Nevsky, in the winter of 1944, shortly after the liberation of Leningrad from nine hundred days of cruel German siege, the street still went by the cumbersome name of Prospect (of) October 25th, the name given it by the bolsheviks in commemoration of the date (1917) they seized power. Now it was just the Nevsky (Prospect) again, as it had been for over two centuries.

The change in the name of the street seemed symbolic of other changes I observed at every turn. The pavement of wooden blocks has given way to shiny asphalt. The electric trams that once clanged along the broad and immaculate avenue have been replaced by gleaming, quietly rolling buses. The gruesome devastation that German bombs and artillery shells had wreaked on the unyielding city was all cleared away. The shattered and gutted buildings had been repaired, and the architectural glory of the famous street again captivated the eye.

The Nevsky was crowded with promenaders from the golden-spired Admiralty to the domed Nevsko-Troitzky Monastery for a distance of over two miles. What first struck my attention was the dress of the people. I had never known Leningraders to be as well dressed as they were now. I was not comparing the Nevsky with Broadway or Fifth Avenue, nor with Helsinki's Alexander Street or Mannerheim Square. I was only comparing the Leningrad of today with the Leningrad I knew in the prewar years, and the contrast was astonishing.

The white-kerchief head covering for women and the shapeless proletarian cap for men were the only articles of apparel that had survived the threadbare prewar years. But only older women wore kerchiefs and only few of the men wore caps. Women and girls carried handbags, wore wrist watches, and gloves too were common, small luxuries they could only have dreamed of in former times. Men also sported wrist watches, which brought to my mind the zeal with which Russian soldiers of World War II detached watches from the wrists of men and women in Western countries. They hadn't spared even Czechs and Slovaks, who greeted them as liberators with songs and cheers, with the result that the Czech and Slovak languages were enriched by the Russian expression *Davai chasui* ("Give me your watch").

Now Russia manufactures her own wrist watches. Windows of jewelry shops gleamed with them. For a country where the average industrial worker or office employee earns from eighty to eighty-five of the new rubles a month, the prices were high, from fifteen to fifty-six of the same rubles ($16.50 to $62.15). But the prices didn't appear to scare away customers. The wrist watch had obviously become a must for the well-dressed man or woman.

Umbrellas, umbrellas! One saw them at every turn, for in Leningrad, as in London, one never knows when it is going to rain, and no longer was there a shortage of umbrellas. Girl after girl wore a plastic raincoat—red, blue, green, gray—lending brightness to the street procession. It was a new sight on the Nevsky, as new to me as the wrist watches and the white gloves.

I was amused to see boys of high school and college age parading around in checked shirts called *cowboika*—derived from "cowboy." Loud and violent had been the crusade against them by Moscow's *Komsomolskaya Pravda* (*Komsomolka* for short), the Communist watchdog of the manners and morals of Soviet youth. To the fighting newspaper, the *cowboika* at one time spelled American vulgarity and even American gangsterism, and it had warned and scolded and shamed young people away from it. But the crusade had fallen flat. The checked shirt was the rage of the moment, rivaling in popularity the Italian-style shirt worn outside the trousers and buttoned across the collarbone. When I was in Kiev, the wife of a college professor spoke so movingly of her son's admiration for both the American- and Italian-style shirt that I presented her with the only checked shirt I had with me.

The girls on the Nevsky were a study in themselves. They weren't pretty, any more than are Moscow girls. To see pretty girls in Russia one has to go to Odessa, to villages in the Cossack Kuban, the Ukraine, and Byelorussia. The Byelorussian girls with their deep and round blue eyes, their luxuriant flaxen hair, are among the comeliest in the country. Nor would the girls on the Nevsky impress a Westerner with their shapeliness. The Russian diet of bread, potatoes, cereals, fat soups, fat meats and sausage, is not conducive to svelte figures. They were broad-hipped, deep-bosomed girls and that's the way Russian men like them.

How often did Russians ask me, "What's the matter with your girls—don't they have enough to eat? Do men really fall in love with them?" Still, there are girls who at last are becoming figure-conscious, and so are their mothers. However slowly, slenderizing is becoming a fashion and a profession in Russia.

Yet the Russian girls, as I passed them on the Nevsky, had attractions that might escape the attention of foreigners who judge girls by their faces and their figures. They had heavy and luxuriant hair and healthy complexions with fresh and often rosy cheeks. They needed little make-up. Girls of high school age wore no lipstick—it's forbidden by the schools—but even older girls of college age didn't always bother with lipstick. In fact, most of them didn't, maybe because educated Russian men, especially college students, take a dim view of painted lips. "I tell my girl," one of them said, "that at her age she can't improve on nature, and why should she even try?" And another, "Don't you think it's disgusting to kiss painted lips?"

One of the greatest appeals of Russian women is their speaking voices; animated and warm and lyrically cadenced, they end a sentence with a dying fall. But the captivating intonation is lost when they speak any other language than the richly voweled Russian. In a foreign tongue, especially English, the voices lose softness and take on a nasal drone, harsh and unmelodious. But on the Nevsky the speech was Russian, the purest spoken in the country, and it was enchanting to catch scraps of dialogue from passing girls and women.

A great change was apparent in the style of women's coiffures. Even high school girls who had been disciplined to demure braids now affected jaunty pony tails. The casual Italian haircut, too, was catching on, having been introduced into Russia by the Youth Festival in the summer of 1957. Russians have lampooned the short haircut as *menginitka* (from "meningitis") or the typhoid style, associating it with patients in hospital wards. Its tousled wind-blown effect has caused it also to be called "the little boy without a mamma."

All along the famous avenue was a parade of permanent waves such as I had never seen before in Leningrad or in any other city. But even to my uncritical masculine eyes, there was something wrong about these permanents: naturally lustrous tresses had been baked to a frizzled stiffness, demonstrating the ineptitude of the new beauty parlors that have mushroomed all over the Soviet Union. The home permanents that can be bought cheaply in any American drugstore have not yet crossed the Soviet frontier. What a happy day it will be for Russian women when they are put on the market, not in driblets but on a mass scale. It will save money, too, for the price of a permanent in a Soviet beauty parlor or barbershop is from two to four of the new rubles without the tip, optional of course, but always gladly accepted.

But, lowering my eyes, I saw that women were better shod than at any time since the coming of the Soviets: round toes, heavy soles, thick flat heels, were visibly out of favor with the younger generation; even spiked heels had come to Leningrad. There was a time when both men and women regarded Czechoslovakian shoes as the height of fashion, but no longer. Even shoes from East Germany are disdained as clumsy and out of style: to be chic in Leningrad a woman must have shoes from farther west. Young men, too, are becoming more fastidious and are demanding the narrow-toed Italian style. Yielding to this insistence, Anastas Mikoyan, Deputy Prime Minister and Moscow's most celebrated international salesman, began to import shoes from West Germany and from Italy. But with the rise of the violent anti-Bonn propaganda, Austria has been favored over West Germany.

In his lively *Inside Russia*, John Gunther writes of such intense Russian addiction to staring at the shoes of foreigners that if Marilyn Monroe were to walk down a street in Moscow "with nothing on but shoes," people would first stare at her feet. I can assure John that nowadays the actress' feet would be the only part of her people would *not* stare at. Now and then as I sauntered along the Nevsky, I passed English-speaking women, obviously American tourists, and nobody paid them the least attention. They were part of the procession and roused neither surprise nor curiosity. A particularly handsome woman, or a woman wearing a flashily styled dress, would of course draw eyes, as she would on the street of a Western city.

Western fashions, improved fabrics, more skilled tailoring, are beginning to catch up with Russian women, and men too, though far more tardily. In the show windows men's clothes looked coarse and tawdry, as though turned out by tailors who had neither the art nor the desire to please customers. But on the stocky backs of Russian men they gave wearers an infinitely more respectable appearance than in former times.

The most sensational thing I encountered on the Nevsky was a display in the window of a women's dress shop: two manikins draped in strapless evening dresses, one green, the other rose-colored. I almost gasped. In all the years I had been going to the theater, the

ballet, the opera, in Moscow and Leningrad and had attended
diplomatic receptions, I had never known a Russian woman, however
highly placed, to appear in such daring dress, with arms and shoulders
bared and quite a bit of bust revealed. Indeed, only a few short years
ago, while the austere Stalin was still alive, *Komsomolka* had thundered against Soviet girls who allowed themselves to be beguiled by
any Western fashions. The official spokesman of Soviet youth denounced these fashions as reflecting the degradation of women in
capitalist countries and fit only for streetwalkers. I happen to be a
subscriber to this most interesting and most intemperate Soviet publication, but of late have rarely read any abusive outbursts against
Western styles in women's dress. I am certain that it isn't because its
scandal-seeking reporters had failed to stumble upon the window
display in the Nevsky dress shop. It could only have been because the
coming of better times had invalidated the old objections. That's
the way the official Soviet mind works: tastes and gratifications that
the tightly controlled economy makes impossible of attainment are
branded degrading; the moment these are within the reach of at
least some citizens, they are acclaimed as proper and distinguished.

There was another display in the same window that startled me:
nylon slips—pink, yellow, green, and blue! I recalled the French
Communist who after viewing the coarse cotton underwear in a
Moscow department store had remarked to a companion, "What
underwear and yet what a birth rate!"

There were no price tags on the dresses, but each slip was tagged
and the prices were inordinately high for a Russian, ranging from
fifteen to twenty of the new rubles.

From all I have observed in Leningrad and later in other parts of
the country, I am constrained to declare that with certain exceptions,
especially among the national minorities in Central Asia, there has
been a revolution in the dress of the Soviet citizenry. Gone are the
traditional Russian and Soviet styles. Gone are the men's short,
long-belted blouses. Gone almost everywhere are the rich-colored
embroidered shirtwaists, aprons, dresses, of the peasantry; only at
parades, on the stage, amateur and professional, do they survive in all
their gay ornateness. Those one sees on Sundays in villages are largely
carry-overs from former times.

Gone most emphatically for men is the outfit that Stalin had made so famous that every party secretary, trade-union chairman, factory director, felt duty-bound to wear it on work and rest days. It was a simple outfit: khaki tunic, khaki trousers tucked inside knee-high leather boots, and a stiff-edged military cap. In style of dress Russia has gone Western with a vengeance.

Khrushchev, as is well known, called on the services of an Italian tailor to dress him up in Western style. Now even village party secretaries have taken to Western business suits. Nor would Khrushchev for one moment think of curbing the newly wakened desire of Soviet men and women to resemble Westerners. He couldn't do it if he tried, any more than the bitter-tongued *Komsomolka*, despite the ferocity of its anti-Eisenhower hate sermons after the breakup of the summit meeting in Paris in May 1960, could quench the yearning of young men for the once execrated American-style checked and hula shirts.

All along the Nevsky were food shops crowded with customers; gone were the sidewalk queues of previous years. I went into one food shop after another and was amazed at the abundance of dairy foods, meats, all manner of delicatessen, pastry, candy, and especially canned foods—stacks and stacks of canned fish, meats, and vegetables. I had never known Leningrad to be so abundantly supplied, though nowhere did I see the piles of imported oranges, apples, pears, tomatoes, that shone in the windows of Helsinki's food shops. Khrushchev's radically revised agricultural policies since 1953 were paying dividends that must have been heartening to Leningraders but only in basic foods. Despite seven cuts since the end of the war, prices have remained high. Here are some of these prices in American money at the new official rate of exchange:

Black bread (1 lb.)	$0.06
Best-brand white bread (1 lb.)	.23
Milk (1 qt.)	.23
Eggs (1 doz.)	1.60
Butter (1 lb.)	1.41
Cheese (1 lb.)	1.31
Ham (very fat) (1 lb.)	1.16
Lard (1 lb.)	1.03
Cow fat (in butterlike lumps) (1 lb.)	1.01

Cow-bone fat (1 lb.)	.91
Pork	1.39
Bacon (1 lb.)	1.11
Boiled chicken (1 lb.)	1.35
Small bar of chocolate	1.82

Significantly, fats were among the most expensive items, pork and beef fat only a little lower than butter. Russians relish fat foods as no other people I know. The fatter the meat, the better they like it; also borsch and soup. I cannot imagine a Russian butcher trimming slices of fat off a cut of meat as American butchers do. To his customers this would be flagrant robbery. Every particle of fat is precious to a people who love fats and who for years have been on short fat rations.

If there were no queues outside the shops, they were everywhere inside. As ever, the Soviet system of service was complicated by bureaucratic procedures. First the shopper goes around, notes prices, does some hard figuring, then queues up by the cashier's window. The cashier, usually a woman, has no cash register. She does all her calculating on an abacus, which of course takes time. Finally the customer pays, receives checks for the kinds and amounts of food he paid for, and drops into another queue by the service counter. If, meanwhile, he has decided to buy a larger amount of sugar, cheese, sausage, anything—or thinks of something he has forgotten—he must go back to the queue by the cashier's window, repeat the procedure of standing and waiting and paying for additional checks, and then go back to the queue by the service counter.

To make shopping easier, Mikoyan has begun to install self-service shops, which do not begin to compare with European or American supermarkets. Nor for some reason do they particularly appeal to Russian women. "I cannot explain the reason," a Russian woman said to me. "Maybe it is because they're so used to the old way that they miss the leisurely browsing, the gossip with other customers, and even the annoyances. When they get into self-service stores, things are too easy. Oh, give them time and they'll get used to it."

The street was more inviting than the shops and so I started strolling again along the Nevsky. More and more people from side streets were swelling the procession of promenaders, and there was nothing in the external scene to suggest dictatorship, terror, East-West feuding, and *Pravda's* vitriolic crusade now against one, now against another Western country. The promenaders appeared as composed and good-natured as are crowds on a comparable street in any Western land. Festively dressed, they were out for companionship, talk, diversion: a girl holding a boy by the wrist with one hand, a bouquet of lilacs in the other, gave a chuckle as I passed her; a tall light-haired young man, a bouquet of lilacs in his hand, walking fast, no doubt on his way to see his best girl; two young men talking animatedly, the words "He shouldn't have missed the goal" falling on my ears, obviously football enthusiasts; a foursome of teen-age girls arm in arm walking fast as though on the way to a party, a foursome of boys walking as fast immediately behind them; a tall man with a goatee—the nearest thing to a beard I had seen—wearing a light summer suit, a gray felt hat, and carrying a cane (obviously a college professor), smiling as he bent his head sideways to say something to a stout woman, probably his wife, walking beside him; a white-kerchiefed woman, evidently a babushka (grandmother), at once servant and patron saint of Soviet households, holding by the hand a pink-cheeked, pig-tailed little girl teasing for an ice cream as they were approaching a white-coated woman selling it from a wheel cart on the sidewalk; wheel cart after wheel cart of ice-cream and soda-water vendors doing a brisk business all along the Nevsky. The Russian appetite for ice cream has risen immeasurably in the years of my absence, and remarkable was the self-discipline of the buyers. They never threw paper wrappers on the sidewalk, but deposited them in the metal urns that were conveniently spaced against the buildings all along the avenue. No wonder the Nevsky gleamed with neatness, with rarely even a cigarette butt soiling the sidewalks.

As I sauntered along I ran into one of those scenes that always enliven a Russian main street. I stopped to buy a brick of ice cream. A knot of promenaders gathered around the cart and were listening to a short stocky man in work clothes, with cap tilted far back on his head and unsteady on his feet, holding forth on the injustice of the woman vendor, who had refused to answer a question he had addressed to her.

"What's the question?" somebody asked.

"An eminently civilized question, *tovarishchui*," the man answered, swaying from side to side. "I asked her if the price of ice cream will go up as did the price of vodka."

"I told him," the woman shot out angrily, "that I cannot answer the question."

"Why not?" the drunk shouted. "Don't you sell ice cream? Don't people buy it from you?"

"But I don't set the prices," the woman snapped back.

"True, true," came a mutter of voices.

"Why didn't you say so?" the drunk demanded, drawing a step closer to the cart.

"Go away, go away," the woman yelled, gesturing with both arms.

"Why should I go away?" the drunk expostulated. "I asked a civilized question and you tell me to go away." He waited an instant, and when the woman paid no attention to him, he rummaged in his pocket, drew out an identification card, and brandished it before her, his hand shaking as with palsy. "Look! Look! I have nothing to hide. I am a respectable worker, a stonemason, if you want to know, and you—you show no respect for me." Addressing the onlookers, he asked, "Is that right?" Laughter greeted his words.

Disgusted, he stuffed the card back into his pocket, and mumbling to himself, "How uncultured you are, all of you," he staggered away, merriment accompanying his departure.

How often have I heard foreigners say that Russians don't smile or laugh. To my mind, people who deny Russians the gift of smiling or laughing are victims of long-perpetuated legends rather than observers of reality. Despite all the horrors they have endured since the coming of the Soviets or throughout their history, the smile and the laugh have been no more alien to Russians than to Americans and Britishers when there is something or somebody to smile or laugh at. Russians are an irritable, quarrelsome, stubborn, argumentative people. They can argue long and hotly over trivial matters, such as who had the right to board a streetcar or bus first, who stepped on whose toes, why the borsch was not as hot or fat as it should be. But they are also a remarkably sturdy and life-loving people, quick to respond to comic or farcical situations in life, as I had just witnessed, and in literature, as those who have attended literary evenings, especially readings of Gogol and Dickens, or have witnessed Russian theatrical performances know so well.

If *Krokodil*, the Soviet humorous weekly, never provokes side-splitting mirth, it is, for one thing, because authority and all its sacred cows, which in the Western world are ever ready targets of wits, are off limits in the Soviet Union. Even so, neither the self-deified Stalin nor the earthy and ebullient Khrushchev has escaped the acid wit of the people, as anecdotes about them circulated by word of mouth unfailingly attest. "Which hell," St. Peter asked Stalin, "would you like to go to, the Communist or capitalist?" "The Communist, by all means," replied Stalin, "I'm sure there will always be a shortage of fuel there." And about Khrushchev: "Go ahead, Nikita, catch up with America if you can, but for heaven's sake don't run ahead. If you do, people will see your bare behind."

On my way back from the Nevsky Lavra (Monastery), I again paused before the window with the display of the low-necked dresses and the nylon slips. It was the only such display on the Nevsky and I could only assume that the state was making a promise that it was not yet in a position to fulfill. Two young men were standing at the window, and by way of starting a conversation, I said, "Paris styles."

"Are you French?" asked one, a tall, broad-cheeked, light-haired youth, wearing a gray sport jacket and black trousers.

"No, an American."

"A delegate?" asked the other, a stocky youth, shorter than his companion and dressed in a dark-blue serge suit. Since most foreign visitors to the Soviet Union are members of delegations, it was natural for the young Russian to ask whether I was a delegate.

"A journalist," I answered.

They didn't draw away, which was a good augury and discredited the rumors I had heard that Russians were afraid to make the acquaintance of foreigners, especially of journalists, whom the Soviet press had again and again described as unconscionable liars. They appeared as eager to talk to me as I was to talk to them. As we walked along the Nevsky, I learned that one of them was a recently graduated engineer working in a shipyard, and the other still an engineering student. We drifted into a discussion of college life in Russia and America, and I asked if at Russian student balls college girls wore low-necked dresses like the ones in the window.

"Someday they will," said the taller one, whom I shall call Yuri.

"Indeed, they will," echoed the other, whom I shall call Dmitry, with a little laugh.

"Do they in America?" Yuri asked.

"Yes, always," I answered.

Before leaving for Russia I had spent several weeks on the campus of the Hampton Institute, the well-known Negro college in Hampton, Virginia. While there I had attended the annual ROTC officers' dance. The girls wore highly fashionable evening gowns of varied styles and colors. Briefly I described the event to my companions and told them that the girl students made a dazzlingly beautiful sight.

"Did you say it was a Negro college?" Yuri asked.

"Yes."

"Do you mean to say there are Negro colleges in America?" Dmitry asked.

"There are many Negro colleges in America," I assured him.

Neither man had heard of this, which didn't surprise me, for the Soviet press never mentions a single favorable or civilized aspect of Negro life in America.

"Do any white students go there?" Yuri asked.

"They can if they want to," I said, "but they don't, not American whites. But there was one white student there, a Hungarian, who ran away during the revolution of October 1956."

Silence followed, neither man saying a word, and I refrained from drawing them into discussion of the Hungarian revolution. I had only met them, and they appeared so sociable that I didn't wish to run the risk of frightening them away. I in fact regretted having mentioned the Hungarian student at Hampton, for my words seemed to have frozen them. But they didn't leave, and presently Yuri asked, "Were you in Hungary October 1956?"

"No," I said.

"It was a terrible mess," he said. "We wish it hadn't happened, but it was Stalin's fault. He treated the Hungarians unjustly, and don't imagine we aren't ashamed of it." Frank words, which I was surprised to hear from a young Russian engineer. But he didn't continue with the subject, nor did Dmitry, and I didn't press on with it. The few words Yuri had spoken were sufficient to convince me that neither he nor his companion believed the Soviet fable that the outbreak in Hungary against Russia was an American-inspired fascist plot to overthrow Hungary's people's democracy. There were others like them, very many others, as I subsequently learned.

We resumed our discussion of American college life, and then Dmitry said, "It would be interesting to visit America. We know so little about it."

Day after day the Soviet press treats its readers to one American rascality after another, and publishing houses turn out pamphlets and books on the threat of American aggressiveness to world peace, on the poverty of the American worker and farmer, and on other social monstrosities in American life. Yet here was Dmitry pleading ignorance of America!

"If you go to America," I said, "do not fail to visit Negro colleges. Go to Hampton. You will be well received. Negroes are a very warmhearted people."

"Why then do you Americans persecute them so?" Dmitry asked.

The old, old question hurled at me by the first Russians to whom I spoke. It is never easy for Americans to discuss this subject with Russians. Whatever their failings, Russians have never been a raceconscious people. They may be anti-Semitic, as is the Kremlin, they may cherish antipathies toward Poles, their army may massacre Hungarians, but the motivation is social, political, and above all nationalistic. It is never racial. I explained as well as I could the nature of the Negro problem in America, the battles of whites and Negroes against other whites for the full emancipation of the Negro, the defeats sustained, the victories won, the battles ahead. My companions didn't argue with me; they listened politely, I thought, and Yuri remarked, "It's a shame to discriminate against people because of the color of their skin."

"Millions and millions of Americans feel the same way," I said.

Then, as we were approaching the once glittering and now faded and ghostly Kazan Cathedral, we saw a crowd opposite it in the middle of the avenue. We walked over and learned there had been an automobile accident. The two automobiles that had crashed into each other were still there, but an ambulance had already removed the victims of the accident, one of whom, we were told, was very badly injured. A policeman was on the scene and didn't attempt to disperse the crowd. People stood around discussing the accident with a sense of personal involvement as though suddenly aware of the precariousness of human life. Russians are easily shaken by a calamitous occurrence, though one would never know it from reading the Soviet press, which never publicizes accidents. However disastrous a mine explosion, a train or plane wreck, a fire, they are never reported in the newspapers. Occasionally one learns about them in Soviet fiction. Nor are murders and suicides reported, except in instances when they serve a social purpose. These are not news, on the theory, I suppose, that they do not or cannot happen in a socialist country that is "in transition to communism." They do not matter, anyway. Nothing of a tragic nature is of any consequence to the official mind. Yet here were these Leningraders lingering on the scene of the accident and talking about it with a keen sense of tragedy, as though it were something that touched them personally. The human responses which the Soviet press and sometimes Soviet fiction deny them, burst out of them as spontaneously as out of children.

"Have you any accidents in America?"

"Very many," I said.

Instantly I was surrounded, and question after question was flung at me. Despite fierce anti-American propaganda, interest in America had not abated since my last visit. How many automobiles were there in America? How much did they cost? How long did a man have to wait for delivery? Did taxi drivers make much money? Were there women taxi drivers in America? Even the policeman, smoking a cigarette (Russian policemen are permitted to smoke), drew close and listened. Then came a question that was repeated to me over and over wherever I traveled. "Why is America so unfriendly to our country?"

As I didn't intend to involve myself in a debate on the cold war on the Nevsky, I merely said, "Americans say it's your country that doesn't want to be friends with them."

Instantly somebody cried out, "Our people don't want war."

"No, we don't, we don't," came a chorus of voices, and the only answer I felt proper to give to these earnest and moving outcries was to say, "Neither do the American people want war."

"Then why can't our countries be friends?"

"Let's hope we shall be," I said by way of ending the discussion.

How could I tell who was in the crowd and what reports would be made of my replies to the eager and earnest interrogators? The street was no place to match argument against argument. Yet I was amazed at the freedom with which these people spoke to a foreign journalist. Had Stalin been alive, they would have been too cowed even to come near me.

Dmitry and Yuri escorted me to the sidewalk and then we parted. It was only a short distance to my hotel and now I wondered if somebody was shadowing me. I turned and looked and saw nobody who seemed to show particular interest in me. But I was wrong. A young couple had been following, and when I turned the corner they approached me. Excusing himself, the man asked if I would answer a question. I replied that I would if I could. I expected them to draw me into a discussion of peace and war, the subject which had stirred the crowd at the scene of the accident. To my surprise the man asked, "We want to know whether women in America do heavy labor."

"No, they don't," I answered.

"My husband," the woman said, pointing to the man, "and I have heard they didn't, but we want to make certain." The man looked solemn, as though disappointed with my answer, and the woman glanced at him with a smile of triumph.

"Please excuse us for intruding on you," she said, and they walked away, leaving me to speculate on why they were so interested in the subject.

I was so hungry when I got to the hotel that I asked the elevator man to take me up to the restaurant. The long dining room was brightly lighted and, it being Saturday evening, was crowded with customers, chiefly young people. Again I was impressed with their clothes, particularly the girls. Never before had I seen such well-dressed girls in the Europa or anywhere else in the Soviet Union, though in the glare of the restaurant their permanents seemed more frizzled than in the white night of the street.

As I was standing by the door observing the people in the dining room, the large orchestra on the raised platform at the other end of the room crashed into a jazz tune. What powerful players they were! The wood winds squeaked, the brasses screamed, the drums thundered. The portly young woman in a black dress with a red rose on her bosom who stepped over to the microphone and crooned the piece the orchestra was playing in a high-pitched and cracked soprano voice, only sharpened the blare that came out of the instruments—

this in the city of Rubinstein, Tchaikovsky, Rimsky-Korsakov, Mussorgsky, Glinka, Glazunov!

It was even so in the prewar years, and not only in Leningrad. Time and again those of us who lived in Moscow's Metropole Hotel pleaded with the management to spare us the earsplitting entertainment during meals so we could hear each other talk. It did no good. The orchestra continued to blare and thunder and set our nerves on edge, even as the orchestra in Leningrad's Europa was now doing. Managers of Soviet hotel restaurants are still as insensitive to civilized music as they were in the prewar years. One of the great Soviet paradoxes—"contradictions" in the Soviet vocabulary—is the spectacle of a music-loving people being subjected to cacophony in a fashionable restaurant.

But I was in the wrong restaurant anyway, so the waiter to whom I showed my meal tickets informed me. Foreigners ate in the restaurant on the roof, he explained, and when I got there I managed to find a seat at a small unoccupied table far from the orchestra.

I waited and waited and no waiter came. Finally I coaxed a waiter into giving me a menu; then he scurried off and forgot all about me. So did the other waiters. Again and again as they passed by I begged for attention, only to be dismissed with the inevitable *seichas* (right away). If it is an ordeal to obtain a meal in an Intourist hotel restaurant, the waiter is the last person to blame. Like shopping in state food shops, the kitchen accounting which the waiter must endure for everything he orders is so encumbered with bureaucratic procedures that the poor man wastes precious time just waiting around.

I waited a full hour and no waiter came to take my order. Finally tiring of the ordeal, I left the restaurant and went down to my room. From Copenhagen I had brought a bottle of tax-free scotch and several bars of chocolate, and as I was refreshing myself with both, the telephone rang. I lifted the receiver but there was no response. Later, after I had gone to bed, it rang again, and again I was greeted by silence. Two telephone calls from nobody! Had it happened in Helsinki, any Western city, even in Warsaw, I shouldn't have given the incident another thought. Now I wondered whether somewhere within the mysterious labyrinth of Soviet Intelligence somebody was particularly interested to learn whether I was in my room, and if so, why? Was it because I was a Russian-speaking journalist who had often visited the Soviet Union and immediately on his return had walked the Nevsky and engaged in conversation with eager-tongued Russians? The calls might have been an error of the operator at the switchboard, no uncommon occurrence in the Soviet Union. But conscious of the all-pervasive secret service, I set to speculating on the possible origin and purpose of these calls.

Still it was nothing to be disturbed about. Once a foreigner obtains a visa he can count not only on correct but on favored treatment, favored according to Soviet standards of hospitality, which are high, and Soviet standards of execution, which are inexpert and sometimes downright nefarious.

I stayed in Leningrad four days and faced no interference with my movements. I went to places I wished to visit, looked up acquaintances I wanted to see, walked the streets at all hours of the day and night, and engaged in conversation with countless casual acquaintances. And how eager Russians were to talk, especially about America, a country that puzzles and fascinates them, which they admire and fear and which despite *Pravda*'s and *Komsomolka*'s torrential denunciations they do not hate.

Once I got caught in the rain in a newly built neighborhood in the Kirov district. Looking around for a place of shelter, I saw a sign of an automat restaurant. How modern Leningrad was becoming! Nobody ever thought of automats in the prewar years. Yet here it was beckoning to me through the sheets of rain that were pelting the street. I hurried there and when I walked inside a plump, white-kerchiefed woman informed me rather severely that the place wouldn't be open until noon. I told her who I was and that I had come not to eat but to see what a Soviet automat was like. Instantly her expression changed and she was all humility and friendliness. Her name was Emma Moiseyeva and she was the director of the automat. She introduced me to her co-workers, who seemed as pleased to have an American drop in on them as she was. Then she took me into the enormous kitchen that faced a rear street green with young trees and grass and flower beds. She introduced me to the two men in the kitchen, the chef, tall, heavy, white-aproned, white-coated, and white-capped, and the baker, a lean and lively man who was dressed like the chef. With pride the baker told me that the kitchen was wholly electrified—cooking ranges, bake oven, Frigidaires, cleaning apparatus, everything. No kitchen could be more modern, more clean, and more sanitary, the wiry and talkative baker, a war veteran, proudly assured me. He had just baked a cake and, of course, I had to taste it and tell him how it compared with American cakes. It was excellent cake and I showered him with praise. Would I have coffee, cocoa? Would I stay for lunch? The specialty for the day was pork chops and I would eat as tasty chops as I would in America. I declined the invitation to lunch but couldn't talk myself out of another piece of cake. The kitchen glowed not only with white uniforms and white lights but with gay and warm sociability.

Only a few dishes were served in the cylindrical revolving containers, and that was because the factory that made them was still experimenting with automatic equipment, the director explained. Most of the dishes were served cafeteria style, a style that is sweeping the Soviet Union—in factories, colleges, offices, and for the general public. The choice of foods in this cafeteria, as in the others I had seen, was, by American standards, severely monotonous. The juices, fruits, salads, dairy foods, meats, fish, desserts, that dazzle the eye in an American cafeteria are unknown anywhere in Russia. But bread, all anyone cares to eat—and Russians are hearty bread eaters—is free. The soups are excellent and so are the kashas; the portions of meat are small and prices are about one fourth what they are in hotels: a plate of pork chops and vegetables costs nowadays only twenty-two kopecks, and a deep bowl of *kissel*—Danish dessert, as Russians call it—which, together with ice cream, is one of the most delicious desserts anywhere one goes in Russia, comes to only five kopecks. A man can eat cheaply in Russia if he knows where to go for his meals; and if he patronizes a cafeteria, he avoids the nuisance and exasperation of the incredibly laggard service in hotel restaurants.

When I left the automat, the entire staff bade me a hearty farewell and invited me to come again whenever I returned to Leningrad.

In Russia, railroad stations are not merely places where a person gets on or off a train. Distances are enormous and a journey may last a long time—nine to ten days from Leningrad to Vladivostok—and tickets are not always readily available, nor are connecting trains for passengers in transit. Again and again people are obliged to lay over at the railroad station, alone or with families. They eat and divert themselves and sleep there. That is why in large cities railroad stations partake of the nature of a clubhouse and a dormitory, and no policeman would think of waking a sleeping passenger, as in New York. Of course, there are no beds, but the benches and floor do as well, and when Russians go on a long journey they often take with them bedding and food, the best food that they can afford or that they grow on their own land. A train journey, whatever its purpose, is always a vacation, a time to relax, to talk, to sing, and above all to eat and drink endless glasses of tea.

I made the rounds of several of the railroad stations in Leningrad. They were cleaner and better lighted than I had ever known them to be. Indeed, in cleanliness and lighting, they compare favorably with any railroad stations in the world, and as I walked around I was struck by the respectable appearance of the waiting passengers. Men, women, and children, wherever they may have come from, were well shod and well dressed in Western-style clothes. Peasants eating raw salted pig fat with thick-sliced bread looked as respectable as cityfolk. Were it not for the pig fat, as favorite a food now as in Czarist days, I couldn't have identified them as peasants. And another striking change about the passengers: few carried their belongings in grain sacks or even in *korziny* (woven reed baskets, sometimes the size of small trunks). Fiber suitcases have displaced the sacks and the *korziny* of even the peasants, and some passengers fitted the suitcases into white cloth casings to prevent damage. Nowhere was there a sight or smell of the muzhik as I had formerly known him: no beards, no home-woven *svitky* (woolen cloaks), no *lapti* (hand-made bark sandals), which I had frequently seen during the war years; and no mother sitting on the floor searching for lice in the hair of a child.

To me these were all significant features of a new culture, to use a hackneyed Soviet word, of which I was getting only glimpses in the railroad stations of Leningrad. New also—astonishingly so—was the use of white bread by waiting peasant passengers, the white bread that had been a luxury of luxuries when I was a child in a Russian village over half a century ago. Russia is rapidly becoming a wheat-bread-eating country, not only in the Ukraine and the Northern Caucasus, which have always been wheat-growing regions, but in Byelorussia and in the northern provinces that had been pre-eminently rye-growing lands. No longer need a village youth save kopecks for a white roll for his best girl on Christmas or Easter, as youths did in my native village in the old days.

The coming of wheat bread to the peasantry is in my judgment a highly significant fact in Russian history. It carries with it among other things a sense of higher status, as do city-made shoes and clothes and gold teeth.

Russia is under compulsion to grow increasing amounts of wheat not only because of its aggressive foreign policy, in which wheat is a weapon of economic and political infiltration, and not only because hens lay few eggs and cows give little milk without grain feeding, but because of fast-growing consumption of wheat bread.

On the eve of my departure from Leningrad I went to see an old friend whom I first met in the middle twenties in a Volga city where he and his wife, whom he had recently married, were teaching school. Because in those days pupils mocked Pushkin, Turgenev, and Tolstoy as bourgeois-aristocrats who couldn't have written anything of importance for proletarians, he gave up teaching, moved to Leningrad, where he studied accountancy, and got a job with an industrial organization while his wife continued to teach school.

The man's name was Fyodor Alexandrovich, his wife's Larissa Petrovna, and in the prewar years during my frequent visits to Leningrad I always called on them in their one-room flat of an eight-room apartment that was inhabited by seven other tenants, all sharing the same kitchen and the same bathroom facilities.

They were living in the same flat and greeted me with the burst of warm exclamations with which Russians greet an unexpected visitor. It took Larissa some minutes to get over the surprise at my sudden appearance. "And you remembered us," she half chanted, "and are actually here—it's incredible—on my word."

Larissa set the table and fetched wine and vodka, ham and sausage, cheese and canned crab, bread and butter, and the inevitable cucumbers, the only fresh vegetable available at the time in Leningrad.

As we drank, ate, and talked Larissa told me about their three children—two sons and a daughter. The oldest son was killed in the war on the Leningrad front. The younger son was a physicist working in Moscow; he was married to a Moscow girl who was a bacteriologist and they had a little girl of their own. Their daughter was the most adventurous soul in the family. She had studied geology, married a fellow student also a geologist, and both were in Siberia working with a large geological expedition in the Krasnoyarsk region.

"We get such glowing letters from her," Fyodor said, "because their expedition is all the time discovering new natural resources. That's where you should go, my friend, and see for yourself what a rich country our Siberia is—it's our America—and think of it—we used to speak of Siberia as a 'prison without windows,' 'a snowy desert.' If I had to live my life over again, I too would study geology, go to Siberia, and join a prospecting expedition—on my word, I would. It's such an exciting life—you are always out in the open, face to face with nature, nature at its wildest as it is in Siberia, and you are always searching for something new and what a feeling of triumph it must give a man to stumble on a hidden treasure. . . . It isn't like sitting in the same office day after day and living in the same"—sweeping his eyes over the room—"wretched hole, year after year—and—"

"Come, come, my dear," the wife interrupted. "No use grumbling now when by autumn we shall move into a new place, only one room but with a kitchen and bathroom all to ourselves. It will be such a delight to have real privacy at last. You have no idea how sick we all are of communal living."

Fyodor Alexandrovich tossed up his head and smiled on his wife as though suddenly cheered by the prospect of living in privacy. "Yes," he said joyfully, "it'll be quite a blessing, like starting life anew, and it's about time we did after all we have endured these many years."

"And no *kerosinka* [kerosene cooker] any more," Larissa said with enthusiasm. "We'll have a gas and an electric range and a vacuum cleaner and a Frigidaire, too. It will be such a joy to keep house, and when our son and his family come to visit us, they won't have to sleep on the floor. We shall have a bed for them. Poor children! The city of Moscow has no living space for them, so they rent a room from a private family, a bunch of parasites, for five hundred [old] rubles a month—think of it—five hundred rubles a month when all our son earns is a thousand rubles a month. If it wasn't for his wife working, they wouldn't have enough to eat."

"Don't forget, my dear," the husband said, "that Moscow too is building new apartment houses and sooner or later our son and his family will have a place of their own in a new apartment house." Turning to me, he went on. "Things are looking up for us in our dear old Russia, and now let's drink a toast to the friendship between your country and ours."

We drank the toast, and then with a melancholy note in her voice Larissa said, "Do you think there'll be war?"

"Nobody wants war," I said.

Larissa shrugged. "I don't understand it—all this writing about American air bases around our country and America's preparation for war. It haunts us, don't think it doesn't. Whew!"—and she gave a shudder.

Fyodor Alexandrovich laughed a little. "Larissa Petrovna takes everything she reads seriously. I don't. Come, come, my dear, don't spoil the evening with silly talk about war."

"I suppose I am silly," Larissa said, smiling cheerlessly. "But all this writing . . . Oh, well—please excuse me."

When I left, Fyodor Alexandrovich escorted me down and walked with me a few blocks. "A strange thing about my wife," he said, "she never talked about war until our grandchild was born—a darling little girl with golden hair and blue eyes like her mother's. She is our only grandchild and means everything in the world to my wife. Over and over my wife has said to me, 'You and I have lived our lives—good or bad—we've lived it. But our little granddaughter—why should anything happen to her?' That's how scared she is of war, scared the little girl will be killed. Imagine it! As though we didn't have an army and sputniks and atomic and hydrogen bombs and missiles. I keep telling my wife that no nation would be mad enough to attack us, but it does no good. She worries herself to distraction and it's all because our press writes so much about American aggressiveness and American preparation for war. Heaven only knows why they do it when we are so strong. I wish they didn't. Would to God they didn't."

3.

MOSCOW
Citizenry on Parade

After Leningrad, Moscow looked like a busy bazaar jammed with people always restlessly on the move. Of course, Moscow, being much larger than Leningrad—over five million people against over three million—has heavier traffic. Yet people in the capital appeared less composed, less disciplined, and far less mannerly. They walked faster and defied traffic signals more recklessly. When a motor vehicle swung into a crowded street or square, pedestrians scattered in all directions like startled chickens, cursing or clucking at their narrow escape.

Like Leningraders, Muscovites were much better dressed than I had ever known them to be, though compared with Leningraders they still looked a little dowdy. When I commented on the contrasts I was observing between Muscovites and Leningraders to the Intourist functionary who met me at the railroad station and drove me to the hotel, he replied a little sharply. "It isn't us Muscovites; it's the provincials who stream daily into the city. They dim the true colors of Moscow."

There was truth in his words, but not the whole truth. Leningrad has a tradition of good manners, an inheritance from the aristocracy of Czarist times, which didn't completely perish in the revolution. Moscow too had its highly cultivated gentry, as readers of *War and Peace* well know. But Moscow was always spoken of as *kupecheskaya Moskva*, "the Moscow of merchants," and the very word *kupetz* (merchant) implied coarseness and cruelty. The aristocracy and the intelligentsia looked down on the *kupetz*, and to the muzhik he was a swindler and a scoundrel. Alexander Ostrovsky, the famous nine-teenth-century playwright, left undying portraits of the greed, the meanness, the brutality, of the *kupetz*, even as Tolstoy left undying portraits of the urbanity, gentility, and generosity of the aristocracy.

"But Moscow has always been the heart of Russia," a Moscow-born college girl once said to me, "and it's a warm heart. I freeze up when I go to Leningrad. People are so cold there." The very coldness of which the girl complained implies a poise and reserve that are the essence of refinement. Where in Moscow is a customer treated with such courtesy as in Leningrad's House of the Book? And where in Moscow are there cafes whose very atmosphere forbids coarseness and loudness as do such cafes as Leningrad and Sever (North) in Russia's second-largest city?

The Moscow of today is one of the most exciting cities in the world, but when I hear Muscovites speak of it as *krasavitsa* (beautiful), which they do all the time, I feel somewhat puzzled. I never shared their judgment, either when I first knew it in the early twenties, when it was a jumble of crooked streets, twisted corners, muddy courtyards, squalid squares, or now, when audacious city planning and energetic reconstruction have made it a remarkably clean city, with broader avenues and more spacious squares than any other city I know. Of course, there is the high-walled sixty-five-acre Kremlin with its fabulous churches and palaces and the ever exciting Red Square with its fantastically colored Cathedral of Vasily the Blessed, a museum now. But without the Kremlin and Red Square, Moscow would be one of the least attractive cities on earth. The seven skyscrapers that were built at Stalin's behest, crude and overornate imitations of the old Woolworth Building in New York, only emphasize the city's architectural banality. In all the years of struggle for a socialist style of architecture that would glorify the age of "the new man," all Russian architects have achieved is a crude and sometimes nightmarish imitation of Western architecture. Khrushchev knows it and the architects knew it all the time, but were timidly silent. At last they are speaking up. "We are reconsidering," writes A. V. Vlasov (*Izvestia*, November 28, 1959), member of the Academy of Architecture, "the concept of beautiful architecture . . . which was associated with superficial ostentatious display." Moscow's Leningrad and Ukraina skyscraper hotels—agglomerations of marble, candelabra, and bronze—Vlasov rightly condemns as "vulgar distortions and extravagances."

But as I strolled the streets of the city, I grew aware of new features in the familiar scene. Never before had Moscow worn so resplendent a green dress. Tall linden trees now shaded the sidewalks outside the Metropole Hotel, and the once bare Gorky Street, which *stilyagy* ("style chasers") have renamed Broadway, was green with sturdy, thick-foliaged and sweet-smelling lindens. Between the trees, flowers in round cement basins made bright splashes of color. So it was on street after street.

Moscow militiamen, except those who direct traffic, love to talk. When I told one of them on a beat at the upper end of Gorky Street of my surprise at finding so much new greenery in the city, he smiled with pleasure and said, "Yes, our Red capital is becoming greener and greener from day to day. This year alone we are setting out a hundred and forty thousand new trees, a million shrubs, and about fifty million flowers. How is it in New York?"

An official of the city told me that already 1677 streets in Moscow were lined with trees and that in the southwest residential section a new park of 300 hectares (740 acres) was planted. There were fifty-five other parks in the city, eleven of them so densely wooded that they were spoken of as little forests.

On a side street off Gorky Street, I wandered into a courtyard that I knew well. In the rear, in a tall brick building, lived a family that I often visited during the war years. Like a village street, the courtyard had been pock-marked with water holes and mud puddles, hazards in the blackout, and I often appeared at my friends' door splashed with mud. Now the water holes and mud puddles were filled up and the yard surfaced with yellow sand. A clump of tall trees shaded the rear of the yard; under the trees stood a long wooden table surrounded by benches. In the center was a sand pile where two little boys and a little girl were playing, while a kerchiefed babushka, snugly ensconced on a bench under a gaily colored beach umbrella, was watching them. The muddy and unsightly courtyard had been transformed into a playground.

The house looked older and more dilapidated than I remembered. I walked up the three dark flights of stairs to find my old friends. Only the old peasant housekeeper was home. We exchanged gossip about personal affairs, and when I told her how impressed I was with the courtyard, she said, "It's so comforting to come out of the house after work hours and sit in the shade of the trees. We all do it; first the older people, who sit around, talk, play cards, chess; and when they leave and retire for the night, young people take over. The poor things have no privacy in their crowded homes, so they sit under the trees and do their courting." So now it's courtyards for courting.

I sauntered into other courtyards and it was the same story—the grounds graded and sanded, set out with trees and sometimes with shrubs and flowers, and so many of them glittering with gaily colored beach umbrellas.

If the trees, the grass, the shrubs, the flowers, with which Moscow courtyards are dressed up, lend the city a fresh radiance, the reappearance of the fat man in the street lends it a comical touch. Originally, in the early years of the revolution, the fat man had been the symbol of the capitalist, the priest, the kulak—in short, the exploiter who swilled the blood and glutted on the flesh of the prostrate proletarian. Cartoons satirized him, the variety stage derided him, orators denounced him. During the lean years of the early Plans, the fat man practically vanished from the Russian scene. In the autumn of 1932, when I piloted the late Alexander Woollcott around Moscow, his paunchy figure drew stares and evoked snickers everywhere we went.

Today nobody on Gorky Street or Red Square would give Woollcott a second glance. Now the fat man is neither novelty nor curiosity. Khrushchev's paunch has inspired some cynical university student to come up with this anecdote: Says one student to another, "Do you know we've already beaten America in the production of meat?" "How do you make that out?" asks the other. "Well, doesn't Khrushchev weigh twenty kilos more than Eisenhower?"

Often enough the fat man in Moscow wears a colonel's or general's uniform. Life seems to have gone well for the high-ranking officers —too well not to disturb Marshal Zhukov, when he was Minister of Defense, with the deterioration of the military posture of his subordinates. Shortly before his dismissal from office he issued a decree ordering those in sedentary positions to exercise vigorously for two hours three times a week. Though Marshal Malinovsky, the new Soviet Minister of Defense, has not revoked the order, it hardly seems to have been conscientiously obeyed, even by Malinovsky himself.

Startlingly new were the flocks of pigeons that strutted about and fluttered over the main streets and squares of Moscow. "How like London!" "How like Paris!" "How like Rome!" "How like New York!"—tourist after tourist exclaims, much to the delight of Intourist guides. The pigeons were accomplishing the purpose for which they were intended, to give Moscow, the most Russian of cities, a Western look, which no foreign visitor fails to observe.

But the Intourist chauffeur who once drove me to the American Embassy for my mail took a dismal view of the innovation. "These pigeons," he scoffed, "are a real pest; they foul up streets and buildings and are a devilish nuisance to automobile drivers; they always have the right of way, so the militiamen tell us, and we must put on the brakes when they pop up in front of us. Pfui on them!" Then he added, "Some morning we shall wake up and see no more pigeons. We'll read in the press that they died during the night from bellyache. That's what's going to happen, and if it doesn't— well—it won't be long before the Metropole Hotel in which you live will be fouled up with their droppings."

Should the Moscow authorities discover that the pigeons are more of a nuisance than an asset—a prestige asset—it won't be beyond them to dispose of the birds by giving them a bellyache. But I don't believe it will happen and it would be a pity if it did. Cruelty to animals is an ancient Russian failing, and despite all Soviet education it lingers on, especially among children. There are very few dogs in Moscow—one can walk for hours in the thickly settled residential districts without seeing or hearing a single dog. It is expensive to feed a dog, and in the cramped living quarters there is no place to keep him. But Moscow has plenty of cats, and incidents of boys tormenting them for the fun of it or throwing them from roofs are not uncommon. But children love the pigeons, and the presence of the birds inculcates in them a much needed respect and fondness for living things.

Getting reacquainted with Moscow brought to view other changes. Rarely did I see a woman smoke in the streets, and when I did she was invariably an older woman, who may have contracted the habit in the earlier Soviet era, perhaps in the golden and tumultuous NEP (New Economic Policy) years (1921–28), when like American flappers of the time, Russian girls flaunted their emancipation by incessant smoking. Now it was out of fashion for women to smoke in public and girls didn't, neither in Moscow nor in any other city I visited.

The men one passed appeared clean-shaven. The daily shave has at last caught on in the Soviet capital, where at best the twice-weekly shave had been the custom. If Muscovite men have taken to this daily ritual, it is in part ascribable to the import of Swedish razor blades, and in part to the success of Soviet industry in at last manufacturing an acceptable home product. The colloquial word for safety razor is *gillette*, and I remember once reading in *Krokodil* the definition of the term as an instrument which in foreign countries detached hair from a man's face but which in Russia detached part of the face together with the hair. No longer could *Krokodil* have reason to lampoon the quality of Soviet blades. I found them eminently satisfactory.

But the land of sputniks still manufactures execrable matches. The sticks are thin and break easily; the light flares up and dies quickly. Once I asked a Soviet citizen why the factories were turning out such a poor product. "We're saving our forests," he replied. I thought he was joking and reminded him that his country had more forests than any country in the world. "Think," I said, "of your Siberian forests alone." But he wasn't joking, he assured me. Forests had been wantonly cut down, timber wastefully used, and the time had come to end the reckless ravage. So they save the forests by wasting wood through the breakage of thin matchsticks. I said so to the Russian, and without another word of sermonizing he said, "If you buy matches with the Sukhum trademark, you'll never regret it. The sticks are as solid as nails. Shop around among tobacconists until you find them. I never buy any other kind."

But Moscow appeared cleared of its beggars, one of its most ancient evils; the lame, the halt, the blind, the deformed, the sore-ridden men and women whining and wailing for a *kopeyechka* (kopeck) for bread, were no longer in sight on any of the streets and squares which I had passed. One Sunday I went to the Church of the Old Believers, where beggars had always swarmed at the doorway. Now not a single one was around. "What has become of your beggars?" I asked an elderly woman parishioner. "God only knows," she replied. "May the Queen of Heaven help them, wherever they are." Queen of Heaven! How rarely one hears the expression nowadays in once "Holy Russia"!

But the beggars had not really gone. On Saturday evenings and Sunday mornings one could see them outside the Church of the Epiphany, to which Intourist takes foreigners, the Devichy Nunnery, and some of the smaller churches in the city. But they were gone from the streets and parks and boulevards, and with them has gone the last of Moscow's luxuriant beards. Actually, Moscow became a beardless city in the early thirties, though the mustaches lingered on. Now even the mustache is no longer fashionable.

Yet now and then as I walked about I passed a man who wore one, but rarely was he a Russian. Usually he was a Central Asian or a son of sunny Georgia. To the dark-eyed, dark-haired, lithe-limbed, gracefully stepping Georgian, the mustache is as much a part of his masculinity as his capacity for wine drinking or his vocal rapture over a pretty girl who catches his roving eye. Moscow may rule him politically and economically, but Moscow's fashions and manners impress the Georgian no more warmly than does Moscow's cookery. It is no accident that the one remaining first-class restaurant in the Soviet capital is the Aragwi, managed by Georgians and specializing in Georgian cuisine, music, and gaiety. The newly opened Budapest, presided over by a chef imported from the Hungarian capital, created a stir when it first opened in Moscow, but the glamor is gone, and so is the quality of its cuisine.

More ostentatiously than in Leningrad, youths paraded around in sport shirts. Hatless, coatless, with shirt collars unbuttoned, often with a crew cut, they appeared to glory in the brilliant plaid and checked shirts. Once I was stopped by two young men, one a technician in a factory, the other a typesetter, both wanting to know if I had sport shirts to sell. What a market there is in Moscow for the beach shirt that Harry Truman fancies! But Moscow girls appeared severely conventional—no slacks, no tapered trousers, no jeans, no shorts, however muggy the weather—not yet, anyway. And nowhere in the women's dress shops did I see a window display of the low-necked evening gowns I had seen in Leningrad. But a saleswoman in the block-long GUM (department store) on Red Square assured me that these were coming: not for Moscow to remain behind Leningrad in display of fashions.

Indeed, GUM had a surprise of its own. Dominating a large window, a tall leggy manikin was dressed up in a white silk gown with a long train that was overlaid with a black silk wrap. This was a sample bridal gown. Already on the old Petrovka a special shop was set up to take orders for such gowns, the GUM saleswoman proudly informed me, and with each gown went a neatly printed booklet explaining in rapturous prose the joy and glory of being a bride and giving detailed instructions on how to wear the gown. The festiveness that brightened weddings in old Russia was at last receiving the attention and the blessing of Stalin's successors in the Kremlin.

Another innovation was the sidewalk bookshop. The great hunger for books is one of the most striking features of Soviet life, and the state seems to spare no effort to gratify it. The sidewalk booksellers almost rivaled in popularity the ice-cream and soda-water vendors. I picked up books on these stalls that I couldn't find in bookshops, and one of the pleasures of walking around the city was the freedom of browsing through them and buying books without the need of queuing up before counters and cashier's windows.

There were no comic books on the sidewalk stalls, no Westerns, no paperbacks with gawdy illustrations of semi-nude, bosomy females. But there were Dickens and Galsworthy, Tolstoy and Chekhov and other classics, and Conan Doyle, whose immense popularity has begun to alarm the *Literaturnaya Gazeta* ("Literary Gazette"), Moscow's guardian of literary tastes and fashions. Once I passed a book table piled high with thick, hard-covered Anglo-Russian dictionaries on the following subjects:

Highway construction
Shipbuilding
Radio technology
Geology
Nuclear physics
Electro technology
A pocket medical dictionary
A collection of technical terms in the English language

Eight highly specialized Anglo-Russian dictionaries in science and technology!

How many more Anglo-Russian dictionaries the Soviet Union

has published, I do not know. But the ones I saw on the book table revealed a rather amusing contradiction between Kremlin-conceived Marxism and Kremlin hardheaded realism. On the one hand, Soviet ideologists are jubilantly proclaiming that Anglo-American capitalism is "rotting away," its capacity for progress in science and technology dying, while on the other hand, Anglo-Russian dictionaries are published at prodigious effort and expense, attesting to sober Soviet respect for the very vocabulary of Anglo-American progress in science and technology.

A Russian cook is no more capable of preparing an unsavory borsch than is an upstate New York farm woman of baking an untoothsome apple pie. But there is borsch and there is borsch, and the steaming plate of soup set before me in the dining room of the Metropole Hotel was a keen disappointment. It didn't even compare in taste with the borsch of the severely rationed war years. Not that it was bad—it was quite good—but some precious flavor was missing, some fragrance had gone out of it.

I searched the menu in vain for an old favorite, a dish to which the late Alexander Afinogenov, the distinguished Soviet playwright who was killed in an air raid during the war, had introduced me in this very dining room. The dish was called *gurievskaya kasha*, a casserole of cereal baked with fruit and rushed to the table piping hot out of the oven. I had made many a light lunch and late supper of this superb dish and a glass of tea. I always recommended it to American tourists, and they were always grateful for the recommendation. When I asked the waiter why it was no longer on the menu, he shrugged and said he didn't know—they just didn't serve it any more.

There was a time when Moscow was famous for its pastry, which sophisticated travelers rated as high as any product of the ovens of Warsaw, Prague, or Paris. Now, even in Intourist hotels, the pastry was flat to the taste, and the compotes I was served consisted of a few acid plums afloat in a glass of colored juice or cherries in a saucer of thin syrup. Beef seemed to have been cut from the boniest part of an aged and undernourished steer; steaks were thin and leathery. As for chicken—in the words of an American housewife in Moscow—"there were two kinds: those about to die from undernourishment and those about to die from obesity." They were either too lean or too fat. Intourist hotels served chicken with more bone than meat. The plump meaty broilers arrayed to catch the housewife's eye in an American supermarket or in a Danish butcher shop are unknown in Russia. But the ice cream is of the choicest in the world.

From the quality of meats served in the best hotels in Moscow, I concluded that Soviet farms either have failed to master the ABCs of feeding livestock or are simply short of fodder and grain—this despite the one hundred million acres of virgin land that have recently been plowed up and seeded to grain. Significantly, in all his optimistic predictions of surpassing America in meat production Khrushchev puts all emphasis on quantity. He never mentions quality.

Being no gourmet, I eat anything set before me. Still, I was conscious of the fact that Russian cooking of today is sadly inferior to that of the years of my previous visits. The old cuisine is gone, a casualty of Russia's muscular civilization. When I asked an elderly waiter whom I have known for many years what had happened to the cooking in Moscow's best hotels, he answered gloomily, "What do you expect? The old masters have gone and the new cooks are ignorant and don't give a damn."

Were Chekhov alive now he couldn't create the epicure Ivan Gurych (in his short story "Siren"), who enraptures himself with talk of dishes that "keep the appetite at pitch." These dishes are a memory now. Foreigners who visit the Soviet Union get more than enough to eat. The caviar, of course, is excellent, and so are the smoked salmon and sturgeon, ancient Russian specialties. But of the celebrated old Russian cuisine they will get barely a taste.

In an effort to develop the housewife's culinary skills Moscow publishes innumerable cookbooks; but except for women whose husbands' earnings can support the family, few have the time or the energy for the preparation of dishes for which Moscow was once famed. There are, of course, training schools that teach mass-production methods of institutional cookery, but an ambitious boy or girl would scorn the career of chef as lacking in glamor and social standing. The revolution that had set out to make labor, however menial, "an honor and a glory" has failed to root out a revulsion against certain occupations: housework, barbering, waiting on table, portering, clerking. Invariably university students looked incredulous when I told them that many American students earned part or all of their living expenses by clerking, waiting on table, baby-sitting, working as garage hands or attendants at filling stations, and felt no disgrace in performing any kind of manual labor. This fear of loss of status is another of the more obvious contradictions that beset the society of "the First Workers' and Peasants' Republic in the World."

But Moscow is in desperate need of good cooks, of armies of them, and to break the resistance of young people and to get them to enter the profession by way of the cooking schools, it has resorted to the one unfailing method at its disposal—material incentive. Even so, the profession doesn't attract status-conscious boys and girls.

On my first day in the Soviet capital I walked for hours and hours from one part of the city to another, and not once did I observe people quarreling in the streets. I marveled at the serenity that had come over the Soviet capital, which I had always regarded as one of the most ill-tempered in the world. Only thirteen years earlier it had seemed to me that one of the favorite pastimes of Muscovites was to pick a quarrel with a neighbor or a stranger. People quarreled not over ideology but over personal affronts, real or fancied. Once I had seen two drunks come out of a beer hall, one threatening to smash the head of the other if he didn't confess that he had deliberately spilled his glass of beer over him. People who were hanging on the steps of a streetcar or bus, like bananas on a stem, were often shouting insults at one another, one citizen accusing the other of choking the breath out of him, crushing his toes, or slipping a hand into his pocket. Those who stood in queues outside shops wrangled with one another over their respective places in line. Common was the sight of a militiaman clutching the arm of a citizen who tugged and squirmed and refused to be arrested; the scene always attracted passers-by, who joined in the verbal tilt between the officer of the law and the victim of his clutching hand.

Now people appeared surprisingly tranquil and good-humored, and it was easy to understand the reasons for the new serenity. Despite still prevailing annoyances and hardship, everyday life had become immeasurably more comfortable. The dread of midnight arrest no longer haunted Muscovites. Conditions that had formerly irritated or incensed them were changed or mitigated. Shining trolley buses rolled along almost one after another and the magnificent subway was substantially lengthened; transportation was no longer the agony it had been.

There were many more food shops and rarely any queues on the outside. Shops were abundantly supplied with basic foods, and such luxuries as pastry and candy and ice cream of course were plentiful. But there was a marked shortage of fresh vegetables, and shriveled egg-sized oranges were the only fruit available. It was the end of June, and May and June are spoken of in Moscow as "hungry months"—months of craving for fresh fruits and vegetables. However, hothouse cucumbers and fresh garden radishes were already on the market.

But then Russians do not share the American appetite for green vegetables. In the words of a Russian woman, they detest spinach, turn up their noses at lettuce, give cauliflower and asparagus a cold stare, make a wry face at artichokes whenever sunny Georgia sends them north. Give Russians cucumbers, cabbage, onions, garlic, potatoes, beets and, with the usual exceptions, they wouldn't care if all other garden produce vanished from the earth. On a farm in Byelorussia I met a plant breeder who was experimenting with early varieties of leaf lettuce (head lettuce is unknown) and onions. A talkative man, he eloquently lamented Russian indifference to his exhortations that they cultivate an appetite for lettuce because it is rich in vitamin *tse* (C). "Do you know what they say to me?" he complained. "They say, 'The only vitamin *tse* we want is *yai-tse* [eggs], *masl-tse* [butter], *sal-tse* [pork].'"

Hearty eaters, Russians are essentially a soup-and-bread, potatoes-and-meat-eating people, and now at the end of June, when radishes and cucumbers were already on the market, though both were expensive—I heard none of the vociferous grumbling that I had heard on earlier visits to Moscow over shortages of vegetables.

For sentimental reasons, I walked over to the Borisoglebsky Alley, north of the Arbat. In the twenties and early thirties, in a house that had been originally leased by the English and American Quakers, who had done relief work in Russia, a succession of British and American correspondents rented rooms and apartments. Henry Chamberlain and his wife lived there; so did Spencer Williams and

Malcolm Muggeridge; and in 1933, fresh out of China, Demaree Bess, then with the *Christian Science Monitor*, and his wife descended on Moscow with two white-gowned, ever smiling Chinese servants, who were the best cooks in Moscow. I too occupied a room there one summer, and I cherished the memories of the lively gatherings in the so-called Quaker House.

I remembered the Borisoglebsky as a dingily lighted, unevenly cobbled street, shiny with mud puddles. Now, though the little street was asphalted and set out with tall trees from end to end, its low brick houses and wooden cottages sagged with age and neglect. Plaster was falling from the walls, windows were aslant, roofs seemed sinking. It is amazing how dilapidated Moscow can look once one gets away from the main avenues. Not even the new greenery can conceal the sad condition of the crumbling houses, too old to be renovated and still needed too much to be demolished—which is what is planned for them for the foreseeable future.

At the lower end of the street was a little park, oddly named Dog's Square. Here were rows of lindens, poplars, and elms, with grass and flower beds under the trees. Gravel paths that crisscrossed the little park were lined with benches. Kerchiefed old women and old men in rumpled caps occupied the benches, staring languidly at nothing or gossiping in low voices. Obviously they were pensioners, for whom the immaculate and shady park was an oasis in an over-crowded neighborhood.

Along the path two young men, coatless, tieless, shirt collars unbuttoned, were wheeling baby carriages, and one of them was wearing a wedding ring! I stared at the ring to make certain my eyes were not deceiving me. But here it was, a gold ring, gleaming in the sun. For years and years it had been execrated as a symbol of middle-class decay and ostentation, a relic of bourgeois hypocrisy and sanctimoniousness. Now it was back, sanctified and glorified as in any capitalist country.

As I watched the men wheel the baby carriages, which I had seen men do on my previous visits, I wondered if Moscow men, who rarely help a woman with her baggage, however heavy, on and off trains or buses or streetcars, were unbending from the masculine prerogative of leaving all housework to women. It always amused Russians, Communists as much as others, when I told them that

American men didn't disdain helping women wash dishes, sweeping the floor, changing a baby's diaper. To them these were strictly women's tasks. Of course, they believed in the equality of the sexes, which the revolution had proclaimed, but this equality didn't include lending a wife or mother a helping hand in household chores. On inquiry I learned that with rare exceptions the Soviet male was not relinquishing his masculine privilege of immunity to domestic duties. I learned it from those who knew best—their wives and mothers.

I had erred when I had first assumed that street brawls were a thing of the past. They hadn't completely vanished, as I learned one evening when I went walking along Komsomolsky Square, which is always crowded. Here is one of the leading subway stations in the city and three of the more important railway terminals: the Leningrad, for trains to that city; the Kazan, the largest in Moscow, for trains to that Volga city and far beyond—to Central Asia, the Urals, Siberia; the Yaroslavl, from which the Trans-Siberian express starts for Vladivostok on the longest train journey in the world, a distance of some 5600 miles.

On the Komsomolsky I saw drunks that brought to mind the Moscow of prewar years. Well-dressed young men staggered around in gay or somber mood, talking or quarreling with one another. I saw a youth lying on the ground flailing away with fists at two companions who were determined to lift him to his feet and walk him away before the militia hauled him off to a sobering station. I saw two young men, arm in arm, wobbling along the sidewalk singing at the top of their voices, so happy that passers-by smiled on them. Then, as I walked along a more isolated part of the square away from the Kazan terminal, I ran into as cruel a scene as I had ever observed in the city.

An elderly woman, wearing a dark dress and a black kerchief on her head, was shouting curses at a young man who was obviously a *stilyaga*. He was short, stocky, broad-shouldered, with long, wavy light-brown hair, and wore a brown sport jacket and blue ski trousers tied around the ankles. He carried a smooth birch stick that reached to his shoulders. The woman was obviously tipsy but he was cold sober. He flourished the stick over his head as though he were about to hit the old woman. She staggered away, frightened, but soon resumed her stream of imprecations against the *stilyaga*. Several men passed by but didn't stop; they might have been in a hurry to catch a train or might only have become calloused to brawls on the square. As I watched, a young girl darted out of a courtyard and stood wide-eyed by the gateway.

Suddenly the *stilyaga* lifted the cane and struck the woman a blow between her shoulders. She dropped to her knees and began to weep. He struck her again.

"Hooligan!" the girl cried out.

"Shut your mouth, you filthy slut," the *stilyaga* thundered, lifting up his cane.

"Hooligan, hooligan, hooligan!" shouted the girl as she darted away.

Turning to the woman, the *stilyaga* asked, "Will you stop now?" She didn't say a word; she only whimpered.

"Let it be a lesson to you, you stinking creature," he said.

The woman rose to her unsteady feet, and laying both hands on her bosom, she wailed, "No man of woman born are you, no woman's breasts ever suckled you; bastard of a she-wolf, that's what you are: a she-wolf's breasts suckled you, a she-wolf's poison is in your blood—"

"Stop, I tell you," the youth screamed back.

"No bastard of a she-wolf can make me stop." Her voice was low, broken but resolute. Drawing near to the *stilyaga*, she turned her back to him, lifted the kerchief from her neck, and went on wailing. "Here—sink your fangs into my neck—break it—drink my blood, devour my flesh—"

He lifted his cane again, ready to strike her, and though I was no match for him and didn't welcome a fight with anybody in Moscow, I touched him on the shoulder. He brushed me off, then turned and gave me a deep look. Meanwhile, gathering passion, the woman cried out, "Come, you bastard of a she-wolf, here is my bare neck, ready for your fangs—here—here—" And she kept pressing closer and closer to him.

I decided to separate the raging young man from the woman with sweet diplomacy. Smiling, I said, "You are a cultured young man—leave her alone. Here, have an American cigarette."

He hesitated an instant, took the cigarette, held it in his hand,

and as though suddenly contrite, he said: "But she isn't giving me any peace. She is my neighbor—an ugly and mean old hag."

The woman heard him and exploded. "A hag, you say, you thrice-cursed bastard of a she-wolf. Don't listen to him—a mother of five children, that's the kind of hag I am—five children—and they all suckled at my breast. Into the big world they have gone and the Lord be with them—" She broke down and cried with despair.

"Come, let's go away," I pleaded with the *stilyaga*.

We walked in the direction of the Kazan terminal, and in self-defense he said, "She lives in a dark hole of a room next to me and she gives me no peace—always asking for money so she can buy vodka and get drunk. The devil with her." Abruptly changing the subject, he asked, "You are an American?"

"Yes."

"Very glad to know you." He pressed my hand. "Can anybody buy a motorcycle in America?"

"Yes, if he has the money."

"Ah, here you have to be highborn, son of a minister or a factory director or an honored worker, before you can buy one, even if you have the money. There's nothing I'd like more than a motor-cycle, so I could travel away wherever my eyes would lead me. But— the devil only knows—" And after a reflective pause he smiled broadly, showing strong white teeth, and went on: "On my word, I'll get a motorcycle yet—nobody can stop me. There are ways—"

"Why don't you go and get yourself a haircut, *stilyaga*?" a voice broke in on us. The speaker was a youth with a bouquet of flowers in his hand—obviously on his way to see his girl.

"Go and —— your mother, you son of a bitch," the *stilyaga* bawled after him. But the youth loftily ignored the insult. "A Komsomol [a member of the Communist youth organization], wanting everybody to be like him—a plague on them all," my companion growled. Suddenly his face livened. "Did you come to Moscow on a motorcycle?" he asked.

"No, I came by plane."

"Maybe you know an American who came on a motorcycle?"

"No, I don't."

"Really? Don't Americans travel on motorcycles? I'll pay a high price for one—very high—in rubles, of course—I've got plenty of rubles. Surely you know some American who came on a motorcycle?"

"I'm sorry but I don't."

He gave a derisive laugh. "You're not telling the truth. I know you aren't. But—I'll get my motorcycle, and when I do, out of Moscow I scoot, far, far away, maybe to India, maybe even to America. Who knows? Nothing like a motorcycle for seeing the world. So you can't help me?"

I shook my head.

Without another word he walked off into the crowd—an unregenerate youth, with romance and wildness in his heart, a misfit and outcast in the sternly disciplined, self-abnegating, work-driven society.

Peasant market places in cities and villages are the only open sectors of private trade that the Soviets allow. But these are more than trading places, even in Moscow. Buyers and sellers are leisurely and sociable, exchange gossip, tell stories and anecdotes, and bargain over prices as they wouldn't in state shops. One can always obtain glimpses into intimate aspects of Soviet life by visiting a market place.

In Moscow the market places have undergone as rigorous a face lifting as the courtyards. They shine with order and cleanliness. Peasants no longer bring eggs yellow with chicken dung or vegetables crusted with dirt. Now they wash their produce before they bring it to the city. Meats and dairy foods are no longer sold from open-air fly-specked stands. In the Central Market, a new high-ceilinged, brightly lighted brick building towers over the bazaar, and meats and dairy foods are sold only there. As I walked around inside it I saw hardly any flies, a miraculous achievement in a Moscow market place.

And yet, as in Czarist times, in Moscow as in the remotest village, the white-coated women offered customers a taste of their butter, cheese, or cream from the tip of a knife—the same knife used over and over without being washed. Despite all the sanitation crusades since the rise of the Soviets, old Russia lingers on in the market place.

In one of the smaller markets I stopped at a stand at which a hefty woman was selling spotlessly clean but very small eggs.

A bareheaded, freckle-faced girl with light hair cut shoulder length was standing beside her. Mistaking me for a customer, the woman urged me to buy her eggs, her daughter (pointing at the girl) having gathered them that very morning, and only eleven (old) rubles for ten. I shook my head and she instantly lowered the price to ten rubles—not a kopeck less—and the reason, she assured me, she was doing it was that she wanted to close up and go home. I told her I was an American and had not come to buy but just to look around. I complimented her on the cleanliness of her eggs and told her it wouldn't be easy to sell them in America because they were so small. Curious, women at neighboring stalls leaned over to listen and to talk. How large were American eggs? What price did they fetch? How many eggs a year did a hen lay? Other questions followed: How many days a year did American women work in the fields and how much did they earn? There were sighs and exclamations of incredulity when I answered that American farm women rarely worked in the fields or milked cows. An elderly man with bushy brows, a stooped back, and a face wrinkled as a prune stopped to listen as he walked by.

"American women must be real *bariny* [ladies]," he said. "Won't even milk cows—think of that! Who then milks cows in America?"

"Men," I said.

"If only our men would do that," exclaimed a portly youngish woman with lively eyes at an adjoining stand.

Addressing herself to the man, the mother of the freckled girl said, "They wouldn't, would they?"

"What would you women do if men did all the work?" the man twitted her.

"We'd be *bariny*, like American farm women," broke in the younger woman.

The man wagged his head and gave a sigh.

"And why not?" interposed another woman. "We'd have no cow smell on us."

"And we'd perfume ourselves every day," the young woman rapped out. She turned to me. "Doesn't your wife perfume herself every day?"

"I have no wife," I said.

"Is she dead?" the man asked with sympathy.

"No, I never married."

Wags of head, sighs of compassion; but the man winked at me and said, "A wise fellow! You must have heard our saying: 'A wife isn't a boot; you can't kick her off your foot.'"

"Shame on you, Nikolai Maximovich," said the woman at the stand. "You wouldn't have said it if you were young."

"I never did—when I was young," the man chuckled. Then pointing to the freckle-faced girl, he said, "There's a fine girl for you. Take her to America and make a *barina* out of her."

"Look at my gray hair," I pleaded.

"She is in love," the mother said, looking at the girl, who blushed and turned away her head. "She'd marry tomorrow if I'd let her. But she is only seventeen."

"Wouldn't you like to be an American *barina?*" the young woman asked.

Firmly the girl shook her head.

"I would—on my word I would," said the young woman. "I would perfume myself any time I wished; I would wear silk dresses and *capron* [nylon] stockings and eat chocolates. Wouldn't you like that?" she again asked the girl.

Again the girl shook her head.

"She's in love, all right," the man said. "But what does she know of love? I'll tell you what love is like. . . ." He addressed the girl. "Love is only there where there is a good life."

"Isn't it the truth?" said the mother, and winking at me, went on. "Take my daughter to America, marry her off to a young American, then she can write and tell us how it feels to be an American *barina.*"

"Oh, mamma, stop," the girl protested.

"When she is my age," the man sighed, "she'll think differently."

"But I'm not your age," the girl flung at him, and gave a little laugh—a laugh of youth at the "wisdom" of age.

These countryfolk were in a jolly mood, ready for chatter and laughter and oblivious of all thought of impropriety in talking to a foreigner. Peasants always were the freest-speaking people in Russia, and it was good to learn that they had not changed.

Nor were young people, or rather boys and young men, though not girls unless properly introduced, inhibited from speaking to foreigners. I was stopped over and over by boys asking for chewing gum, young men asking if I had an American suit, shirt, shoes to sell. The hunger for higher quality or newer style of apparel than Soviet shops offer has never been so intense. *Komsomolka* may daily proclaim that Soviet youth are the happiest in the world; but though much better dressed then their fathers ever were, Soviet youth are discontented with the clothes Soviet factories manufacture. They want brighter colors, more stylish cuts, neater fits, and they disdain the flapping bell-bottomed trousers that until recently were as distinctive a feature of male Soviet attire as the highly padded shoulders.

Once, on returning to the Metropole Hotel, I saw a cluster of lively bareheaded boys around an American woman who was distributing pennies, pieces of chewing gum, and Life-Savers to them. The boys in return gave her badges and pins. When the woman had exhausted her supply of gifts, the boys asked if she had safety pins, cellophane bags or wrappings. I translated the question and the woman said, "I do have safety pins." She went up to her room and soon returned with several rings of pins, and after they were gone, she held up her hands and said, "I'm sorry, I have nothing else to give away." I translated her words, and amid loud chatter and laughter the boys thanked her for the gifts, requesting me to tell her to bring a suitcaseful of chewing gum next time she came to Moscow. "I will, I will," the woman answered, smiling, and turning to me, she said, "How hungry these charming boys are for trivial things." They couldn't possibly have been hungry for safety pins— Moscow shops were well supplied. It was only the sense of adventure in getting something from *zagranitsa*.

Knots of Russians gathered around American tourists are a daily sight all over the streets and squares of Moscow, especially outside the Metropole Hotel. Some of them come around to brush up on their English, which is exceptionally poor, even among high school graduates who have studied it for six years. It is an error to assume, as certain American educators have done, that in a Soviet school all subjects are adequately taught. Instruction in foreign languages is as incompetent as in American high schools. In all my travels in Russia I never met a high school graduate who could carry on a simple conversation in English without making most elementary blunders. I must have missed those whom other foreigners say they have met.

In general, only graduates of the Institute of Foreign Languages attain fluency in other tongues, but then only high school graduates with linguistic ability are admitted to these advanced colleges. The courses continue for five years; the classes are small—from ten to fifteen students; the teachers are excellent and demand strenuous application on the part of their students. Every important city in the Soviet Union maintains one of these institutes, whose graduates are in constant demand by factories, schools, ministries, and other institutions.

I often joined in informal street seminars, gatherings of young Russians eager to try out their English on any American tourist they could press into service. These meetings were usually lively and invariably illuminating. If the Russians blithely butchered the English language beyond recognition, their exceptionally expressive faces and graphic gestures made their meanings clear. Questions never stopped.

Have you an automobile? Is it new or secondhand? Is it a Buick, a Ford, a Chevrolet? How much did it cost? How much did you pay for your suit, your shirt, your necktie, your shoes? What do you do for a living? How much do you earn? Can you travel any time you wish? Must the government give you permission to travel out of your country? Can I come to your country as freely as you come to ours? Why is there so much unemployment in your country? How do the unemployed live? Why are you so unjust to Negroes? How do you like our "high structures" (skyscrapers)? Our subway? Our parks? Why don't you sell us your secondhand automobiles? Do you sell secondhand clothes as you do automobiles? Can a married couple always get a room after they are married? What's the legal amount of living space in America? Do you know Benny Goodman? Do you know Satchmo Armstrong?

I never knew questions to be concerned with ideology, Marxist or capitalist. Invariably they pertained to the details and amenities of daily living. Russians may be naïve and personally inquisitive, but they are neither patronizing nor bellicose. They do not heckle, unless the American is tactless enough to heckle them first, or to touch on such sensitive subjects as the Hungarian revolution, Kremlin-Yugoslav quarrels, or Soviet policies that belie Soviet professions of peace. The street is never the place publicly to discuss explosive subjects. The Russian has no choice but to defend the Kremlin or to remain silent. But in non-political matters Russians show overwhelming curiosity about foreign countries, especially about America. Wandering around the streets one can learn infinitely more about Russia and the Russians than by making escorted tours of parks and theaters, exhibitions and museums, including those inside the Kremlin walls.

In my exhilaration over personal encounters with people in the streets and squares, I almost forgot the Moscow that always frustrates and exasperates the working journalist, which I used to run away from whenever possible. One afternoon I telephoned a distinguished Russian writer, saying that I wanted to see him. I have known this writer for nearly twenty-five years; I have been in his home and taken meals with his family. He is in high standing with the Kremlin, and I saw no reason why he should be wary about meeting me again. Though in speaking to me on the telephone he was as friendly and courteous as ever, I concluded from his equivocal words that he would be happier if I didn't press him for an appointment. Naturally I didn't.

Nothing like this happened to me in Leningrad, Kiev, or any other city I visited, with the sole exception of a Jewish professor in Leningrad. His case was understandable. In the anti-Semitic atmosphere that emanates from the Kremlin and has infected many of the party functionaries, the Soviet Jew has become keenly conscious of himself as a Jew. But though the Moscow writer was a Russian of Russians, he didn't feel as free to talk to me as did peasants in the market place, policemen on their beat, casual strangers I met during my walks, or the clusters of boys and young people that daily gathered around Americans all over the city.

I refrained from telephoning any other of my old acquaintances among writers and intellectuals. I just dropped in on them and if they were home I was warmly received. When I asked a highly educated elderly Russian woman to explain the strange behavior of the writer I had called, she said, "I didn't think *he* would refuse to see you, but I can understand it. You see, we of the older generation remember the purges. It makes us shudder to think of them: the abject confessions, the cruel punishments. We are happy that things are quiet now, but we have no assurance the purges won't recur. We can only hope. And remember also that you are a writer, and writers cannot help making use one way or another of whatever they see and hear."

"But young people have no such fears," I said. "They stop foreign tourists all the time and speak freely to them."

"Why shouldn't they?" came the answer. "They are a new generation. They care nothing for the purges, and being young, they are spirited and adventurous and don't think of possible consequences. But we of the older generation have memories we cannot bury and no longer have the spirit and energy to take chances. So caution is the watchword. That's the way it is, and you must understand it."

But one must say this for Moscow—one never knows when he will stumble into a situation that will dramatize a new aspect of Soviet humanity that makes one forget all Soviet aspiration to create a new man.

On my last evening in the Soviet capital (July 19, 1960), an American woman who had been living there for some months invited me to go with her to Van Cliburn's farewell concert. Tickets had long been impossible to obtain and the indoor Luzhniki Stadium, with a seating capacity of seventeen thousand, was jammed to the doors.

I had often attended concerts in Moscow, but never had I seen an audience like the one before me. It was composed overwhelmingly of women, from teen-age girls to grandmothers, many of them carrying bouquets of wild or garden-grown flowers. There was a hum of excitement in the air, and before the concert started girl after girl made her way down the aisles and laid her floral offering on the edge of the platform. When finally the tall and bushy-haired Texan appeared he was greeted with roaring applause while from the upper tiers a rain of bouquets fell over and around him. I had never witnessed such an ovation anywhere in the Soviet Union.

But this was a mere prelude to the scene that erupted at the conclusion of the first half of the program. The pianist's feminine admirers (worshipers would be the more correct word) pushed into the aisles, holding their bouquets high to prevent their being crushed by the jostling crowd, and swarmed around the platform. Smiling and bowing, the young Texan gathered up as many of the tributes as his long arms could hold. But there was no end to the offerings. Fresh-faced schoolgirls and gray-haired matrons held up and waved their bouquets for him personally to take from their hands. "They want to feel the touch of his hands," my companion said. "They are absolutely mad about him. The girls would all like to marry him and the mammas and grandmas would all like to mother him."

I said I thought her a little cynical.

"Not at all," she replied, "He's a wonderful person and a great pianist, and I'm happy he's so popular here. But—and I hate to say it—this kind of an exhibition makes me think of Liberace's audiences in America and England. It's not his fault, but women have made him into Russia's Liberace."

4.

MOSCOW
Voices of Dissent

One evening a celebrated American judge and his wife invited me to go with them to a visiting Polish circus in Gorky Park. We came early, and on our way to the tent we were caught in a surge of young people, festively dressed. The girls wore bright-colored summer dresses and some of them were so fashionable that they wore or carried white gloves. There was a holiday spirit in the air, as there always is when Russians go to a concert, theater, opera; a football game, the circus —any entertainment.

Observing these well-dressed and spirited young people, the judge and his wife remarked that they didn't answer the descriptions of a drably dressed public they had read about in books on Russia by American writers. The descriptions, I explained, held true for the Stalinist years, but the young people who surged about us were living testimony to the brighter life that Khrushchev's era had brought about.

The audience in the packed tent furnished ample evidence of the Russian gift for gaiety when the occasion calls for it. One of the acts was particularly spectacular. It was a soccer game played by dogs. The players didn't seem to know which side they were on, but they were cannily trained to shoot the ball to the goalie—a dog tugging at the leash inside the goal cage. Yelping and barking, dog after dog leaped high into the air and bumped the ball with his head, another dog immediately bouncing the ball back. The audience rocked with delight, and whenever the ball fell inside the cage, the tent thundered with hilarious applause.

Winter or summer, there is always a prodigal amount of entertainment in Moscow, now more than ever: theater, sports, concerts, song fests. This, together with the better dress people wear, the better food they eat, the cleanliness of streets and courtyards, the lush greenery that adorns both, gives Moscow an appearance of well-being and brightness that the Soviet capital has not shown in all the years I have been visiting it.

Yet beneath this façade of well-being and cheer, there surges a new restlessness that is never reflected in the press and that never flashed out in all the official interviews I had with leaders in one field of endeavor or another. High or low, these leaders are so preoccupied with immediate plans and tasks that they have neither the time to ponder nor the disposition to explore the inner perturbations of the individual citizen. Men of action, armed with a vocabulary of optimism and a spirit of militancy, their minds, like those of soldiers, are set on battle and victory whether in industry, agriculture, education, sports, or diplomacy. Their attention and energies are engaged by one project after another or, to use a favorite Soviet term, by one offensive after another. From Khrushchev down they care little or nothing for the vagaries of human nature or for the demands of the citizen's inner self, so long as he doesn't slip dangerously out of control, which in my judgment cannot happen.

But like an underground stream, the demanding inner self persists. Despite George Orwell's predictions, it has neither atrophied nor been congealed in a Kremlin-contrived mold. Of course, reading the Soviet press and hearing Soviet oratory, one might easily conclude that Soviet humanity is imbued with one mind, one will, one inspiration, one set of answers to all questions under the sun—the mind, the will, the inspiration, the answers, of the one man who rules the Kremlin roost. But nothing is further from the truth.

The remarkable aspect of the voices of dissent today is the fact that they come largely from the Soviet-born, Soviet-educated, and Soviet-indoctrinated generation. The Kremlin hasn't conquered their minds as decisively as official pronouncements so ecstatically proclaim. The postwar generation, notably university students, brims over with doubts and questions, with hopes unfulfilled and yearnings thwarted, which is the principal reason why they so eagerly corner foreigners and engage them in conversation. They do it more openly than I had known them to do since the rise of the Plans, and I shall set down several of the more provocative encounters in the streets of Moscow.

The Laughing Taxicab Driver

He was thirty-two years old, he told me, and his name was Kostya. He was driving me from the Arbat to a remote part of the city to see an old friend. He was an astonishingly handsome man with flaxen hair, deep blue eyes, a strong ruddy face, and a ready laugh. Once a pigeon stopped in front of his cab and he hurriedly stepped on the brake. Instead of swearing at the pigeon as drivers usually do, he gave a hearty laugh. To him there was something comical about a strutting pigeon holding up his cab.

"You're a very happy person," I said.

"Why shouldn't I be?" he replied. "Life is fun, lots of fun."

"Has it always been fun for you?"

"No, not until I did some hard thinking about it. It's amazing what a man can accomplish inside himself once he sets his mind on it." He laughed again, an infectious boyish laugh. I had not met a man like him since my arrival in the country—a man who was so cheerfully disposed toward life that he laughed at the least provocation. When I asked him if he was married, he answered, "I was," and laughed once more, as at an amusing episode in his life.

"Are you divorced?"

"No," he answered, smiling. "My wife got up and left me." After a pause he added seriously, "Our women are getting terribly spoiled. They don't want to work. My wife didn't. After she had her second child, she kept saying, 'Liberate me from my job.' I was earning nine hundred [old] rubles a month and I asked her how she expected the family to live on my earnings. Her answer was: 'You're good with tools and you can pick up a lot of repair jobs and earn extra money. Other men are doing it.' But I wouldn't make a slave of myself, working at my regular job and then working evenings and rest days. So one day when I came home from work, she told me she was leaving me for another man. I was heartbroken, but there was nothing I could do to stop her. She left me and went down to Baku to live with an oil worker. Oil workers earn high wages; and now you see what I mean when I say our women are getting spoiled?" He was of course generalizing, but that more and more Russian women want to be liberated from work is an incontestable fact.

Continuing his story, he told me that after his wife left him he felt so broken up that he quit his job and went down to his native village in the province of Tambov to visit his widowed father. The year was 1952. Before the revolution his father had been stableman on a large landed estate. But he had lived in his own house and had cultivated a garden and a beautiful small orchard. He loved fruit trees and cared for them as tenderly as though they were animate things. After he joined the kolkhoz he continued to tend his little orchard, the best in the village. "Well, I had been away from home for seven years, and now that I was approaching my father's house I saw no fruit trees. There were only stumps in back of the house. Do you know what happened? The state taxed those trees, even in non-bearing years, so extortionately that my father cut them down. That's what happened. My father was over seventy, almost blind, and he wept like a child when he told me that with his own hands he had to 'kill' the trees. 'Kill'—that's the word he used. So here I was, my wife and children gone, my father in the last days of his life—he died soon afterward—and I alone, all alone again, but luckily with a room of my own outside Moscow. I went back to Moscow but I was so wretched I couldn't stay there, so I went to Kazakhstan. Well, you wouldn't believe it—the poor toiling Kazakh peasants were cutting down their fruit trees too —green, healthy fruit trees fell under the ax like weeds under a sickle, and only because, like my father, the Kazakh peasants couldn't afford to pay the taxes that the state slapped on them.

"I went through the war, I saw what the Germans did to orchards in our country. But I tell you that our own state destroyed more fruit trees than the Germans did. And to what purpose? To prevent peasants from becoming 'capitalists' out of a dozen or so fruit trees they had through the years lovingly grown in their back yards. Could anything be more silly, I ask you?" He gave a laugh, but not of bitterness. "Do you see now why I made up my mind to get fun out of life, all the fun I can? Let others do the worrying. I've done my share of it. A man lives only once and why not get all the joy one can out of it?" He paused and laughed. Then he resumed: "Why is a man worse than a pigeon? The pigeons in Moscow get wonderful protection—they are fed and played with. They have lots of fun—all the fun they want, and how ready the militiaman is to jump on you if you spoil their fun, even when they get right under your wheel! Such stupid creatures—but they have a good life, the very best of lives right here in Moscow. If they have it, why can't I have it? You see what I mean?" He laughed again.

"Isn't it different now that Stalin is dead and the cult of the individual has been denounced?" I asked.

"*Ekh!*" and he gave a laugh. "Let them do as they please, and I'll do as I please. I'm a happy man now. My job is lots of fun. Day after day I meet Uzbeks, Kazakhs, Altaians, Georgians, people from far-away regions in my country, and foreigners too; Chinese, Koreans, Indians, yes, and Americans. Sometimes they speak Russian and I learn something new from them, something I never would learn from our newspapers. The whole world comes to Moscow and I rub shoulders with people from many faraway lands, as I never did before. Oh, Moscow is a wonderful town, and I love it! I wouldn't want to live anywhere else in our country—no, sir, I wouldn't." His face livened and his deep blue eyes beamed with pleasure.

"Aren't you going to get married again?" I asked.

"No, sir, never, not I!" he answered with a chuckle.

"But you're so handsome, I bet women won't leave you alone," I teased.

"They don't," and he laughed uproariously. "But they aren't going to trap me. Let them go after richer game—oil workers, miners, others who earn high wages and can afford to liberate their wives from work. All I want is my own liberation, and now that I've won it I'm going to enjoy it."

The Baffled Agronomist

Once on my return from a journey south, Intourist put me up at the Leningrad Hotel, one of the three skyscraper hotels in the Soviet capital. Twenty-six stories high, with spacious lobbies and lounges, immaculately clean white dining rooms, large high-windowed living room, faultless plumbing and no shortage or stoppage of hot water day or night, its one failing is the incredible slowness of the elevators and the blithe absent-mindedness of the girls and women who operate them. Fortunately there are upholstered chairs on the landings by the elevators and I could plant myself in a chair with a book or newspaper while I waited.

Once the elevator let me off two floors above the one on which I lived, and instead of waiting for the return trip I decided to walk down. I searched for the stairway but couldn't find it, so I asked the floor woman where it was. To my amazement she told me that it was locked. Did she have the key? No. Who had the key? She didn't know.

"Do you mean," I said, "nobody can walk down the stairway?"

"That's right. You go up and down only in the elevator."

"What would happen if a fire broke out?"

She shrugged and remained silent.

"Do the city police know the stairways are always locked so if a fire broke out lives would be endangered?"

Irritated, she answered, "How should I know what the police do or don't know?"

Yet staying in this hotel was a rewarding experience. Most of the guests were Russians from all parts of the country, and it was easy to get acquainted with them, especially in the dining room. Late one afternoon I took a seat at a small table far away from the blaring orchestra. Opposite me sat a little man with squinting eyes, a pinched, sunken face—the small triangular face of a man who appeared not to have grown to his natural size. He sat with chin in hand, elbow propped on the table, a cigarette in his mouth, and appeared too occupied with his own reflections to be interested in my presence. He had finished eating but the dishes were still before him, as were those of another diner who was missing from the table. I shall call this man Vasily; and when he saw me pass to the waiter my booklet of meal tickets, he suddenly wakened to my presence and

asked where I came from. I told him, and he said I was the first
American he had ever met. He was an agronomist on a large state
farm in the province of Kursk, where Khrushchev was born in the village of Kalinovka. "It may interest you to know," he went on, "that
corn—in which America specializes—is a great success in our province,
and this year we have pledged ourselves to raise a record crop and
have challenged other provinces to match or surpass our pledge."
He spoke in a grave and measured voice. When I told him that in
June 1955, at a diplomatic reception in Belgrade, I presented Nikita
Khrushchev with an excellent American manual on corn growing, he
gave me a serious and friendly look.

"I'm sure," he said, "Nikita Sergeyevich appreciated the present.
He knows more about corn than all our agronomists and scientists
put together."

Out of courtesy I didn't tell him that I doubted Khrushchev had
read the book, that otherwise he wouldn't be strenuously popularizing
the checked row for all cornfields. But I did tell the agronomist that
the checked row has long been going out of favor in America. The
information surprised him. How then did American farmers plant
corn?

"Farmers in upstate New York," I said, "where I once worked on a
farm, plant corn in one-way rows, dropping one seed every eight
inches. It saves time and work in cultivating because they cultviate
only one way and they get much better crops."

He had never heard of it, he admitted, and instantly pulled out a
notebook and wrote in it. He asked other questions about corn and
ensilage and made notes of my answers. Then he put the notebook
aside, laid his elbows on the table, leaned over, and said, "I wish
you'd tell me something. Why does your country and mine quarrel?"

"Why do they?" I tossed his question back to him.

Ignoring this, he said, "And we were such good friends. You helped
us so much when we desperately needed your help. And now—how
did it all get started?" He looked piercingly at me, his eyes narrowing
to pin points. But I wouldn't discuss the issues of the cold war with a
casual Russian acquaintance, however sincere and importunate he
might be. All I said was: "You say we are the aggressors and we say
you are the aggressors."

For some moments he continued to stare at me. The light of his cigarette was out, but he sucked on it absent-mindedly. Finally he said with a sigh, "In the next war there'll be no place to hide. Nobody can hide, neither our Khrushchev nor your Eisenhower. We'll all blow up. In one minute up blows New York. In another minute up blows Moscow. America can always find a way of striking at Moscow, and don't imagine we don't realize that."

He paused to stub his dead cigarette into an ash try, sat up straight, and said, "You say we are the aggressors, but I say people are people. They don't want to die. They want to live, and—"

The waiter brought my soup and Vasily paused until the waiter had gone. Then he resumed. "It isn't people who quarrel. It's only leaders who quarrel. I only wish I knew why."

I didn't say anything, and soon he spoke again. "Once when Stalin was still alive, I heard a lecturer say that only leaders make history, and he was right. Leaders do everything." He lighted another cigarette, and puffed and puffed away until a cloud of smoke veiled his face. Then impatiently he quashed the cigarette and waved away the smoke.

"Think," he said, "what your country and mine are spending on armaments, of the factories that turn out nothing else, of the millions training for war, of the generals, admirals, other officers, drawing high salaries, living better than working people, and teaching more millions how to fight and kill and destroy. It makes no sense."

"I quite agree with you," I said.

Then he lowered his head, gave a deep sigh, and murmured as if to himself, "It's all the fault of leaders. It can't be anything else. People don't quarrel. Only leaders quarrel."

I wondered if he realized how heretical his words were, he a member of the Communist party! *Pravda* would have excoriated him for daring to imply that Kremlin leaders were not blameless for the fierce tensions that were shaking mankind.

The missing man returned to the table and sat down. "An American," the agronomist introduced me. The newcomer, whom I shall call Fedya, pressed my hand. He was a handsome man, with a round face, pink cheeks, light wavy hair, and he radiated a cheer that was in striking contrast to his companion's moroseness.

"We were talking," said the agronomist, "of why America and the Soviet Union keep quarreling."

"That's what I'd like to know," Fedya burst out excitedly. "I fought all the way from Moscow to Germany. I never got to Berlin. It's just as well I didn't. I hate racists. A plague on racists. We Russians never were racists, we like all peoples, so your country and mine cannot possibly be quarreling over racial problems. Can we?"

"No," I said.

Vasily, looking dejected, leaned back in his chair and stared into the distance. But Fedya brimmed with loquaciousness and good humor.

"Why then are we quarreling?" he pursued excitedly. "People love to live. I love to live. I love music. I love poetry. My favorites are Esenin, Pushkin, Lermontov, and Nekrasov. I don't care for our modern poetry. I don't like Mayakovsky. But ah, how I love Nekrasov. Wait." He arose, darted across the room to the orchestra, where I saw him exchange words with the leader. By the time he returned the orchestra had struck up the tune of "Korobochka." He sat down, hummed with the music, looking very pleased with himself.

"Nekrasov wrote it," he said when the orchestra finished the song. "Beautiful, isn't it? I love all our old songs; I love all our old poetry; and I love Tchaikovsky and Rimsky-Korsakov and all the other old composers. They speak to the heart, that's why I love them. By profession I am a veterinarian, and when I am through with my work I read poetry, sing songs, and listen to records. So you see, I love life and I love to spend my leisure in entertainment that speaks to my heart and that uplifts me. On my word, I do. So why do we have this threat of war hanging over us?"

"It's too bad," I said. "We feel it as deeply as your people do."

"Well, then—" He paused abruptly, and with a wry face he made a sweeping motion of the hand as though to drive away a thought that was troubling him. Smiling, he said, "I wonder if you can do me a favor? You see, I brought from the war souvenirs of German and French money." He drew out his wallet, lifted from it two neatly folded pieces of paper money, and passed them to me. "But I have no souvenir of American money. Maybe you can spare me one."

I offered him a dollar bill. He examined it with the delight of a child favored with a bright toy. Then he said, "I'll give you twenty [old] rubles for it."

"Forget it, please," I said.

"Fifty rubles."

"I don't want your money."

"A hundred rubles."

"I can't take your money. It would be illegal," I protested.

"How about a bottle of champagne?"

"I don't drink champagne."

"What do you drink—vodka? Cognac? I'll get you a bottle of the best Armenian cognac."

"Forget it, I'm giving you a present," I said.

His face clouded. "Here," he said, and passed the dollar bill back to me.

"Please keep it," I begged. "You offend me by returning it."

"But I cannot take a present from you if you won't take one from me."

"But I don't need anything, and it gives me pleasure to present you with a souvenir you want."

Like a hurt boy, he shook his head. "I don't want your souvenir." And after a pause he shrugged and said, "You're such a strange man. You don't want money, you don't care for champagne, you won't take cognac. How do you expect me to take your souvenir? No, I won't take it. It wouldn't be right if I did."

"But it's such a small thing," I said.

His face suddenly sparkled and he said, "A box of candy! Surely you eat candy?"

"Let's settle for a bar of chocolate," I said.

"Two bars!" He leaped to his feet, darted away, and when he returned he held two bars of chocolate in his hand. Without his telling me I knew that he had paid the equivalent of some four dollars for the chocolate—an extravagant outlay in return for the small souvenir I had given him. But the cost was of no consequence, and wouldn't have been if he had spent every ruble in his wallet. At last he could reciprocate my favor and that gratified his pride. He beamed as he gave me the chocolate, and turning to the dream-lost agronomist, he gave him a slap on the back and exclaimed joyfully, "Look at my new souvenir!"

The sight of the dollar bill evoked no emotion in Vasily. He scarcely glanced at it. His mind was preoccupied with his own thoughts. Fedya spread the bill on the palm of one hand and with the other he smoothed it out and then carefully tucked it into his wallet.

"The American here," said the agronomist, "presented our Nikita Sergeyevich with an American book on corn."

"You did?" Fedya's baby-blue eyes glowed with pleasure. He reached over, grasped my hand, and pumped it hard. Then he wanted to know the details of the presentation, and I described them briefly. "You're a real friend of our people," he said.

"It's easy to be a friend of your people," I replied. "Americans who meet them always praise their kindness and their friendliness."

"We are a simple people," Fedya said. "We don't demand anything from anybody and we wish nobody any harm."

"Yes," interposed Vasily. "We have everything we need in our own country—land, forest, minerals—everything. Why should we demand anything from any other country? If we have peace and work as hard as we do, our country will bloom like a flower garden."

The ebullient Fedya struck the table with his hand. "That's it," he said with enthusiasm. "Peace—peace with all the peoples on earth—is all we want. Let's drink a toast to peace and friendship between America and the Soviet Union."

We drank the toast and then, as though it were the refrain of a song that haunted him, the somber-faced agronomist droned again, "Peoples don't quarrel, only their leaders quarrel," and after a lengthy pause he gave a sigh and added, "That's the trouble with the world, the real trouble, leaders not peoples!"

The Questioning Son

"Where is your country from?" I heard a voice behind me as I was sauntering along the Gogol Boulevard. Turning, I saw a finely built youth, about twenty, with dark hair neatly brushed back, smiling on me. He was coatless and wore a gray shirt without a necktie, the collar unbuttoned. "American, yes?" he asked as he caught up with me.

I nodded and suggested that we speak Russian.

"Isn't my English terrible?" he said with a laugh. "That's because it was so badly taught in the ten-year school I graduated from. We crammed grammar and vocabulary, but we learned little of how to use them in conversation. I'm glad you speak Russian."

He was in the university now, in his third year, studying chemistry, and his one great wish was to be selected as an exchange student to America, preferably to the University of California. He had always dreamed of going to California because that was where Jack London had lived, and since his earliest years in school Jack London had been a literary idol of his. What a writer! How he fired the blood with zest for adventure! Even his father, an old bolshevik and a pensioned railroad worker who wouldn't retire from work, loved the American author, and it would be an inspiration to live and study for a while in the author's home country and to see with one's own eyes the wild and exciting scenery of which he wrote so beautifully. Had I ever been in California? What did I know about the University of California?

On and on we talked, and then he said, "Will you pardon me if I make a request of you? It embarrasses me to make it and you will pardon me, won't you?"

"Of course," I said.

"You see, I'd like—I'd like—" He fumbled for words. "Well, I mean, I'd like to buy a suit from you if you have one to sell."

I told him I regretted I couldn't accommodate him.

His face fell, and I tried to solace him with the observation that I never knew people in Moscow to be as well dressed as they were then.

He lapsed into thought for a few moments and then said, "It's a funny thing about us. We thrilled the whole world with our sputniks, but we can't tailor a decent suit of clothes. I know. I see students from foreign countries in our university and they are all well dressed, even the Poles. But we Russian students have to wear clothes that hang like sacks on our backs. When I ask my father, who as I told you is an old bolshevik, why our suits are so badly made, he laughs at me and says that I dress luxuriously compared to the rags he wore in the early years of the revolution. But I tell him that those years are far behind us. 'Think of it,' I say to him. 'Next to America we are the most highly industrialized country in the world; we manufacture sputniks and jet planes; so why shouldn't we be as well dressed as students in other countries, as are Polish students, when Poland is so

much poorer than we are?' And do you know what he says? He says
that when I am his age we shall all have better clothes than Poles,
Americans, any other people in the world. But who wants to wait
that long? I am twenty, I have a beautiful girl, she too is studying
chemistry, and we're very much in love, and when we go walking or
to the theater, we want to feel that we are culturally dressed. My girl
is lucky, she makes her own dresses! Give her a stylish pattern and
she produces a stylish and handsome dress that fits her perfectly. But
I can't tailor my own suit. I have to wear what our factories turn out,
what our stores sell; and our fabrics are coarse, our styles ancient,
our tailoring shoddy. You just don't feel cultured wearing our store
suits."

He paused, and for a few moments we walked in silence. Then he
resumed. "My mother isn't at all like my father. She is a precious
darling, and she tells Father that he mustn't expect my generation to
share his tastes and be content with his satisfactions. Young people
nowadays, she tells Father, have a right to demand greater satisfactions than he ever knew. But Father—well—he's very kind. He is very
proud of my older sister, who graduated from college and is now a
schoolteacher; and of me, studying chemistry in our great Moscow
University. But he's old-fashioned. He lives in the past and doesn't
understand that his children have a right to a new joy in life, a new
pride of person."

"I don't suppose," I said, "you're a Komsomol?"

"Of course I am. In my younger years I was in the Pioneers [the
Communist organization for children between the ages of nine and
fourteen] and now I am a Komsomol."

"Don't they accuse you of being an individualist, a philistine,
thinking only of yourself and not of Soviet society?"

With an ironic smile, he answered, "These are all phrases. We hear
them every day. But what kind of philistine am I—or my girl—
when last year we toiled for a month on a state farm and are again
going to spend a month on the same farm in Moscow province? Duty
is duty, and neither my girl nor I shrink from performing it. But what
has that got to do with the wish to be culturally dressed, to feel a joy
in wearing clothes that fit your person instead of making you look
like a scarecrow? We have plenty of discussion on the subject when

we students get together. Don't imagine that we live like monks in cells, cut off from the finer things in life."

"And aren't you afraid to speak so openly to a foreigner?"

My question surprised him, and he gave me a piercing look. "Why should I be?" he finally answered. "I'm not divulging state secrets. I have none to divulge. I am only a student, and I shall devote my life to working for my people, and I'm a loyal Soviet citizen. If there's war, I'll fight for my Motherland, I'll die for my Motherland. But— it's about time we dressed as well as the foreign students we see in the university. I tell it to Father all the time. Why shouldn't I tell it to you?"

And after another pause he added reflectively, "But Father—well —he'll soon be sixty-six, and there are a lot of things he doesn't see as I do."

He had spoken of his father as being old-fashioned, living in the past, and now he let slip the fact that he and his father didn't agree on "a lot of things."

He didn't elucidate and I felt it inadvisable to urge him. We talked of America and of countries in which I had traveled. Suddenly he asked, "Have you ever been in Yugoslavia?"

"Yes, I was there when Bulganin and Khrushchev came to make peace with Tito."

"Were you? How interesting. I saw Tito when he was here—all Moscow saw him—and we were happy the feud was at an end. And now—" He gave a shrug and lapsed into silence. Then he spoke again. "I wish I were like my father. Nothing disturbs him. Everything we do is always right, everything. It's wonderful to be an old bolshevik like him."

"Are you disturbed over the new conflict with Tito?" I asked.

"It's a mess, and a lot of us wish it didn't happen."

A gray-haired elderly woman wearing a black hat and leading a wolfhound by the leash walked into the boulevard—a rare sight in Moscow. We followed her with our eyes and so did other passers-by. "Such a beautiful dog!" my companion exclaimed. "Have you read Jack London's The Call of the Wild?"

I told him I had.

"What a dog! Oh, how I'd love to go to California and study in the university there. But—" He gave a shrug and paused, then resumed. "If only we have peace with America! On my word—we'd then have peace of mind—and I'd somehow get to the University of California. It's the great dream of my life."

The Angry Young Man

I was looking into the display window of a bookshop on the Kuznetsky when a young man stopped to look into the same window. Soon we engaged in conversation, and on learning I was an American writer, my fellow window-shopper asked whether I knew William Saroyan. He was disappointed when I replied that I had never met the American-Armenian author. "If you meet him," came the request, "please tell him that we in Soviet Armenia are very proud of him."

Intense is the feeling of kinship that Armenians in the Soviet Union have toward their blood brothers in foreign countries, and they expand with pride when any of them attains distinction, especially in the arts. The highly publicized Anastas Mikoyan, or General Ivan Bagramian, whose breast glitters with medals won during the last war, is not the hero among Soviet Armenians that Khachaturian, the composer, is. Or William Saroyan.

My new acquaintance told me that he was a student in a scientific institute, and I shall call him Aram. He was of medium height, and spare, with thick black hair, thick black eyebrows, sparkling black eyes, and a a good-humored expression on his smooth, long, light-brown face. He seemed to have a high regard for correct dress and wore a necktie, a gray necktie, with his brown suit. As we walked along Gorky Street, he asked if it was true, as he had read in a Moscow newspaper, that there were eight hundred thousand unsold new automobiles in America. I replied that I didn't know the precise figures of unsold new automobiles but that showrooms all over the country were bursting with them.

"Think of that!" he exclaimed in wonder. "We can hardly imagine it—going into a showroom, picking out the automobile you want, and buying it right there, with no more trouble than buying an ice-cream brick on this street. Incredible! Here, even if you have the money, you wait from two to five years before it'll be delivered to you. What a contrast! And yet they tell us that millions and millions of people in America haven't enough to eat! They must be starving as they drive around in their automobiles!" He gave a contemptuous laugh and went on. "When we students read of the eight hundred thousand unsold automobiles in America, some of my mates and I amused ourselves wondering which automobile we'd buy if we were there. We had great fun imagining ourselves getting into a newly bought Ford, Chevrolet, Plymouth, Buick—and driving away, the proud possessors of our own automobiles."

Obviously, the propaganda intent of publicizing the large number of unsold automobiles in America had failed of its purpose, which was to dramatize the enormity of the American crisis. To Aram and his fellow students it revealed only the tremendous output of the American automobile industry, and I very much doubt that it conveyed anything else to many Soviet citizens, to whom the automobile has come to symbolize the height of material welfare. In recent years Russians have become extravagantly automobile-minded, and when they read of a country that manufactures more automobiles than it can sell, they can only marvel at the high productivity of the country's industry.

"It's silly," Aram said, "to speak of America as a country where millions of people are starving. I'll tell you something. My father was killed in the war, my father's younger brother was killed in the war, and I grew up on American powdered eggs, condensed milk, and smoked bacon. So did millions of other fatherless children. How do they expect me to believe the fables they tell about starving Americans?"

Suddenly Aram halted, nudged my arm, and pointing to a tree ahead of us, said in a half whisper, "Look, something is happening there." In the shadow of the tree a paunchy man wearing a straw hat and a spring coat was talking to a black-kerchiefed woman who was hugging a cluster of roses. A knot of passers-by was forming around them. Soon the woman, her head bowed, walked away, and the man followed immediately behind her. "The fat swine," Aram said in subdued angry tones, "telling the peasant woman she couldn't sell her roses here, and then following her like a dog to see that she doesn't!" We resumed walking.

"Maybe there's a city ordinance forbidding it," I said.

"There may be, I really don't know," Aram replied. "How silly if there is. All along Gorky Street there are these ice-cream and soda-water carts, right on the sidewalk—look at them—and the woman was standing under the tree. She wasn't interfering with traffic like the women at the carts. Isn't it silly to allow passers-by to buy an Eskimo ice cream but not a rose? The militiaman didn't tell the woman to go away, but the fat swine, who is no doubt a big shot, did. He looks like a gentleman but at heart he is a swine. What does he know of the beauty of a rose or of the joy it gives a fellow to buy one for his girl? Look at all the young couples promenading up and down, dressed in their best clothes. That peasant woman was doing them a favor by offering her roses so that a boy in love with his girl could stop and buy her one. It's so beautiful to give flowers to the girl you love. Sometimes I go without my lunch to save for flowers for my girl. I forget hunger when I think of her. But the fat swine who drove away the woman rose peddler has no more romantic feeling in him than a pig."

"You are a romantic fellow," I said.

"I wouldn't be Armenian if I wasn't," he said with a smile. "That's what I love about Saroyan. He's an American, but in his soul he is an Armenian, always aglow with romance, always searching for romance in the people he writes about. Oh, Armenians cannot help being romantic."

"Russians, too, are a romantic people," I said. "Turgenev and Tolstoy wrote some of the most moving love stories in all literature."

"Of course, of course," Aram nodded with enthusiasm. "Those endearing Turgenev girls and Tolstoy's lovable Natasha! You wouldn't believe it but it's true—whenever I read a Turgenev novel I cry, and I feel uplifted after I've had my cry. But there are Russians and there are Russians. The trouble with the Russians today is that they are so arrogantly Russian. Not all of them, of course, but too many, especially among the big shots, not to make a non-Russian like myself laugh at them or curdle with resentment. But Turgenev wasn't like that. Tolstoy wasn't like that. Chekhov wasn't like that. Those Russians knew the virtue of humility. But the Russians of today don't know the meaning of humility. Their heads are swollen with conceit. Do you know who are among the brainiest people in the Soviet Union?"

He paused as though waiting for me to answer, but I didn't say anything.

"The Armenians and the Jews," he resumed in his soft, clear voice. "Yes, Armenians and Jews are among the brainiest people in the country, and Russians have the gall to call us Armenians and the Jews ugly names. I hear it all the time, even among university students. Think of it—the Armenians and the Jews were highly civilized peoples when the Russians were still barbarians, and yet they dare to insult Armenians and Jews with slimy epithets. That's the kind of 'internationalists' they are. Have you heard the anecdote about the sputnik being a Jew?"

I shook my head. Aram gave a laugh. "'Why is the sputnik a Jew?' one Soviet citizen asks another. 'Because it wanders around the earth and has no place to stop' is the answer. I don't know who originated the anecdote. It must have been a Jew. Only a Jew could speak of himself as having no place here, and the reason he does is because Russians make him feel that way. But Armenians don't. Indeed, we don't. Jews in Erevan [capital of Soviet Armenia] feel at home as they don't in Moscow."

We walked on in silence, both of us deep in thought; I reflecting on the nature of the rebellious spirit of the young Armenian beside me. I had been in Soviet Armenia in the prewar years and hadn't met Armenians there or elsewhere in the Soviet Union who spoke so acidulously of Russians as Aram did. Armenians spoke harshly of Soviet repression but not of Russian arrogance or Russian national prejudices. Yet here was Aram, of the postwar generation, privileged to study in Moscow, living on state stipend, and indicting Russians on both counts, his voice dripping with scorn and derision. He may have been overly sensitive, as members of minorities are the world over. Even so, he spoke a language that was at sharp variance with *Pravda*'s rapturous chants of the happy brotherhood of all peoples living under the Soviet banner. Aram symbolized the deep-felt reaction of a sensitive non-Russian to the Kremlin postwar glorification of Russia as a superior nation, which, though not as blatant under Khrushchev as it had been under Stalin, nonetheless colors Soviet writing, both fiction and non-fiction.

A passing couple hailed Aram. The Armenian waved back cheerfully. "Students, good friends of mine, already married," said Aram, smiling. "They are both Russians, wonderful young people. Tolstoy would have been proud of them. They always stand up for the rights of others. There are many Russians like them, so I don't want you to think that what I said about Russian arrogance applies to all Russians. Of course it doesn't. But why should any Russians insult Armenians and Jews? It burns me up whenever I hear them do it. What right have any Russians to feel superior to other peoples? But they do. It's even official."

"Not since Stalin died," I interposed.

"Not as blatantly, no. But—Russians are the only people in the Soviet Union who are always spoken of as 'the great people.' Ukrainians, Armenians, Georgians, Uzbeks, are never spoken of as a great people. But Russians are, all the time. You see what I mean when I say it's official?"

"Aren't you yourself intensely nationalistic?" I asked.

"Of course I am. That's why I resent Russians calling themselves great, implying that they are greater than others, greater than are my people, one of the oldest and most civilized peoples in Europe. Do you know who Shamyl was?"

"Yes," I said. "I used to see his portrait everywhere I traveled in the Caucasus."

"You won't see it now. First they made a hero of Shamyl because for forty years he led a rebellion of the Mohammedan mountaineers in the Caucasus against the Czars. But after the last war they made a villain out of him, branded him a robber, a bandit who was in the pay of English imperialism. That's what they did to Shamyl—one of the most beloved figures in the Caucasus."

"But they have rehabilitated him," I said, "after Stalin died, haven't they?"

Aram gave a sarcastic laugh. "I want to tell you an anecdote about this business of rehabilitating people who were shot or historic characters who, like Shamyl, were denounced as villains and reactionaries. One student says to another, 'What's the difference between an idealist and a materialist?' 'You tell me,' answers the other student. 'An idealist,' explains the first student, 'is a man who believes in life hereafter, and a materialist is a man who believes in rehabilitation after death.'"

"You amaze me," I said.

"Why?"

"You speak so openly to a stranger right on crowded Gorky Street."

"It does a fellow good to talk himself out, and we students do it all the time. Of course, we have to be careful whom we talk to. You should have heard our heated debates during the Hungarian rebellion. Such nonsense to tell us it was a fascist plot to overthrow Hungary's people's democracy! A child wouldn't believe it and we students are no children. We study mathematics, chemistry, biology, physics, astronomy, other natural sciences. We learn to reason scientifically, to draw conclusions from known facts, from established laws of nature. If we didn't, we'd blow up our laboratories. How then can we believe the fable that the Hungarian rebellion was provoked by fascists when it was Communists and not fascists who for ten years ruled Hungary, ruled it with an iron hand? It makes no sense to our logical, scientific minds. No, it doesn't, and nobody believes it, nobody who does any thinking."

As we walked on, two men coming from behind slowed their steps and gave us such a piercing look that I grew disconcerted. One of the men was tall, broad-shouldered, wore a spring coat, and carried a Caucasian cane; the other was short, bald, bullet-headed, and was dressed in a rumpled dark suit. Aram returned their look and didn't say anything. He appeared completely unruffled. I wondered what would happen. I would have spoken in English to Aram had he understood the language; the inquisitive prowlers might then have taken us for foreign tourists and passed on. Foreign tourists may say anything they please as loudly as they choose in whatever language they speak without invoking suspicion. I had no reason to fear for my own safety, but I was growing panicky for the security of my angry young friend. Soon the bullet-headed man lost interest in us, but the other continued to glare with an intensity that heightened my uneasiness. Seconds seemed hours, but Aram never betrayed the least hint of disquiet. He glared back as intently as did the man with the cane. Finally the man turned and walked away with his companion. Wordlessly Aram watched them until they were lost in the procession of promenaders.

"Scoundrels," he remarked. "Snooping around like hungry dogs hunting for prey. I can spot them like this—" snapping thumb against forefinger.

"Were you frightened?" I asked.

He gave a nervous chuckle. "Armenians don't scare easily." And after a moment's silence he added weakly, "I couldn't say I felt comfortable. Oh, well, it isn't as bad as it used to be." Suddenly growing animated, he went on. "The Youth Festival [July 1957] changed everything. What a holiday it was, what a gala time we had! To the end of my life I won't forget it. For once our boys and girls could mingle freely with girls and boys from all over the world—we felt a common bond of brotherhood that we had never before known. We were like children on a picnic, the most wonderful picnic in our lives. It was the only time we understood what real internationalism was— freehearted and joyful comradeship with young people from all continents, all nations, from capitalist and Communist countries—no bad blood, no insulting epithets, no barriers at all—nothing but good fellowship, the most innocent and most joyful, as though we had all grown up together and known one another all our lives. There was laughter in our hearts and tears in our eyes—tears of happiness. Yes, I wept with happiness, and I wasn't the only one. So let scoundrels eavesdrop on our talk—memories of the festival give us strength to stare back at them as hard as they stare at us, so they know we aren't afraid of them. Oh, the unforgettable festival!"

Suddenly we heard singing floating toward us. Soon three trucks loaded with young people drove by, one after another. The trucks were decorated with freshly cut birch and evergreen twigs, with wild flowers, red banners and red bunting. Large white-lettered legends streamed out from the broad bands of bunting:

"For Our Beloved Motherland!"

"For a Rich Harvest!"

"Beat America in the Production of Milk, Butter, Meat!"

"On to the Virgin Lands, Lads!"

Pedestrians stopped, smiled, waved their hands. The boys and girls in the trucks waved back, smiling and singing, the voices lusty and gay. Aram, too, waved. He appeared visibly moved, and after the trucks rolled out of sight, he said, "Out-of-towners going East to help in the harvest. Wonderful boys and girls! So much spirit! So much will to sacrifice! Something great must come out of it all. It must, it simply must."

He paused and we walked on in silence. Then he spoke again. "If only the big shots didn't treat us like children who don't know anything and can't do any thinking at all. You'd imagine we hadn't even learned to read and write, from all the fables they tell us." He gave a sneering laugh. "The fools! They deceive nobody but themselves, if they believe their own words, which of course they don't."

As we parted, Aram said, "When you see Saroyan, please tell him that his blood brothers in the Soviet Union are proud of him and wish him well."

PART II

FOUNDATIONS

5.
BOOKS
The Grand Contradiction

In Leningrad I introduced an American college student to an attractive Russian college girl who spoke fluent English. Captivated by her, the young American proceeded to engage in an American-style flirtation, bantering with her as he would with an American girl student. But such banter is alien to the Russian college girl; least of all does she expect to be approached with familiarity, however innocent. And the more lively the American student became, the more he confused and antagonized his new acquaintance. Finally the girl arose and walked away.

"Beautiful but dumb" was the American's verdict.

"I'm afraid," I said, "she thinks you are dumb."

Then I ventured to give him a little practical advice. "Next time you want to start a flirtation with a Russian college girl, begin by asking her if she has read Mark Twain, and you'll catch her interest. Your next move is to tell her that you admire Tolstoy's *War and Peace*, and your battle will be half won. But," I went on, "be sure you know your Mark Twain and *War and Peace*, because she does."

My counsel may sound high-brow, but the truth is that the subject of literature never fails to establish an immediate *rapprochement* between a foreign student and the most retiring Russian college girl. She is probably the best-read college girl in the world. She may be preparing herself for a career in mathematics, medicine, physics, chemistry, biology, but she knows her Pushkin and Lermontov, her Dickens and Dreiser, her Balzac and Galsworthy—to mention only a few authors who have attained enormous popularity in the Soviet Union.

The passion for literature is as old in Russia as writing itself, and neither Czarist nor Soviet dictatorship ever attempted to curb the right to read. Czarist and Soviet totalitarianism have both striven to shackle the mind and imagination of authors, the Soviet so ruthlessly that the Czars by comparison were models of tolerance, indeed of benevolence. But readers have suffered from no such shackling, though their choice of books has necessarily been limited to those offered by library and bookshop. Yet—and this is the grand contradiction in the Soviet scheme of things—the prodigality with which the Soviets have made available the great literature of the past, Russian and foreign, is in staggering contrast to the restraints they have imposed on Soviet writers in their efforts to depict life as they observe it and portray character as they envision it. They have applied one set of standards to writers who died before the revolution, especially Russian, and another to those who survived it or who came up after the revolution had triumphed. Though you, Gogol, exalted Czarism and Orthodoxy during the last years of your life, your sins shall not count against you. You can sin no more. But you, Leonid Andreyev and Ivan Bunin, fled from the revolution and cursed it, and you shall have to wait a long time—you, Andreyev, until long after your death —before your literary genius shall bring forgetfulness of your sins; and you, Boris Pilnyak and Isaac Babel, living in the Soviet Union and found sinning against the dictatorship, shall pay with your lives or with oblivion.

The tolerance of the twenties, followed by the terror of the thirties, which abated during the war years, heightened afterward until after the death of Stalin, then subsided again—such have been the ordeals of living Soviet authors. But the reader was left unmolested. He could pick and choose at will—from all that was available to him.

That is why on the Soviet literary scene the reader has been a more consequential personage than the writer. The reader might laugh at socialist realism, and how often have I heard him do it, but the writer could no more escape its interdictions then he could the censor who passed on his manuscripts. It is the reader and not the writer who has kept alive the transcendent humanism of Russia's nineteenth-century golden age of literature; indeed, the humanism of the ages as reflected in literature because so much of it has been placed at his disposal.

Under Czarism, with more than half the population illiterate, the reading public was made up largely of intellectuals. Now it is counted in the millions. In my boyhood days in a Russian village, muzhiks rarely heard of Pushkin. Now everyone there, young and old, has not only heard of the poet but has sat enthralled at public readings of his poetry. Through the years I have attended many such readings in village after village, and I have always marveled at the rapt attention of the audiences. Love of poetry seems to be innate in the Russian, and amateur and professional elocutionists who travel the literary circuits, which bring to mind the old Lyceum lecture circuits in America, never need worry about attracting a packed and enthusiastic audience.

Years ago I wrote that when a Russian had nothing to do, he shelled pumpkin and sunflower seeds. Now I am constrained to write that when a Russian has nothing to do he reads a book. In subways and on streetcars, in parks and boulevards, in railroad stations and on trains, in courtyards and hallways, one always sees people reading books.

Books, books, books! In Moscow they are sold in countless bookshops, in factories, colleges, public schools, subways, railroad stations, hotel lobbies, newsstands, corner bookstalls, on sidewalk tables, at special book fairs that circulate from place to place. A Soviet factory without a bookshop or library is as unthinkable as one without machinery. Once I spent several hours wandering the busy shopping streets in Moscow in search of a stationery store that carried wrapping paper, twine, manila envelopes. It was a vain search, but all along these streets I passed one bookshop after another.

"Do you ever advertise books?" I asked the assistant director of Leningrad's House of the Book, the largest bookshop in the Soviet Union and the only one that fairly sparkles with elegance.

"We don't have to," replied the slender, high-cheeked, gray-eyed assistant. "By the time the advertisement appeared in the press we might be out of the stock. If the author happens to be a favorite, we'd sell out in two hours. It's happened again and again, especially with a foreign author. We recently brought out a new edition—250,000 copies—of Longfellow's *Hiawatha*. The supply we got from the publishing house we sold with lightninglike speed."

One reason the Longfellow poem is a favorite is because of the masterful translation (1903) by the late Ivan Bunin, one of the great stylists in Russian literature. I can still enjoy reading the poem in Russian as I no longer can in English.

As we wandered around the immense, brightly lighted two-story shop in the old magnificent Singer Sewing Machine Building on the Nevsky, my escort told me that a selection of Edgar Allan Poe's poems and stories would soon be published in an edition of 225,000 copies. "It will include, of course, *The Raven*," he said, "*The Bells*, and *Annabel Lee*, poems we love. We'll sell our supply in no time," he predicted. "It will be the same with the new edition of Homer's *Odyssey*, the tragedies of Sophocles, and the two-volume selection of Hemingway's writings."

The House of the Book carries over 30,000 titles, a stock of 2,000,000 books, and averages a daily sale of some 30,000 copies, one fourth of which are sold on the sidewalk tables. "Our sales in 1932," said the assistant director, "amounted to 225,000 rubles. In 1959 sales rose to 21,000,000 rubles a year." In American money the sums are equivalent to over 56,000 dollars for 1932 and 2,310,000 dollars for 1959. About 24,000 people visit the bookshop daily.

"Do you read much Dickens in America?" he asked.

"Usually," I answered, "only when we're in school and in college."

"Is that so?" he said, with an incredulous lift of the eyebrows. "Our people read him all the time, of all ages and all occupations. We're bringing out a new edition in thirty-volume sets and are offering it to the public on a subscription basis. It's the most complete edition of Dickens, we believe, that has ever been published anywhere, including England."

Then he told me that they were republishing Theodore Dreiser in an edition of 450,000 fifteen-volume sets and Mark Twain in an edition of 300,000 twelve-volume sets. Other well-known foreign authors whom they were republishing in sets and in huge editions were Thomas and Heinrich Mann, Maupassant, Molière, Heine, Capek, Balzac, Jules Verne, Jack London, Anatole France, Dumas *père*.

"Our people love to buy the collected works of authors in sets," said the director proudly.

Indeed they do. In home after home, even in villages, I saw these collections, stacked on benches and even on the floor, because it was impossible to buy bookcases. I shall believe in the success of the Seven-Year Plan when the Soviet woodworking industries put on the market all the bookcases that customers are frantically demanding.

When my escort and I passed a fiction counter, he picked up a book in gray hard covers and showed it to me. "Do you know the author of this novel?" he asked. "He's an American." The novel was a Russian translation of Mitchell Wilson's *My Brother, My Enemy*. I had never heard of the novel, hadn't in fact heard of Mitchell Wilson until a few days before my departure for Moscow, when Doubleday's Ken McCormick told me that Wilson was in Moscow gathering material for a novel on Russian and American scientists.

"I'm sorry," I said, "I don't know the author and never read any of his novels."

A young woman who was standing by the counter introduced herself as an Intourist interpreter. "I've been guide to many American tourists," she said, "and I've yet to meet one who has heard of Mitchell Wilson. It's very strange," she added, with a note of sympathy for another American who knew nothing of Mitchell Wilson.

"Here," said my escort, turning to the back of *My Brother, My Enemy*. "It was published in Sverdlovsk, at one of our regional publishing houses. Moscow and Leningrad are out of stock and we were glad to get a shipment from Sverdlovsk. Look at the figures: first edition of 75,000 copies sold out, and this is a second edition of 75,000."

It's only a slight exaggeration to say that Mitchell Wilson is as much a literary as Van Cliburn is a musical sensation in Russia. Two of Wilson's novels, the one I mentioned and *Live with Lightning*, are read by workers as much as by intellectuals. When I was in Kiev and called on Mikola Bazhan, the poet, he too asked whether I knew Mitchell Wilson. "He's an extraordinary writer," Bazhan said. "He makes great drama out of science, out of man's struggle to unlock nature's secrets for the good of all mankind. You start reading his novel and you can't put it down until you finish it. We're impatiently awaiting his sequel to *My Brother, My Enemy*."

To appreciate the reason for Wilson's sensational triumph in Russia, it is well to record that since the first sputnik has soared into space, the scientist has become a fabulous personage. Mitchell himself, as I learned when I met him in Moscow, is a physicist who had studied with Enrico Fermi. His heroes are scientists. In *Live with Lightning* he tells the story of American scientists struggling to make use of atomic energy. In *My Brother, My Enemy* he tells of American scientists pioneering in television. It fascinates Russians to read detailed descriptions of scientists actually at work in laboratories, of their hopes and failures, their anguish and triumphs.

An Intourist girl interpreter whom I introduced to Wilson was so excited that when we left she said, "How my friends will envy me when I tell them that I shook hands with Mitchell Wilson."

"Why do you like reading him," I asked, "when he's so non-ideological?"

"Ah," she answered, "but he tells me much about America that I never knew, how people live, what they are like, the good and the bad people, and he makes scientists so human—they flirt and fall in and out of love, suffer when their love is unanswered and thrill when it is—just like the rest of us."

Yet not a single publication has ever carried a line of advertisement for either of Wilson's novels. Russians learn of new books from announcements in the press and on the radio, from catalogues which they read in bookshops, from window displays, but chiefly from one another. They are the most enthusiastic word-of-mouth advertisers in the world, provided it is a book that excites them.

Until about the end of the war, the millions of new readers read practically everything that was published and bookshops were never troubled with remainders. Now they are. The market, when I was last in Moscow, was glutted with Dickens, Stefan Zweig, Feuchtwanger, and some of the fiction of socialist realism, even as it was with the translations of poetry from Tadjik, Kazakh, Byelorussian, and other minority languages. Not that there is any national prejudice against these poets; it is only that they are vastly inferior to Pushkin, Lermontov, Nekrasov, Mayakovsky, on whom Russians are brought up since their earliest school years.

"Salesgirls," a Moscow woman said to me, "are trying to shove the poets of our minorities down the throats of customers, but people refuse to buy them. Our readers have become too discriminating to have any books shoved down their throats, but especially poetry. This is one of the most astonishing things that has happened in our country since your last visit here."

Even Dostoyevsky has not escaped a certain apathy toward his novels. A complete edition of his fiction was brought out between 1926 and 1930. With the coming of the first Plan, Stalin had all but disinherited him, though certain of his short stories were included in school textbooks. When, after the death of Stalin, a new complete edition was announced in 300,000 ten-volume sets, the public hastened to subscribe. "You cannot imagine the excitement that swept not only Moscow," a schoolteacher told me, "on the day subscriptions were opened. I myself stood for hours in a long queue in freezing weather. But long before my turn came, all subscriptions were exhausted. I was furious and so were the others who had vainly been shivering in the long queue."

But the rage for Dostoyevsky soon subsided. He has his eloquent partisans, chiefly among intellectuals. The broad reading public has cooled toward him—"because," as a highly literary woman explained to me, "he doesn't fit the spirit of the times. He belongs to the past and to the future, but not to the present. We're so busy with construction that we're impatient with his endless digging into the innermost recesses of the human soul. This is particularly true of the young generation. They do not even like his love stories; they find them boring and irritating, nothing like the love stories of Turgenev and Tolstoy, which they read over and over."

Now Dostoyevsky can easily be bought everywhere, and if there are remainders they are disposed of among the ever growing chain of libraries. From Moscow's Book Chamber, which performs the functions of the American Library of Congress in registering new publications, I learned that there were in the Soviet Union 407,000 libraries, 1000 in Moscow alone!

The libraries range in size from Moscow's block-long Lenin State Library with its 17,000,000 volumes to mud huts or timbered cottages in villages that count their collections in only four figures, but which are continually being enlarged. New libraries are being opened all over the country, and when I visited the Ukrainian collective farm Motherland, I discovered a novel type of library: a side room in a newly built cow barn, decorated with banners and potted flowers and furnished with a long table covered with a red cloth, chairs, writing materials, and shelves of books that included novels and poetry. "We come here," said a milkmaid, "during rest hours and evenings to divert ourselves with a book. The trouble is we don't have all the books we want to read."

Literature, ancient and modern, Russian and foreign, plays so transcendent a part in the life and education of the Soviet citizenry that I applied to Moscow's Book Chamber for information on the literary output in the Soviet Union since the rise of the Kremlin dictatorship. In response to my request, T. Gorbunova of the statistical department, supplied me with appropriate statistical records covering the period from 1918 to July 1960.

The records do not include the literature of Scandinavia or the Low Countries, or of Spain, ancient Persia, Greece, Rome; not even of China and India, though literature of these countries has been translated and published in large editions. The information at my disposal covers Russian literature, past and present, and translations from the French, English, and German languages, embracing the literature of France, Austria, England, America, Canada, and Australia. Limited as it is, it tells a vivid tale of reading tastes and habits that, save for Soviet fiction, in no way answer—that indeed controvert—the Kremlin's ideological demands and purposes.

Of the Western countries, France holds first place in popularity: 441 authors have been translated and a total of 182,376,000 copies of their books have been published.

England holds second place: 324 authors translated, 103,290,000 copies published.

America comes next: 239 authors translated, 96,540,000 copies published.

Germany holds fourth place: 324 authors translated, 69,340,000 copies published.

Canada holds fifth place: 7 authors translated, 6,386,000 copies published; over 3,000,000 of which are credited to Ernest Thompson Seton, whom Russians regard as a Canadian author.

Austria follows Canada in popularity: 11 authors translated, 4,480,000 copies published.

Australia comes last: 5 authors translated, 3,453,000 copies published.

But the figures tell only part of the story. The quality of the translated literature may be judged from the lists that follow. In the instance of France and Germany, I have presented those authors who are credited with the publication of a million or more copies, listed in the order of their popularity.

France

Jules Verne, Victor Hugo, Honoré de Balzac, Charles Perrault, Guy de Maupassant, Emile Zola, Stendhal, Romain Rolland, Dumas *père*, Anatole France, Alphonse Daudet, Prosper Mérimée, Gustave Flaubert, Henri Barbusse, George Sand, André Stil, Alfred de Musset, Voltaire, Louis Bussanar, Molière, Hector Malot, Louis Aragon, Rosny *aîné*, Pierre Béranger.

Except for Louis Aragon and André Stil, both of whom are Communists, all the above authors, including Barbusse, were well known in Czarist times, though they never attained the mass circulation that they have now.

A surprising feature of the Book Chamber's list is the presence of the name of François Mauriac, the well-known Roman Catholic novelist. Nor is the output of his translated works negligible—589,000 copies.

Germany

The brothers Grimm, Lion Feuchtwanger, Heinrich Heine, Wilhelm Gauf, Erich Remarque, Heinrich Mann, Goethe, Thomas Mann, Schiller, Bernhard Kellermann, Anna Seghers, Rudolph Raspe, Willie Bredel, Ernst Hoffmann.

Here it might be mentioned that East Berlin was so resentful that Remarque's popularity was greater than Anna Seghers', the leading German Communist novelist, that in a protest to Moscow it charged Soviet publishers with favoring a non-political writer over "an active fighter against fascism." There was even a rumor in Moscow that in deference to the protest a new collection of Remarque's stories, which was already set into type, would never be brought out. The rumor proved false, no doubt because Soviet publishers are no less profit-minded than capitalist publishers, and Remarque is an established best seller, as Anna Seghers no longer is.

Some of the British authors popular in the Soviet Union, with their sales figures as supplied by Moscow's Book Chamber, are:

Charles Dickens	18,441,000
H. G. Wells	7,271,000
Rudyard Kipling	4,855,000
Thomas Mayne Reid	4,827,000
Sir Arthur Conan Doyle	4,751,000
Jonathan Swift	4,518,000
Daniel Defoe	4,223,000
William Shakespeare	4,128,000
Sir Walter Scott	3,969,000
A. J. Cronin	3,926,000
John Galsworthy	3,841,000
Ethel L. Voynich	3,398,000
James Aldridge	2,838,000
Robert Louis Stevenson	2,654,000
Jerome K. Jerome	1,739,000
Ouida	1,364,000
Thomas Hardy	1,353,000
Joseph Conrad	1,336,000
Charlotte Brontë	943,000
William Makepeace Thackeray	933,000
George Gordon, Lord Byron	819,000
Robert Burns	678,000
Henry Fielding	619,000
Graham Greene	514,000
Enid Blyton	512,000
George Bernard Shaw	476,000
Jack Lindsay	430,000
Richard Aldington	403,000
Rafael Sabatini	396,000
Oscar Wilde	354,000
J. B. Priestley	320,000
Emily Brontë	265,000
Tobias Smollett	261,000
Sean O'Casey	240,000
Richard Brinsley Sheridan	164,000
Percy Bysshe Shelley	110,000

Dickens tops the list of British authors, but then, even under the Czars he was one of the great favorites of the Russian reading public. A long time ago, when I was a pupil in a Russian elementary four-year school, we read Dickens and Mark Twain with as much enthusiasm as both authors are read by school children in the Russia of today. *The Cricket on the Hearth* and *Pickwick Papers* were dramatized and presented by Moscow's Art Theater in the prewar years. Both plays are in the repertory of this theater and remain favorites of the theatergoing public.

Through the years, when Soviet ideologists and politicians grew furious with England, Soviet writers and propagandists hastened to remind readers and radio listeners that "the masses" in the capitalist England of today suffered as dire misery and want as they did in the days of Oliver Twist. If there are Soviet readers who believe the propaganda, one doesn't meet them. Russians read Dickens for the same reason that they read Tolstoy and Turgenev—for the joy of reading novels that interest and move them.

Interest in English literature is constantly growing. Christopher Marlowe, for example, was published only in Czarist times. *The Tragical History of Dr. Faustus* was first translated by a woman named Minayeva and was published in St. Petersburg in 1899. Another translation of the same play was made by the well-known Russian poet Konstantin Balmont and was brought out in 1899. *The Jew of Malta* was rendered into Russian by M. Shelgunov and was published in 1882. Now Soviet publishers are wakening to the fact that they have ignored one of England's foremost playwrights— "the remarkable contemporary of Shakespeare." An edition of Marlowe is scheduled for publication.

Thackeray was immensely popular with the Russian intelligentsia in Czarist times. In the Soviet Union he is known chiefly for *Vanity Fair*, though *Henry Esmond* and *The Virginians* were also published. Now there is renewed interest in Thackeray. The *Literaturnaya Gazeta* has chided publishing houses for neglecting him, an author who "side by side with Dickens is one of the major representatives of English critical realism of the nineteenth century."

In 1959, Moscow's Maly Theater mounted a production of *Vanity Fair*. It was one of the theatrical sensations of the season and has heightened interest in Thackeray. There can be no doubt that he too will be published in a set and in a very large edition.

For contemporary English writers who, one way or another, directly and indirectly, parody or disdain Soviet intellectual freedom or the Soviet way of life, Moscow has only hot scorn. "The literature of disintegration," writes the *Literaturnaya Gazeta* (April 12, 1958), "saturated with hatred for everything that is progressive, is represented by T. S. Eliot, by the novels of Aldous Huxley, by the anti-Soviet slanders of George Orwell, who died in 1950, and by, to this day, *still healthy* [my italics] Evelyn Waugh." So drop dead, Evelyn Waugh!

Contemporary British authors commanding the attention of Soviet publishers are Joyce Cary, C. P. Snow, Somerset Maugham, and, of course, the "angry young men." Ever hungry for literature that serves immediate propaganda purposes, the *Literaturnaya Gazeta* perceives in this "galaxy of poets and prose writers . . . the frame of mind of broad sections of the postwar young generation which was deceived by the promises of *social revolution* [the *Gazeta*'s italics] so prodigally made by the Labour party when it came to power." Kingsley Amis, John Wain, John Osborne, are singled out as spokesmen of the youth that is particularly angry over the failure of "the social revolution" to materialize. Needless to add that when the *Gazeta* speaks of social revolution, it means first and foremost Russian-style "proletarian dictatorship" and all that it implies.

The predisposition of the official hierarchy in the Soviet writing profession to see others as they see themselves is one of their conspicuous failings. Hence their dismay and anger over John Wain's "Open Letter to My Russian Hosts," which appeared in the London *Observer* of August 7, 1960.

One of Wain's novels, in an edition of 250,000 copies, sold out promptly and two others were scheduled for publication. During his stay in Moscow, Wain was of course hospitably received by writers and editors, and his hosts never counted on the ironic rebuke with which he would repay them for their hospitality.

"I am the kind of person," Wain writes, "who is adversely affected by propaganda. The more persistent the efforts to sell me a thing, the more churlish and suspicious I become. Imagine what happens to me when I go to a country where the resources of publicity are concentrated in the hands of the state, and are used day and night to hammer home the official view of everything, the past, the present, the future, the destiny of man."

This paragraph alone was a bombshell that shook up Wain's hosts. Instead of being a comrade in arms, as they had imagined he was, Wain gave them a piece of his angry mind over his disillusionment with the Soviet political and intellectual scene.

S. Smirnov, then editor of the *Literaturnaya Gazeta*, devoted two long articles (August 13, 16, 1960) in reply to the British author, and called him not an angry but a "frightened young man," who "flaunts his anti-communism like a visiting card of bourgeois loyalty."

Alexey Surkov, who was first secretary of the Soviet Writers' Union from 1956 to 1960, followed with a full-page reply in the *Observer* of August 28, 1960. When one remembers Surkov's ideological orthodoxy and the savagery of his attacks on non-conformists, one must admire the restraint with which he addresses himself to an English audience. "You must have been attacked," he writes, "by a knight of the cold war, and when unable to resist the attack, you were pushed into the beaten track of previous slanders."

Neither Smirnov nor Surkov chooses to remember what the *Literaturnaya Gazeta* had written about Britain's "angry young men," and how woefully it had misjudged the source and the nature of their anger. Trapped in a "contradiction" of their own making, the Soviet writer-ideologists do not say a word about it and strike out with the old weapon of personal attack. Mitchell Wilson was astute enough to say to his Moscow literary hosts, "Please don't fall in love with me. Let's just be friends. If you fall in love with me, it may end in your killing me."

One cannot agree with Wain that "no Western book is published among you unless it can be made to yield the message that Western society is dying—or so evil that it deserves to die." Soviet publication of Western classical literature in enormous editions contradicts the Britisher's charge, though the *Literaturnaya Gazeta*, like *Pravda*, is continually and gloatingly predicting the imminent demise of Western society.

The United States

Below is the list of favorite American authors, with their sales figures, as given by the Book Chamber.

Jack London	20,726,000
Mark Twain	11,551,000
Theodore Dreiser	10,948,000
O. Henry	4,641,000
James Fenimore Cooper	4,495,000
Upton Sinclair	4,167,000
Bret Harte	2,109,000
Harriet Beecher Stowe	1,736,000
Albert Maltz	1,677,000
Ernest Hemingway	1,362,000
Mitchell Wilson	1,190,000
Sinclair Lewis	1,171,000
Erskine Caldwell	1,139,000
Edgar Allan Poe	1,029,000
William Saroyan	872,000
Joel Chandler Harris	818,000
Henry Wadsworth Longfellow	702,000
James Oliver Curwood	629,000
Washington Irving	499,000
Mabel Dodge	477,000
Agnes Smedley	364,000
Frank Norris	358,000
Lucy Sprague Mitchell	304,000
Walt Whitman	285,000
Sherwood Anderson	233,000
William Faulkner	225,000
Langston Hughes	214,000
Konrad Bercovici	188,000
Nathaniel Hawthorne	176,000
Edgar Rice Burroughs	137,000
John Dos Passos	122,000
Ira Wolfert	74,000

Soviet editors and publishers are beginning to interest themselves in several other American authors whom they have hitherto neglected. Herman Melville, for example, is known only by his *Typee,* which was first published in 1929 and republished in 1957. Now

Moby Dick is scheduled for publication. Thoreau's *Walden* was published in 1910, but Soviet publishers never republished it. Now *Walden*, too, is to be reissued. So are the works of Edward Bellamy.

Upton Sinclair has had a curious reception in the Soviet Union. In the twenties and early thirties he was almost as popular as Jack London. Then, rather suddenly, interest in him flagged. Russians were tiring of his muckraking novels. He was not saying anything new about America, was the opinion I heard over and over. America was then at the height of her popularity in the Soviet Union, as the teacher from whom Russians must learn how to build and operate factories and power plants and to modernize their agriculture. But to the Kremlin, Sinclair was still the author who "mercilessly exposed the sufferings of the exploited American proletarian."

Then, after World War II, aroused by Stalin's aggressive foreign policy, particularly by the Communist *Putsch* in Czechoslovakia in February 1948, Sinclair denounced the Soviet Union. Instantly Moscow retaliated with a string of vitriolic epithets, branding Sinclair a "careerist, a Wall Street lackey, a warmonger who chose his weapons from the arsenal of Churchill-Goebbels." I had assumed that Sinclair would never again be published in the Soviet Union.

To my amazement, as I browsed around Russian bookshops, I saw *King Coal* and *Jimmie Higgins* back on the counters. It is not in the nature of Moscow to ignore authors who depict the seamy side of American life, even when written by an author who has been dubbed "a Wall Street lackey." But the novels do not sell. "The public is not interested," a saleswoman in a Moscow bookshop explained.

The case of John Steinbeck is equally illuminating. His *Grapes of Wrath* was originally hailed as a literary masterpiece and as an indictment of American civilization. Then, about 1950, somebody in Moscow discovered that Steinbeck had written a book bearing the title *Bombs Away*. The book was written in 1942 as a tribute to American fliers in World War II. But the discoverer of the title had obviously not read the book. He assumed that Steinbeck was advocating the bombing of Russia, and to make the attack on Steinbeck particularly sensational, Dmitry Shostakovich was selected to anathematize him. In *Izvestia* of July 6, 1950, the composer execrated Steinbeck as "a reactionary, a barbarian, a cannibal." Like Sinclair, Steinbeck the hero had become a villain.

Yet in Leningrad's House of the Book, I saw copies of a fresh edition of *The Grapes of Wrath*. The renewed interest in the novel was obviously actuated by the same motive as the republication of Sinclair's novels and of Moscow's enthusiasm for Graham Greene's *The Quiet American* and *Our Man in Havana*. Russians were surprised when I told them that both Greene novels were published in America and were widely read.

Russia

Most enlightening is Russian reading of their own literature. The Book Chamber presented me with two separate lists, one of best-selling Soviet writers, the other of best-selling classics—writers of the past who have won a permanent place in Russian literature.

SOVIET WRITERS

A. N. Tolstoy	51,239,000
V. V. Mayakovsky	40,688,000
M. A. Sholokhov	32,834,000
K. M. Simonov	18,631,000
A. A. Fadeyev	16,650,000
M. M. Prishvin	14,966,000
V. P. Katayev	14,785,000
A. S. Serafimovich	13,692,000
N. A. Ostrovsky	13,058,000
P. P. Bazhov	12,695,000
B. N. Polevoy	11,701,000
D. Bedny	10,681,000
A. C. Novikov-Priboy	10,541,000
B. L. Gorbatov	10,068,000
F. I. Panferov	9,685,000
I. G. Ehrenburg	9,374,000
N. S. Tikhonov	9,374,000
V. A. Kaverin	8,119,000
P. A. Pavlenko	7,940,000
V. Y. Shishkov	7,790,000
K. G. Paustovsky	7,327,000
A. C. Makarenko	7,240,000
S. N. Sergeyev-Tsensky	7,109,000

D. A. Furmanov	6,990,000
F. V. Gladkov	6,306,000
A. T. Tvardovsky	6,073,000
L. M. Leonov	4,989,000
G. E. Nikolayeva	4,479,000
V. V. Ovechkin	3,838,000
S. A. Esenin	2,698,000

A glance at the figures brings out the significant fact that the best-selling Soviet authors are the poet Vladimir Mayakovsky and the novelists Mikhail Sholokhov and Alexey Tolstoy. Lenin, it is well known, never cared much for Mayakovsky, but Stalin glorified him, which in some measure accounts for the immense sales of his poetry. As for Sholokhov, his *And Quiet Flows the Don* is regarded even by apostles of socialist realism as the greatest masterpiece that has come out of the Soviet era, and Soviet readers have paid it the tribute of exhausting one edition after another. No other Soviet novel has been so avidly read and reread. Neither pro- nor anti-bolshevik, it is as untainted by ideological partisanship as is the raw and tumultuous Cossack life it depicts. In vastness of scope, liveliness of dialogue, creation of character, fidelity to the realities of life, it properly belongs in the pre-Soviet golden age of literature.

And so do Alexey Tolstoy's two best-known novels—the *Road to Calvary* and *Peter the First* (the Great). To this day Russians read these novels as they rarely do the socialist-realist fiction of the past.

But Soviet authors as a group do not command the fervor of the reading public that the classics do. The figures speak for themselves:

PRE-REVOLUTIONARY RUSSIAN WRITERS

Leo Tolstoy	94,791,000
Maxim Gorky	92,895,000
Alexander Pushkin	91,787,000
Anton Chekhov	55,542,000
Ivan Turgenev	46,024,000
Nikolai Gogol	36,841,000
D. N. Mamin-Sibiryakov	29,148,000
Nikolai Nekrasov	28,818,000
Mikhail Lermontov	28,454,000
Ivan Krylov	28,222,000
Vladimir Korolenko	24,340,000

Mikhail Saltykov (N. Shchedrin)	21,142,000
Alexander Kuprin	16,969,000
Alexander Ostrovsky (playwright)	12,121,000
Nikolai Leskov	11,481,000
Ivan Goncharov	11,306,000
Fyodor Dostoyevsky	9,746,000

Shortly after I received the statistical lists from Moscow's Book Chamber, I was in Kiev, and as I sauntered the streets I came on a block-long queue, made up largely of young people of high school and college age. I thought they had lined up to buy rugs or some other article in short supply. On inquiry I learned that they had come to subscribe to a newly announced five-volume edition of the poetry of Sergey Esenin, who shot himself in 1925 at the age of thirty.

A small group gathered around me, and one after another complained that favorite authors were brought out in editions inadequate to the demand. An engineering student spoke with disappointment over his failure to obtain the collected works of Mark Twain. The edition was oversubscribed. A girl medical student said that her mother was subscribing to the new twelve-volume edition of Chekhov in commemoration of the hundredth anniversary of his birth, but there was no assurance the subscription would be honored; too many people were subscribing to the Chekhov edition. Another girl complained that she had been searching the bookshops for the two-volume edition of Hemingway, but they were always sold out. "And look at all the people standing in line—three, four abreast," she continued, "to subscribe to Esenin's poetry, and how many of us will get it?"

Unquestionably the Soviet Union is something of a paradise for book publishers and booksellers, but only for books that meet with popular appeal.

It is not my purpose to evaluate the statistics of Moscow's Book Chamber in terms of literary criticism. My concern is with the literary tastes of what may properly be called the largest book-reading nation in the world. When one sets the Chamber's sales figures of Soviet literature against those of France, England, Germany, America, and old Russia, one becomes instantly aware of the fact that Soviet literature constitutes the much lesser part of the nation's reading fare. The Kremlin may be demanding of Soviet authors that they infuse their writings with *partiinost* (party spirit). But the public reaches out in ever mounting numbers for the writings of authors, Russian and foreign, who had never heard of *partiinost*.

In these writings the reader can roam freely and at will over the vast range of human experience. He can lose himself in a world that is officially shut out of his daily life. Neither Soviet cultural isolationism, which has only in recent years been mildly fissured, nor imposed ideological conformity can restrain the Russian mind from delving into "the best that has been said and thought in the world" as long as the old Russian classics and world literature are freely accessible. They keep alive a world view of humanity which the literature of socialist realism is intended to obscure and to distort.

The one book that one never finds in a Soviet bookshop is, of course, the Bible. I know that university students who study literature have been demanding it. But the demand has consistently been refused. To Soviet ideologists the Bible is a clutter of superstition and evil—a book that has for ages been a weapon in the hands of the "exploiting classes," which was used "to tame and enslave the toiling masses." But the very violence of the condemnation has roused keen interest in the Book of Books. A Russian woman in Moscow told me of an experience which demonstrates how alive is this interest. "I was walking along the Dzherzhinsky Square," she said, "when I was attracted by a strange sight: a crowd clustering around a sidewalk book table and then melting way, to be followed by another crowd which likewise melted away—crowd after crowd acting in a similar manner. I had never observed anything like it in Moscow. So I walked over to find out what it was all about, and there on the book table lay stacks of a newly published book that bore in large letters the title *Bible*. That's what attracted the crowds. But underneath the title in small print was a subtitle explaining that it was the atheist Yemelyan Yaroslavsky's interpretation of the Bible. Of course people melted away. Had it been the real Bible they'd have bought it. I'd have bought it myself. Lots and lots of people would buy it, if it were on sale, just to find out why it is so loudly denounced."

"The book," wrote Alexander Herzen, Russia's most celebrated nineteenth-century literary exile, "is the spiritual legacy of one generation to another." That this literary inheritance from Russia's and the world's past has been made available to the Russian people on a gigantic scale has always seemed to me one of the splendid achievements of the Soviets. The achievement is all the more remarkable because of the irreconcilable contradiction between the broadly humane spirit of this inheritance and the intellectual obscurantism of the authoritarian Kremlin mind.

6.

RELIGION
Ordeal of Orthodoxy

The long-haired, bearded monks at the caves of the famed and ancient Pechorskaya Lavra in Kiev, the oldest sanctuary of Russian Orthodoxy, made a pathetic sight. Pale-faced, unkempt, their heads hung low, a large pectoral cross shining on their greasy black robes, they stood statuelike, their hands cupped together in expectation of alms. The group of young people I joined for an excursion through the caves eyed them curiously and coldly. Not one of them proffered a copper coin to the cupped hands. Almsgiving was obviously a custom they detested.

Lighted candles in hand, we walked through the dark narrow tunnels, passing one cloth-covered casket after another holding the remains of saints, 252 of them, including those of Nestor, the celebrated Russian chronicler, who died early in the twelfth century. When we came out of the caves, a monk was as if waiting for us. I slipped him a ruble note, and when we were beyond his hearing, the leader of the group, a hefty young woman with thick black hair and deep dark eyes, chided me for my action.

"But he looked so poor," I said.

"Poor?" she exclaimed. "That's what you think. Come, I'll show you something." She led us to a garage with three shining automobiles inside. "That's how poor these monks are. I don't know for certain how many automobiles they have. Six, I think. Once I counted four in this very garage."

The other excursionists were as astounded as I was to see these symbols not only of wealth but of privilege.

"I'll show you something else," the group leader said. She led us up a path to the foot of a hill that was fenced around, the wicket gate under lock. Crowning the hill was a magnificent orchard of apples, pears, plums, cherries. "The monks are expert fruit growers," the girl said. "I'll say that for them, and they make a lot of money selling their fruit."

In Czarist times, monks and rural priests were among the most celebrated orchardists in the country. The largest and finest orchard in a village was usually the property of the parish priest. On their rise to power, the bolsheviks expropriated church and monastery lands, including the gardens and orchards of the rural clergy. Nowhere in the Soviet Union have they been returned to the parishes. But here in Kiev, a magnificent orchard of the oldest monastery in the country, though officially nationalized, was still in possession of the monks.

"And think too of the money they make," the girl leader went on, "from the sale of candles and church emblems and from the contributions of the faithful. And don't forget they pay no taxes on these incomes. It's a shame that any of them are permitted to beg."

These monks were the only beggars in clerical garb that I saw in all my travels in the Soviet Union.

At the famed monastery of the Holy Trinity in Zagorsk, founded in 1337, about forty-five miles from Moscow, the monks were exceptionally well shod and robed. Gone is the time when an Orthodox priest had to beg for a living. (Protestant clergymen never did.) The bedraggled *batushka* (little father) standing at a city street corner or in a bazaar, hat in hand, abjectly soliciting alms, is as much a memory now as the flamboyant atheist posters that caricatured the Orthodox priest as a fat-bellied monster glutting himself on the flesh and blood of the poor. Just the removal of the tax from church incomes, not as calculated by the priest or the parish officials but as deliberately inflated by the *fin-inspector* (representative of the Ministry of Finance), has lifted a ruinous burden from the Church. Nowadays, rural priests in European Russia and in Siberia appear better fed and dressed, more composed and dignified, than I ever knew them to be since the coming of the Soviets. In private conversation the term *pop*—colloquial for "priest"—may still be an epithet of ridicule, but the sting of hatred has gone out of it, and however atheistic a party member, he no longer addresses himself contemptuously to the *pop*. The November 10, 1954, ordinance of the party Central Committee outlaws rudeness in word or act toward the clergy or religious institutions.

So high has the official prestige of the Orthodox clergy risen in recent years that a major diplomatic reception in a foreign embassy in Moscow would seem as incomplete without the presence of the augustly robed Metropolitan Nikolai Krutitzky, as foreign spokesman of the Moscow Patriarchate, as without the presence of the Soviet Foreign Minister. When I saw the high-ranking churchman at the Canadian Embassy on the occasion of National Canadian Day and at the American Embassy at the celebration of Independence Day, it seemed incredible that the Kremlin could have so abated its onetime official fury against Orthodoxy that it not only sanctioned but made it a matter of diplomatic propriety, if not of obligation, for foreign embassies to invite the church dignitary to major receptions.

Yet those of us who were eyewitnesses of anti-religious crusades in the early years of the revolution have vivid memories of the savagery of bolshevik attacks on the Orthodox Church and its representatives. The theory was (and still is) that religion is no innate urge in man, but is imposed from without by the master class to facilitate and sanction the exploitation of the many by the few. Though all religions were under attack, Orthodoxy and its officialdom from Patriarchate to village priest were the primary targets. I need only mention the major reasons for the violence and virulence against them: for centuries they had dominated the religious scene in the country and had identified themselves with Czarism and landlordism; they commanded the largest following among the people and had arrayed themselves in full force against the bolshevik dictatorship which had confiscated their enormous landholdings and their other properties, including the jewels in church icons and archives. To the bolsheviks they constituted one of the most powerful reactionary forces in the country, and they proceeded to break down their resistance and to disgrace them before the public. Thousands of priests were thrown out of their homes and left to the mercy of parishioners, who more often than not had no mercy left to show. Thousands of priests were jailed, and who knows how many of them were shot, how many succumbed to hunger and heartbreak? Thousands of churches were converted into clubs, schools, apartment houses, garages, granaries, henhouses, pigsties. Traveling about the countryside in those years, I frequently passed churches that had been "decapitated"—crosses torn from cupolas and sometimes cupolas demolished too, indicating that they were closed to worship, though local officials had not yet put them to any practical use.

The decree of January 23, 1918, guaranteed freedom of worship but did not protect the clergy against persecution, and during the campaign for collectivization of the land, if a priest evinced the least antagonism, however indirect, he suffered merciless punishment.

The cruel campaign dragged on until about 1936, by which time the Orthodox clergy had become so impoverished and so impotent that the Kremlin no longer regarded it a political menace. The time came for an official change of attitude, and the Kremlin went about it rather deviously. The Kamerny (now Pushkin) Theater in Moscow, with a fanfare of exciting publicity, presented an operetta called *Bogatyri* ("Knights"). The libretto was by Demyan Bedny, then the popular Communist poet, the music by Alexander Borodin (1834–87), famed for his opera *Prince Igor*. The Art Committee, official censor of theatrical productions, set its imprimatur on the text and approved the dress rehearsal. The first-night audience applauded it with extravagant enthusiasm. The newspapers paid it glowing tributes.

Then, with the suddenness of a thunderclap, came a Kremlin-inspired and scathing attack on Demyan Bedny, on Tairov, director of the theater, and the production was banned. Kremlin authority denounced it for portraying Russian folk heroes as vulgar louts and for representing the Christianization of Russia (in 988) as a drunken debauch. The new theory viewed the Christianization of the people as a progressive influence in Russian history, because it brought Russia into close communication with a more advanced civilization. Soon afterward school children read in the history textbooks of Anna Pankratova that "by comparison with paganism, Christianity was a step forward . . . Christianity helped to spread among Eastern Slavs the higher civilization of Byzantium. Under its influence Kiev began to build stone houses, decorating them with paintings and mosaics . . . Education began to spread."

Suddenly Byzantine Christianity ceased to be the unmitigated evil it had long been depicted. No more was it to be fiercely damned.

The new Constitution of December 1936 enfranchised the clergy. The priest was neither outcast nor pariah any longer. He was a citizen with the right to vote and hold office (theoretically, of course) and to send his children to institutions of higher learning. For the first time since the coming of the Soviets, the *batushka* could lift up his head and feel a new pride in his person. I happened to be in the village of Reshetilovka in the Ukraine and called on the local priest. He welcomed me cordially, though formerly he would have been afraid to receive a foreigner in his house. He felt so secure that he was about to appeal to higher authorities to stop the kolkhoz from using the larger part of his church for a granary. The happiest member of the priest's family was his twelve-year-old son. He had set his heart on becoming an aviation engineer, an ambition that was now a possibility. Let it be noted that some of the most distinguished literary and scientific figures in Czarist Russia came from the clergy. Nikolai Dobrolyubov and Nikolai Chernyshevsky, literary critics and social philosophers; Sergey Solovyov and Vasily Kluchevsky, the historians; Alexander Popov, whom Moscow credits with the discovery of radio; and Professor Ivan Pavlov, the physiologist, were sons of priests.

But it was Nazi Germany's invasion of Russia in June 1941 that laid the real groundwork for coexistence between the Kremlin and Orthodoxy. The invasion inflamed Russian nationalism and patriotism and created a mood and a political situation that made inevitable the union of the Cross and the Hammer and Sickle in the common struggle against the most ferocious foe Russia has ever fought. The Church had always been passionately nationalistic. In all Russia's wars, whether against the Swedes (1240) and the Germans (1241) in the time of Alexander Nevsky, against the Tatars (1380) under Dmitry Donskoy and again (1547–52) under Ivan the Terrible, against the Poles (1612) in "the time of troubles," or against Napoleon in 1812, the patriotic record of the Church was unblemished. It had always striven to rally the people in defense of the Holy Motherland. In 1941–45 it did so again. It collected clothes and other gifts for the soldiery. It amassed a sum of 300,000,000 rubles for a tank column, named Dmitry Donskoy, for the Red Army. It called on parishioners to help the wounded and the disabled on their return from the front. The most stirring patriotic speech I heard in those days was delivered by the Bishop of Yaroslavl, a magnificent orator, whose name I do not recall, but who moved his audience to tears.

Most significant was the performance in Moscow's Maly Theater of the dramatization of Tolstoy's *War and Peace*, which from beginning to end was a highly emotional sermon on patriotism. The most spectacular feature of the performance was the scene of Marshal Kutuzov at High Mass, staged with reverence and grandeur. The marshal knelt before the miracle-working icon, kissed it devoutly, and humbly accepted the blessing of the high priest for a triumphant campaign against Napoleon. Not even in the grand finale of Glinka's opera *Ivan Sussanin*, first produced in 1939, was the public privileged to witness on the stage so exalted an Orthodox service in all its mystical majesty and theatrical splendor.

For the first time, on November 7, 1942, on the occasion of the twenty-fifth anniversary of the revolution, the Church, in the person of the aged and bearded Metropolitan Sergey, addressed a letter of salutation to Stalin, hailing him as "the God-chosen leader of our military and cultural forces." The foremost and most ruthless atheist in the world was now sanctified as a "God-chosen leader"— precisely as the Czars had been!

Some ten months later, in a spectacularly ritualistic service, Metropolitan Sergey was elevated to the Patriarchate. Not since 1925, when Sergey's predecessor died, had the eminent office been filled. This was a major triumph for the Orthodox Church. Nothing that had yet happened had conferred on it the dignity and prestige of a traditionally national church.

And the very Germans against whom the Church was thundering anathemas were ironically reinforcing its position: in conquered territories they were opening churches which Moscow had closed. In the summer of 1944, when I made a journey to the liberated Cossack Kuban, I drove through village after village in which churches were functioning again. In the summer of 1958, when I revisited the Kuban, I observed that despite renewed anti-religious propaganda, Moscow had not reclosed the churches the Germans had opened. On the conclusion of the war, the Moscow Patriarchate, with the Kremlin's blessing, ruled a domain that in the prewar years had seemed hopelessly beyond its reach.

The Kremlin did more: in 1946 it drove the Uniat Church of Galicia, which it severed from Poland, with its over three million parishioners into the fold of the Moscow Patriarchate. The Uniat Church had been an affiliate of the Roman Church since 1596, or for 350 years. Nor did the Kremlin stop there. It forged fresh bonds between the Moscow Patriarchate and the Orthodox churches in Albania, Rumania, and Bulgaria. As the Kremlin expanded its empire, it inevitably strengthened the empire of the Patriarchate, trusting it to do its patriotic duty in combating in its own way the political recalcitrance of Orthodox worshipers in the countries that had been reduced to Soviet dependencies.

Yet the war-fashioned reconciliation between the Kremlin and the Patriarchate did not save the Orthodox Church from fresh and heavy-handed encroachments on religious landmarks. In 1952, in the village of Ushtshelye, Archangel province, an old and architecturally distinguished church was taken apart because the kolkhoz needed bricks. In the spring of 1954, a sixteenth-century monastery in the province of Kaluga was turned into a repair shop for agricultural implements. The Joseph Volokamsky Monastery, Moscow province, built in the sixteenth century, in the tower of which Vasily Shuisky, Czar between 1606 and 1610, had been imprisoned, was turned into a pigsty! In June 1956, on order of the mayor of the city of Ufa, dynamite blew up an old cathedral. The Church was powerless to prevent the depredations. But the protest (*Literaturnaya Gazeta*, August 23, 1959) of distinguished writers and academicians against the reckless desecration and destruction of "monuments of culture" has halted the offensive actions of local officials.

When I was in Kiev, I passed the Roman Catholic cathedral, which has been closed for about a generation. It was all scaffolded with steel and timber. The long neglected cathedral was in process of restoration, and Mikola Bazhan told me that it was the only Gothic-style building in Kiev and they wished to preserve it as an architectural monument. Built in 1910, the cathedral is one of the most beautiful structures in Kiev, the city that had first witnessed Russia's conversion to Christianity.

Considering the position of the Orthodox Church nowadays, one must conclude that never since the rise of Sovietism has it been so prosperous or so respected as a purely national institution.

At the office of the monastery of the Holy Trinity of St. Sergius in Zagorsk, one of the monks presented me with the latest figures on Orthodox affairs. There were 20,000 functioning churches in the country, presided over by 35,000 priests, and from 40,000,000 to 50,000,000 people came to services, regularly or irregularly. About seventy monasteries and nunneries were open again, chiefly in Byelorussia and the Ukraine. The Patriarchate was maintaining eight theological seminaries (fifty-seven in 1913) and was preparing to open a ninth in Novosibirsk, Siberia. Among the subjects studied was not only Old Slavonic, the official language of the Church, but Latin and Greek and one modern language—German, French, or English. Applicants for admission were graduates of ten-year schools, though some too were college graduates: engineers, schoolteachers, and even army officers. On graduation from the seminary, students were privileged to enter one of the two theological academies (four in 1913), one in Leningrad, the other in Zagorsk.

Since my interview with the monk, the Moscow Patriarchate has modified its estimate of Orthodox churchgoers. In December 1959, the five-man delegation from the World Council of Churches was told that the figure was between 25,000,000 and 50,000,000. In truth, nobody knows the correct figure. The latest census takers didn't query citizens on their religious affiliations.

In the light of forty-three years of incessant and vigorous atheistic propaganda, even the lowest estimate of the Patriarchate appears impressive but does not tell the story of the weakened position of the Church as compared with its strength in Czarist times. The number of churches now open is only about one fourth of the 80,000 that flourished in the pre-revolutionary years. In Moscow, with a population of over five million, there are some 50 churches and chapels against 450 in 1912, when the population was less than one third of what it now is.

Of the millions that are now counted as Orthodox churchgoers, who can tell how many of them come out of curiosity or out of love of liturgical music? On the Sunday that I went to the St. Nicholas Cathedral in Leningrad, there were several groups of young people who were out-of-town excursionists. To them the church was a museum of historical interest. Some of them were entranced by the singing, particularly by the deep-throated bass soloist. The soloists have always been a stirring feature in Russian Orthodox services. On Sundays one often sees even Komsomol excursionists come to church, some of them only to pick up information that they can interpolate into anti-God lectures.

Aside from the excursionists, the only young people I saw in the largest church in Leningrad were mothers who brought babies to be baptized. There were about twenty such mothers, and each was accompanied by her own mother or grandmother, but not by a father or grandfather. There was not a single man among them, which struck me as strange, because Soviet law demands the consent of both parents for the baptism of a baby. On inquiry I learned that the mothers bring written consent from the fathers, accompanied by their passports, or that the law is winked at by the police.

Some years ago, the late Yemelyan Yaroslavsky, who had headed the militant atheist crusade in the country, told me that if it were not for mothers and grandmothers, the Orthodox churches would have to close their doors. He was of course exaggerating, but the fact is that the chief supporters of Orthodoxy are the older generation of women. This is as true of the village as of the city. If older women broke away from the Church, Orthodoxy would find itself in the most sorrowful plight in its history. The historic battle that is now waged on the religious front, as Soviet ideologists choose to call it, between Orthodoxy and Soviet atheism, is over the young generation—and it is the mothers and grandmothers who are firmly standing up against the press and the party, the playground and the schools, the Pioneers and the Komsomol—all of them staunchly and relentlessly atheistic. A mother or grandmother may teach a child to recite prayers, to bow before icons, to look to God as the ruling force in the world, but once the child ventures into kindergarten, the playground, the school, the summer camp, he is inevitably subjected to a many-sided anti-religious teaching. But the grandmothers are dying off, the mothers are growing older, and one can only wonder about the young women who must take their place in the age of sputniks and moon rockets.

Indisputably one of the appeals of Orthodoxy is the resplendent theatricality of its services, especially on solemn holidays, and more particularly on Easter Sunday. The glittering vestments of the clergy, the majestic performance of rites, the ceremonious blessing of the Easter cakes, the rolling chants of priests and deacons, the magnificent singing of the choirs, never fail to bring out the crowds in Moscow on the day of the Resurrection. This is Orthodoxy's most triumphant day, but there is only one Easter in a year!

Orthodoxy has invested birth, death, and marriage with dramatic rites which are in striking contrast to the bleak performances of *zags*, the Soviet registration office. Red funerals can be very solemn and very moving, but Red marriages and birth celebrations are insufferably commonplace affairs. Many girls, especially in villages, insist on church weddings. Mothers and grandmothers may inspire the insistence but they evoke a ready response in the bride. Other girls insist of their own volition on a church marriage. "I'd no more marry in a *zags* than in a garage," said a young woman schoolteacher in a Byelorussian town. Her fiancé, also a schoolteacher, was a Komsomol and refused to be married in church because it was against his "principles." This has been the quandary of many young couples all over the country, and more often than not the Komsomol or even the party member in the village swallows his "principles" and consents to the church marriage.

In the early years of the revolution, the Soviets had attempted to glamorize civil wedding ceremonies, but the coming of the Five-Year Plan had diverted all their energies into production and nothing came of the experiment. The times were too grim for emphasizing romance and festivity; nor were there suitable fabrics for gowns and veils. Now there is time to spare for the amenities and the textile factories are rolling out ever increasing yardage of silks and satins, and the Soviets have resolved to compete with the Orthodox Church in the festiveness of marriage ceremonies. In some of the large cities bridal salons have been opened to teach prospective brides the art of dressing for the exalted event, and custom-dressmaking shops have been instructed to give priority to orders for bridal gowns. The Leningrad Palace of Marriages, the first to be

established in the Soviet Union as a model for others, to take the
place of *zags*, has been extravagantly publicized—and couples from
all over the Soviet Union have deluged it with telegraphic requests
for an opportunity to be married there. Other such palaces are scheduled to open in the cities, and even towns and villages are to set
them up as ornately as they can so that the wedding ceremony can
be performed there without priestly participation and sanction.

In Leningrad I witnessed the marriage of a dark-haired sun-tanned
sailor to a pretty blond girl in the newly opened palace. It was a
festive but rather hurried affair with not a glimmer of the pageantry,
the symbolism, the drama, of even a village Orthodox church
wedding.

Yet one need not doubt that the new effort to infuse formality
and gaiety in civil marriages will draw couples away from the
church. But if only because of the influence of mothers and grandmothers, other couples will solemnize their marriages in church,
especially in villages. To older village women, their daughters and
granddaughters would not seem married without the exalted church
ceremonies and the blessing of the little father.

Yet one wonders about the future of the Orthodox Church under
the Soviets. If its stress on colorful rites, glittering pageantry,
mystical ceremonial, and solemn music have been a powerful means
of keeping its hold over the Russian peasantry for centuries, it is
now a fatal weakness. The late Paul Milyukov, in his scholarly
Outlines of Russian Civilization, charges the Orthodox Church with
"indifference to the spiritual content of religion." It had concentrated on form instead of substance, on symbol instead of spirit.
The late Dr. E. J. Dillon, whose remarkable career in Russia as
correspondent to the London *Daily Telegraph*, as editor of Russian
publications and lecturer on philosophy at Kharkov University, was
spread over a period of twenty-eight years (1886–1914), called the
Russian Orthodox Church "a museum of liturgical antiquities"—
a resplendent museum, but still only a museum.

I shall permit myself to quote with some slight changes an elabora-
tion on the subject from an earlier book of mine, *Humanity Uprooted*.

The Orthodox Church "didn't seek to fit itself into the varying
mold of an expanding civilization with its power to stir new ideas,

new questions in the human mind. It hardly heeded the challenge of science, the humanities, and the rising social movements. It barely took cognizance of them. It seldom engaged in combat with intellectual and spiritual adversaries as did the Roman Catholic Church. It did not have to. It was shielded from outside encroachments and questionings by the strong arm of the state. It never, therefore, acquired the intellectual and spiritual stature of the Roman Church.

"Nor had it suffered the strengthening agony of an inner purgation. Self-doubt, self-criticism, it vigilantly suppressed. . . . It conceived of itself as the beginning and the end of spiritual wisdom and verity for all time and all mankind. Now and then a waft of . . . questioning would blow into the mind of some monk or layman, and a voice of dissent would rise from some monastery or some scholar's study. But it was stifled soon enough."

In the middle of the seventeenth century the Orthodox Church went through a turbulent schism which resulted in a split, the Old Believers breaking away from the official church. The leading protagonists of the schism were Patriarch Nikon (1605–81) and the priest Avvakum (1620–80), who resisted the patriarch's church reforms. The conflict transcended the immediate practical aspect of the reforms, such as the corrected spelling of church books and making the sign of the cross with two instead of three fingers. It was essentially a conflict between tradition and innovation. Avvakum passionately upholding tradition. One of the most remarkable churchmen in Russian history, a great orator, and a brilliant writer, Avvakum was brutally persecuted by church and state. His autobiography is a classic in Russian literature, which, despite its religious fervor, the Soviets republished in 1934 and again in 1960.

But the ancient schism didn't bring enlightenment to official Orthodoxy. The spiritual forces outside of the confines of the church, it chose to ignore. Hence it didn't grow in spiritual stature. With its conversion into a state church by Peter the Great in 1721, it lost all semblance of independence and became an instrument of political control in the hands of the Czars, with its doors even more tightly shut to the invigorating influences of the outside world. It not only quarreled with Leo Tolstoy, who was searching for meanings in Christianity to which the hierarchy was indifferent, but

excommunicated him in February 1901. In his reply to the edict of
excommunication Tolstoy wrote, "I became convinced that the teaching of the Church is theoretically a crafty and pernicious deceit,
while practically it is a collection of the grossest superstitions and
sorcery completely concealing the whole meaning of the Christian teaching."

In Czarist days the peasantry made up over 80 per cent of the
population, but the Church never strove to shake the muzhik out of
superstitions that had come down from pagan times. The clergy
was apathetic to the witches, sorcerers, magicians, incantation
charmers, that infested the village and preyed on the muzhik's
gullibility and ignorance. The village *batushka* was often himself an
ignorant man, addicted to vodka and not averse to seducing an
attractive woman parishioner. Unlike the Catholic priest and the
Protestant minister, he did not establish close personal bonds with
parishioners. His was an official administrative task—to perform services, and when necessary or called upon to do so, to report on the
political behavior of parishioners. There were exceptions—one of
the most noted of whom was Archbishop Feofan Prokopovich, a
favorite of Peter the Great—but it is not of these I am writing.

As for the peasant, Christianity had through the centuries re-
molded his personal and family life. But he came to associate
religion not with an inner mood so much as with an external act,
"something vital and indispensable," to quote myself again, "but
aloof and detached, residing not within but without himself—a
ceremony to perform, rituals to observe: not an ideal, a revelation to
meditate upon, to absorb, to transmute into communion with the
invisible spirit of the Deity, which constitutes at once the essence
and florescence of religion." With rare exceptions "the individual
psychological experience," of which Harry Emerson Fosdick speaks
as the fountainhead of religion, "was alien to the muzhik."

True, he was a pious churchgoer. He went on pilgrimages to nearby
shrines and faraway monasteries. Slavophiles and the foreigners
whom they influenced had perceived in him the Christian par excellence, forever in quest of Christ's truth and Christ's mercy. They
venerated him as the great carrier of the tenets and ideals of Russian
Orthodoxy, "the Rock of Ages" of the one true Christian faith.

But a strange thing happened after the Soviet dictatorship established firm control of the country. In 1923, when I visited the Kiev Monastery, the monks who still remained there complained bitterly of the muzhik's sudden apathy to Orthodoxy. I wandered the countryside for over a year, often stopping for the night with a village priest, and harsh was the language I heard of the muzhik's indifference to the faith of his fathers. On Sunday mornings I would see crowds of people sitting outside their houses, promenading the streets, gathering in some public square, instead of going to church.

Many churches were already closed but many others were still open; yet the muzhik no longer flocked to services as he did in Czarist times. Except for conspicuous groups of young people, they had not become atheists, but the old compulsion to attend church services had weakened or died out among large masses of them. The very fact that the *batushka*, hounded and terrorized by the Soviets, was helpless to perform a miracle on his own behalf, was powerless to invoke the wrath of God on his persecutors, did something to the peasant's centuries-old piety, eroded his faith in the formal ministrations of the priest, in the execution of mystic ceremonials. The mysteries behind the ceremonials ceased to overawe or inspire large bodies of muzhiks, especially men.

In the old days when through some inner or outer experience the muzhik grew aware of the deficiencies of Orthodoxy, the poverty of its spiritual content, he broke away and formed dissident sects. Czarist Russia was a land of non-conformist religious communities. Some of them, scorning the glittering ceremonials of Orthodoxy, indulged in some form of self-mutilation. The Skoptsy believed in castration, the Khlysty in self-flagellation, the Pryguny in jumping while they prayed. Others, like the Molokans, the Dukhobors, the Evangelican Christians, the Seventh-day Adventists, the Pentecostals, the Baptists, strove for a new interpretation of religion and for fitting their lives into a framework of spirituality that Orthodoxy had failed to provide. Russia is still a country of dissident religious sects, the latest arrivals being Jehovah's Witnesses.

But the muzhik, chief pillar of the Church if only because of his overwhelming numbers, remained in comparative ignorance of the faith into which he was born. Rarely was he a Bible reader. Overwhelmingly he was illiterate. He learned more about good and evil from the tales and ballads of wandering beggars and pilgrims than from the parish priest. The arrival of one of these wanderers in a village was always a joyful event, and in the evening the home where he stayed was crowded with visitors who came to hear not only the news of the outside world but words of wisdom and enlightenment. He may have been as illiterate and superstitious as the darkest muzhik. But there was a sense of uplift and justice in the ballads he sang and the tales he told of ordinary men and of folk heroes, secular and religious, who triumphed over temptation and evil. Unlike the priest, he was always in personal and intimate relationship with the muzhik, lived in his house, ate his food, collected bread, eggs, pork, for his family or for sale in the bazaar. He was not beholden to the state as was the priest and was bound by no commitment other than what came out of his own experience, his own imagination, his own inner light. He was in truth a free man, and the muzhik cherished no misgivings about his person, as he often did about the priest.

One doesn't see these wanderers any more in Russia, either on country roads, in bazaars, or in villages, and the rich body of folk wisdom, folk piety, and folk sense of good and evil which they kept alive, however primitively conceived and expressed, has gone with them.

Memorable is the passage on the Russian Orthodox Church and clergy, as distinct from religion or Christianity, in Vissarion Byelinsky's famous letter to Gogol. The author of *The Inspector General* and *Dead Souls* had in his later years made public his correspondence, in which he eulogized Russian autocracy and Russian Orthodoxy. At the time (1847) Byelinsky was in Salzbrunn, Germany, fatally ill with tuberculosis. Gogol's pronouncement had so enraged him that he wrote Gogol an excoriating letter in which, among other things, he said:

"The Russian Church has always been the pillar of the rule of knout and the abettor of despotism. . . . Why do you drag in Christ? What have you found in common between Him and any church, especially the Orthodox Church? He was the first to enunciate to mankind the doctrine of liberty, equality, fraternity, and with His martyrdom He has set the seal on the verity of His teaching. . . . Is it possible that you, the author of *The Inspector General* and *Dead Souls*, can with all your heart chant a hymn of praise to the heinous

RELIGION—Ordeal of Orthodoxy

Russian clergy? Of whom do the Russian people tell ribald tales? Of the Orthodox priest, his wife, his daughter, his hired man. In the eyes of all Russians is not the priest the living symbol of gluttony, miserliness, sycophancy, shamelessness? As though you didn't know it all. How strange! According to you the Russian people are the most religious in the world. It is a lie. The basis of religion is piety, reverence, fear of the Lord. But Russian folk will pronounce the name of the Lord even while they are scratching themselves. . . . The Russian says about the icon, 'If it does you good, pray before it; if not, use it as a cover for cooking pots.'"

Violent as this is, such denunciations were not exceptional among the intelligentsia. Those of them who had attempted to give Orthodoxy a new direction failed of their purpose. This was as true of Khomyakov, Samarin, Aksakov, Soloviev, Florinsky, Bulgakov, the brothers Troubetzkoy, as of Merezhkovsky, Berdyayev, and others. In 1914 the Holy Synod started proceedings against Berdyayev—and had it not been for the outbreak of World War I, there is no reason to believe that he would not have been excommunicated.

The fatal liability of the Russian Church was its complete subordination and subservience to the Czarist state, which in the words of Milyukov "paralyzed all living buds of religion." After many years of close firsthand observation of the Orthodox peasantry I can only conclude that they were never truly Christianized, that deep in their hearts they have remained more pagan than Christian. Even Nikolai Berdyayev in his book on Dostoyevsky is constrained to say that the author of *The Brothers Karamazov* was wrong in holding the view that "the intelligentsia was defiled with godlessness and socialism, but that the people [meaning the peasantry] would remain faithful to the truth of Christ." But, Berdyayev goes on, "it is the people who have given up Christianity."

Meanwhile, the Church of today renders unto Caesar the things that are Caesar's with no less zeal than it did under the Czars. A Kremlin-sponsored peace congress is as unthinkable without the oratory of Metropolitan Nikolai Krutitzky as without the oratory of Ilya Ehrenburg. The Moscow Patriarchate denounced the Korean War as "an American aggression." The Hungarian revolution was "unleashed by certain foreign circles . . . and the working people of Hungary with the help of the Soviet Army put an end to the anti-patriotic mutiny." The Constitution bars the Church from politics, limits its function solely to religious observances. But when called upon by the Kremlin, it readily responds with its blessings on Soviet foreign policies, whatever they may be. Though the Kremlin no longer speaks of Russia as holy, to the highly nationalistic Church, Holy Russia is always right and its enemies, real or imaginary, as determined by the Kremlin, are always wrong.

Nonetheless, there is a visible reaction against the harsh materialism that pervades all aspects of Communist philosophy. The Soviet press is riddled with stories of young people in search of satisfactions that materialism fails to gratify, of Komsomol boys and girls and even of party members who tear up their membership cards and join the Orthodox Church or some other religious group. But it would be foolhardy to speak of it as a popular movement. Overwhelmingly, Soviet youth is either atheistic or completely apathetic to Orthodoxy. Even in the Cossack Kuban, historically one of the most pious sections of the country, churchgoing has practically ceased among young people. While driving through Cossack villages on Sunday morning, I saw crowds of young people promenading the streets, playing in parks, but not going to church. Not in a single church did I see a significant number of young people, not even in Krasnodar, capital of the region, with a population of over 300,000.

But weak as is the movement for return to Orthodoxy, it has provoked a fresh atheist crusade. The Kremlin has not brushed aside Marx's words, that "religion is the groan of the downtrodden, . . . is the opium of the people." It has only forsworn the rough tactics of the earlier years of the revolution. *Kommunist* (April 1958), the supremely authoritative doctrinal journal of the party, cautions propgandists against arrogance and insolence, and counsels them to argue with believers "calmly, wisely, patiently . . . without hurting their sentiments, which will only drive their faith deeper inside them." Reason and reason alone, derived from "the materialist-scientific interpretation of nature and life," should guide the atheist crusader. Outside this interpretation, it holds, all is fable and fraud—and once believers come to understand it, they will forsake all religious faith and will sunder all association with church or meeting-house.

When one reads Soviet anti-religious literature, one is overcome with the impression that it is on the intellectual level of the American village atheist: God couldn't have created the earth in six days; the whale couldn't have swallowed Jonah; Joshua couldn't have stopped the sun; Jesus couldn't have changed water into wine; He couldn't have raised Lazarus from the dead or performed any other miracle. Jesus never lived anyway. "The gospel stories of the life of Jesus on earth," reads a sentence in a Soviet atheist textbook, "are compounded of historical error, stupidities, and contradictions which deprive them of all credibility." In another anti-religious textbook, the author writes: "There was no resurrection of Christ, because He never died and was never born. Christianity grew up without Christ. But for the exploiting classes the legend of the martyr-God was always advantageous."

Whoever they are, even if members of the Academy of Sciences, Soviet atheist spokesmen never rise above a purely materialistic concept of religion, interpreting it in terms of the physical impossibilities of the events recorded in Holy Writ. They scornfully repudiate any and all moral aspects of religion. Quite the contrary: they perceive in it a force destructive of moral values and ruinous to personal happiness and social fulfillment. "Religious beliefs in God and the hereafter," writes *Kommunist* (December 1958), "signify the helplessness of man's mind, sow distrust in man's power, rouse a skeptical attitude toward science and a hopeless, pessimistic view of life; they weaken creativity and are aimed at distracting people from social interests, from political and cultural living."

Thus the militantly atheistic *Kommunist* sets up religion as a bogeyman, a Soviet-style Evil One, who ensnares innocent souls into depravity and doom.

Even the *Literaturnaya Gazeta* has spoken out vigorously against this type of anti-God teaching. "Our times," it wrote (July 9, 1960), "demand highly educated atheist propagandists," who would intelligently answer the arguments of educated churchmen. It favored the establishment of special courses in the universities to train such propagandists. One can only wonder what would happen were students exposed to the writings of religious thinkers and philosophers of our own and of former times.

The Orthodox Church still has a large following, though chiefly among the older generation, and in the political climate of the post-Stalin era it no longer faces the fierce hostilities of the past. The lingering hatreds against it as the former tool of reactionary land-lordism and Czarist despotism burned out in the fires of the battle of Stalingrad. While, since the rise of the Seven-Year Plan, atheist propaganda has been growing increasingly acrimonious, the clergy is not subject to persecution. Like all religions in the Soviet Union, it is barred from proselytizing outside of houses of worship. But within the incense-scented, candle-lighted, icon-gleaming house of worship, it is free to propagate its faith, and its communicants are free to instruct their children at home.

Though the Church of course repudiates materialism, it has become reconciled to the economics of communism and teaches that the accumulation of riches and property is sin. It points to Christ as the first real communist, who denounced exploiters and drove the moneychangers from the temple. In its favor in this period of fervid nationalism is the fact that historically it is as Russian as the Kremlin walls, and its unswerving patriotism, past and present, has won it not only respectability but prestige. Orthodoxy may be attacked and reviled in the press, but the Church has no more quarrels with the Kremlin over domestic and foreign policies than it had with the Czars. Whoever occupies the seat of power in the Kremlin has its blessing, now as in the past.

But can Russian Orthodoxy transform itself from a "museum of liturgical antiquities" into a religion of "spiritual content," in which not only Milyukov had pronounced it lacking?

The great surprise of our age on the religious scene of the atheist Soviet Union is not the Orthodox but the Baptist religion.

7.

RELIGION
Triumph of the Baptists

On Sunday morning I attended services in the Leningrad Baptist church. Although the brick building was large, it was clearly too small for the congregation; an overflow of worshipers had gathered around the open door.

This was an amazing sight in atheist Russia—a church overcrowded with worshipers, not on the occasion of some festival like Easter or Christmas but on an ordinary Sunday in midsummer when many people were away on vacation. I had observed nothing like it in the Orthodox churches I visited, neither in European Russia nor in Siberia. Whatever else it might have meant, it attested to an overpowering faith among the people of this particular denomination.

As I hesitated at the door a middle-aged man came up, and greeting me cordially, assured me that a few seats were always reserved for foreign visitors. To his question I told him that although I was not a member of the Baptist Church, I had graduated from a Baptist college in America—Colgate. No, he had never heard of the college; had any well-known Baptist preacher studied there? I told him that one of our most famous alumni was Dr. Henry Emerson Fosdick.

"Fosdeek!" he exclaimed. "Do you know Fosdeek?"

I told him I did.

"A man of God and a great advocate of peace among men," he said reverently. "Peace" is a magic word in Russia, and Fosdick's writing and preaching on the subject had obviously penetrated to at least some Baptists in Leningrad. "I know that our minister, Orlov, will want to speak to you," said the man, "if you can remain after services."

I told him I would be glad to.

The church building had been an unused Orthodox cathedral, which the city government had turned over to the present congregation in 1946. The Baptists rebuilt it, stripping it inside and out of all Orthodox symbols and ornamentation. They installed chairs so that worshipers need not stand as in Orthodox churches. The congregation was made up overwhelmingly of white-kerchiefed women, though here were more men and young people, including soldiers in uniform, than I had seen at the Orthodox Cathedral of St. Nicholas, which I had just visited. But here, too, I saw no children, and no mothers carrying babies to be baptized as in the cathedral. To be baptized in the Russian Baptist Church one must attain the age of eighteen, when young people are by Soviet law permitted to join a religious congregation.

I was finally ushered to a seat in front. Facing me on a platform sat the large choir of both men and women; on the wall immediately behind the choir, framed in tarnished gilt and printed in tall black letters, hung the legend "God Is Love."

The minister, a sturdy broad-shouldered man with a thick mustache and bearded chin, announced that his text was from the Second Epistle of John, verse 12: "Having many things to write unto you, I would not write with paper and ink; but I trust to come unto you, and speak face to face, that our joy may be full." He spoke in a deep resonant voice; and the substance of his sermon was the joy of life for the man who takes Christ to his heart—so great the joy that even the fear of death is overcome.

On the conclusion of the sermon the congregation arose and sang a hymn so fervently that it made me think of the singing in the church at Hampton Institute, the Negro college in Virginia.

While the congregation was singing, the man who had ushered me to my seat wrote a note and laid it on the table before the minister. After we had sat down, the minister read the note and announced that present in the church was an American who had studied at a Baptist college. Instantly the congregation arose, hands went up, and from every hand a white handkerchief waved toward me, until I found myself saluted by a sea of fluttering white, while the hymn "God Be with You till We Meet Again" welled up around me.

After the service, the minister invited me to his office, a small room lined with books. Several other churchmen dressed in Sunday clothes, even to neckties, which Russians don't particularly regard as fashionable, joined us.

Minister Orlov presented me with some of the latest information on the Baptist Church in the country. In 1944, the northern and southern branches, which had hitherto functioned separately, merged into the Union of Evangelical Christian Baptists. The churches were under supervision of the Council of Religious Cults, the official Soviet agency that deals with the affairs of non-Orthodox religions, the Orthodox Church being under the supervision of a separate council. To qualify for registration with the council, a Baptist congregation must meet two conditions: have a minimum of twenty members and have a pastor. Only then may they petition the council for a meetinghouse. Communities that failed to meet these requirements gathered for services in the homes of members. How many such groups there were in the country, nobody really knew. They were scattered all over, and as Baptists they were independent of any centralized authority, such as bishops and archbishops, and functioned on the basis of self-determination. But the number of registered congregations came to 5400 with a membership of 540,000. Together with non-members who chose to worship in Baptist churches, they had a following of over 3,000,000.

No, they had no seminary or Bible school of their own, but six young men, among them Orlov's son, were studying theology in England: three in London and three in Bristol. Their ministers "learned from Christ," and were chosen for their special "gifts"— knowledge of the Bible, warmth of heart, spiritual experience, and talent for preaching. No, they suffered from no shortage of pastors.

In Leningrad they held services five times a week, mornings and evenings on Sundays, and evenings on Tuesdays, Thursdays, and Saturdays.

Young people? Well, like other religious groups, they were forbidden to preach outside the church or to conduct religious classes for children and young people under eighteen. But in their homes they were free to teach religion, and Baptist fathers and mothers taught the Word of God to their sons and daughters so intensely that outside pressures didn't easily shake their faith. There were, of course, exceptions.

No, they had no quarrels with other religions or with science. Like all patriotic Russians, Baptists were immensely proud of their country's scientific achievements. But science alone could not satisfy all requirements of man's nature. Nor had they any quarrels with the state. After all, the state permitted them to send six of their members to study theology in England. The state gave them their church. In 1956 it allowed them to publish a hymnal of 402 pages containing 550 hymns, only a fraction of the hymns of the Union of Evangelical Christian Baptists. One of their leaders, the late Ivan Prokhanov (died 1936), who had studied in England, had during his life composed about 1500 hymns, which was more than twice as many as Luther composed. In 1957 the state allowed them to bring out a new Russian edition of 10,000 copies of the Bible, and they also published a journal—*Brotherly Messenger*—six times a year, with a circulation of 10,000.

One wouldn't expect a man in Orlov's position even to mention the difficulties that any religion encounters in the Soviet Union. The Bible and the hymnal are as indispensable to Baptists as candles and incense are to the Orthodox. But there are not nearly enough of these two books to meet the great demand. Orlov could only feel grateful to the Soviet Government for at last permitting his church to bring out a modest edition of the Bible and the hymnal, the first in thirty years.

Continuing our conversation, the minister informed me that the Baptist membership was continually growing. But applicants, he emphasized, were carefully chosen. They had to subscribe to the faith and to its code or morals, which among other things banned smoking, drinking, gambling, sexual laxity, and other ungodly and debasing practices. More people applied for membership than were received. Baptists welcomed only those who were permeated with the spirit of Christ and to whom the motto "God Is Love" meant a way of life. The motto, incidentally, is conspicuously displayed in every Russian Baptist church I have ever visited.

As I listened to the minister and his associates, I was struck by the quality of the Russian they spoke. Only men well educated and well read in Russian literature speak so. It attested to the fact that they were no narrow religious partisans, but men of broad culture who obviously knew their Pushkin as well as their Bible.

The most significant fact about the Russian Baptists is their phenomenal growth since the overthrow of Czarism and the rise of the impassioned atheism of the bolsheviks. Russian Orthodoxy, Mohammedanism, Judaism, the leading religions in bolshevik territory when they seized power, which no longer included such Roman Catholic countries as Poland and Lithuania, have suffered disastrous losses. The Baptist faith is the only religion that has triumphantly breasted the turbulent tides of atheism. According to the volume of the pre-revolutionary *Entsiklopedichesky Slovar* ("Encyclopedic Dictionary") that was published in 1912, there were in Czarist Russia 515 Baptist communities, with a membership of 61,500. Now, according to Orlov's figures, there are over ten times as many registered congregations, and while the number of followers makes up less than 1½ per cent of the entire population, it attests to a dynamism in the Baptist faith that the assaults of Soviet atheism have been powerless to smother or neutralize. Like a plant that withstands the vagaries of a hostile nature, it holds within itself remarkable powers of survival and growth.

There can be no doubt that if Russian Baptists were allowed to proselytize and to publish all the Bibles and hymnals they needed, they would make sensational inroads into both Soviet atheism and Russian Orthodoxy. Next to the group in America, they are already the largest body of Baptists in the world, larger than in all European countries combined. Another striking feature about them is that they are the most prolific composers of Protestant hymns in the world and that they accord hymn singing a major part in all their services. Russians are an exceptionally music-loving people, so it is natural for them to do so. But it is also a reason, though only incidental, for their rise in a country whose political dictatorship is committed to the uprooting of all religious belief from the consciousness of the citizenry.

The Baptist movement is comparatively young in the religious life of Russia. The first Russian to have been baptized into the faith was a merchant whose name was Nikolai Voronin. The place was the Kura River in Tiflis, capital of Soviet Georgia, and the time was August 20, 1867. The man who performed the rite was a German worker named Martin Kalweit, who had himself been converted in East Prussia in 1858. But Voronin must be spoken of as an indigenous Russian Baptist, for even before he met Kalweit he had already committed himself to the rite of Baptism as Baptists the world over understand the term.

Yet the chief sources of the new religion in Russia are of Western origin: the Plymouth Brethren in England and the Stundists, the German colonists whom Catherine the Great had invited to settle on the fertile southern steppes and set an example of advanced farming to Russian peasants. The Germans proselytized in the South, the English in the North. Lord Bradstock converted the first Russian in 1874. The converts in the North called themselves *Yevangelisty* —Evangelical Christians; those in the South went by the name of Stundists or Baptists. Since converts came from the Orthodox Church, both the Czarist police and the Holy Synod persecuted them. They were jailed, beaten, exiled to Siberia. But the movement kept spreading, even in Siberia.

Perhaps I can best explain some of the reasons for their astonishing rise since the coming of the bolshevik dictatorship by relating my personal experiences with them. These date back to 1923, the year of my first journey to the Soviet Union. It was a great day of Soviet oratory, and in city and village, indoors and outdoors, orators were always holding forth on one subject or another. But in the bazaar in a Byelorussian town I heard a new type of oratory on the Russian scene. From an earlier book of mine (*Broken Earth*) I shall quote a pertinent passage of the orator's appeal:

"No parasites for us, citizens. We evangelicans eschew form. God doesn't need form. He doesn't need ikons and He doesn't need priests either, or even churches. Christ didn't build temples, did He? He preached in the wilderness, in the fields, in the streets. God, citizens, hears you everywhere. He needs no man in robes and long hair to deliver your prayers to Him. He can hear you Himself. He always does. He loves to, just as a mother loves to hear the voice of her own child. Read the Bible, citizens; all that counts is the Bible, it came from Him, from Christ and the great prophets. Christ gave his life for us, citizens, for you and me and for those who have died and all those that are to come into this sinful world of ours, and we ought to follow Him, His words, and not those of the long-haired Orthodox priests of ours, who live off your toil and are mortal sinners just like you and me. There is nothing mysterious about

God and Christ, His Prophet. The Bible alone can save us, citizens, the Bible, God's Word, Christ's message; and remember, He died for us and He said that every man must earn his own bread and help his fellow men and never hate his enemies and never kill any human being. That's what Christ said, citizens, Christ Himself, God's own Son."

The evangelist had come from somewhere in the South and was wandering from bazaar to bazaar and village to village, preaching his gospel. All over the Soviet Union there were others like him, and in those days the Soviets permitted them to go their way as freely as any bolshevik orator.

Shortly afterward, while traveling through the province of Saratov, I came to a village where the chairman of the local soviet put me up for the night with a Baptist family, because, as he said, "they have a very clean house." Indeed, it was one of the cleanest peasant homes I had ever seen: the board floor untracked by mud, the walls neatly whitewashed, white curtains at the windows, and—miracle of miracles—hardly a fly in the house and no bugs in my bed.

I lived with this family for several days and observed that the man was extraordinarily polite to his wife, that he was kind to animals, even to pigs, and that he was a more advanced farmer than were other muzhiks in the village. He was a new type of peasant in the Russian countryside, scrubbed free in speech and manner of the barbarisms that had for centuries been degrading what Russians call the byt—the mode of daily life—of the peasantry.

In my further travels in villages, I always inquired whether there was a Baptist family there, and if there was, I stayed with them, knowing that I would live in a clean house, in a tranquil family atmosphere, where the man would defer to his wife with a sense of chivalry that was as new as it was refreshing in Russian peasant society.

My greatest surprise was the discovery of a family of Baptists in my native village, a man and his wife who had been my boyhood playmates, and of course I stayed with them. At the time, I wrote of them: "Piously they fulfilled the tenets of their faith as propagated in Russia. They never smoked and never allowed anybody to draw a breath of tobacco in their house. No liquor ever passed their lips or their threshold. They never sat down to a meal without saying grace, and their speech was free from the obscenities that spice peasant talk. Their house was the cleanest in the village—the floor always scrubbed, the walls whitewashed, the windows wiped. No chickens strutted in their living room and no pigs ever tumbled in for a feeding, as in other peasant homes. It was the only house in the village where one could sit down to a meal without being obliged to engage in a perpetual battle with flies. 'When flies gather inside,' explained my hostess, 'we carry out our food, darken the room, open the doors, and the flies fly out!'" An effective method of riddance but requiring constant repetition. Nobody else in the village was doing it, and my hostess wouldn't have done so had she not been converted to the new faith.

There were several weddings in the village, and my host and hostess and myself attended one of them. They never touched a drop of the homemade vodka which flowed freely in the home of the bride, where the wedding dinner was served. Firmly they resisted all importunities —as I didn't—to drink to the health and good life of the newlyweds. This seemed an incredible performance by muzhik wedding guests. Not a drop of vodka for them—the vodka that had for centuries been the solace and the damnation of the muzhik.

In 1944, soon after the Germans were driven out of my native village, I journeyed there to see what had happened to it. The Baptist community, I found, had grown from one to about half a dozen families, the leader of whom was the woman who had been my hostess. She was a widow now, and the chairman of the soviet jestingly spoke of her in her presence as "the Baptist *pop*." Instantly the woman shot back, "We Baptists have no *pop*. We commune with God without a *pop*. God hears us everywhere, in our homes, in the field, in barns. He not only hears us but blesses us."

The chairman gave a laugh and said, "A strange thing about these Baptists; summer and winter, rain or snow, they all come to her house"—pointing to the woman—"and sing and sing."

No, the soviet didn't interfere with their services. "Why should we?" the chairman said. "They don't do anybody any harm. We always like singing in our village, and people gather outside the house and listen to the singing."

Actually, Baptist congregations that are too small to qualify for registration with the Council of Religious Cults are not sanctioned by the state. But to the best of my knowledge, village authorities never make an issue of it, and for a reason that reflects a virtue in Baptists which village Communists, however atheistic, do not lightly dismiss. In Moscow's daily newspaper *Sovietskaya Rossiya* ("Soviet Russia") of August 19, 1959, there is a story of a battle that the Soviet militia and Soviet social organizations are carrying on in the Volga province of Ulyanovsk, where Lenin was born, against the drinking sprees of peasants during certain Orthodox religious holidays. V. Kuznetsov, the writer of the story, complains that these sprees result in absenteeism from work on collective farms, in family brawls, and in waste of sugar, grain, and potatoes, which members of collectives use in the home manufacture of vodka and beer.

Such charges can never be leveled against Baptists. They are total abstainers and do not celebrate Orthodox holidays. Neither the police nor party functionaries would think of raiding a Baptist peasant home in search of pipes, kettles, or other equipment used in the manufacture of alcoholic beverages. Baptists do not absent themselves from work and do not use sugar, grain, and potatoes for illegitimate purposes. Village Communists, always under pressure to fulfill production plans, appreciate the work habits of Baptists and refrain from interfering with their unsanctioned meetings in private homes.

The very history of Russia, with its cruel suppression of the peasantry, seemed to have prepared the ground for the new faith. On the purely human side, it introduced immediate remedies for centuries-old evils. That is why since its earliest days it has been a movement of the common man, especially among peasants, then spreading to factory workers and small traders, who in Russia were themselves peasants fresh from the village or linked with the village by bonds of blood and custom. Instances of landlords who in Czarist times were converted to the Baptist faith and encouraged muzhiks on their estates to follow their example and even preached to muzhiks, are too insignificant to be of any account. A grass-roots movement, it had never reached the intelligentsia, the aristocracy, the merchant and official classes, from whom the peasantry was always sundered by cultural and social walls.

Because of their humble social origin, in the early years of the revolution the Soviets treated Baptists not only with tolerance but with magnanimity. With rare exceptions they did not belong to what the bolsheviks called "the exploiting classes." Nor were bolsheviks—at least some of them—unmindful of the fact that in Czarist times they championed land reform, basing their thinking not on pronouncements of Karl Marx or any other mortal ideologist, but on the will of God as recorded in Holy Writ:

"The land shall not be sold forever: for the land is mine, for ye are strangers and sojourners with me." Leviticus 25:23.

"For I mean not that other men be eased and ye burdened. But by an equality, that now at this time your abundance may be a supply for your want; that there may be equality." 2 Corinthians 8:13.

"Woe unto them that join house to house, that lay field to field till there be no place that they may be placed in the midst of the earth." Isaiah 5:8.

These are only some of the verses which inspired Baptists to advocate land reform. In the city of Stalingrad (then Tsaritsyn), the Baptist minister told me, in 1924, that the Soviet administration allowed him free use of the city theater for afternoon services. Nothing like this is even thinkable nowadays.

There were other reasons why the Soviets were originally benevolently disposed toward them. In Czarist times they were a persecuted minority, which alone qualified them for special consideration. The decree of January 23, 1918, separating church from state, lifted the disabilities that the Czarist government had imposed on them. At last they were free not only to practice but to preach their faith whenever and wherever they chose. The first edition of the *Bolshaya Encyclopedia* (Vol. XXVI), published in 1926, when Soviet encyclopedists had not yet come under complusion to disregard or falsify facts, tells us that with the passing of the new decree the Baptist faith "spreads widely." Indeed it did, as I observed everywhere I traveled, especially in the countryside.

But at the time, the growing popularity of the Baptists didn't alarm the bolsheviks, violently atheistic as they were. The Baptist attack on Orthodoxy, which had been the primary target of Soviet atheism, made the Baptists in a sense bolshevik comrades in arms against the power of the Orthodox Church. Baptists decried icons;

they denied the power of relics to perform miracles; they scorned the opulent ritualism and the mystical symbolism of Orthodoxy; they stripped away age-old superstitions, thus helping to emancipate the muzhik who came under their influence from his fears of the Evil One in whatever form; they denounced the celebrations of the endless Orthodox holidays as conducive to idleness and drunkenness; they glorified work as a command of God and as a rich source of personal fulfillment. The bolsheviks could only welcome these attacks on old established beliefs and usages.

But there was more to the Baptist faith than a denial and repudiation of Russian Orthodoxy. As already noted, the faith carried with it a new way of life—a set of disciplines and values that were anti-feudal and that transformed the everyday life of the convert. Not only did it forbid drinking, smoking, cruelty to animals, but it forswore idleness, marital infidelity, personal dishonesty, wife beating, abuses of children, prevarication, vituperative language—all of which in varying measure were darkening the lives of masses of muzhiks and was the reason for their having been called "the dark people." To Baptists these and similar practices were an offense against God and ruinous to personal fulfillment. Fellow communicants became brothers and sisters who were in honor and duty bound to help one another to rise to a new life and to succor one another in times of need and misfortune. They visited one another, read the Bible together, discussed it, sang psalms and hymns together, and there was no discrimination between the sexes. The woman in my native village was not the only one who headed the congregation. I met others like her in other villages.

Long before the Soviets came along with their gospel of "cultural living," the Baptists had made it the core of their faith and their way of life. In their theology they were (and still are) fundamentalists, taking the Bible literally. But I never heard a Russian Baptist pastor thunder hell-fire at sinners, as I did years ago in the Baptist church in a village in upstate New York where I worked on a farm. Their emphasis is not on the punishment hereafter for sins committed on earth, but on the immediate rewards for those who fulfill the will of Christ, as they interpret it in the light of the cruel history they have endured.

In their morality they were and are puritanical. They oppose birth control, abortions, divorce—all of which bolsheviks in the early years of the revolution had made as free as air. But they never were ascetics. They disapprove of dancing, but as a young pastor said to me, "We won't expel a member just for going to a dance." Nor, he might have added, for going to movies, the theater, or the ballet, though some of the very old folk still frown on these. "When I first came to England," the young pastor said, "I knew very little English, and do you know what I did? I spent three hours every afternoon in a motion picture theater—a wonderful place to learn English."

Russian Baptists have always believed in the joy of living, clean living, as they understand the phrase. That is why in the early years of the revolution they organized clubs, mutual-aid societies, picnics, festivals, musical gatherings, literary evenings, sewing circles, lectures, which made a strong appeal to youth, especially to girls. They had even formed a youth organization called Baptomol (Baptist Youth), obviously copied from the word "Komsomol" (Communist youth).

In the summer of 1927, when I visited the cities of Poltava in the Ukraine and Stalingrad on the Volga, I was astonished at the crowds of young people they attracted. They were the only organization in the country that was effectively competing with the Komsomol for the allegiance of youth, which sooner or later was certain to bring down on them the wrath of the bolsheviks. In fact, at a literary party on my return to Moscow, I ran into the late Nikolai Bukharin, one of Lenin's closest associates, whom Stalin executed, and when I told him what I had observed in Poltava and Stalingrad, he said, "Yes, we know Baptists are attracting young people and we'll have to do something about it."

But the first serious clash between Baptists and bolsheviks had already occurred, and it was not over their youth organization or over their widespread social work. Baptists had adhered to the doctrine of non-resistance and demanded to be treated as conscientious objectors. Soviet courts ruled against them, the Soviet argument being that their demand for military exemption couldn't be an article of their faith, for their co-religionists in foreign countries never refused to bear arms and fight wars. Why then should Russian Baptists be exempted from service to their country? In consequence, at a conference in 1923, Baptists dropped their demand for military exemption.

But they continued to thrive. They were attracting followers among miners in Donbas, textile workers in Ivanovo, builders in Moscow; in other words, the very class of people whom the bolsheviks had glorified as the "true soldiers of the revolution" and in whose name they had seized power and established their dictatorship. The bolsheviks grew so alarmed that Nadezhda Krupskaya, Lenin's widow, pointed to them as a more sinister danger to the revolution than Russian Orthodoxy. Nikolai Bukharin, addressing a conference of Komsomols, called on them to exert their influence to prevent Baptists from dominating the youth of the country; and Yemelyan Yaroslavsky, who only a few years earlier had hailed the Baptist decision to drop the demand for exemption from military service, now fiercely denounced them. "Whichever front of our struggle you take, whether for a new manner of living or anything else, everywhere we clash with the *sectanty* [Protestants]. Not only are they against anti-religious but against non-religious training of children, against the Pioneers, the Komsomols, the party." In cartoons, posters, pamphlets, Baptist and other Protestant leaders—but chiefly Baptists —were derided side by side with "wreckers" in industry, priests, kulaks, bootleggers, speculators, as active and dangerous foes of the revolution.

The years 1929–31 were a period of continuous intolerance and persecution. These were the years of the forcible drive for collectivization, which roused the hostility of Baptist village folk. More advanced farmers than the average muzhik, they beheld in collectivization a blow to their material welfare and an encroachment on their individual way of life. The fight was on, violent and bitter. I recall an afternoon when Sherwood Eddy, the American YMCA leader, burst into my room at Moscow's Metropole Hotel weeping. He drew a blood-soaked handkerchief from his pocket and told me he had just come from a Baptist friend who was still bleeding from the beating he had got from GPU agents.

In April 1929, a decree was passed which, while upholding the principle of freedom of conscience, forbade all forms of religious activity outside the church. Only anti-religious propaganda was permitted; no longer could Baptists evangelize in the market place or anywhere else outside the church or the home.

The years 1937–38, years of the Big Purge, brought fresh onslaughts against Baptists, though nowadays Baptist leaders do not even care to talk about it. As one of them in Minsk said to me, "It's a finished chapter in our history and in the history of our country. Khrushchev himself has denounced the excesses of the Big Purge, and others suffered from it more than did our people. We must look forward instead of backward, live in the future instead of in the past."

But only on the outbreak of World War II did the Kremlin make peace with the Baptists as well as with the Orthodox. They were all Russians now, fighting a common enemy for survival. Like other Russians, Baptists fought and died in the Patriotic War, as Russians speak of World War II. Jacob Zhidkov, president of the Union of Evangelical Christian Baptists, had four sons in the war, three of whom never returned.

Now, though there is peace between Baptists and the state, which has even allowed them to send six of their students to study theology in England, there is no peace between the Baptists and the party. Hostile as ever to religion, the party ideologists in their renewed atheistic crusade have centered special attention on Baptists.

One of the most virulent outbursts I have read against them appeared in *Izvestia* of October 21, 1959. The article is made up of letters to the editor interpolated with editorial comments. Baptists are accused of "stupefying the weak and the backward with religious mysticism." They are charged with breaking up families, setting parents against children, wives against husbands. A schoolteacher named U. Yakimchuk, from a town in the Ukraine, writes of a woman, Lukerya Shevchuk, who was drawn into the Baptist sect and proceeded to press her new faith on her two daughters, Nina and Natasha. Nina stubbornly resisted, but Natasha, who had been a worker in a porcelain factory, was ill; and when, according to the writer, she could no longer endure the naggings and the threats of her mother and of another Baptist woman, named Anna Bondarenko, she committed suicide. Natasha is alleged to have left a letter for her mother which, as given in *Izvestia*, reads: "You snake, now bring your Stundists to the house, nobody will interfere with you. Go ahead, torment me, devour me—now that I'm dead."

Another writer, a schoolteacher named V. Mironov, a war invalid from the town of Armavir, brands Protestant preachers as "more dangerous than bandits and thieves."

The editor of *Izvestia* is Alexey Adzhubei, Khrushchev's son-in-law. He personally may or may not have written the comments on the letters which feature the article in question. The commentator informs the reader that "the dastardly activity of Protestants rouses the indignation and wrath of every honest person." He calls for renewed and "well-organized anti-religious campaigns."

In the Soviet Union you do not write back to *Izvestia* on such a delicate issue as religion. You do not dare to ask for an impartial investigation of the actual cause of Natasha's suicide or of the authenticity of the letter she is alleged to have written to her mother, however absurd it may sound.

If you are a Baptist, you take it all in your stride, because you know it isn't anything new, and that the charges leveled against an individual member of your faith may or may not be true. But you cannot accept them as proven facts, because you know that they are a violation of every tenet of your faith.

On my most recent journey in the Soviet Union, in the summer of 1960, I picked up pamphlets in Kiev and Odessa that supposedly expose Baptists as being among the wickedest people in the world. When I spoke of it to Ilya Orlov, the son of the pastor I met in Leningrad, who had just returned from two years' study in Bristol, England, he said, "We know all about it. Baptists too can go wrong and betray their faith in their everyday life. As soon as we learn of it, we expel them. Then they say terrible things about us. But it doesn't disturb us. We are careful about the citizens who apply for membership. They are on probation for two or three years before they are accepted into the Church."

A cheerful man, who, in addition to being one of the ten pastors of the church in Moscow, is also a distinguished dental surgeon, he appeared unconcerned over the intensified campaign against the Baptists. I was present when he held a conference with a group of religious American university students, among whom were a Nazarene, a Lutheran, a Congregationalist, a Presbyterian, a Methodist. He astonished me by requesting the students to send him some recent publications of their respective denominations. "We want to know," he said, "what is happening in the Protestant world outside our country."

When I asked him if it wasn't dangerous for pastors to receive foreign religious publications, he replied, "Why should it be? We want these publications for ourselves. We never distribute them as propaganda. No, it isn't dangerous." He gave the students the post-office address of his church.

What amazes the student of the Soviet Union is that in the forty-third year of the revolution, and despite official pretensions of fighting religion with facts and reason, Soviet atheists persist in using the old weapons of billingsgate and horrifying tales, even against Baptists who are well known for their high personal morality and for the correctness of their political behavior.

I know of a Baptist who held a responsible and highly paid position in a factory. One day he was approached by factory propagandists and presented with the alternative of breaking with his co-religionists and publicly denouncing them or losing his position. Father of a family with several children, he submitted. Even if such instances are rare, they light up the difficult position of Baptists in the Soviet Union. As Baptists, they are automatically barred from membership in the Communist party, unless they conceal their faith, which their Church forbids. Officially, admission to the university is as open to the son and daughter of a Baptist as to the son and daughter of a member of the Communist party. Applicants are not required to answer questions concerning their religion. But nowadays, the recommendation of some official organization—the local soviet, the trade union, the party, the Komsomol—attesting to the character, the social interest, the political reliability, of the applicant is filed with the application and is usually a determining factor with the committee on admissions. For a Baptist, it is not easy to obtain such a testimonial.

Still, it is inconceivable that a university would deny admission to a Baptist boy or girl especially gifted in mathematics or the sciences. But it is equally inconceivable that a Baptist would be permitted to teach in public schools, to enter a military academy or the college of diplomacy, or be appointed to any significant political office. Professions in which political policy or the molding of the mind, especially of children and young people, is of strategic importance are automatically barred to Baptists. Only on the technological level are the opportunities fully open to them.

Still, the membership in the Baptist Church keeps growing and the militant atheist is at a loss to combat this growth. Anti-religious propaganda is so primitive that it carries no conviction to the Baptist who has no quarrel with science but who reaches out for meanings in human life that Communist materialism scoffs at as mere superstition. As an atheist lecturer in Irkutsk, Siberia, once said to me, "You don't have to argue with Baptists as with Orthodox about icons, relics, incense swinging. They repudiate these as firmly as we Communists do. Nor is there anything you can tell them about the evils of drunkenness, hooliganism, wife beating—oh, they're strongly against it and teach it to their children. When you throw scientific facts at them, they do not dispute you. They're all for science, they tell you, and for all the good it does for mankind. But they always tell you that the laws of science are God's laws, and when you ask them whether they have ever seen God or spoken to Him, they tell you that God is within them, they feel it and rejoice in it, it inspires them to be good and to do good and to live not only for themselves but for others. They're so stubborn about feeling God inside themselves that you cannot root it out of them."

In truth, the Baptist is the despair of the Communist propagandist. He resents a faith that rivals his own and the essence of which is contained in three simple words: God Is Love. In his arsenal the Communist has no weapons to combat a faith stripped of ancient superstitions. So he employs vituperation and slander.

In the market place of the city of Krasnodar, I heard a young Cossack woman who was selling melons say to a customer, "When you marry a Baptist you know that he isn't going to stink up the house with the smoke of *makhorka* [cheap tobacco]. You know he isn't going to come home drunk and foul up the house with dirty language, and you know he isn't going to be charmed by another woman." No horrifying tales of the wickedness of Baptists can shake a woman like this out of her religion.

Russian Baptists liken themselves to the primitive Christians in early New Testament times. Though they live in an age of rockets and spaceships, they do suggest similarities with Christians in Paulist times. They too are a sect in the first century of their activity; they too live in a hostile world; they too profess a simple faith and are drawn into a closely knit fellowship, share common joys, and offer one another succor in times of stress and misfortune. Well or ill, a Baptist is never lonely. He can always count on the comradeship of fellow communicants. They constitute a collective of their own within a society that is based on collectives.

At the time I was in the Leningrad church and was greeted by the congregation, I saw an attractive middle-aged woman wave a white handkerchief toward me with one hand and with the other wipe tears from her eyes. Like all Russians, Baptists are a sentimental people, easily moved to tears. I spoke to the woman, and when I asked her why she appeared grief-stricken when she waved to me, she smilingly replied, "It wasn't grief. Oh no, brother American. That's the way I always am when foreign friends visit our church. I cannot hold back the tears of joy. Yes, of joy. We Baptists are a cheerful people."

In Moscow I became acquainted with a young woman who was a university graduate and a member of the Komsomol. At an early age her mother died, and the woman who had been her nurse since the day she was born was a Baptist. Several years before I met the young woman, her father, an engineer, also died. She was an only child and was living with her nurse. "You know," she said, "I am an atheist. I think it's silly to believe in God. Who has ever seen God? Who has ever spoken to God? But I love my nurse. She has been a mother to me and as fine a mother as I could have had for all the years of my life. I would share my last crust of bread with her."

"Don't you, an atheist," I asked, "feel strange to be living with a Baptist woman?"

"Of course not," she shot back. "I wouldn't think of living without her, even when I get married. The man who marries me will have to accept her as he would my mother." And after a pause she added contemplatively, "You know there's something admirable about these Baptists. My nurse's friends often come to our apartment and we have long talks together. They are simple and honest and kind. It's really too bad they are religious."

8.

MORALS, MARRIAGE, AND FAMILY

Shortly after my arrival in Kiev I went to see some old friends, an elderly couple and their widowed daughter, who all lived in a single room. I found them entertaining two visitors from another town, who at night were somehow bedded down in the same room. However crowded their living quarters, Russians always manage to accommodate overnight guests. They have never been a prudish people, and to them it is as natural for men and women to sleep in the same room as to eat at the same table. On Russian trains men and women who are complete strangers to one another share the same sleeping compartment, and it is only Westerners who lift an eyebrow when they hear of the custom.

Yet officially the Soviet Union is one of the most puritanical countries in the world, in complete reversal of the original sexual morality of the bolshevik revolution. For a real shocker to those who knew or have read of Soviet sexual morality in the early years of the revolution, I present the story of Galina Komarova from the town of Kovrov, Vladimir province. After graduating from a ten-year school, Galina studied in a trade school and then went to work in a factory in Kovrov. An energetic and eager girl who loved music and dancing, she joined the amateur talent activities of the factory Komsomol. She also persuaded a talented fellow worker, a married man named Anatoly Knyazev, to join in these activities. She had a sweetheart named Victor and was very happy with his companionship.

But then tongues began to wag, tongues of fellow workers, one whispering to the other that Galina and Anatoly were having a love affair. The tales reached Rita, Anatoly's wife, but he only laughed at the factory busybodies and urged his wife to dismiss their tales as idle prattle. But Rita was too hurt to act on her husband's advice. One day when Anatoly came home from work, his wife pointed to a bundle in which she had packed his personal belongings. "Go to your sweetheart," she told him.

"But you are my only sweetheart," Anatoly protested. There was a scene between husband and wife, and finally Anatoly picked up the bundle and his radio and went off to live with his mother.

Galina was outraged and heartbroken. How could fellow workers indulge in such scandalous tales about her and Anatoly when they were both members of the Komsomol and their relationship was confined to mutual interests and activities within the Komsomol collective? Can't a married man, she asked them, take part in Komsomol plays and other entertainments in the factory? Must he shut himself off within the private circle of his family? Is it a crime for a girl to be on comradely terms with a married man? She pleaded and argued, but few of her detractors, supposedly imbued with "Communist morality, the most advanced man has ever known," showed any sympathy for her.

In despair she went for counsel to the Komsomol organizer of the factory.

"I can't stuff up the mouths of people with handkerchiefs," the organizer said to her. "But you yourself can prove your innocence."

"Tell me how," the girl asked.

"Very simply. Go to a clinic, have yourself examined, get a certificate [of virginity], and show it around."

When I read this story in the *Komsomolka* of August 23, 1958, I couldn't help thinking of an age-old custom that prevailed in certain villages in pre-revolutionary times, when muzhiks were spoken of as "the dark people." On their return home from their wedding in church, bride and groom retired to the haymow in the barn to consummate their marriage. When they came out, the mothers of both asked whether in the course of the relationship the bride showed blood. If she did, she was acclaimed a virgin. A red cloth was instantly mounted on the roof chimney of her house and the whole village knew that the bride was a virgin. If she showed no stain, she was supposed to have forfeited her virginity to another man. Then a white cloth was mounted on the chimney and the whole village believed that the bride was no virgin.

Nowadays peasants have become too enlightened to subject a bride to the humiliation of a public announcement of her virginity or lack of it. Yet in the forty-first year of the Soviet revolution, a high placed Komsomol functionary in a factory advised a tormented girl to do just that—to obtain a medical certificate of her virginity and to "show it around."

Had a Komsomol official proffered such advice to a girl in the early years of the revolution, she would have laughed at him or spat in his face. She would have denounced him as "a hopeless counter-revolutionary" and an enemy of Soviet society. But now all Galina could do was to write an angry and pathetic letter to the editor of Moscow's *Komsomolka*, the Communist youth daily, and beg for help.

The editor disapproved of the functionary's advice and told the reader how he should have acted. He should have called a mass meeting, summoned the more articulate gossipers, and said to them, "Tell us what our young Communists are guilty of . . . and if you can prove their guilt, we shall punish them. But if your charges are idle gossip, you shan't escape retribution."

Here then is the official arbiter of the morals and manners of Soviet youth, laying down a procedure that wouldn't have spared the girl the ordeal of a public demonstration of her innocence or guilt. Nothing like it was even conceivable in the early years of the revolution.

It is not my purpose to pass judgment on Soviet sexual morality. I am concerned solely with the Kremlin's spectacular reversal on the subject. In terms of human self-expression it is the most sensational somersault in all Soviet history. It jolted Communists all over the world and outraged many a sympathizer of the bolshevik revolution, especially those who had come to regard sexual freedom as one of its most triumphant achievements. To appreciate fully the significance of the change, it is well to make a survey of sexual mores from the earliest years of the revolution to the present time.

Having set out to uproot the old civilization, the bolsheviks, by the laws which they passed between December 1917 and November 1920, demolished the conventions and compulsions that had governed pre-revolutionary sexual morality and family stability. The principle of equality of the sexes, implemented by free divorce and free abortions, carried with it the principle of freedom of sexual selection. "Down with bourgeois morality" became the slogan of the times.

As for the family and the practice of monogamy, on which the family was based, didn't Friedrich Engels, Karl Marx's closest collaborator, in his *The Origin of the Family*, declare that monogamy "was not in any way the fruit of individual sex love"? It grew out of the institution of private property to guarantee man, master of the household, the inheritance of his possessions by his own offspring.

But the revolution smashed private property. "The means of production" were nationalized, thereby destroying "the economic foundations of monogamy" and thus opening the way for "the private household [to use Engels' language] to change into a social industry." The New Economic Policy of 1921 had brought back certain forms of private enterprise, but the backbone of capitalism was broken, and while the new regime was in no position to convert the private household into a social industry, all talk of the sanctity of the family was bourgeois prattle. Besides, as Bukharin wrote in 1924, the family was a stronghold of "all the scum" of the regime the revolution had overthrown. Wherever I traveled in those days I heard over and over, especially in villages, that the family was the seat of reaction, holding back the progress of the revolution.

Under the new dispensation, sex and marriage were thus officially liberated from the conventions and coercions of pre-revolutionary times. No longer would women be subjected to the double standard of morality by which, under capitalism, men had arrogated to themselves privileges that they denied to women. In sex as in all other aspects of personal and social life, there would be complete equality of the sexes, the women, like men, would be governed by their own tastes, their own romantic fervors, their own sense of ethics.

The leaders of the revolution didn't advocate and didn't encourage promiscuity, least of all the austere-minded Lenin. "Does a normal man," he said, "under normal circumstances, drink from a glass from which others have drunk?" He admonished his followers to remember that "the proletarian revolution is in no need of the intoxication that excites and stupefies. He needs neither the intoxication of sex nor that of alcohol."

Intoxication or not, the Russia of the twenties and early thirties was, to all intents and purposes, a society of unhampered freedom in sexual selection. The most eloquent apostle of this freedom was Alexandra Kollontay (1872–1952), one of Lenin's closest associates. She denied that she favored free love, but in her work *Love and Friendship* she wrote, "I would put it the other way: I was always preaching to women, 'Make yourself free from the enslavement of love to a man.'" In her pamphlet *Communism and the Family* she didn't mince words about her dislike of the individual family. "The narrow and exclusive affection," she wrote, "of the mother for her child must be made to grow and broaden until it embraces all children of the great proletarian family. In the place of the individual house groups there will arise a great universal family."

A highly educated and fascinating woman, she captivated men, but as she admitted to her friend Zoya, her "love affairs ended in the breaking down of romance." There is an apocryphal story about her that reveals something of the nature of her romantic life and of Lenin's good-humored tolerance of her romantic indulgences. According to the story, she had once failed to come to a party meeting because she was away on a romantic adventure. Party leaders demanded that she be severely punished for her breach of discipline. Lenin intervened with a proposed punishment that would fit the misdemeanor she had committed. "Let us sentence her," he supposedly said, "to a week of solitary confinement in the country with her lover."

True or not, the story reflects her widely discussed attitude toward sexual morality. In 1923 she was transferred from party work to diplomacy, first as ambassador to Norway, then to Mexico, and subsequently to Sweden. Though, according to Moscow rumor, she was sent out of the country because of her influence on the young generation, her real sin was her support of the so-called workers' opposition, which demanded an independent trade-union movement.

But the fat was on the fire anyway, and the young generation, especially the student youth, was carried away by the new sexual morality which branded the cult of virginity as a survival of the dark ages of mankind. "What fun we girls had," a Moscow woman physician who had been a student in the late twenties said to me, "mocking the cult of virginity. We used to say to one another, 'What do we need it for—to hide in the cellar or to hang up in a museum?'" Birth control and abortions were legal and free, so women could protect themselves against unwanted pregnancies. Bookshops and newsstands all over the country sold a vast amount of literature on birth control.

I recall an interview I had sometime in 1923 with the late Yemelyan Yaroslavsky (1878–1943), the Siberian-born bolshevik who was a member of the Central Committee of the party. He headed the then fashionable and violent anti-God crusade and was a prolific interpreter of the new sexual morality. A handsome man with deep blue eyes, a firm mouth, a reddish tint to his thick wavy hair, he sat at his long green-covered table looking straight into me as he assured me that only an atheist-socialist country like Russia could emancipate women from the sexual fears and frustrations that had plagued them for centuries. To him, birth control and abortions were the supreme test of the real emancipation of women. No capitalist country, he proudly declared, would dare to place at the disposal of women these measures of protection against pregnancy so that they would be as free from fear of it as were men. Yaroslavsky was absolutely certain that the new socialist morality had come to stay, because to him it was as indispensable a component of the new freedom as was the overthrow of the capitalist system.

Yet Yaroslavsky, like other leaders, was becoming uneasy over the prevalence of abortions, which many women preferred to birth control. Still, the state exerted no restraints on sexual relationships or on marriage and divorce. No couple was required to register their marriage, and the more educated classes and party members didn't bother with registration. They looked on it as a symbol of the execrated *meshchanstvo* (middle-class usage) that thwarted human happiness in the capitalist world and had no place in Soviet society. Nor was divorce beset with legal or other difficulties. If the marriage was unregistered, couples separated at their own discretion. If the marriage was registered in *zags* (the registration office), either party could, without telling the other, step into any *zags* office and get it unregistered—as divorce was then spoken of. The acting member didn't even need to inform his partner of the breakup of the union. A postal card from *zags* brought the news. Divorce was as simple as that, and the cost at that time was three rubles, or seventy-five cents in American money.

But if there were children in the family, the state did not absolve a man from responsibility in contributing toward their support. "Get together, children," wrote the late Nikolai Semashko (1874-1949), then Commissar of Health, "and separate at your will, but do not forget your little children; if you do—well—by the ear we shall drag you into the sun of the People's Court." They did, too, quite mercilessly. If there was one child in the family, the man paid one third of his earnings toward the support of the child until he attained his eighteenth birthday. If there was more than one child, he paid one half of his earnings until the children reached eighteen. In the very rare instance when the father was entrusted with custody of the children, the wife paid him alimony toward their support in the same amounts that she would have received had the children remained with her. Equality of the sexes was rigidly observed by the courts in the enforcement of alimony for the support of the children.

This system continued until the summer of 1936, or for nearly nineteen years. Then came a radical change, which, however, was preceded by nation-wide discussion in the press, at public meetings, and in private conversations. The opposition to change was widespread and vigorous. But it didn't count. The law of June 26, 1936, banned abortions, and though birth control remained legal it was firmly discouraged. The literature on the subject suddenly disappeared from bookshops and newsstands. I happened to be in the city of Tiflis at the time, and when I asked the manager of the largest Russian bookshop in the city whether he still sold literature on birth control, he grew angry and replied, "We don't need it any more." He cut short the interview and dismissed me as an intruder on his busy hours. Yet in clinics, at least in Moscow, the walls were hung with posters giving information on the subject and physicians didn't hesitate to offer it to women who asked for it. Nor were contraceptives removed from drugstores.

The abruptness with which the new law was promulgated caused countless tragedies. The waiting rooms of clinics and private offices of physicians were crowded with pleading and weeping women and girls, especially girls, vainly seeking relief from unwanted pregnancies. "*Nyet*" was the sole reply they received to their despairing importunities. The law was stern with a physician who violated it, sentencing him to two years' imprisonment for performing the operation. The woman who underwent it was subject to public censure for the first offense and to a fine of 300 rubles for a second. If the man who had cohabited with her persuaded or coerced her into a secret abortion (if a physician was willing to risk it for a high fee—and there were such physicians), he suffered a sentence of from one to two years' imprisonment. Once discovered, all parties involved in an abortion suffered the penalties the law prescribed.

As an aftermath of the sudden enactment of the new law, there were suicides in the country, though not a word of it appeared in the press. There were girls who were too agonized and too frightened of their future to give birth to an unwanted child, though such a child would suffer from no legal and social disabilities. They took their lives because they wouldn't face the risk of being looked down upon by eligible men and spoiling their chances of a good marriage. It was well enough for Yaroslavsky to assure me that the double standard of morality had vanished forever from the Soviet scene. Men remained men, and young men in particular to this day have second thoughts about marrying a girl burdened with a child fathered by another man. No law could wipe out the biological advantages of men over women, and it was the woman and not the man who paid the price for bearing a child out of wedlock. Who knows how many young women at that time died from the illegal operations performed on them by the *babki* —the old women who made a profession of it?

The new law put an end to easy divorce. No longer was the clerk at *zags* permitted to grant it freely, even if both parties appeared and asked for it. Actually, the tightening began in December 1932 with the bringing back of passports. But now it was mandatory on the clerk to strive for a reconciliation of the applicants for divorce, to persuade them to continue their married life for their own good, for the good of the children and the new society. Only in the event of failure to change their minds was he under obligation to grant a divorce. The fee was raised to 50 rubles for a first divorce, 150 for a second, 300 for a third. The law mentions no fee for a fourth divorce, presumably because there was to be no fourth.

On my return to Moscow from my journey south, in the summer of 1936, I again sought an interview with Yemelyan Yaroslavsky. I wanted him to explain how he reconciled the new law with the assurances he had given me that the original principle of freedom of sexual love had come to stay, and that only an atheist-socialist country had the courage to grant this freedom. I telephoned Yaroslavsky's secretary and was requested to set down in writing the questions I wished to address to him. I did as requested but never heard from him.

The law of 1936 was the beginning of the Kremlin's return to conventional Western sexual morality and to emphasis on the strong family. More than that, Communist spokesmen burst suddenly into spirited panegyrics of the new morality, while (tongue in cheek) denying that it in any way compromised with the bourgeois morality of the outside world. "Fatherhood and motherhood," wrote *Pravda*, "have long ago become a virtue in the land of the Soviets. . . . The birth rate is continually rising, the death rate is falling. . . . Marriage and divorce are of course personal affairs. [But] in Soviet society the playboy who marries five times a year cannot command public esteem, nor can the girl who flits with the ease of a butterfly from one marriage to another. . . . So-called free love and disorder in sexual life are completely bourgeois and have nothing in common with a Soviet citizen."

Bourgeois moralists could only say amen to *Pravda*'s sentiments, which *Pravda*'s editor would never have thought of penning at any time during the years that preceded the passage of the new law.

By 1936 the playboy of whom *Pravda* spoke had practically disappeared from the Soviet scene. He had never been particularly conspicuous anyway. In the villages, where the vast majority of the population lived, he had rarely made an appearance, and when he did public sentiment stingingly censured him and he either changed his ways or fled to the city. Besides, village girls, though always free in their social relationships with men, were not easily seduced by arguments for sexual freedom. Actually, the family in city and village had remained unshaken, as the late Havelock Ellis in an interview with me had predicted it would under the Soviet system of freedom in sexual love.

Stern practical considerations growing out of purely national circumstances, far more than the damage abortions were causing to the health of women, motivated Stalin in his sensational reversal on the original pledges and promises of the revolution. Determined to pursue the industrialization of the country at an unprecedented pace, he set out to achieve—among other things—two immediate purposes: to discipline and drive the people to work, with no interference from distracting personal situations, and to speed up the birth rate, high as it already was, so that the flow of workers into industry and of soldiers into the Army would be continually increasing. Besides, a woman worker needed from one to two weeks to recuperate from an abortion, and that too interfered with production.

The shock the new law would cause to the people, though principally in the cities, didn't deter the master of the Kremlin. The dismay it would provoke among Communists the world over who had patterned their own morality on the Soviet principle and practice of freedom of sex, and who had always brandished this freedom as proof of the superiority of Soviet over capitalist civilization, likewise left him unperturbed. Nor was he moved by outcries to exempt from the law those who were pregnant at the time the law was announced, so that women and girls who found themselves "trapped" by pregnancies could be saved from torment and suicide. His one overriding goal was to industrialize backward Russia and to strengthen her militarily. Nothing else was of any significant account.

That was why he also began to subsidize large families. According to the law of June 1936, the mother of a seventh child was granted the sum of 2000 rubles a year for a period of five years. A similar subsidy was awarded a mother on the birth of the eighth, ninth, and tenth child. On the birth of the eleventh and each subsequent child, the sum was raised to 5000 rubles for the first year and to 3000 for each of the following four years.

The heavy toll of war, which the Kremlin has never made public but which, in the light of the population census of 1959, was perhaps double the figure of 15,000,000 that Russians I knew had estimated on the conclusion of hostilities, prompted the Kremlin to begin subsidizing mothers on the arrival of the third child. By the law of July 8, 1944, a mother was awarded a lump sum of 400 rubles for a third child. For each additional child up to and including the tenth, the award was increased to a lump sum of 1300 rubles and 80 rubles a month for a period of five years. On the arrival of the eleventh and each subsequent child, the lump sum rose to 5000 rubles and the monthly subsidy to 400 until the children reached their fifth birthday.

The monetary subsidies were supplemented by medals and titles, such as Mother Heroine, Glory of Motherhood, Motherhood Medal. The special honors continue to the present time, but the subsidies were reduced by the law of November 25, 1947. The lump sum for the third child is now 200 rubles; for the fourth child it is 650 rubles and a monthly allowance of 40 more for a period of five years. With each succeeding child both sums are increased, so that on the arrival of the tenth child the immediate payment is 1750 rubles and the monthly allowance for five years is 125 rubles. For each subsequent child the immediate payment is raised to 2500 rubles, but the monthly allowance remains unchanged.

Having started on the road of conventional morality by the law of June 1936, the Kremlin made a leap in a new direction, by the law of July 1944. This time the state armed itself with fresh powers to control marriage and divorce. The common-law marriage, as it is known in Anglo-Saxon countries, while not outlawed, was completely discredited. The mother of children born out of wedlock had neither legal nor economic claim on the father; no longer might she legally impose on him fatherhood or sue him for the support of the children. Again, the state blithely disregarded the biological disadvantages of a woman. She paid the penalty for what the Soviet press speaks of as her "frivolous behavior," while the man was relieved of all responsibility for the same "frivolous behavior."

I was a war correspondent in Moscow at the time the new law was passed, and I remember vividly the dismay of men and women I knew at its enactment. They resented the state's further intrusion into their private lives by making registration of marriage virtually mandatory. They resented even more bitterly the dual standard of sexual morality, which bolsheviks had for years been condemning as an outrageous by-product of capitalist civilization and which the Soviet state was practically legalizing. A man might father all the children he wished out of wedlock without incurring any responsibilities other than those his conscience might impel him to assume. Russians openly spoke of it as "a law for men."

It must be noted, however, that Russia was seeking to increase the heavily depleted population. Millions of men were killed, millions of young widows would never be remarried, if only because of the shortage of men. But these women were capable of bearing children, and men would have been frightened away from them had the old law holding them responsible for the support of offspring remained in force. Instead, the state came to the aid of the unwed mother. It offered her the alternative of placing her children in a state home or receiving a subsidy for their support. The subsidy was originally modest—100 rubles a month for the first-born, 150 for the second, but never more than 200 for the third and each subsequent child until they attained their twelfth birthday. But by a law of January 1, 1948, the single mother became eligible to the same subsidies as other mothers on the arrival of a third child—this in addition to the gratuities granted her by the law of July 1944.

The provisions of the law relating to the unwed mother were regarded as an emergency measure. They have stimulated the birth rate but have not saved the mother from certain perplexities and perturbations that are peculiarly Russian. Men and women are addressed by their given name and their patronym. A child therefore must have a patronym. In registering a newly born child the unwed mother may give him whatever patronym she chooses or leave the question of fatherhood unanswered; which is what many mothers usually do, thus leaving a blank space on the birth certificate. When the child grows up he begins to ask questions about the man whose patronym he bears or why he has no patronym as other children have. The mother either refuses to answer the question, which heightens the child's curiosity, or tells the truth or lies. In either instance the mother is faced with a painful situation, which the unwed mother in Czarist times never knew. Then, an illegitimate child was registered with the patronym of the godfather. But godfathers are out of fashion now, and there have been instances when clerks in registration offices conferred on the child not a patronym but a matronym—the mother's name. If the child was a boy named Vasily and the mother's name was Marya, he was known as Vasily Maryevich. If the child was a girl named Nina and the mother's name was Irina, she was known as Nina Irinovna. To Russian ears matronyms sound oddly comical— nothing like it had ever been known before. Yet "the grief and the tears" of mothers who protested against the clerk's arbitrary and unprecedented procedure were of no avail (*Literaturnaya Ga-*

zeta, June 4, 1960). That the child would be mocked and tormented by playmates was of no concern to the registration clerk.

The law of July 1944 has lent itself to other cruel injustices to the child and the unwed mother, who often enough is a girl in her late teens. Despite all ideological teaching and the moralizing that goes with it, men are men. Exempted from penal and financial responsibility for a child fathered out of wedlock, men, both single and married, have taken advantage of the privileges the law accords them. A man may tell a girl he is in love with her, take her to movies, the theater, write her passionate love letters and promise to marry her, and then on the arrival of a child, or even before, inform her under one pretext or another that he cannot accept her as his legal wife. The girl is left with the burden of her sorrow and the man escapes completely. No wonder that Russians speak of the law of July 1944 as "a law for men."

A woman physician in Moscow was so wrought up when she discussed the subject with me that she angrily exclaimed, "I know of no capitalist country that perpetrates such an injustice on the unwed mother!" She told me that factory girls have been warned not to indulge in a love affair with a man who promises to marry them without demanding to see his passport, where his marriage and children —if he has any—are registered. This is a protection against willful deception by men.

Significantly she spoke of the warning to factory girls. In the villages, girls know boys and men too well to be easily deceived by them. Besides, the peasant mamma has regained her role as a protector of her daughter's welfare, especially in her relations with men. Party secretaries not only encourage this role but eulogize the peasant mamma, however old-fashioned and religious, for the strict supervision of the moral behavior of children and especially daughters.

Yet, contrary as it may seem, Soviet sexual morality today demands of young people continence until marriage and associates sex with children and family. Woe to the young factory worker or college student, man or woman, who is discovered to have had an affair outside of marriage. The event is publicized and all the ignominy that stinging rebukes or Komsomol resolutions can evoke is leveled at the guilty one, though since 1955 abortions have again been legalized, so no children need result.

Once I was discussing this subject with a group of men students of Moscow University. "If things happen," one student said, "it's strictly a private affair. The important thing is not to be discovered."

"How is it in America?" asked another student.

"About the same," I said, and we all laughed.

Divorce in the Soviet Union, as enunciated in the law of July 1944, is beset with more restraints, direct and indirect, than in many a state in America. No longer can a man or woman obtain it in the registration office, even if, as the previous law had stipulated, both parties present themselves in person and ask for it. As in capitalist countries, divorce may be obtained only through court action.

First there must be an application to the People's Court, and the cost of the application is 10 of the new rubles, or twice as much as a first divorce under the law of June 1936. The announcement of application must be published in the local newspaper and paid for as an advertisement by the person making it. The charge is 30 of the new rubles. But newspapers, which are usually published in four pages, have little space for such advertisements. In Moscow, with a population of five million, only *Moskovskaya Pravda*, the city morning newspaper, and *Vechernyaya Moskva*, the city evening newspaper, accept them, and they devote approximately one fifth of the last page to publishing them in small print. Months may pass before space is available. That is why Muscovites, if they are lucky enough to find a room or the corner of a room for sleeping in a town outside of the city, establish residence there and contrive to place their announcement in the local newspaper, which is not so crowded with divorce notices.

Even when the case comes up before the People's Court, the actual divorce is still far off. This court has no right to grant it. It performs the functions of a domestic-relations court in America. All it does is hold hearings, ascertain grievances, and attempt to reconcile the contending litigants. Nothing more. If the People's Court fails to effect a reconciliation, the case may be carried to the next-higher or to the highest court in the country. Only couples without children find it comparatively easy to obtain a divorce. Those with children count themselves lucky if the divorce comes through within nine months, or after as long a period—Muscovites jestingly say—as it takes a woman to produce a child. The fee for a divorce is from 50 to 200 of the new rubles, or from 55 to 220 American dollars, for one or both of the parties involved. And yet Lenin had said, "It is impossible to be a democrat and a socialist without permitting at once complete freedom of divorce."

On my last visit to Moscow I quoted Lenin's words to a judge in a People's Court, and his reply was: "Lenin meant it only for the abnormal conditions that prevailed in the early years of the revolution." This is the present ideological interpretation of Lenin's commitment to free divorce. But there is not a shred of evidence to justify this interpretation. Soviet ideologists have never scrupled to interpret Lenin or Marx to suit their purposes, however contrary these may be to the original pronouncements of either man.

The law of July 1944 does not specify grounds for divorce. These are left to the discretion of the courts. But in the years since the enactment of the law, the experience of the courts has again and again been summarized in juridical writings that set down the philosophy and the motives that guide courts in their decisions. The basic philosophy is no different from that in capitalist countries; namely, that the family is the cornerstone of society and therefore it is the duty of the courts to preserve it, if at all possible. In all ideological and juridical literature, indeed in all Soviet writing and oratory, the phrase *krepkaya semya* (the strong family) is continually and vigorously emphasized. Fathers and mothers must under all circumstances attempt to subordinate personal pleasures or perturbations to the preservation of a solidly unified family. The Soviets demand it because "the functions of the family embrace the Communist upbringing of children, mutual help to one another in the cultural uplift of all, in high productivity of labor for the welfare of the Motherland, and in the joint satisfaction of material needs."[1]

The family is now a sanctified institution, and the Soviets have mobilized public sentiment against its dissolution. The party, the Komsomol, the trade unions, the local soviets all over the country, bring into play persuasion and pressure to prevent the breakup of the family. It just isn't the thing to do, least of all for a member of the party. He is to set an example of devotion to family life, even as is a

[1] N. V. Rabinovich, *Rol sovietskogo prava v ukreplenii semii* (Leningrad, 1958), p. 3.

church member in the outside world. He must endure his personal unhappiness, and no party member would contemplate a divorce without first obtaining the sanction of the unit with which he is affiliated.

Since the rise of Khrushchev, the party has softened its attitude toward a member who seeks a divorce, though it is still common practice for him to discuss it with the party committee before taking action. "You know," a party member in Moscow laughingly told me, "we even have an anecdote about it. One man asks another the difference between a French, a German, and a Russian girl in their judgment of a man. The answer is that a French girl judges a man as a lover, a German girl as a homemaker, and a Russian girl by the opinion of the *partcom* [the party committee]."

Still, Russian city courts are kept busy with divorce cases; crowded living conditions alone stir up antipathies, recriminations, abuses, that tax the patience of husband or wife, and one or the other or both decide to terminate their marriage.

Usually, if the court is convinced of hopeless incompatibility between them, it grants a divorce without much delay. But there are other grounds, which have been summarized in seven general classifications by M. T. Oriodoroga, a woman jurist.[2]

1. Childlessness of couple (impotence or sterility)
2. Serious illness
3. Conjugal infidelity
4. Desertion
5. Offense against one's personal dignity
6. Absence of free agreement to the marriage, or concealment of a serious pre-marital illness
7. Mental illness, disappearance without trace, imprisonment for not less than three years

Think what one will of the Soviet attitude toward marriage and divorce, it is obvious that in substance and in spirit it differs little from that in non-Catholic capitalist countries. Though in the instance of serious illness contracted after marriage, it is much less humane. "Usually," Oriodoroga writes, "if the disabled party consents to the divorce, the decree is granted." In the event that he doesn't consent,

[2] M. T. Oriodoroga, *Rastorzheniye braka* (Moscow, 1958).

"the court must consider not only the interests of the disabled party but those of the other members of the family. The serious and prolonged illness of husband or wife may so upset their normal relations and the peace of the family that the preservation of the marriage is inexpedient."

Nor is infidelity necessarily a cause for divorce. If the court can prevail on the guilty party to agree never to sin again, and if the party sinned against can be persuaded to trust the sinner's word, no divorce results.

The divorce law of July 1944 has been under such severe criticism that a new law is certain to take its place, sooner or later. The unreasonable interpretation by Soviet courts of "disappearance without trace," the Soviet equivalent of the Enoch Arden law, will presumably be corrected, for it has resulted in endless grief to one or the other of the couple involved. Here is Galina in the city of Smolensk. At the age of nineteen she fell in love with a man named Oleg Kuzmin. The marriage lasted only three months. Oleg left and told her not to look for him. She fell in love again and had two children by the man with whom she lived. But she was still married to Oleg, and though five years had passed since his disappearance, the courts insisted that she keep on searching for him. Her passport bore his name and she was obliged to register her children as his. "And my children," she writes, "are growing up. Their nominal father they never saw and know nothing about. But the time will come when they will ask why they bear the name and patronym of the man who is not their father. What shall I tell them? Shall I reveal to them the sorrowful story of my first marriage?"

Also there has been such an outcry, not only by women but by men, against the exemption of the male from all responsibility for fathering a child out of wedlock that the new law is certain to do something about it. Writers in particular have again and again voiced their indignation publicly and privately at the injustices the law of 1944 levels at girls and young women. "Sixteen years after the promulgation of the law," writes V. A. Kaverin, the well-known novelist (*Literaturnaya Gazeta*, April 2, 1960), "fathers write, mothers and grandmothers write" in protest against the law; and soon, he continues, children will be writing. "Judges who do not wish to act against their consciences demand a change in the law. Why then do these protests fail to make an impression on the Ministry of Justice?"

Thus the Soviets have come full circle. The cult of virginity is again officially glorified, however caustically students may privately speak of it. Continence before marriage is the official command, and when violated "the important thing is not to be discovered." The family is no longer left to its own inner powers of survival, as it had been in the early years of the revolution. The state has beset it with external pressures and coercions at least as strong as in any bourgeois Protestant country.

In all Soviet writing—legal, fictional, journalistic, ideological—there is always the insistence that the Soviets have brought into being "the most advanced morality" ever known to man, and "a new and higher type of family." If they have done so, this writer, like so many others, has been unable to discover it in the forty-third year of the revolution and in the new epoch of the grandiose Seven-Year Plan. The usual Soviet argument is that while, to quote a Leningrad ideologist, "in capitalist countries, marriage is *almost always* [my italics] from calculation, in the Soviet Union it is always a consummation of true love." In the Soviet Union, the argument goes further, a girl doesn't have to marry a man she doesn't love, because she earns her own living and doesn't have to depend on him for his support.

"So do millions of American girls," I remarked to a party functionary in Kiev, with whom I had involved myself in a discussion of the subject. Then I said to him, "Surely you have read prerevolutionary Russian literature. Would you say that the heroines of Pushkin, Turgenev, Tolstoy, sacrificed love to calculation? Think of Anna Karenina. Didn't she sacrifice everything for love?"

It was a futile discussion, as such discussions usually are with party functionaries when the sanctity of party precepts and the validity of its presuppositions are questioned. Loudly and dramatically they boast that they have achieved the one true and pure morality that the world has ever known. Actually, Soviet parents are no less elated when their daughter marries a man of position and high earning power than are fathers and mother in non-Communist countries. Nor are Soviet girls less immune to the blandishments of social position and high earning power of a prospective husband than are girls in other countries. Now that an increasing number of Soviet men are enjoying an incomparably better life than others—in respect to food, clothes, living quarters, motorcycles, automobiles, other material satisfactions—an increasing number of girls are coveting them as husbands. The college graduate, be he only a school-teacher, is regarded as a particularly good catch.

In private conversation all this is readily admitted. How often does a Soviet girl marry a man because he has a room to himself when at home she shares the one-room living space with other members of the family? How often does a man marry a girl precisely for the same reason—because she has inherited or acquired a room to herself? How often does one hear people say, "You should marry so-and-so—he (or she) has a large room all to himself (or herself)"?

A cartoon which appeared in Moscow's daily *Sovietskaya Rossiya* of June 11, 1960, speaks for itself. It shows a girl with a jaunty pony tail deep in thought over an automobile, and a country house with a tall frigidaire on the outside. The quatrain beneath the cartoon reads:

> *To get married? Yes, but to whom?*
> *Yasha has a Volga [automobile]. Shall I marry him?*
> *But Sasha has a country house . . .*
> *A difficult problem.*

The Soviet revolution has liberated girls from the marriage deals that parents had in pre-revolutionary times imposed on them. This custom was prevalent not only among the Mohammedan peoples; it often happened in Slavic Christian villages and among town merchants. The abolition of parent-contrived matches and the right of a girl to keep the money she earns, which is the practice nowadays, have left her free to choose her own life-mate. But the Soviet revolution has not chastened girls of motives and temptations that are common to girls in non-Soviet countries. In the last analysis it depends on the girl. Some marry only for love, others marry for a good life as they envision it, with or without love.

The marriage of a girl to an older man because he is well-to-do and distinguished is no more nor less an exceptional occurrence in the Soviet Union than in other countries, as any foreigner who has attended dinner or any other parties in Russian homes in Moscow,

Leningrad, any Soviet city, well knows. The party and the press may discourage and denounce such marriages, but there is no law against them. In fact, a humorous journal once published a biting cartoon on the subject. The cartoon shows a doddering academician standing by his chauffeur-driven automobile with a bouquet of flowers in his hands and saying to a pretty girl, "How would you like to be my widow?"

Academicians are the highest-paid citizens in the country, earning at the official rate of exchange a minimum of 2500 American dollars a month.

9.

NATIONALISM
Russia above All

Through the years I have attended many of Moscow's diplomatic receptions in honor of the anniversary of the October (1917) Revolution. The most memorable of these was the one held on November 7, 1944—the twenty-seventh anniversary of the bolshevik seizure of power. Never before had I seen the Foreign Office mansion of the Spridinovka so thronged with celebrities, foreign and Russian: among them bemedaled Soviet generals in full dress and such members of the Politburo as Mikoyan, Voroshilov, and even Kaganovich, whom I had never before seen at any of these gatherings. Jubilant over the spectacular victories of the Red Army, the guests celebrated gaily, bibulously, and a few of them, especially Molotov, who as Foreign Minister was host of the occasion, somewhat stormily. Molotov had imbibed so generously of the vodka that he loudly insulted the Swedish ambassador and had to be carried away like a boy who had been naughty to a house guest.

But the most striking feature of the celebration was the uniforms which all members of the Foreign Office were newly wearing. Our censors, whom we were seeing daily in rumpled business suits, suddenly blossomed out with braid and epaulets. Except on the stage of Soviet theaters, such uniforms, copied from Czarist models, had not been seen anywhere in the country since the rise of the bolsheviks. It was particularly startling to see such bolshevik intellectuals as Ivan Maisky, who had been ambassador in Great Britain, and Maxim Litvinov, who had been Foreign Minister and ambassador in Washington, arrayed in the swank and splendor of Czarist autocracy.

"You're witnessing," remarked an American, "the birth of a new Russia."

"No," replied an Englishman, "you're witnessing the rebirth of old Russia."

Birth or rebirth, in the early years of the revolution neither the worldly Maisky and Litvinov nor the provincial Molotov and Stalin could have imagined that the time would ever come when bolsheviks would bring back so flagrant a symbol of Czarism as the old-style uniform. But here it was, risen phoenixlike out of the ashes of "the international revolution" of 1917.

The international revolution had of course misfired, or, as an elderly muzhik at a village meeting I had once attended had expressed himself, "It got stuck in the mud of our Russian roads." It couldn't rise above the ugly primitiveness of old Russia, out of which it had exploded. The highly industrialized and truly capitalist nations, which, according to Marxist philosophy and prophecy, should have been first to "ripen" for the world proletarian revolution, remained unshaken by the social storm that had heaved up in the land of the Czars.

In 1914 Lenin wrote an article bearing the title "The Nationalist Pride of Great Russians," in which he declared, "We are full of the sentiment of nationalist pride, because the Russian nation too has created a revolutionary class and has also demonstrated that it is capable of giving mankind great examples in the struggle for freedom and socialism." It is this revolutionary class of which Lenin was especially proud. But nationalist sentiment of itself meant nothing to him. He regarded himself an internationalist with a vision of the common brotherhood of workers of the world that would transcend all nationalist barriers and rivalries. He fervently believed the Marxist assertion that "workingmen have no fatherland."

To him the worker's sole enemy was the capitalist, regardless of nationality. During World War I, he came out with the slogan

"Convert the imperialistic war into a civil war." He didn't care what might happen to Russia as a nation. For him there was neither a Russia, a Germany, an England, a France, an Austria, an America. There was only the proletariat, soldiers of the international revolution. So confident was he of the triumph of this revolution that in his letter to the Swiss workers of April 8, 1917, on the eve of his departure in a sealed German train from Zurich for Petrograd, he wrote, "Russia is a peasant country, one of the most backward of European countries. Socialism cannot triumph there directly and at once." But once the Russian worker, singlehanded, started the revolution, "the European and American socialist proletariat would fight the decisive battles." Of one thing Lenin had not the least misgivings: *"The German proletariat is the most trustworthy and most reliable ally of the Russian and world proletarian revolution."* The italics are his, not mine, and emphasized the strength of his conviction.

History has made a joke of Lenin's words. He was so obsessed with the doctrine of world revolution that he couldn't envision the rise of a Hitler, whose gospel of blood and soil would suck into Nazi ranks the "most reliable ally of the Russian and proletarian revolution," an ally who at Hitler's bidding would kill Russian fellow workers as mercilessly as a hunter kills his game.

Those of us who were in Russia during World War II will always remember the tears and the wails of old and young, especially of old women, over the bestialities the Germans, including workers, perpetrated on the civilian population during the invasion and occupation. No wonder that Stalin proclaimed the slogan "Death to the German invaders." Not Nazi or Fascist, but German! On August 20, 1942, Moscow's *Komsomolka*, in an editorial captioned "Kill the German," wrote:

"Kill the German! is the plea of your old mother.

"Kill the German! is the plea of the girl you love.

"Kill the German! whispers the very grass of your native land."

In still another editorial, *Komsomolka* exclaimed: "You and the Germans cannot live on the same earth . . . so kill the Germans!"

Lenin might never have left his native Simbirsk on the Volga for all he learned about the psychology of the German or any Western worker during the seventeen years of his émigré life in Western countries. He could no more rid himself of the hatreds that Czarist barbarism had inflamed in him, and of the passion for violent revolution which the hatred had inspired, than he could recast the shape of his nose or his eyes. No truer words were written about him than those of Trotsky: "Lenin was not an accidental element in the historic development, but a product of the whole past of Russian history. He was embedded in it with deepest roots."[1]

To him, workers the world over appeared to have come out of the same mold as the Russian worker. He could perceive no differences in them that "class-consciousness" couldn't overcome. He never seemed to have taken to heart Byelinsky's famous declaration, written in 1847, that "one of the greatest intellectual triumphs of our time is the fact that at last we have begun to realize that Russia has her own history, in no way resembling a single European state." Lenin imputed to the German worker, indeed to all Western workers, including the American, the revolutionary psychology of the Russian worker. To borrow a line from the contemporary Armenian poet Sevak, he had "only one key to all hearts"—all workers' hearts, and minds too, the world over. But he lived to see the defeat of his "international workers' revolution" wherever outside of Russia it had arisen—as in Hungary and Germany, or in the Baltic states of Latvia, Estonia, and Lithuania, which detached themselves from Russia and which in 1940 only the might of the Red Army drove back into Moscow's fold.

Yet Lenin was so obsessed with his detestation of all nationalism that he and his collaborators made a clean sweep of symbols and practices identified with the nationalist Russia they had overthrown: passports were abrogated; uniforms in schools, colleges, and the civilian service were abolished; epaulets were torn off army and police uniforms; the policeman was renamed "militiaman"; army officer ranks were designated by the single term "commander"—whether of platoon, battalion, regiment, division. The private was no longer a *soldat* (soldier), he was a Red Army man; and the sailor was no longer a *matros*, he was a Red Fleet man. The military oath was purged of all hints of nationalism. It vowed "all deeds and actions

[1] Leon Trotsky, *History of the Russian Revolution* (Simon & Schuster, New York, 1937), I, 330.

to the great goal of emancipating workers . . . to fight for the Soviet Union, for socialism, for the brotherhood of peoples."

Ministries became commissariats, and ministers became commissars. The Christmas tree was abolished, though for religious reasons, and Grandfather Frost, the Russian equivalent of Santa Claus, was denounced as the puppet of kulak and priest. The study of Russian or any other history was derided as a putrid survival of capitalism. In the words of Anatoly Lunacharsky's Commissariat of Education, written in 1923, "The teaching of history can only rouse national pride and nationalistic sentiments and neither must be permitted. . . . I do not know what a healthy love of the Fatherland is. . . . We need an internationalist all-human education."

In all the schools I visited in those years, history was reduced to an age-old struggle between classes. The very words "Russia," "nationalism," "fatherland," "motherland," "patriotism," were anathematized. The old national hymn, "God Save the Czar," was of course discarded, but no new one was created. All national hymns were denounced as a perversion and a profanation of the true spirit of the proletarian. All over Russia—in army barracks, in schoolhouses, at party and other meetings—they were singing the "International":

> Arise, ye prisoners of starvation,
> Arise, ye wretched of the earth,
> For justice thunders condemnation,
> A better world's in birth.

Yet as I wandered the country, I thought the international indoctrination of the bolsheviks as artificial as the pronouncement I had heard from the long forgotten Glebov, party secretary in the Commissariat of Education, who denied that Tolstoy was a great writer because he came from the landlord class and in his writings reflected the interests and the soul of his class. Intellectuals like Lenin, Bukharin, Trotsky, and others never shared this judgment, but it had penetrated the schoolroom. How often did I hear Pushkin's Tatyana, heroine of *Eugene Onegin*, denounced by pupils and sometimes by teachers as an idler and parasite and nothing more, because she was of gentle descent. Pushkin himself was only an aristocrat, and of what use were his writings to proletarians, the class that had risen to build a new world in which nationalism should have no more place than aristocracy? The little church in Moscow in which Pushkin was married was converted into a machinery-repair shop. "Throw Pushkin off the ship of history" was a widespread slogan.

Yet people read Tolstoy and Pushkin as avidly as they had ever done. Russia was still Russia, wherever I traveled. The smells in peasant cottages and the speech of the people, their complaints and quarrels, their songs and sayings, their foods and fashions, were as intensely Russian as the Russian landscape.

Stalin thought himself a spokesman of proletarian internationalism, but he knew that the problems he was facing were as tragically Russian as the muzhik's *lapti*. How well he knew it he demonstrated in his speech of February 4, 1931, at the conference of industrial managers. The strains and sacrifices of the first Plan, the managers argued, were too arduous for the people, and the pace of industrialization, they pleaded, should be slackened. In reply, Stalin said:

"To slacken the tempo means to fall behind. And the backward are always beaten. . . . The history of old Russia is the history of defeats due to backwardness. . . . military backwardness, cultural backwardness, governmental backwardness, industrial backwardness, agricultural backwardness. She was beaten because to beat her was profitable and could be done with impunity. . . . We are fifty to a hundred years behind the advanced countries. We must cover this lag in ten years. Either we do or they will crush us."

I have always thought that this was the most harshly realistic and prophetic speech Stalin ever delivered. But it was a purely Russian speech, concerned with the ancient problem of Russia's backwardness. Stalin didn't even hold out to his audience the consolation that if Russia was attacked, the proletariat of the world would rise up in her defense. Russia would have to forge her own weapons of warfare and fight with her own flesh and blood or "they will crush us." There was no alternative, he warned, but to go on with industrialization at accelerated speed.

Ten years and four months later the Nazi Wehrmacht flung itself on the Soviet Union.

Yet official anti-Russianism and anti-nationalism endured for nearly seventeen years, until 1934. Sooner or later these were destined to crumble under the impact of traditional native forces which the party and its bolshevik internationalism were helpless to avert and of outside forces which Lenin had not foreseen. The most powerful traditional force was the innate Russian love of their homeland and their culture. The party might insist they shouldn't think in terms of homeland, but they spoke and sang of their forests and steppes, their rivers and wild flowers, their sun and their skies, their birch and their nightingale, with unquenched ardor. Always a nature-loving people, they instinctively responded to the appeal of their natural surroundings. Always a book-loving people, even peasants and factory workers, when they began to read books, turned to the Russian classics with increasing zeal. Always a music-loving people, the new audiences that crowded the concert halls and opera houses learned to love the old composers as intensely as had the old intelligentsia. Russians could only feel Russian, whatever the party secretary might tell them, and wasn't the secretary himself Russian?

Stalin, it must be noted, never shared Lenin's high hopes of world revolution or Lenin's trust in the German worker as a revolutionary ready to tear up the capitalistic German Reich. In his *History of the Russian Revolution*, Trotsky quotes Stalin as having declared in the course of a debate of the Central Committee on January 11, 1918, "There is no revolutionary movement in the world. We have no facts. There is only a potentiality, and we cannot count on potentialities." These prophetic words are not included in Stalin's published writings. Having arrogated to himself the pose of always having been Lenin's closest comrade in arms, he deleted any and all pronouncements that contradicted the self-assumed and self-glorified role.

But by December 1924, having been confirmed in his original mistrust of the possibility of Western or even German workers joining the bolshevik revolution, Stalin proclaimed the doctrine of socialism in one country. The doctrine marked a new epoch in Soviet history; it signalized above all else the exploitation to the full of resources in nature and man for the upbuilding of a new society in a country which had never known the age of chivalry, had never been touched by the Magna Charta, the Renaissance, the Reformation, a Declaration of Independence, Bill of Rights, a country that had known only the absolutism of the Czars.

Forcibly sundered from Western nations, Soviet Russia developed in a historically Russian setting, and leaders, notably Stalin, were under compulsion to deal with immediate Russian realities and consciously or unconsciously to draw in Russian historical experience for guidance, strength, and inspiration. Outside of Western industry, which supplied them with blueprints for their industrial revolution, Western experience—least of all in parliamentary government and trade-unionism—was of no use to them. They hated it as intensely as they hated Western capitalism, with which they identified the one and the other. Even those of them who had lived in the West saw and judged it with their Russian eyes, the eyes of men with the passions and the hatreds, the extremisms and fanaticisms, the theories and inspirations, they had brought with them from Czarist Russia. As for Stalin, who had been only on brief visits in Western countries and knew not a single Western language, he couldn't have been expected to draw lessons from Western history and from the development of Western labor movements. Western labor leaders who didn't share his Marxist theories, he pilloried as reactionaries and traitors. Only violent Russian-style bolshevik revolution and Russian-style proletarian dictatorship would, he always insisted, usher in the golden age of socialism.

Once I discussed the subject of Kremlin-conceived revolution with Karl Radek, once of the wittiest and most cynical men I have ever known. I told him I was writing a new book (*The Great Offensive*) and would include a chapter on the inapplicability of Soviet-style revolution to a Western country. He laughed and insisted that a proletarian dictatorship was inevitable even in America. Nikolai Bukharin, the best-mannered and in many ways the most cultivated of the old bolsheviks I knew, was as rigidly opinionated on the subject as was Stalin himself. But the fact is that Lenin's and Stalin's Comintern and Zhdanov's Cominform failed to shatter or even to shake "the fortress" of capitalist Europe with a Moscow-contrived proletarian dictatorship.

But in the early thirties, Stalin sensed the fierce nationalism that Hitler was arousing in Germany and that Mussolini had stirred in Italy. Though he had underestimated Hitler's military threat to the Soviet Union (he lightly dismissed the warnings of an impending Nazi attack that Sumner Welles of the State Department and Winston Churchill had transmitted to him until the very moment the Wehrmacht began to pound Soviet fortifications), he was impressed by the success of Hitler's appeal to German nationalistic sentiment.

In June 1942, when I was in Teheran on my way to Kuibyshev on the Volga to report the war, I had a long interview with Andrey Smirnov, then in the Soviet diplomatic service in Teheran and previously in Berlin. Among other things, he told me that in 1936 the Nazi Foreign Office had called him in and, to his surprise, questioned him at length on the rise of nationalistic and patriotic trends in the Soviet Union. The Nazis, Smirnov said, had not expected it and were perturbed by it. Well they might have been, keenly aware as they were of the power of nationalism to sway the minds of men everywhere.

Thus the pressures of the Russians' love for their homeland and its culture, of the doctrine of socialism in one country, of the rise of nazism in Germany and of fascism in Italy, spurred the Kremlin into a rediscovery of old Russia and into embracing many of the very usages it had rejected.

On June 8, 1934, the law of "treason to *rodina* (the Motherland)" was promulgated. To the best of my knowledge, this was the first time since the end of the civil war and foreign intervention that the bolsheviks used the term *rodina*, though they did not then capitalize it as they do now. Thus the concept of nation, which had never died in the people, was officially acclaimed. In July of the same year, *Izvestia* published an editorial bidding the people "to love their Fatherland." Soon afterward Intourist guides and interpreters overwhelmed foreign tourists with sentimental avowals of love for their Fatherland. They were infuriated when some of us teased them for having this love after Marx had said the worker has no Fatherland.

One after another, old usages were officially restored: titles in the Army, though originally only of lieutenant, captain, major, and colonel; passports, which everybody hated; the Christmas tree and Grandfather Frost—though only on New Year's Day, so as to strip them of religious connotations—which were welcomed with delight, and not only by children. The old school discipline and the study of history came back, and Lunacharsky—who died in 1933—carried with him to his grave all the misgivings he had felt over "the national pride and nationalistic sentiments" that the study of history would arouse in the young generation. The Glebovs who had sneered at Tolstoy because of his social origin disappeared from the Soviet scene, and nobody any longer gauged the gift of imaginative writing by the social origin of the writer. Nor did anybody any longer scoff at Pushkin's Tatyana as an idler and parasite. In a village school in the province of Tambov, the teacher of Russian called on one pupil after another in her class to recite for me by heart Turgenev's famous tribute to the Russian language: "In days of doubt, in days of heavyhearted contemplation of the Fatherland, you alone, O you great, mighty, truthful, and free Russian tongue, have offered me support and solace. It is impossible to believe that such a language was not given to a people that is great."

Yes. Russians, and not only proletarians, were a great people now, and if you, Bukharin, though editor of *Izvestia*, dare to bring up the old charge that Oblomov, hero of Goncharov's novel bearing the hero's name, symbolized the universal laziness of Russians, you'll have to prostrate yourself with humiliation and write an apology and say frankly (*Pravda*, February 10, 1936): "I unwittingly deceived many and am sorry I did."

No longer did the word "Russia" carry connotations of a land under the whip of Czarist despotism, that "prison of peoples," as Lenin had called it. It had become an accepted and honored term, evoking pride in the great culture that had come out of it in the past and its historic military accomplishments, the conquest of one territory after another. Whether one called the country Russia or the Soviet Union, it was still the Motherland; and had not Lenin himself once said, "We love our language and our Motherland"?

In the summer of 1936, on my return to Moscow I was struck by the popularity of a lively new song called "Broad Is My Native Land." Composed by Lebedev-Kumach, a well-known lyricist, and set to music by Osip Dunayevsky, it went:

> In forests, fields, and rivers it abounds,
> Another land like it I do not know. . . .
> Like a bride we love the Motherland,
> Like a sweet mother we cherish it.

Communism is a Western idea. How the idea, with its slogan "Workers of the world unite, you have nothing to lose but your chains," would have evolved and expanded in practice had the German worker justified Lenin's faith in him as a true ally of world revolution, may prove an exciting subject for debate and speculation.

But history went its own way. Communism struck roots in Russian soil, and try as hard as they might, the bolsheviks couldn't keep it from drawing its sustenance from this soil: from the history and geography of the country and the character of the people, overwhelmingly illiterate or semi-literate muzhiks at the time of bolshevik seizure of power.

Once started, the process of nationalizing bolshevik internationalism rapidly accelerated. Alexey Tolstoy spent sixteen years in writing his novel on Peter the Great, or the First, as he was now called. In superb detail, Tolstoy re-created the speech, the manners, the political tensions, the social atmosphere, of the age of the mighty, ruthless, and farseeing Czar, glorifying his person and his deeds. The author's "depiction of the growing might of the Russian state," writes the second edition of the *Bolshaya Encyclopedia*, "is imbued with patriotic pride in his people."

Patriotic pride—that was what counted now, and those of us who knew Alexey Tolstoy, drank wine and vodka with him in his spacious and brightly ornamented studio, and listened to his brilliant monologues on Russia's past and present, will always remember him as one of the proudest Russians—not bolsheviks, but Russians—in the Soviet Union, despite his official obeisance to the Kremlin dictatorship and the eloquent language in which he phrased the obeisance.

He came from the province of Samara, which was renamed Kuibyshev, and he hated the new name. He hated no less the change from Tver, the ancient Russian city, to Kalinin. To him the very words Samara and Tver, he once told me, sounded melodiously and romantically Russian, while Kuibyshev and Kalinin grated on his ears. He also glorified Ivan the Terrible in a play, though not so eloquently as he glorified Peter in his novel.

In history textbooks, school children learned nothing of the bloody orgies of Ivan. He was no longer "the Terrible." The cruelest of all Czars was simply Ivan IV, "a talented and wise man. In the internal and external life of Russia he skillfully and correctly formulated the problems and purposes and pursued them with consistency and perseverance." He won victories against the Tatar hordes in the battles of Kazan and Astrakhan, and cleared the Volga River of the enemy. He annexed vast Siberian lands to the Russian empire. He consolidated the state and centralized power in his own hands. He butchered the boyar gentry who fought his dictatorial powers. All this made him in Stalin's eyes one of the greatest figures in Russian history, and didn't he himself maintain power and drive the people through the Plans by similar methods?

In private conversation, Russian intellectuals likened Stalin to Ivan far more often than to Peter. Cynically they spoke of Ivan (meaning Stalin) not as the Terrible but as the Good; of the great painting by Ilya Ryepin showing the Czar embracing his son, whom he killed with his own hands, they said (again with Stalin in mind), "Ivan the Good giving first aid to his son."

I was well acquainted with Vsevolod Pudovkin (1893–1953), the noted motion picture director. When I first met him in the middle twenties he told me that he had studied in Moscow University for a career in physics and mathematics. But after witnessing Griffith's *The Birth of a Nation* he lost all interest in physics and mathematics. The crowd scenes in the American picture so excited him that he decided to produce pictures in which he would create great crowd scenes. His picture *The End of St. Petersburg*, with its tremendous crowd scenes, won him world fame. Like others in his profession, he was in time charged with "formalism," and when I saw him in 1937 he was a disconsolate man. Sensitive to criticism, he was pained by the charge, although he was not without hope. Patriotism had become fashionable, and he would produce patriotic pictures on historical themes. *Minin and Pozharsky*, named for the Russian military leaders who in 1612 drove the Poles out of Moscow, won him back his lost standing with Stalin. Then followed *Suvorov*, named for the legendary marshal (1729–1800) who had vastly expanded the Russian empire during the reign of Catherine II.

Sergey Eisenstein, the most noted of all Russian motion picture directors, was in deeper political trouble than Pudovkin and he too redeemed himself, though only temporarily, with his production of *Alexander Nevsky*, named after the Novgorod prince who in 1240 won a victory over the Teutonic Knights.

Patriotism became one of the most marketable ideological commodities, and quite often literary and artistic heretics could absolve themselves of sin by glorifying love of the Motherland. The people welcomed it, not only the older intelligentsia but the student youth. It gave a new dimension to living, something to which they could respond with genuine emotion. On revisiting the city of Ivanovo, I heard students in a textile institute speak a new language. They no longer had to pretend to be internationalists. Neither did the teachers. They were living in a non-capitalist society; private enterprise had vanished; but they were Russians, and unashamedly, indeed proudly, they could now profess their love of Russia and all that it meant to them. They loved the new song "Broad Is My Native Land," and sang it joyfully. So did school children. I saw them parading the streets of Ivanovo and singing it, and no longer did I hear them singing the "International," as children had done on my previous visits to the well-known textile city.

When the war broke out, it unleashed fresh torrents of patriotism. Hanging on the wall of my study is a framed and now faded poster I had picked up in Kuibyshev, which had become the temporary capital of the Soviet Union. Arrayed in their dress uniforms, the figures of conquering military commanders in Russian history—Alexander Nevsky, Dmitry Donskoy, Kuzma Minin, Dmitry Pozharsky, Alexander Suvorov, Mikhail Kutuzov—adorn the poster, and in bold black letters is inscribed Stalin's invocation, "Let the valorous example of our great ancestors inspire you in the war."

Inspire it did, officer and soldier, despite the multitudinous defections to the enemy. I never shared the widespread opinion among Russian émigrés, ex-Communists, Western journalists and politicians, that if Hitler had treated Russian war prisoners and the civilian population in occupied territories with respect and magnanimity, he would have won the war, would even have been welcomed by the people as the deliverer from Stalin's tyranny. Let it be remembered that throughout Russian history it was chiefly the muzhik who did the fighting and the dying. He was the rank-and-file soldier, he and the Cossack, who, though a highly privileged person under the Czars, was of muzhik origin. Yet Czar after Czar, however brutal to the muzhik, won monumental victories on the battlefield, even though the muzhik was only a serf. Neither Ivan the Terrible nor Peter the Great nor Catherine II had manifested the least regard for the lowly, impoverished, and illiterate muzhik serf. But he always fought valiantly for his country. He might have hated the landlord and the Czarist officialdom, who whipped taxes out of him, thrashed him for the least misdemeanor, exchanged him for a horse or hunting dog; but when he faced a foreign enemy on the battlefield, he fought with courage and desperation.

During the decisive battle of Poltava—Peter the Great's Stalingrad of 1709—Mazepa, hetman of the Cossacks, was in collusion with Peter's enemy, King Charles XII of Sweden. And even as Peter was fighting the Swedish king, "his rear areas," writes the historian Kluchevsky, "flamed up with a Bashkirian revolt which seized the Volga regions of Kazan and Ufa, and afterward the Don, . . . whence it spread to Tambov and Azov." So defections were not anything new in Russian history, though never before were they so numerous as during World War II. Yet despite defections and revolts, Peter won his war, and high on a hill outside the Ukrainian city of Poltava stretches the so-called Swedish Cemetery, which has been preserved to this day as a memorial to Peter's victory.

In World War II the Red Army was not fighting for Karl Marx or for international communism. It was fighting a war "not of life but of death," as the slogan of the day proclaimed, to save the Motherland. The original military oath pledging the soldier to fight for the emancipation of workers had already been scrapped and the new oath pledged him to obey his officer and to battle for the Motherland. The epaulets that the bolsheviks had torn off the officers' uniforms were restored in all their old-style hardness and splendor. The swankiest of all uniforms was that of Russia's age-old warrior, the Cossack, and it was brought back in 1936.

"Soldier," wrote Ilya Ehrenburg during the war, "together with you marches Russia! She is beside you. Listen to her winged steps. In moment of battle she will cheer you. If you conquer, she will embrace you."

And the poet Nikolai Tikhonov, immured in besieged Leningrad, was moved to write: "Russia is our joy and our future, our heart and our soul. Russia was, is, and shall be. Her life is our life, and as our people is immortal, so Russia is immortal."

By the time the war ended, Russia was singing what is officially termed the "Soviet *National* Anthem" (my italics):

> *Unbreakable Union of freeborn Republics,*
> *Great Russia has welded forever to stand;*
> *Created in struggle by will of the peoples,*
> *United and mighty, our Soviet Land!*
> > *Sing to our Motherland, glory undying,*
> > *Bulwark of peoples in brotherhood strong!*
> > *Flag of the Soviets, people's flag flying,*
> > *Lead us from vict'ry to victory on!*
> *Through tempests the sun rays of freedom have cheered us,*
> *Along the new path where Great Lenin did lead.*
> *Be true to the people, thus Stalin has reared us,*
> *Inspired us to labor and valorous deed.* (Etc.)

Significantly, since about 1956, the year of Khrushchev's denunciation of Stalin, the anthem is no longer sung, although at parades and on official occasions bands and orchestras play it. The tribute to Stalin has proven an embarrassment and may yet be deleted when the anthem is sung again.

But Stalin didn't stop with the resurrection of old symbols and even some of the terminology of traditional Russian nationalism. On May 24, 1945, at a victory celebration in the Kremlin attended by party functionaries, generals, and admirals, he pledged a toast to the Great Russians (the Russians proper), hailing them as "the outstanding nation of the nations that formed the Soviet Union . . . the leading people in the country, gifted with a lucid mind, a staunch character, and a great patience."

Stalin's tribute would have been richly deserved had he limited it to the fighting spirit and skills of the Great Russians. After the Germans had occupied the Ukraine, Byelorussia, the Kuban, and other territories in European Russia, they bore the brunt of the fighting. But Stalin singled them out for special gifts of "mind, character, and patience," which nature itself had supposedly denied to the other peoples in the Soviet Union. This was strange language for the leader of international communism, which theoretically draws no distinctions between peoples and races. All the more strange is this language when one remembers that not a drop of Russian or Slavic blood flowed in Stalin's veins. He was a full-blooded Georgian.

Stalin's tribute to the Great Russians was a spark that exploded a fantastic burst of purely Russian chauvinism. Academicians, poets, novelists, editors, journalists, party secretaries, vied with one another in their loud acclaim of Russian superiority over all peoples in the world. Russians were the greatest scholars, scientists, inventors, who ever lived. Russians invented the tractor, the combine, the automobile, the airplane, the electric light, radio, the submarine, the adding machine, and countless other products. They even discovered penicillin, though Britain's Sir Alexander Fleming, the original discoverer of the fabulous new drug, was invited to come to Moscow to help Russians manufacture it.

Russian fathers and mothers were sternly reprimanded for giving children foreign names, which "do not fit the Russian spirit" (*Literaturnaya Gazeta*, August 26, 1952). Then there is the remarkable prediction by David Zaslavsky, renowned for his mastery of vituperative epithets. French, Zaslavsky proclaimed, was the language of the aristocracy and English the language of capitalism. Therefore both (the languages of Diderot and Voltaire, of Shakespeare and Shelley) were doomed to extinction. But Russian was the language of socialism and therefore the language of the future!

I have gone to some length to sketch the transformation of Lenin's international communism into Stalin's nationalist socialism and Russian chauvinism, because it is in my judgment the key to an understanding of the nature of communism in theory and practice as evolved by Moscow and as in its postwar drive for expansion Moscow imposed it on one country after another. If Lenin failed to lift backward Russia to international communism, Stalin shackled communism to the Russia he had prodigiously transformed. He permitted no Marxism, no socialism, no nationalism, no internationalism, no art, no science, no politics, no economics, no philosophy, no sociology, to any Communist anywhere except such as fitted the policies and the dogmas he had fashioned and refashioned in his own Russian environment to suit Russian realities as he had conceived them. To the end of his life, he clung staunchly and murderously to his onetime declaration that "an internationalist is he who unreservedly, unconditionally, without hesitation defends the Soviet Union." All others were heretics and traitors, fit for the firing squad if only they were within reach of his executioners. Russia always came first as teacher and leader and in all of the dictator's aims and calculations, all his plans and purposes. The Soviet Motherland, as Andrey Zhdanov (1896–1948), powerful Politburo member, had once declared, was "a model for the whole of advanced mankind."

Stalin didn't know, didn't trust, and wouldn't countenance any other model of communism and internationalism in any country which through the power of the Red Army fell victim to a Communist dictatorship. He staged one purge trial after another—in Hungary, Bulgaria, Czechoslovakia—to brush out of the way Communist leaders whom he suspected of questioning or opposing his Russia-fabricated model of socialism or communism. The trials, with their attendant confessions by defendants of unlimited guilt, the defendants' eagerness to implicate one another in the plots to which they confessed, without a single word of counter-testimony, were from beginning to end Moscow-staged spectacles.

Russia above all was Stalin's passion and obsession, and when Tito challenged him, he stirred up border skirmishes and a war of nerves with Communist Yugoslavia that endured for five years. Tito won the war and inflicted on Stalin the most disastrous defeat he had ever suffered. Tito's own nationalist socialism triumphed over Moscow's.

This is all past history now, of which in the Khrushchev era Muscovites, as I learned, do not even care to be reminded, even as they do not relish being reminded of their own purge trials and of the Stalinist terrors that racked their bodies and souls. But while Khrushchev has banished the nightmare of Stalin's dark age, he has not unshackled the Communist movement, save where it is beyond his control, as in Yugoslavia and China, from the Russia which he inherited from Stalin. His methods are different but the aim has remained unchanged—Russia is "the elder brother," the source of all wisdom and all authority and still the model for the Communist countries which Moscow dominates.

I was in Belgrade in June 1955, when Khrushchev came to make peace with Tito. Khrushchev subscribed to the doctrine of "different roads to socialism," and at the Belgrade Press Club, debates were loud and spirited as to whether Khrushchev would honor the doctrine. Those of us who argued that Khrushchev couldn't and wouldn't honor it, because to him Russia always came first, were not—as time proved —indulging in idle speculation. A more cautious man than Stalin,

Khrushchev has refrained from provocations that might lead to a renewal of the war of nerves, to border skirmishes, or to severance of diplomatic relations. But the heated denunciations in the Soviet press of Yugoslavia's revisionism of Marxism-Leninism have not ceased, nor have Yugoslavia's cool rejoinders that it is Moscow which is the arrant sinner against Marxism-Leninism disappeared from the Yugoslav press. The conflict is unresolved, and it cannot be resolved as long as Moscow insists on being "the leader of the socialist camp." But in truth it is not Yugoslavia but the Soviet Union which is the original and classic land of nationalist socialism—a socialism that is impregnated with historic Russian forces and aspirations.

In Poland the Kremlin was under compulsion to make concessions to the fighting spirit of an ardently patriotic people. In Hungary the Kremlin smote down rebellion with the might of the Soviet Army, and Hungary is once more a subservient dependency of Moscow, as are all the other satellites. The Kremlin will have it no other way. It is like a surgeon who has mastered a single operation and performs it on all patients, regardless of their needs. The exaggeration of the analogy only lights up its essential truth: the Kremlin enforces on all its satellites, regardless of their historical and cultural development, its own methods of rule and its own way of life.

Highly industrialized and highly cultivated Czechoslovakia is without doubt the most tragic victim of the Kremlin's operation. Moscow has stripped it not only of sovereignty but of the freedoms and the culture, the dignity and self-expression, the people had achieved for themselves. These survive only in the privacy of their minds and souls. The subject of Czechoslovakia belongs to another chapter. But it is well to re-emphasize here that, however more flexible the Kremlin of today is than it was under Stalin, its own experience and practice, its own aims and plans, always come first, in industry as in agriculture, in literature as in art, in political administration as in foreign policy, in personal behavior as in moral values.

The great strength of the Kremlin on the international scene is the techniques it has evolved within its own borders for transforming a backward peasant country into a modern and powerful state. It is no accident that the Kremlin is directing major attention to Asia, Africa, Latin America, all in varying degrees peasant and backward and "awakening from the long sleep of primitive life," as Henry Cabot Lodge once expressed himself. One need not underestimate the allure the Kremlin accomplishment within its own country has for the awakening nations.

But though *Pravda* speaks of Moscow as "the torchbearer of international proletarianism," there is nothing international about the Soviet capital; it is in fact one of the most parochial capitals in the world. A foreigner in London knows that he is in England, but he is never aware of being cut off from the outside world. A foreigner in Moscow only knows that he is in the Soviet Union, and after two or three days, even if he reads and speaks Russian, the outside world is completely blanked out for him. Moscow newspapers either ignore or so distort news that the foreign visitor knows nothing or precious little of what may be happening in his own and other countries.

I once asked a Russian party member how he, as an apostle of international proletarianism, could explain his country's closed door to "the starving unemployed" in America, whose fate *Pravda* is always lamenting. Indignantly he replied, "Let American workers build up their own socialist society. The socialist Soviet Union is no boardinghouse." Another Communist in reply to the same question informed me that the housing shortage alone made it impossible for the Soviet Union to invite the American unemployed to come and settle there. This was a practical but eminently unenlightening reply in the light of the Kremlin's pretensions to solicitude for workers the world over.

I do not know what answer a member of the Kremlin Presidium would make to the question. But if only to demonstrate the genuineness of its "international proletarianism," Moscow could easily accommodate a token number of America's unemployed in its mammoth new housing projects. The guarantee of steady work, of free education for children from kindergarten through the university, of free medical service, of social security, might persuade some of America's unemployed to try their luck in the country of "international proletarianism." But Moscow is not opening its doors to them, and not only because Soviet wages are low compared with those in any Western country. Moscow knows that an American worker would feel smothered in the Soviet environment. The Soviet discipline of the mind alone would rouse bitter discontent even in the non-intellectual worker. He would soon discover that he couldn't "shoot his mouth off" as he did at home. He would chafe under the compulsion to submit uncritically and unquestioningly to *Pravda's* version of any and all Soviet national and international issues. He couldn't even say that Anastas Mikoyan lied when, in April 1960, in reply to a question by a Norwegian student in Oslo, he blamed America for the Hungarian rebellion. He would soon be running to his embassy and begging to be sent home, even as did the Austrian socialist workers to whom Moscow offered asylum after Engelbert Dollfuss, the Austrian Chancellor, turned guns on them in 1934. The young Soviet generation has not even heard of the Kremlin's onetime benevolence to Austrian socialist workers and of their gruesome disenchantment with Soviet socialism or internationalism.

Moscow is not even opening its Siberian doors to Chinese migrants. Anyone who has traveled in Siberia has learned that the country is in desperate need of millions of workers. The Chinese peasant or worker from the northern provinces would have no difficulty in acclimatizing himself to the Siberian winter, and living standards in Siberia are much higher than anywhere in China. Housing, especially in Eastern Siberia, would be no problem at all. The Chinese immigrant could easily build himself a cottage from available building materials, especially from lumber. But Moscow is keeping the Siberian doors closed to Chinese immigrants. Moscow is actuated solely by nationalistic motives—it doesn't want a Chinese minority in Siberia, not even of party members.

Officially Moscow excoriates nationalism as "bourgeois-reactionary ideology and politics," which has no place in a socialist society. Yet in no country in the world are love of country and patriotism so assiduously and so passionately cultivated as in the Soviet Union. In posters and in picture books, in songs and in stories, children from their earliest years are taught that the noblest virtue and most sacred duty of the Soviet citizen is love of his Motherland.

From the bitter experience of the early years of the revolution and the years of war, the Kremlin has learned that there is no substitute for pride in one's country, for the élan it rouses in people, for the self-sacrifice to which it may spur them in time of peace and even more in time of war. In all the drives for the fulfillment of the Seven-Year Plan, the Soviet press and Soviet oratory never cease to invoke love of country as an incentive and inspiration to hard work and self-abnegation. The flamingly patriotic posters and banners that greet the traveler everywhere he goes would give an American the impression that the Soviet Union is perpetually celebrating its own Fourth of July. In the Red Corner of a cow barn in the Ukraine, I saw a red banner strung across the wall bearing in large white letters the legend "Milkmaids! Be passionate patriots and beat America in milk production."

A Russian girl, who attended a ten-year school in Moscow and is now studying in an American college, told me that for some time she was amazed at the lack of patriotism among her American classmates. In Moscow she had become so accustomed to patriotic symbols and banners, and to daily orations on love of country, that their absence on the American campus and in the American classroom manifested to her an insensibility to the emotion of patriotism. Only when she became closely acquainted with teachers and students did she become aware of the error of her assumption—Americans just didn't sing and shout about it as Russians did.

But the Kremlin does strive to keep the emotion flamingly alive, in factory and on farm, in classroom and in army barracks, in the hearts of old and young. Of course, there is the Marxist-Leninist theory of society, which, as an instrument of action, has churned up and transformed Russia as it never has been in all Russian history and which the Kremlin avows is destined to sweep the world. But the concept and the emotion of Motherland color and crown Marxist-Leninist ideology, with its slogan "Workers of the world unite," as gold leaf colors and crowns the domes of Czarist cathedrals inside the Kremlin yard. These lend powerful dynamism to Kremlin policy inside the country and to its quest for world power. The Soviet Motherland is the most sacred thing on earth, and the whole world shall be remade in its image, as Khrushchev also affirmed on January 6, 1961.

Stalin executed foreign Communists who challenged the relevance of this image to their own countries. Khrushchev merely denounces them.

The Soviet poet Vladimir Semyonov writes:

Oh, Motherland,
You—all there is to my destiny.
And I your son
Dare say to you:
Here is my life—
Take it unto you.
What a pity
Nothing greater have I to offer you.

PART III

PEOPLE

I0.

PROLETARIAN
Man Reforged

In the summer of 1933, when the late William Allen White of the Emporia (Kansas) *Gazette* and his wife were in Moscow, they asked me to take them to see a factory. I suggested the newly built Stalin Automobile Works, in the construction of which American engineers and American equipment had played an important part. All I needed to do to arrange for a visit to the plant was to telephone the office of the factory's trade union. Moscow had not yet become so entangled in bureaucratic red tape and so ridden with suspicion of foreigners that it required, as it does today, an official Soviet agency to arrange for a visit to a factory, a school, a college, any institution.

At the factory, the Whites and I were cordially received by a secretary of the trade union. The plant was then producing three-ton trucks, 25,000 a year. We followed the assembly line from end to end, and the Whites were surprised to see so many young women working at machines. Then our host showed us through nurseries, kindergartens, schools, restaurants, the polyclinic, and the club-house, or Palace of Culture, converted from the onetime celebrated Simonov Monastery. Among the more impressive features of the clubhouse was a theater with a stage large enough to accommodate a Moscow theatrical or small opera company. Then we visited homes of workers and ended up with a meal in one of the factory's better restaurants. It was a lean meal, for Russia was just beginning to recover from the famine of the previous winter and spring.

One of the newest factories in the country, the Stalin Automobile

Works constituted a self-contained community. A worker born there could go from kindergarten all the way through an engineering institute without leaving it. He didn't even need to go to the city for entertainment; the factory provided him with theater, music, motion pictures, lectures, sports, dances, and companionship. He could fall in love, marry, raise and educate his family, and live out his years there. Jokingly I asked the trade-union secretary if a worker could be buried there too. No, he replied seriously: a worker would have to be buried in the city cemetery.

What was particularly striking was the intense political education of the worker. The party, the Komsomol, the trade union, the clubhouse, separately and jointly, strove to mold his mentality in conformance with Kremlin doctrine and Kremlin policy. After the visit with the Whites, I went back to the factory several times, and the more I learned about the system of political education, the more evident it became that the Kremlin was sparing no effort and no expense to make the worker, the key man in the social structure, unquestioningly obedient to all its purposes. Flattered at being called "the vanguard of all advanced mankind," he was, however, sternly dealt with when he deviated in thought or deed from the way of life laid out for him to the smallest detail. He was the mass man, a new type in the world.

In the summer of 1958 I revisited the factory. It no longer bore the name of Stalin. Instead it was called the Likhachev Automobile Works, after the man who between 1926 and 1939 and again between 1940 and 1950 had guided its destinies; a peasant by birth and a rather unassuming man, Likhachev proved to be one of the most brilliant industrial executives in the Soviet Union. In the intervening quarter of a century the plant had grown enormously, having pushed deep into the surrounding countryside. Now it was manufacturing not only trucks and buses but bicycles and electric refrigerators. The streets were crowded with traffic; bicycles—few in the old days— weaving in and out of trucks, buses, passenger cars. Blocks of new apartment houses, some twelve stories high, had risen on land that had been field and forest. They were still rising, crowding out ancient peasant cottages fenced in and with trees and shrubbery in the courtyards. This is a familiar scene all over Russia, towering modern apartments supplanting age-old village dwellings.

Again I was received by a trade-union secretary, named Safronov. I made my way through a maze of courtyards to reach the two-story building with its wooden stairway leading to his office. He was in his early forties, smooth-shaven, neatly groomed, wearing a dark gray business suit and a bright blue-and-white necktie. In any Western country he could easily have passed for a business executive, and he was quite a contrast to the unshaved, shabbily dressed man who had guided the Whites and me through the plant twenty-five years earlier.

On the walls of his exceptionally neat office hung large framed portraits of Lenin, Khrushchev, Mikoyan, Voroshilov, but none of Stalin. Nor did I observe any of the flamboyant anti-God posters that on my earlier visit had stared down from inside and outside walls. Like the boisterous anti-God demonstrations, the anti-God posters are out of fashion now.

Safronov told me that there were 40,000 workers in the factory, 30 per cent of them women. The average wage was 1000 (old) rubles a month, or 111 American dollars at the new official rate of exchange. This is higher than the average in industry, which in terms of wages makes this factory one of the most select in the country. With the exception of a few shops that kept open day and night, work went on in two shifts of eight hours each and six hours on Saturdays, or forty-six hours a week (since reduced to forty-one hours). When I mentioned the American forty-hour work week, Safronov hastened to inform me that Soviet industry would within a few years convert to the forty-hour work week and then go on reducing work hours until the Soviet Union had attained the shortest work week in the world. Though the details of the Seven-Year Plan had not yet been published, he appeared to know of the provision about "the shortest work week," six or seven hours a day five days a week, to be introduced in 1964.

There were twenty restaurants and many canteens in the shops, and the prices of meals, as I figured, were from one fourth to one third those in hotels. Dental and medical service was free for workers and their families. The dental clinic was staffed with fourteen dentists and their assistants. Yes, patients had to pay for the luxury of gold crowns themselves, but how much, Safronov didn't know. Opening his mouth to show his own strong white teeth, he said, "I've had no experience, but I can find out if you wish." Prices for gold crowns were the same here as everywhere else in the Soviet Union.

There was a medical staff of 120 physicians and 380 attendants, including nurses. The factory hospital was small—only ninety beds —but was well equipped, even for emergency surgery and blood transfusions. They needed nothing larger because the best of Moscow's hospitals, Safronov explained, were close by and they had their own ambulances to carry patients to them. "Oh yes," he said as an afterthought, "if a worker loses all his teeth, we consider him an invalid and he may retire on a pension if he chooses."

Safronov admitted that the housing crisis was acute. However, the factory was putting up huge apartment houses with its own building department; others were being built by the state. There were elevators only in houses over five stories high, which is standard practice all over the country. "We're doing something for newlyweds," Safronov pursued, "putting up a special five-story house for them. The apartments are small, but after they have two or three children we shall move them to another building with larger apartments."

All the new houses were equipped with gas and electricity, and the apartments ranged from one to three rooms, exclusive of bathroom and kitchen. Rent amounted to 5 or 6 per cent of wages; the rent did not include utilities, for which tenants paid by the meter, but the cost was nominal. The house committee had to look after janitor service, and only structural repairs were paid for by the factory or the state, depending on whose house it was. Other repairs were looked after by the workers themselves. They also repainted their own apartments.

Turning to the subject of children of working mothers, Safronov candidly acknowledged that there was a shortage of nurseries and kindergartens, which he hoped would be remedied within two years. But they maintained summer camps on their own 3000-acre farm, raising their own meat, dairy foods, and vegetables. Parents paid one third of the cost. For adults they operated a seaside resort on the Baltic and a resthouse in the village of Voskino, Moscow province.

"Isn't it arduous for mothers with three or four children to work in the factory?" I asked.

"Well—some of them quit—yes, they quit," was the curt reply. He didn't elaborate. He didn't have to. The fact is that the mother of a large family can quit working and still make ends meet only if there is a grown son or daughter to supplement the family budget. Very few men, unless they have risen to executive position, or greatly exceed norms of production, earn enough in any Soviet factory to support their families.

I brought up the subject of strikes, knowing beforehand what the answer would be. Safronov smiled at the question. "Why should a Soviet worker strike?" he asked. No capitalist was exploiting him. The factory was his and it was to his interest to keep working well and uninterruptedly. Arguing this subject with a Soviet trade-union official is always futile, so I dropped it. Yet it is well to note that one of the primary functions of Soviet trade unions is to prevent strikes, though there is actually no law against them.

The factory, Safronov continued, did everything it could to foster the technological education and the cultural development of the workers. There were more schools here for general and technical education than when I had first known the plant. Some workers took correspondence courses, others attended night schools in the factory or went to night colleges in Moscow. But a worker could study for an engineering degree or for a degree in economics in factory institutes. If after graduating he wished to work elsewhere, the factory interposed no objections. Nor was he required to pay to the factory the cost of his training.

The factory also maintained twenty general libraries in the shops, and the trade union encouraged workers to read books, especially fiction and books on politics and technology. The libraries had 23,000 borrowers, and soon they would celebrate their own book week, with special sales of books in all the shops and with meetings between workers, authors, and editors.

As we were talking we were joined by a slight, wiry man with a long sun-burned face and large, serious gray eyes. He was a chemical engineer and one of the eighteen unpaid members of the trade-union committee. He had been in England, he said, and had visited automobile factories. Yes, he liked England, a highly cultivated and exceptionally well-mannered country. But English food was not for a Russian. He didn't mind eating white bread one day, two days, even three days, but not every day. He got terribly hungry for real Russian black bread and never got it in England. And those English steaks eaten almost raw, the blood oozing out of them! Ugh! How could they eat such steaks? Did Americans eat them that raw too? They did? Ah, ah! He couldn't. No Russian could. He liked his steak thin and cooked through and through so that not a drop of blood showed. And the way they fried eggs in England—always with those crisp strips of bacon! Eggs should be fried in pork fat, so they would melt in the mouth. And that wretched English pudding! How could they stand it? No, English food was not for a Russian, not at all, not at all!

"And there's something else about the English that struck me as peculiar," the chemical engineer went on. "Everybody saves for a rainy day. I suppose they have to because they are never sure of their jobs. It's the same in Sweden. A rich country which hasn't had a war in two hundred and fifty years, basking in prosperity, and yet everybody you meet is saving for a rainy day. Save, save; that's the psychology of the English and the Swedes. It's different with us. We don't have to worry about a rainy day because we're always certain of our jobs."

"What you mean," I said, "is that you have a spending instead of a saving psychology."

"That's it," he snapped back. "When we have money we like to spend it."

But the cause and implication of the spending psychology had escaped the engineer: it is not, as he had assumed, solely a result of the absence of unemployment. For years there had been inflation and people hastened to convert the ruble into goods—anything they could buy. But even now, when the ruble has been stabilized, it is only the high earners in the professions who can afford to save. Rarely can a worker do so. Wages and the salaries of office employees are comparatively low and prices are universally high. As already noted, the average monthly wage in the "rich" automobile factory, as Muscovites speak of it, is, in terms of the new money, 111 dollars, which is the price of a suit of clothes or an overcoat of none too high a quality. The price of a pedal-powered sewing machine is over 96 dollars; a standard refrigerator, from 165 to 222 dollars; a motorcycle, the dream of young factory workers, from 605 to 888 dollars. When Russians save, it is to accumulate enough money for something they particularly need. Now that an increasing number of them are moving to new apartments they save for tables and beds, which are not

easy to buy, for refrigerators and sewing machines, which, though
more readily available, are expensive.

Materially, the living standards of workers in this factory do not
begin to compare with those of workers in similar factories in Great
Britain, in West Germany, least of all in America. I drove around the
length and breadth of the community and nowhere did I see a single
parking lot. So few workers own automobiles that there is no need
for any—the term "parking lot" is not even in their vocabulary. Yet
evidence of a marked rise in living standards since I first knew the
factory struck the eyes everywhere.

The rise is particularly evident in the social and cultural life of
the community, centered in the vastly enlarged Palace of Culture.
Nikolai Baranov, the director, was a bespectacled stocky man with a
large finely shaped head and the leisurely manner of a good-natured
schoolmaster. A peasant by birth, he loved conversation and favored
me with a story about his father, who had been a landlord's gardener
in Czarist times. "Fifty years ago, when I was nine years old," he
said, "my father tried to interest our peasant neighbors in tomatoes,
a new crop on the landlord's estate. I remember vividly Father offering them red juicy tomatoes to eat. They would bite into a tomato
and spit it out, swearing horribly. They called it 'the devil's apple.'
Imagine that!" His broad ruddy face wrinkled with mirth. "Now—
how they love tomatoes! They eat them with anything, even with
potatoes, which are our second bread. Quite a change, isn't it?"

He told the story, he said, by way of preparing me for some startling
changes in the institution he was directing since I had last seen it.
"In our furious outbursts against religion in the early years of the
revolution, we banned every reminder of religion, even the Christmas tree. That's the way it was, but not so any longer. We brought
back the Christmas tree, though now we put it up at New Year's
and call it the New Year's tree. Here in the Palace we set it up
toward the end of December and let it stand decorated and lighted
up until about the middle of January. We don't sing Christmas carols,
but we have plenty of other songs as merry as carols. During Easter
we baked old-fashioned *kulichi* [Easter cakes]. During *Maslianitsa*,
the festival which precedes the Orthodox pre-Easter fast, we bake old-
fashioned *blini* [griddlecakes], which symbolize the sun. Then, a
short time ago, on Youth Day, June 29, to be precise, our young peo-

ple drove into the forest and came back with a truckful of freshly cut
birch branches to decorate the halls of our Palace. That's how the
Orthodox decorated their homes during the festival of the Holy
Trinity, which occurs early in June, when birch leaves are full-grown
and sweet-smelling. It's a beautiful custom and we have brought it
back. You see, it's a mistake to think of folk customs as related solely
to God and church. They have reflected the joy and romance of our
folk life since ancient times, long before our people became Christianized."

So customs that had once been despised and taboo have come
back: new Russia turning to old Russia for gratification of the growing urge toward joy and romance—an urge that had long been held
down by the stormy rush into a technocratic civilization. This was
one of the great changes that had occurred in the Soviet Union in
the years that I had been away and which signalized something new in
bolshevik psychology.

"D'you play much football in America?" asked the director.

"Yes, but we don't play soccer, which is what we call your brand
of football, as much as you do," I answered.

For a few minutes we discussed the difference between soccer
and American-style football. Then the director said, "Our automobile
workers are the greatest football enthusiasts in the country, and we
have the second-best team in the Soviet Union—the Torpedo—did
you ever hear of it? The players are all workers, and whenever they
play away from home, everybody—even children—sits by the radio
and listens to the broadcast of the game. That's how football-mad
our people are. We are building a new stadium of twenty-five thousand seats. It's wonderful how loyal our people are to our great football team."

"You talk like an American fan," I said.

"Good," he said. "It's better to talk about football than about
atomic bombs."

"Aye, aye," I agreed, and we shook hands. Ordinary Russian people talk warmly about peace. If only they had a voice in the policies
that make for it!

"What other games do you play?" I asked.

"Well, we have twenty-seven sports clubs with a membership of sixty-five hundred. But the games we like best, after football, are basketball, volleyball, hockey, water polo."

"Do you play baseball?" I asked.

"No, we don't play baseball. But we're beginning to play tennis and some of our boys have taken up boxing. Then in winter we pour water on our front yard to make a skating rink. We have dances on ice and classes in figure skating. I tell you, there is nothing more beautiful than to watch young people dance on ice—it makes your blood tingle with joy. Some of our figure skaters are the best in Moscow."

All over Russia it is the same—the factory and not the college is the great popularizer of sports. The college teams are far behind those of the factories in strength, skill, and drama. The names of the games are the same in Russian as in English, attesting to Russia's indebtedness to the Anglo-American world for its major sporting events.

Then the director showed me through the block-long clubhouse surrounded on all sides by boulevards, lawns, and flower beds that were not too neatly kept. It was much larger than when I had first seen it, with a library—the largest in the community—a reading room, a chess room, and a theater with 1650 seats, where in the course of the year professional theatrical companies from Moscow put on from twenty-five to thirty plays and professional musicians gave about as many concerts. No, the performances were not free. Workers had to pay admission charges so that the artists could be paid their fees. When not in use for drama and music, the theater put on movies and was open every afternoon at four o'clock. Three smaller auditoriums with from 250 to 300 seats were for lectures, meetings, and children's plays presented by children. During the past winter the young people's dramatic club had put on several plays: Tolstoy's *Natasha*, Gogol's *Taras Bulba* and *The Inspector General*, Shakespeare's *Romeo and Juliet*. Most impressive was the dance hall, bright with color, with upholstered chairs along the walls, and large enough for 500 couples, one of the largest and most attractive dance halls in Moscow.

"Now I want to show you what we do for children between the ages of eight and fifteen," the director said. We walked into a large room that was stocked with birds in cages, with rabbits, frogs, hedgehogs, hamsters. "This is the nature room," Baranov explained. "Children love to come here and observe the animals and care for them. It develops a strong feeling of kindness for all living things."

Then we walked through one toyshop after another, where children made miniature balloons, buses, trucks, planes, and, in one shop, boys and girls fashioned mosaics out of broken glass and broken phonograph records. There were also studios for painting and sculpture. "We cater," the director explained, "to every conceivable taste and talent—sports, science, music, drama, dancing, painting, modeling. The party spares no effort to educate our children and young people to be well-rounded citizens, prepared to live in a collectivist society."

"The party does everything?" I said.

"Of course. That's the way it is in our country. Without the party"— he paused and made a wide sweeping gesture—"all this land would still be a primitive wilderness. The automobile factory in Czarist days didn't amount to much. Right here was the Simonov Monastery —and see what the party has made of it. Oh yes, the party does everything. That's why our people love the party as they do their father and mother."

The party has officially taken the place of Stalin as the benevolent father of the worker, the giver of all joys and blessings, the inspirer of all hopes and aspirations—the party, and not Khrushchev. With all the adulation that has been conferred on Khrushchev, he has not been elevated to the godlike stature which Stalin assumed. Now the party does everything, and therefore to the party must go the worker's complete loyalty and unquestioning obedience.

The party has done well by the workers of the Moscow automobile factory, with its ministrations to their social and cultural well-being. Other factories follow the same pattern, but the Moscow factory is a model of efficiency and achievement. In newly industrialized regions, social and cultural work is often neglected or is grimly inadequate. The *Literaturnaya Gazeta* (August 16, 1960) presents a dire picture of what is happening in the forested district of Vaya (Perm province), where there is a highly developed timber industry. In the communities of Beryozovka and Zolotanka, there is no hospital, and when two workers were in desperate need of surgical operations, they had to wait until a surgeon and nurse from a distant town came on horseback to operate on them. The roads were so muddy that an automobile couldn't get through and the weather was so inclement that a helicopter dared not risk the journey.

In three communities in this district where there were hospitals, there were no physicians—the eleven "men in white" ran away. Workers in one town after another could buy plenty of vodka, but shops were short of radios, skates, ski boots, footballs, children's clothes, sewing machines, sport shirts, bathing suit, men's suits. Rare was the clubhouse—wherever there were such—in the whole district that was kept clean or offered any "cultural" diversions for workers. In consequence, the turnover of labor was enormous. One often hears of more or less similar conditions in the newly opened industrial communities.

Nor are there many of the older industrial districts that can compare with Moscow's automobile works in their social and cultural ministrations. But if the factory, wherever it may be situated, smothers the urge for independent thinking, it does offer workers the opportunity to attend classes and schools, to cultivate new skills so they may rise to higher earning power, even to prepare them for the university for whichever profession they may choose. Under the new system of education, the factory is a direct road to any higher institution of learning.

There can be no doubt that one reason for the sudden change in the Soviet educational system is the determination of the Kremlin to hold fast to the proper indoctrination of the fifteen-year-old boys and girls who come to the plant fresh from the school bench. During the three or four years that they work in machine shops in preparation for the university, should this be their goal, they will be more tightly bound to the party in their thinking than they would be had they gone straight from the ten-year school to the college classroom. The Soviet factory, it cannot be emphasized too vigorously, pursues a double purpose: to turn out goods and to mold the mentality of the worker, and the party devotes as energetic attention to the one as to the other.

The party's solicitude for the worker and its control of his mind and destiny reveal the essentially Russian nature of the bolshevik revolution. Despite its avowed internationalism and its glorification of the proletariat, "the most advanced class in society," the party is

ever aware of the historic heritage of the Russian worker, and what a
dismal heritage it was!

In the twenties and early thirties, I frequently visited the textile
city of Ivanovo, of whose revolutionary proletariat I had read much.
On my first visit to the city in 1923, I couldn't find a room in a hotel
and the *izvoshchik* (horse cab) drove me to the home of a textile
worker who rented a spare room to strangers. The family of five
lived in a five-room clapboarded house with no running water or
other modern improvements. A high board fence enclosed a courtyard set out with fruit trees. Back of the house was a dovecote and a
barn for a cow, a pig, chickens, and rabbits. Behind the barn was a
large kitchen garden and more fruit trees. Obviously the textile
worker was as much a peasant as a proletarian. So it was all over
Ivanovo, which, like so many provincial cities in those days, was only
an overgrown village with mud puddles in the streets where pigs
wallowed.

Whenever I returned to Ivanovo I stayed with this same textile
family. The last time, in 1934, the late H. R. Knickerbocker was with
me. Around a steaming samovar we sat up late into the night,
listening to the laments of our host and his wife over the impending
destruction of their house and loss of their farmstead. New apartment houses would rise in the street and they would have no garden,
no pig, no chickens, no fruit trees any more. Here was a proletarian
who rebelled against becoming a man with no roots in the land, who
would have to depend solely on the factory for his livelihood. There
were multitudes like him all over the country.

In the early years of the revolution, if you scratched the Russian
worker you would find a peasant linked to the village by more than
the bonds of blood. He could work on his land in summer and in the
factory in winter. In time of unemployment he could always go
back home for bread and shelter.

Trade unions were legalized in Russia in 1906, but they were under
such rigorous police surveillance that the factory worker never gained
any significant experience in union organization. But the pressures
of life had made him a fighting man, conscious of his grievances,
waiting to strike at the opportune moment and to battle for a better
life. It was in his name that the bolsheviks proclaimed and fought
for dictatorial power. But if it had not been for the peasant soldiery

in the newly recruited Red Army, the proletarian would have been drowned in blood in 1917 as he was during the revolution of 1905, when the muzhik infantryman on the command of Czarist officers turned his gun on rebellious workers. According to academician Strumilin, the population in the Czarist empire in 1913 did not exceed 163,000,000, and the number of workers in big and small industry came to 4,295,000—or less than 3 per cent. This was a far cry from the majority to which, according to Marxist theory, it should have risen to be ripe for a proletarian dictatorship.

In moments of candor ideologists even today, in the forty-third year of the revolution, blurt out unpleasant truths about the Russian worker as he was on the eve of the revolution. In a pamphlet I picked up in Odessa, I read the following passage: "The life of workers in Czarist Russia differs but little from the unenlightened and hopeless condition of the peasantry. Depicting the life of workers in pre-revolutionary times, A. M. Gorky in his novel *Mother* wrote, 'Returning home, workers quarreled with their wives—and often beat them, unsparing of fists. Young people sat in taverns or arranged parties in one another's home, played and sang vulgar songs, drank and indulged in vituperative language. Exhausted from work, people got drunk quickly, yielded to incomprehensible sickly irritations, flung themselves on each other with the ferocity of beasts, . . . swore and beat their children.' "[1]

Manifestly not all workers answered Gorky's picture. Metalworkers, especially in the Czar's capital, were the elite of the elite. But in 1913, out of 216,000 workers in St. Petersburg—"cradle of three revolutions"—only 40 per cent were metalworkers. In 1918, Lenin spoke of the St. Petersburg worker as constituting "a small part of workers in Russia. But—they are of the best, the most advanced, most conscious, most revolutionary, most steadfast, the least inclined to be impressed by the empty phrase, to yield to despair and to intimidation by the bourgeoisie."

At the conclusion of the Red-White civil war, there were at most 2,600,000 workers within Russia's truncated borders, and large numbers of them fled to the village, to claim their share of land or

[1] V. G. Sinitsyn, *Rozhdeniye kommunisticheskogo byta* (Moscow, 1960), p. 6.

to live and work with the family. Everywhere I wandered in the countryside in those years, I met these "proletarians" who appeared glad again to strike roots in the land. Peasant fashion, they imagined that their immediate problems were solved forever by the bolshevik land reform. Disillusionment came when they discovered that an allotment of land, if they had no horse or cow, or lived with an overcrowded family, held no promise for the future. At mass meetings they were among the most vociferous grumblers, and when, about the middle twenties, there was need for workers in industry, they began to track back to the factory.

It would be the wildest of dreams to imagine that men of the Russian worker's background, many of them half literate, with no political or administrative experience and still largely rooted in the village, could possibly be competent to guide, rebuild, and rule the vast shattered nation. From the very beginning, the dictatorship organized in his name was a dictatorship, not of, but over the industrial worker, as Trotsky in 1904 had predicted it would become if Lenin's theory of a secret, professional, tightly disciplined elite leadership were put into practice.

But Lenin had counted on a world revolution, or at least on a triumphant uprising of German workers, who with their superior skills and education would come to the rescue of the Russian revolution. It was a prodigious gamble and it failed completely and ignominiously; Lenin found himself with a proletarian dictatorship in a country where over 80 per cent of the people were muzhiks and where the proletarian himself was overwhelmingly a muzhik at heart, utterly unprepared and unfit to fulfill the goals of the revolution. Lenin had called Russia "Asiatic, barbarous and backward," and it has always been my conviction that he never would have conceived the theory of a revolutionary elite ruling in the name of the proletarian had Czarist Russia developed a class of factory workers comparable in education and skill, in trade-union and political experience, in personal discipline and social manners, to those in the industrially advanced Western countries. Yet though the bolsheviks sublimated the proletarian into the Messiah who was destined to redeem mankind from all its woes, they could not escape the dire heritage of the Russian worker. To save the revolution from collapse, he had to be ruled with an iron hand. In 1924 and 1925 strikes were rampant in one state-owned industry after another—267 in 1924, 198 in 1925. Strikes had to be stopped, and in time they were.

And what a blight the proletarian exercised on Russian letters and arts! In his fury against the old regime he smashed cultural monuments in city after city. Had it not been for Anatoly Lunacharsky, Commissar of Education, he would have blown up the Kremlin during the fight for bolshevik power in November 1917. With tears in his eyes Lunacharsky resigned from his office, so appalled was he at the reckless bombardment of Russia's most sanctified architectural and artistic treasure. He withdrew his resignation after the bombardment ceased.

The spirit of so-called "proletarian culture" was vividly expressed in the poem *We*, written in December 1917 by Vladimir Kirilov, whom Stalin subsequently purged, though not for his poem. In part the poem reads:

> *Today, in the name of our tomorrow,*
> *Let's burn Raphael,*
> *Let's sack museums,*
> *Let's trample art's flowers.*

Early attempts to put workers in charge of factories proved a dismal failure. Whenever anything went wrong in a shop, they called mass meetings, argued and wrangled, smoked endlessly, and wasted precious hours of work. As a director or manager of industry, the highly eulogized Russian proletarian demonstrated that he would just as soon argue as work. There were exceptions of course, but too few to be of any real help to the bolsheviks. "Science, technology, knowledge, art," said Lenin "are in the heads and hands of specialists." Therefore the defamed and execrated managerial and technological intelligentsia had to be restored to administrative positions. Mistrusted as they were, worker-commissars stood guard over them.

Here, then, was the great quandrary of the bolsheviks. The giant they needed to fulfill the creative tasks of the revolution was not there: Russian history had not evolved him, or only in such small numbers that he was not of much account; the one they expected from Germany never arrived. So they set out to create a new proletarian, largely out of muzhiks from the village. The process of converting the raw peasant fresh from the village—often illiterate, untrained in the use of modern tools, undisciplined in work habits, likely to be light-fingered with bolts, screw drivers, hammers, and other tools— was an arduous affair.

Nor was Stalin, who with the beginning of the first Plan and even earlier drew millions of muzhiks into industry and construction, the man to pamper the newcomer from the village. With speed and ruthlessness he drove the muzhik through his paces. Everywhere I journeyed in those days—Sverdlovsk, Magnitogorsk, Kharkov, Stalingrad, Bryansk, Minsk—I saw masses of muzhiks, some still wearing *lapti*, crowded into barracks, living on soup and bread, on potatoes and sometimes kasha, with little or no meat, but working like Trojans, grumbling and wailing, but working and working, smashing precious imported tools and learning from the smashing—learning well with the passage of time.

The muzhik was hardy and strong; there seemed no limit to his patience and endurance; he could eat anything, sleep anywhere. Yet if he heard of a factory where he could buy a pair of boots, a shirt, a package of tobacco, more easily than in the one where he worked, he picked up his bundle of belongings, his wife and children, and moved. The turnover of labor was enormous. During the first six months of 1930, 29,000 workers arrived in Magnitogorsk, where a gigantic steel plant was in process of construction, and 20,000 left: even muzhiks couldn't endure the rigorous living conditions there. But the one thing they rarely did was return to the village, as they had so often done in Czarist times and in the early years of the revolution.

With collectivization in full sweep, the muzhik saw no life and future for himself on the land. Rather he fled from the village to the factory, uprooting himself forever from the land. Of itself this brought about a radical change in his psychology, hastening the process of his proletarianization. All his traditional love of "the little mother earth," "the dear food giver," as he had for ages past sung of the land, withered away like a flower nipped by frost.

He was a new man on the Russian scene, groping and struggling for a new orientation in life, the road back blocked, the road ahead bewilderingly foggy. The theme of the transition of the muzhik from the soil to the machine—millions of them between 1926 and 1940—

with all the uncertainties and heartbreak that accompanied the move, awaits a young Gorky to do it epical justice.

To check the mass turnover of labor in industry and construction, the Kremlin came forth with the most draconian labor laws Russia or any other country had ever known. Between 1930 and 1940 one decree after another was promulgated to prevent the constant migration. Offenders were publicly pilloried, denied food and rationing cards, expelled from the factory, and evicted from the factory's houses. By the decree of June 1940, workers were frozen in their jobs and made liable to criminal prosecution for quitting their place of work without permission and for infractions of labor discipline or dereliction of duty. They might be demoted to lower-paying jobs, fined 25 per cent of their wages up to six months, or sent to jail for from two to four months. The industrial revolution achieved gradually in Western countries was pushed with fierce speed, and no mercy was shown to the man who obstructed its course, yet without whom it could not drive ahead.

At the conclusion of the war, the application of the laws was softened and in 1956 they were abrogated.

Officially, in the press and in oratory, in poem and story, in the theater and cinema, the worker was eulogized as the new man, the builder of a new world, the emancipator of mankind from all its ancient evils. Actually, the millions of peasants that poured into industry were treated with merciless severity. They were only the raw human clay that was kneaded into the kind of proletarian that the Kremlin's blueprints and specifications called for.

This is not the place to tell the story of the transformation of the Soviet trade unions from defenders of the interests of labor, which they were or attempted to be in the early years of the revolution, into defenders of the sole employer of labor—the state. Production and still more production became their chief purpose. At the twelfth congress of the trade unions in March 1959, the Central Committee of the party enjoined them "to mobilize the energies of the broad masses of workers . . . for the fulfillment of the Seven-Year Plan ahead of time." They have responded energetically by promoting more competition and introducing more speed-up systems throughout the country's booming industrial and construction projects.

But the trade unions have also been the educators of the peasant worker. On them especially devolved the task of training him in technology and even refining him in his manners. Once, between the acts at a theater performance in the city of Minsk, I saw a trade-union official mount the stage and deliver an exhortation to the audience of workers to stop spitting pumpkin and sunflower seeds on the floor, calling on them to act not like boors but like "cultured citizens." I witnessed similar scenes in other theaters and in audi-toriums of workers' clubs. Nowadays sunflower seeds are no longer a problem, but in many a factory alcoholism is.

The trade unions have ministered to the personal and social welfare of the worker. They operate factory clinics, health resorts, clubhouses, social insurance organizations. They encourage workers to read books, to attend trade schools, engineering institutes, or schools of general education. If masses of onetime peasants or sons of peasants have become engineers, directors of factories, professors in colleges, scientists, they owe it in large measure to the encourage-ment and help of trade unions.

But having come from the village, the peasant worker knew noth-ing of the rights of labor as understood in the Western world. He still doesn't. He has been subjected to disciplines, physical and mental, that no Western trade unions would tolerate. The most closely sheltered ward of the state and the party, he lives in a community which, though not always as self-sufficient as the Moscow automobile works, is yet a world of its own, with the party, the Komsomol, the trade unions, always on the alert to fashion and re-fashion his mentality according to Kremlin lights and convictions. Theoretically, as Soviet ideologists have again and again assured me, these are derived from the *Communist Manifesto*, which, written over a century ago, must be spoken of nowadays as the orthodox Communist faith. A rigidly formulated faith, as interpreted by the Kremlin, it grants no concessions to ideas and movements which Marx and Engels could neither have foreseen nor predicted. It allows for no doubts and deviations, and factory personnel charged with the political education of the worker spare no energy and elo-quence to keep his mind from straying into forbidden fields of reflection, and in fact barricade him against all knowledge that would rouse distrust in their words.

In the city of Minsk, which is roaring with industrial construction, a woman teacher in a factory would not believe me when I told her that married women in England were *not* barred from teaching school, as she had been officially informed and as she was telling her classes. In the same city a highly personable graduate of a party school who was lecturing in factories on ideology and foreign affairs, didn't know of the forty-hour work week in America, of paid holidays, of unemployment compensation, of pensions. He did know of Social Security and interpreted it as a form of capitalist deception, insisting that workers paid for it through deductions from their wages. It was news to him that employers paid one half of the Social Security tax. Likewise it was news to him that after retiring a worker might receive both a pension from the trade union and Social Security from the government. I told him I knew such workers, but he wouldn't accept my word for it. He knew nothing of free medical service in England nor of the ban on child labor and on the employment of women in heavy industry in both England and America.

One evening in Moscow I went by subway to the automobile community and wandered the streets, which teemed with pedestrians and bicycle riders. Passing a newly built house, I stopped to talk to a group of men outside. They seemed eager for conversation, and their first questions were about the prices I paid for my shoes, my suit of clothes, my shirt, and even my necktie. I translated dollars into rubles at the official rate of exchange, and they marveled at the comparative cheapness of shoes and clothes in America.

Then they asked question after question about the life of automobile workers in America, of which I knew almost nothing and was good-naturedly reprimanded for my ignorance.

"Do you know if there are any automobile workers among American tourists in Moscow?" one of them asked.

"Unfortunately I do not," I said.

"It would be interesting to meet them," another remarked, "just to sit around a table over a glass of tea and talk to them."

"If we met them," another worker said, "we'd ask them why they don't stop American imperialists from plotting war against our Motherland."

The others nodded agreement. They were so steeped in *Pravda's* myth of American imperialists eager to wage war on their country that they expected American automobile workers to support Kremlin foreign policy. As I didn't wish to disturb the friendly spirit of the occasion, I didn't bring up the subject of the Soviet Army's suppression of rebellion in East Germany and the slaughter of workers in Budapest, but merely came up with my stock reply: "The trouble is that you think America is aggressive, and Americans think your country is aggressive."

"Do workers in America think so?"

"Yes, except when they happen to be Communists, of whom there are very few in America."

"Ah!"—an exclamation of disappointment, perhaps of disbelief in the light of the information doled out to them in the factories.

I was treated to lengthy earnest sermons on the wickedness, cruelty, and futility of war—an ever haunting specter to Russians, and I said amen to the words of these sturdy and innocent workers.

As we were talking a young couple came out of the house—a tall light-haired young man and a buxom dark-haired girl. They greeted us and walked past, hand in hand.

"My nephew," one of the men said. "An engineer in our factory," he added with pride. "The girl is his bride, and when the house where they'll live is finished they'll get married."

"In church?" I asked.

"Nowadays," another man said, "young people don't need a priest to marry them."

"We have no church here," another broke in, "and we don't need one. It's better to build a new school, a new apartment house, than a church."

"Don't any of you go to church?" I asked.

The question touched off a flow of lively remarks.

"We let the babushkas pray for us."

"You should see them on Sundays, dressing up and rushing to the subway to go to church in the city."

"These babushkas—they are beyond all reason. I say to our babushka, 'If God can do everything, why doesn't he stop wars?' and she says, 'Because man is wicked,' and I say, 'If man is wicked, then why doesn't God make him good?' And she says, 'God gives man a chance to be good or wicked, and it's up to man to choose; and if man chooses to be wicked, God punishes him.' Try and argue with her!"

"Why only babushkas? I have a cousin who got converted to the Baptist faith, and you know he can no more stay away from his church than a bee from a blossom; and his son, who is only twenty-three, is the same—steeped in religion, yes, steeped in it like a monk."

"That's because they haven't got the right ideology."

"What's the right ideology?" I asked.

"A worker's ideology: no capitalism, no exploitation of man by man, workers of all countries getting together, living in peace and brotherhood so there can be no wars and no country need be afraid of being attacked by another. When a man has the right ideology he doesn't need any belief in God."

"It's all in the *Communist Manifesto*," another worker remarked.

The *Communist Manifesto!* The alpha and omega of all justice and wisdom!

When I left, one of the men said, "Take our greetings to the automobile workers in America. Tell them to come and visit us. We have much in common and we'd like to talk things over with them."

"I'll tell them," I said. "But don't expect them to agree with you."

"It'll do no harm to talk things over as workers to workers."

If only it could be arranged without the pomp and festiveness that usually surround gatherings between Soviet and foreign workers, with activists always present to guide the spirit of the conversation and the nature of the discussion! The Russian workers might then learn from American fellow workers of the irreconcilable views they respectively hold on the rights of labor, especially the right to strike, the functions of a trade union, speed-up methods of work, the relations of workers to a totalitarian state, a totalitarian party, and the compulsive political self-abnegation all these impose on workers on all issues and all problems, whether voting for a single list of candidates in an election or denouncing at a mass meeting the Hungarian revolution as an American-inspired fascist plot.

But there would be no meeting of minds between Russian and American workers, any more than there was between Khrushchev and American trade-union leaders when they met in conference in San Francisco on the evening of September 21, 1959. "You have your point of view," Khrushchev said, "we have ours. They are irreconcilable." All that is of consequence to Khrushchev, as he has repeated in speech after speech and as he told the American trade-union leaders, is that "there is no private ownership [in the Soviet Union] of the means of production." This concept has sunk so deep into the mind of the Russian worker that I do not believe there is a force in the world that can root it out of him. That is why all talk of a possible return to private ownership of "the means of production" in the Soviet Union has always seemed to me futile.

The Russian worker must be judged in terms of his own history, his own social environment, the faith he has been taught by the party, and above all by his peasant origin. The grinding, indeed gruesome, period of his transition from the soil to the machine is over, and however low his standard of living compared with that of the American or British worker, it is higher in the Khrushchev era than it has ever been. You walk along the streets of the Moscow automobile community or attend a dance in the clubhouse, and you observe that the girls are as well dressed as the girls on Gorky Street.

Needless to say, the armies of young workers on the new construction projects in Central Asia and Siberia do not begin to command the living standards of the automobile workers in Moscow or of the workers in any other established and competently managed industrial plant. Even while Khrushchev was traveling in Siberia in October 1959, he faced workers who complained of high prices and of shortages of supplies. In Temir-Tau, Kazakhstan, where a metallurgical plant is in process of construction, workers staged a strike in protest against wretched living conditions.

The young generation of workers is too well educated to endure in silence the hardships to which incompetent and callous management and party secretaries subject them. They feel more free than did their fathers and mothers and do not hesitate to speak up to party leaders and managers, to write letters to the Central Committee, the Presidium, and the metropolitan press in protest against maltreatment, against inadequate housing, shoddy clothes, poor food, and other privations. They are a new voice, clear and rather bold, among Soviet proletarians. But I feel constrained to dissent from those interpreters of the Soviet Union who perceive political undertones in this voice. Nothing, in my judgment, is further from the truth.

It is a voice of indignation against bureaucratic and managerial failings, but not against Kremlin ideology or Kremlin policy: in no way does it suggest or augur political rebellion. Whoever the master of the Kremlin, the one thing he need never worry about is a possible political demonstration of workers against him or the theories of communism he may expound and the internal and external policies he may pursue.

Late one afternoon—the time was the summer of 1960—while I was having dinner in Moscow's National Hotel, a young man in a sweat shirt came over to my table and asked for permission to sit down. We soon engaged in conversation. He came from a village in the Bryansk Forest, and during the war, when he was only a boy, partisans saved his life. He was now a foreman on a housing project in Moscow and was earning 1200 (old) rubles a month. Though he was twenty-nine years old, he was not married, a rather unusual thing for a Russian of his age. When I asked him why he wasn't married, he replied, "I am attending evening classes to prepare myself for admission to an architectural institute. I have almost completed my secondary school education, and in the autumn I shall take my entrance examinations. If I were married, I wouldn't have the time I now have for study. I must make of myself an architect. I won't be happy if I don't."

A taxi driver in Moscow who drove me one evening to my hotel told me that he worked fourteen hours every other day and kept the intervening days free. On these days he was going to school to prepare himself for entrance examinations to a scientific institute. He was the father of two children, and his wife, too, he said, was going to school educating herself to be a midwife. "It's hard on us," he admitted, "but we are determined people—we'll get what we want."

Of all the educational drives in factories and on farms, in fact for adults everywhere, that I have through the years witnessed in the Soviet Union I do not recall any that was so intense as the one that has swept the country since the rise of the Seven-Year Plan. From every possible direction come slogans and exhortations intended to rouse in adults a desire to study, to advance themselves in their specialties, or just to learn grammar and composition, algebra and geometry, German or English, for the sake of being more educated.

All education is free, which of itself fosters loyalty to Kremlin rule.

My journey to Minsk, once a city of slums, was particularly revealing. In the mammoth new factories that have sprung up since the end of the war, most of the workers are only one or two generations away from the village. They have not yet become as urbanized as the workers in Moscow's automobile works, and not even the tractor plant has a Palace of Culture comparable to that of the Moscow factory. But their children enjoy privileges in play and education that their fathers and mothers had never known. Above all, they and their families are accorded a cradle-to-grave security that they likewise had never known. Of course, they work hard, but they always did. Speed-up systems do not irk or harass them as they would Western workers, especially as these yield higher monetary rewards. Civil liberties mean nothing to them—the expression is as alien to them as it had been to their muzhik ancestors.

As in Moscow, Kharkov, Stalingrad, Irkutsk, any factory town, workers have been trained and molded in Kremlin ideology in all its ramifications: in politics as in economics, in individual rights as in social attitudes. They know nothing else. The age of Western enlightenment has never touched them and never can, except as it may seep through the party and the state, if it ever does. They are in truth the most reliable and most powerful bulwark of Kremlin ideology and Kremlin policy.

II.

PEASANT
Calm after the Storm

By the grace of Khrushchev, the Soviet milkmaid has been lifted to the status of a new heroine on Soviet farms. Never before had I heard chairmen of collectives speak with such adulation of any accomplished farm workers, even of tractor drivers, as I now did of "our glorious milkmaids."

Of course, they have to be accomplished; by which I mean they have to coax out of the cows entrusted to their care ever increasing outputs of milk, so that they can help beat American dairymen in milk production. If they fall behind prescribed norms of milk output, out of the barn they may go. But if they attain or, still better, surpass the norms, their deeds are exaltedly acclaimed in farm bulletins and at public gatherings, in verse and song; above all, they are by Soviet standards munificently paid in cash and produce.

To a onetime farmhand like myself, they hold the choicest jobs on farms, the easiest to perform, and the most rewarding in glory and money. If they milk by hand, they have only ten or twelve cows to care for; they milk them three times a day, feed them, clean them, bed them, shovel out the manure. If they milk by machine, twenty or twenty-two cows are allotted to their care. They do nothing else all day long. On an American farm a hired man who did no more work than a Soviet milkmaid would at most earn the cost of his "vittles."

I first learned of the new heroine on the Soviet farm at the Ukrainian collective Motherland, one of the best in the Ukraine. The chairman, who is general manager, was a tall, stocky, ruddy-faced, light-stepping man in his late forties, named Anatoly Vladimirovich Jurkov. The first question I put to him was how long he had been chairman of Motherland.

"Eighteen years," he replied.

I at once took him to be an exceptionally competent man. The rapid turnover of chairmen on Soviet collectives was one of the more pronounced evils the Kremlin inherited from Stalin. Jurkov had obviously grappled successfully with the Stalin-made difficulties in agriculture. Hence his remarkable durability.

In his address of September 3, 1953, before the plenum of the Central Committee of the Communist party, Khrushchev, who always lightly sheds his own responsibility for Kremlin misdeeds during Stalin's years, gave a devastating though incomplete account of Stalin's woeful mismanagement of agriculture. Among other things, he pointed to the sorry state of livestock, especially of milch cows, whose milk yield in province after province was shockingly low—no higher, as I figured it, than that of a goat. No man to leave setbacks unremedied, he called on the party, on farm leaders, and on workers to build new barns, to grow increasing acreages of forage and grain crops, especially of corn, and to improve in every way the care and feeding of livestock. Milk and meat, meat and milk, became the battle cry that thundered from one end of the country to the other. It still does and is invested not only with the flamboyant rhetoric of a fighting crusade but with practical directions.

In consequence, there began an orgy of barn building and feed raising all over the immense Soviet Union, including Siberia. It is, of course, axiomatic that the better dairy cattle are fed, the more milk they produce. All the milkmaid needs to do is "to shovel it out" to the cows and the output of milk rises immediately. The rise is credited to her skill and enterprise, her patriotism and her love of the party, though she doesn't lift a hand to raise the feed crops. Nor does she determine the good luck of being allotted cows that may be superior producers, which is a decisive circumstance in her accomplishment.

On the Motherland kolkhoz the milkmaid is among the highest-paid wage earners, averaging 800 labor days (units of labor) a year against 350 by male field workers (other than those who are skilled machine operators). In cash alone, at the rate of 10 (old) rubles a day, she earns 8000 rubles a year—more than twice as much as a male field worker. Then come the premiums.

"When a champion milkmaid gets married," Jurkov told me, "we present her with a handsome dowry, sometimes a dairy cow, sometimes three thousand rubles in cash." Handsome indeed, when the cash equals almost a whole year's earnings of a male field worker. "But," the manager continued, "we attach one condition—that she abstain from a church wedding."

"Suppose," I said, "she refuses the condition?"

"But she doesn't," the manager replied with a hearty laugh. "Her mother might be upset about it—it's mothers who push daughters into church weddings anyway—but the bride, she is too excited and overjoyed with the dowry to turn it down. If she did, we wouldn't, of course, deny her a dowry, but it would be less generous."

"Your milkmaids," I said, "must be the most sought-after brides by the most sought-after men."

"They are quite choosy, and why shouldn't they be?" replied the manager, beaming.

This was the first collective I visited, and merely being in the countryside brought a feeling of great release, as it always did when I left the city and came to the village. Unencumbered with the lumbering bureaucracy, away from the political tensions, the schizophrenic psychology of the city, the rural social scene is refreshingly simple. Officials, including party secretaries, are down-to-earth people, and the foreigner who speaks the language of farmers, and especially if he communicates with them in their mother tongue, finds them pleasantly companionable. Besides, wandering around fields and barns, one perceives the true condition of things, which no boastful rhetoric of officials—were it proffered, which it rarely is in the village—can embellish or tarnish.

"I suppose you know," said Jurkov, "that our Nikita Sergeyevich has called on us to beat your country not only in per capita output of milk and butter but also of meat."

"Excellent," I said. "Let the best system win. But," I added, "I believe you have a long row to hoe." He laughed good-naturedly when I explained to him the meaning of the farm expression.

I always viewed Soviet agriculture in terms of its own history and development. But since Khrushchev's challenge of May 1957 has resounded all over the world, a comparison—however inadequate—is inevitable. In his address of December 1959 before the meeting of the Central Committee, Khrushchev proclaimed that the Soviet Union had already outmatched the United States in per capita output of butter. Whereas the Soviet Union, he declared, produced 8.8 pounds per person in 1959, the United States output was only 8.14 pounds per person. Prolonged applause greeted the announcement, though neither then nor at any time since did Khrushchev, who is an expert on figures, mention the fact that the Soviet Union obtained its butter from twelve million more cows than did America. Nor did he or anybody else ever make an effort to explain why America, as recently as 1938, produced more than one and a half times as much butter as it now does. That Americans eat more margarine and other vegetable fats in place of butter is never mentioned in Soviet writing and oratory. American food habits never enter into Soviet calculations when they can point to what is to them so momentous a victory over America as the per capita output of butter. Even so, city after city suffers, especially in winter, from shortages of milk and butter.

In his jubilation over the Soviet triumph over America, academician Strumilin, the economist, peering into the future, predicts that by 1975 Americans, unlike Russians, will consume butter in amounts "almost twice less than physiological norms demand."[1] To him it is a reflection of "the well-known doctrine that guns come before butter."

But Russians will have their anecdotes, and a new one came up in 1960 about Soviet boasts of the triumph over America in milk and butter. Khrushchev, according to the anecdote, went in disguise on a journey to Siberia. In one village he asked the chairman of the kolkhoz how things were going. "Wonderful," replied the chairman. "How is your milk production?" "We are 'way ahead of America." "How is your corn?" "We are already beating Iowa." "And pigs?" "Bigger and fatter than in Iowa." Thereupon, according to the anecdote, Khrushchev said to the chairman, "Look here—why do you boast so much? Do you know who I am? I am Khrushchev." "Oh, you are Khrushchev!" the chairman supposedly replied. "That's different. I thought you were an American correspondent." Yet in terms of Soviet agriculture and Soviet life, the rise in the output of milk and butter since 1953 need not be underestimated.

There are, however, other circumstances which significantly count in the Kremlin's self-proclaimed rivalry with America in agriculture. The most important of these is the per capita productivity of the farm worker.

"When I worked on a farm," I said to Jurkov, "I tended ten cows mornings and evenings, fed them, milked them by hand, cleaned them, bedded them, shoveled out the manure, did all the work that one of your milkmaids is doing, and in addition worked a full day in the field."

Jurkov had never heard of anything like it, nor had any other kolkhoz managers I met. Nor do they know that in America men do the milking, that barns are cleaned with push-button equipment,

[1] S. G. Strumilin, *Na putiakh postroyeniya communisma* (Moscow, 1959), p. 74.

that the milk parlor is as much a part of a modern American dairy as the cows that are milked.

For a long time Moscow was secretive about the number of farm workers in the Soviet Union. Neither foreign journalists nor invited foreign agricultural delegations could pry the information out of Moscow's Ministry of Agriculture. At last, in 1960, in a newly published statistical manual[2] of 666 pages on all aspects of Soviet agriculture, the long concealed figure has been revealed. During 1959, 33,000,000 full-time workers were occupied in agriculture. According to this manual, the officially estimated population of the Soviet Union as of January 1, 1960, was 212,300,000. One Soviet farm worker, therefore, fed 6.43 persons including himself. One has to go back to the pre-tractor year of 1900[3] to find a somewhat similar figure for the American farm worker, who then fed 6.95 persons including himself and fed them much better than the Soviet farm worker feeds his countrymen today. But as of July 1959,[4] the American farm worker fed 23.69 persons including himself—a figure that never appears in Soviet ideological or agricultural literature.

Even so, America is burdened with surpluses not only of wheat and corn but of cotton, and feed grains, while the Soviet Union suffers from shortages of meat and eggs, of milk and butter, of cereals for kasha, of fresh fruits and vegetables outside of the growing season, and even Moscow and Leningrad, the best-supplied cities, endure periods in winter and spring when even apples are scarce or unavailable. Nor does Russia grow the large variety of fruits and vegetables that America does. Citrus fruit, for example, a major crop in America, is a comparatively negligible crop in Russia. It always astounded Russian agricultural leaders when I told them that California alone grew some two hundred crops.

On a man-to-man basis, the Soviet Union has indeed a long row to hoe—so long that at present the terminal end is completely out of sight: to equal, not to say surpass, the American farm worker in productivity. But neither leaders nor working farmers in the Soviet

[2] *Selskoye khosiaystvo* (Gosizdat, Moscow, 1960).

[3] *Changes in Farm Production and Efficiency* (U. S. Department of Agriculture, Washington, D.C., 1960).

[4] Ibid.

Union begin to appreciate, through no fault of their own, the task the Kremlin has assigned to them of outdoing America in productivity of farm labor.

In his address on September 19, 1959, before the Des Moines, Iowa, Chamber of Commerce, Khrushchev admitted that the output "per farm worker is today much higher on your farms than in our kolkhozes. I must say, however, that some of your economists are mistaken when they compare, mechanically, the output figures of your farms to those of the kolkhozes in terms of output per worker. In so doing they fail to consider the fact that farming in the Soviet Union and farming in the United States are based on absolutely opposite principles."

Principles or not, figures are figures, whether or not they favor the one country or the other. Russia has her quota of inefficient and lazy farmers and so has America, which doesn't in any way invalidate the arithmetical estimates of productivity per worker on the basis of official figures, especially as the Soviet press, the party, the Komsomol, and Khrushchev himself never tire of drives to rouse and to inspire the farm worker to boost his productivity. There is and there can be no other way of arriving at such an estimate, and I never met a Soviet farm manager who voiced any complaint against it, even if Khrushchev in an address before an American audience spoke of it as "mechanical" and therefore unjust.

The challenge to America aside, the conditions of life on the Motherland kolkhoz at the time I visited it, viewed in terms of its own setting and development, were much richer than I ever knew them to be anywhere in the Ukraine since the rise of collectivization. Khrushchev's reforms, particularly the drive to foster economic incentive for farm workers, bore visible fruit. The cash payments of ten (old) rubles a labor day gave workers new and substantial purchasing power. In addition, there was payment in produce: three pounds of wheat, seven pounds of potatoes, one pound of cabbage and much smaller amounts of other vegetables, and honey for each labor day. Then there was the individual farmstead of from one half to one third of an acre for a kitchen garden, which peasants have always cultivated with particular care and interest. Only a little more than half of the families owned their own cows, and the cowless families bought milk from the kolkhoz at a reduction of 25 per cent from the market price. Every family had a small flock of hens, from ten to twenty birds; the chairman himself had twenty-four; and every family averaged two hogs a year—fat, potato-fed hogs.

Because peasants earned more cash than they ever did in the kolkhoz, the local general store was far more amply stocked than village stores in the Ukraine have ever been since the rise of the Soviets, even in the prosperous NEP years, when the consumer-goods industries were not as highly developed as they are now. By American standards the village store in even the most prosperous collectives I visited—such as in the Kuban—was a mere sample shop, and a poor one too. Neither in the multiple variety nor in the quality of goods did it begin to approach the glittering opulence of an American chain store, however small, or the American general store in a rural community. But by Soviet standards, the Motherland general store was something new on the Soviet scene. There was an abundance of dry goods and footwear, of which there had always been a shortage in villages. Rubber boots had never before been known. Neither soap nor salt was a problem any longer. Nor were tea, sugar, socks and stockings. There were even shelves of canned foods, an innovation in a peasant community. There were sweaters for men and women, dresses for women, and suits for men. The suits were clumsily tailored and sold at from 90 to 110 dollars, an exorbitant price for a peasant, indeed for any Soviet citizen, to pay. On display were radio and television sets, and people were buying them, Jurkov assured me. There were shelves of vodka and wine bottles and the inevitable counter of candy, another of gaily colored boxes and bottles of cosmetics.

"Do you sell many of these?" I asked a kerchiefed and white-gowned saleswoman, pointing to the cosmetics.

"The way some girls buy them," she said, a little resentfully, "you'd think all they live for is dolling up."

"Girls are girls," said Jurkov. "There's nothing wrong with their wanting to look pretty, is there, auntie?"

The woman shrugged and didn't reply. An unsmiling woman, she waited on customers with an attentiveness that would have pleased even Moscow housewives.

We went to the newly built barn—a mammoth solidly built structure for 208 cows. The windows were tall and the ceiling was exceptionally high. But there was no hayloft, and hay and other feed had to be hauled in ox-driven wagons, the ensilage from a trench some distance away. There were, of course, drinking cups for each cow and the barn was exceptionally clean, with hardly any flies buzzing around. As I watched the milkmaids prepare cows for milking, I complimented Jurkov on his perfectionism: the milkmaid washed not only the udder but the fleecy end of the tail so that when the cow swished it around and slapped the milker's face, no drops of urine stung the eyes as they had mine in my farm years. Presently I was surrounded by milkmaids and several men who worked with livestock, among them the tall bony-faced *zootechnik* (livestock expert), a man of middle age with deep gray eyes that teared from the strong wind outdoors. They were all well shod, the milkmaids wearing shiny rubber half boots over their shoes. I saw no barefooted people on this kolkhoz, not even among children. "You see," said Jurkov, "at one time, when our people worked they went barefoot; now it is no longer regarded as respectable to do so." I heard the same thing in other parts of the country, even in Byelorussia, where I was born and where men and women who in the old days had shoes, wore them usually on Sundays and holidays. Now and then in various parts of the country one still sees children playing barefooted, not because they have no shoes, but because "it's easier to run without them," as a boy in a Byelorussian village told me. The old custom lingers here and there among older women because it makes them feel more comfortable. But I never saw young people anywhere in the countryside working or walking around barefooted. The unshod peasant has practically disappeared from Soviet villages.

One pretty milkmaid with big dark eyes, pink cheeks, and a mass of black hair done in a knob on the back of her head, looked so young that I asked her how old she was.

"Seventeen," she replied, smiling and disclosing a gold front tooth.

"You look no more than fifteen," I said.

"She thinks she is old enough to get married," Jurkov broke in.

The girl blushed and gave the manager a chiding look.

"These young girls nowadays," the livestock man said broodingly; "look at her—wears lipstick even when she works in the barn.

There's feminine vanity for you. Do American girls of her age wear lipstick?"

"Even younger ones do," I replied.

The girl gave a triumphant laugh and the man looked perplexed.

"And I thought American girls had more sense than that," he said. "If she was my daughter—" He didn't finish the sentence.

"She has a good mother," Jurkov said, "knows how to handle her —won't let her get married until she's of age."

"Do you mind your mother?" I asked the girl.

"She'd better," Jurkov interjected, "or—" turning to the girl, "you know what I mean."

We all laughed, but the girl blushed and mumbled coyly, "Anatoly Vladimirovich!"

"It's the truth," Jurkov said to the girl, "and you know it is. These old-fashioned mothers—they'll stand for no nonsense."

"Yes," the livestock man sighed. "That's the way it is with girls nowadays—their mother's milk has barely dried off their lips, when some boy turns their heads and off to the altar they want to go."

"The altar?" I inquired.

"If it isn't the altar it's *zags*. It's all the same," the man explained.

"Will you have a church wedding?" I asked the girl.

She shrugged and didn't say anything, but Jurkov shook his finger at her and said, "Remember your kolkhoz dowry," and turning to me, "Her mother is an enlightened woman, and she," pointing at the girl, "doesn't care. All she wants is to get married."

"And why not?" an older milkmaid broke in. "She is ripe for it; look at her eyes—fiery eyes."

"You stop," the girl remonstrated softly and with a smile of seeming pleasure.

"It's the truth," the older girl went on gaily. "Our Ukrainian girls—ho-ho—no water flows in their veins, no milk either." Unlike the retiring blue-eyed, light-haired Byelorussian girls, the dark-eyed and dark-haired Ukrainian girls have always been more assertive and have never underestimated their own feminine virtues.

They were a lively crowd and went on bantering and laughing, and then Jurkov showed me the Red Corner in the barn, which was a reading and rest room. One of the milkmaids complained that they didn't have enough books on their shelves. She wanted more books

—yes, novels, and why not?—must only city people read novels? the amiable Jurkov agreed that they could use more books and promised to do something about it.

As we left the barn the milkmaids followed us to the door, chattering and laughing, thanking me for coming and bidding me to come again soon. "We want Americans to come and see how we live," one of them said. Friendly, freehearted souls, wearing shiny rubber half boots and wrist watches, unabashed of their lipstick even in a cow barn, literate enough to read magazines and novels—a new type of milkmaid in the Soviet countryside.

"You should see them on Sundays," the manager said, "when they put on their best dresses and their best shoes. They could walk along the Kreshchatik and hold their heads as high as any girls in Kiev."

Other new things caught the eye as we rambled around the muddy streets: men and women wearing city clothes, all of them; a movie house for pictures three times a week; a hall for amateur musicals and dramatics; antennas over roofs for radios and television sets, and the roofs over new houses no longer thatched with straw but covered with tile. The ancient fire hazard, when flames leaped from one straw roof to another and burned much or all of a village to ashes, was becoming a thing of the past. But Jurkov spoke nostagically of the old straw-thatched houses. "I'm an old-fashioned man in some ways," he said. "I loved the old straw-thatched cottages. The straw kept the house cool in summer and warm in winter, and it lasted a long, long time. But we harvest with combines and there is no straw for roofing, and no time either. That's the way it is—the old times are going, never again to return."

We drove down to the truck farm. Women and girls were gathering the last of the garden strawberries and red raspberries, their white- and red-kerchiefed heads bobbing up and down like corks on a green sea. The berry field spread over seventy acres and was as level as a floor. "We get big income from this field," the manager said, stretching out his arm at full length as though to encompass the green-clad bottomland all around us. "Next year we'll plant fifteen more hectares [thirty-seven acres] of strawberries; the more income we have, the richer will be our kolkhoz, the more services we can offer our people; and the more socialized our community becomes, the less need there will be for individual members to toil in their own gardens, to bother with their own cows, pigs, chickens. They'll have more time to themselves for books, music, other cultural diversions. We are moving from socialism to communism and we won't stop until we get there."

Jurkov was only expressing the eventual Kremlin aim, which is to rid the peasantry of any and all forms of individual property, and to make them dependent on the kolkhoz for the good life they are promised.

As we passed a wooden shed with built-in stands that were set out with baskets of freshly picked berries, Jurkov picked up in one hand a half-bushel basket of strawberries and in the other a similar-sized basket of raspberries and presented them to me.

"I can't possibly eat all those berries," I protested. But protesting against the generosity of a Russian or a Ukrainian is useless. Jurkov loaded the baskets into the baggage compartment of the automobile that was to take me back to Kiev.

"Well," he said in parting, "Nikita Sergeyevich has called on us to beat you in farm output and we'll have to do it."

"On a man-to-man basis in production," I said, "the American farmer is so far ahead of you that Khrushchev's call sounds to me somewhat fanciful."

"We're making great progress, very great," Jurkov shot back jovially, "and we simply have to beat you."

We shook hands, and I started on the drive back to Kiev.

The countryside we passed through was familiar to me: I had been here both before and after collectivization. The very look of the land told of the revolutionary change-over from individual to collectivized holdings, from scattered strips of land separated from one another by dead furrows or grassy ridges to immense and contiguous fields which can be worked with tractors and other mechanized implements, as the individually managed strips rarely could have been. Nowhere was there the sight of horse or ox—not animal but motor power now cultivated the land.

The countryside was tranquil, and the men and women we passed appeared composed, some of them singing, as is the way of Ukrainian village folk when they are on their way to or from work or even while working. But how they stormed with fury in the years of the drive for collectivization! How bitterly they fought it—a prolonged, tragic, futile fight.

Ever since the beginning of the bolshevik revolution, the Kremlin leaders had proclaimed a so-called *smychka* (alliance) between the peasant and the proletarian. The alliance held through the civil war, when the peasant was fighting not for bolshevism but for land. Afterward the very word *smychka* was a rhetorical artifice to conceal an irrepressible conflict between the highly individualized peasant and the individualism-hating Kremlin.

The individualism of the peasant was becoming increasingly menacing for economic and political reasons. There was first the continual fragmentation of the land as it passed from fathers to sons, individual farms having grown in number between 1917 and 1923 from twenty to twenty-five million. Despite all Kremlin efforts to persuade peasants to merge individual holdings into one form of producing co-operative or another, by 1928 only 1.7 per cent of the families yielded to persuasion. The others, including the *bedniaky* (poor folk), by which I mean essentially those who were without horse or ox, over seven million of them in 1928, stubbornly clung to their personal farmsteads, however inefficient they might be. Readily muzhiks joined credit, trading, and even small manufacturing co-operatives. But even *bedniaky* would rather live poor than yield to the rhetorical blandishments of a rich life in the collective. I say rhetorical because the collectives in those days were no invitation to prosperous living.

Besides, the muzhik cherished his independence too profoundly to shake himself loose from it even if he tried, and he didn't try. He was what he was—a hopeless *sobstvennik* (property holder), as Lenin had branded him. Nothing was more alien to his traditional method of work, his manner of living, his habit of thinking, than to submerge his independence and his individual self in a mass organization, as did and could the factory worker. The peasant women were particularly vociferous in their hostility to joining collectives.

The constantly growing number of landholding peasant families might in time rise up against the Kremlin dictatorship. Since the Red Army was made up overwhelmingly of peasant soldiers fresh from the village, there was risk that the uprising, were it to eventuate,

would smash the dictatorship. The political risk was too real and
too great for the Kremlin to tolerate.

Least of all was the Kremlin inclined to tolerate the reluctance
of the peasant to sell his grain and other foods if in return he
couldn't be adequately supplied with the groceries and manufactured
goods he demanded. In the summer of 1927 and again in 1928, in
the very part of the Ukraine where I was now traveling, and in the
neighboring province of Poltava, I had heard endless tales of peasants
burying their grain in the ground, lowering it in sacks and baskets
into wells, or hiding it under manure piles—the grain which the
Kremlin desperately needed to feed the ever growing army of city
workers. The first Five-Year Plan, with its crash program of industrialization, was approaching and the muzhik held back his grain, feeding
it to his own livestock to provide himself with more milk and meat
or, if he was a kulak, sowing his fields so thinly that the crop would
be poor. In 1927 the marketable grain in the country was only 37 per
cent of what it had been in 1913.[5] Forcible grain procurements were
no answer to the problem. Cleverly and audaciously the muzhik
was on strike against the city, which couldn't supply him with the
consumer goods he demanded in exchange for his grain and other
foods.

To settle the conflict with the peasant once and for all, the
Kremlin set out in the winter of 1929–30 to drive the peasant into
collectives and to get rid of the kulaks. Even earlier, especially in
1928, the muzhik had already begun to slaughter livestock rather
than sell it or have it seized by the state. Now, in retaliation against
forcible collectivization, he struck back vengefully and ferociously:
he slaughtered livestock on a monumental scale. By the end of
February 1930, about one half of the cows, calves, pigs, sheep,
chickens, and horses were gone. In his ignorance of peasant psychology, Stalin had not even taken the precaution of assuring the peasant
that he might keep a cow, a pig, chickens, some sheep, and cultivate
a kitchen garden for his family. I knew of instances when even
sheepskin coats and homemade blankets were collectivized, so un-
restrained and furious was the drive for collectivization. I was in

[5] G. E. Lyapshina and A. S. Pikin, *Torzhestvo kolhoznogo stroya*
(Moscow, 1960), p. 37.

villages where women in their ignorance had even imagined that home life would be collectivized and husbands and wives would no longer remain true to each other.

To halt the catastrophe, Stalin on March 2, 1930, called a stop to the drive and charged collectivizers with "dizziness from success," which to him was the reason for their blindly reckless methods of collectivization. Thus he sought to absolve himself of all guilt for the tragic consequences of the crusade to drive the impotent and bewildered peasant into the kolkhoz.

But four million kulak families were "liquidated": their properties were confiscated and they were exiled to remote parts of the country or thrown on some barren plot of land within the vicinity of their own villages.

In the summer of 1932 I was back in the Ukraine. The late Oregon-born Ralph Barnes of the New York *Herald Tribune* accompanied me on the journey through villages in the Kiev and Poltava provinces. In the village of Reshetilovka, as we walked the streets peasants came out of their houses and wailed their hearts out over the threat of famine. "Winter will come," one after another told us, "we shall have no bread, and we shall die."

Winter came, they had no bread, and they died, at least two million of them in the Ukraine alone, according to estimates I heard in Poltava in the summer of 1934.

Officially the Kremlin denied there was a famine, though everybody in Moscow talked about it. Foreign correspondents were not permitted to communicate the news to their agencies and newspapers, or to travel outside of Moscow and Leningrad. But one American correspondent, Ralph Barnes, defied the censorship. He telephoned the story to the London office of the *Herald Tribune*. The next morning he was called to the Press Department and was threatened with expulsion. Fortunately for him the late William Allen White of the Emporia *Gazette* was in Moscow at the time. After White wrote a letter to Maxim Litvinov, then Commissar of Foreign Affairs, telling him that the expulsion of Barnes would hurt Moscow-Washington relations, the Press Department dropped all action against the correspondent of the *Herald Tribune*.

In his *The Hinge of Fate*, Winston Churchill reports a conversation with Stalin on the subject of collectivization. Stalin admitted that it had been "a terrible struggle." "I thought," Churchill told him, "you would have found it bad, because you were not dealing with a few score thousands of aristocrats or big landowners, but with millions of small men."

"Ten millions," Stalin replied. "It was fearful. Four years it lasted. It was absolutely necessary for Russia, if it were to avoid periodic famine, to plow the land with tractors. . . . We took the greatest trouble to explain it to the peasant. It was no use arguing with him."

This is the only record we have of Stalin ever having acknowledged the powerful resistance of the peasantry to the crusade for collectivization. In all his pronouncements on the subject and in all the accounts that have been published in textbooks on ideology and history, the myth is maintained that peasants joined the collectives voluntarily and gladly, and that only kulaks battled against it.

Nor did Stalin tell Churchill the truth when he said that "it was no use arguing" with them. Collectivizers—many of them young Komsomols—didn't argue, but acted at Stalin's command. But there was one man in the country who didn't follow Stalin's methods, and he averted the catastrophe of famine and the slaughter of livestock. His name was Betal Kalmykov, party secretary of the Kabardino-Balkarian region in the Northern Caucasus.

I met Kalmykov in the summer of 1934 in Nalchik, capital of the region. He told me that during the collectivization campaign he had always assured the peasants, which Stalin's agents rarely did, that they would be allowed, in private ownership, their gardens and orchards, a cow and calf, a sow, six head of sheep, and all their fowl, which eased their anxiety for the future. He didn't liquidate kulaks. He gave them the choice of remaining in their homes with gardens and orchards of their own and the amount of livestock that all the others were allowed, or suffering confiscation of all their property and banishment in the North. Naturally they chose the lesser punishment. Kalmykov urged me to visit a model village he had built some four miles outside of Nalchik, a village of new homes with bathtubs and a garage for every family. When I asked him why he took the trouble to build garages when it was impossible to buy automobiles, he replied that he wanted to fix in the minds of the people that the day would come when they would have their own automobiles.

Betal Kalmykov was acclaimed as the most successful collectivizer in the country—the "Peter the Great" of his region. He was idolized in the press, and a never ending stream of journalists and authors journeyed to Nalchik to interview him and wrote glowing tributes to his person and his leadership.

In 1938 Stalin executed him.

In commenting on his conversation with Stalin, Churchill writes of "the strong impression I sustained at the moment of millions of men and women being blotted out or displaced forever. A generation would no doubt come to whom their miseries were unknown, but it would be sure of having more to eat and bless Stalin's name. I did not repeat Burke's dictum, 'If I cannot have reform with justice, I will not have reform.'"

But Stalin was no Burke, nor was Lenin, any more than the civilization out of which they came was like the civilization that produced a Burke or a Churchill. Lenin never cherished any illusions about the peasant's love of bolshevism. I can best illustrate it by an incident which the novelist Boris Pilnyak once related to me. Gorky had invited Pilnyak and other Soviet authors to his home to meet Lenin. Lenin arrived late and was so fatigued that he retired to the bedroom and lay down in the bed. Pilnyak and several other writers were called into the bedroom, and Lenin burst into talk about the peasant. According to Pilnyak, Lenin, putting his hand to his throat, said, "Either we choke him or he chokes us!"

How Lenin would have tamed the peasant, it would be idle to speculate. He might have followed the course that Betal Kalmykov pursued. He might have shaken out of his mind an original idea that would have compromised the individualism of the peasant without plunging the country into one of the most catastrophic famines in its history. But fanatical Russian Marxist that he was, he couldn't have avoided a final decisive battle with the very muzhik whose guns during the civil war had rescued his proletarian dictatorship from imminent collapse—a dictatorship, it needs to be repeated, that never was and never could be proletarian, because the proletariat constituted a hopeless minority in the country.

Stalin fought the battle in his own way, but he won the most crucial internal victory of his life: the political threat of the peasant was smothered; the scattered strips of land were lumped together into large areas which could easily be cultivated with tractors and other mechanized implements; most important of all, he obtained control of both production and distribution of food. He could push on with the program of industrialization on meager rations but with no more obstruction from the cowed and crushed peasant. When the war broke out, the control was particularly helpful—peasants couldn't hoard grain and other foods at the expense of the Army and the civilian population. And with the addition of all the Lend-Lease aid the Soviet Union obtained from America, the many-millioned Army was well fed and the civilian population somehow pulled through, except in besieged Leningrad, which—cut off from the rest of the country—suffered a disastrous famine.

In the summer of 1934 I revisited Poltava, and the chairman of the city soviet didn't deny the collectivization famine as did the Kremlin and as it still does. He spoke of it with real horror. But he kept repeating over and over that never again, except possibly in time of war, would the country be devastated by hunger. Under the new system of farming, he assured me, with the state in control of vast reserves of "bread" (a synonym for grain) gathered from state and collective farms, the peasantry will be guaranteed against hunger in years of drought.

The periodic famines of which Stalin spoke to Churchill are one of the most tragic facts in Russian history. As far back as 1024, old chronicles speak of famine. Volume IX of the pre-revolutionary *Entsiklopedichesky Slovar*, published in 1892, informs the reader that, beginning with the eleventh and ending with the sixteenth century, droughts and famines recurred on the average every thirteen years, and that in the seventeenth, eighteenth, and nineteenth centuries they were even more frequent. The famine of 1891–92 affected a population of thirty-five million. Since the rise of the Kremlin dictatorship, Russia has suffered two devastating famines: in 1921–22, as a result of economic disorganization and drought, and in 1932–33, as a result of brutal methods of collectivization. Since then there have been food shortages but no famine, though in 1946, a year of one of the severest droughts in Russian history, UNRRA food supplies were of much importance in averting famine. But in 1948 all food rationing was abolished.

Future generations may or may not bless Stalin for having more to eat. But, barring war, the threat of periodic famine, which for centuries had been ravaging the peasantry, has vanished from the Russian land. But at what a price!

Ghosts hovered over the peaceful and well-tilled fields as I was driving from the kolkhoz Motherland to Kiev—ghosts of the past; but the chairman of the kolkhoz, who was old enough to remember the collectivization famine, had evinced no awareness of it. Nor had the merry milkmaids or anybody else to whom I spoke. Nightmarish as the famine had been, it survives only in the memories of the older generation. To the young people it is at best a catastrophe that happened a long time ago; a chapter in Soviet history which they have not experienced and of which they may have heard, but of which they never read in history books or any other textbooks.

Nor did I hear much talk at the kolkhoz of the more recent German occupation, with all the devastation of burned villages and slaughtered livestock it left in its wake.

Within the memory of a single generation, the Ukrainian countryside had been ravaged by two tremendous catastrophes—famine and war—and, observing the people, one never would have known it.

Now new homes and barns had risen out of the rubble, and the fields were green again, greener with their new stands of corn than I had known them to be in the prewar years.

But agriculture is still the number-one problem in the Soviet Union.

12.

PEASANT
Unanswered Questions

"You say one American farm worker takes care of seventy-five thousand chickens all by himself?"

"Yes," I replied. "I was in Kiev the other day and ran into a delegation of farmers from our state of Indiana and got the information from them. The chickens are for meat—broilers, we call them—and one man raises four crops a year, or about one million pounds of meat."

"One million pounds of meat?" he repeated as if bewildered.

"Yes," I said, "and the chicken house is so mechanized that the man never touches a single bird."

"*Zdorovo* [remarkable]!" he exclaimed. "Did you hear that, comrade?"

Lying on the upper berth, absorbed in a book, the man to whom the question was addressed didn't answer—he seemed not to hear his companion. My questioner gave me a quizzical look from his deep gray eyes under a wide and lofty forehead. A cultured, thoughtful Russian, he looked more like a man who was spending his time in a cloistered study rather than in barns and fields ministering to livestock. A veterinarian by profession, his name was Pyotr Stepanovich, and had it not been for the conductor's error, I wouldn't have met him and would have missed the acquaintance with a remarkable peasant intellectual.

After examining my ticket before allowing me to board the train, the conductor demanded additional rubles for my first-class accommodation from Minsk to Moscow. Intourist had bought the ticket, but there was no time to call the office. As I didn't have rubles on me and the conductor wouldn't take a traveler's check, he put me into a compartment in a "soft," or second-class, car with two other occupants. On trains, as nowhere else, Russians are as approachable as children. If you don't speak to them, they are certain to speak to you, and Pyotr and I struck up an immediate acquaintance. When he informed me that he was a veterinarian on a state farm, I said I was glad to know him because I was particularly interested in Soviet farming. At once and with complete good humor he sprang on me Khrushchev's call on Soviet farmers to outdo America in the production of milk, butter, and meat. I countered by reminding him that in man-to-man output Soviet farming didn't begin to compare with American farming. In proof, I cited the accomplishment of one man on a highly mechanized poultry farm in Indiana.

We were deep in discussion when the door of the compartment opened and the conductor reappeared, smiling with embarrassment. He apologized for making an error about my ticket. He had consulted the railroad fare manual, and after figuring all the charges for a first-class accommodation to Moscow, he was happy to inform me, he said, that I didn't need to pay additional rubles. He would move me into the sleeper just behind the "soft" car. Thereupon the veterinarian began to berate the conductor for "subjecting a foreign passenger to insulting treatment."

Russian arguments are always passionate and stubborn, the man on the defensive never at a loss for an explanation, which the man on the offensive rarely finds acceptable, the threads of reasoning becoming so tangled that an outsider soon loses track of who is accusing whom and of what. If there are any more formidably argumentative people than Russians, I have never heard of them.

Finally the conductor left with my baggage, and I remained with the veterinarian to continue our discussion.

"It's amazing," I said, "how much your milkmaids are earning; eight thousand [old] rubles a year in cash alone on the Motherland collective in the Ukraine."

"You think that's a lot?" he countered. "On some millionaire collectives they pile up from ten to fifteen thousand rubles a year, aside from all produce and premiums."

This was an astounding figure, lifting some milkmaids into the highest category of wage earners in the country. More than ever did the glamorized Soviet milkmaid symbolize to me the incredible waste of manpower, accomplishing so little and receiving so much. I said so to my companion, adding that from an American standpoint she was the least productive farm worker, performing a task which to an American farmer was merely a morning and evening chore, leaving him free for a full day's work in the field.

For some moments the Russian was silent. The information was new to him. Then he said, "Yes, it's something we must think about. There are a lot of things we must think about after all the damage the cult of the individual did to our agriculture." By the cult of the individual he meant, of course, Stalin.

"Have you read Khrushchev's report to the September [1953] Plenum of the Central Committee?" he asked.

I nodded.

"There you have the whole story, as plain as the palm of your hand, of the wretched state of so many of our collectives. You may recall that Nikita Sergeyevich mentions the province of Kostroma as being in the lowest category of milk producers. Well, I was born in a village in this province. It's a wonderful region—big forests, lots of streams, excellent pastures, and as good potato and flax land as there is in our country. But our greatest pride is the Kostroma cow. There's a cow for you, the finest dairy cow in the whole Soviet Union, and I don't say it out of chauvinism either. No, I don't. We have a state farm—Karavayevo is its name—stocked with a herd of about four hundred purebred Kostromas, and d'you know what their average output of milk is? Seven thousand kilograms [14,140 pounds]!" He paused as though to allow the significance of the figure to sink into my mind.

"Any American farmer," I said, "would be happy to have a herd like that in his barn."

"Who wouldn't be?" he shot back. "But—with some exceptions, the records of the Kostroma collectives were too grim for words, and how well I know it. You see—" Suddenly distracted he paused and looked up. The man in the upper berth was snoring over his book, the snores crescendoing into resonant honks, followed by bars of whistled tremolos. "What music!" my companion exclaimed with jovial admiration. "A whole orchestra—cornet, drum, and flute!" and he laughed heartily, the laugh of a Russian, who, despite Western reporting to the contrary, can leap from gravity to gaiety as naturally as anybody on earth.

He gestured toward our sleeping companion and said, "Let him sleep. He deserves to—a remarkable fellow. I'll soon tell you about him." Straightening up in his seat, he went on. "I don't work in Kostroma now, I work in the Moscow province. But I frequently go back to my native village—I can't help it—it draws me like a girl I might love—and I'll never forget my trip there in the winter of 1952. There was no hay and they fed the cows straw, which they cut up and soaked in warm water, with not a sprinkling of concentrates. They just didn't have any. Horses were so hungry they nibbled the moss between the timbers of the stables; pigs with backs as thin as knife blades . . . that's how bad it was; and the young people were running away to factories and trade schools. There was nothing to keep them at home. They got so they hated the smell of a cow barn. Older people wailed their heads off over the disaster. They weren't getting any cash at all—not a single kopeck—and the chairman became so disheartened he took to drink. It was a nightmarish collective and others were even worse—yes, worse; they had no fodder and no feed and livestock died—horses, cows, pigs, calves. It makes me shudder to think of it." He paused and ran his hand over his forehead as though to wipe away sweat, though there was no sweat.

"Then, after Nikita Sergeyevich became First Party Secretary," he resumed, "the party sent in a new chairman, a wise and stouthearted fellow. He got a state loan for hay and kept the livestock going until spring pasture. He got another loan and distributed it among the people as advance payment for their work. They cheered up immediately. They drew the accumulated manure piles into the fields; with borrowed seeds they planted a large acreage of flax, a high-priced cash crop. They planted another large acreage of potatoes, and the new chairman told them that if they raised good crops of flax and potatoes they would get real money when the crops were sold, so they worked hard to raise good crops. Well, to make a long story short, the kolkhoz is thriving now. They grow plenty of good feed for livestock, and cows give an average of two thousand kilograms a year. That is not so very much, but it is three times as much as they gave in 1953. A chicken would laugh at the amount of milk they gave then. Yes, a chicken would laugh!"

He paused. The man on the upper berth kept on snoring, but the veterinarian didn't seem to hear him. Absorbed in reflection, he remained silent for some moments. Then, rubbing the back of his head, he said, "Did you hear of the thirty thousand party men we mobilized to rehabilitate the rundown collectives?"

I nodded.

"Well, my comrade"—pointing to the upper berth—"is one of them. He's a man with a good head on him and with the patience of a mule, which is what you need when you become chairman of a tottering collective. The earth is not like a machine which, when broken, can be repaired or replaced by another and set immediately to work. It takes time to heal its wounds, and meanwhile demoralized people crowd around you, shout their demands, and oh, how our peasants can shout, especially the women! But if you have a clear head on you, you don't shout back. You know it won't do any good. A chairman without a clear head on him is like a bird without wings. But my comrade is like a bird with powerful wings—a real eagle.

In his mind he can soar above the sordid realities about him and see the whole thing in perspective; see everything—the wounds in the earth and the wounds in the hearts of people, always remembering that until the wounds in the earth are healed the wounds in the hearts will continue to fester."

He paused again and meditated, then resumed. "We have an old saying, 'A field without a master is like an orphaned child.' Only an understanding master can make a neglected field flourish again, and he"—raising his eyes to his sleeping companion—"is such a master. He's built a new cow barn, a new piggery, a new henhouse, and he's still building, oh, how he is building! And best of all he's infused the people with a new morale. They know their labor will be rewarded. They get advance cash every month, and if he hasn't got it, he'll fight with the bank to get it, and in the end he gets it; he won't go back on his word to the people. They'd shout and laugh at him if he did. And something else—no more delivery in kind to the state by individual farmsteads—neither in milk, meat, potatoes, anything; so peasants have more produce to sell in the open market and still more cash comes to them. Morale, that's what people need. Without morale they're like plants without water—they wither away—wither inside themselves"—pressing both hands to his chest—"right here, all over inside themselves. That's what my comrade up there"—again raising his eyes to the upper berth—"understood, how well he understood it. If only all chairmen of collectives were like him! But they are not. That's our real misfortune."

He paused once more, reflected, then gave a wry little laugh. "How stupid it all was—the director of the tractor station and the chairman of the collective quarreling with each other over who was the real master! It was like two men in the driver's seat of a horse and carriage fighting over who was to hold the lines and driving the carriage into a ditch or stream. That's what happened, I saw it over and over, and nothing was done about it—absolutely nothing. Everybody was afraid, yes, everybody. Why hide the sin? And when you're afraid, you might as well have a rope tied around you. But—we're finished with that now, because collectives are buying machinery from the tractor stations and—"

"They can't all afford it, can they?" I interrupted.

"No, not all, but the vast majority can. The others—well—they're a serious problem. But we have a saying, 'Patience and toil overcome everything'; our people have never been wanting in patience and strength nor in will to work, when they have something to work for, and they have it now, they know they have it if the kolkhoz is well managed. How different things would have been if it wasn't for the cult of the individual!"

Not once did he mention Stalin's name. Nor did I bring it up, lest it disconcert him and shut off the free flow of his speech. The picture he painted was black enough, giving the lie to *Pravda*'s many-columned daily front-page stories, replete with figures, during Stalin's postwar years, of monumental achievements in agriculture in one region after another.

"How did people live on the broken-down collectives?" I asked. "Did they starve?"

"No, no!" He firmly shook his head. "Nobody starved."

"Nobody?"

He peered at me with wide-open eyes, as though resenting the implied aspersion on his integrity. Then, slapping his breast with his long-fingered hands, he cried out, "I swear to you that people didn't starve. There were shortages, lots of shortages, but nobody starved. Livestock died—cows, calves, pigs, sheep, horses—yes, they fell from hunger. Nikita Sergeyevich gave figures—grim figures. I don't remember them, but when you get to Moscow you can easily find them. But people didn't die from hunger. On my word they didn't. Our Soviet Motherland isn't Czarist Russia, with millions of people in years of drought dying from hunger. Our state has plenty of reserves, and when calamity comes, people aren't left helpless. No, they aren't. Plenty of collectives year in and out never met their quota of grain deliveries. They didn't have it. They ate it up, most of it anyway. They borrowed seed from the state or from a strong neighboring collective. They got hopelessly in debt, and there was only one thing to do—cancel their arrears in grain and let them start anew, which is what they are doing, thousands of them, yes thousands." Suddenly pausing and throwing up his head, he asked, "Do they say abroad that our people have been starving? Do they?" There was resentment in his voice, and I hastened to assure him that I hadn't heard or read such reports.

He smiled wanly as though with relief, and continued. "People couldn't starve. They might have had little meat or been short of bread, but they didn't and couldn't starve. Every family had a big garden, and leave it to our women to cultivate every span of it lovingly. A family can raise a lot of food in a garden, especially potatoes and cabbage. And every family in the worst of times had some livestock, a pig and chickens if not a cow—it's easy for a family to raise a pig in our countryside. Then—then—" he raced on, "our little mother earth is rich in nature-grown foods—mushrooms, berries, sorrel leaves, wild onions, nuts; and leave it to our women and children to gather plenty of these for themselves and for the bazaars. Take my native Kostroma—it's a treasure house of wild berries—strawberries, raspberries, currants, cranberries, an ocean of them. I myself began picking them almost as soon as I began to walk, following my mother to the field and wood, and what a wonderful adventure it was—to be out in the sun, birds singing, a breeze blowing in your face, dashing from one berry patch to another." He paused, as though looking longingly back to those days, and then went on. "Do you know what the main trouble was on the broken-down collectives? Instead of working in the field, people spent their time working their farmstead and gathering nature-grown foods, taking them to the bazaars and exchanging them for rubles, for sugar, herring, sausage, and even bread—for anything townfolk brought along. That's what they did. The bedeviled chairman couldn't stop them, and for a very good reason—he had no rubles to give them, sometimes not a single kopeck. 'Go and work yourself,' people said to him, and what could he do? *Ekh!* How terrible things were! It was like a mountain sitting on our necks!" As if to release himself from an inner tension, he struck a clenched hand against the palm of the other. "Yes, a mountain sat on our necks!" he repeated dolefully.

I didn't say anything, and watched him as he stared at the door as though waiting for his discomposure to ease. Then, livening, he swerved around and said, "But Nikita Sergeyevich has lifted the mountain. I want to tell you something. I have a niece who graduated this year from a ten-year school. She's a pretty and lively girl, and during the years of the cult of the individual a girl like her would have sneered at the suggestion of doing any work on a farm. Young people got demoralized—that's what happens when they have no incentive to stay on the land—and a girl like my niece would have run off to the city, worked in a factory, or entered a technical school or an institute. And d'you know what she is doing now? She is a milk-maid—yes, a milkmaid—and she earns more money than she would in a factory. There are lots of girls like her, and boys too. They don't run off to the city and factory like they used to. This is the best thing that's happened to our collectives. Young people are now content to stay and work, and on well-managed collectives they do very well. Maybe, as you say, we are paying our milkmaids too much for the work they do; but we're getting results—our milk supply is increasing and so is our meat and that's what counts."

My companion braced up, opened a bottle of port wine, and treated me to a glassful. Then he gave me a thick slice of bread and a thick slice of sausage, both of excellent quality.

"Have you been in the Kostroma province?" he asked.

"No," I replied.

"If you went up there you'd see what we're doing to remedy past mistakes. We still have run-down collectives, we have them all over the country. The trouble is we don't have enough leaders like my comrade up there—good leaders don't grow in a field like cabbages. But put a good leader in charge of a run-down collective, and give him a free hand, and land and people begin to thrive. If you go to Kostroma, you'll see it with your own eyes. Why don't you go up there?"

"I'm afraid it's impossible," I said. "Foreigners aren't permitted to go to your province."

He gave me an incredulous look. It's amazing how few Russians know of Kremlin limitations on travel for foreigners.

For some moments he was silent. Then he gave a deep sigh. "*Ekh*," he said. "How prosperous we'd have been if we hadn't made so many mistakes, such terrible mistakes."

"Why did you allow it?" I asked.

He gave me a sharp penetrating look as though I had encroached on forbidden territory. Finally he said, "Let's have another drink of port."

The veterinarian was the only farm functionary I met who spoke with candor and grief of the agricultural crisis during Stalin's postwar years. Others dodged replies to queries, contenting themselves with the declaration that that which was past was no longer of interest to anybody.

Yet soon after Stalin's death, the story of the agricultural crisis, which had been wantonly suppressed, burst out in a torrent of facts and figures. In 1951 hunger took a heavy toll of livestock: 850,000 cattle, 1,043,000 pigs, 4,846,000 sheep. In 1953 there were 4,000,000 fewer milch cows than in 1916, and the average yield per cow was only a little more than 2000 pounds a year, this in a country which, in the Kostroma purebred, possesses one of the prize dairy cows in the world.

I do not wish to clutter these pages with statistics, but the few I have presented tell a sorrowful tale. Yet Khrushchev didn't tell the complete story. Nor did he tell it in human terms as the veterinarian did, or as have Soviet writers who, in the Turgenev manner, have rambled the countryside and reported honestly and brilliantly all they saw and heard and felt. Students of the Soviet Union who have read Yefim Dorosh's *Country Diary*, Vladimir Soloukhin's *Country Roads*, or Valentin Ovechkin's *Country Weekdays* must have been astonished to come at last on Soviet non-fiction writing that rings with truth and is invested with poetry. Fields, birds, trees, flowers, streams, above all people, not alchemistically transformed as in so much Soviet fiction, but as they are in daily life—however wretched —pass by in full and vivid review one after another, laying bare the Russian countryside in all its beauty and ugliness, in all its light and blight. Whatever Khrushchev's purpose in permitting such honest writing, it tells the story of Stalin's mismanagement of land and people, which no tables of figures can match in color and truth, in warmth and penetration.

"A mountain sat on our necks!" As soon as he rose to power and while disregardful of failings inherent in collectivized agriculture, Khrushchev proceeded to lift the mountain, as his many practical reforms attest. Whatever the nature of these reforms, whether the abolition of the machine tractor stations, the cancellation of arrears in produce, the cessation of deliveries in kind by individual farmsteads, the increased prices of farm commodities, the advancement of state loans to collectives (to mention only some of them)—the end result is that cash has been flowing into the village, to the collectives alone some eighty billion of the old rubles more in 1958 than in 1953. In 1959, a poor year for grain and forage crops, the income of the collectives was some five billion of the old rubles more than in the preceding year, which was the best in Soviet agriculture.[1]

Cash, cash, cash! I never had previously heard so much talk of it by local officials, who were always ready with figures on the rise of farm income, though in the summer of 1960 the talk was somewhat muted, especially in the Ukraine. There is, of course, the ever clamorous propaganda of love of the Motherland, the party, and the people, of the eventual triumph of communism, and of inevitable economic victory over America, as stimulants to work. But cold, hard cash, or "the Leninist principle of materialist incentive," as it is ideologically phrased, has been the chief energizing force of the collectives. But it is well to bring out that, except for high earners, the chief source of cash, now as never before, has been the sale of surpluses from the individual farmstead and the share of produce that is paid by the collectives. The open markets all over the country are doing a thriving business. As the veterinarian had said, it is easy to raise a pig in the Russian countryside, and pork sells in the open market at the equivalent of $1.50 a pound. Manifestly members of laggard collectives need not be included among those who have substantial surpluses to sell.

Despite all the troubles the collectives are still facing, evidence of rising welfare was abundantly manifest in every village I visited, drove, or walked through, on every train I traveled on, in every country railroad station I sauntered into. Village stores, for example, are better stocked with manufactured goods than I ever knew them to be. It matters not that the quality, particularly of wearing apparel, is inferior to that of Western countries. What counts with the peasant is that the shelves are not empty, that he can buy necessary groceries, kitchenware, a new shirt, a new pair of boots, a new handkerchief, a bicycle, a phonograph, and even a camera, a radio, a television set—though it is not easy to buy paint, a rake, a hoe, or an ax.

There are, of course, exceptions, largely a result of the inefficiency of the highly bureaucratized Soviet wholesale and retail trade organizations. One often hears and reads of villages that are short of tea, sugar, cigarettes, and even salt, of premises that are dingy and littered

[1] *Selskoye khoziastvo,* p. 64.

with rubbish, of sales staffs that maltreat and cheat customers. After the announcement in May 1960 of the new monetary reform, there were villages where women, fearful of the devaluation of the ruble, made a run on shops and left them almost empty of goods. But the one thing the peasant is no longer afraid to do is to complain, loudly and angrily, and it would be an error to assume that the complaints remain unheeded.

One of the more surprising features of Soviet rural life is that people dress better than they ever did in all of Russian history. Particularly is this true of the youth, though one would scarcely be aware of it observing them on workdays. In some parts of the country, notably in Siberia, the Ukraine, and the Kuban, seen on Sundays at a dance or just promenading the streets, boys and girls in the village are virtually indistinguishable from well-dressed boys and girls in the city. Nor is there anything anomalous about it in the light of the cash that has been flowing to farm workers. The produce earned by boys and girls is usually turned over to the family, but they keep the cash. They have no rent or food bills to pay and they have more money than village youth has ever had, and sometimes even more than city youth, for clothes and for other material gratifications.

Yet Soviet agriculture is a sick enterprise, sicker than Khrushchev or any other Soviet leader had imagined in 1958, a year of favorable weather and of bumper crops. Otherwise it is improbable that they would have set the high goals they did for the Seven-Year Plan. In 1959 and 1960 the weather was bad—drought, early autumn frosts, snows, rains, and dust storms in 1960. While during these two years meat and milk production was somewhat higher than in 1958, it fell far short of the target figure, by three million tons of meat and over ten million tons of milk in 1960 alone. Grain production in 1960 fell by some ten million tons from what it had been in 1958 and by over twenty million tons from the figure the Kremlin had envisaged. In Kazakhstan in the winter of 1960, 3,306,000 sheep and goats perished from hunger. Meanwhile the population of the Soviet Union rose by over eight million from what it had been on January 1, 1959.

Bad weather was only in part responsible for the serious setbacks, as was abundantly revealed in the discussions at the plenum of the Central Committee in January 1961. Mismanagement, malfeasance, shortage of machinery and spare parts, lack of competent personnel, failure to apply advanced methods of crop rotation—these and other old failings were threshed over and over with much breast beating by high party leaders and much anger by Khrushchev, who bears no small part of the blame. For one thing, in his concentration on heavy industry he failed to accord proper attention to the manufacture of much needed agricultural machinery and spare parts. For another thing, by virtue of the authority vested in them, local party and state leaders, often inexperienced in farming, thwarted efficient production. Determined at any cost to attain statistical targets, they were not of a mind to permit flexibility of policy when the emergency of bad weather or faulty planning demanded it. They overruled knowledgeable managers and advisers to the detriment of the harvest. They deceived the state and falsified the origin of produce they delivered as procurement quotas. They bought butter in state shops and offered it as of their own manufacture. They slaughtered heifers and milch cows, even purebreds, to fill or overfulfill meat quotas.

In a burst of anger Khrushchev told his audience that statistics do not bake griddlecakes. He threatened expulsion from the party, and even arrest, of leaders, however high their position in the state and the party, if they persisted in the abuses that were frankly and dramatically aired at the plenum. A host of organizational and structural reforms were adopted to combat prevailing failings.

But there are aspects of Soviet collectivized farming which were barely touched upon and which raise questions that remain unanswered. There is, for example, the question whether giant farms in all branches of agriculture lend themselves to the efficiency that the Kremlin presupposes and has for years been predicting for them. In 1950, 250,000 collectives were merged into 95,000, and subsequent mergings have reduced the number to 54,800 as of January 1, 1960. Politics aside, the essence of the Kremlin boast that the Soviet Union will outproduce America in agriculture reduces itself to the proposition that the Soviet giant farm will prove more productive than the much smaller American family farm.

That is why in March 1958, with a fanfare of world-wide publicity, the Cossack Kuban, Russia's richest agricultural territory, a natural corn belt, challenged the state of Iowa to "friendly competition" in Iowa's own specialties of corn and hogs and also in milk production. The challengers, as is the way of the Soviets, set down their own conditions of the contest, basing it not on human effort but on land, on output in milk and meat per 100 hectares (247 acres).

Five months later I was in the Kuban, which I knew well from previous journeys there. I again marveled at the excellence of Cossack cookery—the best bread and borsch in the Soviet Union, the best homemade jams and home-baked pastries. The bazaar at Krasnodar, capital of the Kuban, overflowed with fruits and with a variety of vegetables that had not yet come to Moscow. But even at the bazaar there were banners calling on farm workers "to beat Iowa" in milk and meat production. Kuban party leaders had set 1961 as the year for catching up with Iowa in the production of meat and doubling Iowa's production of milk per 100 hectares of land. I learned that somebody had even composed a quatrain in glorification of the inevitable triumph over Iowa. Freely translated, the quatrain reads:

> Ekh, *the skies are high*
> *Iowa is far away.*
> *More milk and meat* [*than Iowa*]
> *Will come our way.*

I drove to Krymskaya, to one of the largest and most prosperous collectives in the Kuban. It cultivates over 25,000 acres and specializes in grains, including of course corn, and livestock, principally cattle and hogs. Officials presented me with columns of figures, but it is not necessary to set them down here. The only figure of real significance is the number of people who work on the giant farm—3691 men and women. Most of the women, I was told, do not work in winter. Even so, the figure is staggering. On the basis of human effort, or the productivity of labor, this select collective does not begin to approach a well-operated Iowa farm.

We drove around fields, inspected barns, and toward evening, when it was time for me to leave, my hosts, the highest officials of the collective, escorted me in two automobiles to the border of the neighboring collective. Cossacks are ever mindful of their hospitality, and the officials brought with them bottles of wine from their own winery for a last drink of friendship and for a final exchange of opinion.

"Now that you have seen our kolkhoz," said the chairman, "please tell us how it compares with Iowa farming. We want a frank and straightforward answer."

I had no information about Iowa, but a few days earlier while in Kiev I had become acquainted with Pharis White, a cattle and hog farmer from Oxford, Indiana, and with John Raber, president of the Indiana Farmers' Union, who also raises cattle and hogs and specializes in broilers. White's farm of 700 acres is worked by two full-time hired men and himself. Because of his poor health White spoke of himself as "one-third worker." Raber's farm of 800 acres in Elkhart County, one half of it planted to corn, is worked by his son, his son-in-law, a hired man during the summer, and some forty days' extra hired labor in autumn. One man, he told me, looks after 75,000 broilers and does it four times a year, producing single-handed 1,000,000 pounds of meat.

In reply to the chairman's question I said that I could not give them any information about Iowa, but that the state of Indiana was also noted for corn and livestock farming. Then I passed on to them some of the information I had obtained from Pharis White and John Raber. For some moments there was silence, and I explained that though some one third of American farms were poorly cultivated, America, unlike the Soviet Union, was faced with the problems not of production but overproduction, with huge surpluses of wheat and corn and cotton and sorghum grains. Again there was silence. Then one official said, "One man caring for seventy-five thousand chickens!" The figure astounded them as it did the veterinarian I had accidentally met on the Minsk–Moscow express train. I am certain that this was the first time the chairman and the others realized the task the Kuban had set for itself to outmatch Iowa in milk and meat production. The confident rhetoric of the party leaders and of the quatrain I have quoted, if they thought of these at all, must have struck a discordant note in their minds.

The year 1961 has come, and for the present anyway the Kuban has ceased to boast of inevitable triumph over Iowa. Actually, 1959 and 1960 witnessed serious slumps in production. "In most of the collective and state farms," wrote Sovietskaya Rossiya (February 12, 1960), "livestock is fed hungry rations. Why? Because the harvest was poor." The newspaper blamed the party leadership for the setback. But its own correspondent quotes an elderly Cossack as saying, "On our own land we act not as masters but as landlords' hired help. We pick up the easy jobs and shun the laborious tasks." Though not a universal condition in the Kuban or anywhere else, the elderly Cossack pointed up a rather baneful aspect of Soviet farming: atrophy of individual initiative.

In speech after speech, even before the Plenum of January 1961, Khrushchev chided party leaders and farm managers for their lack of vision and enterprise. While traveling in the province of Chita, Siberia, and observing the fine pastures there, he asked local leaders why they never thought of putting thin-fleeced sheep there. He visited Moldavia and scolded grape growers for overirrigating vineyards only for the purpose of adding weight to the grapes so they could make more money. By diluting the sugar content of the grape, he warned, they made it less palatable for the table and spoiled it for the manufacture of quality wines.

While visiting his native village of Kalinovka, Kursk province, he told fellow villagers that it was absurd for them to grow vegetables for the distant Moscow market when sugar beets would be much more profitable. He told the plenum of the Central Committee (December 25, 1959) that it was uneconomical for the provinces of Tula and Orlov to ship milk to Moscow. They should, instead, plant more late potatoes for the capital and thereby liberate lands in the Moscow province for crops that would increase the output of milk which could be shipped fresh to the market. If the soybean, he complained, grew so well in Manchuria, why did leaders in the adjacent province of Amur neglect to plant it on a large scale? And why, he asked, did farm managers persist in cutting down the acreages of millet and buckwheat? "How can Russians and Ukrainians live without kasha?"

In August 1960 he revisited Kalinovka, and while he was gratified by the progress the collective had achieved since his previous visit, he was displeased by the many things that had remained undone. Why, he asked, didn't the farm grow peas, beans, buckwheat? He reminded fellow villagers that in his boyhood women baked pea and bean pies and that "buckwheat kasha was regarded a festive dish for holidays." He was glad the socialized garden grew plenty of cucumbers, cabbage, beets, but "you have a poor variety of vegetables." Kalinovka, he reminded his audience, must set an example in developing new vegetable crops, "but you must treat vegetables with skill. You cannot cultivate cabbage with an ax." And why in setting out a new orchard did they concentrate on the Antonovka—a good apple—but variety was needed in the new orchards and why had they not thought of it?

He went to the newly built cow barn, looked around, and said. "Look at this building. It has a solid foundation, a well-built roof. With some additional expense the walls could have been raised . . . and there would have been a second story for grain or for poultry. This is not the first time I have spoken of this."

The landlord in the old days, the Premier continued, kept his cattle scattered in five different villages so they would be close to food stores and to fields to which the manure could be hauled out. "Now you have nearly the same area, but you wish to keep your cattle in one or two places. This is unwise. A wise farmer follows the principle of keeping cattle close to food supplies and to fields."

On and on Nikita went, pointing out one flaw after another in the management of one of the best collectives in the Soviet Union. He was, of course, addressing himself not only to fellow villagers but to farmers, especially to managers, all over the country. But who in the old days needed to remind the muzhik that if he grew buckwheat and millet he would have excellent kasha, and that if he grew dried beans and peas he would have tasty and high-calorie cereals for soup and pies? The muzhik did it anyway. In the country that has internationalized the word "kasha," the ingredients for it, even in Moscow, are rarely available.

When one reads Khrushchev's speeches on agriculture, one wonders what has been happening to the thousands of agricultural planners, scientists, and other experts, who should know, without Khrushchev needing to tell them, certain elementary facts about farming and the marketing of farm produce. Khrushchev scolded and prodded leaders into a display of greater initiative in the solution of their respective farm problems. But only leaders; the masses of farm workers have barely been touched by the scoldings and exhortations—nor can they be, under the prevailing system of giant farms. They only carry out orders, some with remarkable skill, others with plodding assiduity, still others with simple indifference.

On a giant farm in Byelorussia, I saw a party of workers return from the fields, and as they passed the unhinged door of a henhouse, it did not occur to any of them to stop and put it in place. They were not concerned with a small chore for which they wouldn't be paid and which didn't enter into their prescribed duties. They knew only their own work, and all else was the task of other workers.

When one observes such insensibility to little things, one becomes aware of a failing that is inherent in collectivized giant farming. The little savings in time and economy that go with individual farming and that the American farmer assiduously strives to achieve, Soviet farming rarely manages to accomplish.

And what American farmer would neglect to repair his tractor and combine in preparation for harvesting? This is precisely what happened in Kazakhstan in 1959. About 4,000,000 acres of grain remained unharvested because 32,000 tractors, 21,000 combines, and 11,000 reapers were unrepaired. The magnitude of the failing in this instance is in part ascribable to the haste with which virgin lands in Kazakhstan had been plowed and seeded. But sloppiness in the care of tools is a widespread phenomenon which in time may or may not be completely overcome. Manifestly it is a failing that one doesn't associate with a family farm except when the farmer is shiftless and is headed for bankruptcy.

Of all the unanswered questions about Soviet farming, the surviving individualism of the peasant is the most worrisome to the Kremlin. The flow of cash to the village since 1954 has reinvigorated the peasant's appetite for rubles. In his speech in Kiev (May 1959) Khrushchev sounded a portentous warning. "I am not," he said, "an advocate of paying out large amounts of money and produce for labor days. Let's give a man all he needs to provide well for his family, so that children are well fed, clothed, and shod, and the family lives in a respectable cottage. . . . But at present there are instances of the rise of an *unhealthy* [my italics] kulak psychology: to pay out more and more money to be put away in saving boxes. What do we need it for?"

Kulak psychology! An old expression, long in disuse, hurled anew at the village to remind the peasants that individual enrichment (such as it is in the Soviet village) cannot be tolerated. Himself the son of a peasant, Khrushchev is noted for his contempt of peasant individualism. In 1950, with Stalin's consent of course, he had set out to smash it by converting the village into an *agro-gorod* (agricultural city). The outcry of peasants against it was so violent that the project was dropped. But the idea lingered on, and in 1959, at the Twenty-first Party Congress, Khrushchev brought it up again. "The party," he said, "is aiming to convert the collective farm villages into urban-type communities with all the latest communal, cultural, and service facilities." In his already mentioned speech at Kiev, he emphasized the importance of increasing investment by collectives in the communal institutions: apartment houses, boarding schools, clubhouses, hospitals, nurseries, kindergartens, restaurants, bakeries, laundries, homes for the aged, other institutions that would minister to individual needs and comforts. This is the *agro-gorod* again, a new way of life, a "transition from socialism to communism." The peasant is to attain his highest living standards, not through individual holdings of garden and cow, pig and sheep, chickens and other fowl, but through communal production and communal distribution. He is to be stripped of all income-yielding property, the one surviving source of his individualism.

In favor of this program is the changing psychology of the young generation in the villages, especially the girls. Again and again I heard them say that they would be glad to be rid of caring for garden and cow and other livestock if collectivized production assured them abundant supplies of food. At the market place in Krasnodar I heard girls speak their minds freely on the subject. As one girl expressed herself, "Why should we workers on the land be different from girls who work in factories? When their day's work is over, their time is their own. They can read a book, go to a dance, a movie, or visit friends. We'd be glad to be like them."

This is new language for a Soviet farm girl, but small is the number of collectives whose productivity would allow abolition of farmsteads without upsetting the food situation not only for farmers but for city people. As of January 1, 1960, the private farmsteads accounted for three fourths of all the potatoes, four fifths of all the eggs, three fourths of all the poultry, over one half of the milch cows, nearly one third of all the pigs, over one fifth of the sheep, four fifths of the goats. Most of the produce of the individual farmsteads was consumed by the producers themselves. But some three fourths of the commercial eggs, over one fourth of meats and fats, 15 per cent of the milk, were sold in bazaars. Though the private garden plots constitute less than 4 per cent of the cultivated land in the Soviet Union, they are infinitely more productive acre for acre than either the collectives or the state farms. Cultivated intensively, principally by women, neither weeds nor drought is a threat to high yields because the weeds are hoed or plucked out by hand and water from a stream or well, carried pail by pail, keeps the ground plentifully supplied with moisture.

Committed as is the Kremlin to the ultimate destruction of all income-yielding private trade and private property, there is the danger of party leaders attempting to "give history a push," as I heard an agriculturist express himself, before the people are prepared for it. This actually happened on the conclusion of the Twenty-first Party Congress in January–February 1959. In region after region party officials set off a crusade to "disengage" the peasant from his individual cow. In the provinces of Vinnitsa and Kharkov and in the Kuban region, the crusade was particularly intense. Peasants were made to sell cows at prices set by party officials when the collectives had neither sanitary—if any—barns for them nor even forage and feed (*Pravda*, March 5, 1960). What was particularly distressing to the peasantry was that the promise to sell them milk at low prices could not be fulfilled. That the action was a violation of "socialist legality" was of no consequence to the party leaders who had instigated the crusade.

Physically helpless to prevent the calamity visited on them, all the aggrieved peasantry could do was to scream their protest. The screams were loud enough to reach Moscow, and *Pravda* condemned "administrative coercion" and "mass purchase of cows."

Since then Khrushchev has cautioned party leaders to refrain from all forms of coercion. He has even softened his once cherished scheme of building many-storied houses in the countryside. He has learned that the peasant, having always lived in a house of his own, wouldn't be comfortable in an apartment house. "Let's start," he said, "by building two-family houses. Time will pass and then we can build more compact villages with multi-storied apartment houses. . . . We must consider the requirements of the kolkhoz members and heed their wishes."

Whether they do or not, the indisputable fact is that as a by-product of collectivization the peasant has lost his ancient passion for land. No peasant today would echo the sentiments of Gleb Uspensky's muzhik, Ivan Afanasyev, when he said, "How can I live without land? Have mercy on me—we all live on the land and how is it possible to desert land?" When circumstances obliged him to desert his land and to migrate to another village, many a peasant took with him a little sack of "his earth"—because no earth in other places smelled as sweet as his own.

Despite ideological denial to the contrary, the peasant of today is not rooted in the land as he had been in the pre-collectivization days. It is not his, and no amount of agitation can instill in him a sense of ownership, social rather than personal; anyway, not as long as the state and the party exercise firm control not only of land and crops but of investment and the division of "the fruits of labor." The average collective is too large, the planning, despite mass meetings, too impersonal, the work of the individual too narrowly specified, to foster emotional attachment.

In Moscow's Yaroslavl railroad station, I became acquainted with two families from Byelorussia who were migrating to Siberia. "Why are you moving?" I asked. "Well," one of the men replied, "man is like an animal—he goes where life is better." New houses were waiting for them on a Siberian state farm and the pay would be much higher than on the collective they had left. So they picked up their families and started on their journey, without regret and without qualm. Such migrations are not uncommon, not only from European Russia to Siberia but within the boundaries of European Russia, despite local effort to discourage and to halt them. The land itself has lost its power to hold a man as it once did.

What is keeping the better-educated and more energetic young people on the farm is not love of land; nor, it must be repeated, is it ideological inspiration. Some of them no doubt love farming and are dedicated Komsomols. But essentially it is the money they earn and the goods they can buy that motivate them. There are "enthusiasts" and "innovators"—workers who come up with a new idea or with a better method of cultivation. There are record-breaking corn growers, milkmaids, pig breeders. But for a huge country like the Soviet Union, with over one half of the population still living in the country-side, these are few and far between.

The socialist competition between one team of workers and another, one collective and another, one province and another, as to who will outproduce whom in cotton, corn, sugar beets, milk, meat, may inject zest into the work; but without the material incentive that goes with the winning or the effort to win, there would be little or no zest. During the years when a "mountain sat on our necks," socialist competition was fostered as energetically as now. But it didn't do much good—it rarely kept the more able and more forward-looking young people on the land.

There is a new generation in the countryside, better educated, more sophisticated, and more demanding than any previous young peasant generation. Many boys and girls have been lured back from the city and the factory, or have never left the farm, because of the higher living standards that Khrushchev's reforms have offered them. They, more than their fathers and mothers, have infused fresh energy into the collectives.

But if in the effort to boost production and to socialize the village, ideologists attempt once more "to give history a push" at the expense of living standards, as some of them did on the conclusion of the Twenty-first Party Congress by their crusade to requisition individual cows, the more ambitious and forward-looking boys and girls are certain to lay down their tools and migrate to the factory or to some new construction project where the higher pay will enable them to attain the higher living standards to which they are irrepressibly aspiring. The very fashion magazines that come to village homes and libraries, the very radio and television broadcasts of new types of consumer goods that are coming into the market, the very boasts of the press and of party leaders, including Khrushchev, of the high living standards they have attained, and of the highest in the world that they are soon destined to command, have created desires and wants that girls especially are determined to fulfill.

At a bazaar in Minsk I approached a portly peasant woman who was holding in either hand a chicken she was offering for sale. Mistaking me for a customer, she half chanted, "Feel of them—very fat—the fattest chickens you can find in the bazaar." Fat—the one quality that counts in chicken, in beef, in other meats!

We started talking and I told her that Americans didn't like fat meat. The information astounded her, as it did passers-by who paused to join in the conversation. "Imagine that!" She turned to a grizzled old man who was sucking on a pipelike cigarette that older peasants still roll in newspaper.

"You say," he asked, "Americans don't like fat meat?"

I nodded.

"Do they like fat women?"

"Shame on you, old codger," snapped the chicken vendor. "You're too old to have such things on your mind."

"The older they are," interposed another woman, "the more shamelessly they speak."

Contrite, the man said, "I meant no offense, my little sisters. I was just curious, and why shouldn't I be? I'm a blacksmith and I read a newspaper every day so that I may know what's happening in the whole world, and here is a man fresh from America and he tells us something I've never heard or read. No, I haven't. If they don't like fat meat in America, maybe it's because they don't like fat women. Maybe they haven't any fat women. Have they?"

Laughter greeted his words.

More and more strollers gathered around, and question after question was shot at me. Most significant were the questions that came from young women. Were there plenty of wall mirrors in American *univermags* (department stores); plenty of tables, chairs, rugs, beds, wardrobes? One blue-eyed girl asked if there were plenty of pianos on sale in America.

The old blacksmith listened and gave a deep sigh. "Such greedy creatures! They want everything at once. When they get married they want to fix up their houses like landlords in the old days. *Ekh*, you!" He turned reproachfully to the blue-eyed girl.

"And why not?" she flung back, giggling.

One cannot agree with those Western observers who hold that agriculture is the Achilles' heel of the Soviet economy. Complete agricultural vulnerability is a thing of the past; and the periodic famines that scourged the Russian countryside for centuries have been conquered. Besides, those who look for an Achilles' heel fail to appreciate the Kremlin's capability to learn from mistakes and failures, however catastrophic. The Kremlin has always pursued its own revolutionary methods of action, the formula being: start big, drive ahead regardless of cost, learn by doing. Witness Khrushchev's drive for nation-wide planting of corn and the breakup of some one hundred million acres of virgin land. The very magnitude of the projects and the speed with which they were executed invited setbacks and failures side by side with incontestable triumphs. Now the new crusade is on, with the lessons of past failures as weapons for a fresh advance in agricultural production. The shake-up of agricultural institutions and the other radical reforms called for by the Central Committee Plenum of January 1961 make progress inevitable.

But one wonders about the Kremlin's commitment to outdo America in agricultural production and to bring to the Soviet people the highest living standards in the world. Too many are the problems immediately related to agricultural output that remain unsolved. The clash between peasant self-interest and Kremlin ideology is far from resolved. Though "the principle of materialist incentive" has been vigorously reaffirmed, it still has to be demonstrated that giantism in all branches of farming yields the best possible results. Though with expert managers production invariably rises, experts, as the veterinarian observed, "do not grow like cabbages in a field." Nor is there any assurance that party leaders have been purged of their zeal to reach out for arithmetical records and win glory for themselves even if they have to subvert the plans of the most accomplished local managers. Soviet agriculture is in a transitional stage, but is not foundering in catastrophe.

One cannot escape the conclusion that until the collectives have been granted the autonomy—which they may well be in the future—that will enable rank-and-file members to feel that they are real partners in the enterprise, Soviet agriculture will be encumbered by inefficiency and wastes. The chain that shackles so much personal initiative and inventiveness must somehow be snapped. Khrushchev of course insists that it is still possible to surpass America in agricultural production by the end of the Seven-Year Plan, in 1965; but let it be remembered that as far back as 1900, before the tractor took over from the horse, the American farm worker fed more people and much better than does the Soviet farm worker today with all the power-driven machinery at his command.

13.

PEASANT
"Turning Today into Tomorrow"

As the automobile turned into a narrow dirt road that wound through a finely cultivated cornfield, a water tower loomed out of the Ukrainian steppe. This was my first glimpse of the village of Gladkoye, some seventy miles from the city of Odessa. There are other elevated reservoirs in the Soviet countryside, but this was the first I had seen; and among other things it signalized the liberation of the women of the village from the chore of hauling water pail by pail from a courtyard well, a communal pump, or a nearby stream, as peasant women have always done.

Gladkoye is the seat of the Budyonovskoye collective, one of the most highly publicized in the Soviet Union, and Makar Posmitny, its chairman, is a nationally known figure. Embracing two other villages, the collective now goes by the name of Twenty-first Congress, in commemoration of the 1959 Party Congress with its proclaimed resolve "to lay out the road to communism." But the public speaks of it by the old name, and so shall I. Supposedly in the vanguard as "a builder of communism," Budyonovskoye is a model of the kolkhoz of the future. "When you get there," an agricultural functionary in Moscow said to me, "you'll see us turning today into tomorrow. The women there don't bake their bread any longer; they have a communal bakery and bread is free to all."

I had read and heard so much about this village and its chairman, Makar Posmitny, that I made a special journey to Odessa so that I could drive out there. Yet in physical appearance, compared with an American or English village, Gladkoye is still a backward community. But in Russia, where the majority of the people live and work in the countryside, its reconstruction is an outstanding achievement, and not merely because of its water tower. The traditional whitewashed cottages of sun-dried mud, with their thatched roofs, typical of the Ukrainian countryside, have been replaced by one-story one-family houses of sandstone brick with tile or sheet-iron roofs. Here, as in the Motherland kolkhoz, the hazard of the whole village burning down from a single house catching fire was now gone.

The main street was laid out as straight as Leningrad's Nevsky, but it was still unpaved. "We'll get to it soon," explained Vasily Chechukov, the deputy chairman. But one side of the street was bordered by a new asphalt sidewalk. So was the other street and the roads to schools, barns, shops, and other communal buildings, miles of shiny asphalt in all directions, delivering old and young from the ancient ordeal of wading through mud during the wet seasons. There was a porch to every house and sometimes a glassed-in veranda, but no wattled fence plaited around wooden posts separated one house from the other. Instead, neat picket fences intersected by concrete posts stretched along both sides of the street.

The houses were modest in size—a living room, one or two bedrooms, a kitchen, a storeroom—and few were as yet equipped with bathroom. Gone was the traditional brick oven; all kitchens were equipped with cooking ranges. Gone also were the traditional *polati* (sleeping platforms); metal beds have replaced them. Even the kerosene lamp has gone; the kolkhoz had its own power plant, and homes and other buildings were all electrified. Gas, too, has come to the village, and in some kitchens I saw both electric and gas ranges. "You have no idea," an elderly woman said, "what a pleasure it now is to cook and how clean we can keep a kitchen."

Chairs, divans, mirrors in living rooms and bedrooms and sometimes even in kitchens, radios, little rugs on the floors, pedal sewing machines, bookcases, now and then a wardrobe, a television set, a vacuum cleaner—these were the furnishings. The convenience of a cellar under the house, as on an American farm, has not yet been discovered; the cellar was outside the house and so was a concrete cistern for catching rain water. The courtyards were set out with shade and fruit trees, occasionally with a vineyard, and were exceptionally clean; no pigs and chickens scratched and rooted around in them, as in the old type of village.

There was a single two-story apartment house, but that was only for schoolteachers. "No," explained Chechukov, "we aren't building apartment houses here, or even two-family houses. Our people like to live in separate one-family homes."

Makar Posmitny, a close friend of Khrushchev, is one of the village leaders who, after Stalin's death, spoke out vigorously against the wastefulness of the machine tractor stations. There is reason to believe that his influence counted in persuading Khrushchev to abolish them. Yet even he has remained cool to Khrushchev's suggestion of building two-family houses as a means of breaking down the peasant's resistance to living city-fashion in multi-storied houses. This fact alone stamps the chairman of the kolkhoz as especially sensitive to peasant psychology.

"I don't see any bicycles around," I said to Chechukov as we strolled around the village. "Is it because the people have spent all their money on houses and furnishings?" The cost of the new houses to members of the kolkhoz is from 2000 to 2500 of the newly revalued rubles, or from 2220 to 2750 American dollars. The land is free and so is the sandstone rock.

"Not at all," Chechukov replied. "You might say that our people are bypassing the age of the bicycle. We have twenty-six individually owned automobiles and fifty individually owned motorcycles. We have been promised twelve more automobiles by the end of the year —everybody here wants to have his own."

Again I thought of Khrushchev, who has committed himself to communally owned pools of automobiles. But in this kolkhoz the members were evidently determined to make their journey from socialism to communism in their own cars.

The secret of the comparative welfare of Budyonovskoye is of course the chairman, always the most strategic functionary in a kolkhoz. A heavy-set man, Posmitny is sixty-six years old, and in his youth, he told me, he had been a *batrak* (hired man) on the estate of a German landlord named Huss. The German had owned all the land of the kolkhoz but didn't do much farming: nearly all of it was a sheep ranch. "I'll tell you something interesting about Huss," Posmitny said. "He had five sons by a servant girl and they are all living here now—excellent workers." This was news—nowhere else in the Soviet Union had I heard of landlords or their sons making common cause with the peasantry. Usually they fled for their lives to swell the flood of Russian émigrés to foreign countries.

Posmitny had been in America, had traveled in agricultural regions in the South and Middle West, including Iowa, the one state that Soviet agricultural managers and experts feel it their duty to visit. "If only," Posmitny said, "we had as much moisture as Iowa; but here we get only about one half as much." Still, in the summer of 1959, a summer of widespread drought, the kolkhoz, he informed me, paid in cash alone fifteen (old) rubles ($1.65) a labor day, which is unusually high. This attested to the effectiveness of modern machinery and advanced methods of agriculture in combating drought.

"This is one of the oldest collectives in our country," Posmitny went on. "We organized it in 1924 just to do our field work together, and right here is the district where the first machine tractor station was founded in 1927 on the Shevchenko state farm. They didn't have enough tractor drivers and they came to us for help. We gave it to them, of course, and it is from here that the machine tractor stations spread all over the country. So you see, you are in a historic kolkhoz."

More historic than Posmitny cared to talk about. One of the earliest champions of the state-owned machinery aggregations, he is also one of the first to have realized their liabilities, and one of the first to have dispensed with their services. He began buying his own tractors and other machinery some two years before Khrushchev delivered his speech in February 1958, at the Gostello collective outside of the city of Minsk, proposing the sale of agricultural machinery to collectives. Posmitny is also one of the first leaders in the dry steppe country to have planted forest belts as a protection against drought and dust storms. "I've lived here all my life," he said, "and have witnessed terrible black storms, so in 1929 we began planting green defenses against them. The trees are beautiful to look at, birds nest in them, and they protect our soil." In 1960 his collective raised the best crops in the Odessa province. No wonder that while thundering against party leaders who gave bad weather as an excuse for setbacks, Khrushchev pointed to Posmitny's record in denial of their excuses.

Posmitny had to leave for a meeting of the *raikom* (district party committee) and on departing said, "Go around, see anything you wish, talk to anybody you choose, and Chechukov will give you all the official information you want."

Chechukov was a blue-eyed, light-haired, athletic-looking man in his late thirties. During and after the war he served in the Army for eight years. Then he married, attended a school for chairmen of collectives, and since graduation has been in Budyonovskoye. He was a good man with whom to check my conviction that the peasant was losing his emotional attachment to land. He said, "It isn't the same as in the old days. Then the peasant bought salt, kerosene, sugar—if he could afford them—but land meant food. The prospect of remaining without land terrified him; it meant starvation. When he went to the city to work and lost his job, he fled back to the land, where he could grow bread and potatoes and cabbage, as he couldn't in the city. But it's all changed now. Take me, for example. I was born and grew up on the land, but I have my technical training, and if I were sent tomorrow to the province of Belgorod or anywhere else, I wouldn't care. I wouldn't lose a thing. It is the same with others. Moving from one village to another now holds no terrors. Under our system there is always land to work, and if you have a feeling for land you always love it, whether in the village in which you were born and brought up or in some other village."

It is the work then and not the land that counts, and when you move to another village you won't think of taking along a little sack of earth because it smells sweeter than land anywhere else.

The Budyonovskoye kolkhoz spread over an area of some 8000 acres, of which 6500 were in cultivation. The remainder was untillable and was in pasture for sheep and fowl. Compared with other collectives, it was small. In the province of Stavropol the average size of a collective in 1957 was over 60,000 acres, or over seven and a half times as large as Budyonovskoye. The question at once arose whether the comparative smallness of Budyonovskoye might not be the very reason for its success. "Well," replied the deputy chairman, "a collective can be too small or too large. For our kind of intensive farming, a collective much larger than ours—say, over three thousand [7410 acres] hectares of tillable land—wouldn't gain in efficiency."

Speaking of course as a practical agriculturist and not as an ideologist with a mania for giantism in farming, he was one more functionary I knew who questioned the wisdom of huge farms, except those which specialize in wheat or other grains.

Wheat and corn were the leading crops on this collective. Oats, barley, millet, alfalfa, clover, grapes and other fruit, sunflowers, sugar beets, garden vegetables, silk, honey, were the other crops. They grew all their own seed and raised all their own feed and fodder. Their chief sources of income were 2100 head of cattle, of which 680 were milch cows, the pig farm of 4100 head, and wine from 250 acres of vineyard. A common cause of wastefulness on Soviet farms is the lack of nearby facilities to process their produce. But in Budyonovskoye they have built their own flour mill, a plant to extract oil from sunflower seeds, a creamery, a winery; a sugar refinery was in process of construction. They also maintained carpentry and machine shops. Whenever a tractor, a combine, any tool, breaks down, it is repaired without delay, and if spare parts are difficult or impossible to obtain, the mechanics are skilled enough to manufacture them in their own shops.

"It's impossible to operate a farm efficiently," Chechukov said, "without trained personnel—and Posmitny has always seen to it that our workers are well trained. We have ninety truck drivers and we have sent three young men to a technological institute to study agricultural engineering. We are paying their expenses and when they graduate they are coming to work here."

Budyonovskoye has also formed its own building brigade, which puts up houses for members, schools, barns, nurseries, silos, and other communal buildings. A singular feature of the brigade is that out of the seventy workers not one is a woman. On the mammoth construction projects in Moscow, Leningrad, and other cities, women work beside men, and being less skilled than men, they perform the heaviest labor. But in this kolkhoz there is a concern for women which to the best of my knowledge is unmatched anywhere else in the Soviet Union. The physician here is a man because, Chechukov explained, it is less of a strain on a man to get up in the night for an emergency call. Between October and May, mothers do not work, and it is the aim of the kolkhoz to liberate them from field work by the end of the Seven-Year Plan in 1965. No such hope of liberation is held out to women in industry. It cannot be, because by 1965 the average worker will still be unable to support a family without his wife's wages. Budyonovskoye can achieve its aim only by making the farm so productive that a husband can earn a livelihood for the family without the wife's contribution to the budget. More automation, more fertilizer, better strains of seed, finer strains of livestock, on all of which the management is centering attention, will no doubt boost the income of the collective, but it is questionable whether it will be raised to a point where a man's earnings can support a family.

By American standards, the farm—as of the present—is heavily overstaffed: 760 men and women doing the work. Dairymaids attend to ten or twelve cows when they milk by hand, to twenty-five when they milk by machines in a milk parlor. There is only one such parlor on the farm now. Still, as one walked around barns and fields, one observed scrupulous care given to crops and livestock. The cornfields were as clean as on the best Iowa and Indiana farms. Inside the immense, brightly lighted barns there was nowhere a cobweb or any signs of neglect and sloppiness. Between the pig barns, long rows of fruit trees were set out. "The girls did it," said the deputy chairman. "It's their idea. The trees beautify the land and when they begin to bear we'll have more fruit."

The most significant aspect of the collective is the gradual elimination of individual enterprise, the process of "turning today into tomorrow," when all services will come free from communal institutions. The individually owned cow has already gone, sold to the collective in 1958. But unlike party functionaries in the Kuban and other provinces, Posmitny refrained from "giving history a push." He acted with caution and foresight. He built up-to-date barns for stabling the cows. He grew plenty of fodder and feed so they would give more milk than they had under private ownership. For a year there were meetings at which the subject was discussed in all its aspects. "I must tell you," the deputy chairman explained, "the women didn't take kindly to the idea. Their cows have meant a lot to them, especially after the war, when three years of German occupation—from July 1941 to April 1944—left the kolkhoz a ruin. But we assured them that not only would they be liberated from the arduous chore of caring for the cows but they could buy milk at seventy kopecks a liter (about eight cents). They trusted comrade Posmitny because in good times and bad he has never made misrepresentations to them."

"How much milk are members allowed to buy?" I asked.

"A liter a day per person in summer and half as much in winter, and we distribute it fresh every day. Children in nurseries and kindergartens get special rations there."

"What's your ruling on individually owned pigs?" I asked.

"We have no ruling. Members raise one or two pigs a year. There are always food scraps around a house and why waste them?"

We visited the newly built bakery—a sunny and spacious structure with up-to-date equipment and a spare oven for emergencies. Bread was baked fresh every day, white wheat bread. "At first," Chechukov explained, "the women were afraid that our bakery bread wouldn't be as tasty as their home-baked, but we bake excellent bread and now women are glad they no longer have to bake their own."

"Is it really given away free?" I asked.

"I'll tell you what our system is. Instead of giving members their share of wheat—two kilograms a labor day last year—we pay them in freshly baked bread. We keep a record of the bread each family receives, and at the end of the year members who have not consumed their share get back the unused wheat to do with what they please. The only charge we make is twenty to twenty-five kopecks (two to three cents) a loaf to cover the expense of operating the bakery, and someday we'll be rich enough to dispense with this charge. But we can't afford it now. Our main objective is to liberate women as much as possible from traditional household chores. That's why we're soon going to put up a new nursery for a hundred children, and a communal laundry."

"Won't it be expensive to send the family wash to a laundry?" I asked.

"No, because we don't intend to make a profit. We'll charge only the actual cost of the service—and someday we'll be able to do it at no cost at all. There are a lot of things we'd like to do free for our people that we can't afford yet."

"When a girl gets married," I asked, "does the collective give her a dowry as some other collectives do?"

"We give her a present of a thousand rubles [one hundred in the new currency]. It helps to pay the expenses of the wedding celebration, which is held in our teahouse."

Medical care and education are, of course, free, though in the new boarding school for sixty children, parents pay one third of the operating cost, which does not include teachers' salaries.

In addition to schools (three buildings and a fourth one to be put up), a hospital, a drugstore, nurseries and kindergartens, though with not enough space to meet the demand, the collective has built an array of communal institutions: a library, a bathhouse, an athletic stadium, a radio broadcasting station, a clubhouse for each of the three villages, a teahouse, a general store, a hostel, a dairy shop. They have a string orchestra, a brass band, and an amateur talent society of over a hundred members. They have invested a sum equivalent to five thousand American dollars in musical instruments and in costumes for the talent society.

Like all collectives, Budyonovskoye has its own pension system. The produce and money that the fifty-four pensioners are paid come out of the so-called cultural-and-social fund, for which 4 per cent of the collective's gross income is annually set aside. "But we must do more for old people," Chechukov said. "Those who are single and are not in particularly good health do not care to be burdened with much housekeeping, so we are going to build them a house of one-story apartments. Let them spend their declining years in as much ease and comfort as we can offer them."

An unexpected feature of the collective is the way they honor their dead. They have a new four-acre cemetery, nicely fenced around. A caretaker, an older man, keeps down grass and brush around graves and grounds. It was the neatest village cemetery I had seen in the Soviet countryside. In a shed at the entrance was a hearse—a four-wheeled black-painted carriage—the only hearse I had ever seen in a village. Nowadays the casket is usually carried on a truck, instead of, as in the old days, on the shoulders of pallbearers. But here a casket is carried in dignity on a horse-drawn hearse, followed by the band, playing a funeral march.

There were some half-dozen graves in the new cemetery, and over one stood a large wooden cross. "If a family is religious," the deputy chairman said, "and they wish to put up a cross over the grave of a beloved member, it is their affair. But this is an irreligious kolkhoz." On further inquiry I learned that there was a Baptist congregation of some seven or eight families in this "irreligious kolkhoz."

Toward evening Posmitny returned. I saw him standing under a tree on the sidewalk surrounded by young people. His manner was informal and responsive. He answered questions and listened to the young people in comradely fashion, and one could sense the respect and admiration in which he was held. No doubt this is one reason for his success as a farm manager and village leader, and for the nation-wide acclaim he has received.

Neither he nor Chechukov spoke boastfully of their achievements. Not once did either of them even refer to the national crusade to surpass America in agricultural output. Neither man was given to loud words or to florid rhetoric. They seemed eminently sensible, down-to-earth village leaders who were making history in the Soviet countryside without any attempt to "give history a push."

To a Westerner, the "tomorrow" Budyonovskoye has so far achieved may not be particularly impressive. The free services that "tomorrow" presupposes are comparatively few. They do not have free movies; they cannot afford them yet and, to cover expenses, must charge admission. Inequalities persist: the house of a stonemason was larger and more attractively furnished than others. A high earner, the mason had spent some thirty-five hundred dollars on it. Even so, it doesn't begin to compare with the houses of agricultural workers I saw in England, is neither as spacious, as modern, nor as solidly and attractively constructed. But to the mason and his wife it was a dream house—they never had supposed they would live in such an up-to-date and comfortable home.

Individualism in Budyonovskoye is not dead, and Posmitny obviously is not the man to kill it with an ideological blow. Garden plots may be set out with fruit trees and vineyards, but they are privately cultivated and pigs and chickens are privately raised. The individualism is best exemplified by the one-family houses, which the people prefer, and by their aspiration to own an automobile or a motorcycle.

Sooner or later the privately owned pigs and chickens are destined to go the way of the individually owned cows. Ideology insists on it—the class division between workers and farmers must be bridged. The collective must then assume the responsibility of providing members with meat and eggs, either free or at a cost low enough to make it, as on many farms in America, uneconomical or laborious for them to raise their own. The only alternative is to establish communal dining rooms to take the place of the private dining table.

But one wonders whether the people will bow to it even if the communal meals are up to the standards of home cooking. Actually, something new is happening to the psychology of people, especially the women, in this highly advanced collective. Pride in the new houses, as was evidenced from the talk I heard from women, fosters pride in homemaking. This, in turn, heightens the sense of privacy, the urge to enjoy the pleasures the new home is offering. Remove the meals, or even only the main meal, from the home, and one of the great pleasures is taken out of it.

While in the wine cellar where we retired for refreshments and talk, I asked Chechukov whether there were divorces in the villages which make up the collective.

"Our people," he replied, "are only human, and conflicts between husbands and wives arise over one thing and another. They always come to our office with their troubles and we do our best to straighten them out. We believe in the strong and happy family. It's terrible for children when a family breaks up, nothing more terrible for them, and we always try to impress this on couples that come to us for advice and help. In the end they become reconciled and we hardly have any divorce in our collective."

A strong family is one more reason for home cooking and home meals, however "middle-class" some ideologists may pronounce it. Devoted mothers as peasant women are, it wouldn't seem right to them to substitute the communal dining room for the home dining table, where in their own way they can cater to the tastes and the wishes of the family. This may be only speculation, but observing the joy and the pride of women in their new homes, in the gas and electric cooking ranges, and considering the constant emphasis of "the strong and happy family"—these are circumstances that one cannot disregard.

This collective is the most advanced I have ever visited or read about—far more advanced than Khrushchev's Kalinovka. The achievement of the most remarkable peasant leader I have ever known, one can only wonder about its future—will it be permitted to remain an independent farming community or, in view of Kremlin passion for giantism, will it be merged with other communities and if so will it lose or gain from the merger?

Budyonovskoye is, of course, a long way from the tomorrow which ideologists envision. But even more important is the fact that it is a long way from the yesterday out of which it has risen.

14.

PEASANT
The Cultural Revolution

In contrast to Gladkoye, the Russian village in outward appearance has by and large witnessed scarcely any changes since Czarist times. There are, of course, new barns and granaries, new schoolhouses and houses of culture, other new public buildings. There are tractors and combines and other up-to-date machinery. But even in villages on the outskirts of Moscow the old *izby* (cottages) droop with decay and age: there are the same slovenly courtyards, the same tumbling fences around them, and after a rain or the spring thaw, the same deep mud.

Rare is the village that has already laid out sidewalks or pavements. The old Russian saying "A mud pond at the gate and bread aplenty" reflected the muzhik's joy at the coming of rain and his utter indifference to the mire at his doorstep. The mire is still there, though nowadays people wade through it not barefooted or in *lapti* but shod in knee-high leather or rubber boots or rubbers over shoes.

The country roads off the main highways are, on the whole, no better than in pre-revolutionary years, with bridges over streams, especially in Siberia, that shake insecurely under automobile wheels and that wash away in floodtime or are so heavily submerged in water that they are impassable. After spring thaws and autumn showers, villages in various parts of the country are for days at a time often as completely cut off from the outside world as was the village in which I was born. My trip from Odessa to Budyonovskoye was postponed a day because it had rained heavily the day before and Intourist wouldn't risk the automobile drive for fear parts of the road would be impassable.

Bezdorozhye (roadlessness), as Russians speak of the state of their country roads, is still the curse of the Russian countryside. How often one sees caterpillar tractors hauling a truck out of deep mud! About three times the size of the United States, the Soviet Union has only about 130,000 miles of hard-surfaced roads, not all of them asphalted, against about 2,400,000 miles in America.

The Seven-Year Plan has charted the construction of 7,000,000 new homes in villages and the electrification "in the main" of the whole countryside. I have seen some of the best new houses on state and collective farms. They are a vast improvement on the old and ever drooping *izby*, with more light and more space, with taller windows and more of them, offering a family anywhere from two to three rooms. Yet only occasionally is there running water; this was still to come, I was told. The outhouse is still prevalent. Not that the peasant is demanding a bathroom and a flush toilet inside the house. I doubt if the bathroom will ever take the place of the steam bath, which the peasant has known for centuries and which intellectuals in cities revel in to this day.

The building boom is on in the countryside, but by the end of the Seven-Year Plan the overwhelming mass of Soviet villages will at best achieve only partial reconstruction, with nothing like bathrooms or flush toilets in houses, or even pavements and sidewalks. Mud will still gleam out of thousands of villages.

Yet the "deaf village" or "bear's corner," as the remote and isolated village was called, is now a mere memory. In all the vast immensities of the Soviet Union there are no longer any villages without a schoolhouse, radio, newspapers, magazines, books; without college men as teachers, agronomists, veterinarians; or where the voice of Moscow does not reach.

Whatever the terrors and agonies the peasant has endured since the rise of the Soviets, whatever the ordeals that may lie ahead of him in the impending Kremlin resolve to root out of him surviving remnants of individualism, he has undergone an explosive cultural revolution, which has shaken up his mind and his personality as no other event in all Russian history. Not even during the years when "a mountain sat on our necks" did the forces of this revolution cease to function, and the peasant could no more escape them than he could his shadow. They pursued him relentlessly and without letup and have transformed him inwardly and outwardly beyond recognition. The lowly, miserable muzhik, serf and rebel, ignoramus and brute, fool and schemer, the man whom the Russian intelligentsia pitied and scorned, blessed and cursed, has vanished from the Russian scene.

Chekhov's *Peasants* and *In the Ravine* and Ivan Bunin's *The Village*, all translated into English, are brilliant literary documents of peasant life in the old days. In his *Peasants*, Chekhov writes: "Who keeps the tavern and encourages drunkenness? The peasant. Who embezzles and drinks up the funds collected for the community, the school, the church? The peasant. Who steals from his neighbors, puts a torch to their property, bears false witness in court for a bottle of vodka? The peasant. Yes, to live with them was terrible; still, they were human beings, they suffered and cried like human beings and there was nothing in their lives for which they could not find justification. Crushing toil that made the body ache at night, beastly winters, sparse crops, overcrowding; and no helping hand from anybody, nowhere to look for succor. Those who were stronger and more well-to-do could grant no assistance. They were themselves vulgar, dishonest, drunken, and swore just as vilely. The most petty little clerk or official treated peasants as though they were vagrants; spoke to village elders and church guardians as to inferiors. In truth, can any kind of help or salutary example be offered by lazy, avaricious, debauched men who come to the village for no other purpose than to affront, mulct, and terrorize?"

More savage is the picture of peasant life in Bunin's *The Village*. One of the characters cries out: "And the songs? The same thing, always the same: the stepmother is 'wicked and greedy': the father-in-law, 'harsh and quarrelsome,' sits on the top of the oven 'like a dog on a rope'; the mother-in-law, no less wicked, also sits on the oven 'like a bitch on a chain'; the sisters-in-law are invariably 'young bitches and tricksters'; the brothers-in-law are 'malicious scoffers'; the husband is either a fool or a drunkard; the old father-in-law bids him thrash his wife soundly 'until her hide rolls down to her heels'; while the wife, after she scrubbed the floor for him, ladled out the cabbage soup, scrubbed clean the household, and baked the cakes, turned to her husband with the words 'Get up, you foul wretch, wake up, here is a dish of water, wash yourself, here are your leg wrappers, wipe yourself, here is a piece of rope, hang yourself.' And our adages, Tikhon Ilych. Could anything more vile and foul be invented? And our proverbs! A man who has been soundly whipped is worth two who haven't been . . . simplicity is worse than thieving."

Bunin's depiction of the barbarities of peasant life are often overdone. His generalizations are not devoid of exaggerations. There were multitudes of upright, decent muzhiks in the old days. There were multitudes of families which despite grinding poverty lived in a spirit of amicability. There were joyful festivals in the village, especially Christmas, Easter, Holy Trinity, accompanied by lively songs, ceremonies, games, and pageantry. Among the most precious memories of my boyhood years are the color and gaiety of these festivals. There was wit and laughter in the village; there was tenderness and compassion, kindliness and hospitality—muzhiks didn't turn away a beggar, or any wayfarer who knocked on their doors in quest of bread and shelter. The muzhik was an extraordinarily human person, and if, unlike Turgenev, Bunin failed to emphasize the brighter aspects of his personality, it must be because these seemed of less moment to him than the darkness and barbarity that pervaded village life.

In the prewar years, during my stay in the Ukrainian village of Reshetilovka, I went to a concert given by a girls' choir, and song after song seemed to corroborate Bunin's melancholy tales. One of the songs, long and doleful, I shall always remember. It told of a young wife who pleads with her father-in-law, her mother-in-law, and her brother-in-law to stop her husband from beating her. In reply each in turn presents the offending husband with an oaken stick or a rolling pin and urges him to strike her again. Only the sister-in-law, who when married might be subject to similiar thrashings, cries out against her brother's cruelty to his wife. Even if the inhumanity the song depicts was exceptional, it is significant that it found expression in an old folk melody.

The lot of women in the old days was particularly dismal. Consider the implications of such sayings as: "A woman's hair is heavy, her brain is light"; "A hen is no bird, a woman is no person"; "Love your wife like your soul, shake her like a pear tree." The man was the master, free to impose his will on the woman, beat her with fists and feet, with cane and whip. There were women who struck back vengefully and powerfully—I knew such women—and cowed men into respectful treatment of their persons. But they were exceptional. Usually all the mistreated wife could do was curse and wail and seek solace from a neighboring woman, to whom she cried out her heart.

The Orthodox priest was of no help. It was not within his function, as it is nowadays within the party secretary's, to untangle family feuds. There were too many of them in the parish, which often embraced about half a dozen villages. Besides, unlike the Catholic priest or the Protestant minister, he held himself socially aloof from his flock. The neighboring landlord and the uniformed officials were more agreeable company for conversation, for card games, and for drinking bouts, if the priest was a drinking man, which he was more often than not.

"Don't choose your groom, choose your mother-in-law" is another old saying that reveals the troubled life of a newly married couple when the bride came to live with her husband's family. The mother-in-law tyrannized over the daughter-in-law, and so did the father-in-law. *Snokhachestvo*—cohabitation with the daughter-in-law when the son went off to the Army, was hired out for the summer season to a landlord, or departed for the city in quest of work—was widespread in many parts of rural Russia. Dark and gory were the deeds that grew out of these abuses, sons beating up and even killing their fathers.

There were other social monstrosities in the old Russian village: the abuse of orphans by stepfathers and stepmothers; the obloquy visited on the spinster by her own parents, who regarded spinsterhood a disgrace for the unmarried daughter and for themselves; the anguished position of older people in their own homes when they grew so sick and feeble they couldn't work and were damned as parasites by their own children.

On my return to my native village in the early twenties, the first man I called on was a muzhik who had been a close friend of our family. His only son had been my playmate. The son was killed in France during World War I. His widowed wife remarried and lived with her new husband in her first husband's home. Now the muzhik was a widower and the young couple was driving him from his own house because he was too old to work in the field. He wept copiously as he spoke of the sorrowful end to which he had come in his old age. Tragedies like his were common in rural Russia in the old days, especially among the poorer peasantry.

The coming of the Soviets brought a violent shake-up of the old social system in the village. The muzhik paid dearly, often with his life, for his resistance to the forms of collectivism that the new regime had mercilessly striven to impose on him. Collectivization of the land alone, as already noted, took an enormous toll of peasant lives. But the assault on the old social monstrosities in the village never halted. It blew to pieces the old social relationships within the family and within the community.

The very word *snokhachestvo* has disappeared from the speech of the people. Were a father-in-law nowadays to attempt to ensnare or to intimidate a daughter-in-law into going to the barn with him, which is quite unthinkable, she would give him a piece of her wrathful mind and wouldn't hesitate to throw a stick or a rock at him. Gone is the meek submissiveness of a young wife to her in-laws, even when they live together. But now a newly married girl usually lives with her in-laws only until she and her husband are able to acquire a home of their own. Whatever the failings of the collectivized village, it is duty-bound to help a couple move into a home of their own. It allots them land, building materials, and often, especially since the rise of Khrushchev, credits.

Wife beating has not died out in the village or in the city. Drunken husbands—in the city they are usually proletarians, "the most advanced class of all humanity"—are not beyond mauling wives in the old-fashioned way. But woe to the offender if the wife complains or if the village soviet discovers it. The man is publicly censured and pilloried and is warned of stern retribution, not barring imprisonment if he repeats the offense.

Gone from the speech of the people are the old sayings reflecting the inferiority of woman to man with the implied justification of man's prerogatives over her, however abusively exercised. The young generation has not heard of these sayings unless they have read them in a book. When I brought up the subject before a group of young people in a Ukrainian village, they all laughed and a girl said, "Such sayings belong to the geological ages." Remote from her mind was all thought of the inferiority of her sex.

The loss of this sense of inferiority to man is of itself an epochal change in the mentality of the village woman. The man cannot throw his weight around the house as he formerly did. His wife knows that she no longer has to fear him, and he knows it too. This alone has made for a more tranquil family life than the peasantry knew in the old days. Walk through a village nowadays and you rarely hear the violent quarrels spiced with maledictions and obscenities (used only by men) that so often rocked it in the past.

"Do peasants still use such expressions as 'May the cholera choke you,' 'May the smallpox blind you,' 'May the French disease [syphilis] devour you'?" I asked an elderly schoolteacher in a Byelorussian village, who as a hobby was making a study of changing social manners in the countryside.

"'French disease,'" he answered, "has completely dropped out of speech. The other expressions you do hear from babushkas and dyedushkas [grandfathers], but not from young people."

I heard more old-fashioned muzhik obscenity in some sections of Moscow than in the village. Indeed, I never knew the speech of village folk—even in bazaars, where haggling over prices is still a pastime—to be so chastened of curses and scurrilities. There are, of course, exceptions, especially among Great Russians and Byelorussians, who have always been noted for the richness of their obscene and vituperative vocabulary. But years of propaganda for "cultured speech" and "cultured manners" have borne both visible and audible results. In this one respect, Chekhov and Bunin would hardly recognize the village of which they wrote with such pain and despair.

Sundays and religious holidays, of which there were so many in the old days, were occasions for drinking sprees, often accompanied by brawls and battles. In many parts of the country, on Sundays and holidays, there were also organized fist fights, one section of the village marching against another, the combatants flailing away at one another with bare fists and scratching one another's faces with their fingernails, fighting and fighting until one side had outmastered the other, and the other vowing to avenge the defeat at some future encounter, which might be the following Sunday.

There is still an appalling amount of drunkenness in the village, peasants without ready cash to buy vodka, or not wanting to spend cash, making their own home-brew, in secret of course. How often one hears and reads of a crowd of villagers, including young people, though rarely girls and young women, celebrating an old Orthodox holiday with an alcoholic debauch. They may not be religious, may not bother to go to church; the holiday is merely an excuse for a drinking spree. So are weddings and funerals.

Now and then a crusade breaks out against home-brewers, equipment is confiscated, offenders are pilloried and punished, but the practice persists. Yet there is nowhere nearly as much alcoholism in the countryside as there was in the old days. For one thing, religious holidays have been officially outlawed, and instead of celebrating, people work or are supposed to work. The drive for production and fulfillment of plans is always intense and cannot lightly be disregarded. For another thing, the campaign against drinking is kept ever alive, and the evils of alcoholism are dramatized in poster and banner, in lecture and movie, in personal confession at public meetings, even as among members of Alcoholics Anonymous, and at the so-called comradely trials, where the offender is publicly tried and may have guardians appointed to watch over him and to protect him from "bad company."

Gone from the countryside are the old-style fist fights. Even in Cossack villages, where they had been a popular sport, they have gone out of favor. "Whenever," a schoolteacher in the Cossack Kuban told me, "I hear my grandfather speak of the fist fights, in which he loved to participate, I realize what a savage people our Cossacks were."

Neither orphans nor feeble old folk are at the mercy of foster parents or relatives. If an orphan is treated unkindly or is not wanted, he is transferred to an institution: nowadays usually to one of the new boarding schools, where he is fed, clothed, educated, and trained to work in a factory or on a farm or for study in a trade school or institute. Nor are dependent old people helpless now. The collectives have pension systems of their own, though it is only the more prosperous collectives that have built up funds which allow adequate payments. The others pay something in kind and something in money, and if an old person is not too ill there is always some light job for him. More and more collectives have begun to build homes for the aged, with enough land for a vegetable garden, an orchard, so that inmates, if their health permits, may occupy themselves usefully.

Were a son or daughter nowadays to drive an old father or mother from the home because of inability to work, they would be disgraced at a public meeting and would be threatened with punishment if they persisted in offending the parent. Among Cossacks, even as among Mohammedan peoples, the problem of the aged never arose. They have always venerated the old, as the muzhik, especially if he was poverty-stricken, rarely did.

In a cow barn in Byelorussia I became acquainted with a milk-maid who was a spinster about forty years old. She was as composed and voluble as the other milkmaids. No doubt spinsterhood was a frustration, but it was not the disgrace that it had been in the old days. No father, mother, any relative or neighbor scolded and taunted her for being unmarried. If they did they wouldn't go unreprimanded privately or publicly by the chairman of the collective or by others in authority, and especially by the younger women in the village. They would wither the offender with censure, as they always do in such instances.

The spinster milkmaid was economically independent, and as a superior worker, had money to buy good clothes and other things that gave her pleasure. She told me she was literate and was taking courses in dairying—had once gone to Minsk to a seminar on the subject. Her great ambition, she informed me, was to rise to an accomplishment that would earn her a free trip to the Moscow Agricultural Exhibition, and the chairman of the collective assured her in my presence that he was planning to make it possible for her to do so in the near future. The village in the old days did not offer a woman in her position, as it now did, the companionship, the opportunity for social acclaim and economic reward, the educational advantages, to foster her self-respect and to lift her above the obloquy and the agony of spinsterhood.

In former times the intelligentsia spoke of the peasantry as *narod* (the people). The village was a world of its own, a dark world, separated from the city by its own way of life, and hostile to the city. Village folk made up over 80 per cent of the population. They and only they performed all the work on the land. They were the bread givers—the city would have starved to death without their food; they were the cannon fodder for all Czarist military adventures —Russia would have remained a shrunken principality had not their flesh and blood been pushed and pitted against one outside people after another. No wonder the guilt-ridden and impotent intelligentsia spoke of the muzhik masses as *the* people.

Now it is all changed. Statistics reveal the astounding social change that has come over the village since the rise of the Soviets. From the census of January 1959 we learn that only slightly more than half the population (52 per cent) lives in the countryside. Beginning with the middle twenties, and more particularly since 1927, the peasant, by the million, has been on the move, uprooting himself from the village and swelling the population of new and old cities. He is still on the move, and the time is not too distant when, as in other industrialized countries, a minority of the population (though a heavy minority) will live on the land.

In the old days the peasant looked on the city with suspicion and contempt. What did he want with city people anyway? They cheated and oppressed him. They acted superior and didn't even condescend to shake hands with him. To them the very word "muzhik" was a term of opprobrium signifying an ignorant, unwashed, stinking creature. He was on guard against them as against an enemy, even when he went to the bazaar to do his trading. He was always glad to return home, to his own milieu, where he knew the people around him, people like himself who did not make him feel inferior, who shook hands with him, and whose thresholds he could cross without formalities, without even knocking at the door.

Now hostility to the city has died out of the peasant, and so has his sense of inferiority in the presence of city people. He knows more about the city than he ever could in the old days—if only because there is so much social and cultural interchange between city and village. People go back and forth all the time—to meetings, on excursions, to seminars, or to work. It is no longer an ordeal to transplant oneself forever from the village to the city; millions and millions of villagers have done it. Letters come and letters go, gifts too, all of which has helped to shatter the peasant's old distrust and contempt for the city. The city man who now comes to the village may be a highly placed party functionary with evil tidings of a new policy. In his heart the peasant may distrust and detest him, but he doesn't doff his hat or kneel before him, as he once did before a highly placed official from the city.

The intelligentsia in the old days grieved over the woes of the muzhik and were ashamed of the primitiveness and barbarism of the village. But what did they know of the muzhik? What did they do for him? They wept and groaned, but the barriers that separated them from the peasantry remained barely shaken. Schoolteachers and physicians, especially since the rise of the zemstvos in 1864, were the bravest of the lot. They did not mind the mud and the primitiveness of the village. But as a class, the intelligentsia stood aloof and looked down on the muzhik, and the muzhik cultivated no particular respect for them, and often hated them for being privileged and for coming from the city, where "the enemy" lived.

To this day college graduates who live in the city loathe to be assigned positions in the countryside. Through trickery and high connections some of them succeed in escaping such assignments, but only some of them. The others may grumble and whine—but go, willingly or unwillingly. Besides, the village has an intelligentsia of its own. In consequence, the old barriers between peasant and intellectual have been breaking down, and the old disrespect toward and detestation of the intelligentsia as a class is vanishing.

The breakdown of barriers between city and village, between peasant and intellectual, is only one of the circumstances that have fostered the cultural revolution in the village. There are others: the smashup of remnants of feudalism (as exemplified by the landed gentry), sports and entertainment, the health service, mechanization of agriculture, and, above all, education.

Lenin didn't inspire in the muzhik hatred of the landed nobleman; he only made use of it to win peasant support for his dictatorship, the nature and implication of which were beyond the comprehension of the muzhik. Memories of serfdom and all the horrors attendant on it survived in song and story. The ever-readiness of Cossacks and gendarmes in Czarist times to protect landlords against peasant uprisings fanned muzhik emotion against them. Though much of the land of the nobleman had already been sold to the peasantry, the old hatred rankled. The landlord, whose very appearance, speech, culture, and customs were alien to the muzhik, sym-

bolized social superiority and rule from above, even as the uniformed
Czarist officials symbolized the instrument by which the superiority
and the rule were maintained.

With the coming of the bolsheviks landlordism and Czarist officialdom crashed into the revolutionary pyre, and the muzhik felt as
though the burden of his centuries-old inferiority was suddenly
lifted from him. Of freedom, as the term is understood in the West,
he had no inkling. But he felt the freedom of a man who no longer
needed to abase himself before the master of the manor house. In
revenge he set the manor house afire again and again, looted barns,
cellars, granaries, cut long protected timberlands and even orchards.

The new rulers treated him mercilessly. But the new rulers were
flesh of his flesh, sometimes a neighbor, sometimes even a son, and
when they came from the city or from another village, they wore
the same style of clothes he did, spoke the same language, ate the
same food, trudged through the same mud. The muzhik didn't
kneel before him or reach out for his hand to kiss, and when he did
he was sternly reprimanded, as I had observed in village after village
in the early years of the revolution. The muzhik feared and cursed
the new rulers, but didn't feel inferior to them and might even address them as "thou." Nowadays when one travels in the Soviet
countryside one hears plenty of complaints, but neither in the speech
nor in the manner of the men and women does one observe any
manifestation of the old obsequiousness and the old self-degradation.

Sports have not stirred up the countryside as intensely as they
have the city and factory neighborhoods. Swimming and wrestling
are not new of course, nor is skating, though even these were never
as organized as they now are all over the country. Volleyball is as
new as chess and dominoes. But the game of games, as in the city,
is football, which, like volleyball, was unknown in the old days.
All over the country, state and collective farms have built, are building, or are planning to build a football stadium. All the blueprints
I saw for reconstructed villages call for it, just as they do for a
clubhouse.

Amateur talent activities are the highest form of entertainment
the Soviets have developed in the countryside, which was always
rich in folk art, particularly in song, dance, and ceremonial. The
Soviets have reorganized, refined, and expanded it and given it a

modern coloration. Amateur entertainment nowadays includes plays, concerts, choral singing, dancing, literary recitations, and the always fascinating *chastushki* (quatrains). Often spoken of as *stradanye* (suffering), these in the old days were lyrical laments of unhappiness, usually in affairs of the heart, and were rich in imagery derived from natural surroundings.

Nowadays the quatrains are often also parodies, inevitably non-political, of local events and personages, of the vanities and follies of friends and enemies, of neighbors, and even of officials. These always provoke loud merriment, and invariably girls outdo boys in tenderness of emotion, in sharpness of wit, in the liveliness with which they half sing and half recite their meaningful quatrains.

But this is nothing new in the Russian village. Women were always superior to men in folk literature. They sang the old ballads and told the old tales to their children. They mourned the dead and solaced the living. At weddings they mocked the groom and glorified the bride even while they lamented the fate that awaited her as a married woman with the husband ever ready to snap a whip over her. In the long winter evenings, when girls gathered in some home to do their spinning of flax and wool, they entertained themselves and the boys who came around with endless songs and stories. Overwhelmingly they were illiterate, but they nurtured their imaginations more than did the boys with ballad and tale, with parody and anecdote, above all with compositions of *stradanye*.

The tradition is continuing in the Soviet setting with all the new changes and problems that village folk are facing. Love is still a major theme and only less so is the ancient rivalry between the sexes. As of old, the *chastushki* are pervaded with a morality that exalts the good and decries the evil in the everyday relationships of people.

Like sports, the phenomenally successful talent performances have been a powerful antidote to the drinking sprees and the fist fights that had been favored pastimes in the old days. They have livened the village with a social and literary atmosphere of a kind that it had not known in times past.

For centuries the Russian village had been scourged by epidemics of smallpox, scarlet fever, diphtheria, mumps, malaria, typhoid, typhus, and occasionally cholera. The battle against epidemics began long before the bolsheviks came to power, and particularly note-worthy was the health work of the zemstvos. But epidemics continued and the death rate was high—30.2 per 1000 in 1913. Now epidemics are rare, and whenever they break out, medical personnel hasten to the scene to combat them. However remote a village from town or main highway, it is always within easy reach of medical service, and since it is free to the people, they readily go to the clinic or call a physician to their home. In consequence, the mortality rate dropped to 7.2 per 1000 in 1958, or to less than one fourth of what it had been in 1913.

One does not meet mothers in villages wailing their hearts out over the death of one child after another. The mortality rate of children up to one year of age dropped from 273 per 1000 in 1913 to 40.6 in 1958. The children one sees in the countryside may not always look as clean as the children in cities, but they appear healthy and gay. The old pastime of mothers—sitting on a bench or a log outside the house and combing lice out of a child's hair in full view of passers-by—has virtually disappeared. Even in villages where there are no nurseries or kindergartens, hygiene has penetrated so deeply that lice are not much of a problem. Nor is eye disease and the blindness that, in the absence of medical care, had formerly re-sulted. Go to any bazaar anywhere and rarely will you see a blind beggar playing a lyre to accompany his songs. Beggars are fast disappearing, even in the countryside. For one reason, there is not much blindness and therefore no excuse, as in the old days, for a man to take to begging—even were it a respectable thing to do, which it no longer is. Another contrast between Czarist and Soviet times is the condition of the faces of people. Except among the older generation, one doesn't observe any pock-marked men and women. Smallpox is rare, and when it occurs, it is properly treated. Stalin was less fortunate, and one of his personal disappointments in life, or so Muscovites would have you believe, was his pock-marked face.

Rare in the old days was the peasant who went to a dentist. The toothbrush was unknown, and toothache was treated with home remedies, with vodka, with hot tea, with a compress heavily packed around a swollen cheek. If a tooth needed to be pulled, some man in the village did the pulling with the tips of two fingers or with a piece of wire. I never heard of a barber-dentist in a Russian village.

Now the toothbrush is a must for every school child, though older people do not bother, and neither do some young people once they get out of school. But when toothache sets in, the peasant rushes to a dental clinic. Invariably the dentists in villages are women. More even than medicine, dentistry is a woman's profession in the Soviet Union.

Party functionaries have been loud in their demand for gratitude from the peasant for the accomplishments of the new health and medical services in the village. But the peasant is chary of gratitude, and even when at a mass meeting he rises and utters the expected words of thanks, he does not feel them, as I have had occasion again and again to check. He knows that he has earned the services with his sweat and his blood and that he is paying for them, however indirect the mode of payment.

Mechanization of agriculture has contributed significantly toward the re-education of the muzhik. It antedated collectivization, though on a small scale and in limited regions. With the coming of the new system of farming, it shot up sharply, growing more widespread from year to year.

Something always happens to a peasant in a backward country when he is suddenly transferred from the age of wood to the age of steel, from the wood-framed plow—of which there were over five million in Russia in 1928—to the tractor pulling an all-steel gang plow; from the wooden harrow—of which there were at least ten million in 1928—to the disk harrow; from the basket or sack over the breast, out of which to sow grain by hand, to the grain drill; from the sickle and scythe to the sowing machine and the combine. Man becomes master of something new in life, and all these machines were new to the overwhelming mass of muzhiks. Particularly impressed were the young people. To them the machine was a great adventure, unfolding a new world, in which a man at the controls performs the labor of a squad of men under the old dispensation.

I observed it in village after village, even in the grim summer of 1932. Boys and girls crowded classes in fields and in open bazaars to listen to lectures on the miracle of the tractor. They watched it taken apart, put together again, and sparked into motion. They followed it as it rolled along a field or a street, crowds of children joining the demonstration. It snapped out of the minds of the watchers many a primitive notion of work and life. It lifted them above the dark mud and the drooping *izby* into a vision of the age of science and the machine. It even challenged Grandmother's faith in the Evil One. Whatever Grandmother might say of "the horseless vehicle"—as the tractor was at one time spoken of—the Evil One had nothing to do with its hidden power to move and to roll along open spaces, as children saw with their own eyes. Styopa and Marya and Anna, sitting on the tractor and steering it around in whichever direction they chose, made a mockery of all Grandmother's tales of the doings of the Evil One, of his very existence. Man himself could perform miracles without the aid of any supernatural force, good or evil.

The greatest civilizers of the village have been the school and the book. At Moscow's Ministry of Education I was told that according to their records 74 per cent of the peasantry in Czarist times was illiterate. The figure, it would seem, is too high. But that the vast majority of muzhiks could neither read nor write need not be contested. Had it not been for World War I, universal education would have come to the village even under Czarism. But the war put an end to all plans for nation-wide schools.

Nowadays, except in scattered sections of Central Asia, illiteracy is a thing of the past. More than that—Pushkin, Lermontov, Nekrasov, Gogol, Turgenev, Tolstoy, Chekhov, are well known in the village. The literary evenings alone during the long winter months, either by out-of-town professionals or by local amateur performers, have made these names as well known as are those of the Kremlin leaders.

The most significant aspect of the Soviet educational system is that for the first time in Russian history the doors of all intermediate and higher institutions of learning and to all professions have been flung open to the village. The doors had not been closed under the Czars. After all, Chekhov was the grandson of a serf, though his father had moved up on the social scale by becoming a trader. The poet Alexey Koltsov was a peasant. The peasant poet Sergey Esenin was a product of the Czarist school system, and so are other well-known Soviet poets and novelists. But usually only richer peasants sent their sons to the gymnasium and the university. Nor were there anywhere nearly as many intermediate schools as there are now to prepare peasant sons and daughters for the university or as many universities and other higher educational institutions to attend. Besides, in the old days, however rich the peasant, he rarely educated a daughter beyond the village school.

Now every village in Russia has its quota of college graduates of both sexes, and peasants have risen to the highest positions in the country. Ivan Petrovsky, rector of Moscow University, is of peasant origin. So is Khrushchev, who loves to boast of the fact that his grandfather was a serf, his father a miner, and he himself a shepherd as a boy and then a miner. So are other members of the Presidium. Mikhail Suslov came from the village of Shokovskoye, Saratov province. Frol Kozlov was born in the village of Loshchinino, Rvazan province. Averky Aristov (appointed Ambassador to Poland in early 1961) is the son of a peasant fisherman from the village of Krasny Yar, Astrakhan province. Nuritdin Mukhitdinov, the Uzbek member of the Presidium, comes from a peasant family in a village near Tashkent. Dmitry Polyansky, chosen to the Presidium in 1960, comes from the village of Slavyanoserbsk in the Donbas country. Six of the topmost political figures in the country come from peasant homes and never would have risen to their positions of power had it not been for the free educational opportunities offered them in their younger years. I am not concerned here with the ideas and policies of these men, not even of Suslov, who—from all one gathers in Moscow—disdains the surviving individualisms of the peasant more flagrantly than does any other Kremlin personage. I am only recording the fact that sons of peasants have risen to supreme political power in the Soviet Union.

Especially impressive is the ascent of former sons of muzhiks to the highest military positions in the country. Marshals Georgi Zhukov, Ivan Konev, Kirill Meretskov, Semyon Timoshenko, Andrey Yeremenko, Alexander Vasilevsky, Vasily Chuikov, Vasily Sokolovsky, Andrey Grechko, Pavel Rotmistrov, Leonid Govorov (died 1955), are all peasants by birth.

The names of these marshals were known the world over during the war years. Though in Russia itself their names were scantily publicized—all the glory of their victorious campaigns was officially bestowed on Stalin—Russians I knew spoke jubilantly of them as "our muzhik generals." Well they might. Except for Alexander Menshikov, son of a peasant coachman, who under Peter the Great became a renowned statesman and military commander, and Kuzma Minin, the butcher from Nizhny Novgorod, who together with Prince Dmitry Pozharsky in 1612 rallied the Russian people for the expulsion of the Poles from Moscow, the commanders in chief of Russian armies were always noblemen. But in the most sanguinary of all wars Russia has ever fought, "our muzhik generals" led the many-millioned armies from triumph to triumph on one front after another.

That top political figures and marshals in the armed services are of peasant origin does not, of course, imply mitigation of Kremlin policy toward the village, except when, as after Stalin's death, there is no other alternative. But the fact that sons of muzhiks have achieved the highest political and military positions in the country, and have risen to eminence in other professions, marks a spectacular turning point in Russian history.

On July 18, 1960, in the course of an interview with Anton Chernikov, chief inspector of public schools in the Ministry of Education of the Russian Federated Republic, I asked whether his ministry or the Academy of Sciences has kept a record of peasants who since the coming of the Soviets have risen to high positions in science and other professions. "We've never kept such a record," Chernikov replied, "nor has the Academy of Sciences or any other organization. It is too common an occurrence, and nobody seems to pay any attention to it. I, for example, come from what you'd call a 'bear's corner' in Siberia—a village that was several days' journey by horse to the nearest railroad station. But I went to a village school, then to college, became a teacher, and here I am—heading my department in the Ministry of Education. Offhand I'd say that at least one half of the people in our country who now hold leading positions in industry, science, and other professions are of peasant origin. I have no figures to prove it, but that's my impression."

The rise of the peasant to eminence, even in literature, might have come about had a non-bolshevik government ruled Russia after the Czar was overthrown, and without the tragedies and catastrophes that bolshevism has again and again visited on the village. One often hears this argument from Russian émigré intellectuals, from Western Sovietophobes, and from sober Western students of the Soviet Union. Manifestly Russia wouldn't have stood still even had the Czar remained in power. New opportunities for advancement, especially in education, would have opened up for the peasantry. But history followed its own course. Who knows what Russia and the world would have been like had the Decembrist revolution of 1825 triumphed over the armies of Nicholas I? With her sturdy manpower, her wealth of untapped human gifts, her vast territories, her rich natural resources, Russia might have become the America of Europe and the world might never have heard of bolshevism. But it did not happen that way, neither in 1825 nor during the revolution of 1905, and in 1917 the bolsheviks triumphed. One may quarrel with history, but one cannot alter it. One has to take Russia as she is and not as she might have been. Russia is no Great Britain, whose Edmund Burke would have no reform without justice. "The fate of the Russian people," writes Nikolai Berdyayev in the *Origin of Russian Communism,* "has been an unhappy one and full of suffering. It has developed a catastrophic tempo through interruption and change in its type of civilization."

Out of the catastrophic tempo incident to the bolshevik revolution has come a new peasantry, whose innate gifts have been unshackled as never before in Russian history. "By terrible violence," writes Berdyayev, "[the bolshevik revolution] liberated forces that were latent in the masses and summoned them to take their share in the making of history; therein lies its significance"—a far greater significance for the future than anybody now alive can possibly envision.

15.

WOMEN
The Heroic Sex

"We willingly agree that nature created women primarily for love; but it doesn't follow that she was born for this alone; on the contrary . . . she is meant to function in the same walks of life as men."

These words were written in 1843 by Vissarion Byelinsky, often called the father of the Russian intelligentsia. The celebrated writer laments the fact that outside the province of love women had no outlet for their gifts and energies.

"The history of civilization would have moved ten times faster had the true, devoted, and powerful mind with which nature has endowed women . . . been allowed natural performance." So wrote Nikolai Chernyshevsky, author of the sociological novel *What Is to Be Done?* which became the bible of nineteenth-century Russian feminism. The novel appeared about the time Susan B. Anthony and Lucy Stone were enlivening the American political scene with their boisterous battle for woman suffrage. But suffrage alone could never have satisfied Vera Pavlovna, Chernyshevsky's heroine. "The most important thing," she says, "is independence: to do as I please, to live as I wish, without asking anybody, without demanding anything from anybody, without being dependent on anybody. That's the way I want to live." Chernyshevsky was advocating the liberation of woman from the prevailing restraints of state, church, parents, society, so that she would be free to fulfill herself in both her professional and her love life.

In 1859 Ivan Goncharov published his novel *Oblomov*, which depicts the apathy, indolence, hopelessness, of a Russian landed gentleman in the last days of serfdom. In contrast to Oblomov stands Olga, the heroine, a woman of initiative, energy, decisiveness. Enraptured with her character, Nikolai Dobrolyubov, the famed literary critic and social philosopher, wrote, "In her we perceive a suggestion of a new Russian life; from her we expect words that will scatter and burn up Oblomovism. A purely personal and family life cannot satisfy her; a tranquil and happy life frightens her . . . like a quagmire that threatens to suck you in and swallow you."

Oblomovism was a malady of the male soul. There is no suggestion of it among women in literature. Quite the contrary: for steadfastness of purpose, devotion to duty or love, courage to act, fearlessness of consequences, it is not the men but the women in Russian poetry and fiction who carry off the honors. To this day Russian eyes moisten when they read Nekrasov's long poem *Russian Women*. Tenderly Nekrasov recounts the stories of Princesses Troubetskaya and Volkonskaya, wives of two leaders, both aristocrats, of the Decembrist revolution of 1825, whose lives Czar Nicholas I spared but who were banished to the faraway Siberian mining town of Nerchinsk. In defiance of the pleas of parents, of the wishes of the Czar, the gentleborn young wives journeyed in carts and sleds over the wild Siberian roads to join their husbands in the faraway mining town. To Nekrasov the princesses symbolized a heroic quality in Russian women; hence the title of his emotion-shaking poem.

No Russian author has so glowingly depicted this quality in Russian women as Turgenev has. I have heard hardheaded Communists speak affectionately of the author's heroines as "Turgenev's beautiful little girls." Exquisitely feminine, pure of heart, movingly romantic, they manifest a moral courage and a strength of character that is in sharp contrast to the glib-tongued, ineffectual men they love or who love them. For love or for a cause, the educated Russian woman, as portrayed in the literature and reflected in the revolutionary movement of Russia's nineteenth century, was ready to sacrifice worldly comforts and pleasures, even life.

Spokesmen of the pre-revolutionary liberal intelligentsia accepted women as their social and intellectual equals. At no time did they regard women as rivals in professional careers or for professional honors. They championed the right of women to cultivate their inborn gifts on a basis of equality with men. This alone precluded the rise of a feminist movement comparable to that in the Western world. There are no Susan B. Anthonys and Lucy Stones in Russia's nineteenth century. In the revolutionary movement women fought side by side with men for the emancipation of all Russian humanity, regardless of religion, race, nationality, or, of course, sex. However violently the revolutionary parties wrangled over aims and methods, precepts and practices, there was no discord among them on the subject of the future position of women once the revolution had triumphed over Czarism: women would suffer from no civil or social disabilities whatever, as they did in Western countries. The political battle of the sexes as it developed in the Western world didn't touch Russia.

I have gone to some length to present what appear to me to be the cardinal features of the so-called woman question in the Russia of the past, because I believe it is essential to an understanding of the position of women in Soviet society.

Article 122 in the Soviet Constitution reads: "Women in the U.S.S.R. are accorded equal rights with men in all spheres of economic, governmental, cultural, political, and other public activities."

The article gives expression to ideas which Byelinsky had enunciated long before Lenin was born. Had the Social Revolutionaries, the Mensheviks, or even the bourgeois Constitutional Democrats won the battle for power after the overthrow of the Czar in February 1917, women wouldn't and couldn't have been denied the rights that the Soviet Constitution accords them.

During my more recent stay in Moscow I discussed the subject at some length with a retired professor of science, an old friend, who had once belonged to the Social Revolutionary party. The gentle, stoop-shouldered, white-haired old man glowed with rapture as he spoke of the great deeds of women in the revolutionary movement in Czarist times. "Sofya Perovskaya," he rhapsodized, "Sofya Leshern, Sofya Ginsburg, Vera Zasulich, Vera Figner—these precious Sofyas and Veras, sacred names in our history—how I love their memory!" Then he added soberly, "Remember one thing, had any other party but the bolsheviks come to power after the fall of the Czar, women never would have been allowed to work in mines and in heavy industry."

"Do they still?" I asked. Toward the end of the war, Muscovites I knew firmly believed that once hostilities ended, women would be liberated from all the arduous and hazardous tasks they performed during the fighting years, and now in Moscow and Leningrad I had been told over and over that women were no longer permitted to work in mines or at any heavy and hazardous tasks. At the office of the Woman's Peace Committee in Moscow I was presented with a book in English which was a report of the international seminar that was held in Moscow in 1956 on the subject of equality of women in the Soviet Union. In this book I had read, "The Soviet code of labor laws prohibits the employment of women in heavy and harmful work (Art. 129, C.L.L.), such as smelting and pouring molten metals, rolling hot metal, cleaning gas mains. Women may not be employed in a number of branches in the railway, sea, and local transport services, as well as in mining, construction, and municipal economy."

Without saying a word, the professor arose, lifted off the bookshelf a blue paper-covered pamphlet, turned the pages, and putting his thumb to a paragraph, said, "Read this." Among other things I read, "On Komsomol work orders over 40,000 boys and girls *went off to work underground* [my italics] in the mines of Donbas, Kuzbas, Kusnetsk, Karaganda, and in the suburban Moscow coal basin." Turning to the title page, I learned that the pamphlet was the published address of the then forty-year-old Alexander Shelepin, first secretary of the All-Union Komsomol, which he delivered on April 15, 1958, at the thirteenth congress of the organization. It seemed incredible that the top officer of the nineteen million Komsomols would publicly boast of a performance which, according to assurances I had been given and the book I had read, was a flagrant violation of the Soviet labor code. Yet only about a month before the opening of the Twenty-first Congress of the Communist party, Alexander Shelepin was promoted to the office of chief of State Security, one of the most strategic law-enforcement agencies in the country.

The Twenty-first Congress has come and gone. Speaker after speaker, including Khrushchev, spoke out vigorously against the employment of women in heavy and hazardous jobs. But in *Pravda* of March 8, 1959, Yelena Konnonenko, a Soviet journalist who for years has had the distinction of being the most sentimental glamorizer of the champion working girl, tells the story of a team of six girls who work in the foundry of the Likhachev Automobile Works in Moscow. Their job is to pour "hot mixtures" into molds. The work, the author tells the reader, "is strenuous . . . requiring no little exertion of muscles, eyes, and nerves." But mornings the girls walk to the foundry "as though carried by the wind." One would imagine, she writes, that "they are hurrying to a ball, a date, a skiing party"— so eager are they to pour more "hot mixtures" into molds. The girls do even more—they decide to contribute a Sunday to work on the construction of a new stadium. But one of them, Svetlana Brykova, "a frail, delicate, white-faced" girl, fails to show up. Neither her fragility nor her pallor saves her from a sharp rebuke by her teammates.

Girls, of course, get equal pay with men for equal work; and to earn a man's wages they have to work like men. When young and strong and even when not so strong, they do not seem to mind heavy work. In the journal *Yunost* ("Youth") for January 1958 there is a story of two Moscow girls who journeyed to Kalym in northern Siberia to work in a gold mine. A photograph shows one of the girls in a miner's outfit with a miner's lamp. The legend underneath reads, "What a proud thing to be a miner!" The author of the article pictures the girl as so attractive and so delicately built that she could play Margarita in Goethe's *Faust*. But while the author extols the girl's courage, the girl herself was frank enough to admit that she and her friend came to Kalym because they could earn more money at gold digging than at working as plasterers in Moscow. With their 1700 (old) rubles a month, they could buy silks and velvets, which they never could afford on their wages as plasterers.

Moscow's *Literaturnaya Gazeta* has been waging a vigorous campaign for the enforcement of the Soviet labor code in the employment of women. It has spoken harshly of journalists and novelists who romanticize the girl who performs and surpasses man in muscular work. But the campaign has not stopped the Komsomol from mobilizing girls for work in coal mines and in the construction of blast furnaces, machine shops, hydroelectric plants, highways, railroads; and it has not thwarted the sentimental Yelena Konnonenko from idealizing feminine muscular achievement.

Besides, there are the girls themselves, feminine enough to yearn for silk and velvet dresses, nylon stockings, polished calfskin shoes, fine perfumes. "Work like a man to become the woman you want to be" might be the slogan of these girls.

The Westerner who comes to Russia for the first time is instantly struck by the sight of women doing what is to him man's work. Women roll the ramp for the arriving plane. They sweep the streets. They wield pick and shovel, spade and crowbar. They lay bricks and carry lumber; they are painters, plasterers, plumbers. They load and unload freight at railroad stations.

It must be remembered that Russia was and still is essentially a peasant country, and peasant women have always done man's work on the land. My own mother did everything from milking cows to pitching hay and carrying heavy sacks of grain. The tradition persists. The girls who lay bricks or carry lumber or work at any other job on construction do not appear discontented or unhappy. Speak to them, and they are lively and cheerful. They work shorter hours than they would on a collective or state farm and make more money. They can buy better clothes and enjoy a gayer life in the city than they would in the village. The unmarried woman, whatever her job in industry and on construction, has no reason to complain of monotony and dullness after work hours. There are always plenty of social and cultural diversions—dances, amateur theatrical performances, concerts, games, picnics. Whatever the failings of the Komsomol or the trade unions, they strive to offer young workers a varied and cheerful social life. But in all my conversations with Komsomol and trade-union functionaries, they never betrayed the least awareness of the fact that the heavy and hazardous tasks which girls were performing were a violation of the very spirit of the revolutionary movement that had for nearly a century been fighting Czarist autocracy.

Yet when a working girl gets married and bears children, she is so burdened with household duties that she has little or no time for a social life. Russian women love children and make excellent mothers. But being a mother in Russia is a strenuous and time-consuming affair, especially as men regard it an indignity to help with the housework. Publicly and privately working mothers have for years been clamoring for help from their husbands in household chores. With the rarest of exceptions, notably among young people, the Soviet male has refused to heed the clamor. Even as I am writing these lines, I have before me the Moscow daily *Sovietskaya Rossiya* (March 16, 1960), which publishes an angry letter, from four mothers who work in the Saratov ball-bearing factory, against the privileged position of husbands in the home.

"In the factory," these women write, "we work like our husbands, often in the same shop. . . . But in the home the duties are unequally divided. . . . Mornings the preparation of breakfast is a woman's affair. Taking the children to school or kindergarten is again a woman's job. To clean the table and wash the dishes—what man would take it into his head to do it? To make the bed and clean the room—again the duty of a woman. And evenings after work—to buy the food, cook dinner or supper, do the washing, ironing, mending—these aren't a man's business. . . . And when you ask a husband to help, the answer is always the same: 'Do you want me to do a woman's work? Why, the neighbors would laugh at me.'"

Ask a Russian working mother which day of the week she works hardest, and invariably she will say Sunday. During the day of rest the husband goes off to visit friends, walk in the park, relax himself any way he chooses, but the wife stays at home to catch up with household chores. Lucky is the working married woman who has a babushka to share the burden of housework. The one certain fact is that she cannot afford a servant, and even when there are nurseries and kindergartens for children while she is at work, she still has her heavy burden of housework when she returns from the office or factory.

True enough, the state surrounds a married woman with special care. Forty-six days before childbirth and for a like number of days afterward, she is on leave drawing the full amount of her wages. All medical care is free, and rare is the woman nowadays who bears children at home. She goes to a hospital or maternity home, which in the village may be only a simple cottage but which is always clean, airy, and hygienic. Then there are the subsidies and honors, presented at length in an earlier chapter, that are conferred on mothers of large families.

But all the aids and subsidies do not solve the working mother's basic problem, which is overwork. No wonder that Maria Kovrigina, Minister of Health at the time, in her address to the Twentieth Party Congress, was constrained to say, "You do not need to tell me that a working mother doesn't have enough sleep, doesn't rest during the day, doesn't rest enough on her days off, and consequently cannot restore her lost energies as she should." She recommended that working women with children work only six hours a day and be allowed two days of rest a week without loss in pay. "I assure you, comrades," the Minister of Health said, "women with children have earned this."

Kovrigina's plea was ignored by the Twentieth and again by the Twenty-first Party Congress. However large the families, working mothers must wait until the work week is shortened for all workers before they can hope for relief from the strenuous double burden they bear—as workers and mothers.

Lenin never had counted on the condition that prevails in the Soviet Union today. In discussing the participation of women in "general productive labor," he wrote (*Pravda*, November 6, 1919), "This, of course, doesn't mean that women must be exactly equal to men in productivity of labor, amount of labor, its duration and conditions." In Lenin's day even night work for women was banned. But Lenin might never have insisted on special consideration for women workers for all the attention the Kremlin even today has accorded it.

To help women take full measure and make full use of the rights that were originally granted them, the Central Committee of the party organized in 1918 a special Woman's Section (*Zhenotdel*). Five of the most eminent women party members were selected to head this section: Alexandra Kollontay, Alexandra Artukhina, Yelena Stassova, Klavdia Nikolayeva, and Iness Arman. To those who remember the Russia of the twenties, the very names of these women bring back an age when the voice of women as women, facing situations pertaining to their sex, was loud and eloquent. But Stalin stilled this voice. In 1929 he abolished the Woman's Section of the Central Committee.

Had it been permitted to function and to exercise the authority that was originally given it, it would not in my judgment have been necessary for the Minister of Health, who incidentally was retired soon afterward and replaced by a man, to inform a Party Congress that working mothers didn't get enough sleep. The Woman's Section was vigilant in defending mothers against encroachments on their physical welfare. But as a woman in Moscow told me, at heart Stalin was anti-feminist. "Oh," she explained, "he wanted us as workers and in careers so we could work hard to help fulfill the Plans. But he kept us in our places, never appointed women to high political office. And who ever saw him with his wife, when she was alive, at the opera or at a public gathering? There was something strangely oriental in Stalin's attitude toward women."

During Stalin's years the only wife of an eminent Soviet personage any of us were privileged to meet at diplomatic receptions was Madame Litvinov, or Ivy Low, as we called her. But then Ivy is an Englishwoman and Litvinov had lived in England too long to emulate Stalin's example in the treatment of his wife.

It was not until Khrushchev rose to power that wives of leaders began to share some of the social limelight of their husbands. But Khrushchev is too impassioned in his drive to surpass America in industrial and agricultural production to act on the recommendations of the former Soviet Minister of Health. The new nurseries and kindergartens he is building are only a partial solution of the problem. In industry women make up 45 per cent of all workers, and in construction, where they do the heaviest work, 30 per cent. Those of them who are married and have children would leave their jobs in droves if their husbands could support their families.

The career woman is in a somewhat different position, and I vividly remember the exhilaration that swept Russia in the early years of the revolution when the doors to all schools and colleges, to all careers and professions outside of the military, were flung wide open for women. It was the first time in Russian history that anything like this had happened on so grand a scale. Women responded with fervor. I can still see the broad-hipped, deep-bosomed girls from the provinces, freshly arrived in Moscow to enter some college. Too poor to hire an *izvoshchik* to drive them to the dormitory, they rode the streetcar or walked, their belongings stuffed into grain sack, wicker basket, or square wooden box slung over their shoulders—strong, apple-cheeked, determined girls, too elated over the prospect of sitting in college classrooms to mind the discomfort of lugging their own baggage, to mind anything, even living in a crowded room, sometimes with boys (as they did in those days), and sleeping on straw mattresses on the floor. The book became the symbol of a new life and a new glory to masses of girls in the humblest circumstances from one end of the country to the other. Byelinsky's dream of a time when women would enjoy the right and the privilege of cultivating their innate gifts, and no longer be obliged to fulfill themselves solely in their love life, had at last become a reality.

After forty-three years of revolution, the achievements of the Soviet career woman are unparalleled in any other country. According to figures as of the beginning of 1960, nearly one third of the teaching personnel in institutions of higher learning are women, though only 6 per cent of them have risen to full professorships.

There are 110,000 women in the sciences; 732,000 women are engineers and trained technicians; 13,000 are directors of industry, chief engineers, or their deputies; 28,000 hold the degree of doctor of science or of candidate of science. Forty per cent of farm experts— agronomists, livestock specialists, veterinarians—are women and a somewhat like number are in forestry.

Women make up about one third of the members of the Bar and 40 per cent of the judges. They dominate the teaching profession in the public schools, constituting 69 per cent, among them 100,000 principals or directors. By an overwhelming majority they also outnumber men in the professions of economics, statistics, planning, and trading.

Unlike women in Western countries, they greatly exceed men in the medical profession: of the 362,000 physicians in the country, 300,000 are women—a ratio of almost five to one.

"Our women," a woman physician in Leningrad said to me, "are very maternal, and ministering to the sick and helpless fulfills their maternal proclivities." Woman physicians are reputed to have a warmer bedside manner than men, though in surgery they do not rival men.

In all the health services in the country which include administrators, *feldshery* (doctors' assistants), nurses, and other attendants, women make up 85 per cent of the personnel.

Men patients manifest no antipathy toward women physicians and consult them as readily as they would male physicians, even in sexual ailments. When I asked a woman physician who practices in a Siberian industrial town whether men who suffer from syphilis come to her for treatment, she was astonished by the question. "Why shouldn't they?" was her reply. "Our men do not choose doctors on the basis of their sex."

The profession of foreign languages—interpreters, teachers, translators, secretaries—attracts women as it doesn't men. To men it is a feminine profession, even more so than medicine, and they usually shun it except when they study science or prepare for academic careers in which the knowledge of foreign languages is of particular value.

But in science, women do not begin to approach men in distinction and achievement. They constitute about one third of the postgraduate students in scientific and research institutes. Yet with some notable exceptions—such as Novoselova in chemistry, Blinova in geophysics, Koshina in mathematics, Prikhodko in physics, Bazarova in biology, and some others—they do not rise to top rank; and it is not because there is male prejudice against them. A teacher in Moscow University told me that the higher realms of science, particularly chemistry, physics, and mathematics, are too difficult for women. An American scientist who has observed the work of women in both Russian and American research institutes ventured the opinion that in science men have greater originality and audacity than women. A distinguished psychiatrist in Leningrad held that it was a question of hormones, and his wife, a biologist by profession, fully agreed with him. But whatever the reason, the Soviet Union has demonstrated that women are no match for men in the natural sciences.

The one profession in which, since Lenin's death, Russian women have not been accorded an opportunity to test their gifts is politics. The real levers of political power have been in the hands of men. Under Stalin not a single woman was represented in the Politburo, the highest functioning body in the country. Under Khrushchev only one woman, Yekaterina Furtseva, has risen to membership in the Presidium of the party, which in 1952 superseded the Politburo as the seat of highest authority. Of the 133 members of the Central Committee elected in 1956, only three were women; of the 122 candidate members, again only three were women.

In each province or region, the first secretary of the party is the man of supreme power, virtually dictator of his realm. Not a single woman holds this eminent position. Thus in the highest seats of party power, though constituting the vast majority of the population —122 women for every 100 men—women are barely represented, or almost excluded.

On the state level the picture is no brighter. In the Soviet Council of Ministers (Cabinet), out of some sixty members there is only one woman, again Yekaterina Furtseva, who was chosen Minister of Culture on May 5, 1960.

Only in the All-Union Supreme Soviet (Parliament), whose function it is formally to approve and to apply party decisions, are women fairly well represented. They constitute 27 per cent of the deputies. Yet of the thirty-five members in the Presidium, the executive committee of the Supreme Soviet, only two are women. Of the four other functioning committees in the Supreme Soviet, men outnumber women in a ratio of twenty to one. Nor is there a single woman ambassador or deputy to the Foreign Minister. The Kremlin prefers to entrust men with the task of wrestling with the ever critical problems of foreign policy.

On January 25, 1960, in her address at Chandigarh, capital of the Punjab, Furtseva devoted the major portion of her speech to the glorification of the position of women in the Soviet Union. She spoke of them as "free and equal members of our society. Whoever has visited our country knows that women command all rights and that . . . in her social and political activities she enjoys unqualified and unlimited equality with men." At no time did she or Khrushchev, in all his speeches in Asia or anywhere else, ever refer to the virtual exclusion of women from the decisions of the highest party and state councils. Consequently, in "political activities" the equality of which Furtseva boasted is a monumental myth.

Only in the lower ranks of state and party organizations do women play a significant role. They are chairmen of village and town soviets, chairmen of collective farms. They are secretaries of district party committees and sometimes second and third secretaries in provinces and regions. They are prominent in trade-union leadership, in the Komsomol, in factory political work—as teachers of party doctrine, lecturers on foreign affairs, and directors of clubs. In these and similar positions they encounter no discrimination.

On both recent journeys to the Soviet Union I was interested to learn whether career women whose husbands earned high enough salaries to support the family were tiring of their careers and preferred to stay at home and look after their families. I discovered that the tendency among those with a college education to abandon their careers is stronger than at any time in the prewar years. But to the best of my knowledge the percentage of those who do so is comparatively small. "Give up work? What nonsense," a woman economist said. "I'd be bored to death." In the city of Minsk an engineer-inventor who earns a very high salary told me that he had several times requested his forty-year-old wife, a construction engineer, to leave her work, but she refused. "I might become so tiresome," he quoted her as having said, "you'd be bored with me." Other women I interviewed expressed themselves the same way. They do not want "to rust away" in the home, as a woman biologist put it. They enjoy being useful and "creative."

Now as in Czarist times the Russian career woman encounters no opposition from men. Not once in all the years I have known career women in Russia have I heard any of them say that men regard them as competitors or resent taking orders from them. Nor have I ever heard a college girl say that being intellectual frightens men away from her. Whatever the historical reasons for it, the fact is that neither Russian men nor women have ever held the view that the woman intellectual is in danger of losing her sex appeal.

My most illuminating interview with a highly placed woman in Moscow was with Madame Bondarenko. She is secretary to the already mentioned Woman's Peace Committee, which is a go-between with women's organizations in sixty-six foreign countries. She is a short buxom woman in her early forties, with pink cheeks, a round face, and dancing blue eyes. She radiated a spirit of ebullience that enlivened the very atmosphere of her large, neat, and brightly decorated office. When I asked her whether the Soviet working mother was not working too hard, she didn't burst into a *Pravda*-style editorial about the joys and glories of labor. "Yes," she candidly admitted, "our mothers work too hard. By right women shouldn't work more than four hours a day. They should have more time for books, theater, music, art, personal care, and comfortable homemaking. The time will come when our women, all of them, will work only four hours a day. But for the present we simply cannot afford it."

I asked her if anything had happened since my previous visit to Russia to liberate women from work in mines and other heavy industry.

"It's forbidden by law," she assured me, "to employ women underground or at any hazardous job, and we are enforcing the law."

As I had not yet read Shelepin's speech at the Thirteenth Komsomol Congress, I didn't dispute her words.

Then I shifted the discussion to another aspect of the subject.

"Toward the end of the war," I said, "while visiting a village in the Kuban, I asked girls at a Komsomol gathering which literary character they would want to be like. With scarcely a word of dissent they named Natasha in Tolstoy's *War and Peace*."

Madame Bondarenko's round blue eyes glowed with pleasure. "Of course," she said. "Natasha is such a precious character that our girls want to be like her. They want to be as feminine, as gentle, as spirited, as well-mannered, and as attractive as Tolstoy's heroine."

"Why, then," I said, "is there no woman heroine in Soviet fiction even remotely resembling Natasha or any of Turgenev's heroines?"

Her face clouded as she answered. "You'd better put the question to your fellow writers at the Writers' Union. We women are very much offended with them for their failure to portray us adequately as women. It isn't enough to show us as heroic workers and patriots. I was in the war. I served with an antiaircraft battery. Artillery shells fell all around us, but we didn't run away. We weren't afraid to fight and die for our country. But we are also women and we are resentful that our feminine nature is so ineffectually presented in our fiction."

I didn't go to the Writers' Union. It wouldn't have done any good. Privately authors may admit that they are doing women an injustice. Publicly they insist (not all of them, of course) as does *Pravda* that in these days of the Soviet march "from socialism to communism" the heroine must be vested with the virtues of "a builder of communism." Translated into American colloquialism, this means a Soviet-style "go-getter"—a woman who outdoes other women, and men too, in laying bricks, cutting metal, fattening pigs. It is these women who make headlines in the daily newspapers, whose pictures accompany the rapturous stories written about their heroic achievements.

One hears Russian readers speak of the heroines in Soviet fiction as "cardboard heroines." Madame Bondarenko didn't use the expression, but her words implied that she was tiring of them; she wanted heroines in fiction to be flesh-and-blood women, and an increasing number of poets and novelists, especially of the younger generation, are bowing to the tastes of the reading public.

I must confess that I have always regarded Russian women superior to the men. They are not only better mannered, they are more dependable. Whenever I arranged an interview with a woman, I was certain she would honor it. Whenever I arranged an appointment with a man, he didn't always keep it.

In peace and war Russian women have been at least as courageous as the men and much more self-sacrificing. Through crisis after crisis, tragedy after tragedy, they held the family together and all the values associated with it. Ironically, the Kremlin, which had once spurned these values, now hails them with fervor. Through the years of industrialization women have stood side by side with men, toiling as hard as men. Without them the Plans never could have been fulfilled, nor could the war against Nazi Germany have been won.

"I do not know what would have happened to Leningrad," P. Kapitsa, a well-known author-editor, told me, "if it hadn't been for our women. They showed greater power of survival than men, didn't die from hunger in such large numbers. They kept the munition factories running day and night. Bombs and artillery shells didn't terrify them, and the flow of munitions to the front lines never stopped."

If during the nine-hundred-day siege of Leningrad, which took a toll of over a million lives from hunger, women showed greater physical vitality than men, they are also, I have always felt, more flexible-minded than men. As a rule they are not as fanatically doctrinaire as men and speak more candidly than men do, whether about the position of their sex in Soviet society, literature and art, or any other subject. A foreigner who speaks Russian need only walk into a Moscow courtyard and engage the women there in conversation to discover how much more he learns from them about everyday life than he ever could from any official interviews with men, however highly placed.

If women had their way, the Soviet regime would be more liberal than it is in foreign and domestic policy, if only because they feel the pressures of daily living more intimately than men do. Women wouldn't be in a hurry to outdo or even to catch up with America in every field of production at the expense of "enough sleep" for working mothers. The reduction of the work day to seven hours has been of slight help to them. They still bear the double burden as mothers and workers. Nor are they exempted from speed-up methods of work.

It is my conviction that the Kremlin's plan, initiated by Khrushchev, to put all children between the ages of seven and fifteen into boarding schools will never materialize. Except for mothers of large families that are poor and live in crowded quarters, women, whether shop workers or college graduates, do not speak well of the plan. Overwhelmingly they do not want to be separated from sons and daughters at the age of seven even if they may come home for weekends and holidays. "Boys and girls," a woman biologist told me, "are so young at that age. They need a mother's affection and a father's guidance all the time. No teachers, however good they may be, can take the place of fathers and mothers for them."

If women had their way, the youth journal *Smena* (No. 13, 1960) never would have published a letter from a girl named Tamara Vsendina, who worked as an engineer in the turret of a high giant excavator and fell to the ground together with the turret. Women wouldn't permit a Tamara Vsendina to work at a job like that. The accident happened only thirteen days after Tamara got married. Doctors had despaired of her life, and for two months she lay motionless in a hospital. Expert surgery finally restored her health.

Soviet publications never report accidents except when a moral or political issue is involved. In this instance the girl complained that her husband, convinced that she would remain an invalid, ceased to call on her at the hospital. But when he learned that she was recovering, he came and asked her to forgive him. She refused to do so and asks the editors whether she acted properly.

If women had their way, not one girl—least of all a mother—would be working in mines or at any hazardous occupation. Madame Bondarenko, like other official personages I queried, assured me that no longer were women employed in these occupations. But a pamphlet[1] I picked up in a Moscow bookshop contradicts the assurance. The pamphlet is a popular interpretation of the new pension law and was published by the Ministry of Finance. On page 37 one reads: "For women who work underground under hazardous conditions of labor, in hot shops, . . . or women who do heavy labor in the oil industry, in geological service, at power stations, the retiring age has

[1] M. Voluisky and E. Maslova, *Pensionnoye obezpechiniye v SSSR* (Gosfinizdat, Moscow, 1958).

been reduced from forty-five to forty years and the length of service from twenty to fifteen years."

Further evidence that contradicts official Soviet propaganda that women have been liberated from work in mines is recorded in Soviet fiction. Here is a short story by the well-known writer Anatoly Kleshchenko (*Zvezda* ["Star"], July 1960). Katya Taravkina, the heroine, goes to Siberia in search of exciting adventure. She comes to a mining town, Prostorny, and the only work she can find is at the pumps in a mine. "Girls," writes the author, "work not only at the pumping centers and at the substations, not only at stop cages and elevators. The specialties of Katya's friends bore names that she had never before known: ore conductor, firing woman, haulage woman. . . . After finishing work the girls rushed into the pumping station to look into the mirror in a well-lighted place—after all, it was improper to come out of the mine with faces smudged and hair uncombed."

For years now, women have been crying out against the law of July 1944, which lifts all responsibility from a man for fathering a child out of legal marriage. Instances of heartbreaking tragedies that result from the injustice of this law are no secret to anybody in the Soviet Union, least of all to readers of Moscow's *Komsomolka*. Here, for example, is a young man named Ivan Vasilyev, in the Siberian village of Kustanay. He isn't just a farm worker; he is a schoolteacher and secretary of the local Komsomol. For a year he had been courting a girl named Shura Kolganova. Shura was so much in love with him that she refused dates with other boys, and when Ivan asked her to marry him she of course said yes. But—she had a son by him before they were married. Twice Ivan came to see her and brought little gifts for his son. Then he abandoned both of them. Pressure on him to marry Shura did no good. So while "Shura sits by the cradle forgotten by everybody, Ivan struts the village street and smiles as though nothing had happened." Who knows how many Shuras and Ivans there are in the Soviet Union? But the male hierarchy has been either too busy or too callous to bother about the woes of the Shuras.

One evening, during my last days in Moscow, I climbed five flights of cement stairs and rang a bell. "Who is there?" a girl's voice inquired. "An old friend of Alexander Dmitriyevich," I replied. I heard the click of a bolt and the turn of a key. The door opened halfway, and a dark-haired, big-eyed girl with thick black hair cut short gave me such a suspicious look that I wondered if I had come to the right house. To make certain I had not erred, I asked if this was where Alexander Dmitriyevich lived. Holding the door half open, as though ready to clap it shut, the girl said, "He is not at home. He and mother have gone to the country."

"You are Lilla," I said.

"Yes," she answered. I told her who I was and her expression changed. "What a surprise," she said. "So sorry Papa and Mamma are not home." She invited me to come inside.

I had become acquainted with the family during the war years and now and then brought Lilla an old copy of *Life* which I managed to obtain from some American in Moscow. Lilla was seven years old when I had come to bid the family good-by before my departure for America in January 1945. Now she was a full-grown young woman, a little statuesque, with long eyelashes and a sun-tanned angular face. There was a friend with Lilla and she introduced us. Her name was Lyuba—a tall, slender girl with reddish hair, a freckled face, and wide-open gray eyes. Lilla explained that she herself had been in the country and had come to town for some library books in biology, in which she was specializing at the university. Lyuba, who lived in the same house on a lower floor, was studying medicine.

A thick book lay open on the table. It was a Russian translation of the poems of Nizami, Persia's celebrated twelfth-century poet. The girls had been reading *Laila and Majnun*, often spoken of as Persia's *Romeo and Juliet*. I told them I had been searching bookshops in Moscow and Leningrad for a Russian translation of Nizami and other Persian poets and had not found a single copy of anything, anywhere.

"You won't," said Lyuba. "People buy up these books as soon as they appear in the stores. Father bought this copy in Baku, and Lilla and I love it."

Lilla served tea, cheese and sausage sandwiches, and Russian-style cookies, and we drank and ate as we talked. Why, Lilla asked, had I not come to the Youth Festival in July 1957? It was such an extraordinary event and would have interested a writer like myself, who specialized in Russian subjects. Both girls spoke with fervor of what the festival had meant to them—freely meeting young people from all over the world for the first time in their lives—talking to them, walking and playing with them, singing and flirting with them—yes, and falling in love, Lyuba with an Egyptian boy, Lilla with a French boy—a passing infatuation, yet something to remember.

Then Lyuba asked whether I knew Eleanor Roosevelt, whom she had seen once in the street in Moscow. "She must be a remarkable woman," she said.

"Your Furtseva," I said, "must be a remarkable woman, too. The first woman to be in the Presidium."

"She isn't popular," Lilla answered.

"No, she isn't," Lyuba interjected. "She is just—well, a cold soul. The popular woman in Moscow is Mironova."

I hadn't heard of Mironova and asked who she was.

"A deputy mayor of the city,"[2] Lyuba answered, "very handsome, feminine, warm, public-spirited—we all adore her."

"When you say 'we,'" I asked, "do you mean girl students?"

"Everybody," Lilla said. "It's impossible not to adore her, she is so beautiful in looks, in character, in spirit, and she helps people so much—an ideal Soviet woman."

"And you don't think Furtseva is an ideal Soviet woman?" I asked.

"She must be very capable or she wouldn't be in the Presidium," Lilla said. "But—I don't know—she doesn't touch you here," laying her hand on her heart.

"I suppose Ulanova touches you here," I said, laying a hand on my heart.

"Oh, Ulanova!" Lilla exclaimed. "She is like somebody above this earth, a dream woman—beautiful, romantic—she breaks your heart in her role of Juliet. We adore Ulanova but in a different way from Mironova. You see, Mironova is so earthly." For some minutes the girls were lost in a discussion of Mironova and Ulanova, and to an observer like myself the significant feature in the talk was the appeal both women made because of their femininity and their character. Both girls, incidentally, were strongly career-minded; Lilla determined to do scientific work in biology, Lyuba to practice medicine, not in Moscow or any other city, which is the aspiration of the usual medical

[2] In July 1959 she was appointed to the Soviet United Nations delegation.

student, but in a village. "That's where I can do most good for my people," the slender girl said simply and sincerely.

As we continued our conversation, I learned that both girls favored the revival of the old Russian custom of men kissing a woman's hand. "It's about time our men were gallant to women," said Lilla. "I hate rudeness in men."

"Men should be *gentlemen*," Lyuba added, using the English word.

"Do men in America kiss women's hands?" Lilla asked.

"No, America never knew the custom," I said.

"No?" Lilla was surprised.

I shook my head.

"The French boy at the festival kissed my hand all the time," she said, "and I loved it. I'm sorry I didn't get to know any American boys."

"An American boy would kiss you on the lips," I said.

"If I'd let him!" Lilla burst out laughing.

"Wouldn't you?"

She reflected and said, "I might if I liked him a lot. I'd have to like him a lot—really."

We shifted the conversation to books, and I asked who was their favorite heroine in Soviet fiction.

The girls discussed the subject between themselves at length and with animation, their emotion-charged voices a delight to hear. They finally chose Axinya, heroine in Sholokhov's novel *And Quiet Flows the Don*.

It was a revealing choice—not of a glorified girl tractor driver or cloth weaver or of a Communist hurrah girl, but of a woman of women, the tender, sturdy, passionate, martyred Axinya, felled by a bullet in her flight on horseback with the man she loved from the triumphant bolshevik armies during the civil war.

Further I asked whether they approved of the new school law that required a heavy schedule of farm or factory labor as a qualification for college.

"Our mothers," said Lyuba, "were more upset about it than we were. It really isn't so bad as it finally worked out. We get a first-class academic preparation for college."

"The trouble is," said Lilla, "that so many of us looked down on physical work. We regarded ourselves as a privileged generation. But I'll tell you this—if I had to work three full years in a factory and study evenings to prepare myself for college, I'd have done it."

"So would I," said the freckle-faced Lyuba. "I cannot imagine myself happy not practicing medicine. I always wanted to be a doctor. When I was a little girl, I played doctor to my dolls, curing them of all kinds of imaginary sicknesses. I suppose it's in my blood."

There is much in the blood of college girls like Lilla and Lyuba that brings to mind Turgenev's "beautiful little girls." They are as spirited, as purposeful, as strong-minded, as intellectually alert, as romantic as Natalya (*Rudin*), as Yelena (*On the Eve*), as Liza (*A Nest of Gentlefolk*)—the difference being that no air of melancholy broods over their persons. Unlike Liza, who, when frustrated in the one true love she has known, consecrates her life to piety in a nunnery, a Lyuba or a Lilla would dedicate herself to science, to healing the sick, not even in a city but in a village, or to some other purposeful pursuit. So if there are Shuras in the Soviet Union, there are also Lillas and Lyubas, even if Soviet fiction writers refuse or find it still impossible to portray them as they are.

Komsomolka's constant outcry for more and more production, for more and more sweat and toil, may muffle their voices. But the voices are there, a fusion of the finest in Russian womanhood of yesterday and today. One can only speculate whether someday in the future the voices will be loud enough to be heard and heeded by the Kremlin male hierarchy that decides the destiny of the nation and that in the person of Shelepin proudly boasts of mobilizing girls in their mid-teens for work in mines and on heavy construction.

16.

JEW
Russia's Stepson

In Moscow I called on an elderly Jewish woman who lives with her widowed granddaughter and five-year-old great-granddaughter in a respectable one-room flat, sharing the kitchen with only one other family. Seventy-five years old, the woman lived on a pension. Observing that her right foot was bandaged, I asked what had happened to it. She explained that one morning she woke up and found she couldn't walk. She immediately called the district doctor, who after examining the foot advised an operation which, if she objected to going to the hospital, could be performed in her home. She preferred to have it done at home, and soon afterward a surgeon and nurse arrived and performed the operation. There was no charge for their services. Nor was there any charge for the nurse who came every day to change the dressing.

On the Moscow–Kiev train, I became acquainted with a middle-aged Jewish woman, a teacher in a public school in the Urals, who was on her way to Kislovodsk for a month's treatment of a heart ailment in a state health resort. She was paying her own railroad fare but the month's stay in the resort, including all medical treatment, would be free.

On a plane in Siberia, I struck up an acquaintance with two young Jews who were members of the Novosibirsk opera company. For Soviet citizens they were astonishingly well dressed. They told me that they were well paid and that their regular salaries were substantially augmented by fees from concerts. One of them had been on a concert tour in China. Though Novosibirsk is one of the fastest-growing Siberian cities and the housing crisis there was distressingly acute, they occupied more comfortable flats than when they had lived in Moscow.

While I was in the city of Minsk, capital of Byelorussia, I read in the daily newspaper of a man named Rabinowitz, chairman of a collective farm, who had raised a record corn crop. He was hailed as a hero who, despite the harsh climate, had achieved a notable triumph in agriculture.

I am mentioning these incidents, which I could easily multiply, because in the study of Soviet anti-Semitism it is well to remember that, as workers, Jews, whatever their pursuits, are accorded the same rights and benefits as non-Jews. In the ministration of social services —medical care, pensions, vacations in a health resort, an apartment in a new house—they face no discriminations. If a Jew attains distinction on the so-called production front, the rewards that go with it, monetary and social, including public acclaim, are bestowed no less generously on a Rabinowitz than on an Ivanov.

Nor are Jews segregated in the new residential sections into neighborhoods of their own. When they move into a new house, their neighbors may or may not be Jews. Minsk, which had been traditionally a Jewish city until the Nazis exterminated most of its Jews, well illustrates the wide intermixture of Jews and non-Jews.

I had visited Minsk shortly after its liberation from over three years of Nazi occupation. The city was more than half destroyed, but by some miracle the welter of narrow muddy streets with their rows of sagging wooden cottages on the outskirts, which had been largely a Jewish quarter, had escaped destruction.

Now the old slums are gone, replaced by tall apartment houses. The new streets are broad, asphalted, and lined with young trees. The reconstruction of Minsk is one of the more notable achievements of Byelorussia. But in the new housing developments, Jews do not live in neighborhoods of their own. They are scattering all over the city in houses that cluster around new plants and factories and in other residential sections. With the rise of new housing projects, the old ghetto, even in a physical sense, is disappearing everywhere.

Actually segregation, in the American sense of the term, did not exist in the Russia of the Czars. Privileged Jews who were permitted to live outside the Pale of Settlement (the territory to which Jewry was legally confined) could live anywhere, even in Moscow and St. Petersburg. The same was true of cities within the Pale of Settlement. Jews could rent or buy homes on any street, in any district of the city, though there were anti-Semites who didn't want Jews as neighbors. But the exceptions need not obscure the reality of the prevailing custom in Czarist times.

Jews were barred from noblemen's clubs, but so were Russians who didn't bear a title. But a nobleman was free to entertain Jewish friends in his club. Merchants' clubs admitted Jews to membership, and as for the intelligentsia, the doors of their homes and their study circles were open to all kindred spirits, regardless of race or nationality.

With the coming of the Soviets, the Pale of Settlement was abolished, and now more than ever Jews all over the country are intermixed with non-Jews in the newly built apartment houses.

And yet—

On my arrival in Leningrad, as I sauntered through the streets, I saw billboards announcing the performance in Russian of *Tevya the Milkman*, a play by Sholem Aleichem, the Yiddish writer, by a theatrical company from Riga, the capital of Soviet Latvia. I learned that the performances were a sellout and that Jews were the chief patrons. But nowhere in the Soviet Union could Jews see the play in the language in which it was written.

When I visited the House of the Book, the assistant director proudly told me of the large new six-volume edition of the works of Sholem Aleichem that the state publishing house was bringing out in honor of the hundredth anniversary of the author's birth, again only in Russian, though later a one-volume edition of stories was published in Yiddish.

As I browsed around the children's book counter, my eyes fell on a volume of children's poems by Leib Kvitko, a Yiddish poet whom I knew. Between 1919, when he first began to write, and 1958 (according to a report I read in the bookshop) over nine million copies of his books were sold in Russian translation. "Our children love his poetry," a salesgirl said, "and his books sell out quickly." But since 1948 his poems have been unavailable in the language in which he wrote them.

Up in northern Siberia lives the Mongol tribe of Chukchi, of whom there are no more than twelve thousand men, women, and children. In 1930 the Soviet Government gave them a written language, opened public schools, a pedagogical college, a medical and a musical institute, all in their native tongue. Since then the publishing house of Magadan in northern Siberia has been bringing out the literary works of Chukchi authors in their native language.

But the 2,268,000 Jews (census of January 1959), over one fifth of whom give Yiddish as their mother tongue, have since 1948 been deprived of all publishing facilities.

One afternoon in Moscow, as I turned the corner from my hotel, I was approached by a little man with a shriveled face and a shapeless cap low over his forehead.

"Are you an American?" he asked.

"Yes."

"Jewish?"

"Yes."

"Maybe you have a *cidur* [prayer book]?"

"I thought," I said, "new prayer books were published here."

"*Ekh!*" he answered with a wave of his hand, "we haven't enough of anything—prayer books, prayer shawls, phylacteries. Don't you believe anybody who tells you our religion is respected."

I told him that I had met Baptist clergymen and Orthodox priests and they didn't complain of lacking indispensable religious accessories.

"Yes," the little man answered. "For Christians there is always enough paper, enough of everything. But we Jews are in *goluth* [exile] here. Maybe you know an American Jew in Moscow who has a prayer book? I need it so badly."

"I'm sorry," I said. "I cannot help you."

Dejectedly he wagged his head and said, "It's too bad Jewish tourists from America don't bring prayer books. Good-by." He turned the corner and walked away.

Well may the religious Jew speak of himself as being in *goluth*— the first time I ever heard a Soviet Jew use the term—when the tattered old religious accessories, mostly inherited from Czarist times, are falling to pieces. The five thousand prayer books newly published in 1956, re-edited to conform to Kremlin power politics, do not begin to meet the demand. Until recently nobody knew how many Jews in the Soviet Union were officially counted as religious. The mystery has at last been solved by M. Voshchikov, one of the five-man Council of Religious Cults. In an interview with Tullia

Zevi, Italian Jewish correspondent of the Jewish Telegraphic Agency (January 14, 1960), he gave the number of "practicing" Jews as 500,000.

The Jewish synagogue is the sorriest house of worship in the Soviet Union. Neither in a Baptist nor in an Orthodox church was I ever made aware of fear brooding over worshipers as I was in the Moscow Central Synagogue. Baptists in particular, despite the violent attacks on them in the press, always appeared serene and self-confident. But after about five minutes in the Moscow synagogue, a middle-aged Jew on learning that I was an American whispered to me to remember that there were "ears" among the worshipers—ears that presumably listened and reported all they heard. I know of no place where the foreigner who may be interested in Soviet Jewry finds himself in so frustrating a situation as in a synagogue. The rabbi and other officials tell him that the Constitution guarantees freedom of worship and that the Jewish religion is treated with no less respect than any other, which is manifestly untrue. I need only cite several examples. Baptist congregations that are too small to qualify for a meetinghouse of their own and so worship in the home of a communicant, encounter no interference from local authorities. I never heard of a single instance of such interference. But in Minsk and in Kiev I was told over and over that when Jews gather in a quorum of ten men for worship in a home, they are often dispersed by local authorities. In Minsk I was also told that synagogues in a number of Byelorussian towns, among them Bobruisk and Baranovichi, have been shut down since the end of the war. How many Jewish congregations have been ousted from synagogues, nobody knows. There is no way of checking the stories one hears of scores of synagogues taken away from worshipers in Byelorussia, the Ukraine, Moldavia. Moscow denies and denounces these stories but doesn't permit foreign journalists to investigate them—the communities involved are out of bounds for foreigners.

But not a single Baptist or Orthodox church or Moslem temple has been closed since the end of the war. Quite the contrary; new houses of worship for these three religions have been opened. The privilege these religions are accorded to maintain national organizations is denied to Jews, as is the privilege of attending a religious conference in a foreign country or of holding one with co-religionists from abroad in Moscow or any other city.

But though much worsened, the problems of the religious Jews in the Soviet Union are not new. What is new in Jewish life, startlingly new to me after an absence since early 1945, is the intensification of Jewish consciousness even among young Jews. Let the following incidents speak for themselves:

In Moscow I presented an American dacron necktie to a Russian schoolteacher. He examined it and pointed to the label stamped "100% washable" and asked what it meant. I translated, and he said jokingly, "Wonderful! If I go broke I can get a fancy price for it. Nobody will doubt that the necktie is American and washable."

When I presented a similar necktie to a Jewish schoolteacher in Moscow, he too wanted to know what the label said. "It's got to come out," he said. "Right away," agreed his wife. She fetched a pair of scissors and snipped out the label.

I told them what the Russian teacher had said, and the wife replied, "There are a lot of things Russians can do that Jews no longer dare to do."

"Why?" I asked.

"If you'd been here in January 1953, you wouldn't have asked the question." That was the month when *Pravda* unbridled its wrath against the Jewish "murderer physicians . . . recruited by the international [Jewish] bourgeois organization JOINT, an affiliate of American intelligence," to assassinate Soviet military and civilian leaders. "We don't even like to talk about it any more," said the teacher.

"But the doctors' plot," I said, "has since been exposed as a fake, and *Pravda* had to swallow its anti-Semitic words."

"But who knows what's going to happen in the future?" said the wife. "Jews have to be careful."

This couple were in their early thirties, Soviet-born and Soviet-educated. Yet they were saying, "Jews have to be careful." The burden of Jewishness was weighing heavily upon them, had eaten itself so deeply into their minds that they wouldn't risk leaving a tiny white label inside a necktie lest it serve as incriminating evidence of their "being in the service of American imperialism," or some other form of disloyalty. The nightmare of the Jewish doctors' plot still haunted them, so they played it safe.

Safer, much safer, than other Jews I knew. In Moscow I met an elderly Australian Jew who had come to visit his daughter. Every day she came to his hotel, or he went to her home. She was a physician; and her daughter, a biologist, was married to a young Jewish physicist, the son of one of the most distinguished scientists in the Soviet Union. One evening I called on the Australian in his room and found him with his daughter, his granddaughter, her husband, and his parents, the scientist and his wife. I was surprised to see the scientist and his wife in the hotel—Soviet scientists and other intellectuals, Jews and non-Jews, except when they are on official missions, do not readily visit foreigners in an Intourist hotel. We spent a delightful evening together, tactfully confining our conversation to non-political subjects. Later I learned that the scientist and his wife had obtained special permission to visit their Australian in-law.

I knew other Soviet Jews who freely invited relatives to their homes and freely called on them in hotels, with or without permission; and I knew still others who would never dream of stepping inside these hotels and who have warned relatives abroad not to communicate with them. In the Soviet Union there are Jews and there are Jews, some more courageous than others, some believing that the Kremlin will never again dare to stage an anti-Semitic spectacle, and others too fearful of a repetition of such a spectacle to risk any action, however innocent and trivial, that might at some future date be dug up and flung at them as evidence of disloyalty.

What a shattering contrast to the onetime faith of the Jew, especially of the young generation, in his complete emancipation by the Soviet revolution from all the disqualifications and abuses to which the Czarist government had subjected him. He could live anywhere he wished, attend any school or college he chose, no longer on a quota basis, as under the Czars, but on a basis of equality with Russians and others. Famished for education, masses of young Jews flung themselves with enthusiasm into the lower and higher institutions of learning all over the country. No career was barred to them. No opportunity for advancement in the Army, the foreign service, the party, the state, in any profession or vocation, was denied them. They were equals among equals for the first time in Russian history.

The Kremlin had recognized Yiddish, "the language of the masses," as the official Jewish language. It banned Hebrew because it associated the language of the Old Testament with religion and

Zionism—both of which it opposed and fought. It started schools, theaters, newspapers, publishing houses, teachers' colleges, scientific institutes, museums, reading rooms, libraries, in Yiddish. The Academy of Sciences in Byelorussia and the Ukraine had opened special Yiddish sections. In the early thirties there were in the Soviet Union thirty-five newspapers, fourteen theaters, four publishing houses, in Yiddish.

Originally there was a rush of children to the Yiddish schools and Yiddish was a flourishing culture, though stripped of Jewish nationalistic ideas and traditions. How often did I hear Jewish fathers and mothers in those days complain that their children were attending Jewish schools but were educated to be *goyim* (Gentiles). This was not quite true. One of the distinctive features of these schools was the extraordinary amount of attention they devoted to Yiddish literature and to folklore in song, story, and dance, which kept alive Jewish sentiment and Jewish sentimentality.

Since most Jews in Czarist times had engaged in some form of private enterprise, if only as peddlers in bazaars, the bolshevik revolution dealt a severe blow to their economic life. The NEP years, 1921–28, when small private enterprise was again legalized, had brought economic relief but were accompanied by disfranchisement and social contumely. The term "nepman," the equivalent of "businessman," like the terms "kulak" and "*bourshui*," was an epithet of contempt. But even Jewish nepmen, despite the disabilities visited on them, rejoiced in the abrogation of pre-Soviet discriminations against their people. The very word "Jew" was redeemed from the stigma with which Czarist Russia had for so long invested it.

Traditional Russian anti-Semitism didn't disappear. In some places it was overtly rampant. But the state and the party fought it earnestly and vigorously. I attended social trials of factory workers who had insulted Jews by calling them *zhid*—the equivalent of "kike." Once in a bazaar I saw a militiaman arrest a peasant who in the course of bargaining with a Jew flung the old epithet at him. Nor was this an exceptional instance. Were a college dean in those days to deny admission to a Jew because of his national origin, he would instantly have been dismissed and might even have been jailed.

Once in a Byelorussian village I visited a bearded blacksmith whose son had married a non-Jewish peasant girl in the village. The blacksmith and his wife were heartbroken over the marriage. But the son and his bride were happy. They were in love and to them their union signalized a new era, when barriers between peoples, even between Jews and non-Jews, had fallen away. All over the country Jews of both sexes were marrying non-Jews.

With each succeeding generation of Jewish school children, there was a marked drop in the attendance at Yiddish schools. In the summer of 1936, the late Hubert Griffith, the British journalist, and I journeyed to the Crimea to make a study of Jewish agricultural villages. We visited schools, and everywhere we observed a striking situation: teachers and pupils speaking Yiddish in classrooms and most of them breaking into Russian once classes were over. Why prepare for the university or some scientific institute in Yiddish when the language would be of no use, was the complaint we heard from pupils and teachers. Yiddish, they held, should be a subsidiary language and the chief language should be Russian—which would throw open to them opportunities for study and work all over the Soviet Union.

But the one thing the children loved was Jewish folklore. In one village the school put on an amateur performance for the benefit of the foreign journalists, and it was as spirited and delightful as any I had seen in non-Russian schools. When the performance was over, we spoke to the boys and girls who had taken part in it, and they were so pleased with our compliments that when the hall was empty, only the schoolmaster and some teachers remaining, they favored us with several more acts—songs and dances and a sketch from Jewish village life.

For the parents, Yiddish was a cherished language, all the more so because it was officially accepted as the language of the "Jewish masses." The exception was the small number of culturally assimilated Jews who neither knew nor cared to know the dialect. For the others, Yiddish was a satisfaction and an inspiration, especially as so many of them were not fluent in Russian. For them, Yiddish was the language of their ancestors, of their folk wisdom, their songs, fables, anecdotes, and of the literature that had flowered under the Czars and that had begun to flourish anew under the Soviets. For this generation of Jews, Russian was no substitute for Yiddish, as it was rapidly becoming for most of their children. They were too conscious of themselves as Jews to sever this living bond with the past, even when they were no longer religious, with all that it had meant to them in personal expression and in romance. Deep in their hearts some of them still cherished the dream of an eventual migration to Palestine; Soviet anti-Zionist propaganda, vociferous as it was, had not killed the dream, though it was dangerous to speak of it in public.

For these Jews, Biro-Bidjan, the Soviet project of establishing a Jewish autonomous territory in the Far East, north of the Manchurian border, was no substitute for Palestine. Nor was Biro-Bidjan the triumph that Khrushchev would have the world believe it had been originally, from all he said about it to Serge Groussard, correspondent of Paris' *Le Figaro*, as reported by him in his newspaper of April 9, 1958. "Jews," Khrushchev is quoted as having said, "left en masse for Biro-Bidjan. They were raving enthusiasts. They rushed there from every corner of the Soviet Union, and I might say from all European countries they could come from, fleeing persecution."

Khrushchev's fancy soars above the facts. The chief enthusiasts were the Jewish Communists, to whom Biro-Bidjan was primarily a means of counteracting Zionist sentiment and of winning prestige for the Soviet Union in foreign countries. I attended mass meetings of Jews that were addressed by Jewish Communists, and on the surface, to judge from the applause of the audiences, it appeared that Jews heartily favored the project. On investigation I learned that while they favored it as a gesture of good will toward Jewry, they didn't want to migrate there. Sometime during 1930 I had a long interview on the subject with the late Mikhail Kalinin, President of the U.S.S.R. Having traveled widely in Russia in those days, I told him that I found little enthusiasm for Biro-Bidjan among the young generation of Jews, who were not interested in a homeland of their own in the Soviet Far East or anywhere else. He replied that there were enough Jews who wanted such a homeland to make Biro-Bidjan a success. He even expressed the hope that American Jews would help their brethren in Biro-Bidjan with industrial and agricultural machinery.

The truth is that *lishentsy* (disfranchised Jews) were the chief volunteers for the project. It offered them an escape from the harassments they suffered in European Russia, not as Jews but as *lishentsy*. The efforts of Jewish Communists to whip up enthusiasm among the Jewish youth for Biro-Bidjan was an unqualified failure.

A comparatively small number of them journeyed to the Far East. Never at any time were there more than 40,000 Jewish settlers there.

Thinking back to those days, I can only say that from the start the Biro-Bidjan project was doomed to failure. Jews had no historical roots in Russia's Far East and felt no sentiment for the place. City-folk, they were neither mentally nor physically fit for the harsh life and the strenuous toil that taming the wilderness demanded, especially as the Soviet Government in those years was too poor to provide them with modern agricultural and industrial tools. In consequence, they began to desert and flee back to European Russia. The purge of the middle and late thirties further disintegrated the Jewish settlement and sapped the faith of settlers in its future. The failure of Biro-Bidjan was officially though indirectly recognized by the editors of the second edition of the *Bolshaya*. In the volume which was published in 1950, the subject is slightingly disposed of in a single paragraph. Of the 163,000 population in Biro-Bidjan, as given by the census of 1959, Jews are a hopeless minority of some 25,000.

Carried away by the idealism of the revolution, young Jews, as I have already related, had no enthusiasm for Biro-Bidjan or for Palestine. They were losing their consciousness of themselves as Jews, and a Jewish homeland inside or outside the Soviet Union held no allure. They scoffed at all talk of a Jewish spirit, a Jewish destiny, a Jewish mission, and at Jewish separateness. The socialist society that was in the making was breaking down nationalist barriers, so they were convinced, and would in time erase from peoples' minds all consciousness of nationalism and separatism. Why, then, they argued, should Jews seek a separate life? Russia was their Motherland and they would exchange it for no other. Soviet Russia had freed them from all their pre-revolutionary troubles and torments and opened up to them, on a basis of equality with other peoples, the right to education and self-realization, to careers in every field of Soviet life. Integration with Russia's new socialist civilization was their slogan and their faith.

In *Humanity Uprooted*, which was written at the height of the heroic age of the revolution and was published in 1929, I concluded the chapter on the Jews with the following sentence: "I cannot escape the conclusion that unless the Soviet Government collapses or anti-Semitism reaches the magnitude of a national epidemic, the bulk of Russian Jewry is destined to assimilation." I could draw no other conclusion from all I had observed and heard in the Soviet Union in those days and from the enthusiasm of the younger generation for the sublime emancipation that the revolution had brought to Russian Jewry.

Not one of those enthusiasts could have imagined in those perfervid days that the time would come when one of them, now a celebrated philologist, would be constrained to say, "What a misfortune it is for my children that they have to bear my Jewish name and that the fifth point in their passports stamps them as Jews." The fifth point! The bane of Soviet Jewry, the ever present reminder to them and to others that they cannot escape their Jewish origin, however non-Jewish they may have become in their thinking, and however deep their resentment at being officially classified as Jews. Soviet law does not allow change of name or nationality, though in the instance of a child born of a mixed marriage the child may be registered by the nationality of either parent.

The fifth point on passports applies to all Soviet citizens and was never intended as a discriminatory measure against Jews. Now Jews regard it as particularly oppressive to them as a minority because it results in one discrimination after another. Cynically some Jews speak of it as a certificate of "fifth-class invalidism."

The son of a brilliant Jewish woman bacteriologist, though he had graduated from the ten-year school with the mark of *otlichnik* (excellent), failed to win admission to Moscow University, while a Russian classmate with a much inferior scholastic record was accepted. In the presence of his mother he tore up his Komsomol membership ticket and vowed never again to have anything to do with the organization. The incident is all the more illuminating because neither the mother nor the son had ever thought of themselves as Jewish. But—there was the fifth point in the passport and there was no escape from it.

The son of a cabinet minister fell in love with a Jewish girl. When the father heard of it, he told the son that while he didn't wish to assert his parental authority in such a personal matter, he felt obliged to warn the son that marriage to a Jewess might cause him serious difficulties in his professional life. The young man gave up the girl.

Once I attended a party in a Russian home. I had no reason to believe that the people at the party, all intellectuals, were anti-Semitic. Yet in the course of the evening I heard them speak of So-and-so married to a Jew, and of such-and-such a Jewish woman divorcing her Russian husband. Never before had I heard such distinctions drawn between Jews and non-Jews. Weekends during the war I frequently visited Peredelkino, the writers' village some twenty miles outside of Moscow. At gatherings there the subject of Jews and non-Jews, whether in marriage, divorce, or any other personal and social relationships, never came up. Intermarriage was still common and nobody gave it a thought. Now they did.

Mixed marriages are not nearly as common as they were even during the war years. Despite the Kremlin's avowed internationalism and its official espousal of the equality of all races and all peoples, Jews and non-Jews have become aware of a barrier between them, the barrier that the revolution had originally set out to demolish once and for all.

The so-called Malakhovka affair illustrates the effects of the barrier. Malakhovka is a suburb of Moscow, with a population of some 30,000, of whom 10,000 are Jews. Early in the morning of October 4, 1959, which was the first day of the Jewish New Year, incendiaries set fire to the synagogue and to the little house of the eighty-year-old caretaker of the Jewish cemetery, which was about a half mile away from the synagogue. The town's fire brigade brought the fire in the synagogue under control, but the caretaker's house burned to the ground, and his sixty-seven-year-old wife was found dead. The whole incident was hushed up by Soviet authorities and the Soviet press, and though the news of it quickly spread in Moscow, no foreign correspondent was permitted to send it out.

It was only through an American Jewish tourist, who happened to be in Moscow at the time, that the outside world learned of it. He drove in a taxi from Moscow to Malakhovka, where he learned the details of the incident, and on his return to New York he broke the story in the New York *Times* (October 13, 1959). He also brought back anti-Semitic leaflets that had been posted on the houses of Jews and that were signed by a committee which called itself *Komitet Bey Zhidov* (Committee to Beat Jews), reminiscent of slogans of Czarist Black Hundreds.

In his interview with the already mentioned Tullia Zevi, Voshchi-kov of the Council of Religious Cults admitted the depredation and laid it to an act of "hooligans." The death of the cemetery care-taker's wife, he said, was caused by asphyxiation from smoke when she attempted to escape the flames. This is the only admission of the Malakhovka affair by a highly placed Soviet official. But not a word of it has appeared in the Soviet press.

In the twenties and even in the thirties, the incident would have been widely publicized and denounced by *Pravda* and other news-papers. A public trial would have served as an occasion for dramatiz-ing the evils of anti-Semitism. In those years, however anti-Semitic individual party members might have been, they kept their sentiments to themselves. The party was then earnestly fighting anti-Semitism, even as it was fighting prejudice against other minority groups.

What has happened since then?

In 1937 one could sense a rising hostility toward Jews because of the prominence of Jewish Communists in the purge that had be-gun to sweep the country. But Maxim Litvinov, a Jew, then Com-missar of Foreign Affairs, was not removed from his high office, nor were some of his Jewish co-workers, among them Konstantin Ouman-sky, who subsequently became Soviet ambassador to Washington. Likewise Ivan Maisky continued his ambassadorship in Great Britain. In the party, the trade unions, the Foreign Trade Commissariat, in other institutions, one found Jews in high positions all over the country. But in 1938 an attack began on Jewish culture. All Yiddish schools were closed. There were, it is true, too many of them, but there were parents who wanted their children educated in their mother tongue. The voices of these parents were disregarded. More significant was the closing of the Yiddish sections in the Byelorussian and Ukrainian Academies of Sciences. All research in Jewish subjects in these academies was brought to an abrupt end.

The Molotov-Ribbentrop "peace" pact of August 1939 intro-duced new anti-Semitic features into Kremlin policy; and it was not until I arrived in Kuibyshev, in June 1942, that I learned some of the details of this policy. Jews were "discouraged"—to quote a Jewish Communist in Kuibyshev—from seeking a career in the foreign services. Molotov, the new Soviet Foreign Minister, though married to a Jewish woman, didn't want them. Non-Communist Jews had begun to worry over possible Nazi influence on Soviet policy toward Jews, and well they might. Barred from diplomacy, Jews were also finding it difficult to enter the profession of journalism. Still, the chief of the Soviet Information Service in Kuibyshev was a Jew named Solomon Lozovsky, one of the few surviving old bolsheviks who was executed in 1952.

Later, when I left Kuibyshev for Moscow, I heard more of the resurgence of anti-Semitism among Russians, including party members. During the confusing and perilous days in October 1941, when the Germans were rolling toward Moscow and masses of Muscovites were fleeing the city, rumors were spread that Jews had seized motor vehicles and rushed out of town, carrying with them untold state treasures. A well-known elderly Jewish writer told me that the janitor of the house in which he lived had warned him to flee or his throat would be cut. He ignored the warning, but he was disturbed, he said, by the wave of anti-Semitism that suddenly surged up in Moscow. The young wife of an eminent artist who was a party member, who had never thought of herself as Jewish, wept as she told me how in one Soviet institution after another she and friends of hers were refused jobs because they were Jewish. At a meeting of poets and composers, a Russian member of the Arts Committee, a party member, solemnly declared that only *Russians* were qualified to compose patriotic war songs. Present at the meeting was Lebedev-Kumach, the author of the already mentioned "Broad Is My Native Land." Lebedev-Kumach arose and all but called the speaker a fascist. There were others in Moscow at the time, chiefly party members, who spoke and acted like anti-Semites.

But after the Stalingrad victory, the late Alexander Shcherbakov, a member of the Politburo and one of Stalin's closest friends, delivered a speech at a plenum of the Moscow Communist party, in which he inveighed against the newly risen anti-Semitism, bluntly telling the assembled party members that the Red Army was not shedding its blood to destroy fascism only to suffer its rise in the Soviet Union. He demanded that the party strike hard at manifestations of anti-Semitism anywhere and everywhere. The speech was never published, but it was widely circulated by the Moscow grapevine. Russians who resented the rise of anti-Semitism were as cheered as were Jews by Shcherbakov's vigorous attack on it.

One of the last men I saw in Moscow before returning to America toward the end of the war was the Yiddish poet Leib Kvitko, whom I came to know in Kuibyshev. A party member and an official of the Jewish Anti-Fascist Committee, the stocky, gentle-voiced poet felt assured that, once the war ended, Stalin would smite hard at any and all forms of Russian anti-Semitism. He asked whether I had seen the officially published figures on war decorations awarded to Jewish soldiers in the Red Army. I told him I had seen the figures and that foreign correspondents had cabled stories on the subject to their respective news agencies and newspapers. He was pleased to hear that the Soviet figures, placing Jews in fifth place among the peoples in the Soviet Union in the number of decorations bestowed, were publicized in the outside world. It only reinforced his conviction that Stalin would fight down the newly risen anti-Semitism. He couldn't have foreseen that seven years later Stalin would send him to his death.

When I was in Leningrad in the summer of 1958, a Jewish schoolteacher, discussing anti-Jewish events since the end of the war, said, "When I heard on the radio of the formation of the state of Israel, I said to my wife, 'Jews must prepare for trouble. We shall be like the Finns during the Russo-Finnish War, when all of them, party members and non-party men, were banished from the province of Leningrad. We're going to be distrusted more and more.' Of course, there was the campaign against cosmopolites, but it concerned solely writers and artists. It didn't touch men in my profession or in my wife's, who is a physician. But after the broadcast on Israel, we grew terribly uneasy. But we never counted on the terrible things that happened afterward."

Terrible things they were, and they broke out soon after Golda Meir, the Israeli ambassador, was accorded an enthusiastic reception by Jews in Moscow, many of them actually expecting that they would be permitted to migrate to Israel. Stalin struck out relentlessly. In December 1948 came the sudden closing of Jewish cultural institutions—publishing houses, newspapers, theaters, libraries, everything but synagogues—the dismissal of many Jews from professorships in universities, from ministries, and from other highly responsible positions. On August 12, 1952, twenty-six distinguished Jewish writers and cultural leaders were executed. In November of the same year came the Moscow-inspired purge trial in Prague, one of the most anti-Semitic trials of the century, when such life-long Communists as Rudolf Slansky, Bedrich Geminder, André Simone, confessed to having always been Zionists and "bourgeois Jewish nationalists," and traitors to communism and the working class.

Most alarming to Soviet Jewry was the Kremlin-contrived "doctors' plot" of January 1953. Jews, I learned, had become frantic with anxiety and anguish. Some of them had begun to sell personal possessions—books, pictures, pieces of furniture—in preparation for forcible deportation to some bleak corner of the Soviet Union.

"Never in Czarist times," an elderly religious Jew in Moscow said to me, "could Jews have been as apprehensive as we were. God only knows what would have happened to us had Stalin lived long enough to bring the unfortunate doctors to trial. They would have been forced to confess to everything, and then what would Stalin have done to us? I remember the Kishinev pogrom staged by the Black Hundreds back in 1903. I was fourteen years old. They killed how many Jews? Maybe thirty, maybe forty—I don't remember— and they injured many others. But the Czar didn't forbid the Yiddish language, didn't close our schools, didn't curb our Jewish cultural life. Who would have imagined that Communists, infidels that they are, would outdo the Black Hundreds? Yes, it was a pogrom, the most terrible, I tell you, Jews have ever suffered in Russia. Think of it, they killed our leading writers, arrested and exiled thousands of Jews, forbade Yiddish, and closed all our cultural institutions, except, of course, a few crumbling synagogues."

The horror is remembered, but unless pressed to do so, Jews prefer not to speak of it to foreigners.

The question I was most frequently asked by Jews was whether there was hope of a revival of friendly relations with America. A Jewish scholar in Moscow ventured to say, "Half of our troubles would be over if the cold war was ended and our country and yours became friends again as they were during the war years. Make no mistake about one thing: They [meaning the Kremlin leaders] are very much afraid of America. The American air bases that surround our country frighten them. They hate America, but they are also afraid of America, very much afraid, and as long as the cold war persists, Jews will be suspect, especially those who have relatives in America."

The scholar himself was demoted to a lower position because, though he never hears from his relatives in America and doesn't even know anything about them, he was mistrusted. So were many of his friends. However, they didn't remain unemployed. The demand for skills is so great that jobs are always available. A Jewish medical professor I met, who was dismissed from his lectureship in the university, was eagerly engaged by a hospital. Engineers, except some of those in defense industries, rarely lost their positions. Neither did teachers in the public schools, not many of them anyhow. Anatoly Isayev, principal of School 157 in Leningrad, one of the finest in the Soviet Union, told me he had never dismissed a single Jewish teacher at any time. "Across the street," he said, "is another school and the director is a Jewess, one of my closest friends. I have eight Jewish teachers on my staff, she has fifteen. No, we do not discriminate against Jews in the public schools."

But a Russian woman physician in Leningrad who had been director of a medical research institution was herself demoted because she refused to dismiss her fifteen Jewish assistants. The new director at once purged the institute of Jews, so two of those who had been purged told me. But they didn't remain without work. They were given assignments in hospitals outside the city.

If the cold war ended and Russian-American relations softened, mistrust of Jews would lessen but it wouldn't disappear. There are other circumstances in Soviet life and politics, both national and international, that would keep it alive and in a moment of crisis it could again be inflamed. As a Jew in Odessa said to me, "We can't help it that we have relatives in America, and even if we don't hear from them, it counts against us."

"But Armenians, too," I said, "have relatives in America."

"That's different," he replied. "Armenians have their Soviet Armenia, where most of them live, and those who don't live there can always go back. But we—we Jews are like unexpected guests who are at the mercy of our hosts."

The upsurge of a vigorous Russian nationalism has of itself erected new barriers between Jews and Russians. The upper intelligentsia are so jealous of Russian prestige that they covet all honors and glory for themselves. They—not all of them of course—have come to regard Jews not as partners but as rivals. No Soviet Jewish scientist of world renown has suffered because of his nationality, not even during Stalin's most anti-Semitic days. But these men grew up and attained their distinction in an age when the fifth point on passports was only a legal formality.

Leningrad University is more liberal in admitting Jews than is Moscow University. But even in Leningrad a Jew must be especially gifted, "something like a genius," as the demoted professor said to me, "to be admitted to *aspirantura* [postgraduate work]." To the best of my knowledge, Siberia is the only part of Russia where the unofficial quota system is given a broad interpretation. Siberia is in the throes of such gigantic development and the demand for specialists in all fields is so pressing that universities and scientific and technological institutes are inclined to overlook an applicant's fifth point.

When I asked an assistant to the rector in Moscow University whether there was a quota system on Jewish students, he denied it. He assured me that Jews are accepted on the same basis as Russians or other nationals. But Jews in Moscow scoffed at the assurance. "Yes," said a Jewish mother, "on the basis of the same qualifications —plus the fifth point."

Without Kremlin direction, and despite their passionate Russian nationalism, the upper Russian intelligentsia, who govern the Academy of Sciences, the universities, the scientific institutes, and technological colleges, never would have dared to impose quotas on Jews in any institution of higher learning. Jews are definitely barred from careers in diplomacy, the party, the armed services except at the lowest rungs, the trade unions, the state administration (again except in the lower ranks), and other politically and militarily sensitive areas. There are exceptions, chiefly in the armed services. In other professions, opportunities have been narrowed but not closed. In the arts, including literature, there are no restrictions, though there are in journalism. In the sciences there definitely is discrimination, though a Jewish youth particularly gifted in mathematics, physics, or chemistry is certain of acceptance.

During my stay in Kiev, I raised the question of anti-Semitism in the Ukraine with Mikola Bazhan. The personable poet appeared startled when I put the question to him. "How can anybody say there is anti-Semitism in the Ukraine? Our greatest mathematician is a Jew. Our most distinguished physicist is a Jew. His name is Brodsky. Another Jew, Leipunsky, is our outstanding authority on atomic energy. A Jew named Hrubach is the leading historian of the Ukrainian revolutionary movement. We all read Sholem Aleichem, and we have translated into Ukrainian the writings of Peretz, another great figure in Yiddish literature. Go to our conservatory of music and see for yourself how many Jewish professors and students are there. Jews have a special gift for music and we do all we can to help them develop it. Why, if you had come half an hour earlier I'd have introduced you to three young Jews who we believe have great literary promise; and we shall help them develop their talents. No, we do not discriminate against Jews."

"But you have no Jewish schools or any other cultural institutions?" I asked.

"No, we don't," he replied. "Jews are so well assimilated that they do not need any of these separate institutions. But please remember," he went on solemnly, "that it's a crime in our country to foster anti-racial or anti-national sentiments. I wouldn't say that all of us have been educated out of our old prejudices, any more than Americans have been. I greatly admire Faulkner, one of your very great writers. We haven't yet translated him into Ukrainian, but Poland has translated him and I read him in Polish. Great writer that he is, he hasn't to my mind rooted out of himself anti-Negro prejudices. Maybe he doesn't even know it. Some of our people are like that. But we fight it. If we heard anybody call a Jew *parkhaty zhid* [mangy Jew] we wouldn't tolerate it."

When I repeated Bazhan's words to a young Jew, a teacher in a Russian school, he said, "Bazhan is a lovable man. No Jew would accuse him of the least ill will toward Jews, but he doesn't make policy. It all comes from Moscow, and what would you expect him to say to an American writer? That's the trouble in our country—people like Bazhan, who know that Moscow treats us like second-class citizens, are helpless to do anything about it. They must acquiesce."

He paused an instant and resumed. "Oh, if only all Ukrainians were like Bazhan! But few of them are, yes, few, especially at the university and at the institutes. Why, even at the medical school they deliberately flunk some of the most brilliant Jewish applicants. You won't find many Jewish girls in Kiev who would think of marrying Ukrainians."

We were walking along Kiev's famed Kreshchatik, the city's main street. Now that it has been rebuilt from the heap of rubble to which the war had reduced it, it is—next to Leningrad's Nevsky—the most attractive street in the Soviet Union, lined with beautiful chestnut trees and livened with flower boxes and flower beds. It was evening and the street hummed with the gaiety of promenaders. But there was no gaiety in the voice or the face of my youthful companion. Tall and athletic-looking, with deep gray eyes, his expression was beset with harassment, as of a man in perpetual inner conflict. "I want to tell you something else," he said in a low quavering voice. "I know very little Yiddish. I am what Bazhan would call a culturally assimilated Jew. But I thrill when I go to a Yiddish concert, and so do many other young people who, like myself, hardly know any Yiddish. It does something to us to hear old Yiddish songs, sayings, stories, and to see old Jewish dances. We really are more Jewish than we thought we were and are only now discovering it."

The popularity of Yiddish concerts, which are variety shows, is one of the more dramatic consequences of Kremlin anti-Semitism. The only form of Jewish cultural activity that the Kremlin sanctions, the performances draw packed houses. According to official figures in 1957, over three thousand such concerts were presented in the Soviet Union, averaging a thousand paid admissions each. The Jew is not only discovering himself but rediscovering his cultural heritage, if only as reflected in Jewish folklore.

But one wonders how long the concerts can continue. The performers are nearly all former actors and actresses in Yiddish theaters. They are advanced in years and there is no school to train young talent. In a country that has earnestly dedicated itself to convert folklore into one of the great arts of our times, Jews are the only people who are deprived of the opportunity to perpetuate their folklore. There is no Jewish clubhouse anywhere in the Soviet Union, not a single theatrical school to train professional performers. When the performers of today pass from life, they will carry with them to their graves the one cultural heritage that the Soviets allow, unless of course the Kremlin permits these performers, before it is too late, to pass it on to a new generation.

The complete collapse of Soviet internationalism and the rise of a flaming Russian nationalism are among the more pronounced causes of Soviet anti-Semitism. In reaction to Russian nationalism, the nationalism of Soviet minorities—which surged up with their cultural and economic development—has only been heightened. They, too, have begun to discriminate against Jews in professional careers. The exceptions are Soviet Armenia and Soviet Georgia, which, though among the most nationalistic peoples in the Soviet Union (or maybe because of that), have visited no discrimination on Jews. But then, the number of Jews in these republics is small: 52,000 in Georgia and about 1000 in Armenia.

One of Khrushchev's more admirable traits is his propensity to blurt out things and sentiments in conversation with foreigners that are never reflected in his official pronouncements, and that *Pravda* never publishes. "The Jews," he told the already mentioned Serge Groussard, *Le Figaro*'s correspondent, "are essentially intellectuals. They never think they've learned enough. As soon as they are able to do so, they go to the university, no matter what sacrifices that may involve." And again, "Jews are interested in too many things; they like to look into everything profoundly; they discuss everything and end up by differing widely among themselves."

Whether Jews are possessed of a more analytical or critical intelligence than Russians or any other people is not for me to say. The indisputable fact is that with the rise of the Soviets they have been striving to make the most of the educational opportunities offered to them. Never in the prewar years did Stalin or any other Politburo member, including Khrushchev, perceive in it anything abnormal or undesirable. Stalin would have checked the rush of Jewish youth to colleges and universities had he judged it hurtful to his power or to Soviet civilization. Now Khrushchev regards it as a specific Jewish failing. One thinks of Caesar's reflection on Cassius: "He thinks too much: such men are dangerous." Khrushchev would have been happier had Jews become workers in the steel, mining, building, lumbering, and other heavy industries, which have attracted insignificant numbers of them. They prefer, he said, individual effort to "collective work or group discipline."

For years I have been particularly interested in Soviet agriculture. Rightly or wrongly, I have never taken as pessimistic a view of Soviet collectivization as have other students of the Soviet Union. On my latest journeys to the Soviet Union, I saw some of the most advanced collectives, and though the results they have achieved are not insignificant, neither in administrative efficiency nor in productivity of labor do these collectives begin to compare with the *kibbutzim* I had visited in Israel; and the *kibbutzim* are completely socialized, as the Soviet collectives are not. It requires a deep sense of "collective work" and "group spirit" to achieve success in socialized farming, which is one of Israel's notable achievements. Yet the Soviet press has never published a single word in appraisal of the *kibbutzim*, though they should be of special interest to the Kremlin, as it is seeking to expand the socialized features of collectives. Nor has the Soviet press yet published a word on the collective effort and group spirit that go into the co-operative enterprises of Israel's Histadrut, the federation of trade unions.

As long as the Kremlin persists in the view that Jews are incapable of collective effort and are lacking in group spirit, widespread mistrust of them is inevitable, feeding as it does on jealous Russian nationalism. Neither *Pravda* nor any other Soviet publication ever reprinted a word from *Réalités*, the French journal, which records (May 1957) an interview between French socialists and Khrushchev. The First Party Secretary frankly acknowledged the distinctions that are drawn between Jews and non-Jews in appointments to high positions. "Should Jews now seek to hold," he said, "the foremost positions in our republic, the native inhabitants would naturally take it amiss." In her interview published in the New York weekly *National Guardian* (June 25, 1960), Yekaterina Furtseva expressed herself in a similar manner. "The government had found in some of its departments a heavy concentration of Jewish people, upwards of 50 per cent of the staff. Steps were taken to transfer them to other enterprises, giving them good positions and without jeopardizing their rights."

When I spoke of these interviews to a Jewish intellectual in Moscow, he said, "This is nothing new to us. 'They' and 'we'—that's the way it is nowadays. I'm surprised Khrushchev and Furtseva admitted it to foreigners. The worst of it is that the notion of 'they' and 'we' has seeped down to children, at least to some of them. Once my ten-year-old son came home from school crying. Russian children ganged up on him, insulted him, and told him he has no business going to their school. He and the likes of him, they said, should go to Israel, where all Jews belonged. The strange part of it is that the boy had never before even heard of Israel and now he wants to know all about it."

How come, one wonders, that the first edition of the *Bolshaya Encyclopedia* mentions Karl Marx's Jewish origin and the second edition fails to do so? Or that the first edition devotes 116 pages to Jews and the second limits the monograph to only two pages? Or that the fighting song of the ghetto Jews in Warsaw whom the Nazis exterminated is forbidden in the Soviet Union? Paul Robeson is the only singer whom Jews and Russians heard sing it in Yiddish in Moscow, when he appeared at the celebration of the one hundredth anniversary of Sholem Aleichem's birth.

Only power politics rivals Russian nationalism as a cause of Soviet anti-Semitism. This is best demonstrated in the official attitude toward Israel, which has refused to subordinate itself to Kremlin foreign policy. The significant role of the Kremlin in the creation of the Jewish state—first by supplying Jews with Czech arms during the war with the Arab nations in 1948–49, and secondly by the vote which Andrey Gromyko, its representative at the United Nations, had cast on May 5, 1948, for the establishment of the state of Israel —has since been expunged from Soviet history. On May 29, 1948, in discussing the Jewish-Arab war, *Pravda* described it as "a military attack of the Arab states of Transjordan, Egypt, Saudi Arabia, Iraq, Syria, and Lebanon, whose rulers have thrown their armies against the young newly created Jewish state." But in Volume XVII of the second edition of the *Bolshaya*, the Jewish-Arab war is presented as having been provoked not by the Arabs but by England and the United States. Not a word is said about the shipments of Czech arms to help Jews fight the war. No mention is made of Gromyko's vote at the United Nations. Instead, the encyclopedia states: "At the end of the Palestinian war, American imperialism further strengthened its activity in Israel, having squeezed out England and converted Israel into a colony and a military strategic base in the Near East and into a bridgehead for aggressive war."

Volume XVII of the encyclopedia was published in 1950, when Stalin was still alive, but subsequent writings on the Jewish-Arab war to this day uphold its distortion of history. Ignoring the original Kremlin policy of aid to Israel, Soviet journalism now depicts the Israeli Government as the tool of American imperialists, the enemy of peace in the Middle East, and even as the enemy of the Israeli Jews themselves—particularly those from the Soviet Union.

Late one afternoon a waiter came to my room in the National Hotel with tea and a copy of *Vechernyaya Moskva*, the one gossipy newspaper in Moscow. It carried a story about Israel, written by a Soviet Jewish tourist. He wrote: "A man of forty can no longer find work. He is, you see, already old. Before a man is hired, the master feels of his muscles and all but looks at his teeth as at those of a horse. The newly arrived immigrant rarely finds work for even one day a week. The common man suffers from all manner of humiliations. . . . People who have come here from the Soviet Union are subjected to torment and moral humiliation, whereas in the Soviet Union they were accorded genuine human rights guaranteed them by the Constitution."

Endless is the stream of such writing on Israel in the daily and periodical press, in books and pamphlets. The obvious purpose of it is to justify Soviet enmity toward the Jewish state and to discourage Jews from migrating there, even if they were allowed to do so.

How many of them would leave, were permission granted, is anybody's guess. But one thing is certain: Jews in the newly annexed Soviet territories—the Baltic States, western Byelorussia, Galicia, Bessarabia, Ruthenia, and former eastern Czechoslovakia—would be among the first to go. They didn't participate in the heroic age of the bolshevik revolution; they never shared the ardent faith of their brothers within the prewar borders of the Soviet Union in the promise of the bolsheviks to deliver them from historic disabilities. The ban on Yiddish hit them hard, for they are overwhelmingly Yiddish-speaking. Deprived of their Yiddish culture and having been drawn into the Soviet empire at the moment when official anti-

Semitism in one form or another—climaxed by the Slansky anti-Semitic trial in Prague and the doctors' plot in Moscow—pressed upon them, they would fervently welcome the opportunity to migrate to Israel. There are about 160,000 of them.

The so-called eastern Jews—those in Bokhara, Daghestan, and Soviet Georgia (and Georgians have always treated Jews with respect throughout the some two thousand years they have lived in Georgia) —would with but insignificant exceptions likewise emigrate. They are the only group of Jews in the Soviet Union who have remained staunchly religious. They do not speak Yiddish but they have not forgotten their Old Testament. To them the centuries-old prayer "Next Year in Jerusalem" has been hope and dream they have always yearned to fulfill.

Though most Jews within the prewar borders of the Soviet Union have become culturally Russianized, the resurgence of anti-Semitism has been such a shock to them that the older generation—those of fifty and over—would by and large pull up stakes and emigrate to Israel, especially if they could take their children with them. But when one speaks to young people one discovers that though their interest in Israel is intense and they want to hear all about it, they rarely feel the emotional ties to the little Jewish state that their fathers and mothers do. Some of them told me that, given the chance, they would gladly emigrate to America, Canada, Australia, the only foreign countries that attract them. They feel that their scientific and technological education would enable them to fit into their industrialized societies.

Still other young Jews told me that they have no desire to emigrate anywhere. Russia is their Motherland. They love the country, the people, the music, the theater, the literature, and all the other cultural privileges that the Soviets offer the citizenry. Despite the annoyance and frustrations they encounter because of the fifth point, they would miss Russia, they said, if they pulled up roots and migrated elsewhere. "There are Russians who are anti-Semites," a young Jewish chemist from the Crimea told me, "and there are Russians who are sick at heart over any form of anti-Semitism. I want to tell you something. If the Yiddish theater was reopened in Moscow, it would be packed to overflowing by at least as many Russians as Jews. You have no idea how pained some Russians are that Jews are the only minority in the country who are not permitted a language and culture of their own."

Jews in Moscow and Leningrad estimate that at least 500,000 Soviet Jews would emigrate to Israel were they permitted to do so. But nobody really knows. There is no Gallup poll in the Soviet Union, and none of course could be undertaken among Jews on so politically sensitive a question as migration to the new Jewish state, or anywhere else. Meanwhile the hate propaganda against Israel continues hot and violent.

There is something pathological about the intensity of this propaganda. It brings to mind the Stalin-inspired hate crusade against Yugoslavia. Of Yugoslavia's defiance of the Soviet Union, Stalin had once said that it was like a mouse nibbling at an elephant. Of Khrushchev's hate crusade against Israel, it may be said that it is like an elephant nibbling at a mouse.

The Kremlin is obviously pursuing a double purpose: to disabuse Soviet Jews of all thought of a good life in Israel, indeed to frighten them of the fate that awaits them there, and to pose as the one true friend of the Arab peoples and the one true champion of their independence and sovereignty. "If there had been no Israel," a European diplomat in Moscow told me, "the Russians would have had to invent it." Manifestly the Kremlin holds it as a club over the Arab states, which it can wield at its pleasure as need arises. The abruptly legalized and then abruptly halted emigration of Jews from Rumania to Israel, which began in September 1958, clearly demonstrated to Arab leaders the might of this club.

For reasons of its own the Kremlin has been uneasy over the Jews in Rumania, the largest Jewish community in the satellite countries, numbering about 250,000. Most of them feel strong ties with Israel and have resisted Sovietization even on Rumanian terms. The Kremlin regards them as poor security risks, whose loyalty it could not count on in time of emergency. It would be happy if Rumania were cleansed of all of them, and so would the Rumanian Government, if only because it would be rid of the ever vexing problem of anti-Semitism.

It would be foolhardy for any student of the Soviet Union to foretell future Kremlin policy toward Soviet Jewry. Lenin never imagined that a Jewish problem ever could arise in a Soviet society.

Neither did any of the other bolshevik leaders, and least of all the
Jews themselves, whose younger generation was so warmly, indeed
idyllically, responsive to the high hopes the bolshevik revolution
had held out. But the problem is there, haunting Soviet Jewry—
even those who have been completely assimilated into Soviet Russian
culture. "You should have been here," a Jew in Leningrad said to
me, "at our last [1959] Simchas Torah—the festival of the Rejoicing
of the Law. Thousands of Jews—students, clerks, soldiers in uniform—young people who never pray, who don't know a word of
Hebrew, gathered in the streets and sang and danced together with
pious Jews. That's how eager they were to demonstrate their identity
with their people."

Whatever the circumstances out of which anti-Semitism has
erupted—the cold war, relatives in America, Russian nationalism,
the nationalism of the non-Russian minorities, the creation of
Israel, Jewish intellectuality—the Kremlin regards Jews as different
from non-Jews, as "peculiar people"—to resurrect an old phrase—
with a propensity "to look into everything profoundly," and, to
quote Khrushchev again, as too individualistic to melt into a collectivist society. Mikoyan, Suslov, Furtseva, Kozlov, Khrushchev himself, may again and again officially deny that there is a Jewish
problem in the Soviet Union; but the problem is there, attesting
to the failure of Kremlin communism to fulfill the original ideals
and promises of the bolshevik revolution with respect to the
emancipation of Jews from all inequalities and discriminations.

There is no evidence that the Kremlin has a realistic approach to
the Jewish problem. It still counts on the eventual assimilation of
Jews with non-Jews. But the fifth point and all the discriminations it
carries has made the Jew, even when he no longer speaks Yiddish
and knows nothing about Jewish history or Jewish culture, keenly
aware of his Jewishness, which of itself strengthens resistance to
assimilation.

Will the Kremlin change existing law and allow Jews to change
their names and choose some non-Jewish nationality, so that the
fifth point will no longer count against them? Nothing is beyond
the Kremlin. It may even allow some Jews to emigrate to Israel or to
other countries. A Russian writer told me he was certain Yiddish

would be restored as a minority literary language. The pressure for the restoration has not abated and, however grudgingly, the Kremlin may permit Jews to rebuild some of their own cultural institutions. In Moscow alone there are some eighty Yiddish writers, members of the Writers' Union, who are clamoring for a Yiddish publishing house. Distinguished Russian writers have been supporting the clamor. It is no consolation to Yiddish writers that now and then their writings are translated into Russian and non-Russian languages in the Soviet Union. Most of their work receives no such recognition and lies tucked away in desks and trunks—symbols of helplessness and torment, of affront to their talents and their persons. The Kremlin can no longer pretend that the Yiddish language and Yiddish culture have died a natural death. It cannot discount the nearly half million Jews who in the census of 1959 gave Yiddish as their mother tongue, any more than it can discount the writers who write in no other language.

As for the Soviet Jews themselves, the one conclusion I allow myself to draw from my own observations in 1958 and again in 1960, is that since Stalin's death their condition has vastly improved. They no longer go to bed fearing a knock on the door, the dread signal of arrest or deportation to some remote part of the country. Skeptical of further improvement in their lot within the foreseeable future, their hope is that it will not worsen.

17.

INTELLECTUALS
The Fathers

"In the time of Stalin," a retired Moscow schoolteacher said to me in 1958, "teaching history was a simple matter: all I had to do was to stick to Anna Pankratova's texts like a fly to paper and no one could make trouble for me. But soon after Stalin's death, academicians, historians, and ideologists began to denounce Pankratova's fables and to wrangle over how best to present our history to the young generation. It was a trying time for history teachers; we didn't know from one day to another what opinions to hold on any subject from Ivan the Terrible to Stalin himself, or what we were to teach our pupils. So when I reached sixty, I retired. Now I draw my pension and teach retarded students—but only in mathematics; there are no ideological implications in the definition of an isosceles triangle."

Because of the perplexities of historians over a new textbook in history, there were no school examinations in the subject in the spring of 1953.

As we were talking there was a knock at the door. A young man, a neighbor, walked in. The teacher introduced us and said to the visitor, "I was just telling the American here how much I miss teaching history and doing my part in making patriots of our young generation. It's a real grief to me that I had to give it up, but I must think of my age and my health."

At another time a woman physician complained to me about the lack of certain drugs for cardiac patients. Her father, who was over seventy, suffered from high blood pressure and a serious heart ailment, and she had read of drugs in America (ansolysen and diuril) which she thought might help him. Would I on my return home air-mail these drugs, addressing the parcel not to her but to her father? Being old and sick, it wouldn't draw on him the suspicion that it might on her. "They are very lenient with old people," she said. "That's one of the best things that's happened since Stalin's death."

"But many Soviet citizens," I said, "are receiving parcels from America all the time."

"Yes, I know," the woman answered. "But I'm a physician, and it wouldn't look well for me to receive drugs from America."

Presently a young woman, an out-of-town guest of the physician, returned from a movie. We were introduced, and, suddenly beaming, the physician said, "I've been telling the American journalist about our excellent health service, so he can write about it. They know almost nothing of it in America."

Neither the schoolteacher nor the physician, both of whom I had known for some years, needed to explain that the respective newcomers were party members or close followers of party policy. They knew I would understand their double talk. I had heard it often before, over and over. Yet after an absence since early 1945 I found it both comical and tragic.

No people in the world are more sociable and hospitable than Russians, yet an American surgeon, who was warmly received by his Russian colleagues, wondered why they didn't invite him to their homes. Was it because, he speculated, they were ashamed to show foreigners the way they lived?

No doubt this is true of some of them. But medical specialists often engage in private practice and charge high fees. Like other high earners among the intelligentsia, they have servants and their own automobiles and command the highest living standards in the country—in food and drink, in clothes and household furnishings, and some of them even in housing. They have the means and, I am certain, the desire to entertain a foreign colleague, and some of them do so, especially if the foreigner is a personage of distinction or has been invited to visit the Soviet Union. The higher the professional standing of a Soviet citizen—a scientist, writer, university professor, academician—the more ready he is to invite a foreign colleague to his home. If others deny themselves the pleasure, it is because they do not care to expose themselves to possibly embarrassing political probings. Above all, they wish to avoid the gossip of neighbors— and Russians, it must be noted, are among the world's most avid gossips. However relaxed the political atmosphere since Stalin's death, these men remember the terror of yesterday and refrain from words and actions which in some possible future crisis might be flung at them as evidence of "conspiracy with agents of imperialism."

"If you had called on me in the last years of Stalin's life," said the afore-mentioned schoolteacher, "I'd have shut the door on you, and if by accident I had met you in the street, I wouldn't have dared speak to you."

"I'm glad I wasn't here during those years," I said.

"Nightmarish years," he sighed. "But the clouds have lifted and now the sun is out."

The sun is out but the clouds are remembered. In the summer of 1960, when I again called on him, and despite the raging anti-American campaign, he was as friendly and talkative as he had been two years earlier. But he wouldn't accept an invitation to dinner at the National Hotel.

However cruel Czarist repression, spokesmen and leaders of liberal and radical intelligentsia never tried to compromise with their own minds and consciences. Men of candor and courage, of honor and compassion, they were true to their inner selves. They chose exile and torment rather than betray their beliefs and principles. One has only to think of Byelinsky, Nekrasov, Chernyshevsky, Dobrolyubov, Herzen, Pisarev, Mikhailovsky—patron saints of Russia's nineteenth-century intelligentsia—to become excitingly aware of their fiercely uncompromising spirit of rebellion against all forms of tyranny over the mind. Falsification of facts, contemporary or historical, they detested as violently as they did the Czars under whom they lived. However rigid the censorship, they manipulated the rich and flexible Russian language with such skill and power that they gave full expression to their faith and their fealties. "If things come to a pass," wrote Byelinsky, "when I have to choose between the independence and integrity of my convictions and hungry death, I shall find within myself sufficient strength to die like a dog rather than allow dogs to devour me."

Not so with the foremost scholars and academicians of the Soviet intelligentsia. Outside the field of science and technology, one searches their public utterances in vain for the integrity and rectitude of their nineteenth-century predecessors.

I happen to be the fortunate possessor of the now discarded sixty-five-volume first edition of the *Bolshaya Encyclopedia* and also of the fifty-one-volume second edition of this encyclopedia. Twenty-three years (1926–49) is the span of time that divides the publication of the first volumes of the respective editions. The introduction to the second edition states that many articles in the first edition "contain flagrant theoretical and political errors" which had to be corrected.

It is both wryly entertaining and sadly enlightening to compare the two editions. For example, the first tells us that George Washington's "personal qualities won him immense popularity and in 1774 he was elected to the National Convention, and in 1775 . . . was appointed commander in chief of the North American armies. . . . On the conclusion of the war in 1783 he handed over his powers to the Congress and retired to Mount Vernon." In 1789, the article goes on, he was unanimously elected President of the Republic. In 1792 he was re-elected but refused to run for a third term. It is a simple, straightforward account that might be found in any reference book anywhere.

But in the second edition, a new and mordant note is sounded: "Under the chairmanship of Washington, the Constitutional Convention of 1787 in Philadelphia worked out, in secrecy from the people, a new constitution, which guaranteed the bourgeoisie and slaveholding plantation owners complete separation of the people from participation in the administration of the state. On the basis of this anti-national Constitution, Washington was elected in 1789 the first President of the U.S.A. He was re-elected in 1792." Not a word about his "immense popularity" or of his refusal to run for a third term.

In the first edition, the article on William James recounts his career as a philosopher and psychologist and in a tone of respect and reasonableness goes on to criticize James's pragmatism and acceptance of religion. To the monograph is appended a bibliography of James's writings, including the Russian translations of his major works made between 1892 and 1910. Of these, *Talks to Teachers on Psychology* ran through six editions and a seventh was brought out under the Soviets in 1921.

The second edition of the encyclopedia denounces James as "an American reactionary philosopher and psychologist, ideologue of the imperialist bourgeoisie, one of the founders of the anti-scientific philosophy of pragmatism, defender of religion . . . The reactionary philosophy of James won him followers among contemporary Anglo-American bourgeois philosophers. One of his followers was John Dewey—the militant obscurantist and incendiary of war against the U.S.S.R. and the People's Democracies." The bibliography of the first edition is omitted and no mention is made of the translations into Russian.

Of Woodrow Wilson the first edition states: "Wilson was sincerely convinced that military action against the Soviet Republic would only strengthen it. 'If action were to cease,' he said, 'the bolsheviks would either collapse because of lack of popular support or would soften their policy toward the Allies.'"

In the second edition, Wilson's Soviet policy has become definitely sinister: "Carrying out military intervention against Russia, supporting all anti-Soviet counter-revolutionary powers, Wilson nurtured murderous plans for the dismemberment of the Soviet state and the enslavement of its people; at the Paris Conference in 1919, Wilson was the initiator of the proposal to cut off the Caucasus, the Ukraine, Siberia, from the Soviet state."

As for James Joyce, the first edition gives a detailed account of the Irish author's life, education, and literary career, and speaks of "the world-wide fame" that came to him after the publication of *Ulysses*. "The novel represents a merciless and cynically sharp arraignment of bourgeois culture, . . . augurs with the farsightedness of a genuine artist the impending revaluation of values, subjects to the hammer blows of his criticism all ideological and moral foundations of contemporary society."

By the second edition, Joyce has become "the representative of the reactionary literary school which is characterized by the subjective portrayal of the stream of consciousness. . . . His principal work, the massive novel *Ulysses*, depicts one day in the life of an ordinary Dubliner. The depiction of the perverted psychology of the petty bourgeoisie, the cynical digging into his lewd sentiments, are subordinated to a reactionary purpose—to show man as amoral and anti-social."

On the subject of homosexuality, the first edition says that it is "encountered in all races, in all classes, and in various professions. . . . In general we may presume that in most instances it is hereditary, though surroundings may favor this anomaly and may even determine its particular forms (fetishism and others)."

The article includes a lengthy ethnographic sketch on the prevalence of homosexuality in its various forms in Asia, in Africa, in ancient Rome and Greece. Among the peoples discussed are the Siberian tribes of Chukchi, Koryaks, and Kamchadals—all, of course, Soviet citizens.

But in the second edition we read: "In capitalist society homosexuality is a widespread phenomenon. . . . Of much importance in the spread of homosexuality is drunkenness and also the sexual impressions of early childhood. . . . In bourgeois countries, where homosexuality is an expression of the moral disintegration of the ruling classes, it is actually unpunishable."

The ethnographic sketch of the first edition has been dropped, leaving the reader with the impression that homosexuality is the inevitable by-product of modern bourgeois civilization and peculiar to it alone.

Such is the "scholarship" of the Soviet encyclopedists who wrote the second edition of the *Bolshaya*. Of course, this edition was largely written during Stalin's postwar years, when official hatred of the Western world had contaminated the political and intellectual climate in the Soviet Union.

On my arrival in Moscow I wondered whether during the mellowing years since Stalin's death Soviet scholars might not have recovered at least some of the respect for their profession that had marked the work of their Czarist predecessors and that had carried over into much of the writing of the first edition of the *Bolshaya*, notably the volumes brought out before the war.

Some of the sharp criticisms aimed at the falsifiers of the Russian past which I had read in *Problems of History*, the most authoritative Soviet journal on the subject, had encouraged me to assume that the recent writings of Soviet scholars on foreign countries would reflect this new demand for greater objectivity. Day after day I browsed through the volumes in the bookshop of the Academy of Sciences on Gorky Street, where new publications about foreign countries are in such demand that passers-by snap them up as soon as a display copy is put in the window. With the aid of a courteous and intelligent saleswoman I acquired a small collection of books I considered significant. I shall draw examples from only three of them, all published in 1958, five years after Stalin's death.

On page 128 of *Collaboration among the Countries of Socialism* I find the following paragraph: "Reactionaries, inspired and supported by imperialists in Western countries, especially in the U.S.A., attempted to unleash an armed struggle against the national governments of European countries. Such attempts were made in Czechoslovakia in February 1948, in Berlin in June 1953, in Poland in 1956, and more particularly in Hungary in October 1956. Everywhere they suffered speedy defeat. In Hungary they succeeded in organizing an armed fascist revolt . . . but the Hungarian people, supported by socialist countries and the peace-loving forces of the whole world, replied with an armed suppression of the fascist mutineers."

In Leningrad and in Moscow rarely did I meet a university student who believed the myth of a fascist rebellion in Hungary, and more than one student spoke of his shame at the sanguinary suppression of the rebellion by Soviet tanks, machine guns, and artillery. Yet here is the Philosophical Institute of the Academy of Sciences, citadel of "high learning," laying on Western countries the Kremlin's guilt for the revolts in Hungary, Czechoslovakia, East Berlin, and Poland.

Another book, *Canada and Anglo-American Contradiction,* is published by the Academy's Institute of World Economy and International Relations. The author, A. Mileykovsky, stigmatizes Canada as imperialistic because, among other things, it participated in the Marshall Plan, joined NATO, and is investing capital in Latin America. He further charges that for the first time in its history Canada is "reaching out its tentacles to the colonial and semicolonial countries of Asia and Africa." This has happened, writes Mileykovsky, because Canada is ruled by an "economic oligarchy" which in collusion with U.S. "imperialist monopolists" is seeking private enrichment at the expense of the peace, prosperity, and sovereignty of Canada.

But the author is not without hope for that country. Toward the end of his 500-page work he advises the Canadian people to elect to power the Progressive Workers' (Communist) party, the only party that expresses "their patriotic aspirations." Only this party, he assures Canadians, can rescue their country from the evil conspiracy of their own and U.S. "imperialist monopolists." The meaning of Mileykovsky's argument is unmistakable: Canada can recover its peace, prosperity, and sovereignty only when it is ruled by a party capable of converting the country into a Kremlin satellite like East Germany, Czechoslovakia, and the others.

Of particular interest to me was the book entitled *The State System and the Political Parties of Great Britain,*[1] published by

[1] *Gosudarstvenny stroy i politicheskiye partii Velikobritannii* (Isdatelstvo Academii Nauk SSSR, Moscow, 1958).

the Academy in its popular scientific series. The editor is Ivan Maisky, whom I knew well during his years (1932–43) as Soviet ambassador in London. Born in Siberia and educated under the Czars in the gymnasium at Omsk and St. Petersburg University, he was thirty-three years old when the bolsheviks rose to power. He therefore has deep roots in Russia's nineteenth-century intellectual tradition, which spurned falsification of facts. As Maisky had lived in England for over a decade and had cultivated close friendships with Labour party leaders, I had anticipated that the book he edited would make amends for the scurrilous 401-page work that the Academy had published in 1950 under the title *The Right-Wing Labourites at the Service of Anglo-American Imperialism.* The book was a symposium on the Attlee Labour government and charged it with being "the defender of rotting English imperialism" and "the deceiver of the working class." It accused the Attlee regime of pursuing policies that resulted in a "further and absolute impoverishment of the English working class," of having dragged workers down "to a state of starvation."

What, then, does the reader learn about Great Britain and the British Labour party from the book that Ivan Maisky, now an academician, has edited?

The first thing that must be said is that it is purged of the scurrilities that drenched the pages of the Academy's earlier work. Yet nowhere in the book is there the least expression of regret or error for this work or serious departure from the dark picture it presented of Great Britain and the Labour party. Let the following passages speaks for themselves:

"Between 1919 and 1934 there were [in England] more sentences for political offenses than in the century of 1817–1919."

"The English bourgeoisie has the opportunity at any given time to limit the democratic rights of the working class or to prevent it from making use of its rights. The ruling classes of England have by legal procedure passed a series of measures which permit it in moments of necessity to constrict bourgeois democratic liberties. Freedom of speech and press are restricted by the fact that the radio and press are in the hands of private monopolies." Not a word about the state-owned BBC, to whose broadcasts in English (which have rarely been jammed) Russians who know the language listen avidly, and which they respect more than other foreign broadcasts. Need one doubt that Maisky himself is one of the listeners?

"Judicial investigation which is conducted by the police opens up broad possibilities for abuse, because in most instances the police are the chief witnesses. . . . The accused brought to trial by the police, especially if he is a working man, is *actually defenseless* [my italics], because the judge, despite evidence in his favor, more readily believes the policeman than the victim of the police." Not a word about habeas corpus, bail, Legal Aid, and the right of any defendant, however penniless, to legal counsel.

As for the Labour party, the book quotes Lenin as having once written that "the leaders are reactionaries, the very worst reactionaries." To Ivan Maisky they still are. "The practice of the Labour leadership during the past thirty years confirms Lenin's judgment." Why?

Because "instead of the promised struggle for peace, the Labour government conducted a policy of organizing aggressive blocs"—such as the Brussels Treaty and NATO. "It participated in the imperialist adventure in Korea, conducted a colonial war against the Malayan people and the Negroes in Kenya. Instead of the promised friendship with the Soviet Union, the third Labour government carried out a policy of enmity, supported 'the cold war,' aided in the split of Germany and the conversion of West Germany into a hotbed of revanchism and preparation for a new war." The Labour government, then, was an enemy because, unlike Czechoslovakia or the province of Tula, it refused to convert itself into a blind instrument of Kremlin expansionism.

In the chapter on the Labour party there is no mention of the Attlee government's granting independence to India, Pakistan, Burma, and Ceylon; not a word about the abolition of mass unemployment, or the National Health Service, which is as universal and all-embracing as Russia's and much more efficient; not a word about Social Security, old-age pensions, about any Labour reform; and only a sniping sentence of fifteen Russian words about Labour's nationalization of coal, steel, transport, gas, electric power, civil aviation, and atomic energy. Instead there is profuse eulogy of the British Communist party, which alone "can transform Britain into a strong, free, happy, and independent country," but not a word of explanation why the mass of British workers refuse to vote for the party.

Five years after Stalin's death and despite Khrushchev's denunciation of the generalissimo as "a common criminal," as I heard Muscovites speak of it, Maisky and the Academy of Sciences with him conform as slavishly to the black-and-white formula as they did when Stalin was alive. Having known well the genial, cultivated, and always approachable former Soviet ambassador in London (most unapproachable in Moscow), I cannot make myself believe that at heart he concurs in the absurd appraisals of British justice and the Labour party as set down in the book he edited. The most charitable judgment one can pronounce on him is that he is a hopelessly divided man, too old and too broken in spirit, or only as chauvinistically Russian as is the Academy, to be true to his inner self.

The Soviet people learned more basic facts about Great Britain from Prime Minister Macmillan's 2000-word television broadcast (March 2, 1959) than from all the tomes and dissertations that the Academy of Sciences has ever published. It was, in fact, the first time in Soviet history that the public was privileged to hear a few simple truths about contemporary Great Britain, and at least some Russians, I must testify, vividly remember them.

Despite the years and years of misinformation and misrepresentation, there is an extraordinary amount of friendliness toward England among cultivated Russians, even among the older academicians. I was especially aware of it in the summer of 1960. English is the most popular foreign language all over the country, and an increasing number of young people read English literature in the original and derive a special appreciation of it. A complaint I frequently heard was that the Soviet Foreign Publishing House was bringing out too few British authors in English. Whatever Britishers may think of the *Forsyte Saga*, it is one of the most beloved novels in the Soviet Union, while *Vanity Fair* is an outstanding triumph in Moscow's Maly Theater. And never before had I heard so many young people tell me that they are saving money for a tourist journey to Great Britain and that one of the first things they would buy there is the one-volume Oxford University Press dictionary. Russian-English dictionaries are difficult to buy and the one published by the Oxford University Press seems to be particularly well known.

It was amusing to learn that Intourist interpreters in Leningrad, which has a tradition of "English" English, are inclined to look down on interpreters in Moscow, which has a tradition of American English. "The Leningrad interpreters," a Moscow interpreter said to me, "affect an English accent and think they speak the language better than we do."

And what shall be said of the Soviet Writers' Union staging an organized moral pogrom on the lone Boris Pasternak immediately after the Swedish Academy had conferred on the author of *Doctor Zhivago* the Nobel literary award for 1958? The persecution, I was reliably informed, was instigated not by Khrushchev, though he no doubt approved of it, but by party-pious officials of the Union and by Nikolai Mikhailov, Minister of Culture at the time. Muscovites speak caustically of Mikhailov for his disparagement of *The Cranes Are Flying,* one of the more distinguished motion pictures to come out of Soviet studios. Had it not won first honors at the Cannes Film Festival in 1957, he might have suppressed it, so Muscovites told me. An anecdote about him illustrates the disrespect in which he was held by the public. A Soviet citizen, runs the anecdote, was sentenced to twenty-one years in jail for calling the Minister of Culture an idiot— one year for offending a state personality and twenty for revealing a state secret.

It was Khrushchev who brought the frenzied campaign against Pasternak to an end. But it was fellow writers (not all of them) who placed the crown of thorns on his head.

Yet what gracious hosts these same people are when one meets them officially! In Leningrad and in Kiev I had occasion to visit the Writers' Union and was pleasantly entertained. My hosts were among the best-dressed people in the country and outwardly the most composed and the most cheerful—brilliant conversationalists, with a ready wit and hearty laughter, with no hint of the *Weltschmerz* that characterized the pre-revolutionary intelligentsia, especially writers. We talked about books and authors in Russia and in America, and as if by mutual consent we refrained from bringing up controversial subjects. To the end my hosts remained models of graciousness and geniality, never once employing the vocabulary of arrogant and boastful clichés that leaps from the pages of Soviet journalism and from the lips of Soviet orators. One wonders how such people, so urbane and sensitive, could publicly and unashamedly applaud the Hungarian massacre, or stage in full view of the whole world the moral crucifixion of the author of *Doctor Zhivago!*

A Russian friend of mine made the pilgrimage from Leningrad to Moscow to attend Boris Pasternak's funeral. He had known the poet well and revered both the man and his work. I quote from his letter: "The veranda and the passageway to the room where he lay were carpeted with pine needles, and the mirrors, according to our custom, were veiled. The darkened room was decked with flowers—roses, lilacs, narcissuses. As I came in two foreign correspondents switched on the lights of a crystal chandelier so they could photograph him in the coffin. By the harsh light I saw how greatly his face had changed. He had known that he was dying of cancer; and just before the end he turned to his wife and thanked her 'for everything.' The cancer had brought on metastasis of the heart, and fortunately he went quickly. No doubt you read in the papers that five Kremlin doctors and nurses were in constant attendance at his bedside. Though a Russian Orthodox service was held in the house, he had a civil funeral. In accordance with his wish he was buried in the little cemetery at Peredelkino. At the graveside I saw his wife and his sons—handsome young men who resemble their father—and his brother. I had thought of bringing the camera, but it would have been of no use—I couldn't have brought myself to use it. So for a memento of that day I tore off a twig from the old lime tree whose branches were softly brushing the window of the room where he lay: the leaves were tender and smooth as the skin of a child. I shall press them between the pages of my inscribed copy of his books of poems *Second Birth*."

History has played a mordant jest on the pre-revolutionary intelligentsia. The men who conceived and engineered the bolshevik revolution came from their ranks. Lenin and Trotsky, Radek and Bukharin, Dzherzhinsky and Pyatakov, Molotov and Krassin and others, except Stalin, were neither peasants nor workers. The Kremlin fable that masses make revolution is too absurd to merit serious consideration. If it were not for the intellectuals among them, notably Lenin and Trotsky, the bolsheviks never could have come to power. But the Russian intelligentsia was a house hopelessly divided against itself. In fiction and non-fiction, Russians themselves have written voluminously of the passion for extremism, or "the flight of fancy," as it is sometimes spoken of among sections of the pre-revolutionary intelligentsia. The bolsheviks were well known for their extremism, and the chief reason they won the battle for power was that, though a small minority, they boldly championed the extreme immediate demands of a long suppressed, politically uneducated, and undisciplined people, by which I mean the peasantry and the industrial workers.

In the mid-twenties I once spent a weekend with a Czarist-educated schoolmaster in the village of Fyodorovskoye, Ryazan province, and my host, his wife (who was also a schoolteacher), and I engaged in a lengthy discussion of bolshevik prototypes in pre-revolutionary Russian literature. It was my host's view that, spiritually speaking, Turgenev's nihilist medical student Yevgeny Bazarov (*Fathers and Sons*) is the truest forerunner of the bolshevik. He read many passages from the novel and read and reread several times the scene of Bazarov's leave-taking from his university mate and disciple, Arkady, in proof of his view. Briefly quoted, Bazarov said:

"And now I say again good-by, for it's useless to deceive ourselves —we are parting for good and you know it. . . . You are not made for our bitter, rough, lonely existence. . . . There's no dash, no hate in you. . . . You won't fight. . . . But we mean to fight. . . . Our dust would get into your eyes, our mud would bespatter you. . . . We want to smash people."

The schoolmaster insisted that this was the language Lenin spoke to the mensheviks and the Social Revolutionary intellectuals. Whether or not one agrees with the schoolmaster, the fact is that the bolsheviks were fired up with dash and hate and were ready "to smash people," smash anybody in the way, with steely resolve and with unfaltering hand. They centered particular fire on the intelligentsia, to whom the new dictatorship was a betrayal of their own lofty vision of man and society. The intelligentsia raged and cursed, struck back and sabotaged, which only heightened the bolshevik onslaught. Having dedicated themselves, as they had loudly proclaimed, to the redemption of the mass of peasants and proletarians, who together constituted almost 90 per cent of the population, the bolsheviks cared nothing for the aspirations and idealism of the small minority of intelligentsia, who under the Czars had risen to a privileged position in material comfort and in social prestige.

It was a tragic time for the intelligentsia. They were scorned and mocked, battered and humbled. They were "wreckers," "counter-revolutionaries," "spies," "traitors"—and they were depicted as such in novels, plays, motion pictures. University professors dared not wear hat or collar and tie for fear of being insulted in the streets. "He puts on his hat and thinks he is a big shot" was a common taunt in those days. The very word "intelligent" had become an epithet of opprobrium, and I knew young people who were heartbroken because they were sons and daughters not of peasants and workers but of the intelligentsia.

But the bolsheviks needed brains, and they set out to tame the intelligentsia and to convert them into unquestioning instruments of service in the state administration, in industry, in the professions—a service which because of their education and experience only they were qualified to perform.

Then an unexpected incident happened. The year was 1930 and I was in Moscow at the time. The Art Theater presented a sensational play, Alexander Afinogenov's *Fear*. For once, from the stage and only from the stage, the intelligentsia—in the person of Professor Borodin—were permitted to speak their minds. "The milk woman fears the confiscation of her cow; the peasant, forcible collectivization; the Soviet clerk, endless purges: the party worker fears accusations of deviationism; the scientific worker, charges of idealism; the technical worker, charges of sabotage. We live in an epoch of great fear. Fear compels talented intellectuals to repudiate their mothers, to falsify their social origin, so as to press on to a higher position. Yes, yes! When you are in a high position the danger of being exposed is frightening. . . . Fear pursues our steps. Man becomes distrustful, secretive, churlish, unjust, and unprincipled. We are all rabbits. How can you work creatively? Of course you cannot. . . . Destroy fear, destroy everything that rouses fear—and you'll see the country flower into a rich creative life."

Afinogenov, whom I knew more intimately than any other Soviet author, told me that Molotov loathed the play and would have banned it, but Stalin approved of it as symbol of a truce, however uneasy, between the Kremlin and the intelligentsia that would permit them to work together creatively. By this time the intelligentsia was beaten into utter submission, and I well remember the current saying expressive of this submission: "Don't read, and if you read, don't think, and if you think, don't speak, and if you speak, be careful what ears hear you."

Yet there was one man among the intelligentsia who refused to make of himself a divided man. He was Professor Ivan Pavlov, who had openly declared he wouldn't give a frog's leg for the bolshevik experiment, because of the methods with which it was carried out. In 1926, through Dr. Horsley Gantt, now a psychiatrist at Johns Hopkins Hospital and at the time one of Pavlov's collaborators, I met the eminent physiologist. Humble of manner but sharp of tongue, he bristled with indignation as he spoke of the cruelty of the revolution and of the squabbles he had had with Nikolai Bukharin, who had vainly sought to persuade him to abandon his hostility. He sneered at Bukharin's presumptuousness in imagining that bolshevik pleas and arguments could recondition his "cerebral reflexes." Pavlov was the only man in the Soviet Union who never watched out for the ears that heard him, and like Tolstoy in Czarist times, he was immune to police recrimination.

But time and circumstances reconditioned Pavlov's intransigency —which was an epochal event in the relationship between the Kremlin and the intelligentsia.

The son of a priest, Pavlov, who had studied theology and shifted to science at the age of twenty-one, never to the end of his life uttered a single word in approval of Marxism. Such phrases as "class struggle," "class war," with their implications of violence and bloodshed, were repugnant to this humane genius. But, being honest, he was finally forced to admiration for the sweeping Soviet educational efforts, and more particularly the energetic Kremlin dedication to science.

Because it had distrusted the old intelligentsia, the Kremlin set out to create a new intellectual class, recruited from the poorer peasantry and factory workers. In 1919 it set up the *rabfaky* (workers' faculties), accelerated secondary schools that prepared students for institutions of higher learning. Nikita Khrushchev and Frol Kozlov graduated from these schools before the one entered an industrial academy and the other a polytechnical institute. In 1932 there were in the country

926 *rabfaky* with an enrollment of 352,700 students, boys and girls whose minds were supposedly uncontaminated by the idealistic traditions of the pre-revolutionary intelligentsia.

At the same time the Soviets were building new universities and other institutions of higher learning. In the pre-revolutionary years there were 105 such institutions within the Russian borders of that time, with an enrollment of 127,000 students. In 1932–33 there were within the shrunken frontiers of the Soviet Union 832 such institutions with a student body of 504,000, the vast majority—about two thirds of them—of peasant and worker origin. Though the Soviets didn't ignore the humanities and social sciences, which they slanted in their own way as they still do, they placed the chief emphasis on the natural sciences and technology. Scientific institutes and research laboratories mushroomed all over the country. Within four years, between 1929 and 1933, their number had grown from 438 to 1028, or more than double. All this was happening under Pavlov's eyes.

An ardent patriot who spoke fervently of the Russia he loved, he deplored the cruelties of the revolution and yet welcomed the efforts to educate muzhik Russia and make it into a modern nation. His own scientific pursuits were lavishly subsidized. Nothing was denied him, neither in personnel nor in equipment, however expensive. His fierce hostility to the bolsheviks mellowed into tolerance, and on August 20, 1935, addressing in the Kremlin the Fifteenth International Congress of Physiologists, he startled his audience by saying, "We, the leaders of scientific institutions, are truly alarmed and uneasy as to whether or not we are in a position to justify all the means that the government is placing at our disposal."

For the first time since the bolshevik rise to power, an assemblage of foreign scientists heard, not from the lips of a Kremlin personage but from their most highly esteemed Russian colleague, of the prodigious investment the Soviets were making in science. But it created no stir in the outside world; it was not the kind of news to make headlines.

Soon afterward, while visiting his native city of Ryazan, Pavlov paid a further tribute to Soviet devotion to science. "In our country," he said, "the whole population honors science. . . . I do not err, I think, when I say that this is to the credit of the government . . . of my country. Formerly science was divorced from life and alienated from the people, but now I see it differently—I see that the whole nation respects and appreciates science."

Again the professor's words created no stir. No foreign observer, including those of us who represented the Western press, had perceived in them anything particularly momentous or ominous for the outside world. Russia, we told ourselves, was only straining to make up for lost time. Never did it occur to any of us or to Pavlov himself that the feverish concentration on science would someday explode into an accomplishment that would dazzle and dismay even America.

Because of his world-wide renown, Pavlov is the most dramatic example I can cite of the changing attitude of the old intelligentsia toward the dictatorship that had wrecked their hopes of refashioning their homeland in accord with their own values and their own concept of the sacredness of the individual. There were, of course, the Zhivagos who perished in the wreckage. They loved Russia intensely, "the incomparable motherland; famed far and wide, martyred, stubborn, extravagant, mad, irresponsible, adored with her eternally splendid and disastrous and unpredictable adventures," as Pasternak has written. But they were too weak-willed to act, or to breast the tide that engulfed them. They could only suffer and mourn, eloquently and beautifully, like Turgenev's Rudin and the galaxy of "superfluous" heroes in so many other nineteenth-century novels and plays.

Yet Pasternak himself was no Zhivago. Those of us who knew him will remember him as a live, excitable, and argumentative man. A dedicated physical culturist, he had always striven to keep himself in excellent health. He was a hardy man, and he loved to swim in any weather, however inclement, until the water in the river was frozen. His *Doctor Zhivago* may not be the literary masterpiece that the Western world has acclaimed it—how many of the thousands who bought the novel actually finished reading it?—but it is news to those of us who knew the author that he was "a hermit crab," as Mikhail Sholokhov, during his interview with American intellectuals in Washington (September 25, 1959), called him. Stubbornly Pasternak clung to his own convictions, but the door of his rambling house in Peredelkino was always open to anybody who wished to call on him. He was infinitely more gracious a host than Sholokhov ever was. Great writer as he is, gallantry of spirit is a virtue which I never heard anybody in Moscow attribute to the author of *And Quiet Flows the Don*.

Like Professor Pavlov but unlike Zhivago, Pasternak didn't flee to the Siberian wilderness for refuge from the storm. He knew there was no refuge from it except in death and he was too intoxicated with life to take that way out, as did other literary personages: among them the poets Mayakovsky, Esenin, and Marina Tsvetayeva, and the novelist Alexander Fadeyev, whom lifelong dedication to bolshevism failed to save from the despair that drove him into putting a bullet into his head.

Like Pavlov, Pasternak remained a man of purpose, energy, and endeavor. Pressures to enlist his poetic gifts for the glorification of "the father of peoples," of the tractor heroine, of "the dear party," he resisted. He wouldn't compromise with his conscience and abase himself before the men who ruled the country, not even Stalin. Denied an outlet for his poetry, he took to translating Shakespeare, Schiller, Shelley, Goethe, and the poets of Soviet Georgia. He remained busy and creative.

So it was with the overwhelming mass of the pre-revolutionary intelligentsia. Patriotic men, they sought salvation in the pursuit of their professional specialties. Professors Romanovsky, Korovin, Uklonsky, Molchanov—to mention only a few of them—from Moscow and Leningrad universities, journeyed to Tashkent in 1920, and in the midst of political turmoil and economic ruin, founded a new university, the first in Russian Central Asia. Between 1918 and 1923, other professors founded universities in Minsk, Nizhny Novgorod (Gorky), Baku, Voronezh, Tiflis, Erevan, Dnepropetrovsk, Sverdlovsk, Irkutsk, Vladivostok—eleven universities, if we include Tashkent, within a period of six years and under the most trying circumstances. There is nothing in Russian history to parallel the heroic achievement of these professors, who laid the foundation of higher education for future generations.

Still other intellectuals organized institutes and research laboratories, and those outside the academic world—engineers, physicians, geologists, agricultural experts, foresters, writers—made what adjustments they could with the new times, however agonizing the compromise with their private beliefs.

One of the most charming men I met in those days (the year was

1932) was Professor Dmitry Pryanishnikov, world-renowned agrochemist. A stocky gray-haired man with a lofty forehead, the inevitable Vandyke beard, and a gentle voice, he lived in Moscow by himself in a frame house with a big garden, in which he loved to work. Once when I came to his house for dinner, he showed me around the garden, taking particular pride in his strawberry beds and the large luscious berries that he picked for dinner. Though the countryside was in turmoil, with peasants sabotaging work in the newly formed collectives and inviting famine in the country, he wouldn't be drawn into a discussion of collectivization. Instead he spoke of Central Asia and of the remarkable agricultural potentialities there.

There were others like him pursuing their careers honestly and indefatigably. Enormous was their contribution to the economic, scientific, and cultural development of the country. But, unlike Pavlov, they were not always immune to distrust and persecution, not even to the firing squad. This was particularly true of historians, philosophers, literary specialists, and even Marxist scholars. But after the presentation of Afinogenov's *Fear* and Stalin's speech of June 1931 calling for a new deal for the intelligentsia, their position visibly improved. They were more at ease with themselves and the world; they had mastered the art of living a double life, one public and one private, one of submission and even obeisance, the other of nonconformism, which they revealed—if at all—only to trusted friends. But woe to those who were overheard and were reported to the security police!

Except for some of the younger generation and some of the young writers who have come to prominence since the end of the last war, the Soviet intelligentsia are still divided men, whether they are survivors from Lenin's and Stalin's times or members of the numerous group that has entered the intelligentsia from the peasantry and the factory workers. I do not include the professional ideologists, the party secretaries, who are the men of real power in the community, the other party and non-party functionaries and white-collar folk—including writers—who are more keenly attuned to the mood and motives of the Kremlin hierarchy than are priests of any denomination to those of the hierarchy of their church. These men are in fact supreme anti-intellectuals, fundamentalists in party doctrine and party policy. They dismiss facts that might shake the ground under their beliefs or that might inhibit them from the execution of a given policy, whether it is liquidation of kulaks, denunciation of the Hungarian rebellion, or the moral crucifixion of a Pasternak. Dedicated men of action, they pursue only the accomplishment of the task at hand. The Plan and its execution is the passion of their lives.

In Moscow I met an editor, a member of the party, who wished me to tell him "frankly" why American publishers were bringing out so little Soviet fiction. In the course of the conversation I could sense that literary men like himself felt humiliated because while Soviet science, music, theater, dancing, and athletics have in recent years won wide fame, Soviet literature has achieved only scanty and unenthusiastic recognition. He impressed me as a man earnestly concerned with bringing glory to Soviet letters. In passing let it be said that if a Soviet writer achieves the distinction of foreign publication, not in a people's democracy, which is taken for granted, but in a Western country, more notably in America, England, or France, he wins fresh laurels for himself—provided, of course, his work brings no dishonor on "the socialist Motherland." Nor are Soviet writers indifferent to the royalties they may accumulate in dollars, pounds, or francs, particularly in these days, when it is comparatively easy for those with a favorable political record to secure a passport for foreign travel. They can count on these royalties, especially from America, where the Soviet Government maintains in New York a literary agency that signs contracts with publishers and collects royalties, a benefit Moscow has consistently refused to extend to Western writers.

Candidly I told the editor that while, to the student of Soviet civilization, Soviet fiction was of no small importance, to the lay reader Soviet "positive" and "negative" characters and the problems and conflicts in which authors involve them were too alien and too artificial to evoke a response. "For one thing," I said, "you are emotionally involved in production and we are not, and very much of your writing is devoted to the problems and struggles in industry and farming, which do not interest American readers. But give us well-written stories in which the reader can identify himself with the lives and problems of the characters, as he can with those of Russian nineteenth-century fiction, and you'll have no difficulty in finding publishers in America."

He smiled ironically and then asked whether I had read Leonid
Leonov's *The Russian Forest*. I replied that I had read the novel but
didn't believe it would interest American readers. My opinion startled
him, and at some length he held forth on Leonov's brilliant writing,
his feeling for people, his skill in complicating plot, his love of
Russian nature, especially of the forest. "And isn't Polya, the heroine,
a lovable character?" he asked.

"Yes," I replied, "but only in the early part of the novel, making a
reader like myself feel that here at last is an author who depicts a
heroine in the tradition of nineteenth-century fiction. Unfortunately,
as the story unfolds, Polya begins to speak in the pious clichés of
Komsomolka's editorials, which alone makes the novel unacceptable
for American publication." Leonov's earlier novels, especially *The
Badgers* and *The Thief*, I told the editor, were well received by
literary America.

He argued with me for some time and then said, "So you wouldn't
recommend the novel to your publisher?"

"It wouldn't do any good," I replied. "Please believe me, it
wouldn't."[2]

The editor was a man of about forty, and therefore a product of
Stalinist education and indoctrination. I am certain that I failed to
convince him that it wasn't the American publisher who, out of
hostility to the Soviet Union, deliberately withheld Soviet fiction
from the American reader.

There was, I thought, something pathetic about his inability to
dissever himself from the tastes and attitudes of the Stalin era; and
I could imagine him fiercely wielding a blue pencil over manuscripts,
striking out everything that affronted his ideological fixations. These
seemed to have become such an organic part of him that to get rid
of them would be like cutting flesh from his own body.

There are others like him in the Soviet Union: bulwarks of anti-
intellectualism, they detest free inquiry and are determined to perpetuate control over men's minds, while declaring all the time that
they are fulfilling the intellectual and spiritual legacies of Byelinsky
and Herzen, of Chernyshevsky and Dobrolyubov, of Turgenev and

[2] I have since learned that the novel made the rounds of leading
American publishers and they all rejected it.

Tolstoy. These men are the hard-shell fundamentalists of Russian communism.

But even they cannot keep down the intellectual ferment in the country. This ferment is not rebellion or anything that threatens the power and security of the party or the state; it is a disillusionment with official ideology, a quest for new ideas, a longing for the acceptance of man as he is in his hopes and sorrows, in his personal defeats and personal triumphs. The ferment crops out over and over in private conversations with professors, poets, writers, scientists, schoolteachers, and laymen who read the literature of the past, Russian and foreign. They are the real intelligentsia of today, men and women who do their own thinking, however conformist they may sound in their public utterances. "Authors—engineers of the soul!" a young mathematician exclaimed. "What tommyrot! Man's soul isn't a mechanism that you can take apart and put together according to a specified blueprint." Mordant is the derision of the idealization of Soviet reality and of the ebullient optimism of the "true" socialist-realist fiction. In Siberia, where the intellectual climate is more equable than in European Russia, an elderly geologist in discussing socialist-realist fiction permitted himself to say that all it was good for was toilet paper. The harsh and unjustified judgment was a reaction to the "sweetness and light" of so much Soviet fiction.

The protest against the pretension to universal happiness in Soviet society, "the most perfect" man has ever known, rings out from most unexpected quarters. In Vsevolod Kochetov's novel *Yershov Brothers*, of which there was much talk when I was in Moscow and which is a thinly disguised indictment of authors who chafe under the demands of socialist realism, there is a debate between Kapa, a medical student and daughter of the town's party secretary, and Andrey, the man she loves. The subject of the debate is a play called *Woman Alone*. Kapa says:

"And that woman loved her husband very much, gave him everything her heart could give, and then he left her for another woman— a younger one. And the author dares to say it doesn't matter; that though you haven't got a husband, you've still got a collective, your work, and things like that. He should have shown us how wrong the assumption is, how wrong and sad. That would have been the truth." And Kapa goes on: "Nothing could replace you as far as I'm concerned—neither the collective nor the sick people I will be healing someday. If you left me, I should weep day and night, and you could never put me into a cheerful little play, if I remained true to life. But the play we saw tonight was hypocritical."

A strange point to be raised by an author who, in his novel, threatens reprisals against "our ideological opponents who have started an offensive against us"—an offensive against the shackling tenets of socialist realism that are so sacred to him. Even he could no longer remain oblivious to the tragedy of women who are fated to live alone and without love. "Nurseries, kindergartens, allowances—yes," Kapa says. "It's easier for a mother to bring up her children. But can all this make up for the loss of love, for the loss of the man you love, who abandons you for another woman?" And again: "I'm very proud to live in a country like ours, but I don't like it when people get hypocritical and mushy over it."

An ideological fundamentalist like Kochetov would never in my judgment have dared to put into Kapa's mouth such words had it not been for the thaw that followed Stalin's death, and more particularly Khrushchev's denunciation of Stalin at the Twentieth Party Congress in February 1956.

That denunciation was like a thunderstorm that cleared away the heavy fog which had darkened the Soviet cultural scene. During 1956 and the larger part of 1957, one could hardly pick up a literary journal, whether published in Moscow or Leningrad, without coming upon poets, short-story writers, novelists, who spoke with a new voice, a voice of protest against the "engineers of the soul" who had for years been fabricating images of men and women in which Soviet citizens rarely recognized themselves. The human being was again looked upon with clear eyes and sometimes with a tender heart. Even the party man was no longer the machinelike demon of duty and accomplishment that he had formerly been depicted as, as is vividly attested to in Nikolai Pogodin's play *Sonnet of Petrarch*. The hero, a construction engineer named Dmitry Sukholodov, a party man of some eminence, falls in love with a girl named Maya, a librarian in the Siberian town where he works. "For twenty years," he says, "I've been building. Isn't it about time that I learned something about love?" But he is a married man, and though he and his wife have no love for each other, he is denounced to the party. Summoned before the party secretary of the province for an explanation of his "sin," he bluntly replies, "I cannot discuss this subject with anybody." When the secretary insists, Sukholodov tells him, "There are things in life that are higher and more complex than ordinary ideas."

"Listen, brother, for the last time I'm asking you to sit down and write your explanation," the secretary demands.

"I shan't write anything."

"Well then, remember . . . and don't cry."

Unperturbed by the secretary's threat, Sukholodov answers, "A Russian classic says that not only for you and me but for father and son it's impossible to discuss one's relations with a woman, even when these are of the purest. Why can't we abide by laws long established by the highest morality?"

"Who said it?"

"Dostoyevsky."

But the party secretary is adamant. "Do you know," he says, "with whom you refuse to speak? You refuse to speak with the party."

Undismayed, Sukholodov answers, "There are intimate sides to a man's life that he won't open to anybody. He simply isn't obliged to do so. There is no law that he must."

The party, then, isn't the universal, infallible, omniscient body before whom a member when called upon must lay bare the innermost secrets of his life. A party member is a man again, with the right to privacy in his intimate relationships with a woman, a right that the party still refuses to honor. But the protest is there, vivid and sharp.

However, the Hungarian revolution and the threatened insurrection in Poland frightened Khrushchev. He perceived danger in the passion for truth that suddenly flowed from the pens of poets and storytellers. The terror of the Stalinist police regime, the frightful mismanagement of collective farms, the privileges that high party functionaries arrogated to themselves, the thwarted lives of children denied parental love, the agonies of men and women in unfulfilled love—these and other themes that had for years been crying for expression suddenly found their spokesmen, especially among the younger poets and writers, who will be discussed in a later chapter. Then, in May 1957, at a gathering of eminent writers in Moscow, Khrushchev called a halt to the exposure of the failings in

Soviet society. The party was to decide what was truth in letters and art, and no author or artist would be permitted to ignore *partiinost* (party spirit).

"When I read Khrushchev's speech," said a literary woman in Leningrad, "I wondered what would happen. But it isn't as bad as I imagined it would be. It did not prevent *Oktyabr* from serializing Galina Nikolayeva's *Battle on the Road*, a wonderful and tragic love story, one of the finest Soviet novels that has ever been published." I could not buy this novel in any bookshop I visited; they were always sold out.

Khrushchev is no Stalin. Pogodin's play has not been banned; it is in the repertoires of leading theaters all over the country. Andreyev, Bunin, Dostoyevsky, whom Stalin had anathematized, are always in print. John Reed's *Ten Days That Shook the World* has been republished. At last the monumental *History of Russia*, by Sergey Solovyov, is being brought out, and there were rumors in Moscow that Paul Milyukov's *Outline of Russian Civilization* may likewise be published.

Pasternak, though expelled from the Writers' Union and the Union of Translators, remained unmolested. The taboo on tragedy has been softened, and at the Third Congress of the Soviet Writers' Union, in May 1959, the ideological fundamentalists, who had girded themselves for battle with "revisionists," as they label their opponents, were constrained to hear some pungent words from two of their most respected colleagues—the poet Alexander Tvardovsky and Konstantin Pasutovsky.

"We cannot go on living in the old way," said Tvardovsky. "We must say this to our literary yesterday and even to our literary today. Nor shall we go on living that way." Then, speaking of the "selflessness and noble disinterestedness" of the literary masters of the past, he told the congress that "their inspired dedication to great art shall serve us as a lofty example." He further admonished writers "to write as your conscience commands . . . and do not fear in advance either editors or critics."

Pasutovsky was too ill to attend the congress and addressed it through a contribution to the *Literaturnaya Gazeta*. He lamented the pretension of writers that there was no suffering or tragedy in the country and scoffed at the obligatory and mawkish happy endings. "We are fortunate," he said, "that Leo Tolstoy wrote *Anna Karenina* before this tradition arose. He could allow Anna to break up her family and pass out of life from purely private, and consequently impermissible, motives"—impermissible under the dispensation of the fundamentalists. "We shout so much and so loudly about truth in literature," the venerable author continued, "precisely because we lack it." He called on the congress to end the never ceasing squabble among writers. "We must at last stop calling friends enemies only because they tell the unpleasant truth. Two roads face the congress: one of consolidation, the other of destructive disagreement."

Khrushchev himself, in his long address to the congress, was remarkably conciliatory. Though he called for literary creations that rouse enthusiasm for "heroic exploits," for "the victory of communism," he adjured the right "to go into an analysis of your works. I am no literary critic, you know, and therefore don't feel myself obliged to analyze your literary work. . . . It is you who do the writing, so it is you who must criticize the writing." He even had a good word to say for Vladimir Dudintsev, whose novel *Not by Bread Alone* had roused the fury of the fundamentalists because he mercilessly depicted the selfishness and the arrogance of bureaucrats in high position who stifle creative effort, even in engineering. "I have said before and think so now," said Khrushchev, "that Dudintsev never has been our enemy and never has been against the Soviet system." Not once did Khrushchev use the expression "engineers of the soul" or "socialist realism." He left writers with the impression that while he expected from them loyalty to the party and its policies, and dedication to "the building of communism," he wanted above all peace with them and among them. Kochetov's call to arms against "revisionists" was officially muffled, and the militant obscurantism which he championed was officially checked.

But there is no peace. The fight goes on, and the spy mania and vitriolic hate crusade against "American aggressors" that followed in the wake of the U-2 incident has given fresh courage and boldness to the fundamentalists. Kochetov is back with his old threats and recriminations. In the weekly journal *Ogonyok* (No. 30, July 1960) he denounces the motion picture *The Cranes Are Flying* as "a low bow to the West." He attacks pictures and plays that "give rise to copious tears in the auditorium but do not light up living horizons before the audience." He centers particular scorn on the literary journal *Novy Mir* ("New World"), whose editor, Alexander Tvardovsky, the poet, is a great favorite of the university youth. Kochetov loathes the fiction *Novy Mir* has been publishing, more particularly a short story, "The Second Night," by the talented Victor Nekrasov, about a valiant simple-minded soldier, Lenka, who silently leaves the company of fellow soldiers because he cannot endure their rough talk about the women in the family photographs of a German he had just killed in battle. Lenka is too human for Kochetov, to whom fiction like Nekrasov's short story is "drops of nihilistic poison, the poison of faultfinding, of freewheeling criticism, of snobbism, petty-mindedness, and mediocrity." If this poison, he continues, drips into "twenty, ten, or even one soul, the result is very bad."

But the fact is that the Soviet reading public is too mature, too sophisticated, too discriminating to be content with the myth that heroic accomplishments in laying bricks and railroad tracks, fusion with the collective, love of country and party, lift a citizen above tears and above all personal unhappiness. Even milkmaids told the late Fyodor Panferov, a novelist of peasant origin who specialized in writing about the village, that he wrote about them without knowing them.

No authors in the world could wish for a more ardent and more challenging reading public. Their reading of the classics, their own and foreign ones, has spoiled them for the schematic "positive" and "negative" characters in socialist-realist fiction. Gladly they read a socialist-realist novelist like Boris Polevoy, because, as a Moscow schoolteacher told me, he has a lively style, he is an interesting storyteller, and his "cardboard" heroes are likable. At the time Kochetov's blast at *Novy Mir* was published, a Moscow woman told me of an incident she had recently witnessed in a bookshop. A girl with a jaunty pony tail asked a saleswoman for a collection of Yevtushenko's poems. "Sold out," said the saleswoman. "Yes," flung back the girl, "trash you have, but good books—you are always sold out."

The grand old men in Russia are the aging and aged pre-revolutionary intelligentsia. The years have taken a heavy toll of them, and in Leningrad, Moscow, Kiev, I had moments of sorrow when I learned that So-and-so had passed away. But those who are still alive are among the most venerated men in the country. The day of Afinogenov's Professor Borodin, who cried out against the fear that was paralyzing the creative efforts of a scientist like himself, are a memory now, except of course to those who are in the humanities and social sciences. But aside from these, the Borodins have free rein in the pursuit of their specialties. In their declining years they hold their heads high and are richly rewarded in comfort and glory for the torments they endured in the earlier years of their lives. In the universities at Moscow, Irkutsk, Tashkent, over and over I heard students pay exalted tributes to "the glorious old professors." They are "the last of the Mohicans"—the galaxy of brilliant minds inherited by the bolsheviks from Czarist times, without whose dedicated services the Soviet Union never could have achieved its spectacular scientific and technological rise in the world.

When I learned in Moscow that Vladimir Nikolayevich, a mineralogist and veteran of the old intelligentsia, was alive, I hastened to his home. He wasn't there, and the old peasant woman who kept house for him informed me that he was in the country visiting his daughter at her *dacha* (country house). I couldn't go to the *dacha* because it was out of bounds for foreigners; so I left a note saying that I was leaving for the Ukraine and would be back in Moscow on a certain date and hoped I could see him.

I first met Vladimir Nikolayevich in the middle twenties in a wayside restaurant on the Georgian military highway in the Northern Caucasus, and afterward, whenever I was in Moscow, I often went to see him. He had been a Social Revolutionary, and everything in his person, his background, his education, his once hallowed ideals of a free, cultivated, and prosperous Russia, cried out against the terror of the bolshevik revolution. Unlike Pavlov, he had not responded to the creative accomplishments of the Kremlin dictatorship. "Dung," I often heard him say. "That's what my generation of intellectuals is—dung with which to fertilize the earth for future generations and if the bolsheviks are still around, rank weeds are all our earth will grow."

But he was no Zhivago; he had the will and the energy to fight for a place for himself in the tempestuous new society. An accomplished specialist, he never lacked work. But he couldn't control his sharp tongue, and again and again he was arrested for blurting out some derisive remark. Fortunately for him, he was desperately needed and he had a high sense of honor in discharging his professional obligations. He neither stalled nor sabotaged and his superiors knew it. Besides, he had connections in high places, among them a ponderous middle-aged woman, a party member, who frequently came to his house and lectured to him as to an unruly child on his "despicable tongue."

It was the war that galvanized Vladimir Nikolayevich into a new person; patriotism at last submerged his hostility to the dictatorship: Mother Russia was in mortal danger and it was no time to be thinking of the evils of bolshevism. This of course was true of hosts of pre-revolutionary intellectuals; now they had a new cause to live and fight for—a cause as precious to them as to Stalin—a cause that roused in them their deepest and most sacred sentiments. Despite the miseries and agonies of war, they felt exhilarated and uplifted —Russians again, gloriously and glowingly Russian—and Stalin's invocation of "the valorous image of our great ancestors," the military commanders of the past, who had heroically and triumphantly defended the Motherland, roused their deepest emotions.

It was Vladimir Nikolayevich who had first called my attention to the fact that the leading generals in the Red Army were sons of muzhiks, and he glowed with pride whenever he spoke of "our muzhik generals." The faith he had lost in his people, whom in pre-revolutionary years he had pitied and revered, as did so many old-time intellectuals, especially the Social Revolutionaries, flamed up again, high and ardent.

I looked forward to meeting him again and on my return from the Ukraine I went to see him. A stately man of seventy-six, with the inevitable Vandyke beard as white as snow, as was his thick, short-cropped hair, he appeared energetic and cheerful with a face as sunburned as a peasant's and with a firm, heavy tread.

"Well, well," he said as he pumped my hand with both of his, "you cannot resist the lure of my country."

In reply I quoted to him what the late Walter Duranty had once said: "Russia is a disease, like love, only you get over love and you don't get over Russia."

He laughed. "A healthy disease to have, and things do happen here, always, don't they?" he said.

We sat down, and as I glanced around the spacious sitting room which I knew so well, I observed no changes except that there were more books than ever, neatly set in wall-length shelves. "Now, tell me how everything is in America," he said.

"As you know," I replied, "millions of us are starving to death." I knew he would understand my allusion to the stream of stories in the Soviet press about the millions of America's unemployed and their misery and hunger.

"*Ekh*," he said with a deprecating swing of the hand, "they don't believe a word they write. We still have our Nozdryovs."

The reference to Gogol's memorable liar-braggart in *Dead Souls* reflected something of the nineteenth-century Russian intellectual, the man of integrity who abhorred falsification and boastfulness. As we continued talking he revealed more and more of the nineteenth-century intellectual: in his literary and musical tastes, his moral and intellectual values, his appreciation of Western civilization, and his spirit of cosmopolitanism, in the refinement of his manners and the purity of his speech, utterly untouched by the coarseness that has crept into the speech of the younger generation. He might never have lived under the Soviets for all the effect it seemed to have exerted on his mind and character. Listening to him, I had the illusion that I was transported back to an age that had never really died.

When I told him this, Vladimir Nikolayevich quickly lifted up his arm in an orator's gesture and replied with emotion: "Ah no, a million times no! I have changed, all the pre-revolutionary intelligentsia have changed. How could we help it? Think of all the blood and horror we've witnessed: the civil war, son against father, daughter against mother, Reds hanging Whites, Whites hanging Reds, corpses dangling from trees and telephone poles; then the respite of NEP—followed by the first Five-Year Plan; terror again, ceaseless houndings of men like myself, in jail and out of jail, yet the people working and building, building and working, and suffering too—God, how we suffered! And then—forcible collectivization, a gruesome famine, corpses again in streets and fields, millions of corpses, and then the purges: executioners busy all over the country, Communists killing Communists, the intellectuals among them, getting bullets into the backs of their heads! Everything, it seemed, was falling to pieces, even the earth under our feet. You know how I felt in those days. But the earth held together, held us together; and then—then the war, our patriotic war, fresh blood and horror, more than our people had ever known and—we got dried of tears, dried of compunction, were carried along by physical instinct, animal instinct, fortified by love of country, a hallowed love of the earth we trod, of our beautiful birches, of our mighty forests and rivers, and—and we won the war! Then came the sputniks—imagine what it has all meant to us—our muzhik Russia—the Russia of my youth—rising to unprecedented heights in the world of science!" Nikolayevich paused to catch his breath. Then with a wry smile he went on. "We've become tough-skinned, hardened like rocks, too hardened to be shocked by anything, to be scared by anybody, to be hurt by anybody. We've changed from the nineteenth-century intellectuals we were and shall never be again. Never! We're finished with dreaming for the sake of dreaming, suffering for the sake of suffering. Cruel things have happened to me; I don't even like to talk about them any more. But I take great pride in my pupils, who have done so much to help build up the strength and the glory of our Motherland, and I can pass out of life with the consolation that despite all the troubles I have endured, I have been a man of action and shall leave behind men I have trained who may have their days of despair over this or that wrong, but who'll go on with their purposeful tasks, on and on. Other things? No, we haven't forgotten them—man doesn't live by mineralogy alone. But we—my generation—don't want to make martyrs of ourselves any longer, not at our age and after winning the bloodiest war in our history and sending sputniks into space. You may think this is our tragedy but it is also our triumph."

I didn't need to ask him whether he regretted the change. There was no throb of regret in his deep voice, no flicker of disappointment in his lively gray eyes. He was a new man and yet a divided man, more divided, I thought, than he knew: forswearing the dreams and confusions of the years of his youth and yet needing the old cultural values as much as the bread he ate.

"Come," he said cheerfully, "let's have a drink of cognac."

18.

INTELLECTUALS
General Staff of Science

Professor Igor Tamm, one of the three Soviet recipients of the Nobel Prize in physics in 1958, in Czarist times had studied in Edinburgh. But the second edition of the *Bolshaya Encyclopedia* does not mention this fact.

Professor Lev Landau, reputedly one of the foremost theoretical physicists in the world, in Soviet times had studied with Niels Bohr in Copenhagen. Nor is this fact mentioned in his biographical sketch in the same edition of the *Bolshaya*.

Most significant is the encyclopedia's omission of the fourteen years (1921–35) that Peter Kapitsa, perhaps the Soviet physicist best known in the Western world, spent in England, studying and collaborating with the late Sir Ernest Rutherford.

The son of a Czarist military engineer, Kapitsa graduated from the Petrograd Polytechnical College. During the revolutionary turmoil and famine his first wife and child died, and in 1921, at the age of twenty-seven, he migrated to England. He was without funds, but Sir Ernest recognized his remarkable ability and never allowed him to suffer from want of food and shelter or tobacco for his pipe. During his sojourn in England he carried off one high honor after another. Awarded a Ph.D. degree, he became Assistant of Research in Magnesium at the Cavendish Laboratory at Cambridge, Fellow of Trinity College, Massel Research Professor of the Royal Society, and director of the Royal Society Mond Laboratory.

In 1935 Kapitsa went to Russia to attend a scientific congress. I was there at the time and remember the excitement among intellectuals when it became known that the young physicist was not permitted to return to England. The rumors that he had been arrested were untrue. Quite the contrary: keenly appreciative of his scientific genius, the Kremlin offered him special inducements to continue his research in his native land. The fixtures and appliances in the laboratory set up for him in Cambridge were bought by the Soviet Government and transported to Moscow, where Kapitsa has lived ever since. The handsome physicist with his pipe and brown tweeds looks more like an English squire than a Russian academician. At the conclusion of the war, an academician I know informed me, he invoked Stalin's displeasure and was exiled for some time to his country home.

But the *Bolshaya* biography reveals nothing of Kapitsa's career in England and never mentions the honors he won there. In the years of Stalin's postwar chauvinism it was heresy to suggest that Russians had anything to learn from foreign science or scholarship.

Sir Ernest, called in the West "the father of nuclear physics" and Nobel Prize winner in 1908, is conspicuously absent from the pages of the *Bolshaya*.

In the monograph on anti-Semitism one reads the following: "In Great Britain, with the open connivance of the Labourite government, there is unbridled anti-Semitic agitation. In August 1947, there were Jewish pogroms in Liverpool, Glasgow, and other cities." The 1958 edition of Smirnitzky's Russian-English dictionary, published in Moscow, defines "pogrom" as massacre; hence Soviet encyclopedists would have readers of the *Bolshaya* believe that in the manner of Czarist Black Hundreds the Labour government connived in the perpetration of Jewish massacres.

I shouldn't have cited these further distortions and falsehoods in the *Bolshaya* had it not been for the glowing tribute of some two thousand words to the unmatched excellence of its scholarship that appeared in *Pravda* of August 24, 1959. This was no ordinary journalistic effusion. It was signed by three of Russia's most distinguished academicians: Alexander Nesmeyanov, president of the Academy, Aksel Berg, the famed radio engineer, and Stanislaw Strumilin, the celebrated economist. They speak of the *Bolshaya* as "the largest up-to-date encyclopedia in the world, larger than the *Britannica*, the *Americana*, the French Larousse encyclopedias." Actually it is some 30 per cent shorter than the *Britannica*. But if the arithmetical misrepresentation may be dismissed as an instance of the juvenile boasting that interlards official Soviet writing and oratory, what shall be said of the claim of the distinguished academicians that "in newness and trustworthiness of information [the *Bolshaya*] excels all foreign encyclopedias."

Nesmeyanov is a renowned biochemist, and it is no secret in Moscow that he and other academicians in the Chemistry and Physics departments of the Academy are striving to lift the science of biology from the depths into which Trofim Lysenko, the botanist and plant breeder, had with Stalin's support degraded it by "outlawing" the Mendelian law. The articles in the *Bolshaya* on Gregor Johann Mendel, biology, and genetics are permeated with Lysenkoism and damn the Mendelian law as "idealistic and reactionary," of which a scientist like Nesmeyanov must be heartily ashamed.

Yet in the *Pravda* panegyric to the *Bolshaya*, Nesmeyanov and his colleagues inform the reader that the *Bolshaya* "has a large circulation and meets with a lively response among intellectuals in foreign countries." Though they quote a letter from a Dr. Giovanni Berlinger in Rome saying, "We welcome the arrival of each volume as a triumph of advanced science and international co-operation against the accomplices of obscurantism," they do not and cannot quote a single word of commendation from any recognized Western scholar or any other non-Communist, be he only a schoolteacher. I have heard Russians themselves speak with disrespect and even ridicule of the *Bolshaya*, especially of the volumes that were published while Stalin was still alive, in which Stalin's anti-intellectualism and hatred of the Western world and Western civilization are glaringly manifest. In truth, it is not an encyclopedia but an instrument of political warfare, waged with malice aforethought.

The *Bolshaya* devotes half its space to the natural sciences, in which, except for biology and genetics, it is doubtless one of the great reference books of all times. But in other fields, especially in the social sciences, it is a testament to the degradation of the Soviet intelligentsia, more notably the academicians who edited the work. Nesmeyanov and his colleagues dismiss the misrepresentations and falsehoods as mere editorial slips, devoting to their criticism only one sentence of eighteen Russian words: "Unfortunately intolerable errors and inaccuracies have been allowed in separate articles in the encyclopedic publications." In 1958 they hurried into print a supplementary volume (Vol. LI), of which I heard Muscovites speak as "the Book of Resurrection," because it resurrects some of the nations Stalin had uprooted and abolished and the names of individuals whom Stalin had executed.

One can only speculate on the motives that prompted Nesmeyanov and his colleagues to trumpet their praise of so execrable an encyclopedia. "Don't expect them," said a scholarly Western diplomat in Moscow, "publicly to dishonor themselves and the Academy before the whole world by repudiating even the volumes that were brought out while Stalin was still alive." A Muscovite who is not a party member said, "It would have been better if they had remained silent and proceeded to correct their falsehoods for a new edition. But maybe the Central Committee demanded the tribute they published in *Pravda*. Why? Nobody knows."

Doubtless also the *Pravda* panegyric is a form of insurance against possible future trouble. Being close to the Kremlin, the trio of noted academicians are keenly aware of the ideological battles among the top hierarchy of the party, struggles of which the public knows little or nothing. How can even academicians tell who will rule the Kremlin after Khrushchev passes from the scene when there are no dependable safeguards for an orderly and legitimate succession? How can they envision the ideological strictures and political coercions that the new master or masters of the country may, in the name of Marxism-Leninism, complete with proper quotations, hurl at them and the country?

In "a house without a roof," it is never amiss to have at hand a protective umbrella.

But whatever the purpose of the *Pravda* panegyric, the older academicians and other intellectuals of their generation must be spoken of as beaten men, cynical of integrity, immune to remorse. Outside of science they are truly Russia's lost generation, lost to the high intellectual tradition to which they were born, lost to disinterested scholarship, to honesty of mind and respect for truth. If ever Soviet scholarship is rescued from the degradation into which it has sunk, it will not be by the academicians of today but by the rising generation of intellectuals.

Yet in recent years, visiting foreigners who have come to know Russian intellectuals have recognized in Alexander Nesmeyanov, despite his signature to the *Pravda* panegyric, a man of real stature.

He became president of the Academy in 1951, when the Stalinist terror was unleasing fresh excesses. He could not save Kapitsa from banishment to his country home. But with the aid of close associates, notably Professor Topichev, secretary of the Academy, he held the staff together and protected scientists from the dictatorship's persecutions. After the announcement of the "doctors' plot," the universities, either out of timidity or on order from above, began to dismiss some of their Jewish professors. But Nesmeyanov stood firm. Under him, Jewish academicians and scientists were free from political and personal molestation.

He has his enemies among his colleagues, and when he came up for re-election in 1956, he was severely criticized for political maneuverings and for having mishandled certain fields of research. In spite of the attacks he was re-elected.

From his predecessor he inherited the redoubtable Trofim Lysenko. But outside of genetics and excepting Kapitsa, the scientist even under Stalin was free in his study and laboratory to pursue his investigations unhindered by political intrusions and restraints. The onetime denunciation of Einstein, he silently disregarded. He was striving for results that bore no immediate relationship to bolshevik dogma and he has astounded the world with his spectacular achievements. On October 4, 1957, the first sputnik broke through the atmosphere and orbited the earth. Less than a month later followed Sputnik II, carrying the dog Laika, the first space passenger, who didn't survive the journey. On May 15, 1958, Sputnik III weighing 2925 pounds, soared into the outer world.

On January 2, 1959, Soviet scientists aimed the rocket Mechta (dream) at the moon and missed by about 4500 miles. But in September of the same year they tried again and succeeded. Mankind had touched another celestial body. Other triumphs followed, culminating on April 12, 1961, in the most sensational of all Soviet scientific achievements: sendng Yuri Gagarin into space and bringing him safely back. In orbiting once around the globe, Gagarin won the Soviet race to be first in man's travel through space.

At first the outside world regarded these Soviet feats with a mixture of astonishment, admiration, and envy. After the initial shock, it pondered how it could have happened at all, and finally had to face the fact that it had persistently either underestimated or ignored

Russia's scientific growth, even as it had underestimated or ignored Russia's immense war potential when the Wehrmacht invaded the Soviet Union in June 1941.

Long ago Lenin wrote that, in a planned economy, the urgent problems of industry and national defense could be solved solely through the utilization of all resources of science. The bolsheviks therefore embraced science as a powerful and sanctified instrument of the revolution. They set about promoting its advancement with all means at their command. They stirred up enthusiasm for science among the young generation, and ambitious boys and girls came to regard science as the most exalted of careers. The bolsheviks subsidized science so generously that even Professor Ivan Pavlov, as already related, was overcome with embarrassment and gratitude.

With their passion for science it was only natural that the new rulers should have devoted particular attention to the Academy of Sciences. With the aid of Gottfried Leibniz, the German mathematician-philosopher, and the French Academy, of which he became a member, Peter the Great drew up plans for a "Russian Academy" that was to be a combination of a gymnasium and a university. Peter died several months before the Academy opened on November 13, 1725. At that time there was not a single university in Russia. Only a generation later (1755), in Moscow, was the first university founded.

Necessarily the Imperial Academy, as it came to be called, was staffed with foreigners, some of whom were distinguished scholars and others alchemists, sorcerers, and other types of charlatans. But as higher education advanced, Russians supplanted the foreigners and the Academy became a center of Russian science and scholarship.

A political conflict between the Academy and the bolsheviks was inevitable. Determined to subordinate its resources and personnel to their own purposes, the bolsheviks in 1930-31 proceeded to pogromize the Academy's social sciences, more notably the History Department. Such noted historians as Platonov, Tarle, Grekov, Bakhruchin, were persecuted and exiled. Nor were specialists in literature, philosophy, archaeology, and even Marxism in the Institute of Marx and Engels spared. The story of Stalin's onslaught on members of the Academy and on other distinguished men in the universities has never been told. But once secure in their control of the foremost institution of science and learning in the country, the bolsheviks proceeded to court and favor its members and to allow them a larger measure of autonomy in the management of their affairs than to representatives of any other institution.

Being under the immediate control of the Council of Ministers, the Academy has never become a political football for the ministries and defense forces. It is well to emphasize that while marshals of the armed services co-operate with the Academy, it is not they but the Council of Ministers and the Academy staff who have planned and produced the space rockets and the "fantastic" military weapons of which Khrushchev boasted. The president of the Academy is always privileged to approach the Council directly or the Premier personally with any of his problems, projects, and requests.

Art, medicine, education, agriculture, architecture, construction, are all under the control of their respective academies, but until April 1961 other sciences were guided by the Moscow Academy. Specifically, the Academy was committed to four primary tasks: to concentrate on problems in the branches of science under its control; to explore the natural resources of the country; to train specialists and to act as adviser to the higher state institutions; and lastly, to digest "the cultural and economic achievements of mankind and to co-operate in their timely and rational exploitation."

No other country in the world ever evolved an institution like the Moscow Academy of Sciences. Mitchell Wilson, the American physicist and novelist, who during his five months (1958) in Russia visited more scientific research centers and became acquainted with more Soviet scientists in their laboratories, offices, and homes than any other foreigner, spoke of it as "the heart and head, beginning and end of science . . . the AEC, Cal Tech, MIT, Columbia, Nevis, Chicago, Harvard, Rockefeller Institute, Mt. Wilson, Yerkes, Woods Hole, Princeton's Institute for Advanced Study, with an additional list of research laboratories too long to mention, all rolled into one." A Moscow friend of mine called it "our General Staff of Science."

To achieve its many-sided objectives, the Academy was divided into eight departments: mathematics and physics; chemistry; geology and geography; biology; technical sciences; history and philosophy; economics and law; literature and linguistics. Each department was divided into separate sections that maintained their own research institutes. Biology, for example, operated institutes in botany and the physiology of plants, forestry, biochemistry, microbiology, genetics, animal morphology, and paleontology, in addition to the Pavlov Physiological Institute, the chief botanical garden, and other institutes.

The Academy works through committees and commissions, and each institute operates its own laboratories, experiment stations, museums. Consider the mammoth responsibility of the Geology and Geography Department, which until recently supervised much of the exploration of over 5000 prospecting expeditions with a personnel of over 300,000 scattered all over the country.

Membership in the Academy is rigidly limited. In 1959 there were only 158 members and 344 corresponding members, against 146 members and 255 corresponding members in 1949. Thus during a decade of history-making accomplishments, the membership increased by only 12 full and 99 corresponding members. Usually new members are elected only to fill the vacancies of those who have died. But now and then the Academy elects members to expand its activities or to honor scientists for distinguished achievements. In 1958, for example, it added to its roster three outstanding astronauts.

The Academy grew so top-heavy with projects and institutes in both pure and applied science, that by a decree published on April 12, 1961, its widely scattered affiliates and many of its institutes, some 200 of them, were transferred to various committees of the Council of Ministers.

A new agency—the State Committee for the Co-ordination of Work in Scientific Research—has lifted from the Academy much of its administrative work and has assumed responsibility for applying science to technology as well as initiating and promoting major scientific and technological projects of its own for the advancement of the Soviet economy.

Henceforth the Academy is to dedicate itself to theoretical research in the natural sciences—in physics, mathematics, chemistry, biology, the sciences of the universe and the earth. It is also to render direction and aid in pure science to its former affiliates, the academies of the 15 federated republics, the universities, and other institutions of higher learning. Now it is the General Staff of pure science only.

Outside the field of natural sciences its functions have remained unimpaired. It continues to train scientists, directs the relationships of Soviet and foreign scientific organizations, and operates all its departments in the arts and social sciences: in history, politics, economics, literature, and the others. Likewise it continues to operate its own sizable publishing corporation and its highly specialized and highly efficient bookshop on Moscow's Gorky Street.

In 1954, soon after the death of Stalin, the Academy founded the Institute of Scientific Information, which has no parallel in any other country. The chief function of the Institute is to read, digest, and write abstracts of foreign scientific publications. It maintains a permanent staff of about 2000 readers, writers, and editors, every one of whom is conversant with one or more foreign languages, European or Asian. The Institute publishes periodic comprehensive surveys of contributions to 6890 foreign scientific publications.

The one thing the Academy never has to worry about is funds. Any project it initiates or is called on by the Council of Ministers or the new state co-ordination committee to investigate or to perfect is amply subsidized. The budget of the Academy has never been made public. Friends in Moscow assured me that it is fantastically high, but nobody knew the precise figure. However discouraging the results of a project, the Kremlin never withholds funds to continue investigations that might prove successful. Nobody knows, for example, how much the Kremlin has been investing in the search for oil in Siberia. For years and years the results were scanty, but the search continued on an ever mounting scale. The Kremlin was willing to abide by the judgment of Academy geologists that sooner or later they would strike rich oil reserves in the Siberian land. The first such strike of "commercial significance," as *Pravda* speaks of it, was accomplished under the direction of academician A. Trofimuk (*Pravda*, July 18, 1960) in the province of Tyumen, at a point where the tributary Mulimya falls into the river Konda. "The oil prospects of the region are enormous," Trofimuk announced.

Membership in the Academy is for life. An academician may or may not be a party member; membership is not obligatory. Nesmeyanov, the president, joined the party in 1944, a year after he became an academician. Ivan Petrovsky, who in addition to being an academician is rector of Moscow University, never joined the party. No scientist or scholar would, of course, be considered for membership if his loyalty to the state and the party was under suspicion. Presumably most academicians are party members. But the primary qualification is distinction and accomplishment.

In the West we say that So-and-so lives like a millionaire. In Russia they say that So-and-so lives like an academician.

As a group, academicians are the highest earners in the country. The honor of being a member of the Academy carries with it an emolument of about 500 of the new rubles a month. A member of the Byelorussian Academy told me that no matter what happens to an academician, even if he goes to jail or is sent into exile, he always receives his honorary salary. "All the time Kapitsa was in banishment in his country home," he said, "he drew his monthly payments." Another monthly sum of from 350 to 450 of the new rubles is paid an academician for being a specialist. He receives further remuneration for his discoveries or inventions, for directing an institute, presiding over a commission, heading a field exploration, lecturing in a university, counseling industry, editing a book, writing a monograph, or for anything else he may specially be called upon or may set out to accomplish. From information I gathered in Moscow, the minimum a member of the Moscow Academy earns is the equivalent of 2500 dollars a month, and some of them earn much more.

Despite earning the highest salaries in the country, academicians, by Western standards, command no life of luxury: the Soviet Union has few luxuries to offer anybody. The head of a department in an American college may not begin to earn as much as a Russian academician. But the American lives in a more modern and spacious house and drives a higher-quality automobile. Only the president of the Moscow Academy, whom the Kremlin has favored with a large and shiny limousine, is an exception to the rule. Others have a modest Moskvich, a Volga, or the now abandoned Pobeda, though always with a chauffeur at the wheel. Some even have two automobiles, one for themselves, the other for the family.

Some academicians, living in old though comfortable homes, are still waiting for new apartments. They all have summer homes, some of them in the village of Lutsino, about forty miles outside of Moscow. Stalin built these houses in the thirties, and though equipped with modern conveniences, they are modest in size and furnishings.

Other academicians have summer places in Istra and other pic-
turesque villages within easy reach of Moscow, or on some island of
the new Moscow-Volga sea. I know of no academician who lives in
the palatial mansion of a Czarist aristocrat, as Khrushchev does.

Still, in money, goods, and services, the Kremlin lavishes on them
more generous attention than on any other group of citizens. But
they cannot begin to spend their money on mere material satisfactions, so they spend it on other gratifications. They are the most
zealous first-nighters at the theater, the opera, the ballet, and concerts.
They buy jewelry for their wives, collect paintings, rare old books,
old Russian porcelain, furniture, and other antiques. Through some
grapevine an academician may learn of the death of someone who has
left art treasures to his heirs. Immediately he descends on the heirs
and buys up the inheritance, often at a fabulous price. Directors of
commission shops in Moscow need never worry about customers for
high-priced antiques or art treasures: they can always telephone an
academician or a high-earning writer and assure themselves of a ready
sale.

I know of one academician whose hobby is collecting inkwells
from the period of the father of Peter the Great; another who collects
eighteenth-century furniture, especially of the period of Paul I, son of
Catherine the Great. I know of others who are patrons of abstract
artists, buy up their canvases, and openly display them in their homes,
despite all official derogation of abstract art.

The elite of the elite, they constitute a society of their own, the
most exclusive social set in Russia. Though they frequently deliver
lectures in factory clubhouses, they do not rub shoulders with the
masses. Now that the trade unions have taken over all health and
vacation resorts—all but those of the Army—academicians have built
summer cottages of their own in some still unsettled and secluded
southern locations, away from the crowds in the public resorts. In
winter some of them fly for weekends to their cottages in the South.

They are the Kremlin's most celebrated brain trust, and outside of
politics they are the key figures in the intensified drive to surpass
America in industrial and scientific accomplishment. By their disciplined, co-ordinated, and unified efforts, they have within a brief
space of time achieved sensational triumphs in supersonic aircraft,

ballistic missiles, atomic and hydrogen bombs, rocketry, and space-ships. If in the humanities and social sciences they have remained largely timeservers, in the natural sciences and technology they are among the most accomplished men of the ages.

On an overnight train journey in the summer of 1960, I made the acquaintance of the academician whom I shall call Anton Antono-vich. When the porter led me to the door of my sleeping compart-ment, I found a gay party going on inside. The little table had been set up for bottles and glasses, and three men and three women sat around it talking and laughing. Feeling an intruder, I started to back out, but one of the men, tall and broad-shouldered with close-cropped black hair and small dark eyes, begged me to join them. To have refused such wholehearted cordiality would have been churlish. He explained that he was leaving on a mission, and his family—his wife, his son, his daughter-in-law, her father and mother—had come to see him off. They were all well dressed and well spoken, obviously of the Soviet intelligentsia.

I shook hands all around and told them that I was an American journalist. Though at that very moment the press was raging violently over the U-2 incident, these people were as cordial and as unreserved as though nothing of the sort had ever happened. We clinked glasses to lasting peace and friendship between our countries.

When the call came for visitors to leave, and the final embraces and kisses had been exchanged between Anton Antonovich and his family, he and I settled down, and as the lights of the city slid past and the train picked up speed we began to talk. My new acquaintance turned out to be an academician and director of an institute. His field was chemistry. Though to be the director of an institute is to hold an exalted and honored position in Soviet society, Anton Antonovich revealed himself as a completely simple and unpretentious man.

I asked him about his social origin. "My father," he replied, "wore *lapti* and was barely literate enough to sign his name; my mother could not. Yes, I'm the son of a lowly muzhik, that's what I am. But under the Soviets all doors were open to me, and now I'm an acade-mician." There was a note of pride in his voice.

He picked up a cognac bottle and held it against the light. "Empty," he announced. "We must have more; and caviar sandwiches. Do you like caviar?" At my nod he went off to the buffet to give the order.

When the buffet woman appeared, I took out my wallet, but Anton Antonovich objected vehemently. I was a guest in his country and Russians consider it a pleasure to honor a guest. "Isn't that so?" he appealed to the woman, who smiled and replied, "Yes, that's our nature." He added a generous tip to the bill, and when the door had closed he said, "Someday I hope to visit your country, then I shall be your guest. Until then . . ."

He started to pour me a tea glass of cognac, but I stopped him when the glass was half full. "This isn't so much," he protested. I won my point and he passed the sandwiches.

For a while we sat listening to the rhythmical clicking of the wheels while the dark countryside streamed past. Finally he said, "I love long train journeys. A comfortable compartment, no telephones to answer, no secretaries to intrude, nothing to do but sit and read or chat or look out the window at our beautiful scenery. I read a lot on trips." He pointed to a suitcase. "It's full of books, mostly poetry. I love poetry, especially sad poetry. There is great beauty in sad poetry, and rapture too." In a country where *partiinost* is held to be the lifeblood of creative writing, his words sounded heretical.

Anton Antonovich replenished our glasses. His little eyes were sparkling and his cheeks were flushed. "I myself write poetry—sad poetry," he confided. "Shall I recite something I composed recently?"

I begged him to do so, and he cleared his voice and declaimed:

> *Autumn is not the time for sorrow,*
> *Save your tears for spring:*
> *For spring prepares for autumn*
> *As life leads into death.*

His deep sonorous voice perhaps gave added meaning to the words, but I sincerely praised the lines.

"Only trash," he said, "but it's the best I can do. Now with your permission I'll recite you a real poem: *Like a Gypsy Fiddle, the Blizzard Wails,* by Esenin, very sad and very lovely."

Esenin was followed by Pushkin and Lermontov, and his compelling voice transmitted his own enthusiasm to his audience of one. "They all died young," he said. "Pushkin at thirty-eight and Lermontov at twenty-seven, both killed in duels, and Esenin killed himself when he was only thirty. Our greatest poets . . . How tragic!" He took up his cognac glass and peered into it. "I'm nearing fifty, but I hope to live to be a hundred. Yes, I want to go on living and working and loving. To love is so important. I'm a happily married man and I have two fine sons; the one you met is a chemist like myself, and when he's my age he'll outshine me in the field. I love my family and I do all I can to make them happy. I buy diamonds for my wife. I buy paintings too, and old candelabra because my wife loves them." He drank and turned to me.

"Yes, I love my wife, I love her deeply. But I need to be *in love* too; do you understand? I need to experience the exultation of being in love, to be on fire with it. And not for the sake of gratifying my lust, but for the sake of my soul, for the strength and the inspiration and even the pain it gives me. Once at a conference in Kiev I fell in love with a young woman from the Ukraine. It was love at first sight and that was my last sight of her too. But for two years I dreamed of her; for two years I lived in that rapturous dream. I never wrote to her, I do not know where she is. But I had the dream; that was all I wanted. And that is the way I want to live, even when I'm a hundred."

"And what does the party think about that way of living?" I asked. "Mightn't it get you into trouble if they knew?"

He looked at me in surprise. "All I can say is that I do far better work when I'm in love."

For a while he looked at the window as though trying to see through the reflection of our lighted compartment into the dark countryside beyond. Then, as if suddenly recollecting my question, he said, "Oh yes, the party—well—I'll tell you something. When I assumed directorship of the institute I was faced with a serious housing problem. I couldn't make the necessary appointments to my staff unless I could offer comfortable living quarters: otherwise scientists from other cities just wouldn't come. So I held several meetings with the local party leaders and they proposed to build a big apartment house for the institute. 'But why build an apartment house,' I said, 'when there's plenty of land all around us for private homes. There would be room on each plot for trees, flowers, and a vineyard.' Well, they scolded me fiercely, called me an individualist—but in the end I had my way. I convinced them that after a day's intense mental exertion a man should be able to relax under his own shade tree or dig in his own garden. There's nothing more refreshing after hours of concentration. My colleagues liked the idea too and supported me. One of them, it may interest you to know, had come across an American journal that carried illustrations of one-story houses; and that's what we are building, low houses of three or four rooms, with kitchen and bathroom and garage, built around a large courtyard that we are planting with trees and flowers. We have to thank America for their design: it's better than anything our own architects drew up for us."

"And do they still call you an individualist?" I asked.

He smiled and said, "What if they do? They know we do good work and that's what matters."

As the train rattled on through the dark sleeping countryside, we continued to sip cognac and talk. Late in the night, when we had at last settled into our berths, Anton Antonovich leaned out for a final word. "Do you know what the great truth, I mean the great fact, of our time is? You think it's the conflict between capitalism and socialism? No, it isn't. You write terrible things about us and we write terrible things about you. But these are only words, dust whirled about by winds of passion. You insist that you are always right and we insist we are always right. But nobody can be always right and nobody can be always wrong. The one great fact of our time"—he paused, stabbed his finger at me—"is this: we scientists have made a world in which there is no place for fools any more, neither in your country nor in mine."

Again he paused, laid his hand on his breast, and exclaimed, "Lord my God! What terrible forces we scientists have released—so terrible that they make fools obsolete. No, there is no place for fools any more: this is the one great fact of our time, and how well we scientists know it. If only the fools discover it before it's too late."

He sighed and drew the cover over himself. In another moment he was snoring softly and I turned out the light.

The next morning when we got up, Anton Antonovich was a changed man. He barely acknowledged my presence in the compartment and had not a word to say.

"Did you sleep well?" I asked.

A stiff nod of the head was his only reply. When the train pulled into the station, he gathered up his bags and dashed out without even the formality of a good-by.

19.

INTELLECTUALS
The Sons

After only a week in the Soviet Union, I was so eager for news of the outside world that when I saw an English tourist walk into the lobby of Moscow's Metropole Hotel with a newspaper under his arm, I asked him if he would lend it to me. He gave me the London *Times,* and as it was hot in the hotel, I walked across to the neat little park and sat down on a tree-shaded bench. I had scarcely unfolded the *Times* when a tall Russian youth wearing a gray open-necked shirt and a dark cap approached me and asked in English, "You Englishman?"

"No. American," I replied.

"You ja-azz baby?"

"Do I look it?"

He gave me a blank stare and shrugged, indicating he didn't understand. I told him I spoke Russian, and at once he took a seat beside me and voiced a harsh complaint against the quality of the teaching of English in the ten-year school from which he had graduated. Then, grinning, he said, "I ja-azz baby, beeg ja-azz baby." He and his friends, he explained, often gathered in a home, played jazz records, danced to *rok* (rock 'n' roll) and the cha-cha. But they didn't have many records, and he asked whether I had brought any from America and wished to sell them. I told him I hadn't. Did I know of any American tourists who had? No, I didn't.

Street conversations between a foreigner and a Russian, unless they keep walking, do not long remain private. Passers-by feel free to stop and participate, and presently a group of young people, including a swankily uniformed student of a naval academy, gathered and we fell into a discussion of American jazz and American band leaders. They knew more about the subject than I ever hope to learn. They asked whether I knew Artie Shaw, Tommy Dorsey, Dizzy Gillespie. I replied that I didn't. Did I know Doris Day, the naval student asked. No, I didn't. Didn't I even know such "grand masters of jazz" as Benny Goodman and Louis Armstrong? No, I didn't. Didn't I like jazz? Not very much, I said.

"And I," rose the voice of a newcomer, "don't like it at all. I'd just as soon listen to a pig squeal."

A loud colloquy ensued; the newcomer, an Armenian, held fast to his opinion and finally left in disgust.

"Why do you like jazz?" I asked.

"We get a lot of fun out of it," replied the first youth, and the others assented. There was nothing in their speech or appearance to suggest the *stilyaga*. They were young workers and students to whom fun in life seemed important.

"If you see Benny Goodman or Louis Armstrong," said one of them, "tell them we want them to come to Moscow. They'll overcrowd the Lenin Stadium." The seating capacity of this stadium is over 100,000.

Russian youths soliciting jazz records from an American visitor is an old tale now. It began with the reappearance of American tourists shortly after Stalin's death. But after my long absence from Moscow it was new to me. Never before had I observed such an intense obsession with jazz. The expressions "jazz baby," "swing," "hepcat," have become a part of the vocabulary of Soviet jazz fans.

Officially jazz was never outlawed; dance orchestras played it all the time. In Tiflis University, I was told, students had formed one of the liveliest swing bands in the country. But then Tiflis is a long way from Moscow and Georgians have a way of slighting Moscow's demands and exhortations.

But jazz is not the kind of fun that the Komsomol, official guardian of the manners and morals of youth, encouraged. Neither murders nor accidents are publicized in the Soviet press, unless they serve an immediate purpose, such as exemplifying the evils of jazz. The much publicized trial in Moscow, in August 1958, of four young workers charged with the murder of a militiaman, gave an illuminating insight into the official Soviet mind on the subject of jazz.

The youths had been listening to jazz broadcasts of the Voice of America. They were so carried away by jazz that they began to dance rock 'n' roll, to wear gay sport shirts and narrow trousers, and to drink cocktails instead of vodka, which they considered "too uncivilized." They had been good workers but had become loafers with an appetite for bourgeois enjoyments. They took to robbery to support their "gay life"; and when a militiaman pounced on them as they were burglarizing a state store, one of them, Victor Shishkin, fired seven bullets into his body. The incident was officially proclaimed a lesson for youth: jazz was an evil that begot other evils, until ruin overtook its misguided enthusiasts. Moscow's *Komsomoletz*, a journal for the youth of the city and province of Moscow, warned that "jazz is the short cut to the pistol."

The Komsomol has since reversed itself on the subject of jazz. The craze continues unabated and is beginning to penetrate the villages. While it may seem only a surface excitement, it is actually a reflection of a restlessness which in part at least is a reaction to the tight official control over the inner and outer life of youth, a control over everything from style of haircut to style of thinking. An example is the case of Alexander Krivonos, a fourth-year student in Kharkov University. Late one evening, as he was on his way home, a Komsomol patrol (voluntary militia out to suppress hooliganism) suddenly pounced on him and without a word of explanation led him to the basement headquarters of the staff. His offense, he was told, was "on his head"—his *polka* haircut, which he admitted he had not trimmed in six weeks. His pockets were emptied, "as though I were a thief," he wrote, and even his personal notebook was carefully read by the Komsomols who tried him. Then the hair was clipped short and he was ordered to "gallop off like a horse."

Incidents like this have occurred over and over. In Sverdlovsk the Komsomol patrol rounded up a group of youths whose haircuts it didn't approve of and clipped their hair. In Irkutsk two students were warned that if they persisted in wearing narrow trousers they would be expelled from the university. In Ulyanovsk, Lenin's birthplace, the Komsomol patrol, with the help of the official militia, seized three young factory workers, clipped the hair off two of them, and tore off the shirt from the third. The patrol branded them as *stilyagy* because two of them wore narrow trousers and the third a checked shirt with a strange design.

The brutal abuses of the volunteer street squads evoked loud protests from the victims, and finally prompted Moscow's *Komsomolka* to devote half a page (October 5, 1959) to a sermon that was headlined over three columns: "How Wide Should Trousers Be?" That the chief spokesman for Communist youth chose to preoccupy itself with a subject that appears trivial, has indeed aroused derisive attention in the Western press, and attests to an official determination to keep firm control of youth lest it stray into ways and pleasures that may corrupt its ideology and dissipate energies needed in the challenge to America.

As caricatured in the Soviet press, the typical *stilyaga*, according to *Komsomolka*, "wears a long plaid jacket, invariably of canary-colored cloth, tight-fitting trousers, loud socks, shoes with soles that are two fingers thick, and a haircut with a shaggy forelock." In all my travels in European Russia and Siberia, I never knew anybody who answered this description, although one often sees youths strutting around in flashy outfits, with their hair worn long or in a Marlon Brando cut. In the coldest winter weather they go hatless, just to attract attention and to flaunt their superiority. They are not the equivalent of American beatniks, for they disdain personal sloppiness. They are Soviet-style show-offs.

The Soviet Union has its share of young idlers, drunkards, thieves, speculators, knife wielders, "angry young men," fops, and fools. Officially Soviet authorities deny that they are faced with serious problems of juvenile delinquency, but now and then a story comes to light that contradicts the denial. Here is an example, from the highly industrialized Ural city of Chelyabinsk: The literary journal *Oktyabr* (December 1959) carries a long story of gangs of hooligans who prowl the streets of the community, where workers of the famed tube-rolling mill live. After dark it is dangerous to walk alone here, and the militia is helpless to prevent "drunken brawls and gangster attacks." L. Tatyanicheva, the journal's correspondent, was warned by a militiaman not to go there after dark.

To combat the wave of delinquency, the factory mobilized eight hundred young workers, one third of them girls and women, as volunteer guards. Wearing red arm bands, they start out at eight o'clock in the evening to patrol the streets. When they find a drunkard they take him home; a rowdy they take to their headquarters for investigation and rehabilitation; an outright criminal they turn over to the militia.

In the whole city of Chelyabinsk, sixteen thousand Komsomols, boys and girls, have joined the volunteer guards. Now and then they meet with stiff resistance from the hooligans. More than once, writes Tatyanicheva, there were clashes that resulted in serious injuries to the guards. "Once a thief was caught and they found on his person a list of names of the more active Komsomols, who were condemned to death."

The writer assures the reader that the volunteer guards "have proven a reliable support of social order." Yet she quotes a worker as saying, "On the streets we now have peace, but in homes behind closed doors there are all manner of disturbances. We must find a tactful way of entering the homes where frequent scandals cripple the life of children, distort and embitter their souls, thereby creating a favorable climate for mischievous influences."

Yet Westerners who travel about the country cannot help being impressed with the prodigious amount of work that young people perform in field and factory, in forest and mine, laying new railroads and building new cities, constructing gigantic hydroelectric dams and huge steel mills. Whatever its failings, by and large the young Soviet generation is not lacking dimension in depth.

But the more intellectual segment of the youth of today is not content with production drives alone or with ideological abstractions. It yearns for a fuller measure of self-expression than it has hitherto been permitted to exercise in matters more important than clothes.

On my second day in Leningrad I struck up an acquaintance with a student, and as we were walking along the bank of the Neva River discussing Soviet youth, he surprised me by saying, "We do not want to be Minayevs." Minayev is a character in a short story of only eight pages by the young novelist David Granin. In thinking back to his youth, Minayev reflects that the years have numbed his crusading spirit for truth and justice. He remembers that he had "voted *for* what his conscience demanded he vote *against*; that he had spoken words he didn't believe; that he had praised what he should have condemned; and that when a situation had become intolerable he remained silent. Silence is the most convenient form of lying."

Though Granin was vociferously denounced for his story, its impact on the minds of young readers has remained strong. "Lost years" is the way the student spoke of Minayev's life.

I have never encountered any young Soviet citizens, workers or intellectuals, who question collective ownership of the "means of production." They accept the Soviet economy without reservations, and I am certain they would battle against a movement to overthrow it. They know nothing else, and to them the term "capitalism" spells depravity and damnation. But they laugh at admonitions that jazz is a steppingstone to banditry and murder, or that "kowtowing" to Western fashions in dress corrupts the mind of a Soviet citizen. Once I complimented an Intourist girl interpreter, a college graduate, on the beautiful dress she was wearing. Proudly she replied, "My father bought it for me in Paris." At another time I was in a home where a seventeen-year-old girl was presented with a pair of open-toed shoes by a relative who had been at the Brussels Fair. The girl was overcome with delight and so was her mother.

Although the Soviet shoe industry is manufacturing attractive open-toed shoes, there is something about the word *zagranichny* (foreign) that still weaves a spell over the Russian mind. It signifies something different if not better, or not readily attainable, and carries with it special prestige. It may be only a form of snobbism, but if so it will require more than the flaming remonstrances of *Komsomolka* to eradicate it.

I shall hazard the prediction that as the Soviet Union grows increasingly prosperous Soviet youth will increasingly "kowtow" to the West for fashions in dress and for new forms of entertainment. Slacks, shorts, tapered or toreador trousers for girls, will, I am certain, become as popular in the Soviet Union as in any Western country. *Shortiki*— a Russian word for shorts—have in fact already caught the fancy of the more privileged women—wives and daughters of writers and scientists. They have even ventured to appear in them in the streets and bazaars of towns near their secluded summer colonies, only to be violently denounced in the local press. The *Literaturnaya Gazeta* has fired a salvo of its own against the very use of the American-derived term when the Russian language has a perfectly good word (*trusiki*) for shorts. But *shortiki* it is with the public.

No word has yet been coined for toreador trousers, but there are already a few brave feminine souls who have defied the ban on them, though only in the privacy of their summer homes. I know girls in Moscow who wear trousers, though again only in their homes. One of these girls told me that the fashion authorities in Moscow were working on designs of trousers for women but only for home wear. She was confident that the time was not far away when it would be proper for her sex to wear trousers in the streets.

In the famed Black Sea resort of Sochi women have been fighting valiantly against a city ordinance that forbids them to wear trousers in a public place, and the street, according to the ordinance, is a public place. The Komsomol volunteer guards, in their battle against *stilyagy*, loafers, and idlers, have been ripping shirts with flower designs off the backs of boys and have dealt sternly with girls who are caught wearing trousers, even cutting off their hair. *Komsomolka* has been deluged with complaints against the depredations of the volunteer guards. An eyewitness named Levitin, lecturer at Leningrad University, writes: "To spoil and to rip up clothes is unlawful . . . and to cut a girl's hair—and there have been such instances— is, bluntly speaking, an act of violence" (*Komsomolka*, December 13, 1960). Now that the scandals perpetrated by the volunteer guards have been brought out into the open by the chief spokesman of Soviet youth, Sochi may yet become the first city in the Soviet Union where girls and women will win their battle for the right to wear trousers in the streets.

Komsomol leaders may speak harshly of girls who dye their hair, but never before had I seen so many bleached blonds and dyed redheads in Moscow and other cities as I did in the summer of 1960.

Before the Bikini atoll was in the news, Russian girls as early as the twenties wore the prototype of the bikini bathing suit. Here necessity was the mother invention. Nude bathing fell into disrepute and there was such a shortage of bathing suits that Moscow girls contrived the combination of homemade brassieres and abbreviated shorts. The fashion spread widely and nobody protested. To this day nobody does, not even when girls wear bikinis in mixed company in winter sun parlors.

On my arrival in Moscow in July 1960, the chauffeur who drove me around, on learning that I had been in the city two years earlier, asked what my impression of it was now. I spoke of several things and then said, "Skirts are getting shorter.

He laughed and replied, "Oh yes, our girls are quick to catch on to foreign styles when they see so many foreign tourists in the streets of our capital."

It was so not only in Moscow and Leningrad but in Kiev and Odessa. Always famed for its pretty girls, a city of great culture and great charm, where—as in Leningrad—the tradition of good manners has survived the roughness and wreckage of the revolution, Odessa appeared more responsive to latest Western fashions than did any other city. Foreign and Russian ships come and go and customs officials in proverbially witty and cunning Odessa seem powerless to check the smuggling of foreign goods. It is the one city where one rarely hears complaints from women of the low quality of Russian lipstick—sailors keep them well supplied with foreign brands.

Another change since 1958: now and then along Moscow's Gorky Street one sees a girl wearing a Brigitte Bardot hairdo. "Do you know what we say of such girls?" a young Muscovite said. "'I invite you into my cave.'"

And still another: the appearance of the sweater girl along Moscow's Gorky Street and Leningrad's Nevsky. Pullovers and cardigans are readily available and the fashion is on—and the Russian girl needs no falsies to fill out a sweater.

As for men, the craze for the gay sport shirts is unabated. No longer is the sport jacket a novelty, and department stores are selling flamboyant neckties and crepe-soled shoes that are supposedly the special fad of the *stilyaga*. Russian casual fashions may in time outdo anything Florida or California has dreamed up. Russians are an imaginative people, and the craving for novelty in dress is beyond the power of ideologists to suppress.

Jazz, of course, has come to stay, and certain Soviet musicologists never shared the judgment of the ideologists that all forms of jazz led to damnation. "We needn't completely ignore the better compositions of jazz music with their harmoniously graceful melodies," writes V. Gorodinsky (*Komsomolka*, June 13, 1959). "We have no reason to reject the blinding variety of rhythms and the dance-provoking samba and rhumba, the facile tango, and the lively and mobile-as-mercury rhythmic jazz dances." Musicologists think highly of W. C. Handy, especially of his "St. Louis Blues" and "Memphis Blues"; and George Gershwin has achieved the distinction of an official biography in pamphlet form extolling his musical genius.

During the Soviet Exhibition in New York, I interviewed the representative of Moscow's Ministry of Agriculture. Sitting at the table were his wife and daughter, a girl of fifteen, and both were chewing gum! Neither would have dared to do it publicly in Moscow. But whatever the official attitude, hordes of Moscow children clamor for gum and follow Americans hoping for the gift of a stick.

When a Muscovite told me that chewing gum was a most vulgar American habit, I informed him, rather to his surprise, that while many Americans agreed, they would never seek to impose their tastes on those who enjoyed it. I also told him that there were Americans who chewed tobacco. He threw up his arms and vowed that never would "so cursed an American atrocity" be permitted to take root in his beloved Motherland. Yet as for chewing gum, I am not indulging in idle fancy when I declare that it is only a question of time before Soviet industry manufactures it. In fact, Moscow's *Komsomolka* published a lengthy dissertation on the subject by a biologist who advocated its use as a means of combating smoking.

I shall even venture the prediction that someday Russia will have drum majorettes who will prance around football stadiums with no less zest and perhaps more artistry than American drum majorettes. Anyway, Russian youth, from factory workers to university students, are fascinated by descriptions of this American *novatorstvo* (innovation).

The Youth Festival in Moscow in the summer of 1957 rocked Russian youth into an appreciation and emulation of many a *novatorstvo* it had never before known. For the first time Soviet youth mingled freely and joyfully with boys and girls from foreign countries, capitalist and non-capitalist. For once activists and agitators remained on the side lines, and the slogan "peace and friendship" was more than rhetoric. Russian boys and girls invited the foreigners to their homes, danced and sang with them, flirted and frolicked with utmost freedom. It was without doubt the most sensational social event that had occurred in all Soviet history, and when it was over it left an aftermath of tastes in fashion and play including rock 'n' roll, the pony tail, the Italian haircut, and even the hula shirt.

Amusing and enlightening is the full-page cartoon in *Krokodil* (No. 3, 1960). It shows two emaciated fungoid creatures who appear to have grown out of a clump of toadstools, their legs the elongated stems of the plants. The girl's pale face is heavily made up; her blond hair falls untidily down her back and over her eyes; she wears a short pink sack. Her gangling partner—they are dancing, though footless —dangles a cigarette from his mouth; his hair is uncombed and uncut. He wears a gaudy Hawaiian shirt of yellow and blue, and from his pocket protrudes a liquor bottle. Dressed somberly, they might be a pair of American beatniks. The quatrain at the top of the page reads:

> *Foreigners! Foreigners!*
> *No! From foot to crown*
> *These toadstools are home-grown,*
> *Our own town's "Broadway"!*

If the Kremlin is yielding, however slowly, to the pressures of youth for a gayer and less austere life, it continues to keep its rigid ideological hold, especially over the intellectuals. How strenuously Soviet educators strive to keep youth from breaking through the framework of official thinking came out in a discussion I had with Professor Petrov, head of the Philosophical Faculty of Irkutsk University. He explained to me that the core of Soviet intellectuality and ideology is dialectical materialism, the infallible guide to all truth and a short cut to thought and action in science and other fields of human endeavor.

"Suppose," I asked, "a student questions the validity of dialectical materialism?"

"You must remember," the professor replied, "that throughout his five years in the university our student takes courses in dialectical materialism and related subjects. Besides, the study of all our courses is permeated with this philosophy. The student cannot possibly question its validity."

"Suppose he disagrees with the professor's position that there is no truth other than what the dialectical materialism he studies reveals to him? In America, students are free to disagree with their professors."

"Then we reason with the student. On the conclusion of a lecture we have from ten to fifteen minutes of questions and the student is free to bring up whatever arguments come to his mind. The professor takes up the arguments one by one and proves them false. It's the professor's duty to set the student right in his thinking. Take my subject for example. We study all schools of philosophy, from the Greeks to Kant and Hegel and such American philosophers as William James, John Dewey, and George Santayana. But with us philosophy is no mere abstraction. It cannot be, because it is based on dialectical materialism."

"Einstein," I said, "was one of the greatest scientists of all time, and so far as I know he never accepted the philosophy of dialectical materialism."

"We have translated the book Einstein wrote with Enfield. We study the book because the authors are great scientists. But we reject their idealistic doctrines."

"Suppose the student perceives merit in these doctrines?"

"We argue him out of it."

"But suppose he remains unconvinced?"

"Impossible. We have the question period and we hold seminars and in the end we defeat our ideological enemies."

"But if the student persists in contradicting the professor?"

"It doesn't happen. It cannot happen. Our arguments are incontrovertible."

"And if it were to happen?"

This time the professor replied solemnly: "Then the student would place himself outside our Soviet society."

The student then knows that there is a limit beyond which he must not permit his mind to wander. If he trespasses the boundary set for him by the professor, he is in danger of reaching the point of no return. So in formal class discussions he has no choice but to bow to the professor's arguments. But when away from the class he may move into an intellectual underground—intellectual but not revolutionary; not an underground where in the manner of students in Czarist times he would conspire and plot the overthrow of the government. Only dismally uninformed Russian émigrés and the Westerners whom they influence indulge in the futile luxury of periodic forecasts of an imminent overthrow of Soviet rule. Their wishful thinking blinds them to the vast and stormy changes in Russia since Chekhov's days. Chekhov's perennial student can only talk of the glory of work and dream of the day when men like him can find a fit outlet for action. The student of today is educated to be a man of action and finds ample outlet for his energies and talents, however much he may dislike the conditions under which he works or the place to which he is assigned. Nor is he unmindful of the benefits the state offers him: free education, free medical service, assurance of employment, to mention only some of them.

The intellectual underground into which the student or any inquiring youth moves produces only talk: protests, parodies, anecdotes, songs for the relief of his frustration; it hides no guns, manufactures no bombs. No Czar in Russian history ever traveled about the country as freely and mingled with people as informally as does Khrushchev. Had there been the revolutionary underground of which groups of Russian émigrés boast so exaltedly, Nikita Sergeyevich would long ago have been lying embalmed on Red Square beside the bodies of Lenin and Stalin.

I am writing of the generation which has come of age since World War II, young people who were infants or children at the time Germany attacked Russia in June 1941. They have no memories of the heroic age of the revolution, the civil war, or the strenuous years that followed to the end of the first Five-Year Plan. Who in those days ever had time to think about the styles in haircuts or the width of trousers? It was a time when the leather jacket and the peaked cap were the height of fashion; and students were so poor that they gave each other haircuts as frequently or as infrequently as they thought of it. Some who came from the villages wore linen wrappers instead of socks on their feet. These things did not matter; students in those days were too intoxicated with ideals and ideas to care what they wore. I was present at endless debates in student dormitories when subjects which in the light of present-day ideology would seem utterly fanciful were excitedly argued over until late into the night. Was it right to fall in love with someone whose parents were members of the enemy class, which in those days included the intelligentsia?

Why should there continue to be families when, under the new dispensation, it was the duty of loyal citizens to love all children alike? Was it ethical for a Soviet youth to dress well or even to wear a necktie when millions of unemployed proletarians in Germany and other capitalist countries were starving? Wasn't jealousy an evil heritage of cursed capitalism? Why was world revolution so slow in arriving?

There were times when I was the kill-joy of these earnest and excited gatherings. Faith in world revolution was as intense as hatred of capitalism, and whenever I was questioned about the "imminent revolution" in America, I invariably attempted to make clear to my interrogators that America never had a land problem like Russia's, never had a peasant like the muzhik, never had a landlord class like the Russian *pomeshchik*. Therefore the type of revolution they were thinking of for America, they had better discount. Few believed me, and those who did were painfully chagrined and often solaced themselves with the conviction that even if America was not yet ripe for a proletarian revolution, European capitalist countries were, especially Germany.

It was an age of great follies and great dreams, of which the student body of today has no comprehension. Recently in Moscow I called on a woman who is now a grandmother but who, when I first knew her in the middle twenties, was a student and an enthusiastic Komsomolka. I asked her what the chief differences were between the mentality of the youth of her day and that of the youth of the present. She reflected and answered, "I think the chief difference is that my generation was passionately selfless and self-sacrificing. I recall how often friends of mine and I would go to pare potatoes in an unheated community kitchen. We had no gloves and our hands were freezing, but we only jested about it. We had a wonderful time. It was the same when we went to unload wood from a freight train. We were cold, but we were warmed by the ideal society that was to come, and we didn't mind the cold at all."

I reminded her of the 350,000 boys and girls, many of them high school graduates, who went off to the virgin lands and of the tens of thousands of others who journeyed and were still journeying East on big construction projects.

"I don't say," she said, "that the youth of today is incapable of sacrifices. But they aren't the same. Remember, they are well paid, better than if they'd stayed at home and worked in an office, in a factory, or on a farm. Who in my day bothered about pay? The most a party member received, even Lenin, was two hundred fifty rubles a month. Take my youngest daughter, Irina, who'll soon graduate from the university. She is in love with a young chemist who works in the rubber industry, and both of them say they won't get married until they have saved enough money to furnish an apartment respectably. Save money! Who ever heard of such a thing in my young years? I know young couples who are saving every ruble they can to buy an automobile. We'd have scoffed at such couples as incorrigible bourgeoisie. No, the young people of today haven't the ardent faith of my generation."

Indeed they haven't. Once I passed the Kazan railroad station in Moscow when it was crowded with young people who were leaving for the virgin lands. They were well shod and well dressed, and they carried their belongings in suitcases. Friends and relatives who came to see them off brought flowers, boxes of candy, bars of chocolate, other goodies. An orchestra was playing and some couples danced.

As I watched I recalled a trainload of boys at a railroad junction in the Urals I had seen over a quarter century earlier. The boys were on their way to build the city of Komsomolsk on the Amur River, in the wilderness of the Far East. They were shabbily dressed and carried their belongings in sacks or wooden boxes. Big loaves of dark rye bread, sausage, onions, garlic, were the foods on the train. Yet while the cars remained on the siding the boys tumbled out onto the platform; the inevitable accordions played, and the boys sang and danced. They were as cheerful and inspired a crowd of youths as I have ever seen in the Soviet Union. They were on their way to the wooded wilderness, not for a specified period of time, as are so many youths who go East nowadays, but to stay there for the rest of their lives. At first only boys went. Girls came afterward. Many of them died from accidents and disease, but they built Komsomolsk, now an industrialized city of 177,000, an unmatched monument to the faith, dedication, and self-sacrifice of the Soviet youth of yesterday.

Having missed the heroic age of the revolution, the young generation of today has also missed the barbarisms that accompanied it. They do not know the hatreds that crackled fiercely from one end of the country to the other and that actuated the barbarisms, hatreds that Khrushchev and men of his generation can never shake off.

Collectivization and liquidation of kulaks are only history to the young people of today; they read about them, but their furies and terrors are unknown to them. They never participated in the gaily tumultuous anti-God demonstrations that were climaxed by the burning in effigy of the crucified Jesus and of the bearded Jehovah. They never practiced marksmanship on rifle ranges where the favorite targets were the lithographed posters of Austen Chamberlain, George Curzon, and Winston Churchill—a trio the Soviets had branded as the most ferocious villains of the times. They never felt under compulsion publicly to denounce their fathers and mothers and to change their names in proof of a repudiation of their "bourgeois" heritage. The blood purges of the thirties are not even a memory to them. They are only history.

These young people grew up in an era when values that had been fiercely rejected were restored and sanctified: love of country, love of father and mother, love of family life, respect for older people. No Protestant tent evangelist I ever heard was more sentimental about mother than is Moscow's *Komsomolka*. In a front-page three-column editorial (August 7, 1958) one reads: "The first word that man as a child learns to pronounce is 'mother.' The word springs from his lips in the hour of danger and in the last minute of his life. . . . The nearest and dearest is contained in this word. To her, our mother, we always owe an irredeemable debt."

Thus the young generation with which I am concerned in this chapter grew up without any internal enemy to hate—no kulak, no nepman, no bourgeois, no priest, no wrecker, no saboteur, not even a capitalist on whom to vent scorn and fury. The violent and heartbreaking battles between sons and fathers, mothers and daughters, were over and the Mosaic commandment "Honor thy father and mother" was once more dutifully obeyed. They were too young to be seriously touched by Andrey Zhdanov's scorching denunciations of cosmopolites and cosmopolitanism, which agonized and terrorized the older generation of intellectuals. They are, indeed, a new kind of generation, more mellow, more secure, and, despite the inevitable ideological pieties, freer.

For, though the war was an agony of childhood, it was also a source of exciting romance. In the summer of 1942 I spent several days in the village of Bolshiya Lipyagi, in the province of Kuibyshev. I stayed in the home of a woman whose husband was in the Army, and as manager of the local co-operative store, she had little time for housework or for looking after her five children, the oldest of whom was a boy of twelve. But the children looked after one another, cleaned the house, weeded the garden, pastured the cow and calf, and together with other children wandered the meadows in search of wild onions and other edible plants, which were widely publicized as foods rich in vitamins. They were bright and cheerful children and their responsibilities seemed more of an adventure than a task. They learned to be self-reliant at a very tender age.

It was so with children all over the country; they matured beyond their years. They listened eagerly to the war stories of invalided soldiers —stories in which Russian soldiers, of course, were the heroes. They played war games and "slaughtered" their enemies. It was their heroic age, but quite different from the heroic age of the earlier years of the revolution. The emotion of patriotism submerged all party and non-party squabbles. Mother Russia became the symbol of a new faith and new dedication. Marshal Suvorov, after whom the new military schools for boys were named, became a historic hero whose portrait adorned the walls of classrooms and clubhouses. Marshal Kutuzov, conqueror of Napoleon, and Admiral Nakhimov joined the long line of other historic heroes who had always loved and always fought for their Motherland.

But the greatest hero of all time was, of course, Marshal Stalin. He and only he had supposedly masterminded the strategy that trapped and destroyed the invading Nazi hordes. Not only was he the bestower of all earthly blessings but he and only he was the savior of the country in the moment of greatest peril. Children intoned a hymn that went:

> Leader, scattering darkness like the sun,
> Conscience of the world,
> Luminary of the ages,
> Glory to him!

Then came the shattering shock—Khrushchev's speech in February 1956 at the Twentieth Party Congress exposing Stalin as a monstrous tyrant. The speech was read at party meetings, and though it was never published in the press, no secret police in the world could keep it from seeping into every home in the country. "You have no idea," a woman schoolteacher said to me, "what a sensational subject of conversation it became even among school children. To us of the older generation Khrushchev's revelations were an enormous relief. We knew that never again would conditions be the same. But for the younger generation it was a knife in their hearts: the idol they had worshiped was proved to be a common criminal. Bewildered pupils kept asking us if it was all true, hoping it wasn't, because to their innocent minds it couldn't be."

The bewilderment of the young generation in those days still awaits its chronicler. But the new language of youth, the questions they began to ask, the demands they began to make, were touchingly —sometimes angrily—recorded in the new poetry and fiction that burst out in the wake of Khrushchev's shattering disclosures. Why had insufferably dull novels been awarded Stalin premiums? Why were textbooks rewritten? Why were foreign scientific discoveries attributed to Russians? Why were French rolls renamed city rolls? Why were American nuts (pecans) renamed southern nuts? Why did newspapermen who interviewed students write the opposite of what students told them? These and similar questions by students star the pages of L. Kabo's novel *The Difficult March* (*Novy Mir*, November–December 1956). "What shall I believe now?" asks Zhenka, one of the leading characters. Here is a groping for truth which had long been denied and which could no longer be suppressed.

In all institutional categories—schools, factories, farms, scientific institutes—youth is organized into collectives. The theory is that the collective inculcates a social discipline, a community purpose, a spirit of co-operation that prevents acquisitiveness and develops a so-called socialist personality, the distinctive feature of which is the subordination of individual to social interests. If a boy or girl falls down on homework, perpetrates mischief in class or at home, indulges in abusive language, the collective is ever ready to cure him or her of the dereliction. If a young factory worker violates discipline, gets drunk and stays home instead of coming to work, maltreats his mother or his girl friend, expresses heretical ideas, the collective is supposed to chasten him. The collective has the right to pry into the most intimate aspects of a member's life, including, of course, his relationships with the opposite sex, whether for immediate pleasure or for "lasting comradeship." The individual is not supposed to withhold any secrets, however personal; otherwise he runs the risk of public censure and disgrace at meetings, in local newspapers, in the metropolitan press, and expulsion from the collective.

This type of socialist togetherness with its intrusion on privacy has evoked indignation and protest from the young generation of today, and the more educated the youth, the firmer is the hostility to the confessional. In Konstantin Lebedev's novel *People and Degrees*, Sheremetyev, the Komsomol leader, calls on a student girl named Bylinskaya to stand up before the the the gathering of her collective and explain herself for a misdeed she had performed. Indignantly she replies, "I shall not stand up and shall not explain myself. . . . Who are you to question me, huh? A militiaman?"

The quest for emancipation from collective control of one's emotional life is boldly enunciated in the poem *An Uneasy Conversation* (*Novy Mir*, June 1956), by the young Armenian poet Pamuir Sevak. After five hours of violent discussion at a meeting of the collective, the chief character in the poem agrees to break relations with the married woman he loves and who loves him. "Family dramas must be avoided." But the poet has second thoughts on the subject. "If there is no love in the family, why preserve it?" He repudiates the reasoning of the mind, for "nothing is wiser than the heart." He knows the woman he loves doesn't and never did love her husband. She married him because the families knew each other and it was the proper thing to do. Some women are like that, just as other women prefer "warm fur coats to the warmth of love. . . . I'm grateful my pocket is empty . . . it will attract few into romance. . . . But you I love—all else is a lie!"

But the hero of the poem will not abandon his love even if he promised his collective to do so. "Oh, people often speak the untruth and think they tell the truth, but there is no soul in such truth— it's truth only for meetings." Why then honor it?

The poem evoked a stormy debate which has not yet subsided. One meets students who in discussing it acclaim it and even recite by heart the more telling lines.

Yevgeny Yevtushenko, who translated Sevak's poem from Armenian into Russian, himself caused a sensation with his long poem
Station Zima (*Oktyabr*, September 1956), which he began writing
at the age of twenty, or soon after Stalin's death. Old friends in Moscow with whom I discussed the subject of youth urged me to read it.
It sounded bolder and more powerful in Moscow than it did when
I read it in New York. It is a long poem and I shall briefly touch
on some of the more relevant issues it raises.

We learn from the poem that Yevtushenko is the grandson of a
Ukrainian peasant whom the Czarist government had exiled to
Siberia. Born in the village of Zima (winter in Russian), Irkutsk
province, the poet presents an account of his return to his birthplace
and what he observed, heard, felt, and thought during his stay
there. The poem is at once a lament and a protest, a confession and
an invocation—a youth newly discovering himself and the village of
his birth.

During the twenty years of his life, he says, he has re-examined
much in his experience and now realizes that "words he had spoken
he should never have uttered, and words he should have spoken had
remained unsaid." His uncle Volodya tells him that people are thinking and cannot quite understand "the when, what, and how." The
uncle mentions the doctors whom Stalin had arrested on charges
that were faked. "Why did they hurt people?" the uncle asks. "What
an outrage for all Europe to talk about."

In a teahouse the poet runs into a newspaperman from Moscow
who came to gather material for a story. The "red-faced" newspaperman speaks of his own young years and of his youthful dream to
become a writer. But—he remained a newspaperman. "And what's
a writer nowadays? Not a ruler but a keeper of man's mind." The
Muscovite doesn't foresee a change, because "we affirm that on
which we were silent yesterday, and are silent about that which we
did yesterday." And what of faith? No, there is no faith, because faith
means love and there is no love. Yet there must be love.

"What do I desire?" asks the poet. "I desire to battle bravely
. . . so truth shall burn up everything I fear."

On his departure the poet hears an invocation from his beloved
village:

Seek, seek. Wander the whole white world.
Yes, truth is fine but happiness is finer,
But without truth there is no happiness.
Wander the world with a proud head
Ever onward—and heart and tears,
And over the face
The lashing of damp needles [of evergreens]
And on the eyelashes tears and storm.
Love people and you'll understand people.
Remember—
　　　　You're within my sight.
Should things get hard—back to me you return. . . .
　　　　Go!
　　　　And I went.
　　　　And I go.

To a Westerner the poet's protests and aspirations may sound somewhat commonplace. But for a Russian youth of twenty they are dramatically daring. They affirm a need to recover faith and truth, honesty with oneself and pride in one's person, love of life and love of the common people—not the love that the ideologist extols or that *Pravda* and *Komsomolka* enjoin, but the love that comes from the heart, unsmirched by power politics and party policy.

Yevtushenko was denounced for his departure from the main stream of Soviet ideology with its insistent optimism. He was branded "a nihilist," "a pessimist," "a revisionist." But under Khrushchev the literary heretic need not fear arrest or banishment. He remains at home; pen and ink are his for the asking, though he has slight hope of acceptance if he continues in his mood of doubt and defiance, as Yevtushenko did in 1956. Literary friends in Moscow told me that the poem couldn't have been published after 1957. But by that time young people had learned parts of it by heart and still recite it to one another in private and at literary evenings.

In speech after speech Khrushchev has exhorted youth to express its search for heroism and romance in "useful performance." Such performance was denied the youth of the nineteenth century, and the youth of today has not failed Khrushchev. It was largely youth that brought under cultivation one hundred million acres of virgin land, that built the Irkutsk hydroelectric plant, that is building at Bratsk and Krasnoyarsk, Siberia, the largest hydroelectric plants in the world. Thousands of young people who went to Kazakhstan and Siberia sickened of the hardship of pioneering in wild country and fled home. Thousands of others are unhappy with the conditions under which they are obliged to live. But thousands of still others keep arriving all the time. Construction goes on, however cold the climate, wretched the food, primitive the housing.

But youth is reaching out for more than the rewards of "useful performance" with its connotation of triumph over stubborn nature and the heightened national pride that comes with it. It yearns for romance in life and is contemptuous of poetry that sublimates the romance of love into tractor driving and cloth weaving. "Love has vanished from our lyrical poetry," wrote the poetess Olga Bergholz only a few weeks after Stalin's death. "I've looked over the poetry for 1952 in the four leading literary journals and have discovered not a single love lyric." And in his poem *Rockets and the Horse Wagon*, Yevtushenko pays tribute to the wooden vehicle which in its day had well served its purpose. But in art its age is still alive. "With sorrow" he looks at a colleague whose novel reflects the horse-and-wagon days. "We have shot a lunik into space, but opera is still in the horse-and-wagon days." Another poet, Boris Slutsky, mourns that while "physics is honored, the lyric is in the doghouse."

Actually this is no longer so. The thrill of the kiss is back in a big way in Soviet fiction, poetry, and drama, and Yevtushenko has written poems that are frankly sexual. He has of course been denounced, but his "bedroom poetry," as Muscovites speak of it, has appeared in the literary journal *Oktyabr*, though it has not been included in the collection of his verse.

When Leonid Leonov, one of the most distinguished Soviet novelists, was in New York, I happened to mention to him that there was a lot of kissing in the thick (literary) Russian journals. With some indignation he replied that he didn't care for such writing, and neither, I am certain, do other writers of the older generation. But youth will be served, regardless of its elders. It is amazing how frequently the physiology of sex tantalizes the imagination of younger novelists, of A. Tunitsky, V. Artsibashev, A. Dimarov, M. Kolesnikov, to mention only some of them. Glowingly they describe the breasts and legs, the throat and shoulders, the curves and birthmarks, the hair and dimples, of heroine and villainess.

The *Literaturnaya Gazeta* (May 14, 1960) has denounced them for debasing "social tastes in beauty" and for their ignorance of "the dialectics of the soul." Whatever the expressions may mean, the *Gazeta* accuses these writers of indulging in "the canons of middle-class literature," another expression that holds no terrors for young poets and novelists. I very much doubt that the *Gazeta* or the Soviet Writers' Union can cow them, though censors may be coerced into deleting the more sensual descriptions in their works.

One of the most brilliant young short-story writers is Yuri Kazakov, who has been violently attacked for his short story *The Renegade* (*Oktyabr*, July 1959) because it is completely divorced from Soviet problems and realities. Yet V. Frolov, the literary critic, has risen to the vigorous defense of the young heretic. To Frolov, Kazakov's gift of "glimpsing into the heart" of his characters is one of his transcendent literary virtues. The very phrase brings to mind Sir Philip Sidney's line: " 'Fool!' said my muse to me, 'look in thy heart, and write.' "

This is precisely what youth, and not only poets and writers, is doing—peering into its own heart and into the hearts of its elders. Out of this concern has erupted a new conflict between fathers and sons, the fathers as usual on the defensive, the sons on the offensive. The conflict is dramatized in much of the fiction of 1959–60, in which the problems of the upbringing and of the yearnings of youth preoccupy storytellers almost as much as do the problems of production. I shall confine myself to only a few of the more impressive works on the subject.

In the short story *The Happy Age* (*Zvezda*, September 1959), by Alexander Rozov, a twelve-year-old boy named Vladik, who idolizes his father, learns from a conversation he overhears between his mother and another woman that he has a brother named Kostya, who has just died in an accident. Neither his father nor his mother has ever told him of Kostya and he wonders why. He is certain that if his father were home he would go to the funeral and pay his last respects to his son. But as the father is away on the day of the funeral, Vladik takes it on himself to attend. He says nothing about it to his mother, and when he leaves the house she is under the impression that he is off on a trip with his friends.

On his arrival in the village in which Kostya and his mother live,

Vladik, carrying a small potted geranium, finds his way to their home. Jostled by the crowd, he drops his offering and the pot breaks. Embarrassed and frightened, he squeezes his way out, hearing as he goes his father spoken of as a "scoundrel" for not once having seen Kostya during the eight years of his life.

On his return in the evening, Vladik invites his father for a "man to man" talk. He tells his father where he has been and "the bad names" he heard people call him. "Why haven't you ever said a word to me about Kostya?" the boy asks. The father dismisses the question by assuring his son that when he grows up he will tell him "with a clear conscience" that everything he did was for him, Vladik.

"But Kostya is my brother."

"Let's not talk any more about things you don't understand."

"Why don't I understand? He is my brother."

"And I say no, enough about it."

"No? Why? Is it because he was illegitimate?"

"Where did you learn that? A small boy and he speaks such nasty things! Aren't you ashamed? Where did you pick it up?"

"I do not mean to speak nasty things. I thought you'd explain. I heard it at the funeral. . . ."

"Ah, at the funeral! So that's it! Impudent nonentities speak and he believes them."

The father grows angry and leaves the son disillusioned and saddened. Late in the night, when everybody is asleep, Vladik steals out of the house and runs off to live with Kostya's mother.

Though a non-political story, the author's glimpse into the boy's heart is not without political implications for the Soviet reader, always alert to read between the lines and to draw his own political lesson. Vladik symbolizes the personal integrity and the strength of character that his father lacks. Vladik is intolerant of the lies and deceptions with which the older generation has been accustomed to shield itself, not only from immoral personal acts but from political embroilments.

The young novelist Nina Invanter, in her novel *August Again* (*Novy Mir*, August–September 1959), presents another conflict between father and son in a direct political setting. The son, seventeen-year-old Boris Bashkirov, is a Komsomol, impatient with people, even close friends, who lie and deceive. He learns from his mother that in the thirties, when his father was a Komsomol, his most intimate friend was a youth named Boris Petrovich, after whom the father named his son. But when Boris Petrovich, an engineer, returns from twelve years of banishment as "an enemy of the people," he and the father are cool toward each other. Though Petrovich lives in a room next door to the Bashkirovs, the father never visits him and he lives a secluded life. He rouses young Boris' curiosity and sympathy and they become friends. Once when Petrovich calls on his namesake, he sees a photograph on the wall and stares at it intently. The photograph was of the father and of other smiling young Komsomols. Suddenly the seventeen-year-old boy becomes aware that there is something amiss with the photograph—one end is cut off and only a hand with no arm lies on his father's shoulder. The boy wonders who the missing man is, and the suspicion grows on him that it is Petrovich; his father had cut him out of the picture. Tormented by the suspicion, the boy questions his father.

"Son," says the father, "what happened concerns only myself. Someday I shall doubtless tell you; and now excuse me, but . . ."

"So you don't want to tell me?"

"Go away."

Never before had the father refused to answer Boris' questions, and Boris cannot understand it. If a man is not guilty he has no reason to hold back an explanation. Yet he dreads the thought of his father having committed an ugly offense against the most intimate friend of his young and happy years. But he must learn the truth, and so he approaches Petrovich and asks him what has happened between him and the father. Mellowed by suffering, Petrovich bears his old friend no grudge and tells the boy that if he holds his father guilty of breaking faith with a friend, he had better go back immediately and beg his pardon. "I tell you your father is guilty of nothing."

Dissatisfied with the answer, the boy asks, "What shall I make out of it all? What? You too don't want to tell me. Father did something—I know he did. Something is wrong."

"He didn't do anything," Petrovich replies. "More than that, after all that had happened and I was no longer here, there was a party meeting and your father didn't say a single word against me. This I definitely know."

"Did he say a good word *for* you?"

"What do you mean? A good word?"

"So he didn't?"

"You see, my namesake—you just cannot imagine. . . . I mean, no good words would have helped me."

"He should have spoken them."

"Do you mean you'd have preferred him to say a few good words in my behalf even if it brought suffering to the family?"

"Yes, yes, yes!" And when Petrovich makes no reply, Boris asks, "Something else—the photograph—was it not you who stood beside him? Wasn't it he who cut you off?"

"Well, it is I. That doesn't change anything."

"Good—but if . . . if there is no guilt, why are you and he—like this?"

"It isn't I. It's he. He thinks I hold him guilty. But nobody can and nobody has the right to do that. Understand, my friend, he couldn't do anything. No man could."

Lying in bed, thinking, Boris says to himself, "No, never again will things be the same between father and me, and I really don't know how I can live like that. . . . If fathers could choose their sons, he never would have chosen me."

On an express train, I became acquainted with three medical students. Two were young women and the third a young man. The young man said that he was on his way south to work in the orchard of a state farm and earn extra money for expenses in medical school. I told him that American college students did the same, but that I had read so much in Khrushchev's speeches and in *Komsomolka* about the contempt for manual labor among Soviet students that I wondered if he was an exception. He admitted that many students did disdain soiling their hands with menial toil. He didn't. Besides, he loved fruit trees and at one time had considered making horticulture his lifework. He and the girls appeared incredulous when I told them that about half of America's three million college students earned part or all of their living by working at one thing or another, and never felt they were debasing themselves by milking cows, shoveling manure, or performing any other common labor. They had never heard of it, they frankly admitted. They had imagined that in America college was a privilege only of the rich.

We went on talking, and in some detail they told of their life in medical school. They paid no tuition and no laboratory fees. They received a stipend of 265 (old) rubles (33 dollars) a month from the state, which was less than for students of science. This they felt an injustice that should be remedied. Why should a student who prepared himself to build machines or even sputniks be paid a higher stipend than one who was preparing himself to cure sickness and to save life? They were certain that the time would come when the disparity in stipends would be abolished. No, they couldn't make ends meet without help from the outside—from the family, from the trade unions, or from work in a dispensary or hospital. But their expenses were low. They lived three and four in a room and paid only fifteen rubles a month rent. Food was cheap, costing from six to eight rubles a day. Girls did their own laundry and boys had it done for them at a cost of from twenty to twenty-five rubles a month. There was television in the dormitory and twice a week there were free movies. Occasionally they had free concerts.

During their first three years they were pinched for expense money, yet somehow they managed to go to the theater, for, as one girl expressed herself, "It's so uplifting to see a good play." Beginning with their fourth year they began hospital duty and were paid an additional 500 rubles (55 dollars) a month. That was when they began "blowing themselves" to better clothes, better food, more plays and concerts.

Then the medical students asked questions about American college life. They were surprised to hear that few American girls studied medicine, to them a natural profession for women. We talked of bull sessions, of football games and the crowds that come to see them. Like other young people I met, they were fascinated by an account of marching bands, of drum majorettes, of cannon volleys, and of the singing and the cheering at American football games. Their curiosity seemed endless, and I even obliged them with a description of the performances of the Kilgore (Texas) College Rangerettes. To them it was a new form of group gymnastics, which is so popular in the Soviet Union. "Tell the Kilgore girls to come to

Moscow," said the young man. "We'll give them a great reception."

They would, too.

We talked of books and authors, and when I told them that I knew Mitchell Wilson, they wanted to know all about him. They asked about Hemingway, but I could tell them little, because I had never met the author of *A Farewell to Arms*, the novel the girl students said they had read and wept over. The name of Boris Pasternak came up and the three of them expressed sympathy for the persecuted author. What particularly impressed them was Pasternak's letter to Khrushchev saying that banishment from his homeland would be equivalent to a sentence of death. "A poet who loved his Motherland," one of the girls said, "as warmly as did Pasternak couldn't possibly have written an unpatriotic novel." One needn't doubt that most university students resented the vilification of the author of *Doctor Zhivago*, whose poetry, though as yet unobtainable in bookshops, is read as avidly as ever, young people copying and recopying it by hand and passing it from one to another.

I know of no young people anywhere who idolize a favorite poet or novelist as do Soviet young people. Eagerly they crowd his readings with pencil and notebook in hand. This is nothing new in Russian history—young intellectuals always idolized their favorite poets and novelists and the tradition lives on.

Significantly not one of the students asked a single question about the Communist party in America or the "imminent" workers' revolution, about which earlier generations of students and young workers rarely failed to ask. When one meets young people like these, the question of whether or not the intensely materialistic Soviet civilization dulls or kills the taste for music, painting, literature, and other arts, answers itself. In fact, a debate on the subject erupted in the Soviet press, and while some of the debaters, interestingly enough mostly men, ridiculed the need of art in an age of spaceships, others vigorously championed the view that Beethoven and Tchaikovsky, poetry and theater, were indispensable to "civilized" and happy living. The crowds that visit picture galleries, and not only in Moscow, that fill concert halls and the better theaters, the enormous popularity of Russian and foreign classics, the incessant demand of youth for more and larger editions of favorite authors, can only mean that young people like the medical students I met on the train are not an exception.

One of the most striking things about them is their frantic desire to travel in the West, of which they know pathetically little. One must dissent from the view of the erudite Isaac Deutscher, who in his *Great Contest* says, "The Soviet people are probably the world's most educated nation." They may be the best read in literature, but they are dismally and exasperatingly ignorant of the outside world. It was news to the medical students that I needed a passport only when I traveled abroad and that if they came to America they wouldn't need to register their passports in every hotel at which they might stop. They were equally surprised when I told them that I subscribed to *Pravda* and other publications and received them regularly, the daily newspapers arriving within three days. They had never heard of the Soviet Four Continent bookshop in New York, which sells Soviet books, including those that specialize in bitter denunciation of America and all other Western countries. The amount of malicious misinformation that is daily planted in the minds of young and old by Soviet ideologists and journalists is one of the grimmest facts of our times.

One has to be cautious when one speaks to Russians on a train, and the medical students, delightful companions as they proved to be, after some gentle probing revealed that they knew nothing of Russian guilt in the cold war—didn't even know that on the conclusion of the war Russia violated the Teheran Treaty of 1943 by refusing to withdraw its army of occupation from Iranian Azerbaijan. They had never heard of the Berlin blockade or of East Germans fleeing in large numbers to West Germany. They thought it was the other way around and appeared perplexed and incredulous when they heard it was otherwise. They credited their own government with the Austrian peace treaty—this after ten years of persistent Soviet sabotage of Allied efforts to sign the treaty.

For some reason it occurred to me to ask whether they knew the Ten Commandments. They didn't; the very expression was new to them. I put the question to other young people, principally college students and college graduates, and with the exception of the very few who came from religious families, they too had never heard of this foundation stone of Western civilization.

But like other educated youths, the medical students were keenly aware of American impact on their Motherland: tractors and combines, corn and Iowa, crossword puzzles and funnies, crew cuts and *cowboiky*, cafeterias and self-service shops, frozen and pre-cooked foods, volleyball and basketball, installment buying and car renting, jazz and motels, a few of which have already been built. When I told them that one afternoon as I was sauntering along Moscow's Gorky Street, I stopped before a newly opened shop that was selling freshly cooked doughnuts, they asked for the address of the shop so that they could go there and get a taste of "the American specialty." When I spoke of hamburger stands, they were all for them.

European intellectuals may deride and detest America's so-called mechanical living, but not Russians, neither young nor old. They glorify gadgetry at least as much as Americans. Even such a trivial thing as a pencil sharpener which I had bought at a Woolworth store for ten cents fascinated a college professor and his wife with whom I became acquainted on a train. At another time, when my companion in a sleeping car saw me polish my shoes with a jet spray, he became so excited that he called in other passengers to see the American *novatorstvo* in shoeshining. There were times when I had the feeling that despite never ending clashes between Moscow and Washington and despite *Pravda's* vitriolic rhetoric against America, the Soviet Union, politics aside, was at least as pro-American as any country in Europe. In fact, ideologists who concern themselves with the Communist society to come predicate their vision of it on the automation and mechanization of the material aspects of life, or the "mechanical living" that so disgusts European intellectuals.

Here is one of the more astounding "contradictions" in all Soviet propaganda. On the one hand, in English-language textbooks, in ideological dissertation, in poster and cartoon, America is depicted as the number-one villain in the world, the country of capitalist colonialism and imperialism, of a handful of billionaires—Vanderbilt, Rockefeller, Du Pont, Mellon—who mercilessly exploit the workingman and are seeking to unleash a world war so they can enslave all peoples. On the other hand, as one travels about the country, one sees even trees and fences hung with banners and posters exhorting the citizenry to "catch up with and to surpass America" in one field of endeavor and another, in the manufacture of steel as in pig breeding, in the construction of houses as in corn growing. America is the target to aim at, the ideal to attain if the Soviet citizen is to enjoy the abundance that Communist society promises him. How more intensely could the Kremlin arouse popular curiosity and admiration for its number-one villain?

The one great dream of the medical students, as of other educated youths one meets, was to visit Western countries. If ever the time comes when Soviet citizens are permitted freely to travel abroad, Soviet youth will outdo American youth as tourists, even if they have to go on bicycles.

The 7000-word decree of the Central Committee of January 9, 1960, calling for a fresh crusade of indoctrination in the faith and philosophy of Marxism-Leninism can never still the hunger of Soviet educated youth for travel abroad and for truthful and responsible information about Western countries. The attraction of the West, not its capitalism but its purely human scene, exerts itself against anything the Central Committee can say or do. Over and over the Central Committee may proclaim that coexistence does not imply an abandonment of the ideological struggle against the West and the battle against the infiltration of "decadent and dehumanizing" Western ideas and practices. But the imagination of Soviet youth, even of factory workers, is stirred by the West infinitely more than by the East—even Communist China.

It is astonishing how infrequently the subject of China comes up in conversation. One would suppose that the very size of China and pride in its Communist dictatorship would excite the mind of Soviet youth. But not even in Eastern Siberia, which has been introduced to Chinese oranges and pineapples and through whose airport in Irkutsk Chinese delegations come and go, was the subject of China ever brought up for any lengthy interval in all my conversations with Russians. There is friendliness toward China, but no visible or audible enthusiasm.

The Chinese students in Moscow University have been a painful disappointment to their Russian classmates. The penuriousness of the Chinese is strange and offensive to the generous-souled Russians, who will readily lend their last ruble to a fellow student for flowers for his girl. The fanaticism and social exclusiveness of the Chinese is utterly incomprehensible to the Russians. "Such grinds," a Moscow student said to me, "and such joyless souls. We really don't understand them."

The chief reason for the comparative uninterest in China is its geographical remoteness and the absence of any social challenge or cultural stimulation. A Chinese motion picture does not pack the theater and rarely do pictures from Bulgaria, Rumania, or even Czechoslovakia, which now and then produces a picture on a historical theme that attracts attention. The heroes and heroines speak a language that is "old junk," as young people express themselves, no matter what the review in *Pravda* said. But let a motion picture from Great Britain, France, Italy, Austria, Japan, America, Sweden, be announced and queues form outside the box office. Young people know that they will see and hear something new in a Western picture. The story may be trivial, the dialogue dull, but the settings —dress and furnishings—the manners and customs, offer glimpses into daily life that fascinate them; it is something immediate and concrete with which they can compare their own life. One reason the American picture *Roman Holiday* has been a sensational success is the personal grace of Audrey Hepburn and her exquisite costumes.

In one respect the youth of today bring to mind the youth of the twenties, especially the intellectuals among them. Now as then they are engaged in *dispooty* (public debates) on the subject of Communist morality and the new man in Soviet society.

Early in the twenties Bukharin and Trotsky delivered lectures on this subject which touched off endless discussions. I attended some of these discussions in universities and invariably students were concerned with the personal and social problems that confronted them. The themes of love, romance, family, the nature of the society to come, were threshed over and over. I recall a stormy debate of students at Irkutsk University on whether or not it was proper for girls to wear lipstick. Ironically there were girls in the audience with painted lips.

Times have changed but the old problems remain. A vast new literature has been published since the rise of the Seven-Year Plan on Communist morality and the new man. From all one can gather from this literature, the Soviet citizen must first and foremost love the Motherland, make work not only the duty but the delight of his life, fuse himself body and soul with the collective, purge himself of selfishness and greed, imbue himself with proletarian internationalism, and dedicate himself to good deeds for the good of his fellow man and society.

Members of the Communist brigades (work teams) that have sprung up all over the country since the end of 1958, are supposedly the latest exemplifications of the ideal Soviet citizen. By their joint and disciplined efforts they have unquestionably helped to reorganize and boost production. But unlike Stakhanovites, shock brigadiers, and other outstanding workers of former times, they also pledge themselves to promote education, mutual assistance, and a code of personal conduct that includes truthtelling, honesty in money matters, renunciation of "the green serpent" (the liquor bottle), politeness to women, to which any Russian Baptist would say amen. But their primary purpose is to boost production, which is still the ever pressing problem, still the front-page story in newspapers all over the country.

But when boys and girls of high school and college age get together for a *dispoot*, they do not talk about love of the Motherland or of a citizen's duty to work as best he can. They take these for granted even as they do loyalty to the Soviet system. Not once did I hear young people, however bitter their resentment against wrongs they have suffered, suggest an alternative to Soviet-party rule. They have no such alternatives, and in the light of their political education and their hopelessly distorted knowledge of the history and the making of Western civilization, they cannot have any. They do not think of political democracy and parliamentary government as known in the West. The angry and despairing writings of 1956 and 1957 were outcries against abuses in the system, not against its validity. Such writings have not in fact stopped, though the spirit is less acrimonious.

The Kremlin bloodbath in Budapest was a shock. Nevertheless, I met students who voiced sincere approval. While they laughed at the myth that fascists had stirred up the Hungarian rebellion, they firmly insisted that the Soviet Union could not permit Hungary to slip away. This might have encouraged other people's democracies to emulate the example of the Hungarians and leave open the highway to Moscow for a future enemy army. The moral issues involved did not perturb them. Westerners will err egregiously if they disregard the sentiments of Yevgeny Yevtushenko, perhaps the most rebellious young poet of the post-Stalin era, expressed in the lines:

For my country
> my life
> > and my death.
> > > I offer everything I have
> > > > Now and forever.

The old doctrine of "my country, right or wrong," is no monopoly of any capitalist country. It is, indeed, a transcendent tenet in Kremlin ideology.

But the young generation is not satisfied with ideological clichés about Communist morality and the personal and social problems that confront it. When a certain I. Svadkovsky, a lecturer on the subject, told an audience of young people that girls whom boys invite to the theater, a movie, a cafe, should pay their own way, girls in the audience sent written protests. In reply the lecturer said that he didn't mean it as a universal rule, but "the boy who pays for you behaves dissolutely . . . because you are in some measure obligated to him." A young instructor in a technological institute in Kiev with whom I discussed the lecture said, "Of course, we don't take such a lecturer seriously. He's too old-fashioned to understand our new young generation. He cannot understand them because our boys and girls wouldn't open up to him."

Confirmation of this attitude is well expressed by Yevgeni Vinokurov in a poem entitled *Didn't They All Preach to Me?* The poet admits that he listens politely to all the sermonizers. "It gives them pleasure, so why not?" But—"The more I listen to my mentors, the more I yearn to be alone."

In his play *Three of Us Went Together to the Virgin Lands*, Nikolai Pogodin, a playwright of the older generation with a keen ear for the language of youth, makes the director of a state farm say, "I know how to assert authority, but I have no time for thinking. What I mean is, we think all the time—but about man, about the boys and girls who come here, their souls, what's inside them as they grow up, we have no time to think of that. Before our eyes we always have these indexes, plans, norms. . . . But character—well—forms outside these indexes."

No truer words have been written about the barriers that stand between the older and younger generations of today. Young people live more within themselves than Khrushchev, Kozlov, Suslov, Furtseva, in their preoccupation with problems of production and power politics, begin to realize. Older ideologists may write glowingly of "the psychology of collectivism" that is transforming the Soviet citizen, but the intellectual youth are revolted by the intrusion of the collective into the intimacies of their lives. They are acquiring a keener sense of privacy than ideologists suspect or care to recognize. The re-education of their emotions, a primary Communist objective, is encountering resistance that I do not believe can be overcome. A healthy, sports-minded, book-reading, fun-loving youth, the Kremlin slogan of "one for all and all for one" in work and play, in thought and aspiration, holds for them severe limitations. Academician Strumilin's outline of Communist society "that is already on the horizon," as Moscow's *Komsomolka* has rapturously proclaimed, when people will eat together, spend their leisure hours together, plan and do everything together, when everybody will be everybody else's keeper and the collective will be everybody's father and mother, judge and jury in disputes and derelictions, is to my mind purely hypothetical. Indeed, in the light of the psychology of today's youth, there is a distinct boundary beyond which the socialization of the outer and inner life of the individual can never be achieved. The high-earning novelists whose stories are sermons not only on love of country and love of work but on "socialist togetherness" and "socialist do-goodism," are poor examples for youth of the ideals they preach. Their private and country homes, the private automobiles they can afford to buy, their free spending on whatever luxuries are obtainable, the opportunities they now have for travel abroad, the gifts they bring home for family and friends, do not inspire the intellectual youth, social-minded as they are, into a literal interpretation of the principle "one for all and all for one" in everything. If there are any among them who do not dream of an automobile of their own, of a country home of their own even if built by the state, of other purely material acquisitions for personal use, one does not meet them.

Unlike the intellectual youth of the twenties, who were fervently revolutionary and lived in the future more than in the present, the youth of today are largely conservative and live in the present more than in the future. That is why they fought in their own way and won the battle for gayer and more fashionable dress, for jazz, which some of them detest, and for a livelier social atmosphere. Volunteer guards in Sochi may seize girls who venture into the street in trousers and cut off their hair, but this will not deter girls from pressing for the right to wear trousers in the street.

The intellectual youth of today are in quest of answers to the old purely human problems of love, romance, family, society, of ethics and aesthetics, of social accommodation and individual self-expression, for which ideological verbal rituals are no substitutes. They are in fact bored by the endlessly repetitious lectures on ideology. "You should see our class," a physics student in Moscow University said to me, "when an ideologist delivers a lecture on Marxism-Leninism. Most of us do not even pretend to listen. We read a newspaper, a book, or pore over our notebooks."

The ardor of the twenties for world revolution is missing from the intellectual youth of today. In all my encounters with them, the subject of "the imminent collapse of capitalism" rarely came up. They may or may not have believed it, but unlike the youth of the twenties, they didn't seem to care one way or another. They lived under socialism, in which they unreservedly believed, but they displayed a lively curiosity in the more positive aspects of life in Western capitalist countries. Unlike *Pravda*'s correspondents in America, who gloatingly depict the American scene as of chaos and disintegration, of cruelty and misery, they sought for factual information about American workers and intellectuals, food and clothes, homes and highways, books and music and other aspects of American culture. It was the same whenever the subject of Great Britain came up. When they talked about books, American or British, their language was singularly free from the ideological postulates that color Soviet literary criticism. They are the most enthusiastic supporters of cultural exchange with Western countries, and while the Kremlin vigilantly guards them against the infiltration of Western ideas—wouldn't even permit the display of the *World Almanac* at the American Exhibition in Moscow in the summer of 1959— they have no scruples about reading anything that may come their way or listening to foreign-language broadcasts, which are rarely jammed.

Among themselves the intellectual youth do not disdain discussing the subject of free love, which had excited the youth of the twenties. It horrified ideologists when in the course of a public debate a girl asked whether it was true that men and women were sometimes sexually incompatible, and if so, whether it wasn't proper for a couple contemplating marriage to discover it before they legalized their union. No wonder that the late Judge Lindsey's gospel of "companionate marriage," which has somehow penetrated the Soviet Union, has been fiercely denounced by Soviet moralists. Yet premarital unions are not unknown though are not talked about.

Above all, and this cannot be too vigorously reiterated, the youth of today, workers as well as intellectuals, do not know the hatreds that molded the minds and the souls of Khrushchev's generation. Nor do they know the fears that made cowards and hypocrites of their fathers and mothers.

The very young and very gifted Siberian poetess Rima Kazakova exhorts her generation:

> Be yourself, be true to your real self.
> Never fear to lose yourself in life. If
> you are where life is with the full richness of your being,
> life is where you are. Live! March on! Good luck!

One can only wonder what the Soviet Union will be like when the young generation of today becomes the ruling generation tomorrow.

PART IV

FRONTIERS

20.

SIBERIA
The Great Transformation

One afternoon, shortly after my return from Siberia, as I was searching for a seat in the crowded dining room of Moscow's National Hotel, I saw a young man sitting alone at a small table at the far end of the room. I sat down opposite him and we exchanged a formal "good evening." From the cut of his clothes and the setting before him—a decanter of vodka, a bottle of beer, a plate of smoked salmon, and a cucumber salad—I knew that my neighbor was Russian. A remarkably handsome youth with flaxen hair, blue eyes, and ruddy cheeks, he seemed ill at ease, as though eating in a hotel reputedly for rich foreigners was a new and disconcerting experience. Now and then he glanced at me, uncertain whether to start a conversation. But diffidence held him back, and he was such a fascinating study of a Russian youth in a social setting unfamiliar to him that I made no effort to resolve his dilemma by speaking first.

Presently a tall, robust, dark-haired waiter passed by and my table companion nudged him by the arm. For some moments the two spoke in hushed voices. Then, when the waiter left, the young man, like a boy bursting with a secret, turned to me and said, "Imagine it, here I am in this hotel for the first time in my life and the waiter is a Siberian like myself!"

"Where do you come from?" I asked.

"Omsk. Have you ever been there?"

"Years ago, and I'll never forget your dust storms."

"Ah, but they aren't so bad now. We are asphalting the streets and squares and setting them out with trees, shrubs, and flowers. We're licking the dust storms."

I told him I was an American journalist and had just returned from Siberia but had seen Omsk only from the air.

"You should see our new Omsk," he boasted. "You wouldn't recognize it. I like it much better than Moscow."

"Don't tell it to Muscovites," I said.

"But I do tell it to them," he snapped back. "I've never before been in Moscow; I came here to take examinations in my specialty —technology in the woodworking industry. But look"—nodding at the darkened rain-spattered windows—"it's only the nineteenth of August and the weather is foul—bleak skies, raw winds, rain and rain. But in Omsk the sun is shining."

He paused and smiled with triumph. "Strange people, these Muscovites. Mention Siberia to them and they begin to shiver. But I tell them we have more sunshine a year in Omsk than they have in Moscow. They laugh at me, but I tell them to look it up in the encyclopedia, and when they do their faces drop."

Again he paused and smiled with pride. "Of course, Siberia is cold in winter. But it's a dry healthy cold, with brilliant sunshine, even in winter. When the ground freezes it stays frozen until spring, so we have few of the sicknesses that come from thaw and slush. Our Siberia is really a land of sunshine."

"I bet," I said, "you have no hotel like the National in Omsk."

"That's the truth. But give us time and we shall have hotels as good as and better than the National. We are the richest country in the Soviet Union."

"What a Siberian patriot you are," I said.

"Of course. Every Siberian is. Where in the world will you find such forests as our taiga, such wild game, such wonderful rivers and lakes, such tasty fish, and such powerful people? I was too young to fight in the war—I'm only twenty-four—but my father saw plenty of fighting and you should hear him tell how the Fritzes feared Siberians, called them polar bears, because however intense the cold and wild the blizzards, Siberians were ready to shoot—and a Siberian always hits his target. Hunting makes us crack marksmen."

"You talk," I said, "like Texans in America."

"Who are they? Indians?"

I was not surprised to hear him speak of Indians—Russians are avid readers of Fenimore Cooper.

Siberians think big, talk big, and tolerate no aspersions on their country or its climate. Ask a European Russian where he comes from and he will say that he is from the province of Tambov, Moscow, Tula, Ryazan, or whatever his native province. Put the question to a Siberian, and whether the province of his birth is Omsk, Tomsk, or Irkutsk, he invariably answers, "I'm a *Sibiryak* [Siberian]." To him Siberia is a single country, a superior land, with its special blessings, breeding a superior type of humanity, more hardy, more adventurous, more fearless than European Russians. Moscow's former psychopathic fear of foreigners, which still haunts many Muscovites —especially the older generation of intellectuals—got dissipated somewhere in the Siberian forests and steppes. The youth from Omsk felt no hesitation in writing down his home address for me in full view of waiters and others whose business it might have been to keep a sharp eye on people in the dining room. He heartily urged me to visit him if I ever came to Omsk, so that he and his wife could treat me to a "real banquet," champagne and all!

Let it be remembered that even in Czarist times Siberia was freer than European Russia. It never knew serfdom. It never was plagued by landlordism. The peasant settler might be too poor to buy a horse and cow, but he didn't suffer from want of land. Siberia always had and still has more land than people to cultivate it. Besides, the Czarist exile system brought to Siberia freethinking political rebels who were among the most highly educated men in the country. They left a heritage of self-assertiveness which, though repressed by the Soviets, has not died out.

It is no accident that Vice-President Nixon was greeted more warmly and spontaneously in Siberia than in Moscow or Leningrad. Siberians felt freer to express their sentiments.

On my first journey to Siberia, in 1927, I traveled by train, and it took five days and five nights to cover the distance of 3100 miles from Moscow to Irkutsk. This time I traveled by Soviet jet plane, and the flying time between the two cities was six hours.

Siberia is no longer the faraway and isolated country that it had been and that the outside world may still imagine it to be. The highways of the air have drawn it close, not only to European Russia but to every country on our planet, more especially to China, Mongolia, North Korea, to which one can fly directly from Irkutsk. "There is five hours' difference in time between our city and Moscow," said Victor Rogov, the athletic-looking rector of Irkutsk University. "If I leave Irkutsk by jet plane at noon, I arrive in Moscow about one in the afternoon, Moscow time. I can transact my business during the afternoon, go to the opera in the evening, and be back in Irkutsk at five the next morning."

The assistant director of the state experimental farm *Rodina* (Motherland) in the province of Irkutsk said, "We now receive frozen semen from the choicest bulls in Holland in less than two days. It's going to revolutionize our dairy industry." The poultryman on the farm, the tallest and plumpest Georgian I had ever known, broke in and said, "I can now get newly hatched chicks of the best breeds from European Russia in one day, and in two days from any country in Europe. We can get anything quickly from anywhere in the world."

There have always been two Siberias: the Siberia of exiles, salt mines, prison camps, torture chambers; and the Siberia that lies outside the barbwired, gun-sheltered camps and prisons. Had Mikhail Suslov, the Kremlin's apostle of Communist orthodoxy, been even scantily acquainted with Western psychology, he would have saved himself the embarrassment he suffered when he spoke of Siberia as he did before the Foreign Press Association of London. The Associated Press report of the event (New York *Herald Tribune*, March 20, 1959) speaks for itself:

"'Two months ago,' he [Suslov] said, 'I visited Siberia. It's a wonderfully rich country to live in, with a dry climate.'

"Laughter came from the newsmen.

"Mr. Suslov went on: 'In place of deserts, new towns and cities have been built. Several million people have been settled. They are full of enthusiasm and all our expenses [of development] have been covered!'

"The laughter of the audience erupted into a roar."

Deeply ingrained in Western memories is the Siberia of labor camps and torture chambers.

Yet there is the other Siberia, "a land of sunshine" and of "inexhaustible riches," as Siberians speak of it. When a young woman in Irkutsk told me there was about twice as much sunshine a year in Irkutsk as in Moscow province, I couldn't restrain a laugh. "You Siberians," I said, "always talk big." But after I consulted the encyclopedia I regretted my laughter. Though the growing season in Irkutsk province, the southeastern farm belt, lasts from 130 to 146 days, "the duration of sunshine," says the encyclopedia, "is almost twice that of Moscow province."

In area, including the Far East, Siberia is much larger than the United States, though one fourth of it lies north of the Arctic Circle. The population of Siberia proper, as of January 1, 1961, was 18,500,000 as against 8,000,000 in 1913. But though still only partially explored, it is one of the richest storehouses of natural wealth in the world. One has to be in Siberia, speak to industrialists, engineers, university professors, above all to geologists, to gain some impression of the prodigious riches that nature has packed into its forests and steppes, its lakes and rivers, its mountains and tundras, its immense, peat-rich swamps.

Here stretches in silent majesty the most gigantic forest in the world, stocked with the richest fur-bearing animals, the most precious of which is the dark-brown sable. About a billion acres in area, the forest constitutes more than three fourths of all of Russia's timber reserves.

Here roll immense areas of tillable land, about twenty million acres of which were newly plowed (1954–58) and seeded, principally to spring wheat. At Moscow's Department of Agriculture a Siberian specialist told me that in Western Siberia alone—the territory that lies east of the Urals up to the Yenisei River—there are about a hundred twenty-five million acres suitable for agriculture, much of it still in wild meadow and pasture, in swamp that can be drained, in dwarf forest that can be cleared. In Eastern Siberia, he went on, there are still other vast areas of virgin lands, especially in the fabulous region of Krasnoyarsk (three times the size of Texas) and east of Lake Baikal.

In 1957 Siberia seeded about fifteen million more acres to wheat than did the Ukraine, Russia's traditional breadbasket. But the wheat harvest was no larger than that of the Ukraine. Poor transportation, shortage of storage space, lack of fertilizer and herbicides, inadequate tillage, slip-ups in calculations on when to begin seeding and when to finish the harvesting, have again and again resulted in huge losses of grain. Still, beginning with 1958, Siberia has been outproducing the Ukraine in wheat. The catastrophic droughts and crop failures that have periodically swept large parts of European Russia, especially the Volga regions, Siberia has not known. "Here in Siberia," an agronomist told me, "we never speak of a crop failure the way they do in European Russia; we speak only of poorer or richer crops." Siberia has been spared the periodic famines that had for centuries devastated the Volga country. Even in the driest years Siberia grew enough food for itself and for export. Siberian hard wheat is world-famous, and in Czarist days Siberian butter and cheese commanded a ready market, not only in European Russia but in Western Europe.

The Siberia of today grows on a large scale crops that it had once cultivated only in kitchen gardens or not at all. Tomatoes, melons, sunflowers, millet, potatoes, sugar beets, turnips and carrots even for livestock, alfalfa, flax, hemp, tobacco, are among these crops. Corn, too, has come to Siberia (1954), though it is grown not for grain but for green fodder and ensilage. Most remarkable has been the acclimatization of fruit, principally apples and pears, though for the present on only a very small scale. I saw what Siberians call "crawling orchards," meaning trees that do not grow vertically —frost would kill them—but whose branches spread over the ground so that the cover of snow will be like "a fur coat" over them, as Siberians express themselves, and will prevent winter kill. "We got the idea," a horticulturist explained, "from observing the way dwarf cedar grows on mountains. It grows outward instead of upward, the branches spreading over the ground. Nature is an excellent teacher, and here in Siberia you must observe nature very closely and put her lessons into practice."

Through the Siberian land flow the mightiest rivers in the Soviet Union, holding within them, so Soviet scientists declare, more potential hydroelectric power than all the rivers of France, Canada, and America combined. Originally the wild Angara alone, so swift-flowing that in winter ice begins forming on the bottom instead of on the surface, was scheduled to be spanned by a cascade of six mighty hydroelectric plants that would yield more power than the four largest rivers in European Russia—the Volga, Kama, Dnieper, and Don. Originally the other great rivers—the Ob, Irtysh, Lena, and above all the Yenisei, mightiest of all Siberian rivers and spoken of as "brother to the ocean"—were to be mounted with gigantic hydro plants, whose output of power would speed the drive to outproduce America within fifteen years.

Then suddenly, on August 10, 1958, on the occasion of the opening of the Kuibyshev dam on the Volga, with a capacity of 2,300,000 kilowatts as against the Grand Coulee with only 1,974,000 kilowatts (Khrushchev's figures), Khrushchev, with an eye on America, announced that the hydro dams cost too much and took too long to build. The one at Kuibyshev took nine years, the one at Stalingrad would take ten years to finish. The water resources would always be there, Khrushchev told his vast audience, but thermal stations would be more immediately profitable, and should be built near sources of cheap fuel supplies, such as gas in Uzbekistan and coal in Siberia.

Yet Siberia is not neglecting hydroelectric plants. The one at Bratsk over the Angara is in process of construction and will have a capacity of 4,500,000 kilowatts. The one at Krasnoyarsk over the Yenisei when completed will generate a larger output, 5,000,000 kilowatts.

The Seven-Year Plan calls for the complete electrification of the Trans-Siberian Railway all the way from Moscow to Vladivostok. This is the longest railroad in the world—some 5600 miles long.

Siberia is above all a treasure chest of mineral resources. It is Russia's richest gold producer, much richer now than under the Czars because of new discoveries and the mechanization of the gold-mining industry. It is Russia's richest repository of coal. The seven bases already explored make Russia, according to Soviet scientists, the richest coal country in the world. The find in the Krasnoyarsk region alone spreads over a territory of 600 miles and the seams reach a thickness of 100 meters. This, like some of the other fields, lends itself to open-strip mining, which is much cheaper than the coal of the famed Donbas in the Ukraine.

Some iron had always been mined in Siberia. Genghis Khan, who pushed out of Mongolia, was known to have forged iron weapons in Kuznetsk, now a metallurgical center. But for years

Soviet geologists vainly searched for iron deposits that would make Siberia independent of ore from the Urals. Now they have succeeded. "We have all the iron ore," a geologist said to me, "that Siberia will ever need, once we get our transportation problem settled." One of the largest deposits was uncovered in the swampy wastes of the basin of the Ob River in Western Siberia. Other deposits were uncovered in the Altai region, in the Khakass region, in the Angara-Ilymsk region in Eastern Siberia. In 1946 a geologist named V. Medvedkov, prowling around the lower reaches of the Angara, stumbled on what geologists regard as the richest of all Siberian iron-ore reserves, lying almost on the surface. In his report of the discovery the geologist exclaimed, "Nothing like it has ever been known in Siberia!" Called the Angara-Pittskoye field, its reserves are estimated to contain five billion tons of ore, though mostly low-grade.

Bauxite, nepheline, tin, zinc, lead, nickel, mercury, cobalt, wolframite, molybdenum, magnetites, titanium, graphite, rock salt, limestone, mica—Siberia is rich in all of these and more, though as yet no large sources of copper, manganese, or potassium have been uncovered.

But the end is not yet. From one end of Siberia to the other, traveling on foot and horseback, on trucks and in planes, on river boats and rafts, and in winter on skis and in dog and reindeer sleds, geologists are scouring the country for hidden treasures. Siberia is without doubt the greatest prospecting country in the world. The adventure of prospecting has attracted high school and college students, and in summer one sees parties of boys and girls, knapsack on back, mallet in hand, often escorted by trained geologists, wandering over hills and mountains, forests and riverbanks, in quest of treasure.

In Czarist days Siberia was famed for three kinds of gold—yellow, which was metal; soft, which was fur; and green, which was forest. Now it is also known as a land of diamonds. These were uncovered in faraway, perpetually frozen Yakutia, whose capital, Yakutsk, is 5500 miles from Moscow. The search was long and arduous, and it was young geologists just out of the university who first conceived the project and carried it through in the face of the opposition from older geologists, who were convinced that nowhere in the Soviet Union could appreciable amounts of diamonds be found.

Alexander Burov, a young geologist in the Urals, was not discouraged. But his expeditions up and down the Urals in 1930 were accompanied by failure. Then another young geologist, Vladimir Sobolev, a graduate of the Leningrad Institute of Geology and a specialist in petrography, spent years in searching for territory anywhere in the Soviet Union with a geological structure similar to that of South Africa. In Yakutia he found such territory, and on August 7, 1949, Grigory Feinstein, a graduate of the Irkutsk Institute of Geology, discovered the first Soviet diamond field on the banks of the Vilyui River. The story related to his find demonstrates Soviet secretiveness about the search for diamonds. Radio messages of the discovery were transmitted in code so that no foreign intelligence would pick them up. In the instance of Feinstein, he had forgotten the code and radioed the message "I lost my reindeer." The receivers of the message took it literally and sent him a fresh team of reindeer for travel in the taiga. The error was corrected but Moscow never published a word of Feinstein's discovery.

On June 13, 1955, two other young geologists, one named Yuri Khabardin, the other Volodya Shchukin, the one prospecting the Yereliakh River upstream, the other 560 miles north, upstream on the Daldyn River, discovered much richer fields than Feinstein's. Two weeks later, the twenty-four-year-old Shchukin, while prospecting upstream on the Alakit River, stumbled on still another diamond field, and a month afterward he came on a third find—three finds of diamond fields within two months by young Shchukin, one of the new heroes of Siberia. It was only then, in February 1956, that Bulganin, who was Premier at the time, surprised the world with his announcement of rich diamond discoveries in Yakutia.

Since then other diamond fields have been located in Yakutia and the search continues. Meanwhile Moscow has set up a Yakutian diamond trust, and at the place where Khabardin discovered his first diamonds at the edge of a fox hole, a diamond city is in process of construction. Khabardin had radioed to geological headquarters the code message "have lighted the pipe of peace [mir] and the tobacco is excellent."

The name of the town is Mirny (which means peaceful), derived from Khabardin's code word, which was mir (peace), and supposedly symbolizing the Kremlin's loudly heralded quest for world peace. Because of permafrost the town is built on sturdy wooden piles, yet within four years, or as of October 1960, the population grew to some 20,000 and is still growing. Situated within dense taiga some 150 miles north of the village of Mukhutya, its nearest neighbor, there is neither railway nor highway connecting the two.

While Mirny is the center of the diamond industry, two other diamond towns, Novy (new) and Udachny (successful), are in process of construction. The Russians have been so secretive about their diamond finds that nobody knows how true is the claim, widely circulated in Irkutsk, that the fields compare favorably with those in South Africa. Anyway, the fact that in January 1960 the Kremlin quite unexpectedly signed an exclusive agreement with the Diamond Corporation of South Africa for the marketing of its diamonds would indicate that they have a surplus to sell, if only for industrial purposes. Thus South African fears that Russia might dump diamonds in the world market have been stilled.

But operations in the wild country of Siberia, in a region of permafrost, far from railroads and highways and from sources of food and other supplies, and the high wages and premiums the state must pay to induce workers to migrate there, make diamond mining prodigiously expensive. For this reason alone, one wouldn't venture to forecast the future of the Soviet diamond industry in Yakutia.

Rich in forest and hydro power, coal and iron, and many other minerals, including nepheline, raw material for aluminum, Siberia is now one of the boom lands of all time. Towering smokestacks and gigantic cranes greet the traveler as his train rolls into a railroad station or his plane circles for a landing. Or, flying over the wooded wilderness, he glimpses the tops of building machinery poking through the trees, and a fellow passenger proudly informs him that down below a new industrial city is rising in Siberia's virgin forest. "Have you heard of our Chulym Necklace?" a fellow passenger at the Omsk airport inquired. "It's beautiful country out there, a forest snaking along the Chulym River, and we are building four new industrial towns along it that aren't yet on the map." Again and again I was to hear the expression "not yet on the map."

Moscow is determined to convert Siberia into a powerful industrial empire, an empire of iron and steel, of machine building and chemical products—fertilizers, synthetic rubber, plastics, all kinds of artificial fibers—and, above all, aluminum. "Our Siberia," an engineer said to me, "will someday become one of the great aluminum centers of the world, and if America would sell us machinery for our chemical industry, then with our cheap coal and timber, the oil we are piping from European oil fields, our Siberia, I tell you, would soon become one of the world's leading manufacturers of chemical products." Of course, Siberians talk big, but the coal and timber are there, and so is the gas, though chiefly in a faraway Yakutia.

For years the search for oil in Siberia yielded no significant results. In the summer of 1958, the year of my journey, the rich strike in the province of Tyumen had not yet been achieved. But when I asked a geologist if he had hopes of discovering substantial oil deposits anywhere in Siberia, he replied significantly, "It took us twenty years to uncover large deposits of iron. Twenty years! Some of my colleagues thought we'd never find it. Now we estimate the known deposits in billions of tons—to be specific, at least thirteen billion. It will be the same with oil. If the Canadian prairies are rich in oil, so our Siberian steppes must be."

I was surprised at the keen and rather friendly interest of Siberians in Canada, due no doubt to geographic similarities between the two countries. A famed hunter wished me to tell Canadians that their muskrat, which was introduced into the forest about a generation ago, has become one of the most prolific and profitable fur animals. "Your American mink is doing exceptionally well too. It's very fecund and its fur is of a higher quality than that of European mink. The only trouble with your American mink is that it has a voracious appetite for Canadian muskrat." With a grin he added, "We seem to have a regular American-Canadian war in our forests."

Moscow's Academy of Sciences may publish a thick volume on Canada's loss of "peace, prosperity, and sovereignty" to Canadian-American imperialists. But the Siberians who queried me about Canada didn't seem to have heard of the book. Nor did anybody ask me a single question about the Progressive Workers' (Communist) party, which the Academy's author has chosen as the hero destined to rescue Canada from vassalage and restore the nation's "lost" peace, prosperity, and sovereignty. Siberian interest in Canada, at least of those with whom I spoke, was completely non-political. They wanted to know about Canada's apple crop and how corn was doing there, and whether Canada had acclimatized watermelons and honeydews as southern Siberia has done. They asked if Canadian farmers sold their winter milk in frozen cakes as Siberian peasants did in the bazaars of Irkutsk.

Siberians proudly told me that they are a *krepky narod* (powerful people) and like to indulge in strong drink, so they asked what Canada's strong drink was and whether Canadians knew about vodka. They asked what hunters got for their fur and whether they had a dog like the Siberian laika? I confessed that all I knew about the breed was that one had been shot into space in the second sputnik, and they told me it was the favorite hunting dog of the country.

There were times when I was sorry I wasn't a walking Canadian encyclopedia. I bogged down when an agricultural expert asked how many sunny days Canada had a year, and like the youth from Omsk, he proceeded to enlighten me on the glories of Siberia's sunshine. "You may not believe it, but it's true," he assured me. "We have as much sunshine in a year as the Crimea." How like Floridians native-born Siberians I met are, the way they exult in their sunshine!

A hunter came forth with a fresh boast of Siberia. "Here," he said, "we have the best deep-freezer in the world, with no failure of electric current. When I come home with a bagful of game, I freeze it outdoors and use it as I need. I do the same with fish. Nothing spoils." It is a fact that peasant women in Siberia popped their weekly batch of freshly baked bread into the natural Siberian freezer centuries before Western housewives had heard of the electric kind.

But among the new arrivals in the big country, one hears woeful complaints. They loathe the climate, the primitive living conditions, and the wildness of nature. "I signed up for two years," a young Muscovite said to me, "and when my time is up they cannot keep me here for anything in the world." The truth is that Siberia is not prepared to care for the trainloads of migrants that keep coming there. For a year or two they live in tent colonies, which are not always properly heated. Now and then there are shortages of food, even tea and sugar, and of soap and cigarettes; there are not enough cots to sleep on and benches to sit on, no closets in which to store one's belongings. The planners appear to be so carried away by blueprints for dams and factories that they neglect accommodations for the young people who come to build them. The press keeps thundering at them, but the stream of migrants outstrips facilities to feed and house them properly, which doesn't in any way depress the native-born Siberian's enthusiasm for his country or the fervor of those newcomers who despite hardship thrill to the excitement of pioneering in the wild and rich country. "I have no use for the whiners," another Moscow youth said to me. "They're mamma's little darlings, are afraid of falling off a rock, hitting themselves with an ax, being eaten by a bear. I just laugh at them. I love the Siberian wildness, the Siberian sun, yes, even the snows. Of course, life is hard, and d'you know what I do when I feel discouraged? I read your Jack London. Lots of us do, because London makes us feel strong and heroic."

One of the more significant accomplishments of Siberia is the great upsurge in higher education. In 1914 there were only three institutions of higher learning, with a student body of 2500 and all located in Tomsk. Now there are 63 such institutions, with a student body of 167,000. There are also 219 scientific institutes staffed with 8244 scientists.

In Omsk the jet on which I was flying to Irkutsk laid over for five hours—a storm in Irkutsk had closed down the airport. It was deep twilight when my plane finally landed at the large Irkutsk airfield, where I saw more planes, including jets, than I could count. The small airport building was brightly lighted and the downstairs waiting room was crowded with people, who milled around as they do at airports the world over—friends and homefolks gaily meeting incoming passengers, fathers embracing wives and children from whom they had been separated, greeting them with bursts of endearments, in which the Russian language is so rich.

The local Intourist representative guided me to the second-floor waiting rooms for foreign travelers, where they sometimes make a prolonged stay. The rooms are neatly kept, furnished with rugs and the overstuffed furniture so dear to Russian decorators. Flowers in tall vases stood on every table in every room. It all seemed the symbol of a new and modernized Irkutsk that had risen out of the primitiveness in which it had sprawled a generation earlier, when I first visited it.

As there was no room for me at the airport, I was driven to the hotel in the city, and the moment the Pobeda rolled into the outskirts

of Irkutsk disenchantment set in. Nothing here had changed. The
unpaved streets still looked like village streets, lined with wooden
hovels, mud puddles gleaming in the dim lights. The Pobeda slid
and slithered and made sharp turns to avoid splashing into mudholes.
This was the Siberia I had known—wooden hovels and mud everywhere, in city after city—Novosibirsk, Omsk, Tyumen, Krasnoyarsk,
Chita, and of course Irkutsk. Yet after a generation of feverish construction, the city to which I had come, capital of Eastern Siberia
and one of the oldest cities in the country, having been founded in
1652, and once renowned for its gold millionaires, still sprawled in
slush after rain, its darkened wooden hovels looking like relics of its
founding days.

But the scene changed abruptly when the Pobeda stopped at the
hotel. Here was a block-long, four-story structure I had not seen on
my earlier visit. So, side by side with the old, there was a new Irkutsk.
The next morning when I went driving I saw block after block of
new brick buildings, yellow and gray; office buildings, apartment
houses, schools, clubs, and of course factories, which gave the city an
impressive new skyline. Many of the streets were already asphalted,
and squads of men and women were tearing up pavements and at
last, after forty-one years of Sovietism, putting through a city-wide
sewage and water system. There were new parks and squares arrayed
in greenery, though Moscow's skilled solicitude for trees was lacking:
dead branches on old trees were uncut, many a young tree was wind-
broken, saplings were wilting from the root. Sensitiveness to beauty
has never been a marked Siberian attribute—a country of peasant
settlers with a sprinkling of exiled intellectuals, the conquest of nature, as in all pioneering countries, transcended all regard for beauty.
Not even the high banks of the broad Angara, which courses through
the city, had been cleared of scrub and debris.

Yet gone from the scene were the scattered little artisan shops and
the small factories with their ancient and largely hand-run equipment.
Instead, over a hundred new enterprises, some old ones rebuilt and
enlarged but mostly newly constructed ones equipped with modern
tools, had risen on both banks of the Angara. Here was one of the
largest tea-processing plants in the Soviet Union; the tea from China
and Ceylon was packaged here for shipment all over Siberia and other
parts of the country. Here were highly mechanized sawmills, wood-

working shops, brickyards, cement factories, food-processing plants, knitting mills, factories for shoes, machine tools, agricultural implements; and towering over them all and over the whole city, high on the bank of the river, stood the giant Kuibyshev metallurgical plant, specializing among other things in machinery for the gold-, coal-, and iron-mining industries in the province.

The city's greatest pride is the newly constructed hydro plant over the Angara. The dam is a mile and a half long, and behind it rolls a new sea all the way to Lake Baikal, some forty-five miles away.

As I stood marveling at this sea, shimmering in the brilliant sun, the young engineer who had piloted me through the plant had ideas of his own on how best to impress me with the grandeur of Irkutsk. "Now that we have finished this plant and are building a much larger one at Bratsk, we shall build more factories still."

They are building them not only in the city but all over the province. Ten miles outside Irkutsk the aluminum city of Shelekhov— named after the famed Siberian explorer—is in process of construction. Forty miles north, the industrial city of Angarsk, with a population of 134,000 (census of January 1, 1959) and growing fast, has mushroomed out of the wooded wilderness within ten years. Still farther north, three onetime villages—Ust Kut, Mama, and Chuna— are in process of being converted into industrial cities. The rising city of Bratsk is to be a complex of industries—metallurgy, lumbering, paper, chemical products, and others. "And only a few years ago," the engineer said, "bear came to feast on berries in the taiga around Bratsk."

The slumbering town of Taishet on the Trans-Siberian Railway is to be the seat of a new and powerful steel industry, while north of it, deep in the forest, bulldozers were set to work in 1959 to clear ground for the construction of the new city of Zheleznogorsk (Iron City) to mine the recently uncovered iron ore for Bratsk and Taishet.

Space does not permit me to catalogue the new industries that are rising or are scheduled to rise in the province of Irkutsk alone. While the industrial output of the Soviet Union as a whole is to increase during the Seven-Year Plan by 80 per cent, in the province of Irkutsk, which could comfortably hold within its boundaries six Englands, it is to be trebled. The same is true of the adjacent Krasnoyarsk region. The reason for concentrating effort in the Eastern Siberian provinces is not fear of China, as some Westerners in Moscow believe. Russians may be antipathetic to the Chinese as a people, may think their Communist leaders are brash and brutal, but they do not fear the Chinese. It is the natural wealth of these provinces and other parts of Eastern Siberia that has prompted Moscow to devote special attention to its development.

Whenever I am in Moscow I never fail to pay frequent visits to the bookshop of the Academy of Sciences. One never knows what important *novinky* (new books) may appear in the windows, whether on the approaching death of Western society or on a purely non-political Russian subject. The books sell out quickly, sometimes within a day or even a few hours. I was fortunate to drop into the shop on the day it was stocked with the first five volumes of the thirteen-volume study of the productive resources of Eastern Siberia.[1] A monumental work, it brings together in great detail all the recent scientific studies of this vast region, which embraces the provinces of Krasnoyarsk, Irkutsk, and Chita and the Buryat-Mongol, Yakutsk, and Tuva autonomous territories. In area the region is almost as large as Australia or the continental United States, but 60 per cent of it is in swampy tundra and permafrost. For once the Russians themselves inform us that the early anticipations of making use of the far northern lands for agricultural purposes have not fully materialized. Less than 0.5 per cent of the land there has been put into cultivation. But 37 per cent is in reindeer pastures, Russia being the largest reindeer country in the world.

But this territory, according to the study of the Academy of Sciences, is—in addition to gold and diamonds—Siberia's richest depository of building materials other than timber, is "rich enough in iron to supply the needs of its own metallurgical plants and in part those of the Kuznetsk metallurgical industry." It holds 80 per cent of all the coal of Siberia and the largest part of Siberia's water resources and forest reserves. From here also come the greatest number and the finest of Siberian furs.

While climatic conditions limit agricultural possibilities even in the southern regions, the scientists believe that much more land than is

[1] *Razvitiye proizvodstvennykh sil Vostochnoy Sibiri* (Academy of Sciences, Moscow, 1960), Vols. I–V.

now in cultivation can be put under the plow. Pastures occupy almost one half of the southern territories, wild or natural meadow over one fifth, and mineral resources about 3 per cent. Already the seeded land is four times larger in acreage than it had been in 1913.

But even in this vast and widely explored region, there are immense "white spots" that still await the geologist.

In Siberia more than in European Russia, the traveler is struck with the great anomaly of the Soviet system: gigantic industrial development alongside primitive living conditions, most vividly symbolized in Irkutsk by the towering Kuibyshev plant on the banks of the Angara and women doing their laundering in the Angara's chilly waters.

The Irkutsk of a generation ago with its small population was an infinitely more comfortable place to live in than now. Food was plentiful, as it was in all Siberia—meat, fish, butter, cream, cheese, vegetables, honey—all of the highest quality. There is no shortage of common staples in the Irkutsk of today; but the variety of food is severely limited, though for a brief spell in winter it is supplemented by imports of apples, oranges, lemons, pineapples, from China.

The Irkutsk of yesterday knew no housing crisis. People lived in houses of their own or in commodious rented apartments. Now the housing shortage is at least as acute as in Moscow. Officials proudly told me that living space has doubled in the past thirty years. But the population has more than trebled and is rapidly climbing to the 400,000 figure. With the industrial boom on, a new influx of settlers is expected, and despite the feverish building of new apartment houses, the average citizen must content himself with only four and a half square meters of living space. Eight square meters is the most he is promised in 1965, on the completion of the new Plan.

As in Moscow, married couples are forever in search of not an apartment but a room to themselves. In speaking of a somewhat privileged woman to whom he introduced me, an acquaintance said, "What a shame she's unmarried; she has such a large living room all to herself."

And yet I heard less grumbling in Irkutsk than in any city in European Russia, far less than in Moscow. For one thing, people felt freer than in the Soviet capital and not only because of traditional Siberian self-assertiveness. Freedom, whatever there is of it in the

Soviet Union, seems to be in inverse ratio to the distance from Moscow, and Irkutsk is farther away than is San Francisco from New York. People were easy to meet and readily came to my room in the hotel, and oddly enough the woman clerk at the hotel had even neglected to pick up my passport, which is inconceivable anywhere in European Russia.

There was no running hot water in my room and mornings I had to wander through lengthy corridors and climb a flight of stairs to fill a teapot with hot water for shaving. Invariably there was a small queue in the hot-water room and we held little seminars there about Siberia, America, the prospect of world peace, and other subjects. One evening a craggy-faced geologist I met while I was waiting my turn for the hot water came to my room. We stayed up late talking, he telling one story after another of his amazing experiences in the Siberian wilderness, where pack on back, rifle over shoulder, and mallet in hand, he had for years been wandering in search of minerals. "Our Siberia," he said, "is our real El Dorado and there are still so many white spots on the map that we haven't begun to know what riches lie hidden in the Siberian earth. That's what makes Siberia so exciting to a man like myself."

That's what makes Siberia exciting also to Victor Rogov, rector of Irkutsk University. A squat man with broad shoulders, a powerful neck, he appears more like a wrestler than an educator. Born and educated in Leningrad, he is a quantum physicist. (Is there a university rector in the Soviet Union who is not a mathematician or a scientist?) Despite the enormous responsibility of administering a large university, he found time to give a course in his specialty and to spend several hours every day in his laboratory. He was happy to be in Siberia, he said, because he felt the challenge and excitement of helping to educate experts for the development of its inexhaustible natural wealth.

Between the university, with its seven faculties, its research centers, and the twelve independent colleges in the city, they were educating students in forty specialized professions. "If you'll read our newspapers," he said, "you'll see columns of advertisements for all manner of experts. We cannot begin to supply the demands, not even with all the help we now get from our affiliate of Moscow's Academy of Sciences, with its departments in geology, chemistry, biology, energetics, economic geography, and ichthyology."

Present at the interview were Professor Petrov, head of the philosophical faculty, and Professor Travilsky, director of the city's teachers' college, which was no longer allied with the university.

"We also have a seismic station, an astronomical observatory, and a museum institute," said Professor Petrov. "Irkutsk is a city of great learning and great science."

"Our polytechnical college [mining and metallurgy] alone has twenty-eight departments and a faculty of two hundred," said the rector, "and it's already too small for us, far too small."

"The more industry we build," Professor Petrov interposed, "the more science we need, and the more colleges and institutes we must open."

"That's why," the rector resumed, "we are building a new student city—a completely independent city—for ten thousand students. You must go and see it. The grounds are extraordinarily beautiful."

"By the time we finish building it," Petrov spoke again, "we shall have to enlarge it or build a new university city. That's how fast we're growing."

Hearing these men speak only strengthened the conviction that the Kremlin is determined to convert Siberia not only into a mighty industrial empire but into a country of great science, with Irkutsk and Novosibirsk, where they are building a "city of science" and a new university, to be the centers of it, the one for Eastern, the other for Western Siberia.

Yet the foreigner who walks the streets of Irkutsk or of Novosibirsk, so many of them dark with mud and flanked by drooping hovels, might never be aware of it. The wretched plumbing in the hotels might even prompt the presumption that the most advanced Siberian cities, which Irkutsk and Novosibirsk are, still linger somewhere in the beginning of the nineteenth or perhaps the eighteenth century. Nothing could be more fallacious. These cities boom not only with industrial activity but with the modern age of science, as modern as any in the world. How significant it is that the Moscow Academy of Sciences is bringing out thirteen thick volumes on the resources and economic development of Eastern Siberia alone.

I shifted the interview to the more personal aspects of university life in Siberia.

"How much does a full professor get a month?" I asked the rector.

"From four to five thousand [old] rubles," he replied.

I had already learned that the province of Irkutsk maintained a State Lecture Bureau with some two thousand lecturers on its roster, so I asked whether professors earned extra money from lecturing.

"Yes, but not much," the rector replied, smiling. "You see, lecturers are paid a percentage of the gate receipts, and professors draw small audiences. People seem to think that professors are dull lecturers."

"The same in America," I said.

"But let a celebrated poet, novelist, actor, dancer, come to town," Petrov explained, "and oh, how people pack the auditorium! The gate receipts are high and the performer draws a rich fee."

"The same in America," I said.

"But if the professor is a consultant to industry," the rector said, "he is exceptionally well paid."

"The same in America," I droned again, and we all laughed. Actually, Soviet professors, whether in Siberia or European Russia, are among the highest earners in the country. They get well paid for every extracurricular service they perform, even for the abstruse articles they write for highly specialized magazines of limited circulation.

I drove out to the site of the projected new university city, and the rector had not erred when he spoke of it as extraordinarily beautiful. Rising high on a steep embankment of the Angara, it overlooked Irkutsk, which lay deep down in a plateau surrounded by chain after chain of high hills. Nearby was the new hydro dam, and beyond, the new sea shimmered away to the far horizon; and at my back rolled the taiga, all the way to Lake Baikal. It was hot in the city, but here a cool breeze blew from the sea, still empty of ships though dotted with a few rowboats, and already, my guide, a recent university graduate, informed me, stocked with the choicest fish from Lake Baikal.

Hills, river, sea, and taiga—here lay concentrated the rugged grandeur and wild beauty of the Siberian land, an ideal site for a university, offering sports-minded students the finest of fishing, hunting, skiing, skating, and hiking in the forest, and with limitless space for a campus.

I walked around the grounds. Several streets were already laid out, shrubs and saplings planted along the curbs. All the streets, my guide said, will be boulevards, with trees, lawns, and flower beds, and the squares will be little parks, with fountains—without which a park is no park anywhere in the Soviet Union. Several rows of residence buildings were already put up, three-story, square-cornered, thick-walled, yellow-painted houses, one like the other, as though all poured from the same mold, which augured no architectural distinction to match the grandiose scenery all around. But my guide insisted that famous architects were at work to create a beautiful city, a real Siberian city, to fit the grandeur of the natural surroundings. The new student community, he proceeded to explain, would have a football stadium, a gymnasium, an indoor swimming pool, hockey rinks, tennis courts, a theater for movies and plays, an auditorium for concerts and balls, an infirmary, and all manner of service shops. All the buildings, he continued, administration, classrooms, library, laboratories, recreation halls, dining rooms, dormitories, will be the most modern in Siberia. Every dormitory, he further assured me, will have its own social parlors, game rooms, television sets. "Oh," he rhapsodized, "it'll be an up-to-date, beautiful city. Come back when it's finished and you'll see for yourself."

Beautiful or not, it seemed to me, as I heard him describe the details of the campus life that awaited students, that somebody in Moscow, or perhaps in Siberia, had made a searching study of an American country college. It might have been Dartmouth. It might have been my own Colgate University.

21.

SIBERIA
The New Farming

On my first journey to Siberia I traveled by mail bus from Irkutsk to the Lena River, a distance of over one hundred miles. It was a rough journey over a bumpy and poorly graded road with long stretches that were washed out of gravel, the mud undried. The country was sparsely settled, and now and then we passed caravans of horse carts, a mile long and longer. Not even on market days had I seen such long processions of horse carts in European Russia, nor horses so small, a little larger than ponies. They were of the Mongol-Siberian breed, noted for their hardihood when fed only on grass.

Horse bells clanging in the crisp Siberian air, the caravans were carrying kerosene, salt, sugar, hardware, textiles, other goods to villages up the Lena River, and the drivers, men and women, walked beside the carts to ease the burden of the plodding beasts. This was old Siberia, as it had been for centuries, horses doing the hauling on country roads over vast distances.

With the coming of night the caravans laid up in pastures and meadows by the roadside; horses were unhitched and fettered so they could graze without straying away, and bonfires were built for cooking and for guards to sit around while the others slept. Whenever we passed a resting caravan, it brought to mind a colony of migrating Gypsies.

Now and then we drove by a tall wooden cross at the side of the road, and the postman explained that each cross marked the place where a murder had been committed. Once three crosses rose before us—three murders in one place! I grew shivery, but the postman was unperturbed. He pointed to his gun and assured me I had nothing to fear. He knew how to handle bandits, should any attack the bus, which they had never dared do yet. Somehow they regarded the mail bus as improper or inadvisable to fall upon.

A talkative man, the postman proceeded to enlighten me on the subject of banditry in the countryside. In the old days, because of its enormous distances, Siberia was poorly policed and there had always been desperate characters there. Criminals sent for hard labor from European Russia often, on being liberated, remained and reverted to their criminal careers. During the civil war their numbers were augmented by convicts who had broken out of jails and mines or had been released and recruited for service in the Red and White armies. With the liquidation of the civil war, remnants of Red and White deserters, fearful of capture and execution or hopeful of the collapse of the Soviet regime, hid in the taiga and lived off depredations on passing travelers, on towns and villages. It was dangerous for freight-carrying peasants to travel alone or in small groups. That was why they were traveling in such long caravans—there was protection in numbers. Though the State Security Police was capturing and annihilating bandits, gangs of them still operated in the wooded wilderness and were still committing murders.

Once when we came to a crossroad, the postman stopped the bus, and pointing in the direction of a branch of the road, he said that the village to which it led was inhabited by former criminals and their descendants. Even the women there were such expert pickpockets that on bazaar days when one was selling you a live chicken or eggs, another picked your pockets and you were not even aware of it. It had once happened to him and he would never go there again.

In 1927, the year of my journey, banditry, of whichever origin, was a serious problem in deep-forested Eastern Siberia.

Late in the evening the bus reached a village and we put up for the night at the inn, and what an inn it was! There were neither beds nor cots. Travelers slept on the floor in their clothes, one beside another. But a huge samovar was boiling and the innkeeper served us a hearty meal of bread, butter, milk, honey, and eggs fried with bacon—six eggs apiece, swimming in sputtering bacon fat. When I protested that I couldn't eat so many eggs, both the postman and the innkeeper assured me that once I started eating I would finish them. That's the way it was in Siberia, they boasted, the appetite was always strong, and no innkeeper put less than six eggs before a customer. How prodigally rich Siberia was in food in those days when it was still a pastoral country, with less than half its present population.

I recalled the memorable journey on the mail bus now, as I drove along the same road thirty-one years later. The rolling hills and the encroaching taiga were unchanged, but the road was asphalted, one of the few links of highway to have been so covered, and the old Pobeda rolled along easily and smoothly. Nowhere did I see a single wooden cross—the murders of yesterday were a memory now. Wild and interminable as was the taiga, the bandits had long ago been hunted out. "Our highways," said the chauffeur, "are as safe as the streets in Irkutsk."

Nowhere did I see a single caravan of freight-carrying horse carts. Trucks were now hauling goods to towns and villages up north that were not serviced by the newly built railroad of some four hundred miles that cut through the taiga from Taishet to the Lena River. We passed streams where people were bathing and fishing, and along the banks were the truck or passenger automobile in which they had come. "City people," the chauffeur remarked, and being a Siberian he added proudly, "There's no finer fishing anywhere than in our Siberian streams."

Horses were so rare that whenever I saw one I gave it a second look. Once one of the great horse countries in the world, Siberia, like the Ukraine, appeared to have outlived the age of the horse. But I was wrong. "We have lots of horses," the chauffeur told me. "But you cannot see them from here, they are 'way out on the range." No, they weren't used much, he replied to a question, but the immense range lands hadn't yet been plowed up and the horses lived off them summer and winter.

"And nobody shoots them?"

"Why shoot them?" came the reply. "Let them live."

There were tribes in Siberia—among them the Buryat-Mongols—who loved horseflesh. I had lived with the Buryat-Mongols and had attended shaman festivities at which horses were killed, the flesh immediately roasted on open fires and served around for the big meal which crowned the festivities. There was a market for horseflesh in the Buryat-Mongol country across the nearby Lake Baikal, yet herds of horses wandered the range and nobody made use of them. The thought came to me that their preservation might be related to the Kremlin's always farsighted military plans. In such densely forested country as Eastern Siberia, were it ever involved in hostilities, the horse would be an invaluable asset, lending itself with particular effectiveness to partisan warfare. I kept the thought to myself—one doesn't allude to subjects of military import in conversation with Russians, whoever they may be.

My destination this time was the village of Khomutovo, where I drove to see the new farming of which I had been told much in Moscow and in Irkutsk. I knew it was one of the best collectives in the province—none by which to judge the others, where in winter shortage of forage still results in death of livestock from hunger. But I wanted to see the new farming at its best so as to estimate, however inadequately, the agricultural potentialities of the faraway Siberian territory.

My first impression of Khomutovo as we drove into it was that it was a lucky village—the asphalted highway wound through the long main street, thus saving people from the need of wading through mud after rains. On closer inspection I observed that the short side streets which sloped down into lowland were shiny with dark puddles that seem never to dry out in many a Russian village.

Khomutovo was an old village and showed its age: the cottages that lined the main street drooped with dilapidation, the boarded roofs sagged, windows were pushing out of timbered walls. Never on my previous journey had I been in a village in Western or Eastern Siberia that looked so weather-beaten and tumble-down. Despite rich forests all around, housing had obviously been neglected, though here and there a roof shone with new red slate, and the few new houses—I counted four in the whole village—stood out of the dark rows of cottages like lone birches in the dark taiga.

But this was a Siberian village, and despite collectivization, it preserved unimpaired the peasant's love of privacy, which the peasant in European Russia never had cultivated. Every courtyard was fenced off by a high board fence and protected the home from the prying eyes of neighbors and passers-by and from possible thieves. Driving by one of the new houses, we stopped to take a look at it. The wicket gate was barred on the inside, but the barking of a dog in the courtyard soon brought the housewife out. I told her what I wanted and she opened wide the wicket gate and invited us to walk in. On sight of strangers, the small black-brown watchdog with a black bushy tail, which was chained up under the yard-long woodshed, flung himself about, barking savagely. The housewife shouted at him, but he kept tugging at the chain and barking. A little girl ran out of the house, darted over to him, slapped him hard on the back, and he curled up, growling with choked rage. Not even in the Ukraine are dogs as ugly as in Siberia, and if the dog be off the chain, heaven help the stranger who wanders into a courtyard without a stick in his hand.

The woman smiled and said, "You must know that in our Siberia the dog is our doorbell." This was the first time I heard a peasant speak of a doorbell. To this day it is unknown in villages, and the use of the word by this woman signalized urban influence on peasant speech and emphasized the Siberian's love of privacy.

Save for the electric lights, there was nothing of the city inside the house, not even running water. Yet a city man, even a Muscovite, would be happy to live in such a house: three spacious tall-windowed rooms, all flooded with sunlight; a separate airy kitchen with an iron wood stove instead of the old-fashioned brick oven, and a glassed-in porch—a new feature in village housing. A baby wearing a diaper was sleeping in a cradle on the porch and no flies disturbed its sleep—a tribute to the Soviet health service even in this faraway Siberian village.

In every room the windows were set with pots of geraniums and dahlias. In the living room, out of an immense dirt-filled wooden tub rose a tall treelike plant that bore a resemblance to a weeping willow, its leafy branches thin and drooping. But it was no willow, the woman said. It was a wild bush that was growing in the woods and they loved it in the house because it was so decorative. They hadn't trimmed it and wouldn't trim it unless it grew to the ceiling. They loved it as it was in its wild state, and the more branches grew out of it, the more they were pleased. The forest reached into the home.

The walls of the living room were hung with rows of dark-framed family photographs, but nowhere was there a single icon.

"Icons," said the woman, who was about middle age, "are for old-fashioned people."

"You never go to church?" I asked.

"No, indeed." And she gave a little laugh, as though I reminded her of a folly she had committed in her young years. "Nobody here goes to church." The little girl spoke up and mentioned names of people who went to church.

"Oh, they are very old people," the woman explained. "We have no church in the village or in the villages around here. But if grandfathers and grandmothers want to go to services, the kolkhoz lends them a truck to drive to Irkutsk. Why deprive old people of a pleasure that doesn't hurt anybody? That's the way I feel and that's the way our kolkhoz administration feels."

The feeling, I must say, is not always shared by chairmen of collectives. I have known instances when they refused transportation for churchgoing. The deprivation is of no moment to Baptists, who gather for worship in the home of a member. But for the Orthodox, who associate worship with churchgoing, it must be a painful disappointment.

It was Sunday afternoon and the sun was hot, scorchingly hot, as it so often gets in Siberia in the daytime. Older people were sitting on benches in front of their houses, children were playing in the street, and young people were riding around on bicycles or promenading up and down village-fashion—girls three and four abreast, boys following behind, rarely walking in couples. They were remarkably well dressed, all in Western-style clothes as in Irkutsk. I had not seen such well-dressed young people in villages on my previous journey. Seldom had I seen bicycles, and the motorcycle was formerly unknown. Now I saw several parked against yard fences. As we were driving around, now one youth, now another, mounted a motorcycle and roared up and down the asphalt street with an exuberance that scared children and young people into scurrying away. Yet nobody seemed to mind. The older people watched from the benches with wide-eyed wonder as at daring feats in a circus, and the children and promenaders appeared to enjoy the adventure of fleeing from the racing motorcycles. They laughed and shouted with glee, like little boys proud of their narrow escapes.

The chairman of the kolkhoz was away from the village and I was received by the deputy chairman, a stocky, smooth-featured, handsome young man named Zuvorin. He told me he was a Tatar, but there was nothing of the Mongol about his appearance. He might have been a Swede or a Dane, with light hair, round blue eyes, and exceptionally fair skin. "My people," he explained, "have been in Siberia for hundreds of years and got mixed up with Russians. But I regard myself of Tatar nationality." He was a living testimony to a rather striking aspect of Russian mentality—an absence of color consciousness. Russians have always readily intermarried with Mongols and other Asians, and some the most handsome people one meets in Siberia are the products of these intermarriages.

As we sat in the kolkhoz office, talking, I mentioned to Zuvorin the reckless riding of the motorcyclists up and down the main street of the village. In reply he said, "Well, there is always danger of an accident, but not really when a man is sober. It is the drunken rider and driver who are a menace. Isn't it so in America?"

I agreed that it was.

Brushing both hands over his silken light hair, he resumed. "You see, I have a motorcycle; I have to have it for inspection trips, as our kolkhoz is so large—twenty-seven thousand hectares [sixty-five thousand acres]—and if motor riders and drivers would do what I do, there would be precious few accidents." Then, resting his elbows on the clean desk and leaning over as though to heighten my attention, he continued. "We Siberians are a hardy people, none more hardy in the whole Soviet Union, and why deny it, we like our vodka. But when I go to a wedding, a birthday party, any celebration, d'you know what I do? After I've had my first drink, I turn my ignition key over to my hostess; always trust a woman not to give it back to a man whose mind is fuzzy from drink."

We laughed; then Zuvorin added soberly, "Pass it on to Americans, and if they do what I do, they'll avoid a lot of accidents."

What struck me as genuinely Russian was Zuvorin's expression "always trust a woman." Russian men of today, even in high positions, have much, very much, to learn about chivalry toward women. Yet it is the women they trust with the choice of furniture for the new apartment into which the family may be moving, with the disciplining of children, with the cultivation of good manners, with the money in the wallet when vodka is beginning to go to their heads, and even—as often happens—with effecting a reconciliation with a friend or neighbor with whom they have quarreled. When a student couple decide to get married and begin to lay away a nest egg in the savings bank out of stipends or special earnings, the bankbook is invariably in the girl's name. The woman is always there with her good sense and her strength of character, and it would be inconceivable for a Russian woman to give back to a Zuvorin or whoever the man might be the ignition key he had entrusted to her keeping if his head was fuzzy from drink. I knew it was so in European Russia and now I was discovering that it was so also in Siberia.

We proceeded to talk of the kolkhoz, and my first question was whether milkmaids were among the highest-paid workers on the farm.

"Yes, indeed," came the reply. "The average woman worker earns two hundred sixty labor days a year, but a milkmaid earns as high as eight hundred. You should see them ride to the barns on bicycles."

"Do you give an accomplished milkmaid a dowry when she gets married? They do that sometimes in the Ukraine."

"Not a dowry, oh no. But we do something else. Every ten or fifteen days we call a meeting to honor the milkmaids who have overfulfilled their quotas of milk output. We make it a festive occasion —speeches, songs, music—and the presentation of sealed envelopes to the honored milkmaids. Inside each envelope is a sum of money, not large, but enough to buy lipstick, powder, perfume. You know how women are."

"Do your milkmaids wear lipstick at work?"

Zuvorin grinned. "They wear lipstick all the time. That's the fashion nowadays."

"How many cows does a maid milk?"

"Fourteen, if she uses a milking machine; ten if she milks by hand."

"And she does nothing else?"

"She has plenty to do to take care of her cows."

So in Siberia as in European Russia, the milkmaid symbolized the enormous waste of human labor in Soviet agriculture. Like other rural leaders I had met, Zuvorin had not heard that milking was only a morning-and-evening chore on an American dairy farm. But the kolkhoz, he assured me, had made astonishing progress since September 1953, when Khrushchev sounded a call to arms for the regeneration of agriculture. "Nikita Sergeyevich has taught us," he said, "that without material incentive you can't get work out of people, and how well we realize it now!" Then he enumerated the bonuses the kolkhoz paid workers for good work and for overfulfillment of norms of output in every branch of field work and animal husbandry. The most subsidized crop was corn. "We're still learning how to cultivate it," Zuvorin informed me, "but we aren't taking chances with sloppy work. So when the shoots come out of the ground, the workers are paid a bonus. Every time they cultivate the fields, they get another bonus. When they fertilize the corn with a liquid ammonium preparation, a still further bonus is paid them, and still another when they cut it and put it into silos."

It was the most "bonused" kolkhoz I had known, and no wonder. In a country like Siberia, where the growing season is short, every day and every hour of the day is precious, and as Zuvorin had said, they were not taking chances with sloppy work.

What was especially remarkable was the number of bonuses the chairman was piling up. He was getting free a house, a cow, a sow, a garden, and a passenger automobile. Though a party man, he was paid a bonus of 1500 (old) rubles the first year and 1300 for two more years for leaving the city where he had worked and coming to manage the kolkhoz. His basic pay was 120 rubles a month and 400 labor days. But he received a bonus for the overfulfillment of plans in every branch of farming. In 1955 alfalfa seed, in which the kolkhoz specialized, did particularly well, and the sum the chairman received as his bonus was 4500 rubles. In 1957 his bonus in milk was 1½ tons, which he sold in the free market. His bonus in pork was 1000 kilograms, which he also sold, at 20 rubles a kilo, yielding him the sum of 20,000 rubles. At a conservative estimate, the chairman earned in cash alone about 40,000 rubles (4400 dollars), which was one of the highest earnings in the country. Of course, he proved to be an excellent manager, otherwise he wouldn't have amassed all the bonuses he was awarded.

Unlike Stalin, clearly Khrushchev wasn't taking chances with Siberian kolkhoz personnel, whether herdsman, milkmaid, pig attendant, corn grower, or chairman. If they produced results, they were, by Soviet standards, handsomely paid. *Pravda* might glorify the Soviet man as a new breed of humanity so dedicated to social purposes that he "toiled rapturously" for the Motherland; but on this kolkhoz, more than on any I had visited or read about in European Russia, the "rapture" was sweetened with material rewards other than bonuses. In European Russia one milch cow and at most one calf are all a member of a collective is allowed to hold in individual ownership. But on this farm he might own as many as six head of cattle: two milch cows and four head of young stock. "Why not?" the deputy chairman explained. "Pasture is no problem here. Kolkhoz members hire their own herdsman and the kolkhoz pays him out of the community fund. But you see, people have to work hard to earn fodder for the winter months. The more incentive you offer them, the harder they work."

I didn't see any horses in the village, and I asked if there were any on the farm.

"So many of them," Zuvorin replied with a lift of both arms, "we can't even count them. I should say there are at least seven hundred, 'way out on the range summer and winter." No, they didn't shoot them; why shoot them when their upkeep cost nothing? That was what the chauffeur had said, and again the question arose in my mind whether there was military significance in the preservation of horses. The kolkhoz could sell them for horseflesh, not only to the tribes who favored it but to the new mink and fox ranches that were springing up in the province of Irkutsk. I didn't ask any questions and can offer no authoritative proof of the correctness of my assumption.

We drove out to the fields that stretched for miles and miles—rolling hills and sweeping steppes. Wheat, oats, rye, barley, buckwheat, always did well in Siberia, but peas and vetch, the deputy chairman told me, were new. Both were seeded with oats for green forage and the fields were thick and green. We passed an immense field of sunflowers breaking into golden-yellow bloom, even as in the Ukraine and the Kuban. This was another new crop, Zuvorin explained, but they didn't wait for it to ripen. It was too sensitive to frost and would soon have to be cut and put into silos. They grew it only for fodder and cows loved it and throve on it.

Alfalfa and red clover were not new, but in Czarist times they were neglected. Now red clover did remarkably well, and alfalfa was "a miracle crop in Siberia"—grew lush and fast, so fast that it "gladdened the heart to watch it grow." They had already cut it twice. "And look at the aftermath," my companion rhapsodized, sweeping his arm over the breeze-blown field thick and green with growth. "We shall cut it again, this time not for hay but for ensilage."

Well might Zuvorin speak of alfalfa as one of nature's great boons to Siberian farming. In 1906 Professor N. E. Hansen, a plant explorer for the U. S. Department of Agriculture, gathered a collection of hardy alfalfas in Irkutsk province. He seemed to have shaken it out of wild hay, and subsequently, when he joined the faculty of the South Dakota Agricultural College, he propagated the seed and developed what is now known as Siberian alfalfa. Indigenous to Irkutsk province, Soviet scientists have obviously made the most of it—developed new strains that now yielded excellent forage for livestock.

Beets and turnips, grown in the old days only in gardens for human consumption, were now grown on large acreages for livestock. The poorest of the new field crops on this farm was corn. They first began to plant it in 1954, and only once in only one field did the ears ripen—small ears which they fed to pigs. But they weren't planting corn for grain. Green forage was what they wanted. Still, in the field we were surveying, the plants came up only to my knees and it was already the first of August. There were only about ten more growing days. By August 12 it would have to be harvested to save it from the threat of early frost.

Wasn't such a heat-loving plant as corn, I asked, a gamble in a country where the growing season was so short and the nights so cool? Firmly Zuvorin shook his head. "If you go to our state experimental farm, *Rodina* [Motherland], you'll see corn as tall as in America. This year on our farm the weather was against us— the shoots were slow in coming up. Frankly, we're still learning how to cultivate it. But at *Rodina*, where they have a lot of scientists, it isn't a gamble. Nikita Sergeyevich isn't gambling. You must go to *Rodina* and assure yourself corn is no gamble in Siberia."

Some American scientists are convinced that Siberia, both east and west, would do better with some other forage crop than with corn. But Khrushchev's faith in "the queen of the fields," as he calls corn, even for Siberia, is so apostolic that he wouldn't hear of abandoning it. "We're pushing ahead all the time," Zuvorin declared, "and with the help of corn we shall continue to push ahead."

Yet in Khomutovo, considering all the bonuses the kolkhoz paid workers in the cornfields, the cost of the "pushing" made corn, economically speaking, an unprofitable crop. But at the moment cost was of no consequence. Milk and butter were what counted, and the output of both was constantly rising.

Then we drove out to the orchard, some miles outside the village. The very word "orchard" sounded romantic in a country that, save for isolated fruit trees in Western Siberia, had never known any. But the orchard here was still in an experimental stage. Except for the transplanted crab-apple bushes which grow wild in Siberia, the fruit smaller than in America, the trees grew horizontally, the branches crawling over the ground like pumpkin or cucumber vines. I followed the tall, lanky, sun-scorched orchardist from tree to tree—apple, plum, pear—all of which he had planted three years previously and which were not yet bearing. He was certain that famous *slavyanka* (apple) would do exceptionally well when the trees grew old enough to bear. He too mentioned *Rodina*, where horticulture was in a more advanced stage than on this farm, and what *Rodina* was accomplishing other farms could accomplish, he assured me. That was why they would plant more and more fruit trees. "Nature here," he explained, "is both kind and cruel, and we've had a lot of experience in fighting its cruelties. Now we have science to help us, a lot of science, and we can't fail. Come, I'll show you what we've done with strawberries and red raspberries."

We walked down the knoll where the orchard was planted into a level field thick and green with vines and bushes. About one half of the two-acre field was in strawberries, the other in raspberries. "We picked over a ton of strawberries and about three fourths of a ton of raspberries," said the gardener, "the most profitable crop we have, and we'll plant at least ten hectares more. And think of it— I've lived in this province all my life and I never knew anyone in any village who even thought of planting berries in his garden. Wild berries were the only ones our people gathered."

As we walked around the field, here and there a raspberry gleamed out from a bush and a strawberry showed in a clump of vines. The sun was hot and now and then I stooped to refresh myself with a berry. They were remarkably juicy and as large as those sold in New York. Garden berries were obviously an unqualified success.

As the gardener was watching me search for hidden berries, he laughed. "That's a hard way to fill up on berries. Let's go up to the house and I'll treat you to a feast of raspberries. I picked the last of the crop this morning."

We walked up a hill, on top of which stood the large house. As I approached the porch, a dog of the size and shading of a German police dog sneaked out unseen from the back of the house, and tugging at a heavy chain, turned on me in fury. I shrank back with a shudder and the gardener instantly chased him back to the tree to which he was chained. But he kept on barking with unabated rage. "He is my alarm clock," the man said. "He wakes me at night when some hooligan sneaks into the berry field. But I never let him loose. After dark I keep him chained to the porch. If he wasn't chained he would tear a man to pieces."

"Not a dog, but a wolf," I said.

"But a most reliable alarm clock!" "Alarm clock," like "doorbell," was a new expression in peasant speech.

We walked into the house and the man introduced me to his wife, a fleshy woman with a sunburned face and radiant gray eyes. "An American?" she exclaimed. "Never saw one before. Welcome to our house." Turning to the husband, she said, "Let's treat the American guest to the raspberries you picked this morning."

"That's what we came to the house for." The man walked out of the room, and the wife said, "How d'you eat raspberries in America?"

"With sugar and cream," I said.

She gave me a puzzled look. "That's not the way we eat raspberries, any berries. We'll show you how we eat them."

The man came back holding in both hands a half-bushel-sized wooden box gleaming with raspberries. Immediately the woman set a large bowl before me, filled it with berries, then fetching a tall glass pitcher of crystal-clear strained honey, she poured it over the berries as unstintedly as if it were water, filling the bowl to the brim.

"Now taste it," she said, and after I had done so I complimented her on the combination. "Tell Americans they must eat berries, any berries, the way we do."

"I will," I said, and she smiled with pleasure. So here I was with two Siberian innovations—how to prevent motor accidents and how to eat berries—to pass on to Americans. When I spoke of it, they both laughed.

The door was open, and as I glanced outside at the rolling hills, falling into steppes that sank into the taiga on the faraway horizon, I spoke of the beautiful view they had from the house.

The woman sighed. "But it's so lonely out here all by ourselves."

"I have a Pobeda," the husband said. "I couldn't move around without it. But it isn't the same as living in the village, where you know there're people around you."

So the Siberian peasant, with all his traditional love of privacy, longed to live among neighbors—good neighbors, with whom to exchange gossip and confidences over a glass of tea or a tumbler of vodka; bad neighbors, with whom he wouldn't sit at the same table and whom he wouldn't even admit into the highly fenced courtyard—but always with and among people, never all alone with only empty spaces to gaze upon.

We drove back to the village. The sun was setting and the asphalt street was now swarming with promenaders, a gay crowd of young people, the girls dressed in vivid colors, even as in the Ukraine, the boys following behind, teasing the girls and making them laugh. But there were few fathers and mothers in the procession or sitting around on benches. "Older people are doing chores," Zuvorin explained. "But the young people would rather be out for a good time. No, they aren't like their fathers and mothers. They don't want to bother with garden and cow if they can help it. We're just finishing our new clubhouse and they are impatiently waiting for it to open so they can go there to movies, lectures, dances, put on plays and musicals. Our young people would rather enjoy culture than bother with gardens and cows."

Enjoy culture! If the kolkhoz economy permitted, which with rare exceptions it does not at present, the young generation in this village, especially the girls, would be glad to rid themselves of the time-consuming chores that now preoccupy their fathers and mothers.

"What we need in Siberia," Zuvorin said, "is people, millions of people. On our farm we could use two thousand more workers if we had them. We have so much land! We've put up three houses for new settlers. They are still empty. We hope they'll soon be occupied by families from European Russia. But we want hundreds more, if we can only induce them to come!"

This is a universal cry in Siberia, and while China is not far from Khomutovo, the doors for Chinese settlers are shut tight.

We came to a grassy field with a tumble-down fence and with upright posts at either end. Zuvorin asked the chauffeur to stop and proudly explained that this was the football field. "Someday soon we'll build a stadium so people can sit down when they watch a game. They love football around here, and this year we had a champion team. They defeated every team they met. But four of the best players have graduated from high school and are going off to college. We'll have to start building up a new team and it isn't going to be easy."

How like America it sounded!

The state experimental farm, *Rodina*, was truly a revelation. Here was one of the choicest dairies I had seen anywhere in the Soviet Union—440 cows, which were a cross between Dutch Frisians and the best Siberian breeds, averaging over 12,000 pounds of milk a year. The twenty-four select producers furnished semen for their own cows and for collectives, including the one at Khomutovo. They were also importing by jet plane frozen semen from Holland, the plan was to fertilize every cow in the province of Irkutsk with semen of purebred stock. Here as everywhere else in the Soviet Union the cry was: "Produce milk, produce and produce," but here milkmaids, using machines, did a respectable amount of work, each milking thirty cows three times a day.

As farms go in Siberia, *Rodina* was not large, some 18,000 acres, of which 13,000 were cultivated. But the farm was headed by a staff of forty-three scientists, all college graduates, five of them holding degrees of candidates of science. Yet here too the waste of human labor was manifest. The labor personnel embraced a thousand men and women. Since 60 per cent of the acreage was seeded to grains and grasses, the number of workers was astonishingly excessive. The scientists admitted it. It was one of the problems that hampered "peaceful competition" with America. But they were putting their trust in the rationalization and mechanization of all processes of work on which they were presently engaged and on the application of new science the *Rodina* staff was developing. In the good-natured discussion that flickered up between the scientists and myself, one of them closed in sportsmanlike fashion by saying, "Let the best system of farming win."

We drove around the fields and all crops looked far more prosperous than in Khomutovo, the corn reaching up to my shoulders. The bunches of dry stalks I had seen from the office were over six feet high, and the scientists who accompanied me to the fields upheld Khrushchev in the belief that acre for acre no other green crop equaled corn in the amount and quality of forage it yielded. Now that they were receiving increasing amounts of fertilizer, they would grow more and more of it. One of the great problems in Siberian agriculture, they explained, as applicable to corn as to other crops, was to regulate the work so as to take full advantage of the short summer with its long days of sunshine. Once things started growing, they grew fast, corn from six to eight centimeters a day. They needed a fast-growing strain that would give them not only tall stalks but large ears with wax-milky grain for ensilage. Experiment stations in European Russia, whence they received all their seed, were working on the problem, and they would solve it, even as they themselves solved the problem of developing a strain of wheat that wouldn't mat down after heavy rains.

On *Rodina* they learned to time every process of field work almost to perfection, and if *Rodina* could do it, so could the state and collective farms, provided leaders were vigilant about the weather. " 'Do not fall behind and do not race ahead of the weather' is our slogan," one of the scientists said, "and now that we are getting increasing shipments of up-to-date machinery, we have a new weapon to fight the weather. We'll lick it too."

I spoke of the rich grasslands for which Siberia was always noted, and the deputy director of the experimental farm replied, "Yes, but in the old days people left it to nature to grow grasses. Now we're teaching nature how to do it, and if understandably treated, nature is an excellent pupil. We're seeding the grasses we choose. We've discovered, for example, that white clover can stand a lot of trampling by cows, and so on our newly reclaimed acreage we've mixed white clover with other grasses for pasture. Imagine the difference it'll make in the output of milk when cows feed on such pasture. We're learning new things all the time, and what we learn we teach the collective and state farms to do. Take root crops for cattle, which were unknown in pre-Soviet Siberia. Now we plant not only turnips and beets but carrots, and they grow big, beets weighing as much as five kilograms apiece. Of course, carrots rot easily, but we salt them away in cement barrels and they keep fresh as long as they last. For vitamins there's no other feed like carrots."

We drove out to the truck farm where *Rodina* grew not only the staples that Siberia had always known but such vegetables as tomatoes, asparagus, lettuce, and kohlrabi. They also grew two crops of cabbage and potatoes, early and late, whereas in the old days they grew only one crop of these vegetables. I asked whether, as in European Russia, they were meeting with buyer's resistance to the new vegetables they have acclimatized. They were indeed. Kohlrabi they couldn't sell at all, so they fed it to the chickens. But they weren't discouraged. They would continue to grow it and in time people would learn to eat it. It would be the same with other vegetables they were planning to acclimatize.

Their greatest triumph, they said, was garden berries, and their harvests were richer than in Khomutovo, according to the figures they cited. They were also confident they could grow fruit—apples, pears, plums, cherries—as well as did Western Siberia.

"We're telling factory workers," the deputy director said, "members of collectives, intellectuals, office employees, everybody with a garden plot, to plant orchards; that's how strong our faith is in the future of fruit in our rigidly continental climate. We're telling them to set out the trees in rows and to plant berries in between the rows. We're also advising them in great detail how to do everything to accomplish the best results. To you it may sound like utopia, because of the reputation of Siberia as a wild and frozen country, but we have great faith in our Siberian soil and sun, in the courage and hardihood of our people. Can you imagine anything more beautiful around a Siberian home than a fruit-and-berry plot, beautiful and beneficial? Old Siberia never knew anything like it. But new Siberia is determined to bring in a lot of new things that old Siberia hadn't even thought of."

He paused, and another scientist said, "When we began to plant tomatoes around here on a large scale, people thought we were wasting our time. But what has happened? We start the plants in a hothouse and transplant them to fields sometime in June. Now we grow remarkable tomatoes. If they don't ripen on the vine we pick them green and they ripen in the sun in homes. Did you see the hothouse in Khomutovo?"

I nodded.

"We want all collectives to build such up-to-date hothouses, where they can start their gardening when there is deep snow and freezing weather outdoors. We have lots of coal and we are going to get more and more electricity, so heating hothouses in no problem any more."

"Do people around here," I asked, "pickle green tomatoes?"

"No, not yet. But they will. They pickle cucumbers, beets, mushrooms, cranberries, mountain-ash berries—have done it for a long time—and there's no reason why they shouldn't pickle green tomatoes as they do in European Russia. We'll teach them a lot of new things that they have never done before."

When one speaks to men like these scientists, one carries away the impression that they are leaders of high purpose and dedication, who with the coming of Khrushchev have been freed from the strangle hold of the Stalinist days and who "dream up ideas," as one of them expressed himself, which they do not propose to keep as "mere paper plans." They didn't underestimate the difficulties—bad roads and shortages of fertilizer, storage space for grain, and up-to-date machinery—that hampered the progress of Siberian agriculture. They were genial and companionable and answered questions fully and frankly, never failing to remind me over and over that they were pioneering for a new Siberia on every acre of land on their farm.

We drove to a new cow barn they had almost finished building. It was the most practical of the new barns I had yet seen, with no waste space as on the Motherland kolkhoz in the Ukraine and in barns I had seen in Byelorussia. Built of brick, with large double windows, it was equipped with modern installations for watering and feeding the 150 cows that would be stabled there. Yet even in this eminently modern barn there was no automatic cleaner. The scientists were surprised when I told them that in upstate New York no dairyman any longer cleaned the barn with fork and shovel. The idea, they said, was not new to them, and they would develop it unless someone else in the Soviet Union got ahead of them. They'll do everything to save human labor and beat America in farming.

"If you do," I said, "we'll come and learn from you, even as you still have much to learn from us."

"Yes," said the poultryman, a tall stocky Georgian with the inevitable curled mustache and the expressive gestures that accompany the speech of Georgians. "We have crossed your white Leghorns with native breeds and we're getting splendid results. The hens average 175 eggs a year. We also have your Plymouth Rocks and Rhode Island Reds, which average about 160 eggs a year and give us much meat. How is it in your country?"

"In America," I said, "the professional poultryman wouldn't keep a hen that laid fewer than 200 eggs a year."

"Oh," exclaimed the Georgian, waving his arms above his head, "we'll catch up with you. We're getting new chickens from the best breeds in Europe—they come here by jet plane in two days. And this year we're distributing one and a half million eggs from purebred stock to hatcheries for collective farms, so they can rid themselves of the scrub hens they're carrying."

As we continued to discuss poultry, I told them of farmers in America who singlehandedly cared for 75,000 chickens for broilers and that they got one pound of meat out of two or two and a half pounds of feed.

This was news to all of them, even as it was to other leaders on collective farms to whom I spoke of it. The Georgian scratched his head and laughingly said, "The devil only knows—you are a clever people. But we'll beat you just the same."

Even as we were walking around the barn and talking, a furious storm broke out. Thunder rocked the earth and lightning flashed blindingly into the barn. "You're witnessing," said one of the scientists, "a real Siberian storm." The rain splashed down in such torrents that it drowned out our voices, and we had to speak loudly to make ourselves heard. The thunder shower lasted only about ten minutes, and when it was over, the roads all around the barn were seas of glistening mud. The Pobeda in which I drove couldn't get started, and a truck had to be "mobilized" to pull it to the main highway. All the way to Irkutsk it slid and skidded and stalled, but the chauffeur managed to bring me back to the hotel.

"Our Siberian roads," he moaned, "are pretty terrible, aren't they? If only we had the people to build new roads!"

The chauffeur was not the only one to complain of the wretched condition of Siberian roads. In a book I picked up in Irkutsk (*Sibirskaya Nov*, Novosibirsk, 1957) the author, G. Pospelov, speaks of truck drivers as performing "a hero's feats" in carrying two and a half times as much tonnage of freight as do the railroads. "I could count on the fingers of one hand the long-distance highways in Siberia that are built on a comparatively high level. . . . Siberia needs many people, millions of settlers from the western regions and republics, to achieve the grandiose plans for taming and developing it. Of course, it is impossible to expect that even in the approaching decades about one fourth of the population of the country, fifty million of them, which is not too many for such a vast and rich country as Siberia, will migrate there."

Only "fraternal" China has these millions to spare. But the Kremlin doesn't want them, not even for building desperately needed highways.

22.

SIBERIA
Romance of the Country

"Have you heard of the drug *pantocrin*?"

The interrogator was a tall, lean, big-boned hunter who was conducting a course on wildlife in the taiga and on the techniques of hunting at the Irkutsk Agricultural College.

"No," I replied.

"It's a cure for sexual impotence and it comes from the taiga."

"From a plant?"

"No. It comes from the maral [a species of Siberian deer]. In the spring its horns are soft and leathery and full of blood. Hunters shoot it then and sell the horns to the state and the state manufactures the drug. It's taken with spirits and is supposed to cure sexual impotence."

"Is it a folk remedy or do physicians prescribe it?" I asked.

"Physicians prescribe it. I understand that it originated in Tibet, but our scientists have discovered that the blood is rich in sex hormones and vitamins. We sell the drug in pharmacies and there is a big market for it in China. But we don't want to exterminate the maral, so in many parts of the taiga we have put up reservations where we capture the animal, cut off its horns, and let it go."

In Siberia hunting is both a popular sport and a profitable occupation. I had searched out this hunter for an interview on the wild game in the taiga, and we spent the afternoon together in my hotel room discussing the subject, on which he was one of the foremost authorities in the country. He brought up the maral and the drug that was made from its horns as an example of the taiga's gifts to man. To Siberians, he said, the taiga was no wild, frightening virgin forest, but an endless source of wonder, adventure, and bounty. One found game everywhere—birds and beasts. They introduced the Canadian muskrat and the American mink and they throve magnificently. They introduced pheasants, but their feet froze in winter. They introduced special rabbits from European Russia, and they were getting easily acclimatized. But the chief game in the taiga was black and brown bear, bobcat, wild goat, wolf, elk, and the precious fur-bearing animals—squirrel, fox, muskrat, nutria, marmot, mink, kolinsky, ermine, and the world-famed sable.

In Moscow I had met American furriers who had come to buy skins at the annual Leningrad fur auction. They told me that in October 1951 the United States Congress put an embargo on seven kinds of Russian furs—fox, muskrat, mink, ermine, kolinsky, weasel, and marten—but that Americans bought about four fifths of the Siberian sables, the costliest of all furs. They had only vague ideas how sable was hunted, so I asked the hunter to tell me. He leaned back in his chair and began: "The first thing a hunter needs is a well-trained laika, a wise and gentle dog, fast on its feet, with a powerful instinct for hunting and easily trained. Man and dog start out in pursuit of the animal, which lives in a hole, sometimes under the roots of a tree, sometimes in a shelter between rocks, but usually in the hollow of a fallen log. If the snow is hard the hunter travels on skis, but if the snow is soft he must go on foot. He can, of course, read animal spoor in the snow—it's a language he knows as well as his alphabet—and when he comes on the trail of a sable he follows it to the hole or until the dog sights the creature. It's a predatory little beast and kills a lot of birds—woodcock, snipe, partridge, and others. Well, when the dog sights it he gives chase and drives it into its hole or up a tree. Then comes the hunter's test of skill in capturing it without damaging its fur. Sometimes with a special gun a hunter will aim for the eye. But a safer way is to catch it in a specially constructed net. If the sable is inside a log, the hunter will fasten the net over the hole and pound the log with a stick until the sable gets scared and rushes into the net. Then the trick is to seize it by the back of the head and strangle it. You must act fast or the sharp teeth will rip your hand. Well, that's about all there is to it."

"What happens," I asked, "when the dog chases the sable up a tree. Do you shoot it?"

"I don't, " he replied. "Few hunters do—won't risk spoiling the skin. What we do is set a ring of tall posts in the deep snow around the tree. Then we spread a special net we have over the top of the posts and tuck the ends of it into the snow. Sooner or later the cunning little creature will come down. But you never know when. It has to be good and hungry before it does, and sometimes it'll stay up in the tree all night. So the hunter puts one or two little bells over the net and goes away out of sight. He may build a little fire, boil himself tea, and just sit and sit and fall asleep. But when the sable comes down, it gets entangled in the net and the bells ring. The more fiercely it struggles to get free, the more loudly the bells ring and wake the hunter. Then hunter and dog hurry over and seize the catch."

The hunting for sable, my companion went on, begins November 1 and ends February 15. "You're in the taiga all the time. You shoot plenty of game for fresh meat whenever you want it—man never starves in the taiga. And you never know boredom, not a moment of it. Every day brings its excitement and adventure, and when you return to the shelter for the night, you turn on the radio, listen to the news of the world, to concerts and opera from Moscow, Leningrad, or some Siberian city. You're a hermit, but always in touch with civilization. It's a rugged life but none more satisfying for those who take to it."

None more profitable or freer either, he might have added. The state pays 100 of the new rubles for a skin, and a hunter may capture from fifty to eighty sables and earn for sables alone the equivalent of from 5500 to 8800 dollars at the new official rate of exchange. But he bags other game too, especially squirrel and muskrat, for which he also gets well paid. And he is always by himself, doing his own thinking and planning, meeting with no censure for laxity of effort, no contumely for ideological perversion—a truly free and happy man, the freest in the totalitarian Soviet Union and one of the most prosperous—too prosperous and too individualistic to suit Kremlin ideology and Kremlin purposes. That is why it has been striving to organize hunters into collectives. But in the Irkutsk-Baikal area the individual hunter and the hunting family—father and sons—are strongly entrenched. For the present the party is leaving them alone, so as not to disrupt the seasonal catch and curtail the flow of foreign exchange to the state's treasury.

When I first drove into the taiga I was no more impressed than by forests around Moscow. Generations of settlers had cut many of the trees, and about the roadside on the way from Irkutsk to Baikal, the taiga was visibly thinned. Between towering old trees, young growth and underbrush grew thick and wild, and here and there weeds and berry bushes shrouded the fallen giants. The sun was bright and the taiga silent; only the faintest breeze stirred the tops of the trees and hardly a bird sang. Of the two hundred species in the ancient forest few are songbirds.

As the Pobeda bounced along the poorly asphalted road, I observed the trees around us. I wasn't surprised to see birch—where in Russia does one fail to see it—the snow-white birch that brightens the dreariest landscape and which the muzhik had celebrated in hundreds of songs.

No broad-leafed trees like oak and maple grow in the taiga, and aside from the birch, the other deciduous trees of which I caught glimpses were aspen, alder, mountain ash. The ash gleamed with clusters of red berries, still unripe but certain to be picked for the many uses to which it lends itself—to be munched raw in deep winter, to flavor sauerkraut, to distill a home-brew that's as pleasant to the taste as it is intoxicating. But the deciduous trees seemed interlopers in this dark world of evergreens. Here were fir, spruce, larch, pine, and cedar, which is no cedar but a species of pine, as its Latin name, *Pinus cembra sibirica*, attests. Nobody could tell me how Siberians came to call it cedar. But it is the most precious tree in the taiga. It's even-grained wood lends itself to a multitude of purposes—the manufacture of pencils, pianos, plywood, furniture, especially wardrobes, which in Russia take the place of clothes closets. No moles ever get into a cedar wardrobe. It is even used in the construction of planes and submarines.

To Siberians the cedar is especially valuable because of the delicious little nuts in its cone. Siberians dry it, shell it, and eat it as a snack, even as European Russians do sunflower and pumpkin seeds. The geologist I mentioned in the preceding chapter told me that the whole taiga feeds on the cedar nut, from birds and bears to mice and men. "In summer," he related, "the taiga is one of the most tranquil places on earth. But in autumn when the cedar nuts ripen pandemonium breaks loose—squirrels chatter, birds scream, bears roar, creatures you rarely see come out of hiding, gnash their teeth at one another, fight and kill one another in a mad scramble for the cedar nut." Scientists figure that in Western Siberia alone about two million tons of the nuts ripen, the largest part gathered by the wildlife in the forest.

Shishkovat (cedar-cone gathering) is a lively sport and a profitable pursuit for Siberians living within easy reach of the taiga. They not only eat the nuts but sell them to the state, which presses out the oil for medicinal and dietetic purposes. Some nut gatherers earn as much as the equivalent of over one thousand dollars a season from the sale of cedar nuts, a source of income European Russians do not have.

"I'll tell you something else about the cedar nut," the geologist said. "Hunters make milk out of it."

"Milk?" I asked, incredulous.

"That's right; much richer than cow's or goat's milk. They beat the nuts into powder, pour water over it, boil it, and there's your milk. It looks like milk and tastes delicious." He further explained that nothing in the cedar nut is wasted—dyes are extracted from the shell, the skin makes excellent stuffing for mattresses, and the oil cake lends special savor to halva and pastry.

The taiga grows other foods too. As we were driving along we passed small parties of kerchiefed women and pig-tailed little girls, all wearing trousers tied at the ankles and carrying boxes, buckets, and baskets. The mushroom season was at its height. Siberians tell you that nowhere else in the Soviet Union do mushrooms grow as bountifully as in their taiga, and everybody, especially peasants, picks barrels and barrels of them to dry or to marinate for winter use or to sell in the bazaar.

My companions on the drive, the chauffeur and the guide, both Siberian-born, kept up a running narrative of other gifts of the taiga. All summer long there are berries; first strawberries, then currants, black and red, then raspberries, then all manner of bilberries, cran-berries, mountain-ash berries—berries and berries, all one cares to pick—to eat as a snack, sometimes with bread, to boil into jam, or to put into a barrel with sugar and water for winter use. "They taste wonderfully refreshing in winter," the chauffeur said.

"Have you heard of our compass berry?" the guide asked.

I shook my head.

"It's our *brusnika* [a species of bilberry]. If you get lost in the taiga you can always find your way. You see, the white side points north and the red side points south. It's always so. It never fails."

Then there is the berry *obleppikha* (the sea buckthorn). It is a soft yellow berry that grows on tall thorny bushes. The bushes are so thorny and the berry when ripe is so soft that it cannot be picked by hand. Peasant women gather it by cutting the stalks, which they lay away until winter, when berry and stalk have dried. Then they beat the stalks against the ice of some frozen stream and the berries fall off. They make jam and jelly out of it which Siberians say taste like the pineapple they get from China.

There is the Siberian *shipovnik* (wild-rose bush), whose petals lend aroma to jam and whose berries in olden times were exchanged for sable, silk, and velvet. The berries were highly prized for their medicinal properties and were supposed to cure every conceivable illness, so old Siberian chronicles relate. Modern science has dis-covered that they are loaded with vitamins A, C, B_2, R, and K. They are sold in drugstores, but why buy them when they can be picked free in the taiga?

There is also the *cheremsha* (wild garlic). "A hunter," the guide said, "would no more think of going off into the taiga without a supply of *cheremsha* than without salt. It prevents and cures scurvy, and when bears first come out of their lairs in the spring, they feed on it."

Later, from a Siberian handbook I picked up in Irkutsk, I learned that the *cheremsha* is spoken of as "bear's fat," because bears fatten on it.

So here is the mighty and majestic taiga, rich in timber and fur, in meat and fish, in mushrooms and berries, in cedar nut and in a variety of edible and medicinal plants, in deer whose horns supposedly hold a cure for sexual impotence. No wonder Siberians speak of it as "little mother taiga."

The chauffeur asked if I would like to take some cedar cones back to America as souvenirs, and I replied that I would. He drew up at the roadside and we walked into the forest. The wild grass and underbrush were so dense that walking was like wading through snowdrifts. Finally we came upon a sturdy cedar. With sticks my companions flailed down more cones than I could carry to America or even to Moscow. They were larger than the ordinary pine cones and heavy as rocks. The nuts were too green to pry loose from the flesh. "In Siberia," the chauffeur explained, "nature works fast; in about two weeks the cones will be ready for picking. You'd better stay over and go with us on a cone-gathering excursion."

"How do you pick them?" I asked. "Do you climb the tree and shake them down?" That was the way I picked apples in my boyhood days in a Russian village.

"Oh no," answered the guide. "We have stout wooden mallets which we strike against the trunk and the cones come flying down."

"Doesn't it hurt the tree?"

"Not the cedar," the chauffeur replied, and glancing up at the tree, he added, "There it has stood for maybe two hundred years and the yearly malleting it gets might be only caresses for all the damage it shows." He gazed at the splendid tree with wonder and pride.

We drove on, the road walled by the forest teeming with its own mysterious life. Then suddenly we were in full view of Lake Baikal, and the Pobeda stopped. Shaped like a half moon, it is the deepest, clearest, coldest lake in the world, about four hundred miles long and with as large a volume of water as the Baltic Sea. Framed by mountains, some grassy, some wooded, it glimmered silver gray and bluish green in the brilliant sunlight.

I remembered the lake from my previous journey, when I had seen it from the window of the Trans-Siberian express. As the train snaked slowly along the shoreline, passengers crowded to the window exclaiming in admiration, as is the way of Russians when they are moved to wonder. They had all, of course, heard of Baikal— what school child hasn't sung "Glorious Baikal, Sacred Baikal," as a popular song venerates it? At some station the train had stopped and passengers tumbled out with sacks, baskets, towels, to load up with the famed *omul*—reputedly the tastiest fish in the Soviet Union. Found in Baikal and nowhere else in the world except in the Arctic Ocean, where its meat is stringy, it belongs to the salmon family. It is rather a small fish, weighing from one to two pounds, and European Russians do not challenge the boast of Siberians that neither the Black and Caspian seas nor the Volga, Don, and Dnieper rivers produce as delectable a fish as the *omul*.

At the railroad station, buxom kerchiefed women sold it, smoked dark and dripping with fat; and everybody, including conductors, firemen, and engineers, bought it. Our coach looked and smelled like a fishhouse as we feasted on the fragrant and tender *omul*.

Now I was seeing the lake again under a cloudless sky, the water gently lapping the nearby shoreline, its silvery expanse losing itself in faraway blue mists.

"Do you know how many rivers flow into Baikal?" asked the guide, a delicately built, dignified youth with blue eyes. "Three hundred and thirty-six, and only one flows out of it—the Angara—and at its 'throat' the flow is so swift that it never freezes."

"And 'way up north there are colonies of seal," the tall, gangling, swarthy-faced chauffeur threw out, as though further to impress me with the Siberian wonder lake. "We hunt them every year from March 15 to June 15."

Some distance away a small one-funneled boat was slowly gliding over the water, and the guide informed me that it carried an expedition of the Academy of Sciences that was permanently stationed on the other side of the lake and was devoting all its time to investigations of the plant and animal life within its waters. "Of the eighteen hundred species of plant and animal life there," he said, "about three fourths are indigenous, unknown anywhere else on earth." Then the chauffeur, pointing toward the fishing village of Kultuk that straggled off the steep southern shoreline, said, "There are no wells in the village. The people prefer the water of Baikal. There's no fresher and purer water anywhere in the world."

Siberians never speak of Baikal as a lake. To them it is a sea stocked with the precious *omul* and colonies of seal, both of which ages and ages ago, before nature sundered Baikal from "the big water," as the ocean is sometimes spoken of locally, had remained within the fresh water of the lake.

The three-hour automobile ride from Irkutsk to Baikal is open to tourists and is one of the most scenic and exciting in the Soviet Union.

We drove into Kultuk, a village of unpaved streets, of dark-timbered cottages and courtyards aglow with flowers. Children played in the streets, chickens pecked underfoot, and, miracle of miracles, the dogs were as tame as kittens! They lay asleep in the shade or perked up their heads and didn't even growl as we passed them. I had never known a Russian village with such easy-tempered dogs.

We stopped at a cottage which was the fishermen's kolkhoz. The chairman was a short stocky man, powerfully built and quite young, in his middle or late twenties. Sunburned, with a sharply chiseled face and glittering brown eyes, the most distinctive feature of his appearance was his thick wavy and lustrous dark-brown hair. He wore it in a neatly brushed high pompadour, a style which Moscow's *Komsomolka* frowns on as improper for "the Soviet man." It might stigmatize the young chairman as a "show-off" or "dandy." But Kultuk was far away from Moscow, and the leading figure in the village obviously took pride in his luxuriant hair and cut it to suit his own taste.

The chairman's name was Victor Demin and meeting foreigners was no novelty to him, but I was the first who spoke Russian and we at once fell into animated conversation. I learned that Mozart was one of his favorite composers and Chekhov one of his favorite authors. He loved music and literature, he said, and now and then dabbled in writing, having had stories published in the Irkutsk newspaper. Then he asked whether I knew Walter Lippmann. I replied that I had met Lippmann years ago but knew him chiefly through his writings.

"I greatly admire him," said Victor, his voice soft and gentle, "as a brilliant advocate of world peace."

Lippmann is probably *Pravda's* most quoted foreign journalist, and reading the cannily selected quotations, which omit any criticism of Soviet foreign policy, readers like Victor might readily conclude that Lippmann is another Ilya Ehrenburg, always applauding Soviet peace crusades. I spoke of it to Victor, and after some reflection he said, "I like to read Lippmann—he writes brilliantly. Now I want to ask you something. I listen sometimes to the Voice of America, and why do they say such stupid things about Siberia? Why don't they come over and see for themselves our great developments here?"

As he did not mention any particular broadcasts, I could only surmise that he was referring to stories of Siberian labor camps, a sensitive subject to any Siberian party member. But Victor was so amiable that I let the matter drop and remarked on the beauty of the country.

"We love it," he said. "Once I spent eight months on the coast of the Black Sea. I liked it fine—the sun, the sea, the flowers, the fresh fruits and vegetables. But I soon got lonely for the taiga. That's the way it is with us Siberians. When we are away from the taiga we long for it as for someone we love. And here in Kultuk we have not only the taiga but mountains and the Baikal Sea. I wouldn't want to live anywhere else."

In reply to questions, he related the history of Kultuk. In 1909 the population was only 400. There was no school, no physician nearer than Irkutsk. The fishing equipment was primitive—rowboats, barges, and hand-woven nets that had to be spread out and dried after each catch. Now the population was 8000. They had elementary and intermediate schools for all children, and 200 of their young people were studying in institutes and colleges. The fishing industry was completely revolutionized. Fishermen had motorboats, hoisting equipment, nylon nets, and a freezing plant for fish. There was a hospital in the village and seven physicians, all women.

I asked how much the fishermen earned a month.

"From eight hundred to a thousand [old] rubles [88 to 110 dollars] the men and the women," he replied. This was higher than the average for factory workers. "They have their own gardens and there is also hunting; around here everybody hunts. I want to show you something."

From the drawer of his desk he lifted out a glossy photograph and passed it to me. It showed a grizzled old man and a boy crouching over the body of a bear that was bound with a stout rope.

"We have black and brown bear around here," Victor resumed. "They prowl around the taiga and the shores of Baikal and you never know when you'll have an encounter with them." Pointing to the old man in the photograph, Victor went on. "Andrian Kobelev is his name, a fisherman, sixty-five years old. He got the bear single-handed and without a gun." Then he told me how it happened. The old man and a party of fishermen, among whom were women and young people, were on their way five kilometers offshore to inspect *omul* nets. Suddenly they saw something black rolling around the nets. At first they thought it was a barrel, then they thought it was a cow. "But the sharp eyes of the *starik* [old man] told him that it was a bear. Quickly he and the boy transferred into a small motorboat while all the others sped away in the larger one. The boy was at the motor and old Kobelev stood up, butcher knife in hand, ready for the bear, who was swimming toward them. It was a big bear and the old man realized a knife would be a poor weapon. So he dropped the knife and picked up an ax. The bear drew close and Kobelev struck him a blow on the head. It stunned the bear, but soon he was up again and flung a paw on the boat. He'd have tipped over the boat had not Kobelev with lightninglike speed chopped off the paw. The bear dropped into the water but soon came up again, laying the other paw on the gunwale. Kobelev chopped that off too. But there was no holding back the big beast, and when he moved close again Kobelev struck him one blow after another on the head. The bear fell into the water and this time Kobelev reached out for a rope, lassoed him, and ordered the boy to go full speed ahead. The boat dragged the bear along, and when he keeled over, Kobelev cut his throat with the knife. That's how the duel between the big black bear and the old fisherman ended. Not bad for a man of sixty-five!" Victor exclaimed.

There was no season on bear, Victor informed me, or on wolf or bobcat. Hunters shot them on sight. Then he asked whether I had heard of the Barguzin sable. I told him I couldn't tell one sable from another. The hunter-teacher in Irkutsk hadn't enlightened me on the different breeds of sable.

"But there is a difference," Victor pointed out. "The Barguzin is the choicest of all sables. It's smaller than the others, with darker and silkier fur, and fetches the highest price in the international market."

What the price was, Victor couldn't tell me. But from American furriers I learned that at the Leningrad fur auction in the summer of 1959 the Barguzin sold at $715 a skin!

"I want you to know," Victor resumed, "that you are in the heart of the Barguzin sable country." Pointing out the window, he added, "Out there is a special preserve of over half a million hectares for the Barguzin."

The precise figure is 570,900 hectares, or over 1,400,000 acres. It is all wild country, mountains and valleys, streams and lakes, overgrown with trees and abounding in cedar nuts, berries, rodents, and birds for the ravenous and omnivorous little creatures.

In the early years of the revolution, Victor explained, rapacious hunters had all but exterminated the Barguzin. That was why, in 1926, the state set up the preserve and banned all hunting for several years. The Barguzin throve so well that the ban was lifted and nearly everybody hunted it, even the railroad workers who lived there. They took their vacations in winter so they would be free during the hunting season, when they usually captured from fifteen to twenty-five sables. At the state price of 100 of the new rubles a skin, a railroad worker would earn from 1500 to 2500 rubles, or the equivalent of some 1600 to 2700 dollars, which is more than his yearly salary.

Victor resumed. "Out here we try to catch the Barguzins alive." This was something else the hunter-teacher in Irkutsk had not spoken about. "You see, for a live sable the state pays three times as much as for a skin alone."

I gasped—the state offering munificent rewards for individual enterprise! But Victor smiled and said, "It's worth it to the state. There are many regions in the taiga where the Barguzins can thrive. So we're stocking them in these regions. Once last winter I was at the airport and I saw about seventy live Barguzins ready to be flown out. The plane takes them to some faraway airport. Then trucks take over, then they're carried on horseback, then man carries the cages on his back and releases the creatures, always in pairs, at some particularly wild and wooded place."

So besides steel plants, power stations, aluminum factories, pulp mills, other industrial projects, Siberia is witnessing the rise of the Barguzin sable. The reason is obvious; it is an invaluable source of foreign exchange.

I went to Victor's house for lunch. The small courtyard that fronted the one-story timbered cottage was ablaze with flowers and there were flowerpots on the window sills. The two spacious rooms were bright with sunlight and exceptionally clean, though modestly furnished with old-fashioned furniture. Here was the inevitable brick oven, running from the kitchen, which was also the living room, to the other room, which was bedroom and parlor—the huge wood-burning oven that has kept the Russian peasant home warm for countless generations throughout the stern winter months. But here the modern age had brought an innovation: the fore part of the oven was converted into a kitchen range, now steaming with cooking pots, the smell of fish thick and fragrant.

An elderly gentle-faced woman with pink cheeks and blue eyes welcomed me with effusions that are so natural and so genuine to Russian peasant women. A relative of Victor, she was his housekeeper. The table was already set and several other guests had come, among them a pale-faced woman wearing a black hat with a narrow brim who was teaching Russian language and literature in the local high school. Of course, the meal started with drinks—where in Russia does it start otherwise when there is a guest in the house? But the drink was not vodka; it was the liquor distilled from Siberian mountain-ash berries. Pink in color, it was a little sharp but pleasant in taste, and since it was the first time I had drunk it, my companions wondered how I liked it, their own Siberian product, made out of the juiciest mountain-ash berries in the Soviet Union. I told them I liked it, but when my host lifted the bottle to refill my tumbler, I put my hand over the top and shook my head. He set the bottle down and nobody else was served another drink—the example of the guest was not to be snubbed. Such is the social ritual I had observed even among some of the hard-drinking Cossacks.

The first course of the meal was an *omul ukha* (fish stew), but what an *ukha!* The traditional Russian dish exuded a fragrance that has gone out of it in Moscow's Intourist hotels. The new chefs there haven't learned what the gentle-faced peasant woman has never forgotten and had so lovingly prepared. I praised her cooking, and by a complicated association of ideas she suddenly mentioned that Victor was unmarried. He smiled but said nothing. The schoolteacher added some remarks of her own on the loneliness of a man living in a state of bachelorhood. Still the young chairman remained silent and smiled.

The housekeeper served us both fried and broiled *omul*, sizzling hot, and then returned to the subject of Victor's bachelorhood.

"Such a strong and handsome man," she told me, "and so highly educated, and can't find himself a wife."

"Well," Victor said, "a man has only one romance in his life and he'd better make certain it is real."

"If you wait too long," the teacher admonished, "you'll find yourself unwanted."

"Such a stickler," the housekeeper complained. "I never knew a man like him."

"Why don't you marry him off to one of your young women physicians?" I said.

"They are all married," exclaimed the housekeeper and the teacher in one voice.

"Do you think anybody is going to wait for him?" the housekeeper added, frowning at Victor.

"Oh well," said the teacher, smiling at the young chairman, "he'll find his romance yet."

"By the time he does," the housekeeper said ruefully, "no girl will want to look at him."

Victor sat up and said soberly, "A bad wife is like a pistol to a man's head."

The woman clucked her tongue and spoke no more.

When one witnesses scenes like this in a home, one forgets that there ever was a bolshevik revolution in the Soviet Union.

After lunch we went for a boat ride on Lake Baikal in a large rowboat to which a motor was attached. The sun stood high and white, and the water, now silver gray, now sky blue, now grass green, rippled gently. All around stood mountains, high and rolling; now and then a wall of brown and shiny granite as upright as a pine, falling sheer into the lake. "Look into the water," Victor said. I did, and saw, as through glass, rock and vegetation on the bottom. "It's about fifteen meters deep here," said Victor, peering in, "and the bottom is as clear as the palm of your hand. Isn't it remarkable?"

Then standing upright, he pointed to the mountains and resumed. "Over yonder we have paths for walking excursions, and over there groves for picnics, and that way sites for camping. With the sea here, the taiga, the mountains—where in the world is there grander country for vacationists? That's what we must do—attract vacationists here, and they'll always want to come back. Wouldn't you?"

"Indeed I would," I said.

The boat glided along deeper and deeper into the glittering lake, a cool breeze blowing into our faces, the color of the mountains, now in shade and now in sun, changing from dark green to misty violet, from pale pink to shiny gray, the surface of the water as calm as the mountains.

"Such a calm lake," I said.

Victor laughed. "You don't know how angry our Baikal gets in autumn, when strong winds lift up high waves that roar and thunder, crash violently against the mountains as though determined to smash them. But to us it's music—music we love. But come winter and the lake freezes and we have weddings here."

"Old-fashioned weddings?" I asked.

"Not with a priest, if that's what you mean," he answered. "Our people love the pleasures of this earth too much to give any thought to the hereafter. Isn't that so?" He turned to the others in the boat. Hearty and laughing assent was the answer to his question.

"In winter," Victor continued, "we have more time than in summer, and we make quite an event of weddings. Why not? One gets married only once in life, so why not make a festival of it to be remembered? You see, Baikal freezes in January and stays frozen until May. The winds sweep away the snow and the sea is as smooth as a skating rink. Evenings, the wedding procession comes here, accompanied by music and plenty of food and drink; we build bonfires on the ice and ride around with bride and groom in the wonderful old-fashioned troikas [three-horsed sleighs]. We have troika races on the ice, too. With the moon shining, the fires burning, the music playing, the people singing, the horses galloping up and down, their bells ringing, our Baikal becomes a fairyland of beauty and joy."

"How long do the weddings last?" I asked.

"Sometimes as long as five days—or, to be mathematically precise, not counting the hours for sleep, which are few, about one hundred hours of gaiety for everybody." "Everybody" meant that no invitations were issued and anybody who cared to join in was welcome.

"You should come here to a winter wedding," Victor said. "I assure you, you'll never forget it."

I'm sure I'll never forget the short, brawny youth standing in the boat, his wavy hair glistening in the sun, his face radiant, as he talked of the revival of one of the gayest ceremonials in the Russian village, with the inevitable troikas lending it the color and the romance of old times. The old wedding bells, which had so long been silenced, are ringing again, not only in the remote Siberian fishing village of Kultuk but in other villages I visited.

We drove back to Irkutsk. The sun was setting and the taiga was growing dark, the lone white birches shining out of the somber evergreens like stars in a clouded sky. Along the road there was no sign of the wildlife or of any of the other precious gifts that the incomparable forest freely and bountifully bestowed on man. But I was to learn something else about the taiga before I left Siberia.

On a Sunday afternoon I went walking the streets of Irkutsk. Sidewalks were crowded with promenaders, chiefly young people walking in pairs and in groups and lively with conversation—the ever gregarious Russians must always talk, especially when they are out promenading, which in Siberia, as in European Russia, is a favorite popular diversion. Snatches of conversation fell on my ears: from a youth saying to his companion, "I can outdo him in molds, believe me I can"; from another youth to a girl friend, "When he twirls his mustache I know he's pleased with my answer, but when he starts grunting I begin to tremble"—doubtless talking about a college professor; from still another youth, "She's too conceited"; from a girl walking arm in arm with two other girls, "But she doesn't love him"; from another girl walking hand in hand with a boy, "I could die when I hear him sing"; from a boy promenading with two girls, "I tell you we'll beat the Chinese team, wait and see"; from a short, stout woman to the man beside her, "Little father mine, how lush it is with mushrooms"; from a man with stooping shoulders to the tall youth beside him, "You shouldn't argue with her, it wouldn't do any good." Talk and talk—not about plans of production, diversionists, the imminent death of capitalism, the glorious Motherland; no hosannas to Soviet superiorities, to the unmatched character and valor of the Soviet man, to the dawn of communism already breaking on the Soviet horizons—subjects that supposedly consume the minds and emotions of the Soviet citizenry, if one were only to believe *Pravda*. It was talk that one might hear among people in any non-Communist country, and with which a foreigner understanding the language could identify himself as readily as with the conversation of his own countrymen.

Finally I turned off an asphalted avenue and found myself on an unpaved street lined with timbered cottages, mud puddles gleaming in the dusk. I wandered around, turning corners, following one street after another, and suddenly found myself in a square with a pretty flower garden in the center. Towering over the square stood the newly built, yellow-painted post office. There was a small fountain among the flower beds and children were playing around squirting water on one another and shouting as gaily when the water missed them as when it struck their faces.

There were no promenaders in the garden, but an elderly man was sitting on a bench, his chin on hands folded over a cane. He wore a cap, a *watnik* (cotton-padded jacket), and knee-high leather boots. But he also wore a long beard, the first man with a beard that I'd seen in Irkutsk or in the countryside I had visited. The beard and the cane seemed so old-fashioned that I walked over, sat down beside him, and we began to talk. I learned that he was an Old Believer whose ancestors fled centuries ago from persecution in European

Russia. When I asked him where he lived, he answered, "I am a *tayezhnik* [dweller in the taiga]."

"A hunter?"

"Of course. If you don't hunt you cannot live in the taiga, and thank the Lord my eyes are still keen, and when I set my sight on game, down it comes." He looked me over and asked whether I was a Muscovite. I told him I was an American and came to Siberia to learn something about the life of Siberians.

"So, so!" he intoned slowly and reflectively. Then he asked, "Have you a taiga in America?"

"Nothing like the Siberian taiga."

"No, of course not," he muttered, and ran his hand through his tangled beard. "There's no taiga like ours anywhere on earth, and a *tayezhnik* like myself doesn't feel at home outside it."

"What are you doing in the city then?" I asked.

He propped his cane between his knees and answered, "I have a son, he hunts in winter and works in a kolkhoz in summer, so I came out to visit him. Today we drove in a truck to Irkutsk and I got so lonely in the crowded streets I came here to this little park to be by myself and to look at the flowers."

"Don't you like people?"

He gave a little laugh, showing a mouth with darkened teeth worn almost to the gums. "When you live in the taiga, you don't miss people, and you don't get sick in the taiga. Sickness doesn't come from trees and wildlife. It comes from people. Often when I come out of the taiga, I get headaches, I cough, I have a fever. But when I go back to the taiga, I get well again. There is no air like that of the taiga; it's got all kinds of medicine in it. The good Lord put it there for the benefit of all living things." He paused and fell into thought. Then he spoke again. "I want to ask you something. Have you ever seen an atomic bomb?"

"No."

"Do you know how big it is—is it as big as this structure?"—pointing to the post office.

"It cannot be," I said, "because it's carried in a plane."

"Maybe it's no bigger than a bear."

"Maybe."

"Ah!" He thought again and said, "I suppose if it was dropped on Irkutsk it would kill everybody?"

"It might."

"But if it was dropped on the taiga, there would be only a few *tayezhniki* like myself to kill. Strange, very strange."

"What's strange?"

"I was thinking," he said, "that nobody would want to drop the bomb on the taiga. It's people they want to kill, and there are more people in Irkutsk than in the whole taiga—many more. That's what's so strange. Ah!" He seemed too bewildered for words.

"Being a *tayezhnik*," I said, "you don't have to worry about being hit by the bomb."

He seemed not to hear me, but kept stroking his beard and thinking. "Do you know much about bear?" he finally asked.

"Very little," I answered.

"There's a creature for you—powerful and wise—and I never shot one of them. Never! Why should I? He doesn't molest me and I don't molest him. Once I saw a big bear run out of a forest fire. He looked scared and wild, but he only sat down on the bank of a stream and lifted up his burned paws to be cooled by the air. I saw him and he saw me. He was content to be left alone, and he left me alone. A bear gets terribly ferocious during the mating season. He tears up the earth, tears up trees, and you can hear his roar all over the taiga. He'll fight another bear for the favor of the female, and that's the time it's dangerous to get within his sight. But after he's had his pleasure, he becomes peaceful again—I mean peaceful to man if you don't molest him. That's his nature and I don't care what other people say. I've seen as much bear in my lifetime as any hunter in the taiga, and I know all there is to know about bear, yes I do. I love the powerful animal—ah, what a majestic animal he is!" He paused and smiled as though the mere thought of bear made him happy.

Then fixing his eyes on me, he resumed, his voice grave and a little angry. "One thing I never saw, nor did anybody else. I never saw bears massing together to fight other bears. Never. It would never occur to them to invent an atomic bomb even if they had the brains to do it. But man—no, I can't say that I understand man now that he's got the atomic bomb to kill other men, kill and kill. Ah!" He groaned as if in pain. As an afterthought, he added, "Maybe God doesn't understand man any more. Maybe man has become an anti-Christ, maybe!" He groaned again.

The children were still playing around the fountain, running and shouting and laughing. The old man turned his eyes on them and said, "There's no anti-Christ in them, and I tell you if they grew up in the taiga they never could become anti-Christs. They'd always be aware of God and thank him for the peace and beauty all around them. And yet there are people who say the taiga is a lonely and cruel place to live. The fools!"

23.

UZBEKISTAN
Show Window in Asia

"These Uzbeks!" exclaimed an executive in Moscow's GUM when I told him I was leaving for Uzbekistan. "What a time we had with their deputies to the Supreme Soviet when they came to Moscow. We opened the department store for them after closing hours and you should have seen them scramble—they bought and bought and just about cleaned us out of refrigerators, washing machines, phonographs, sewing machines, other things. I never saw anything like it."

"Where did they get the money?" I asked.

"Money?" he chuckled. "Uzbekistan is first in cotton, first in rice, all high-priced cash crops, and it is first in Persian-lamb skins. It's our richest republic."

I remembered these words when I arrived in Tashkent, capital of Uzbekistan, some two thousand miles southwest of Moscow. The seventh-largest city in the Soviet Union, with a population, according to the latest census of 991,000, it was nowhere nearly as well supplied with manufactured goods as Moscow or Leningrad. Still, Uzbeks told me, never before had shops been so plentifully stocked and from month to month stocks were increasing. Better times, they assured me, had come and would grow even better, though voices were not lacking to express resentment over favors bestowed on Moscow and withheld from Tashkent.

I soon learned that the Kremlin has chosen Uzbekistan as the Soviet show window of Asia, a demonstration more particularly for Asians and Africans of its power to transform a backward and illiterate country, as Uzbekistan had been in Czarist times, into a modern, industrial, and highly scientific community.

"Will you stay over for the Asian-African film festival in August?" a young Uzbek asked.

"I shall be in Siberia in August," I said.

"Maybe you can come back in October for the Asian-African Writers' Congress," the young man said.

"By October," I replied, "I shall be out of the Soviet Union."

"Too bad," he said as if with commiseration. "The leading Asian and African writers are gathering here and you'd have had a chance to become acquainted with them. We'll have great celebrations."

They did, too. Representatives from fourteen Asian-African nations came to the Tashkent film festival and from thirty-nine nations to the literary congress, which the Soviet press hailed as a gathering of "the flower of the Asian-African literary world," dedicated to "the breaking of the chains of colonialism . . . to the struggle for progress of humanity, for national independence, for peace." On the conclusion of the congress, the participants journeyed to Moscow, where in the evening of October 22 (1958) a gala banquet was held in the Kremlin. Nearly all the members of the Presidium, including Khrushchev, attended the banquet, and speaker after speaker spoke glowingly of "the spirit of Tashkent," a spirit of battle for the liberation of "the enslaved peoples" of Asia and Africa.

The fact that the Kremlin chose Tashkent for these gatherings attests to its confidence in the appeal the capital of Uzbekistan would make to Asians and Africans, in the desire and dedication it might stir in them to strive for the Sovietization of their homelands. In the East-West rivalries and battle for influence in Asia and Africa, Uzbekistan and Tashkent in particular are destined to play an increasingly important propaganda part.

My first impression of Uzbeks as I wandered the streets of the new and old parts of Tashkent was what a clean people Uzbeks were. No

Soviet lecturer, I was told, needed to instruct them, as they did muzhiks and Russian factory workers, in such rudimentary rules of hygiene
as washing hands before eating. As Moslems, Uzbeks would no more
touch bread without first washing their hands than they would let
chickens strut into their houses, as Russian peasants in Byelorussia, for
example, still often do. It is a sight to watch an Uzbek, even a peasant, wash his hands. He doesn't merely rinse them as I have seen
peasants in other Mohammedan countries do; he rubs and scrubs
them almost like a surgeon about to perform an operation. Bread to
him is such a sacred thing that he wouldn't defile it by soiled hands.

The living room of an Uzbek peasant mud hut is as spotless as
a mosque; the gaily colored rugs and embroideries on the floor and
walls, the cushions and settees, give it the charm and the glow of a
little oriental museum. Expert in needlework, Uzbek women are also
indefatigable housekeepers. Mornings on arising they clean their
rugs as conscientiously as though it were a part of a Mohammedan
rite, except that now many of them, even in remote villages, no
longer use a broom, but a vacuum cleaner. Sweeping the courtyard
every morning is another chore the women do not neglect. Cleanliness is to them indeed next to godliness.

When I spoke with some enthusiasm to the porter of my hotel of
Uzbek love of cleanliness, he smiled with pleasure and said, "Yes, we
are a clean people. That's why we don't eat pork. We regard the pig
as an unclean creature unfit for human consumption. But we love
chicken, a bird that swallows everything it can peck its beak into. So
you know what our peasants do? Before killing it, they shut it away
for about five days and feed it only pure food—wheat, barley, corn—
and serve it only pure water. Only then do they regard it fit for eating.
Here, have some tea."

Unlike Russians, who fill the glass to the brim, the porter poured
mine only half full. That's the Uzbek style when he drinks tea out of
a glass, something he usually doesn't do. Like the Chinese, he prefers
his tea in a cup without a handle—a *piala*. The porter didn't take
sugar, but he offered it to me. When I asked him why he didn't
sweeten his tea, he said, "We have a saying: 'Where will you find
strength if you don't drink tea?' Why then dilute the strength that
tea gives you with sugar, milk, or jam, as Russians do? Oh no! In
the morning an Uzbek starts and finishes his breakfast with tea.

In summer when it is hot, he drinks tea. In winter when it is cold, he drinks tea. When he has a bellyache, he drinks tea. When he has a toothache, he drinks tea. When he is happy in love, he drinks tea. When he is unhappy in love, he drinks tea. Well or ill, happy or unhappy, tea always gives you strength. But remember—only green tea, without sugar, milk, jam."

"Do you ever take a sip of vodka?" I asked.

"Not I, oh no. But some Uzbeks do, mostly in the city, rarely in the village. You see," he went on with a knowing smile, "this is the way they justify it. The Koran forbids the fermented juice of the grape. But it says nothing about wheat or barley, from which vodka is made. Not bad?" He laughed amused at the casuistry of his vodka-drinking countrymen.

Most amazing of all, Uzbek men like to cook. Russians, as already reported, regard it something of a disgrace to lend a hand in any kind of housekeeping. But not Uzbeks. The men not only love to cook, they fancy themselves better cooks than women. Borsch? Not for them. Hardly any Russian cuisine at all. Even their bread is different, being baked in round, flat cakes with raised rims. Shashlik is their pride and glory, and the men boast that nobody can cook it as expertly as they do. "Tell it," I once said to an Uzbek, "to a Georgian or an Armenian." "Well," came the reply, "we might challenge Georgians and Armenians to a socialist competition on who the best shashlik cooks are and let foreigners act as judges. We would win."

Having eaten shashlik in Georgia and Armenia, as well as in Tashkent, I need only say that the judges would be hard put to render a decision. They are all expert shashlik cooks—which is more than I can say for the new chefs at Moscow's leading hotels.

Plov (pilaf) is another Uzbek specialty. "Don't say just *plov*," an Uzbek cautioned me. "Say *Uzbek-plov*. It's different from any other." Different or not, as Uzbeks cook it it is one of the most delicious dishes I have ever eaten anywhere in Asia: the heaping bowl of hot rice richly mixed with lumps of mutton, carrots, and raisins, fattened with butter and seasoned with spices. Even on Russian menus one reads *Uzbek-plov*, to distinguish it from any other.

The Uzbek girls one sees in the streets and parks of Tashkent or in villages, with their lush black hair plaited into waist-long braids, their heads crowned with the snug-fitting, gaudily embroidered *tubeteika* (skullcap), are among the comeliest in the Soviet Union, and also among the most retiring when confronted by foreigners. The women, except those who have been completely modernized, wear long sack-style dresses, and once, while in a village store, I jestingly remarked to the Uzbek who accompanied me on the trip that the latest Western fashion seemed to have struck the fancy of Uzbek women. "It must be the other way around," he replied. "This is the home of the sack style." Nudging me aside, he whispered, "Our women regard it as improper to show their breasts. That's why they wear the sack-style dresses, as you call them." So the Western cult of the bosom, unadvertised but amply demonstrated in Russia proper, has left Uzbekistan untouched, except in the cities, where the younger girls have taken to modern-style dress.

If Uzbeks had reason to envy Moscow its shops, Muscovites could only envy Uzbeks their bazaars. Toward the end of July—the time I was there—they overflowed with peaches, apples, grapes, melons, green peppers, eggplants, that had not yet reached Moscow. There was a superabundance also of tomatoes, carrots, garlic, wild mustard, beets, everything it seemed but cucumbers. Those I saw were small, scabby, and shriveled. I doubt whether, unlike Russians, Uzbeks would miss cucumbers if they were never grown.

But Uzbeks must have their tea and shashlik, even in the bazaars. At the central market place inside an open-front restaurant, chefs in white caps and white coats were as busy broiling shashlik over glowing charcoal in long tin troughs as are Coney Island dispensers roasting frankfurters on a hot summer day. At the oilcloth-covered tables, skullcapped customers lingered over the savory repast. Uzbeks are a leisurely people, especially at the table.

Never anywhere did I eat shashlik as cheaply as in this restaurant —the equivalent of some twenty cents for a sizzling skewerful fresh off the fire. But it was too hot for tea, so I asked for beer. A startled stare greeted my request. Who would want beer when he could get hot tea? Never would it occur to an Uzbek visiting the bazaar to ask for beer, however hot the day and however thirsty he might feel. So it had to be tea.

Babies, babies, babies! One sees them everywhere in city and village, even in the bazaars—clean-faced, raven-haired, bright-eyed babies. In fecundity the Uzbek woman can probably outmatch her sisters anywhere in the Soviet Union. Moscow never needed to offer her premiums for bringing large families into the world. The premiums are welcome, but without them babies would come anyway. They always have. "Nothing so agonizes an Uzbek woman," a Russian schoolteacher told me, "as to be incapable of bearing children. Fortunately such women are rare in Uzbekistan."

Uzbeks are an ancient Asian people. According to the *Entsiklopedichesky Slovar* of 1902, they are "a conglomerate of Turki, Iranian, and Mongol stock." In the days of Tamerlane (1336–1405), the ancient capital of Samarkand was a city of great culture and science, especially noted for its magnificent shrines, mausoleums, palaces, and other architectural monuments. But through the centuries the river-watered valleys and upland grasslands brought on the country one invasion after another.

In the sixth century B.C., Persia swept over them and for large sections of the population the Zoroastrian *Avesta* became the Holy Book. In the fourth century B.C., Alexander the Great brought his armies there and left some Greek influence in his wake. Early in the second century B.C., the Chinese broke into the fertile Fergana Valley, but met with such resistance that they were obliged to withdraw, taking with them to their own country the grape and alfalfa. In the eighth century A.D. the Arabs conquered them and the Koran became the Holy Book. Turki armies swept over them in the ninth century and Genghis Khan in the thirteenth. The Czars seized the country in the late sixties of the nineteenth century, having first occupied Tashkent on June 29, 1865.

Having known war after war and the disasters that accompanied them, the Uzbeks didn't escape the influences ("the good and the bad," as an Uzbek expressed himself) of their conquerors. Yet they remained essentially a primitive pastoral people, far off the highways of Western civilization.

Dark-eyed and dark-haired, there is barely a trace of the Mongol among them, and very rare is the Uzbek with such slanting eyes and high cheekbones that one would mistake him for a Mongol. The Mongol-looking people one sees in Tashkent are usually Kazakhs, who are a mixture of Turki and Mongol tribes. Yet Tashkent is a city of striking faces, white, brown, and yellowish, with round, oval, and slanting eyes, even as it is a city of striking dress—conventional

Western styles parading side by side with richly embroidered ancient Asian styles, with the inevitable *tubeteika* for both sexes, usually black and white for men and gaudily embroidered for women.

Sturdy and light-footed, Uzbeks gesture extravagantly, and once they start laughing—the start is slow—they laugh with the abandon of children at a circus. At an outdoor variety performance by Uzbek artists, the large audience that filled every seat and stood rows deep appeared as solemn as at a religious service. But when two dancing girls appeared there was a titter of delight that grew into loud laughter which still echoed in the intermission that followed. To my Western eyes there was nothing amusing about the slow-paced panto-mime dance, and when I asked an Uzbek in the seat next to mine what had provoked the loud merriment, he tossed his head and laughed. A Russian woman who overheard the question interposed with an explanation of her own. "You never know when an Uzbek will laugh, but once he starts he doesn't stop." She turned to the Uzbek. "Isn't that so?" The Uzbek laughed gaily but said nothing.

"You see what I mean?" said the woman. The Uzbek laughed again. Yet when one observes them promenading in the streets and parks, they appear reserved—some even holding in check any urge to gaiety, as though to indulge in it publicly were a display of bad manners. Young or old, they seem—unlike Russians—even aware of decorum. Whatever the provocation, they do not explode into quarrels and brawls as easily as do Russians. However jammed a street-car or bus, they neither scold nor scowl at a neighbor who may jolt them or step on their toes. Despite its growing population, critical housing, and wretched transportation, Tashkent is a city of excep-tional good temper and tranquility.

The Soviet Republic of Uzbekistan was carved out of Russian Turkestan in Central Asia in 1924. In area it is about the size of California. The census of January 1959 gives it a population of 8,113,000—more than two thirds of it still living in villages. Sixty-two per cent of the population is Uzbek; 13.6 per cent is Russian, its largest minority. The other ethnic groups are Tadjiks, Tatars, Turk-menians, Kara-Kalpaks, Gypsies, Jews, and others. The city of Bo-khara shelters one of the oldest Jewish communities in the world, the Jews having been brought there by Tamerlane from Mesopotamia.

If one were to believe Soviet historians, the overwhelming mass of Uzbeks, like those of the other peoples in Russian Central Asia, welcomed the bolshevik revolution as their liberation from all the ills they had ever known. There is not a word of truth in it, though there were small groups of bolshevik enthusiasts, especially Moslem intellectuals, in their midst—even as there were larger groups who fought the bolsheviks. These peoples had always regarded Russians as aliens and conquerors who, through the years of Czarist rule, had thrust upon them over two million land-hungry settlers from European Russia. But they were all primitive peasant peoples with no experience in self-government, no significant intelligentsia, no proletarians of any consequence—only about eighteen thousand of them in Uzbekistan, half of whom (and the more skilled) were Russians.[1] They were without military training, as the Czars had exempted them from military service, and when they were mobilized for the home front in 1916, they broke into rebellion.

It is idle to speculate on what would have happened to them had the bolsheviks honestly fulfilled their pledge of nationalist self-determination. But the Red Army fought to hold the Czarist empire together, as would any Russian army. In Central Asia the native peoples were overwhelmingly suffering spectators of the civil war which the bolsheviks won.

Originally Samarkand had been the capital of Uzbekistan. But Uzbek restlessness with Russian rule caused Moscow to move the capital in 1930 to the more Russianized and more controllable Tashkent. Resentment against Moscow's policies didn't die but never menaced Kremlin rule. Nobody in Tashkent would discuss the purges of the late thirties—when, as in other parts of the Soviet Union, Communist leaders were shot. Khojayev, who had been chairman of the Council of Ministers, and Ikramov, who had been first secretary of the party, were sent to their death on the charge of pan-Turkish sympathies. Abdul Hamid Suleiman, who wrote under the pseudonym Cholpan, the most distinguished Uzbek poet in the early years of the revolution, disappeared in 1937 and has not been heard of since. Other literary figures who, like Cholpan, resented Russian domination, have likewise disappeared. Among them were Fitrat, Ramasan,

---

[1] A. Alimov, *Zavtrashny den Uzbekistana* (Moscow, 1959), p. 5.

Elbek, Ramys, Synnun, Syndig, Tahimi, Batu—names that are unknown in the Western world and that lent honor and grace to a rising school of letters in the small Asian country.

How many other Uzbeks, Communists and non-Communists, fell victim to Stalin's wrath, the outside world doesn't know, and neither Uzbek nor Russian Communists, who rule Uzbekistan now, would say a word on the subject. One of them became so irritated with me for bringing it up that he charged me with "searching for dirt to help the cause of imperialists."

Another fable Soviet historians and academicians have been at pains to promulgate is of the progressive nature of Czarist imperialism. "By becoming members of the Russian empire, the non-Russian peoples were protected from the danger of foreign enslavement and were guaranteed the fruitful influence of the advanced Russian economy and culture. All this was of *enormous* [my italics] progressive significance in the development of these peoples." This pronouncement occurs in Volume XXXVIII of the second edition of the *Bolshaya,* which went to press in 1955, two years after Stalin's tempestuous Russian chauvinism had already subsided.

But only Czarist imperialism was and still is accorded the accolade. Chekhov thought differently. In a letter to Alexander Suvorin (December 9, 1910), editor of the highly influential and reactionary *Novoye Vremya* ("New Times"), Chekhov, on his return from a long journey east which took him to Hong Kong, wrote: "I grew indignant as I listened to my Russian fellow travelers abusing the English for their exploitation of the natives. Yes, I reflected, the Englishman exploits Chinese, Sepoys, Hindus; but he also gives them roads, canals, museums, Christianity. You Russians exploit and what do you give in return?"

What indeed? The heritage of Czarist imperialism, even in the vastly re-created Tashkent of today, stares at the visitor from across the gurgling green-watered Anchor and Boz-Soo canals, which divide the city into two parts: Old Town and New Town. New Town was built by Russians for Russians. The streets are wide, the houses, mostly of one story, are of brick, the windows are high; there is space between the houses and the courtyards spill over with greenery. Old Town, though much of it has already been razed, is made up of mud huts with flat roofs, the huts so close together one has to look sharply to tell where one ends and the next begins. The streets are crooked, unpaved, and so narrow that two horse carts cannot pass each other. Under the Czars all but the few rich Uzbek traders lived in Old Town, in a congested ghetto, ever aware that Russians were their rulers and the most privileged persons in the city. As long as any part of Old Town endures, no rhetoric of ideologists and academicians can blot out of the visitor's sight the blighting neglect of Uzbeks by Czarist conquerors.

By Moscow's own admission, at the time of the bolshevik revolution only 2 per cent of the Uzbek population was literate. In 1914, again by Moscow's admission, there were only about a hundred physicians in the territory that is now Usbekistan. The railroads that the Czars built connecting Uzbekistan with European Russia facilitated the exploitation of the Asian land; its cotton, chief source of its wealth, was shipped to factories in Ivanovo, Orekhovo-Zuevo, and Moscow. There was practically no textile industry in Uzbekistan. Nor, save for the importation of American cotton seed, did the railroad usher in an age of enlightenment—it brought in few new tools to ease the toil of Uzbeks in the cotton fields; the wood-framed plow was the only one the average peasant could afford; the donkey rather than the horse was his common beast of burden.

Even Khrushchev seems to have sickened of the sublimation of Czarist imperialism into "a progressive influence." In his address at the banquet of the Asian-African writers, he pilloried imperial Russia as "a prison of peoples," which Lenin had termed it. But Kary-Niazov, the "learned" Soviet historian of Uzbek civilization, persists in the Stalinist legend that the Czarist conquest of Central Asia was of "exceptionally important and positive significance"; it put an end to "feudal" internecine wars and averted the danger of British subjugation!

But it is not what the Czars had failed to do but what the Soviets have done that makes the Uzbekistan of today, and particularly Tashkent, the Soviet show window in Asia. Not that even the reconstructed New Town holds any wonders for the Western visitor. The streets are broad, lined with trees—chestnut, poplar, elm, oak, walnut, mulberry, acacia, and others that canopy the sidewalks and protect pedestrians from the hot Central Asian sun. The twenty-five squares are spacious and the thirteen parks are finely wooded, though not as expertly cared for as in Moscow. Shallow irrigation ditches water the trees all over the city, and Uzbek love of flowers brings the Persians to mind. New Town gleams with flowers—daisies, marigolds, cockscombs, asters, hollyhocks, peonies, dahlias, and even carnations brought all the way from Armenia and hyacinths and gladiolas imported from the Caucasus. The trees, shrubs, and flowers give the city a freshness all the more pleasing because of the broiling sun.

But save for the old mosques there is nothing particularly distinctive about its new architecture, with only now and then a design reminiscent of the grandeur of ancient Uzbekistan. The Soviet spirit of harsh and ungainly austerity shines out of the mammoth new post office, the new schoolhouses, and the blocks of new apartment houses.

Yet Uzbekistan, and Tashkent in particular, furnishes a demonstration of the dynamic creativeness that the Kremlin unleashes when it sets out to reconstruct a backward and illiterate country. The philosophy that actuates the Kremlin and the methods it pursues have nothing in common with those of Homer Atkins, the engineer hero of the best-selling American novel *The Ugly American*. A forthright and vivid presentation of the problems and struggles of a backward country, the novel evokes a warm response in the reader, because Atkins sounds so eminently sensible and earthy. "You want big industry," he says, "you want big TVAs scattered all over the countryside. That takes skilled workmen and lots of money and a whole lot of production-minded people. Of course you've got hard-working people who are plenty savvy. But they don't want what you want. It takes time for that. That's why I recommend that you start small, with little things. Hell, we could build dams and roads for you—but you don't have the capacity or need for them now."

Atkins is a gradualist, who believes in building up a backward country step by step, advancing from stage to stage along with the advancement of the education and the skills of the people, never subjecting them to material privation, to shock of mind, indeed enabling them to reap immediate material rewards for their labor.

But the Kremlin rejects the philosophy and the methods of the Atkinses, whoever they may be, engineers or statesmen. It cares not for small things that bring immediate rewards to people. It aims to start big, big industry, big TVAs, big everything, whether the people want them or not. It will not wait for them to acquire skills. Learn by doing, however costly and painful the process, is the law it lays down, the command it enforces. Nothing else is of any consequence, neither material privation nor shock of mind nor agony of heart. Time, it holds, is of the essence and time doesn't wait. The backward must race against time, race and race until, at whatever sacrifice, they have made their way into the twentieth century, into the thick of the machine age and the scientific revolution of our times. Hence the accelerated Plans, the crash programs, the excruciating pace of execution, a pace that would horrify Homer Atkins but which Uzbekistan could no more escape than did any other part of the Soviet Union.

Still, Uzbekistan is a non-Slavic Asian land, and at the beginning of the Soviet revolution it was one of the most backward in Asia. This is what lends the Kremlin formula of its development global significance. Ideology aside, the formula, roughly speaking, embraces the problems of land, education, emancipation of women—always a special problem in a Moslem country—health, exploration of natural resources, electrification, industrialization, and entertainment. Though to the Kremlin the components of the formula are all of one piece, inseparable from one another, all accorded simultaneous direction, I shall survey each one separately.

Land

The climate of Uzbekistan is arid and continental, with only from three to six inches of annual rainfall. The soil is rich, but as an Uzbek saying has it, "Where the water ends, the earth ends." Without water there is no growth. Given water, Uzbekistan would bring to mind Egypt—its abundance of sunshine, about 250 days a year, its rich variety of crops: fruits, grasses, grains, with cotton as the king of crops, spoken of in Uzbekistan as in Egypt as "white gold."

The land in Czarist days was largely landlord-owned. About two thirds of the peasantry were landless or land poor. Between 1925 and 1927 the landlord estates—land and water—were confiscated and distributed among the peasantry at no cost to them. Land hungry, the peasants could only acclaim the land reform. Nothing like it had ever happened to them in all their history. They worked the fields with primitive tools. Of commercial fertilizer they knew nothing, and the only fertilizer they used was manure from livestock. But the market for cotton was ready at hand, prices were good, as they were also for silk, rice, Persian-lamb skins, for which Uzbekistan is noted.

Hardly had the peasants begun to reap the rewards of the land reform when they were driven into collectivization. At once they realized, as did the peasantry in other parts of the Soviet Union, that land reform was only a bait, heady and irresistible, at which they had snapped with the hunger of starved creatures. But once entrenched in power, the Kremlin scrapped the original commitment of individual landholding. For the Uzbek peasantry this was the most anguished moment since the rise of the bolshevik revolution. They felt cheated and betrayed. But they were helpless against the formidable forces arrayed against them, helpless to stop the confiscations and liquidations of those who were labeled kulaks, though they might only be *bedniaky* (poor folk) who raged against the forcible dispensation.

For the Kremlin, agriculturally speaking, collectivization was, of course, a means to an end, the end being state control of production and distribution, and large-scale mechanized farming.

Now, a generation later, there are in Uzbekistan 1350 collectives, some larger than others, the average encompassing 3600 acres. Plowing, seeding, cultivating, and harvesting of grains and grasses have been completely mechanized. But there is still an appalling amount of hand labor around barns, vegetable fields, above all in weeding and picking cotton.

Since the Soviets have come to power, nearly 2,000,000 acres of desert land has been newly watered. At the Irrigation Institute of Tashkent, the Uzbek assistant director told me that by 1965 water will be channeled into about 1,700,000 more acres in the so-called Hungry Steppe—the big desert within a short distance of Tashkent. He also told me that they hoped to bring water to millions of acres of pasture lands. "Do you think," he said, "that such gigantic irrigation projects could even have been conceived if our peasants had held their lands in individual proprietorship and worked only small farms, as they did before the coming of collectivization?"

A dedicated party man, he could think of state irrigation projects solely in terms of state purposes. That in other countries the state irrigated vast acreages of land that is held in private ownership or is distributed to individual farmers, was of no particular consequence to him. "Look at our results. We now plant three times as much cotton as we did in 1913, when we gathered only 518,000 metric tons. This year we'll harvest at least 900,000 metric tons, which is more than the combined harvest of Turkey, Brazil, Iran, and Pakistan. With all the new land we shall irrigate by 1965, our harvest will rise to about 4,000,000 tons. Never in the world could our peasants hope to gather such a rich harvest if they grubbed for a living with their old tools on their own small farms."

A visit to the Kyzyl kolkhoz, one of the largest and richest in Uzbekistan, brought to light the usual failing of Soviet collectivization: inefficient utilization of human labor. The kolkhoz cultivated 5880 acres, about one half in cotton, the rest in silk, grain, alfalfa, clover, sorghum, fruits, and vegetables. The labor force came to 3000 men and women! So despite tractors and other agricultural implements, one worker averaged less than two acres of cultivated land.

Even so, the cash pay for each labor day came to the equivalent of some three dollars, the highest I have known not only in Uzbekistan but anywhere in the Soviet Union.

Supplementing the cash income on the Kyzyl collective was the payment in kind for each labor day: seven pounds of grain, two and a half pounds of vegetables, eighty grams of meat—which is precious little. But each family had a kitchen garden, a small vineyard, which is as much a part of an Uzbek homestead as the house itself. Not all families had their own cows, though all were possessed of sheep and chickens.

The surprising feature of this kolkhoz was the pig farm. Moslems raising pigs! But it was chiefly for the Russian market, I was informed. To this day few Uzbeks, except some who live in the city, eat pork.

"Do many of your collectives raise pigs?" I asked.

"More and more of them are beginning to do so," the secretary answered. "Pigs bring good income," interposed another Uzbek functionary, "and the more pigs we raise, the sooner we'll beat America in the production of meat." He ended with a triumphant smile.

Education

"Do you know how our peasant signed his name in the old days?" said Dr. Abid Sudakov, the Uzbek rector of the state university of Tashkent. "He pressed the tip of his thumb to the paper. Our people were among the most neglected in Czarist Russia. Only about 2 per cent of them were literate. Now rare, very rare, is the Uzbek even in our most remote villages who cannot read and write."

A tall, slender man with lively dark eyes and thick black hair cropped short, almost like a crew cut, the rector was himself a symbol of the new age of learning that has come to his country. The son of a shoemaker, he had worked as his father's apprentice for three years. Now he is a doctor of science, his specialty being chemistry.

"Had it not been for the revolution," he said, "I would have remained a shoemaker. I could look forward to nothing else, absolutely nothing. Czarist Russia was not interested in educating Uzbeks." He paused, then resumed slowly and soberly. "When our state university was founded in 1920, we had no intelligentsia to speak of, not a single professor. Lenin sent us professors from Moscow and Leningrad to start our university, and our people were so hungry for education that we now have two state universities, one here, the other in Samarkand. We have three medical schools, independent of the universities, and thirty-six other institutions of higher learning with a total student body of seventy thousand. We train all our own specialists—physicians, teachers, engineers, scientists, scholars, agronomists, yes even writers and musicians, actors and ballet dancers. We have ample facilities to enable our boys and girls to prepare themselves for whichever profession they wish to pursue, and at no cost to themselves, not even for their keep. The stipends they receive pay for that."

A secretary entered and presented the rector with freshly arrived mail. He glanced at the envelopes, one by one, laid them aside, and dismissed the secretary. "I could talk to you for hours and hours," he resumed modestly, "of the great revolution in education since the overthrow of the Czar. It is something that I do not believe your country knows much about." He leaned back in his chair, intertwined his hands on his breast, and continued amicably. "We now have our own Academy of Sciences, our own Academy of Agricultural Sciences devoted to research in all phases of agriculture. Our Oriental Institute is stocked with one of the largest collections of oriental manuscripts in the world, over sixty thousand of them. The institute specializes in the study of Hindi, Persian, Arabic, Chinese—not only the languages but the literature and the history of the peoples who speak them."

Uzbekistan alone, preparing scholars and, no doubt, also potential political and intellectual leaders for other oriental countries! How little do the Homer Atkinses, who are honestly convinced that the step-by-step build-up of a backward country is certain to save it from Communist dictatorship—how little do they know of what is happening in this faraway Asian land!

Dr. Sudakov enlightened me on one more significant fact about Uzbekistan. "We now have over a hundred scientific institutes in my country, all doing research in every conceivable field, but with special emphasis on metallurgy, hydrology, geology, engineering, microbiology, geophysics, atomic energy, chemistry, irrigation, and other subjects that are directly related to the advancement of our material and cultural development."

"How many of your research workers are Uzbeks?" I asked.

"The overwhelming majority of them. At present we count in our country about seven thousand Uzbek scholars, two hundred of whom have doctor's degrees and two thousand of whom have degrees of candidates of science. The presidents of our two academies are Uzbeks. The rector of the University of Samarkand is, like myself, an Uzbek. The chairman of our Supreme Soviet is an Uzbek. The chairman of our economic council is an Uzbek, and surely you have heard of Mukhitdinov."

Born in 1917, Nuritdin Mukhitdinov, son of a peasant from a village on the outskirts of Tashkent, has since December 1957 been a member of the Kremlin Presidium, the highest party ruling body. An Asian and of Moslem origin, he is despite his atheism an ideal Kremlin spokesman in dealings with Asian and African countries and nationalist movements.

"We have gone a long way," said the rector as we were parting, "a very long way in education in my country."

Indeed they have. There are over 5500 public schools in the country, staffed by over 72,000 teachers, attended by 1,300,000 pupils. There are also about 100 trade and technical schools with a student body of 60,000 boys and girls.

For Uzbek children the basic language in school is Uzbek, but Russian is compulsory; so if they stay in school long enough pupils grow up to be bilingual.

One evening I made the acquaintance of an Uzbek schoolteacher and his wife, who was also teaching school. Both told me that from one end of the country to the other, men and women in their profession were making the rounds of communities and homes, in village and city, to obtain a record of older people who were still illiterate. "It's up to us teachers," said the woman, "to teach reading and writing to those who haven't yet learned it. By the time we finish our campaign we shall have 100 per cent literacy in the country."

Emancipation of Women

Walk along Old Town, the exclusively Uzbek section of Tashkent, and you will observe that most of the mud huts have no windows facing the street. In the pre-revolutionary days women were so completely segregated from men outside their own households that they were not supposed to sneak a look at any man passing the house or make it possible for him to see them, if only through a window.

Marriages were arranged by parents and the groom was obliged to pay a *kalym* (dowry) for his bride. Polygamy among the upper class who could afford it was widespread, and so were child marriages; rich men, however old, could always buy themselves young wives, often girls in their early teens.

Women, of course, wore black horsehair veils and were wholly illiterate. Only the nomad women went unveiled. They rode around the pasture lands on horseback as open-faced as men.

The revolution tore the veil off women's faces, banned polygamy, fought the *kalym*, which often enough was the whole reason parents gave a daughter in marriage to the man they chose as her husband. It was a purely monetary transaction. Now women were ordered to school.

"My grandmother," an Uzbek woman related, "cried bitter tears on the first day I went to school." That was the way it had been in many Uzbek homes. For girls to go to school and sit in the same room with boys seemed to devout Moslems "the height of sinfulness." There were times, the Uzbek woman continued, when men set their dogs on school representatives who came to enforce the new school law. "It seems incredible that such things happened, but they did. That's how powerful the resistance to the education of girls was."

Once school was opened to women they took to education almost as eagerly as men. Now Uzbekistan counts 27,000 women schoolteachers, 7000 women physicians, 2000 women engineers. Fourteen women have won the degree of doctor of science and 400 more that of candidate of science. Ten women are ministers or deputy ministers of the republic, and Yagar Nasriddinova is President of the Uzbek Republic.

Dr. Sudakov told me that his wife is a botanist and teaches in the university. They have three young children, and when I asked him who cared for them when their mother was away from home, he replied with a gay grin, "Our babushka." So in Uzbekistan, as in European Russia, the babushka lifts a heavy burden from the career woman who is away from home eight to ten hours a day.

The Uzbek family is a closely and warmly knit unit, and to this day rare is the girl, however highly educated, who—if only out of deference to her parents—will marry a man without their blessing. But once married, especially if she is a career woman, she has an easier time than her Russian sister, because Uzbek men love to cook.

Health Service

In pre-revolutionary years trachoma, malaria, diphtheria, smallpox, were widespread. These and other scourges Soviet preventive medicine has practically wiped out. The sore-eyed children with rings of flies around their eyes that are a common sight in Persian and Egyptian villages and that were equally common in Uzbek villages in the old days, one no longer observes in Uzbekistan. Children everywhere appear clean and healthy.

In 1914, on the territory that is now Uzbekistan, there were about 100 physicians and 200 assistants and some 100 hospital beds. Now there are 8800 physicians and 26,000 assistants, including midwives, which makes twelve physicians and about thirty-six assistants for every 10,000 persons. The number of hospital beds has increased to 44,500. There is not a village without some medical service or far removed from a hospital. There are in addition thirty-six health resorts and fifteen resort houses for vacationists. Medical service is free.

Exploration of Natural Resources

No iron has been discovered in Uzbekistan; it has to be imported from the Urals. Coal was known in Czarist times, but the mining of it was neglected. The quality of the coal is poor, and the Soviets too had neglected to develop the industry until the outbreak of World War II, when European industrial enterprises were transported to Uzbekistan. Now, in the basin of the Angren River, where the chief source of coal is located, the mining town of Angren has arisen and coal is being mined on an ever increasing scale, 2,860,000 tons in 1956 against only 34,000 tons in 1940. In recent years another coal basin has been uncovered and put into exploitation in the Surkhan-Darya province.

In the old days nobody had suspected that Uzbekistan was rich in copper and polymetals. "Nobody really cared," said an Uzbek scientist, "to explore our underground treasures seriously. Now in copper and polymetals we hold one of the first places in the Soviet Union." Tungsten, zinc, lead, molybdenum, antimony, are among other minerals that have either been newly discovered or are being newly mined.

Oil was discovered in the Fergana region in Czarist times, but it was feebly exploited—only 13,200 tons in 1913. With the coming of the Soviets fresh searches were made for oil and its output has been constantly rising—1,150,000 tons in 1957. Prospecting for oil never stopped. On September 27, 1960, Tass, the Soviet News Agency, announced to the world that the richest oil deposits in the whole Soviet Union have been uncovered in ancient Bokhara.

Ancient Bokhara is also the location of the most fabulous gas deposits in the Soviet Union. The discovery was first made known in 1953, and there is so much of the gas that, in addition to supplying ever growing local needs, it will be piped to the Urals, to Western Siberia, and to adjacent Central Asian Soviet republics.

Electrification

Though an arid country, the rivers that wash or flow through Uzbekistan have been spanned by networks of hydroelectric dams, and other power plants have been built that are fueled by coal. New ones that are being built are fueled by gas. About three fourths of the villages have already been electrified, a record unmatched by any other republic in the Soviet Union.

Industry

The impressive feature of the Soviet industrialization of Uzbekistan as distinguished from the Czarist, feeble as it had been, is the use of raw materials on its own territory in its own factories. Uzbekistan's raw cotton and silk are no longer shipped almost exclusively to European Russia as it had been in Czarist times. Uzbekistan has its own cotton and silk mills, among the largest in the country, and in fact holds second place to the Russian Federated Republic in the manufacture of cotton goods.

Since the rise of the Soviets 1300 large manufacturing plants, specializing in 70 industrial products, have been built in the country. Uzbekistan manufactures practically all the implements for its cotton fields. It manufactures machinery for its textile, mining, building, and chemical industries. Excavators, scrapers, cranes, bulldozers for its immense irrigation projects, are largely manufactured domestically, as is equipment for the expanding electrical industry. The Seven-Year Plan calls for an increase of 80 per cent of industrial output.

Entertainment

In the old days Moslem rites and customs forbade social relationships between the sexes, which alone was a barrier to the forms of
entertainment that had always enlivened the Russian village. Now
boys and girls mix freely and, as everywhere else in the Soviet Union,
folk singing, folk dancing, and folklore are vigorously promoted.
There are over three thousand clubhouses in the country, two thousand of them in villages, and home talent groups put on amateur
performances in song and dance, in theatricals and concerts.

Modern athletics were unknown. Now there are athletic teams all
over the country. There are football stadiums in every city and in
some villages; the one in Tashkent has a seating capacity of 60,000.

Theaters, too, except for the one semi-professional Russian theatrical company in Tashkent, were unknown. To the devout Moslem
population, theater was a house of impiety and wickedness, and so
was the cinema. Now there are twenty-six theaters in the country
for drama, musicals, variety shows, children's plays; and the inevitable
puppet theater and the no less inevitable circus. Tashkent has an
opera company, a symphony orchestra, a ballet. Uzbeks are as avid
theater- and concertgoers as are Russians.

Nor are they less avid readers of books. One sees people reading
books everywhere in Russian and in Uzbek. In 1913 there were fourteen libraries in the country. There are four thousand now. They
have their own publishing houses and their own socialist-realist literature. Yet the Uzbek reader's taste in literature seems almost as cosmo-
politan as that of the Russian reader, who prefers the old to Soviet-
style poetry and fiction. Ali-Shar Navoye (1441–1501) is to Uzbeks
their foremost poet and one of their most celebrated historical personages. If they do not know Russian they may read in their own
language Pushkin's *Eugene Onegin*, Tolstoy's *War and Peace*, the
works of other Russian classics, and some of the writings of Homer,
Euripides, Dante, Shakespeare, Goethe. *Arabian Nights* is being
published in Uzbek in ten volumes and the poetry of India's Rabin-
dranath Tagore in eight volumes.

Here then is Uzbekistan, a small Asian nation, once almost wholly unlettered, primitive, fanatically Mohammedan, living its own sequestered life, far removed from the highways of modern civilization and from the achievements of science. Now after forty-three years of revolution, it has become almost totally literate, highly industrialized, with a largely mechanized though still grossly inefficient agriculture, with its once veiled and subjected women lifted to a level of equality with men, with an impressive health service, with a network of schools, colleges, scientific institutes which—in numbers if not always in quality—rivals and possibly surpasses those in any Western country with a comparable population. Nor are the achievements of today to remain at a standstill. For the further development of Uzbekistan during the Seven-Year Plan (1959–65), the Kremlin has allotted the prodigious sum of 35,000,000,000 (old) rubles, which even at the former tourist rate of exchange of ten rubles to the dollar amounts to 3,500,000,000 dollars!

Russians, of course, have been the pioneers and the energizers, the planners and the masters. They have driven themselves and the natives without letup and without mercy, riding roughshod over age-old traditions, ruthlessly smiting down all resistance, inflicting—especially during the years of collectivization—untold misery and death. They have always been mindful of their own supreme goal: to destroy all forms of private enterprise and to convert Uzbekistan within the limits of its resources into a modern country, tightly subject to Moscow's own far-reaching purposes, internal and external. Everywhere one is continually aware of Moscow's vigilant and all-powerful domination. Uzbekistan has no voice in foreign policy, defense, security, economic aims, political control, general and specialized education. The school and college textbooks, the courses of study, the aims and methods of education, are Moscow-made. The ideology that permeates and regiments all intellectual and artistic life is Moscow-made. The newspapers and magazines, the lectures and the broadcasts, the slogans and banners, are as monotonously alike as everywhere else in the Soviet Union, and woe to the Uzbek who dares to question Moscow's omniscience or to challenge Moscow's supremacy. The "sovereign state" of Uzbekistan is no more sovereign than the province of Tula in the Russian Federated Republic.

Yet Moscow is so confident of the impression the reconstructed country produces on representatives of backward nations that it has converted Uzbekistan into a secular Mecca for them, a place that is supposed to inspire them with the justice of its own faith and the wisdom of its own methods for transforming their diseased, impoverished, superstition-ridden homelands into healthy, lettered, industrialized nations.

Both Nehru and Nasser visited Tashkent, and Moscow is keenly aware that neither India's nor Egypt's leader would sacrifice his own and his country's independence for all the cultural and material progress that Uzbekistan has achieved. With his repudiation of the precept that the end justifies the means and his faith in democratic processes, Nehru can only shrink from the relentlessness of Moscow's dictatorial rule, while Nasser with his religious ardor and his flaming spirit of nationalism can only disdain Moscow's atheism and Moscow's suppression of nationalism and sovereignty.

But with its long-range view of history and the world, Moscow is looking beyond Nehru and Nasser and nationalist leaders like them, and the question is whether Moscow is miscalculating.

One afternoon as I walked into the small dining room reserved for foreigners in the old hotel in Tashkent where I stayed, I saw seated around a table a tall, light-haired, buxom young Russian woman and three young Asians neatly dressed in Western-style clothes. The table was decorated with flowers and was set out with refreshments such as are never served to tourists who pay thirty dollars a day for accommodations. Here were platters of choice cream-colored apples, platters of grapes, platters of candy and cakes, and bottles of brandy and champagne. Speaking in low voices, the foursome seemed engaged in lively conversation, and each time they took a drink they clinked glasses, bowed and smiled to one another. Obviously the young Asians were being treated not like ordinary tourists but like cherished guests.

Later, in the lobby of the hotel, I introduced myself to the young men. One of them, who spoke excellent English, was from India, the other two—whose English was less fluent—were Indonesians. They told me they had heard so much of Uzbekistan that they wanted to see it. They had come as tourists, and as we walked along they spoke glowingly of Tashkent, the clean streets, the healthy-looking people, the absence of beggars, of men and women in rags. They knew no city like it in Asia. Then the young Indian burst out emotionally: "What do you in America know about poverty? What do any Europeans know about poverty? You all talk and write about it, but have you ever experienced it or even seen it? For real poverty you have to go to Asia or Africa—see people there in all their filth and misery, sleeping on sidewalks, eating on sidewalks, when they have anything to eat, and dying on sidewalks. What do such people care whether a country is capitalist or Communist? They were born to live, as you and I, and they cannot live. They can only suffer and die. And here—look at them, look at them"—pointing to the procession of promenaders we were passing. "Look at their clothes, their shoes, their faces. Look at the old people, the young people, the children. There is nothing like it among the natives anywhere else in Asia or anywhere in Africa."

The Indonesians didn't utter a word of dissent. I asked them if they were Communists and they all said they were not, which may or may not have been true. But the impact of Tashkent on their young minds was as powerful as it was understandable.

Yet all is not well in Uzbekistan.

24.

UZBEKISTAN
Nationalism Awake

On my first evening in Tashkent I strayed into a square which in the old days had been a noisy and smelly bazaar. Under the new dispensation it had become a neat little park, shady with trees and bright with flower beds. In its center a huge fountain cooled the air with a multitude of high-spurting jets of water, which after dark concealed lights transmuted into living rainbows. I joined the crowd around the basin, where entranced children watched wide-eyed the fairyland of light and color.

Sounds of commotion drew my attention from the gay spectacle.

A young man, a Russian and very drunk, was staggering along a path shouting, "Donkeys, that's what you Uzbeks are, and it's we Russians who are civilizing you." Some of the bystanders only laughed at him, but others responded with taunts: "Hooligan, *Samarsky*." "Shame on you, *Samarsky*." "Go home and sober up, *Samarsky*." A few muttered something about calling the militia.

It seemed incredible that a young Russian, born and educated under the Soviets, and supposedly indoctrinated with the spirit of "proletarian internationalism," should—even in drunkenness—insult Uzbeks so openly. I also wondered why Uzbeks called him *Samarsky*, obviously an epithet of contempt.

Two young men seized the drunk by the arms and led him away, and I turned to a middle-aged Uzbek who was accompanied by a boy of about ten and asked what *Samarsky* meant. He looked me up and down and asked who I was. When I told him he dismissed my question with a wave of the hand. His reluctance to answer it only heightened my curiosity, and as he appeared not unfriendly but only cautious, I stuck to him and we fell into conversation. Finally he consented to enlighten me. Uzbeks, he explained, had always been a supremely honest people; stealing was unheard of among them. That was why merchants in the bazaars didn't lock their shops and stalls for the night, and produce on stands they covered up with sacks and boards and left it unguarded. But when, in 1891, Russians from the famine-stricken province of Samara (now Kuibyshev) flocked to Tashkent, where there was food in plenty, they took to looting the bazaars, night after night. Outraged, Uzbeks began calling Russians *Samarsky*, a synonym for "thief." "It isn't a nice word," the Uzbek said, "and people shouldn't use it. But when a Russian insults us—well—you saw what happens."

That the opprobrious epithet has not fallen into disuse can only signify that old tensions have not died out. A proud people, Uzbeks obviously resent an assumption of superiority by any Russian; though nowadays, my companion begged me to believe, only uncultured Russians looked down on his people as inferiors. He might have added that official propaganda spurns the theory of inferior and superior peoples. But official insistence on Russians being "the elder brother" to racial and national minorities carries with it the implication of superiority, a concept that the average Russian does not accept but which the Kremlin persists in promulgating, though not as bumptiously as did Stalin during the postwar years.

As we walked on, the Uzbek asked how I liked Tashkent and how it compared with New York. Did I know that the American President had visited here? It turned out he meant Adlai Stevenson. Also the great American lady Eleanor Roosevelt, India's Nehru, and Egypt's Nasser had come to Tashkent. Celebrated people from all over the world were coming to the Uzbek capital, because it was such a beautiful city. I must see the new lake the young people had made with their own hands, and the new schools and the new parks and the new factories—all the things that made Tashkent such a modern and handsome city.

"Did you see the pigeons in Moscow?" asked the boy, who was the man's son.

"Yes."

"I wish we had pigeons in our streets," the boy said longingly.

"We shall, we shall," the father assured him. "If Moscow has pigeons, Tashkent shall have them. Tashkent must have the best of everything."

I had always thought that Georgians and Armenians were the most nationalistic of all non-Russian peoples in the Soviet Union. But here was an Uzbek, not an intellectual, but a worker, speaking of the Uzbek capital with the fervor of a Georgian speaking of Tiflis, the Georgian capital, or of an Armenian speaking of Erevan, the Armenian capital. Nor was he an exception. Hardly an Uzbek I met but one of the first things he asked me was how I liked "beautiful Tashkent."

Whatever may have happened to the ancient Uzbek people in Central Asia since their conquest by Russia nearly a century ago, they have remained intensely aware of their separate identity. In the course of a jovial tilt with his Uzbek interpreter, a young man fresh out of college, an American tourist, a hotelkeeper in California, jestingly remarked, "You're like all Russians."

"I'm an Uzbek," the interpreter snapped back. "Don't call me a Russian."

About one third of the population in Tashkent is Russian, and yet to this day there is little intermarriage between Russians and Uzbeks. I asked the head of the Intourist office, a scholarly Kazakh, why this was so. "You see," he replied, "there are cultural differences and it takes time to dissolve them. Uzbeks, like Kazakhs and other peoples in Central Asia, have had over a thousand years of Moslem civilization and only a short period of Soviet civilization."

A Russian woman, a schoolteacher in a Russian school in Tashkent, was more enlighteningly specific. "Older Uzbeks," she said, "oppose intermarriage. They haven't outlived the Moslem precept that non-Moslems are infidels. Though most of the young people are completely irreligious, the old feeling against intermarriage persists. I know an educated Uzbek girl, a college graduate, who was deeply in love with a Russian, a classmate in the university. But her mother strongly opposed the marriage, didn't think a Russian would make a good husband, and so the girl obediently gave up the Russian. This is all a survival of the past and it will take time to overcome it."

The impact of Russian culture is strong on all minority peoples. But neither this impact nor Kremlin political, economic, and intellectual domination necessarily means Russification, still less assimilation. True, of course, the Kremlin has defaulted in its original pledge as voiced in the declaration of the Council of People's Commissars on November 5, 1917, which among other things promised "equality and sovereignty of the nations of Russia" and the right "to free self-determination, including the right to secede and form independent states." These are hollow words, which the Kremlin has never honored, except when it was powerless to prevent it, under Lenin as well as under Stalin and Khrushchev. Russian guns have always been ready to smite down the least stir of secession, and many a Communist leader, not only in Uzbekistan but in the other four Soviet republics of Central Asia, paid with his life for evincing his displeasure with Moscow's dictatorial rule.

Nor, in moments of crisis, did the Kremlin shrink from uprooting whole nationalities from their homelands and deporting them to faraway regions. I was in the Crimea shortly after the Red Army had reconquered it. I stayed overnight with a Tatar family. The man of the house was under arrest, and his wife, a mother of three children, wept as she spoke of the impending deportation. Why, she wailed, should she and her children be punished for what had happened during the German occupation? She denied, of course, that she and her husband had co-operated with the Germans, which was the

Kremlin charge against the Crimean Tatars. But her tears were of no account to Moscow. The Crimean Tatars, the Chechen-Ingush, Balkar, Bacharay, Kalmuk peoples were forcibly deported and nobody knows of the lives that were lost during the process of deportation and resettlement. It took place in 1944, at a time when transport for civilians was disorganized, food supplies limited, and housing, even in regions untouched by war, tragically inadequate. The Volga Germans had been deported much earlier.

Soviet writers and academicians have written endless volumes about the cruelties of Western imperialists to colonial peoples and of Americans to Negroes. But not a single word have they dared to pen of the Kremlin vengeance on some of their own subject peoples, old and young, even babies in swaddling clothes. Officially these peoples ceased to exist; the second edition of the *Bolshaya* doesn't even mention them. Only after the decree of January 9, 1957, rehabilitated all but the Crimean Tatars and the Volga Germans did the *Bolshaya* in a supplementary volume (Vol. LI) resurrect them.

In time of peace and war, the Kremlin has summarily smothered the least manifestation of independence on the part of any of its non-Russian and supposedly sovereign peoples. But though leaders of these peoples speak of Russians as their "elder brothers," neither Uzbeks nor any other minority peoples have been Russianized. They insist on being what they are, members of their own national group. Despite Communist doctrine, the Soviet Union is neither a universal state nor an international community. It is an amalgamation of diverse nations, over one hundred of them, European and Asian, with Russians constituting only a little over one half of the population (55 per cent); and while the onetime internecine national feuds have been held in check or extinguished, the nationality problem still awaits a solution acceptable to the minority nations.

There is, of course, the Kremlin formula of "nationalist in form, socialist in content." What has happened in practice is that while the formula smothers the independence of non-Russian nationalities, it kindles their nationalist spirit: the urge to preserve their national identity, with a distinct history and culture of their own, in the face of the monolithic political and economic system under which they all live.

An unfailing mark of the disintegration of the nationalist spirit of a minority people is a growing disinterest in the native language, foreshadowing its eventual disuse, as is happening among the American-born children of immigrants. But this is not happening in the Soviet Union. Language in fact is the one aspect of nationalism that not even during Stalin's flamingly chauvinistic postwar years was under attack. True enough, the Russian language was glorified as "great and mighty . . . the language of socialism and therefore the language of the future." But excepting Jews, not a single minority was obliged or encouraged to abandon its native tongue.

For political reasons the Kremlin changed the Arabic alphabet of all Central Asian peoples first into Roman and later into Cyrillic, the Russian alphabet. The Kremlin thus broke an old bond with Moslem pan-Arabism and Moslem pan-Turkism and forged a fresh bond between Russians and Central Asians. Manifestly this was a form of Russification. But as an Uzbek scholar said to me, "It leaves unchanged the content and spirit of our ancient language." If the Uzbek tongue has been heavily interlarded with Russian words and expressions, so has the Russian language been with Anglo-American words and expressions, as in athletics, technology, jazz music, modern dancing, sportswear.

"What language do you speak at home?" I asked an Uzbek university instructor who spoke flawless Russian and whose wife, he told me, spoke it as flawlessly as he.

"Uzbek, of course," he replied. "It's our mother tongue. It's the first language our children learn. It's the language we love to speak among ourselves."

As I strolled among Uzbek crowds in the bazaar, the streets, the squares, the playgrounds, I heard them speak only Uzbek, though when I approached them in Russian, they readily answered me in Russian.

"I'll bet," I once twitted an Uzbek militiaman, "you cannot swear in Uzbek as you can in Russian—you know how rich Russian is in swear words."

"So is Uzbek," he replied. "It's a rich language, oh how rich!"

Rich enough for the latest Russian-Uzbek dictionary to include 50,000 words, packed into 1046 pages. Under the Czars the only dictionary was published in Samarkand in 1899 and was limited to 4000 words.

Uzbek parents may send their children to Russian schools, but even in Tashkent few do so. They prefer schools where the primary language is Uzbek. Russian is compulsory, but only those students who graduate from the ten-year schools or who have Russian playmates ever acquire a fluent knowledge of it. It is amazing how many Uzbeks, even young people, speak a broken and faulty Russian.

Significantly, Hindi is the other foreign language that school children now study. When I asked the Uzbek director of a newly built school why Hindi was taught, he replied that the pupils demanded it.

"The pupils, children—how do they know which foreign language is best for them?" I asked.

"They do," he answered, "especially the girls. They love Hindi."

One need be no diplomat to perceive in this "love" Moscow's own far-reaching aims in Asia. Now that the New Delhi Constitution has made Hindi (1950) the national language of India, it suits Moscow to make it the required foreign language in Uzbek schools.

The rector of Tashkent University informed me that students represent thirty-eight nationalities, including Chinese, and they all had to learn Russian if they didn't know it on admission. But many of the courses are in Uzbek. "I myself," he said, "teach a course in advanced chemistry in Uzbek. But we haven't textbooks in our language for all the courses we teach. We're a very large university." Uzbek applicants for admission must pass examinations in both Uzbek and Russian.

But Russian is not crowding out the native language, either in the public schools or the universities, in daily speech, in journalism, or in any other aspect of Uzbek life. Uzbek is the predominant language. In Czarist times there was only one small newspaper in the Uzbek tongue. Now, of 208 daily, weekly, and biweekly publications, 162 are in Uzbek or in Kara-Kalpak, the language of a small minority in Uzbekistan. In Tashkent the newly built opera house is shared by an Uzbek and a Russian opera company. But Uzbeks have their own Hamza drama theater, their own Mukimi musical-comedy theater, their own motion picture studios, which specialize in Uzbek themes, modern and historical. They also have their own publishing houses, which in 1958 brought out twenty million books and pamphlets, overwhelmingly in the Uzbek language.

Again and again I was asked, "Have you read our great poet Ali-

Shar Navoye?" and each time I had to confess that I had only heard of the poet but never had read him. My interrogators appeared as astounded as Russians would be had I told them I had never read Pushkin. To them, Navoye is their greatest literary hero, and one of the most distinguished figures in their history. A leading street in Tashkent is named after him; so is the state opera house and the university at Samarkand. Abiak, who translated Pushkin's *Eugene Onegin* into Uzbek, wrote a long novel on the life and times of Navoye, and the playwrights Uigin and Sultanov jointly wrote a play on the same theme. Not a peasant or factory worker, I was told, but knows by heart Navoye's verses, and at the *chaikhana* (teahouse) Uzbeks recite his poetry and quote verses to support this or that argument. In conversations with Uzbeks, even with intellectuals, I rarely heard any mention of Pushkin. Navoye was their Pushkin.

In like manner the Kremlin not only sanctions but fosters Uzbek folklore, though it vigilantly censors derogatory references to Russia and Russians, glorification of nationalism, and any allusions to independence. These reservations aside, the Kremlin has made a cult of folk arts, in whatever form, and especially in song, story, and dance. Children respond to it as readily as adults, intellectuals as spontaneously as peasants. The one performance I witnessed in an outdoor theater in Tashkent drew an enormous crowd, and while some of the numbers were beyond my comprehension, the audience was rapt with attention. The brilliant costumes, the chants, the dialogues, the pantomime of the dancers, the ancient musical instruments, the sensational solo beating of the drum, evoked an enthusiastic response from the spectators. They were getting glimpses into their history, their culture, their arts, into the wisdom and the foibles of their people, presented by their own inimitable performers, and how could they help warming to it all? By its very nature, folklore, in whatever form, is the most universally nationalistic mode of self-expression and only heightens the nationalistic sentiments of a people.

What further intensifies these sentiments is the passionate attachment of Uzbeks to their country. An instructor in mathematics who had studied in Moscow assured me that he could never be happy living in the Soviet capital. Unlike Russians, to whom Moscow is the country's glamor city, in which they yearn to live, Uzbeks are not lured by it. They love the sun, the scenery, the trees, the flowers, the customs, the cuisine, the rich variety of fresh fruits and vegetables of their land to the exclusion of other parts of the Soviet Union. To them *rodina* is not the Soviet Union, but their own homeland, in which they have roots, deep down in its very soil and in its history.

But it is not only language, folklore, customs, love of country, historical origin, and tradition that have kept alive their national spirit. Official propaganda that Uzbeks, like any other minority, like Russians themselves, are "an independent and sovereign" people heightens the awareness and deepens the sentiment of a separate and distinctive identity. The disparity between verbal commitment and practical fulfillment on the subject of nationality remains an unresolved contradiction.

Uzbeks are in fact much more nationalistic now than they were under the Czars. In those times, backward as they were, they thought of themselves as apart and different from Russians by reason of their racial origin, their history, their religion, their way of life, the very food they ate and the clothes they wore. Now that they have attained a level of economic and cultural development more or less comparable to that of their "elder brother," their sense of nationhood has taken an intellectual and emotional turn that is new to them. I could sense it in all the conversations I held with Uzbeks, official and unofficial; in the pride with which they spoke of "our" factories, "our" schools, "our" theaters, "our" great Ali-Shar Navoye, whom they know and cherish now as they had not done for centuries. These are all new features, in truth high marks in their civilization, which they couldn't have envisioned in pre-revolutionary times. Education and industrialization, even as in Western countries, have given nationalism a fresh meaning and a fresh strength. Nuritdin Mukhitdinov, the Uzbek member of the Kremlin Presidium, may boast, as he did at the Twenty-first Party Congress, that the citizenry in all Soviet republics is educated "in the spirit of proletarian internationalism," but in his own country, as in all other republics, nationalism rides high, uncomfortably high for the Kremlin.

One evening as I was sauntering around a park, I became acquainted with a Russian oil engineer who worked in the Uzbek oil fields. We talked about Uzbeks, and in the course of the conversation he said, "They're a very clannish people." Elucidating, he went on. "They favor their own in promotions to better jobs."

"You mean," I said, "they discriminate against Russians?"

"That's precisely what I mean," he answered. "Nationalism has gone to their heads."

Another Russian, a schoolteacher, confirmed the engineer's arraignment, though without rancor. "Let Uzbeks," he said goodnaturedly, "take over everything. The Soviet Union is so big that a Russian can always find work to suit his skills and his gifts."

Moscow, of course, controls all political, economic, and military affairs. The first secretary of the party, the Premier, the chairman of the economic council, all but two members of the Politburo, are Uzbeks. Even the Minister of Internal Affairs is an Uzbek. Moscow appoints them, though not always directly, and Moscow purges them when they fail to obey its commands or achieve its aims. But a multitude of other positions, rich plums in the economy and culture of the country, are locally controlled. Uzbeks covet these plums for themselves and get them because Uzbeks usually favor Uzbeks—blood being thicker than the water of proletarian internationalism. Moscow is fighting this favoritism, and not only in Uzbekistan, but the practice persists.

The real man of power in Uzbekistan is not the first but the second party secretary, and he is a Russian. Roman Melnikov held that position for ten years (1949–59). Fyodor Titov, who has replaced him, was first party secretary in the Ivanovo province, famed for its textile industry. During Melnikov's term of office there were four changes of first secretaries, all of them Uzbeks. The Uzbeks went but the Russian remained, though in the instance of Mukhitdinov, who was first party secretary in 1955–57, the replacement was occasioned by his advancement to membership in the all-powerful Kremlin Presidium.

Ever since the founding of the Uzbek Republic, it has suffered its share of purges, not only of the first party secretary but of other high functionaries and of eminent literary figures, on the charge of "bourgeois nationalism." The latest purge occurred in March 1959, when Sabir Makalov, first secretary of the party, and Mizra Akhmedov, the Premier, were ousted from office. Only two months earlier Makalov was one of the heroes of the Twenty-first Party Congress. Suddenly he fell from grace, fell into oblivion, as did Akhmedov.

It appears now that whatever their executive or ideological short-comings, Makalov and Akhmedov were scapegoats for a nationalist unrest that was beyond their control. That was why in August 1959 the Central Committee of the party called the most extraordinary conference that has ever been held in Uzbekistan. The Central Committee invited 1200 foremost leaders, not only in the party but in the Army, education, industry, journalism, the arts and sciences, to condemn and smite down "bourgeois nationalism" for the nth time since the rise of the Uzbek Republic. But the beast refuses to stay smitten. "The most important problem," reads the resolution of the afore-mentioned conference (*Pravda*, August 13, 1959), "is . . . to further strengthen the monolithic unity of the Uzbek people with the Great Russian and other peoples in the country—to educate workers in the spirit of the Leninist ideas of proletarian international-ism and to promote an attitude of intolerance toward the least demonstration of local loyalty."

The resolution dramatizes strains between Tashkent and Moscow, whose contrived "proletarian internationalism" has neither absorbed nor transcended local loyalties. In his speech at the Twenty-first Party Congress, Mukhitdinov laid the blame on "the pernicious in-fluence of imperialist propaganda"; but he didn't explain how in the face of rigorous Kremlin censorship and of the enforced geographic isolation of the country from the whole outside world, the message of the imperialists reaches the ears and the minds of the Uzbek or any other people. Nor did he explain how it happens that it is more persuasive than all Soviet teaching in and out of school, in factory and on farm, in laboratory and office, through the written and spoken word, on the sin of "bourgeois nationalism" and on the virtues of "proletarian internationalism."

The fact is that Uzbeks are now an educated people and are asking questions and indulging in actions, openly and covertly, that annoy and anger the Kremlin. Students in particular are harshly critical. "Moscow decides everything," a student complained to me. "Why should it? It makes us Uzbeks feel as though we haven't yet learned the alphabet."

Another student said, "Moscow has opened our country to foreign tourists and we're happy it did. For the first time in our lives we see

Westerners in the flesh and they see us in the flesh. But what do we know about the West? What do we know about America?"

"*Pravda*," I said, "writes a lot about America; it has its own correspondents there."

"That's not enough," he protested. "Lots of Americans are coming to our country, but we cannot go to America and see for ourselves what the country is like."

There is no danger of Uzbekistan breaking away from the Soviet Union. The Soviet army in Central Asia, which goes by the old name of the Turkistan Army, is under Russian command and would quickly suppress an insurrection, were it ever attempted, which to me is inconceivable. Uzbekistan is so tightly linked to the economy of the Soviet Union that it wouldn't be easy for it to replace the Russian market for its cotton, its prodigious deposits of natural gas, and the newly discovered oil in Bokhara.

If there is a separatist movement in the country it must be confined to the older generation, the dying generation, who may still cherish vivid memories of pan-Moslemism or pan-Turkism. But the young generation knows little or nothing of these movements. I never heard any young people allude to them. But it is increasingly resentful of Moscow's tight control of their country and their lives.

Nor is Uzbekistan the only nationalist minority that shares this resentment; witness the periodic purges of leaders now in Turkmenistan, now in Kazakhstan, now in Latvia, now in Moldavia, now in Azerbaijan, now in some other minority country, on the charge of "bourgeois nationalism."

One can only conclude that despite Moscow's achievements in industrializing and educating the nationalist minorities, it has failed to solve the nationalist problem on terms that gratify these minorities. In truth, the more industrialized and educated they become, the more they are driven to ask challenging questions to which Moscow has only rhetorical answers. But the questions persist and cannot, in my judgment, be answered until the distant day—should it ever arrive—when the Soviet Union becomes a genuine Commonwealth of Nations.

PART V

IMPERIALISM

25.

POLAND AND CZECHOSLOVAKIA

The moment the twin-motored plane from Moscow to Warsaw rose above the airport, I felt that I was already out of the Soviet Union. Here inside, the contrast between the two Communist cultures, Polish and Russian, was vividly manifest; and the immediate cause of my awareness of the contrast was the Polish stewardess, a tall slender girl with sparkling brown eyes and wearing a Western-style uniform with pilot's cap.

Unlike the Russian stewardess on the plane from Helsinki to Leningrad, the Polish girl was at ease with herself and with the passengers, most of whom were Germans and Americans. There was grace in her carriage, friendliness in her manner, self-assurance in her smile. She didn't hold aloof from foreigners as the Russian girl had done. Though a poor linguist, speaking neither English nor German fluently, she gladly answered our questions, whether about the flight itself or about life in Poland. When I told her I had once been in Zakopane and liked it, she appeared pleased and urged me to revisit the well-known Polish year-round mountain resort. She was as free from the self-imposed restraint of the Russian stewardess as any American or British stewardess. Once she came over and we spoke at some length of Warsaw, Moscow, New York. Whatever the indoctrination she had received, it was obvious that warnings to be on her guard against "foreign spies," "ideological enemies," and other villainous foreigners had not been a part of it.

Once on Polish soil, other contrasts showed up at every step. At the Warsaw airport the inspection of my baggage was as perfunctory as it had been in Leningrad. But the inspector, wearing civilian clothes, lingered over my baggage to chat with me, which his counterpart in the Soviet border cities would never have done, even with Russian-speaking foreigners. The uniformed Russian official is always aware of his position and is always conscious of the foreigner, giving him the feeling that some invisible wall stands between them.

As the customs inspector and I were talking, a young woman came over and, introducing herself as a representative of Orbis, the Polish tourist agency, smilingly inquired whether I was a tourist. I replied that I was a journalist, and she asked whether I had a hotel reservation. I told her I had. Did I expect to travel in Poland? Yes, I did. "Get in touch with us," she said, "and we'll be glad to make all arrangements for you." No, there were no forbidden zones in Poland, she assured me, and as she left she again reminded me that Orbis was at my service and would do all it could to make me comfortable. Ordinary business courtesy was not a lost art in Warsaw as it was in Moscow, whose hopeless Intourist hadn't even troubled to inform me that it had been instructed by the Press Department to extend my visa for an additional month. I was already prepared to leave the country when, on the insistence of a veteran correspondent in Moscow, I telephoned the Press Department and was informed it had instructed Intourist three days before to extend my stay.

The Orbis representative managed to look chic in a simple cotton dress. Her coiffure, a pile of carefully tousled hair, was copied from Brigitte Bardot, whose frank flaunting of sex makes her pictures taboo in Moscow. As I drove to the hotel I observed that, poor as Warsaw was, with war-bombed buildings still awaiting demolition or rehabilitation, and somnolent as the city appeared compared to the crackling vitality of Moscow, young women in the streets were smartly dressed. It is not because Poland manufactures higher-quality textiles than does the Soviet Union, but because Polish girls are more shapely than Russian girls and because their dresses were attractively cut and fitted to their figures. I also observed that Brigitte Bardot's coiffure had caught the fancy of a conspicuous number of Polish young women.

White-collar men, too, were neatly tailored. It would be unthinkable for a Polish Communist newspaper to give space to disquisitions on the proper width of trousers, or for young vigilantes to seize youthful workers and college students on the street, ripping up their trousers because they disapproved of their style or clipping their heads because they disapproved of their haircuts. Here young men wore blue jeans and snug-fitting trousers, and now and then a girl appeared in slacks, but nobody cared. There was no talk of kowtowing to the West, because Warsaw had always been Western and in the prewar years its women were among the most fashionably dressed in Europe. In the Polish capital style of dress or haircut, jazz, rock 'n' roll, cha-cha, hula hoop, were no ideological problems. They were matters of personal taste and discretion. Even on the surface Warsaw appeared more mature than Moscow.

On my arrival at the Bristol Hotel, I saw non-Communist French and English newspapers. After two months of travel in the Soviet Union, the sight of these papers gave cheering reassurance that I was no longer isolated from the outside world.

I went walking, and passing a bookshop on Nowy Swiat, one of Warsaw's finest avenues, I saw in the window a display of Bibles, something one never sees in Moscow. In the bookshops here I was free, as I was not in Moscow, to roam around the stacks as at Foyle's in London or Brentano's in New York; salespeople were friendly and knowledgeable; Camus, Kafka, Simone de Beauvoir, Joyce, and Proust —whom Moscow officially execrates as decadent and reactionary— were on display; at the Russian sections of two bookshops there was not a single customer. On inquiry I learned that Poles were buying Russian scientific and technical books but not much fiction. "Our people prefer to read Soviet fiction in Polish translation," a saleswoman said, "because they know that we translate only the best." Within only one year, from 1956 to 1957, the publication of translated Soviet works dropped from 9,500,000 to 2,800,000 copies, and it is still dropping.

In Moscow an American woman had requested me to look up a Polish friend of hers in Warsaw. I telephoned the man and he came over to my hotel room, where we spent several hours talking as freely as we might have done in any Western city. Other Poles whom I invited readily came to my hotel. Intellectuals, they were free of the pressures which inhibit most Russian intellectuals from visiting foreigners in hotels.

As I am not fluent in Polish, I requested one of my visitors to telephone the Press Department of the Foreign Office for an appointment for me. "Oh," he said, "you don't have to telephone. Warsaw isn't Moscow. Get into a cab and drive over there and someone will see you."

I did as told, and when I climbed out at the Foreign Office Building there wasn't a single police guard to be seen. Nor was there a doorman or anybody else to ask for a pass or to look at my passport. This might have been a hotel, so free was it to visitors. Passing an open door, I inquired of a typist for directions to the Press Department. She gave me the number of the room, and when I reached it and knocked on the door I was invited to enter.

Nothing like this was possible in Moscow. The personal association of foreign journalists with officers of the Press Department, including censors, that I had known on all previous visits came to an abrupt end during Stalin's postwar years and has not been revived. At diplomatic receptions the officers are friendly and even genial. They exchange pleasantries and jests. They profess good will and friendship. They make promises which you know they have no intention of keeping. Still, it is good to see them in the flesh and to hear their amiable voices. But once they are swallowed up by the labyrinthine skyscraper of the Foreign Office, which is always guarded by police, they transform themselves into what a correspondent called "machines." "When you speak to one of them on the telephone, you feel that you are speaking to a machine, and so you yourself become a machine. It's pretty dreadful, but there's nothing we can do about it."

Though Yuri Zhukov, chairman of the State Committee for Cultural Relations with Foreign Countries, has called for the clearing away of "the pernicious cold-war accretions," the Moscow Press Department has remained solidly frozen within the Stalinist cold-war mold. Why, nobody knows.

But in Warsaw, with no prearranged appointment, I was cordially received by an officer of the Press Department. He called in several officials from other departments to answer questions which he felt were beyond his competence. As we were sitting around the table talking, I asked whether any of them had read the blistering attack on Polish cultural life that had appeared in the Leningrad literary journal *Zvezda* (July 1958). The attack is headed: "On Loss of Faith in Man, on Nihilism, on the Philosophy of Despair," of which Polish intellectuals—according to the author, a certain A. Gozenpud —were unpardonably guilty.

The young Poles chuckled and told me they had read the *Zvezda* indictment, then asked whether I had read the reply in *Tribuna Literacka* ("Literary Tribune"), the weekly supplement of *Tribuna Ludu* ("People's Tribune"), the Communist daily. I replied that I had not, and they said they would mail it to me. It came the next morning, and reading it so soon after my arrival from Moscow was an enlightening experience. Despite the repression Gomulka was already imposing on the Polish intelligentsia, Communist literary spokesmen were not overawed by Russia as they had been in the years preceding their own October revolution of 1956. The rebuttal was earnest and trenchant and revealed the deep gulf that separated Communist literary spokesmen in Poland from their comrades in Russia, if comrades they are in more than name.

Among other things, *Zvezda* complained that "works of decadent bourgeois contemporary art are widely presented in the theater and on the screen in Poland and are sold in bookshops." Even a motion picture made from such a "pornographic" book as D. H. Lawrence's *Lady Chatterley's Lover*, *Zvezda* pointed out, was shown to the public.

In reply, the writer in the *Tribuna Literacka* said, "What shall we say of this judgment? . . . The sternest censor wouldn't classify the inferior and rather innocent picture *Lady Chatterley's Lover* as pornographic." Obviously, Polish Communists have no desire to emulate Moscow's official puritanism, which, incidentally, the historically non-puritanical Russian people and least of all the Soviet intelligentsia have never truly embraced.

Zvezda was particularly angered by the popularity in Poland of certain Western non-Communist writers. "Many novels, short stories, plays, by Beckett, Ionesco, Sartre, Camus, Simone de Beauvoir, Sagan, not to speak of such 'classics' as Joyce and Proust, are being translated into Polish and are published in weekly and monthly journals and books. The book market is glutted with works that popularize the philosophy of despair and hopelessness and disbelief in man, that are anti-humanistic and deny spiritual values."

"It is difficult," replied the Polish spokesman, "to agree with the author. I do not regard the translation and publication of the works of Proust, Camus, Sartre, and others as a crime against socialism. . . . Ostracism is unjustified and so is cultural autarchy. I do not esteem it proper to treat an adult reader like an adolescent who is enjoined from reading 'improper' or 'difficult' books. The fact that passages in Sartre make nasty reading is no reason for outlawing him. . . . Nobody can apply the label 'fascist' to writers like Camus, Sartre, . . . Moravia, or even to a pessimist like Beckett."

Five or six years earlier, the author went on, Polish writers had shared *Zvezda*'s attitude toward Western non-Communist writers. "Fortunately for us, we reject it now."

As a further instance of Poland's cultural degeneration, *Zvezda* pointed to the reproduction of brightly colored hotel labels in the weekly picture journal *Przekrój* ("Profile"), the most widely circulated publication in Poland. It presents the news of the world in pictures free of ideological remonstrance or exhortation, and usually sells out on the day it makes its appearance on newsstands. To *Zvezda*, the reproduction of hotel labels signalized "provincial kowtowing to the West."

But to the Polish writer in *Tribuna Literacka*, the denunciation of the picture magazine was "only an example of the way [*Zvezda*] makes truly satanic the practices of our publishers and editors. . . . Some people collect matchboxes; I do not. I laugh at the snobbery of those who collect hotel labels. But, by heaven, must I for that reason gird myself in armor . . . and throw myself into an anti-label crusade, hallowing it with loud-sounding rhetoric about the social mission of culture and art? Why should we put our nose into it? Incidentally, among the labels *Przekrój* reproduced are those of hotels in China and Hungary." Incidentally also, Moscow has not banned the sale of *Przekrój*, publishes Moravia, is at last bringing out Sagan's *Aimez-vous Brahms*, and in Odessa I was given hotel labels for my baggage.

It seemed incredible to read *Zvezda*'s denunciation of Joyce and Proust as "anti-humanistic." This was not always the Soviet attitude. Parts of Joyce's *Ulysses* were published in the Soviet Union in 1925. *Dubliners*, in a somewhat abbreviated edition, came out in 1928, and I learned that because Joyce is difficult to render into Russian, his translators were paid one and a half times as much as for any other translation from the English. As for Proust, a four-volume edition of his works, with an introduction by the late Anatoly Lunacharsky, was published as late as 1938.

I feel confident the time is not too distant when both authors will again be published in the Soviet Union. This is inevitable in the light of the rising literary standards of the reading public, which is quietly pressing for closer acquaintance with Western literature, particularly with authors whose names, like Joyce and Proust, appear—though derogatively—in Soviet literary criticism and—not so derogatively —in private conversation. Soviet ideologists still have to learn that the more violently they attack a foreign author, the more they incite the reading public to become acquainted with his work.

It is ironic for *Zvezda* to execrate Sagan and Camus when in secondhand bookshops in Moscow one can often find used French copies of their novels. Russians who read French eagerly buy them and pass them on to friends. How the novels get into bookshops is of no consequence, though it is surprising that the Security Police has not brought the bookdealers to account.

Zvezda's acrimonious denunciation of Polish cultural life stems from the assumption of Soviet ideologists that they alone have the right to interpret Communist doctrine as it applies not only to politics but to literature and other forms of art. They are "the elder brothers," and only they know what is proper and just for the people's democracies and for Communists the world over. Poles have no right to question them or to disagree with them. Only when they put their stamp of approval on Joyce and Proust may Poles read their writings, and not until then.

At a dinner party in Warsaw, I became acquainted with a Polish writer who spoke bitterly of Wladyslaw Gomulka for his persistent encroachment on the intellectual freedom of the country. "For nearly ten years," he said, "Russia kept us locked up in a jail. We broke the lock, thank God we did, but I am pained by Gomulka's retreat from the promises of our revolution of October 1956. I find it increasingly difficult to place manuscripts with our editors. I am convinced that the Russians are pressing Gomulka to lock us up again. But I do not believe that, in spite of his being a Communist, Gomulka will stand for it."

"Why do you think that?" I asked.

"Because," he replied, "we are a Western people; we have been Westerners since 966, when we were converted to Roman Catholicism. The Russians cannot remake us in their own image. Stalin tried it and failed disastrously." After a brief pause, he added, "Of course, the Russians can always turn their guns on us as they did on Hungary."

At another dinner party, I asked a Polish drama critic who was having trouble placing his articles what he thought would happen in Poland now that Gomulka was retreating from the promises of their October revolution.

Throwing up his hands, he exclaimed, "God only knows! I cannot even tell you how long the *modus vivendi* Gomulka has worked out with Khrushchev will last. But Gomulka won't live forever, nor will Khrushchev, and what will happen when either or both go—well, who knows? We don't even like to think about it."

In October 1956, Poles were ready to fight and die, even without hope of victory. Now they are merely disillusioned, especially the intelligentsia. They talk freely but they cannot write freely. The phrase "socialist realism" offends their ears, as do the rest of Moscow's dogmas about socialism, nationalism, abstract art, modern music, and religion.

"We're a hard-working people," said the drama critic, "but we don't want to be made into tools of production for Moscow or even ourselves. We're not Russians, and heaven protect us from becoming like Czechs."

There was soft music in the dining room of the Bristol Hotel. If only Moscow's Intourist hotels would follow the example! In the sidewalk cafes people were reading American and British paperbacks. The waitresses in the cafes had a ready smile for customers and served delicious pastries, which Moscow has lost the art of baking. In night clubs the atmosphere was gay, and young couples danced the cha-cha with high-spirited abandon.

Two tall, handsome African students in Warsaw went with me to several night restaurants. They spoke with admiration of the friendliness of Poles, of the charm and beauty of Polish girls, of the gay times they had at student theatrical performances and dances. "But Poles are not a happy people," one of them said. "They hate and fear

Russia." "Yes," said the other, "they are a worried people, very much worried about their future."

The indisputable fact is that Stalin's highhanded effort to force Poland into the Soviet Russian mold failed hopelessly and tragically. With the exception of the small group of hardheaded Stalinites, it antagonized every class in the country—peasants, workers, women, youth, and above all the intelligentsia. The forcible imposition on them, in the name of the brotherhood of workers, of what they regarded as a Russian-made civilization pressed painfully on every aspect of their lives. *Zvezda*'s silly reproach of *Przekrój* for reproducing hotel labels provoked widespread laughter and indignation. "You see," a Polish journalist said bitterly, "how completely they want to control us."

When I remarked that probably Russians themselves would laugh at the reproach, he replied hotly, "But you don't understand one thing about Russians: once they hold power over you, they wield it like a club. We Poles know it—how well we know it."

I reminded the excited young Pole that whenever Poles held power over Russians, they too wielded it "like a club."

"We had no Marshal Suvorov," he flung back resentfully, "who butchered our people, even the women among them, after our army surrendered in the insurrection of 1794. The Russians would like us to forget it, but we never will."

"But Khrushchev," I said, "didn't use a club. Otherwise you wouldn't be speaking to me as freely as you do."

"Khrushchev knew better," the young Pole snapped back.

In December 1959, at the time the Congress of the Polish Writers' Union witnessed the imposition of fresh curbs on creative writing, the Polish youth journal *Sztandar Mlodych* ("Banner of Youth") poled young people on a number of subjects, among them their favorite living author, painter, and motion picture actress. Hemingway was the first choice as novelist, Camus second, and Sholokhov third. They did not permit their hostility to Russia to obscure their appreciation of Russia's foremost living novelist.

Picasso was their favorite painter, and Brigitte Bardot ran away with the honor of being the most exciting girl in the world. Polish youth seem to have no more intention of yielding their beliefs than the peasant has of abandoning his Roman Catholicism. Actually, despite the new pressures on intellectuals, Poland is the freest of all Moscow's satellites. People speak freely. The peasant has been permitted to keep his land. The Communist regime has made peace with the Church, though the relationship is so uneasy that early in 1961 a new conflict erupted between Gomulka and Cardinal Wyszynski over the issue of religious instruction in the schools. Gomulka is fighting anti-Semitism, as Khrushchev is not; nor has Gomulka sundered his country from the West. On February 22, 1960, Poland renewed her agreement with the United States for the import of American books, newspapers, movies, television material, theatrical rights, musical recordings, to the amount of 1,200,000 dollars, to be paid in Polish zlotys. No other member in Moscow's "socialist camp" would dare to do this. Nor has Moscow's fierce crusade against Boris Pasternak deterred Poland from republishing his poetry, and Poland's Ministry of Defense brought out in 1960 a Polish translation of Eisenhower's *Crusade in Europe.*

The prime example of what Moscow's home-grown socialism accomplishes when imposed on a Western country is Czechoslovakia. A highly cultivated and highly industrialized country, Czechoslovakia had demonstrated, as Poland had not, remarkable capacity to rule herself by Western-style parliamentary government. Besides, by a decree for which even the Catholic party voted, it nationalized in 1945 key industries, banks, insurance companies, mines. I was in Prague at the time, and Klement Gottwald, the outstanding Communist leader, and Rudolf Slansky, the party secretary, then in Stalin's good graces, welcomed the country's evolutionary road to socialism. I interviewed both men many times, and as late as June 21, 1947, in an authorized interview with me which was published in the New York *Herald Tribune,* Gottwald said, "Dictatorship of the proletariat and the Soviet is not the only road to socialism."

Obviously neither he nor Slansky meant a word they had said in all the interviews I had with them and in all the public pronouncements they had made to the people. But the people, especially the peasantry and the intelligentsia, had taken them at their word and were firmly convinced that they were entering an era of evolutionary socialism without benefit of dictatorship, class struggle, labor camps, secret police, gallows, hate campaigns against the West, with only the friendliest sentiment for Slavic Russia, reinforced by a military alliance.

But it was not the type of socialism of which Stalin approved, or of which Khrushchev or any other Moscow bolshevik leader can approve. For one thing, Czechoslovakia remained independent of Moscow's political, intellectual, and economic domination. For another thing, a large section of the country's economy, including agriculture, remained in private ownership, which contradicts Moscow's own brand of nationalist socialism.

This is not the place to tell the story of the Communist coup in February 1948. But once the Communists seized power, they hastened to convert the country into a Soviet-style police state, fortified with formidable instruments of suppression, including the gallows. Step by step they proceeded to wreck the structure of Czechoslovak civilization and to erect in its place a Kremlin-conceived society, closely modeled on the Soviet Union. The trade unions were completely stripped of power and forged into tools of the state, and, as in the Soviet Union, were used to promote the very speed-up system of work the Communists had loudly decried prior to their rise to power. Josef Kionka, the powerful Communist trade-union leader in the city of Zlín, seat of the world-famous Bata shoe industry, had told me again and again that Bata had been cruel to workers by enforcing on them speed-up systems that damaged their health. Once the Communists rose to power in Zlín (renamed Gottwaldov) socialist competition and other speed-up systems, as everywhere else in the country, became the rule and were proclaimed "the glory" of the working class. The free communication with the West that, save for the six years of Hitler's occupation, the people in all their history had never been denied, and which they had always cherished as an inalienable right, was brought to an abrupt end. Gun towers, electrified barbed-wire fences, and mine fields along the country's western borders attest to the forcible sequestration of the people from the Western world.

Education, the judiciary, political institutions, the press, literature and art, the relationship of the individual to the state, the Communists have re-created in the Soviet Russian image, with the powerful secret police always on the alert to enforce obedience and conformity.

The Czech peasant is no muzhik. He is highly literate and one of the most skilled farmers in Europe. But like the muzhik, he was driven into the collective, and to this day, despite huge investments in machinery and fertilizer, agricultural production has barely attained the level of 1938, the last free year of the first Czechoslovak Republic.

The Prague Communists boast that between 1949 and 1959 they have more than trebled the output of heavy industry. A country of only 13,500,000 people, Czechoslovakia has become a gigantic machine shop and is constantly growing. Its export trade is the highest in its history, having attained the sum of 24,000,000,000 koruny in 1959, or approximately 3,400,000,000 dollars at the official rate of exchange.

The booming industry and the Jáchymov uranium mines should have insured the people one of the highest living standards in the world. Yet if a citizen wishes to buy high-quality consumer's goods, including home-manufactured woolens, he must have dollars, pounds, or some other hard currency to pay for them in the specially established state stores called Tuzex. Other stores may or may not have these goods, but Tuzex always has them in unlimited supplies, and the price is from six to ten times lower. Neither the first nor the second Republic had ever known anything like it.

Moscow has proclaimed that its new ruble is the hardest currency in the world. But no amount of these rubles can buy a handkerchief or a pair of shoelaces in a Tuzex shop.

At one time the Soviet Union too maintained domestic export shops, called Torgsin. For gold, foreign currency, Soviet citizens might buy in Torgsin unlimited quantities of choice foods, textiles, shoes, other goods. But Moscow abolished them in 1936, and the new generation doesn't even know the meaning of the word. The second edition of the *Bolshaya* doesn't mention it, nor do the dictionaries. The word has been expunged from the Soviet vocabulary. Moscow is now too proud to acknowledge operating shops in which the ruble was of no account. But in Czechoslovakia, Tuzex is a household word signifying privilege for those who have friends or relatives in capitalist countries. Despite its stupendous foreign trade, the Prague government is continually short of foreign exchange and must coax as much as it can from the relatives of citizens in hard-currency countries.

I have before me the Tuzex 1960 circular for Christmas gift parcels, which its New York office has mailed out to prospective clients. Impressive is the list of goods which highly industrialized Czechoslovakia, whose factory workers are far more productive than Soviet workers, offers to those citizens lucky enough to obtain dollars from their American friends and relatives. I shall set down only a partial list of these goods: cocoa, coffee, sugar, rice, sardines, milk chocolate, lard, export ham, tea, fruit juices, walnuts, almonds, special pork sausage, imported olive oil, *slivovice* (plum brandy), figs, dates, walnuts, raisins, and even lipstick, nylon stockings, and Gillette razor blades.

The list of textiles and clothes includes: waterproofs, pure-wool pullovers, cardigans, overcoats, suits, trousers, pajamas, leather coats, tweed jackets, cashmere scarves, socks, shirts, pure-silk and cashmere dress materials, woolen blankets, pure-woolen cloth, cotton or linen sheeting.

For dollars the state store will sell to a citizen, without need to wait for a priority: gasoline coupons, motor oil, domestic and foreign automobiles, typewriters, building and construction materials, furniture, motorcycles, electric appliances, accordions, pianos.

A paragraph in the circular reads: "The price list gives only an indication of the large selection of merchandise available. Actually, thousands of items could not be listed for lack of space."

It was strange and exciting to find myself back in Prague, in July 1960, after an absence of thirteen years. In the days before the Communist seizure of power, Czechoslovakia had been my favorite European country. I had many friends there and had written three books about it. But after the *Putsch* not one of my friends dared to send me even a Christmas card, and at the Slansky purge trial I was denounced as "an American spy." I had resigned myself to the conviction that never again would I be permitted to set foot in the little country I loved; but with the advent of Khrushchev, the Prague Communists, ever responsive to the winds that blow from Moscow, followed the Kremlin's example and opened the country to tourists, even to those whom they had denounced as spies.

On the Moscow–Prague plane I became acquainted with a young Catholic priest from San Francisco. Like myself, he had paid for his tour in dollars. We were in the hands of Cedok, the state tourist agency, but when we came down at the airport there was no one to meet us. An official there told us to take the bus to the air terminal, where a Cedok representative would, he assured us, be on hand to look after our needs. But no one was expecting us at the terminal either, and we were advised to take a taxi to the agency's office. The priest and I agreed that Cedok was even more incompetent than Moscow's Intourist, which at least never fails to meet arriving foreigners and assign them to their quarters.

When we drove up to the Cedok office, we asked the taxi driver what our fare was. "An American dollar, if you have one," he said. We gave him a dollar and to our surprise he pressed it to his lips. For the dollar he could buy something in a Tuzex store that was unavailable elsewhere, or was much cheaper.

Later I asked an old friend what was happening to Czech trade balances and where the profits of their enormous foreign trade were going. He smiled ironically and replied, "Do you suppose we sell for dollars? In my country it's politics, not dollars, that counts. Do you understand what I mean?"

The meaning was unmistakable. Moscow is exploiting Czechoslovakia for the promotion of its foreign policy and its quest for world power. It is Moscow's mighty arsenal of armaments for nations which it is to Moscow's interest to arm. It is a gigantic manufacturer of machinery, not only for the Soviet Union and other satellites but for underdeveloped countries that Moscow is seeking to draw into its own political orbit. Moscow's will and Moscow's goals are more important to the Prague Communist dictatorship than is the hard currency that might be obtained in exchange for products from its ever expanding, highly organized, and efficiently managed industries. "Colonialism" is a dirty word in the Soviet vocabulary, but a taxi driver kissing an American dollar bill which he could spend in a Tuzex store only dramatizes the magnitude of Moscow's exploitation of the small Slavic country.

"Tell me," I asked my friend, "how was it possible that Czechs, of all people, could have staged before the whole world such an orgy of anti-Semitism as the Slansky purge trial?"

Immediately on the defensive, he replied, "Don't blame us, blame Moscow. The NKVD did it. From a list of some fifty political offenders, they deliberately selected eleven Jews and only three non-Jews. But I can assure you of this—Moscow hasn't infected us with anti-Semitism. Look here," he continued excitedly, "we translated Ann Frank's *Diary* and played it before packed audiences all over the country. Go to the synagogue and on the walls you'll see inscribed the names of seventy thousand Jews who lost their lives in Hitler's gas chambers. We're constantly adding new names as soon as we learn of them." Suddenly he arose, walked to the bookshelf, and took down a volume. It was handsomely bound and well printed, with fine color plates. The book was an English translation of poems and prose writings, illustrated with drawings and paintings, all the work of Jewish children awaiting the end in the Terezín concentration camps. "Every one of these children died in the gas chambers. But we're honoring their memories so that something of them shouldn't die. You've just come from Moscow: did you see anything like this there?"

He sat down and was silent for a while as I went on turning the leaves of the lovely and tragic book. Then he said, "The Slansky trial stirred up no anti-Semitism among us. It sickened us. Even the Communists are ashamed of it. That's why they published this book and translated it into English, French, and German. They want the world to forget the anti-Semitism in the Slansky trial. But—" He lifted his hands in a gesture of helplessness. "What could we do? Moscow wanted it, and what Moscow wants here, Moscow gets." Then, jabbing the air with a forefinger, he went on. "Do you suppose we Czechs would have embalmed Gottwald's body and put it in a glass case for the public to admire? Absurd, absurd!"

The conversation took place in my friend's home on the outskirts of the city. When I telephoned him to announce my arrival in Prague, he immediately and with cordial insistence invited me over. Without exception all my old friends behaved the same way. Without the slightest hesitation they invited me to their homes and came to my hotel, though they had to leave their red identity cards with the porter. In New York I had been told that Czechs were cautious about associating with foreigners. Manifestly this was no longer true. But I was saddened at listening to a highly educated Czech apologize for his countrymen while placing the blame for all the unpleasantness on Moscow. I recalled the remark of a friend in Warsaw who had said, "The difference between us and the Czechs is that while we Poles are willing to die for our country, the Czechs are only willing to live for theirs."

Widespread is the opinion in the Western world that, unlike Poles and Yugoslavs, Czechs appear as if born without a fighting spirit. But I was in Prague during the fateful Munich days in September 1938, when the French and the British issued an ultimatum to Beneš: unless he agreed to the severance of the Sudetenland from the Republic, they wouldn't support him in the event of attack by Nazi Germany. Beneš yielded, and as soon as the radio broadcast the news of Beneš's submission, the people swarmed into the streets of Prague, shouting, clamoring, and begging for arms, ready to stand alone against the Wehrmacht. They had no hope of help from Russia, the Kremlin having declared that it would not send aid if France reneged on its military alliance with Czechoslovakia—which, in joining the British in the ultimatum, France had done. Yet not only in Prague but all over the country, the people were ready and determined to fight; they lacked not spirit but guns. But the Beneš government stood by the agreement with the British and the French, and the country was first dismembered and then occupied by the Germans for six years. The Czechs never recovered from the blow. The fighting spirit went out of them and they became resigned and submissive.

Yet one cannot dismiss as mere fantasy the remark of the Pole that, unlike his people, Czechs do not easily grow desperate and take to guns against an oppressor. By telling Khrushchev that his people, including workers, were ready to fight when the Soviet Army was closing in on Warsaw, Gomulka frightened Khrushchev into retreat. But the Czech Communist leaders are the most servile of any in Moscow's satellites, and the people have acquiesced in the servility.

When I spoke of this to an elderly Czech woman who on my previous visit to Prague often invited me to her home for dinner, she replied significantly, "I want to tell you something. German tourists come for weekends to Karlovy Vary [Carlsbad] and quite often leave Nazi stickers in their rooms. How do you suppose we feel about it? Of course the Russians exploit us, and our Communists keep saying all the time their hearts are in Moscow—they wouldn't even take down the monstrous statue of Stalin. But the Russian Army will defend us. We have no choice but to stick with the Russians." And how remorselessly Moscow takes advantage of Czechoslovakia's understandable fear of Germany.

Not even at the select Alcron Hotel, where I stayed, was an orange, a lemon, a pear, a peach, or even an apple to be had. A city that had always been plentifully supplied with fruits during the summer months was now even more without fruit than Moscow. The cherry season was over, and the Prague dictatorship wouldn't spend foreign exchange for the import of fruits, not even for guests who paid dollars for their hotel accommodations. Otherwise there seemed plenty of food in Prague. Prices of bread, potatoes, milk, were low, but butter was 40 koruny a kilo (or the equivalent, at the tourist rate of exchange, of $1.80 a pound). Chicken was 23 koruny a kilo (or $1.05 a pound), and the famed Prague ham, whenever it was available, 60 koruny a kilo (or $2.70 a pound). Since the average wage of industrial workers was some 1325 koruny a month, the head of a family couldn't feed his household unless his wife worked. Never before in Czech history did married women work in such large numbers as they now do.

"Eating," an old acquaintance said to me, "is our national disaster —we love it so much. We have to have our meat and dumplings, our sausage and pastry." There was no shortage of either in the automats —Czech-style cafeterias, which were always crowded.

"At Christmas time," the man went on, "we even get oranges and lemons. So you see, we don't do too badly. But the one thing we miss and don't forget is freedom to travel. Oh yes, some of us can get visas to Vienna or can join a conducted tourist group to Paris, but we can't go to Yugoslavia's sea resorts as we used to do in the old days. How we loved to go there for our vacations! But— Yugoslavia is 'revisionist,' and leave it to our Communists to outdo even Russians in their hostility to Yugoslavia. But remember this: no matter what *Pravda* or our own *Rudé Právo* ["Red Justice"] writes against Tito and his people, they cannot make us hate them, no they cannot."

By comparison with Moscow, Prague was better fed and better dressed. But the expert tailoring of men's clothes for which Prague was formerly noted was nowhere in evidence: suits were baggy and ill fitting. In the lobby of the Alcron Hotel I heard a Czech-American garment manufacturer say he couldn't give away the kind of clothes they made in Czechoslovakia: the cloth, he said, was coarse and the tailoring shoddy. The best home-manufactured cloth goes either to Tuzex stores or is exported, and Czechs who have only koruny can rarely buy it.

"What's happened to your famous tailors?" I asked an old friend, a retired schoolteacher.

"The older ones have retired and the younger ones have gone into factories," came the reply, "where their skills don't count, and frankly they don't give a damn."

The poor tailoring was further emphasized by neglect and sloppiness. "The men look," I said, "as though they slept in their clothes."

"That's because they don't really care," replied the teacher. "We've become indifferent to the finer things in life." Other Czechs made similar replies.

As the teacher and I walked along, we passed men who were unshaved. At a corner a tourist bus stopped, and the driver's face was dark with stubble and his hair uncombed. "Czechs were never like that," said my companion. "Food is the one thing they care most about, and as long as our workers and peasants have their five meals a day, often very poor meals, neither Moscow nor our Communists have anything to worry about. Of course, there are shortages of meat, except for those who get dollars from American relatives, and the new farming system has created havoc with the supply of fresh vegetables, even in Prague. People grumble all the time, but in the autumn we get vegetables and grapes from Bulgaria and we have our own apples. So we get along, better this year than last. As for myself, the one thing I miss most is the books I'd like to read. Recently one of our magazines published a novelette by Henry James—*The Aspern Papers*. I liked it so much that I'd like to read James's other works and so would my friends. We'd read them in English, but we can't get them. We have plenty of bookshops in Prague, but they'll take no orders, as they did in the old days, for foreign books. The same, of course, goes for non-Communist foreign newspapers. But thank God for the BBC. We'd be living in a wilderness if it wasn't for foreign broadcasts, especially the BBC. We're not supposed to listen to them, but we do."

A party member whom I knew in the pre-Communist days spoke at some length on the achievements of the Communist regime: of nurseries and kindergartens for working women; of peasants in the mountains who didn't always have shoes but were well shod now; of the benefits that intensive industrialization of backward Slovakia was bringing to the people there; of the new dignity of person that has come to workers; of the schools and colleges that children of workers were now attending and of the high positions to which they were rising. On and on he talked, and when he stopped I said, "But your workers couldn't support their families if their wives didn't work, and before your party came into power there was no Tuzex, where even your famous Prague ham and your best brands of *slivovice* can be bought only for hard currency."

"I assure you," he replied, "it's all temporary. Remember that a revolution requires sacrifices which in the future will pay high dividends."

It was sacrifices all along the line, not only in the freedom the people had known but in living standards, which, though higher than in the Soviet Union, have dropped substantially for the mass of the population since the Communists have been in power, notably in food and clothes, in housing and transportation. "It used to take me four hours to get to my native village from Prague," a matronly woman said. "Now I'm lucky if I get there in nine hours, and most of the way I have to stand. Our railroads are just terrible." This is a common complaint, and though Czechoslovakia manufactures some of the finest automobiles in Europe, the taxis in Prague are as dilapidated as those in Warsaw. Czechoslovakia also manufactures elegant buses, but the old-fashioned electric streetcars still clang along the Václavské Náměstí—Prague's leading street—as they no longer do along Leningrad's Nevsky and Moscow's Gorky Street.

It was strange to walk along the Václavské and not see a single non-Communist foreign newspaper—either on newsstands or in the lobbies of hotels. I browsed around bookshops: Moscow-approved books and none other. What a contrast to the Václavské I had known: stands piled high with newspapers and magazines from France, England, America, Germany; bookshops selling the latest publications in French, English, German, and sometimes in Italian and Spanish. Russian publications, too, were always available for readers who knew the language and cared to buy them, and so were Communist publications in foreign languages. An intellectual and book-loving people, never afraid of new ideas, always glad to welcome new movements in literature and art, Czechs were now at the mercy of Moscow's censors. The only foreign literature they may read is what Moscow permits. In one bookshop after another I was told that when a new foreign novel is published, it is immediately sold, precisely as in Moscow. But the hunger for modern foreign literature is so intense, a hunger that was always amply satisfied in pre-Communist days, that it was pathetic to hear Czechs talk about it. Books in English, French, German, that are mailed to them from abroad do not always pass the post-office censor.

In a chapter on Communist Czechoslovakia in one of his pamphlets,[1] Ilya Ehrenburg writes: "The cultural life of Czechoslovakia brings to mind a roaring mountain stream. New spectators are bursting into the theaters. The book has become a primary necessity. In Prague at every step there is a bookshop with many customers and outside several people are inevitably looking at the displays of new publications in the windows." Ehrenburg would have the Russian reader believe that this was something new in Prague, a city always famed for its bookshops, its artistic bookmaking, and its book-reading and book-buying public. Nowhere does Ehrenburg inform the reader that gone from Prague's bookshops are the racks and shelves that were once piled with new publications from Western countries. Nor does he tell the reader that even Karel Capek, Czechoslovakia's most distinguished playwright, was banned by the Prague Communist dictatorship until *Pravda* wrote a favorable article about him. The only books in English that one now sees in Prague are those published in Moscow.

On my last day in Prague an old acquaintance said, "*Pravda* has proclaimed us 'a socialist country,' so now we are no longer 'a people's democracy.' It may be that Moscow is planning to convert us into a Soviet republic. You see, we're supposed to have finished 'building socialism' and to be about ready to 'build communism,' which

[1] Ilya Ehrenburg, *Nadezhda mira* (Sovietsky Pisatel, Moscow, 1950), p. 49.

theoretically would put us on the same level as the Soviet Union. The next step is to become a Soviet republic. I can assure you that people are talking about it."

"I doubt," I said, "that Moscow will dare to do it."

"Maybe not this year or next. But people are uneasy about it. Oh well . . ." And he dismissed the subject.

But I picked it up again. "Suppose," I said, "I were to write a story for an American journal about the talk in Prague of Czechoslovakia's becoming a Soviet republic and part of the Soviet Union: what would the reaction be here?"

"You would certainly be denounced as a slanderer of both countries and as an enemy of socialism, and *Rudé Právo* would scorch you with its choicest vituperation. But when Moscow sees fit to absorb us, *Rudé Právo* will hail it as the greatest favor the Kremlin is ready to confer on us and will assure the Russians that we have always been yearning for it with all our hearts. Let me explain to you how these things work—something I've learned from my own experience. If, in a discussion with a Communist, he tells you that something is black and you reply, 'No, it's white,' he'll say, 'You don't see well; it's black, I tell you.' You assure him that there's nothing wrong with your eyesight and he'll insist that you don't see well. In the end you give in. But the next time you meet him and discuss the same subject, he'll call the identical thing white. You laugh and say, 'But last time you said it was black.' He stares at you and says, 'I'm not talking about last time, I'm talking about now and I tell you it's white.' You have no choice but to give in again. So you see that it would be quite in line for *Rudé Právo* to denounce you for being right and then to turn around and applaud Moscow for the very thing it blasted you for predicting. Truth has nothing to do with facts; truth is what Moscow tells us."

In his speech at the United Nations on September 3, 1960, Khrushchev, in his violent outburst against colonialism, cried out: "People in the colonial countries have not only been deprived of the right to independence and self-government, but their national and human feelings and dignity are insulted and flouted at every step."

Of no other country in the world is this so true as it is of Communist Czechoslovakia. "The physical man is all Moscow cares about," remarked the afore-mentioned schoolteacher. "All else is of no account." As with a surgeon's scalpel, Moscow has been striving to slash out of the minds and souls of the people their Western heritage, which Russia has never known and which holds no meaning for any Kremlin personage or Soviet ideologist.

Webster's New International Dictionary defines imperialism as "the policy, practice, or advocacy of seeking, or acquiescing in, the extention of the control, dominion, or empire of a nation." Where on the map is there an imperial power that exercises such totalitarian control of a foreign nation as does the Kremlin hierarchy over Communist Czechoslovakia? Of course, the Kremlin acts through the Prague dictatorship. But it is the Kremlin that selects the top men, holds the reins over them, and Stalin even hanged them. Had the top men in the dictatorship been party secretaries in the provinces of Stalingrad, Voronezh, Vologda, Kaluga, they couldn't have been more loyal to Kremlin behests and purposes. "When Moscow frowns our Communists jump," is the way another Czech friend phrased the servility of the Communist leadership to Moscow. So the difference between Moscow's and the old-style imperialism is purely technical.

One of my last book purchases in Moscow was the third volume of *The History of Czechoslovakia*,[2] which was published by Moscow's Academy of Sciences. On my last night in Prague I picked up the thick, richly illustrated, handsomely bound volume, which is devoted to the history of the first and second (postwar) republics and to the Communist dictatorship since its rise to power in February 1948. In the introduction I read: "Under the impact of the revolutionary ideas of the Great October [Russian] Socialist Revolution and in the setting of the disintegration of the reactionary Habsburg monarchy, the workers in the Czech and Slovak lands achieved the formation of the new national Czechoslovak state." Not a word about Tomaš Masaryk (1850–1937) and the decisive role he played, even while living in exile, in the restoration of Czechoslovakia's independence after three centuries of subjugation to the ruling house of Austria. Instead, the editors write: "The Czechoslovak bourgeoisie seized control of the new state and established a regime of cruel exploitation of workers." Throughout the book Masaryk is

[2] *Istoria Chekhoslovakii* (Iazdatelstvo Akademii Nauk SSSR, 1960).

pictured as an enemy of his people and the Communists are exalted into the true patriots who rescued workers from "capitalist exploitation" and restored the sovereignty of the country.

Masaryk was no capitalist. Son of a lowly peasant coachman, he had in his youth worked as a blacksmith's apprentice. Architect of the first Czechoslovak Republic, he was the most beloved man in the country. But however offensive it is to the nationalist sentiments of the people, Moscow's Academy of Sciences degrades him to the position of a tool of "capitalist exploiters," and the Prague Communist dictatorship is determined to obliterate his place in the hearts of his countrymen. Day after day *Rudé Právo* execrates him as "poison" for the minds of the people. While the massive statue of Stalin towers high over Prague, the memorials to Masaryk, even in villages, have been removed. Hodonín, Masaryk's birthplace in Moravia, is one of the few places where his monument still stands, and a Czech-American tourist who drove through Hodonin told me that mounted on a steel pole in front of the monument is a sign that reads: "In 1918 Masaryk contributed 200,000 koruny for the purpose of assassinating Lenin."

In all Soviet writing on Czechoslovakia, whether by the Academy of Sciences or Ilya Ehrenburg, one never reads this significant fact: A Czech worker cannot buy high-quality home-manufactured cloth for a suit for himself or a coat for his wife unless a friend or relative abroad sends hard currency for a Tuzex store; but when a shipment of the finest Czechoslovakian woolens comes to Moscow's GUM, a Russian worker, any Soviet citizen, needs no hard currency, needs only rubles, to buy all the yardage he may need.

On entering and leaving Prague, my passport was examined and stamped by "green caps," the Czech security guards. They wore identically the same uniforms as the Russian "green caps" who had passed me in and out of Leningrad and Moscow. As I was boarding the Prague–Paris plane, a "green cap" at the foot of the ramp examined my passport again, as he did that of every passenger. Another "green cap" had stationed himself at the top of the ramp and closely scrutinized every ascending man, woman, and child. In Moscow I had not observed such vigilance over departing passengers.

The plane climbed; Prague, with its river, bridges, castle, church spires, and the gigantic statue of Stalin, fell away in mist and distance. I could only think of *zlatá Praha* (golden Prague) as the saddest city I knew.

26.

IRAN AND THE BATTLE AHEAD

On the plane from Prague to Paris, I became acquainted with a young American of Czech origin, a postgraduate student in a noted American university, who was returning home a grief-stricken man. Two years earlier, while on a visit to Czechoslovakia, he had fallen in love with a girl whom the dictatorship would not permit to leave the country. For two months he had knocked on the doors of one office after another, pleaded and argued, but all in vain.

The personal ordeal of the young student high-lighted afresh the contrasts between the Czechoslovakia I had known in pre-Communist days and the Czechoslovakia I had just left. Of all the grievances one hears in Prague against the Moscow-cowed dictatorship, the ban on free travel is most bitterly resented.

On my way to Moscow I had stopped for a few days in Copenhagen. By sheer industry and intelligence the Danes have transformed their comparatively poor country, not nearly so rich in natural resources as Czechoslovakia, into one of the freest, most prosperous, most cultivated, and most agreeable in the world. Neither monarch nor university professor, neither farmer nor worker, neither shopkeeper nor clerk, has any fear of ideas, wherever they might originate, whether in the Soviet Union or in America. Like the Prague of yesterday, the Copenhagen of today hospitably receives the thoughts of all men everywhere.

Fresh from Prague, I couldn't help reflecting on what would happen to Denmark were a Moscow-dominated Communist dictatorship to seize power and rule the country. Where would Danish exports of pork and ham, of butter and cheese, of eggs and broilers, go and who would be in control of its highly efficient merchant marine, one of the largest in the world in proportion to the population? To ask the question is to answer it—Moscow would have the final say on the disposition of Danish exports and the use of its merchant marine. Living standards would no doubt remain higher than those in the Soviet Union or any of its satellites, but they would drop from what they now are, even as has happened in Czechoslovakia. Gun towers, electrified barbedwire fences, and mine fields would guard the frontiers of Denmark as they do Czechoslovakia's western border, and traffic with the free world and the civilization that has always nurtured the Danish people would come to an abrupt end. A Danish girl who might fall in love with a foreigner would suffer the torment of a thwarted love. Nor need one doubt that Moscow's Academy of Sciences would hasten to rewrite the history of Denmark as it has done that of Czechoslovakia. The new history would present the past as a time of "brutal exploitation of workers" and the sacrifice of the nation's sovereignty to "the greed of Western monopolist-imperialists," from both of which the Communist party has at last rescued the country.

Any Westerner who visits Prague can see, as in a mirror, what would happen to him and his country were a Moscow-ruled Communist dictatorship to ascend to power.

But if Czechoslovakia is the prime example of a Western country continually degraded and exploited by Moscow, Uzbekistan is an example of an underdeveloped Asian country which within a brief space of time—as time is reckoned in history—Moscow has lifted to an advanced stage of industrial development, of science and technology, skipping, as Soviet ideologists never fail to emphasize, generations of "capitalist development." The Asian, the African, the visitor from any underdeveloped country, who comes to Tashkent can only compare the miseries of his homeland with the achievements of Uzbekistan: the health of the people, the rise in living standards, the upsurge of education, technology, industry, and science. Moscow smothers the advanced Western civilization of Czechoslovakia but elevates the backward Asian civilization of Uzbekistan.

Westerners who visit the Uzbek capital may be depressed by the absence of freedom; they may be amused or sickened by official insistence that the country is freer than any non-Communist country anywhere. But in underdeveloped countries, with some notable exceptions, the primary problem is not freedom but bread.

The United Nations Review (Vol. IV, 1957) writes: "Probably half of mankind is permanently hungry. Perhaps two-thirds are illiterate, miserably poor and with a life expectancy of thirty years. . . . Until quite recently vast numbers of people in Asia, Africa and Latin America accepted these sufferings as an inevitable part of their life. Now, however, a new spirit is stirring among them"—a spirit of defiance and rebellion.

The problems in underdeveloped countries are monumental, and first and foremost is the problem of food. But food begins with land, and in most of these countries, which are preponderantly peasant, the man who works the land doesn't own it.

Long ago James Joyce wrote in *Ulysses*: "The movements which work revolutions in the world are born out of the dreams and visions in a peasant's heart on the hillside. For them the earth is not an exploitable ground but the living mother." Out of such dreams and visions exploded the bolshevik revolution in Russia and the Communist revolution in China. I must again quote Leon Trotsky, who was frank enough to admit that "if the agrarian problem as a heritage of the barbarism of old Russian history had been solved by the bourgeoisie . . . the Russian proletariat couldn't have come to power."

Land reform is still the mightiest weapon, in fact the time bomb, in the Communist arsenal. In the light of what has happened in both Russia and China, where the peasant was dispossessed of the land he was allotted and forced into state-controlled collectives or communes, the Communist pledge of free land is a travesty and a deception. But to an impoverished peasant it nevertheless spells deliverance from want; land is the "living mother" whose breast will feed him. Poorly lettered or completely illiterate, he doesn't think beyond the misery of today, beyond the acres that lie all around him that the Communists promise him free of any obligation to the landlord, and more, too: the cancellation of all his debts, whether to the landlord, the moneylender, or a bank. The appeal is too powerful to resist.

One of General MacArthur's greatest achievements in Japan was agrarian reform. Within three years (1947–49) absentee-landlordism practically disappeared from the Japanese rural scene and three million share croppers, or about one half of the nation's farmers, became landowners without battle and blood, with the expropriated landlords guaranteed indemnity. MacArthur's action wrenched from the hands of the Communists the one powerful weapon they held in their effort to win the support of the peasantry. Highly significant are the election returns for the Japanese House of Representatives of November 1960. The Communist party nominated candidates in each of the 118 electoral districts, and despite the riots they had helped to rouse against President Eisenhower's visit to Tokyo, they elected only 3 out of 467 deputies.

But in Japan, MacArthur was master of the situation and the Japanese Government honestly co-operated in terminating the heritage of land tenancy.

In contrast to Japan is Iran, the scene of a tense diplomatic duel between Washington and Moscow. For Washington, Iran is a strategic link in the chain of Western defenses against Moscow's expansionist drives. For Moscow, it is the road to the Persian Gulf, an old Russian aspiration, and also the highway to the Arab Middle East and to Africa, an undeveloped continent of untold natural wealth. America has assumed the burden of protecting the land of the Shahs from aggression by its Soviet neighbor, and Moscow is naturally striving to undermine America's strong position there. So the battle is on, though without guns, which Moscow has not dared to bring into play for fear of American retaliation.

But Iran is a sick country. Of its twenty-one million people, about 75 per cent are peasants, and those of them who live on the land have for ages been at the mercy of a feudal landlord class that has stubbornly resisted any effort at land reform, and some of whose members haven't to this day troubled to provide healthy drinking water for the people who cultivate their acres.

I have traveled widely in the Iranian countryside and must say that the condition of the peasantry is more dismal than that of the Russian muzhik in Czarist times. A larger percentage are not only illiterate but landless, without draft animals, horse or ox, without steel plows, often without wagons or carts to haul crops from the fields and without bed or table in their homes. In the rich Caspian province of Ghilan I have been in villages where people live on earth floors with mats or little rugs over the ground. There the people eat and sleep, pray and entertain; there they are born and there they die.

I was once a guest at a Christmas party given by a wealthy landowner in Teheran. My host was a charming and handsome young man, gracious as only a highly cultivated Persian can be. But I shall always remember the shock I received when I heard him speak of the villages he "owned." Though the peasant is no serf, he and his family are so bound to the land that the landlord refers to them in the same proprietary manner as to his fields or his automobile. It was so in Isfahan, in Shiraz, the most charming of old Persian cities, and everywhere else I traveled.

The forty-one-year-old Shah is a hard-working, well-educated, and enlightened ruler, with a profound sense of justice and an overpowering sympathy for the peasant. Keenly aware of the pressing need for land reform, he has begun to distribute the crown holdings of some 1,300,000 acres among the people who have been cultivating it. By the middle of 1960, about one half of the crown lands had passed into ownership of the peasantry. But the Shah, it must be said, is no General MacArthur, with neither the resolution nor the drive of the American general. Nor are there at his disposal the honest and competent administrators that served MacArthur so well in Japan. Still, his earnest effort to make a landowner of the peasant by distributing not only the crown lands but those held in public domain, is an unprecedented event in ancient Iran.

But the landlords refused to follow his example. Finally, in March 1960, the *Majlis*, or lower house of Parliament, passed a Land-Reform Act. But it is not the act that the Shah had striven to achieve. The powerful landlord group that dominates the *Majlis* has so mutilated it that one can only wonder how much of their holdings will be distributed among their share croppers. The landlords are permitted to hold 1000 acres of irrigated and 2000 acres of dry land. Nor are they obliged to sell the remainder to tenants at the price that is based on the taxes they have been paying. Since they have been among the shrewdest tax dodgers in the country, such a price would, of course, be much lower than the price in the open market. Contrary to the wishes of the Shah, they have inserted a provision into the Land Law that holdings over and above the permitted acreage may be disposed of in the open market. But as a concession to the Shah, the law obliges them to pay to the Development Bank one half the price they receive from their private sales, while the Shah contributes to the bank all payments from the sales of the crown lands. The bank in turn loans funds to peasant co-operatives at 9 per cent and finances whatever projects it seeks to promote for the advancement of agriculture.

Other provisions in the law favorable to landlords give them the right to distribute holdings among their heirs, the right to hold virgin land they plow, and to acreages which they modernize and mechanize. The Shah is dissatisfied with the Land Law of March 1960, and is determined to continue his battle against the so-called "thousand families," whose political power is enormous and who, in their effort to debase genuine land reform, have enlisted at least part of the Mohammedan clergy.

But the passage of the law, such as it is, is one thing and enforcing it is something else. Iran has an excellent income-tax law on the statute books, but the King of Kings has trouble enforcing it. There is a law making universal education obligatory, but of the some 47,000 villages in the country, only about 10,000 have primary schools and 85 per cent of the soldiery who come from the peasantry can neither read nor write their native language.

The Constitution presumes an honest judiciary, but the courts are riddled with corruption. "You can do nothing in this country," a resident German businessman told me, "without greasing someone's palm." I once asked a wealthy Iranian textile manufacturer why merchants, manufacturers, landlords, evaded the tax laws, and he replied, "Because we know the money will go down the sewer." This may have been only an excuse, but the fact is that the monied people in Iran are among the most cunning tax dodgers in the world. Speaking on Edward R. Murrow's television program (CBS) on December 18, 1959, Abdul Ebtehaj, one of the ablest and most public-spirited men in Iran, was constrained to say, "The tax laws are all right, but they are not carried out. People don't pay their taxes and I don't believe that sufficient efforts are made to collect taxes, especially from the wealthier classes."

How to root out the cancer of bribery and corruption from givers and takers is as vexing a problem for the Shah as is the modernization of the village. A man of courage, he is discharging corrupt officials and bribe-taking army officers all the time, but he is doing it more or less singlehandedly and is only partially successful.

Nor is there anything America, Iran's most powerful and most benevolent ally, can do about it. American advisers may counsel and persuade, but they can neither make a public issue of domestic derelictions nor exert pressure to correct them. Were they to attempt it, the press and influential personages would cry out the charge of "imperialism," "interference in internal affairs," "encroachment on sovereignty." This alone makes America's position in Iran, or in any underdeveloped country that may be sodden with corruption and enchained in feudal landlordism, indeterminate and uncertain.

America has already invested vast sums in economic and military aid to Iran. Only in Formosa does America maintain a military mission larger than the one it has in Iran to train the Shah's army of 160,000 men. The Shah has requested additional financial assistance to strengthen his defense forces and to equip his air squadrons with the newest jet fighter planes in order to offset the MIGs which Moscow had provided for the air force of neighboring Afghanistan. In the televised broadcast with Edward R. Murrow, the Shah declared that the MIGs are so superior to the American planes in his air force that an encounter with them "would be as if we tried to fight with bows and arrows against a modern tank. If we are weak, it's like an invitation to a waltz."

But while a more powerful army and more modern planes may strengthen the Shah's position in his own country and enable him to meet an attack by Afghanistan or Iraq, two unfriendly neighbors, it would solve no internal problems. Neither planes nor tanks are substitutes for schools, hospitals, land to share croppers, an incorruptible judiciary, an honest civil service. There is no military solution for the problems and conflicts that burden any underdeveloped country anywhere in the world.

One of the finest American achievements in Iran is the cleanup of the malaria-carrying mosquito which had for centuries been infecting and disabling large masses of the rural population. Point Four officials, in co-operation with the Ministry of Health, have struck hard at the pestiferous insect and are on the alert to prevent its return. But on the constructive side, the achievement of the American Near East Foundation in rural rehabilitation is an event of singular significance. Here the "ugly American" is at his modest and creative best, fulfilling his mission with energy and skill, with devotion and selflessness.

Invited in 1946 by the Shah and the Council of Ministers, the Foundation was assigned for its program five share-cropping villages in the Varamin Valley, some twenty-five miles southwest of Teheran. Fortunately for the Foundation, the lands in these villages were the property of an orphanage, so that the ever suspicious, gossipy, and impetuous Iranians, peasants and others, couldn't accuse it of having come to help landlords get richer and richer.

Only a little over a year after the work had begun, I visited the village of Mamazan, where the Foundation maintained its headquarters. To me, fresh from wandering in the Caspian countryside, Mamazan presented a new face in rural Iran: no insects in houses, no children with rings of flies around their diseased eyes, pure drinking water, sanitary latrines, irrigated and flourishing kitchen gardens, chemicals to kill ticks and other vermin on sheep and goats, imported well-laying Rhode Island Reds and Plymouth Rock hens, the traditional bathing pool sanitized, and a new school rising, the first the village had ever known. The village sparkled with new life and hope. Yet all the representatives of the Foundation did was to direct and supervise the application of new techniques in working and living, Iranian peasants themselves doing the work honestly and earnestly.

"How did you win the confidence of these suspicious Iranians?" I asked Dr. Lyle Hayden, from Pittsfield, Illinois, who was the directing head of the project.

"We didn't win it," Dr. Hayden replied, "we earned it. That's what you have to do in a country like this. People have to learn to trust you, and once they do they will not spare themselves in co-operating with you."

During the fifteen years of its work in the Varamin Valley the Foundation has ministered to 360 villages, made up chiefly of share croppers, devoting its major attention to agriculture, education, home and family welfare, sanitation, and community development.

The income of the peasantry has trebled and quadrupled. Not only men but women are becoming increasingly literate and have mastered basic rules of hygiene and prevention of disease. The tractor and the disk, sometimes co-operatively owned and sometimes hired from an individual owner, are beginning to displace human labor. More and more peasants are building new houses, which they can now afford —the Foundation has worked out special architectural plans for them. Credit co-operatives have practically banished the moneylender and the usurer. Here and there a peasant buys a table or bed or both for the first time in his life. The great rage is for radios and bicycles, and for an understandable reason: the bicycle brings nearby towns and even Teheran within reach of the rider, and the radio brings news and entertainment into the home instead of only to the teahouse.

The Foundation has demonstrated that with comparatively little money, safeguarded from grafters and under efficiently directed teamwork of villagers, a backward peasantry can make its entry into the twentieth century without political upheaval, without turbulence and bloodshed. But the Foundation has ministered to only 360 out of about 47,000 villages. Point Four, too, has made its contribution to rural welfare, and so has the Shah in villages that have benefited from the distribution of crown lands. But all these are at best only islands of comparative well-being in a vast ocean of misery. Neither the Foundation nor Point Four officials, by the nature of their foreign origin, have struck at the root of the rural problem, which is an equitable land reform.

"Do you want us to commit economic suicide?" a landlord in Isfahan once said to me when I pointed to Russia as an example of what may happen to landlords when a landless or land-poor peasantry rises up against them under the leadership of a Communist party.

It was a legitimate question, and yet in Japan landlords were paid for the land that was distributed among share croppers. But in Russia and in China, too, landlords lost not only their homes and their lands but often enough also their heads.

Not that land reform alone, even when honestly planned and efficiently executed, ever performs miracles. I have been in Iranian villages where, though peasants owned their land, they mortgaged their crops in advance to the man who sold them seed or provided the ox for field work. Without cheap credit, even landowning peasants are often obliged to place themselves at the mercy of the usurer without advanced methods of agriculture—selected seed, proper rotation of crops, modern implements, improved breeds of livestock, all of which the Near East Foundation introduced to the Varamin Valley— the peasantry is still at the mercy of intractable nature. And without an industrialization program to draw surplus population from the fields to the factory, the agrarian crisis, as population increases and families subdivide holdings, must sooner or later reassert itself with growing intensity.

In his interview with Edward R. Murrow, the Shah expressed the hope that within ten years Iran would lift the per capita annual income to some $1000 as against $120 in 1958. Were he to achieve this miracle of economic salvation, non-Communist Iran could compete effectively with Communist Uzbekistan as a show window in Asia. Though neither industry nor education nor science would be as highly advanced as in Uzbekistan, living standards would rise and the Shah would sit on a secure throne as ruler of a sovereign country whose citizens would enjoy a freedom of self-expression that Uzbeks are denied. Neither the Shah nor anybody else would ever need to bow in gratitude to an "elder brother," and delegations of representatives from Asia, Africa, and Latin America would flock to Iran for guidance and inspiration.

But the stern fact is that the land of the Shah is afflicted with illiteracy and corruption, with misery and want. The peasantry, though at last rescued from the ravages of malaria, work their land in overwhelming numbers as their ancestors did ten centuries ago, and with some notable exceptions the landed gentry hardly wish it otherwise. The modest social welfare and industrialization program that the Shah has been promoting and the project of irrigating the Khuzistan Desert, admirable as they are, are ameliorative and not transforming measures.

"Suppose," I asked Dr. Hayden, executive director of the Near East Foundation, "the Iranian Government or Washington or both of them offered your organization the sum of a hundred million dollars for the purpose of covering rural Iran with projects like the ones you've worked out in the Varamin Valley. Do you think that you could achieve similar results all over the Iranian countryside?"

"Yes," came the reply. "I'll go along with that. It would take about fifteen or twenty years, but we could do it."

The Shah would no doubt welcome such a move, but would the "thousand families"? A healthy and literate peasantry, knowledgeable in modern methods of agriculture and enjoying higher living standards, would be a new political power. On election day they would cast their ballots, not as the landlord's agent or the landlord himself might direct, but as their own interests would dictate. They would break the political power of the landed gentry, and the *Majlis* would no longer be in a position to emasculate a genuine land reform and other measures intended to lift the countryside from centuries-old stagnation and adversity.

It would be fatuous to assume that a Communist *Putsch* is inevitable in Iran. All one can say is that with conditions as they are, with poverty, disease, a high death rate, illiteracy, corruption, landlordism, however modified by the law of March 1960, pressing on the many-millioned peasantry, and with the ever growing number of high school and college graduates unable to find a place for themselves in Iranian society, the country is not invulnerable to a Communist or some other social explosion. In August 1953, when Dr. Mohammed Mossadegh was Premier, uprisings erupted and the Shah was compelled to flee his homeland. Loyal generals came to his rescue and brought him back to the throne. But the internal tensions and conflicts persist, however valiantly the Shah may be struggling to ease or subdue them.

The prestige of the King of Kings among the people is enormous. But prestige alone, as foreign journalists have not hesitated to tell Iranian diplomats, solves no problems, cannot, for one thing, allay the restlessness of the educated youth who find no adequate outlets for their talents and energies in the landlord-ridden country. Unlike Egypt's Nasser, the Shah has failed to rouse in this youth a spirit of national mission, a sense of dedication to high national purpose. A floundering and frustrated youth, one never can tell when despite a rigid police system an emergency will arise that will inflame them into rebellion, which may or may not be allied with the Communist movement. In any backward country the student youth of today is one of its most explosive social forces.

Ours is a century not of proletarian but of peasant revolutions. That is why Moscow has been zealously championing the cause of colonial and backward countries, which are predominantly peasant. The non-Communist national leaders in these countries, if they are at all enlightened, cannot be ignorant of the fate that would befall them and their countries were a Kremlin-dominated dictatorship to sweep into power: independence, sovereignty, national self-determination, which the Kremlin is eloquently and sometimes frenziedly upholding, would become words empty of meaning. The principle that what is good for Russia must be good for others, the Kremlin would ruthlessly enforce and it alone would decide the meaning of the principle and the methods of application. As a first step it would barricade the country against all outside influence and association: the challenge of ideas, movements, historic experience in conflict with its own, the Kremlin never tolerates unless driven by circumstances, as in Yugoslavia, which it is powerless to master.

One cannot take seriously Khrushchev's declaration of January 6, 1961, that "all Communist parties are equal and independent," and that it is no longer necessary or even possible for Moscow to lead other Communist parties. That the Communist movement is no longer the monolith it had been in Stalin's time is incontestable. China pursues her own highly nationalistic interpretation of Marxism-Leninism. Enver Hoxha, the party secretary of remote and primitive Albania, which has no common border with the Soviet Union, vehemently supports Peking's instead of Moscow's Communist gospel. Poland in its internal policy, at least for the present, has departed markedly from Moscow's road to socialism.

But wherever Moscow has power, it tolerates no deviations from its own policies and practices. In the very speech in which he proclaimed the Communist parties as "equal and independent," Khrushchev struck out violently against Revisionists-Communists who refuse to bow to Moscow's dictates. "It can be stated with satisfaction," he said, "that the Revisionist scum has been exposed and cast out of the Communist parties." And again, "The Communist parties have unanimously condemned the Yugoslav type of present-day revisionism." In all Soviet doctrinal writing, Yugoslavia is the *bête-noir* of the Communist movement.

To assume that the Kremlin is motivated solely by an altruistic desire for the redemption of underdeveloped and colonial peoples from the historic ills that afflict them would be blindly to disregard the facts. One might argue that such was the motive in Lenin's time, but the idealism that championed "the disinherited and the downtrodden" has long ceased to govern Soviet international policy. One has only to remember Stalin's brutal attempt to subjugate Yugoslavia and Khrushchev's breakup of the general strike of workers in Hungary and of the bloodbath he unleashed in Budapest, to realize the utter mockery the Kremlin has made of its pretensions to the brotherhood of the poor the world over. Power politics alone, and first and foremost the destruction of Western prestige and influence among emergent nations, dominates Soviet policy toward Asia, Africa, and Latin America.

But it would be equally self-deluding to disregard or underestimate the Kremlin's proven ability to mobilize the energies and resources of a backward country for the solution of the ever pressing problems of bread and work, of health and education. The "thousand families" or their counterparts would have no say. They could only run for their lives. The voice of non-Communist leaders and intellectuals would be stifled. The Kremlin has had abundant experience in taming intellectuals: witness the moral and intellectual corruption of Moscow's Academy of Sciences as reflected in its published writings on foreign countries, Communist and non-Communist; witness the utter subservience of Czechoslovakia's highly developed intellectual class to Moscow precepts and demands.

But the poverty-stricken peasant is no more an intellectual than the muzhik was in Czarist times. Engaged in a perpetual struggle for physical survival, he doesn't think in terms of the political philosophy and political institutions, Western or Eastern. He is raw clay for the hands of the Kremlin-dominated Communist, eager to shape him into the Kremlin concept of the social and economic man.

Were the Westerner to apply himself to the task of regenerating the world's backward peasantry with the passion and determination the Communist gives to the effort, he could meet the challenge of the situation with infinitely more grace and humaneness than does the Communist, Russian or Chinese, and with none of the Communist's demand for sacrifice and self-abnegation and for hos-

tility to Western civilization. The unpublicized accomplishment of
the Near East Foundation in Iran is a salutary example of what Western modesty and integrity, intelligence and skill, can achieve, despite
limited funds, in a dismally backward corner of the world. In Iran's
Varamin Valley, bread and health are no longer problems to be
solved; poultry and sheep and other livestock are well protected
against the diseases that ravaged them. Primary education, so long
denied to boys and girls, is spreading through the Varamin Valley.

But these accomplishments in economic and social reconstruction,
one must repeat, are too localized to affect the national picture,
though, as previously noted, only a comparatively small outlay of
finances would be required to apply the effective pattern of reconstruction on a nation-wide scale. It would yield so much for so
little, and were the Shah to find a way of enforcing the existing
tax laws on landlords and merchants, Iran itself could raise part or all
of the funds that would be needed to execute the project.

Indeed, a project of such momentous importance could under
proper direction be exalted into an Iranian type of populism—
dedication to the redemption of peasant humanity. It would offer
the educated youth the high purpose in life which it is so sorrowfully
lacking. One needs only to spend an evening with college students
in Teheran to realize how disillusioned, indeed disgusted, they are
with the greed and the corruption they observe all about them,
and how profoundly they yearn for something to happen that would
shake youth into a transcendent national purpose. But nothing
of the kind is happening. There is no leadership to rouse the
idealism of youth, and even those who study in foreign universities
and return home eager to put their acquired knowledge and skills
to some high purpose, find themselves more often than not thwarted
by the state bureaucracy.

The Shah himself, well-meaning and earnest a ruler that he is,
has become increasingly impatient with foreign journalists who report on the more unsavory features in the Iranian national picture.
He would prefer them to write of his efforts to redeem the country
from the evils that beset it, which no honest foreign journalist
ignores. But one only has to read the beautifully written story of
the village of Sarbandan, some fifty-six miles from Teheran, by

Najmeh Najafi,[1] a highborn, American-educated young Iranian woman, to become startingly and painfully aware of the sordidness of village life. The young woman went to Sarbandan, a community of some of 1600 peasants, to help the people rise out of their poverty, superstition, and ignorance. The peasants were so poor that they couldn't afford soap and women washed clothes with polluted white sand. Eggs were a luxury, vaccination and immunization were unknown, and even in winter there were children who had no shoes and wrapped their feet in rags. "Villagers fear three things: hunger, disease, and the government agent." The government agent was, of course, the gendarme, whom the people feared as they did "the evil eye or a ghost." Of hunger she writes that "in the villages of Persia . . . it sits like a howling dog at every doorstep." Some of the peasants were share croppers, others were landholders, but they were all overawed of the landlord.

No foreign journalist could have written a more devastating picture of village life than did this highly educated, social-minded young Iranian woman.

As for unemployment in cities and villages, only a national program to promote the exploration and development of natural resources, always a primary objective in a Communist program, could grapple with it. Manifestly the Western world is in command of the equipment and the skills to match and surpass the Kremlin in the pursuit of this objective. Gifts of money, however large the sums, especially to states that are sodden with corruption, accomplish little or nothing, as America has learned. But unlike America, the Kremlin is not granting monetary gifts even to friendly non-Communist nations. Whatever the form of its aid—credits, barter, technological and scientific assistance—it is a political investment. But once a Communist dictatorship comes to power, the Kremlin makes the most of native resources and manpower, as it has done within its own borders.

But can the Western world unite and organize for the historic challenge it is facing in backward peasant countries as does the Communist world, whether under Moscow's or Peking's domination?

[1] Najmeh Najafi and Helen Hinckley, *Reveille for a Persian Village* (Victor Gollancz, Ltd., London, 1959).

The peasant, whether in Latin America, Asia, Africa, has long been the forgotten man in history. He has wakened from his centuries-old torpor, and it is his needs and demands, far more than conflicts of ideology, that have stirred up the sharp struggles between East and West.

In a rational world, both sides would join hands and hearts to bring bread and health, work and education, to the long neglected and long-suffering peasantry in backward areas. But as the Belgian Congo alone has demonstrated, Moscow flouts efforts at co-operation; it rushed planeloads of experts and technicians to the scene in the hope of seizing immediate advantage and attaining ultimate domination of the newly emerging and disorganized African nation. That the precipitate action resulted in the expulsion of the newly arrived Soviet emissaries, including the ambassador, will not halt Moscow's drive first for the sympathy and eventually the control of underdeveloped countries.

Moscow is tough-skinned and takes the long view of history. An immediate rebuff, however ignominious, may cause Khrushchev to explode with rage and into a torrent of rhetoric and fist banging that any village Komsomol would denounce as "uncultured." But it will not abate Kremlin zeal in the pursuit of distant goals. Frustrated in the West by the very worker whom it has for forty-three years striven to cajole and embrace, the worker whom it has never understood and is neither socially nor intellectually equipped to understand, it has set its sights on the lowly peasant in backward countries. This peasant it well understands—was not Czarist Russia overwhelmingly a backward peasant country, and are not Khrushchev, Kozlov, Suslov, and several other members of the Kremlin hierarchy of muzhik origin?

So the battle is on, and no scheme of coexistence, however amicably achieved, can stay it until such time as the Kremlin either accomplishes its purposes or realizes the futility of the struggle.

EPILOGUE

The middle-aged Russian at my table in the lobby buffet of the Ukraina Hotel asked if I could tell him who "the distinguished-looking foreigner" was standing there in the center of the lobby surrounded by a group of Russians. I turned to see and told him that it was the American scientist Norbert Wiener.

"The *kibernetica* professor?" asked a young man at an adjoining table who had overheard us, and I assured him that it was indeed the father of cybernetics.

The two men with whom I had fallen into conversation were educators who had come to Moscow from the provinces to attend a teachers' convention. They gave the M.I.T. professor a long and interested look.

During his brief stay in Moscow in July 1960, Norbert Wiener was dined and wined everywhere, even in the privacy of the homes of Russian scientists. Whenever he appeared in the lobby of the hotel, Russians who recognized him from newspaper pictures came up to him and shook his hand. The spy-scare incident to the U-2 affair which the press had whipped up had chilled the always uneasy relationships between Russian university students and their foreign non-Communist classmates, more notably the Americans. But it didn't, as during Stalin's postwar years, frighten away from foreigners the public at large, not even in Moscow, least of all from the highly publicized Professor Wiener.

"Do you know him?" asked the older educator.

"Yes," I said, "I met him and his wife right here in the lobby." Then I added, "It may interest you to know that his father was my professor in Russian literature when I was doing postgraduate work at Harvard University."

The educator at the next table moved his chair closer. "Was his father Russian?" he asked.

"Yes," I replied. "He was a famous Russian scholar and translated Tolstoy's major works into English." Questions about the late Professor Leo Wiener led to questions about Russian authors who were popular in America, about those American universities that were giving Russian courses, and about general American interest in Russian culture.

"We are pleased," said the older man, "to know that Americans show an interest in our language and culture. The more you learn about us, the better you'll understand us. But tell me, please, why our countries can't be friends? Why must they go on wrangling with each other?"

"Yes, why?" echoed the other.

This is the eternal question one hears from ordinary Russians, sincerely and urgently asked. But here one is always at a disadvantage, because the issues and complexities of the cold war are difficult to discuss with people whose information on the subject has been deliberately limited and distorted. With few exceptions, Russians take it for granted that all the onus for the cold war rests with the West, especially with America; and while one may feel free to discuss the subject with old friends in the privacy of his home, one feels tongue-tied in a hotel lobby among strangers.

Evasively I replied, "Americans are as sick of the cold war as Russians are."

"Then why can't we get together?"

Purposely vague, I said that many unresolved conflicts separated us.

"What conflicts?" demanded the younger man. "The Soviet Union is socialist, America is capitalist. We couldn't impose our system on your country if we tried, nor could you impose yours on us. So why can't we have a genuine and friendly coexistence?"

This time I decided to be less evasive. "Well, there's the knotty problem of West Berlin, for instance."

To my surprise this remark did not elicit an explanation of the merits of Khrushchev's proposal for a free and demilitarized city; instead the older educator said, "What? The Germans again? Haven't they made enough trouble already—plunging the world into two wars in this century? Millions of our people died to keep them from enslaving our country, and here they are again with their West Berlin. How ridiculous to think that your country and mine would blow each other off the face of the earth over Germans anywhere."

"Our country," said the younger man, "is very big and very rich in resources. All we want is to live in peace so we can work, develop our resources, raise our living standards, and build our new society."

"War over West Berlin," the older educator exclaimed. "Preposterous! Unthinkable! It must never happen!"

It was obvious that the educators, like other Russians one meets, knew nothing of the Berlin blockade, of the flight of more than three million East Germans to West Germany, of the results of the West Berlin elections in December 1958, when the Social Unity (Communist) Party polled less than two per cent of the vote. They had no realization of the sharp contrast of life in East and West Berlin, of the gay and crowded Kurfürstendam and of the dreary emptiness of the Stalin Allee, a contrast that strikes even the most casual tourist who takes the rigidly regulated bus trip to East Berlin. They appeared quite unaware of the danger that a free and prosperous western sector holds for Kremlin policies and purposes, a danger pointed up by Khrushchev himself when he called West Berlin "a thorn in the heart of Europe." They knew only one thing, that there must be no war. It would be no solace to them that war, as they have been told over and over, would bring about the death of capitalism and the triumph of communism. They knew only too well that hydrogen bombs and missiles do not distinguish between ideologies, and didn't Khrushchev himself tell them that "the use of the new means of mass annihilation threatens unprecedented destruction and the doom of millions and millions of people"?

The foreign visitor who talks to Russians everywhere he travels comes to feel that, if left to decide for themselves, they would refuse to sacrifice a single Soviet-built tractor as the price for imposing a Moscow-directed Peoples' Democracy on any country in the world. The crusading spirit of the twenties is dead; the generation that would gladly have fought for world revolution has long ago passed from the scene; the fervent slogans of the twenties ring empty to a long-suffering people who only want to go about their own affairs and enjoy life in their own way. The sentiment is deeply felt and is a powerful deterrent to war. But whether it is powerful enough to deter the Kremlin from a bold step from which there can be no return, either over "the thorn in the heart of Europe" or over some other area of conflict, one would not venture to say.

Professor Wiener was leaving the lobby as we rose from our table. The two educators from the provinces looked after him.

"Please tell the American people that we want to be their friends," said the younger man.

"The very best of friends," said the older man, and we shook hands.

INDEX

Mukhitdinov, Nuritdin, 273, 485, 501, 502, 503
Murrow, Edward R., 535, 536, 539
Music: in hotels, 25–26, 64; jazz, 372–74, 379–80; national anthem, 169–70; religious, 108, 123
Mussolini, Benito, 163
Muzhiks. See Peasants
My Brother, My Enemy, 85, 96

NEP, 140, 304
NKVD 520–21
Najafi, Najmeh, 544
Nakhimov, Admiral, 387
Nalchik, collectivization in, 219
Napoleon I, 104, 105
Nasriddinova, Yagar, 487
Nasser, Gamal Abdal, 492, 540
National Guardian, 319
Nationalism: and anti-Semitism, 314–15, 318; Armenian, 70, 73; Russian, 72 ff., 104, 156; Siberian, 412–13, 422; Uzbekistan, 493–504; World War II and, 163 ff.
Navoye, Ali-Shar, 490, 500
Nazis, 104–6, 156, 161, 163–64, 310–11, 522
Negroes, 22, 23
Nehru, Jawaharlal, 492
Nekrasov, Victor, 277, 352
Nesmeyanov, Alexander, 358–61, 365
Nevsky, Alexander, 104, 167
Nevsky Prospect, 11–12 ff.
New Economic Policy (NEP), 140, 304
Newspapers: Czech, 525–26. *See also* Press; Specific papers
Nicholas I, 277
Nikolayeva, Galina, 350
Nikolayeva, Klavdia, 283
Nikolayevich, Vladimir, 353–56
Nikon, Patriarch, 111
Nixon, Richard M., 413
Nizami (poet), 293
Not by Bread Alone, 351
Novosibirsk, 429
Novy (Siberia), 420
Novy Mir (periodical), 352, 389

Oblomov, 165, 276–77
Odessa, 246 ff. 379

Oil, 365, 421, 488–89
Oktyabr (periodical), 350, 375
Old age, 265–66. *See also* Pensions
Omsk, 411–12
Omul (fish), 458, 459, 464
Orbis (tourist agency), 508
Orchards, crawling, 416, 443
Origin of the Family, 140
Oriodoroga, M. T., 152–53
Orlov (Baptist minister), 121–22
Orlov, Ilya, 121, 133–34
Orthodox Church, 100–18, 128–29
Orwell, George, 92
Osborne, John, 92
Ostrovsky, Alexander, 33
Oumansky, Konstantin, 310
Our Man in Havana, 96
Outlines of Russian Civilization, 110, 350
Ovechkin, Valentin, 231

Palace of Culture, 187–88
Palace of Marriages, 109–10
Panferov, Fyodor, 352
Pankratova, Anna, 103, 325
Pantocrin, 451
Passports, 5th point on, 308
Pasternak, Boris, 336–37, 342–43, 398, 516
Pasutovsky, Konstantin, 350–51
Patriotism. *See* Nationalism
Pavlov, Ivan, 104, 340 ff.
Peasants, 29–30, 51; Baptist Church and 125 ff.; collectivization and, 204–22, 222–45, 246 ff.; converted into proletariat, 195 ff.; cultural revolution and, 258–75; Czech, 517–18; individualism of, 239–42; Iran, 533 ff.; Kazakhs, 59; literacy and, 84; market places and, 49–50; marriage, the family and, 138 ff.; Orthodox Church and, 112–115; and Revolution, 192–94; Siberian, 435 ff.; Uzbeks, 481–84; World War II and, 168–69. *See also* Villages.
Peasants (Chekhov), 259
Pechorskaya Lavra Monastery, 100–1
Pensions, 254, 264, 291–92
Pentecostals, 113
People and Degrees, 389

866-1680

947
H662H

AUTHOR

Hindus, Maurice

TITLE

House without a roof.

DATE DUE	BORROWER'S NAME
FEB - 2 197	Elliott Zah

ARCTIC
NORWAY
SWEDEN
FINLAND
N
W
E
S
NOVAYA ZEMLYA I.
Ostrov Bely
L. TAIMYR
Arkhangelsk
Naryan-Mar
Amderma
Dickson
Ust Tsilma
Salekhard
Dudinka
Norilsk
U.
S.
Igarka
Kirov
OB
URAL MTS.
S I B E
YENISEI
Izhevsk
KAMA
Molotov
Yanaul
Khanty-Mansisk
NIZHNYAYA TUNGUSKA
Sverdlovsk
IRTYSH
Ufa
Tyumen
Podkamennaya Tunguska
Chelyabinsk
TOBOL
Kurgan
OB
ANGARA
Kustanay
Petropavlosk
Tomsk
Omsk
Novosibirsk
Krasnoyarsk
Bratsk
Kemerovo
Taishet
Akmolinsk
IRTYSH
YENISEI
Barnaul
Stalinsk
Karaganda
Angarsk
Irkutsk
Semipalatinsk
Dzhusaly
SYR DARYA
Balkhash
L. BALKHASH
Tashkent
Alma Ata
Frunze
MONGO
Leninabad
Miles 0 100 200 400
Samarkand
Stalinabad
CHINA